Revolutionary Patriots

of

Montgomery County

Maryland

1776-1783

Henry C. Peden, Jr.

HERITAGE BOOKS
2014

HERITAGE BOOKS
AN IMPRINT OF HERITAGE BOOKS, INC.

Books, CDs, and more—Worldwide

For our listing of thousands of titles see our website at
www.HeritageBooks.com

Published 2014 by
HERITAGE BOOKS, INC.
Publishing Division
5810 Ruatan Street
Berwyn Heights, Md. 20740

Copyright © 1996 Henry C. Peden, Jr.

All rights reserved. No part of this book may be reproduced or transmitted in any form or by any means, electronic or mechanical, including photocopying, recording or by any information storage and retrieval system without written permission from the author, except for the inclusion of brief quotations in a review.

International Standard Book Numbers
Paperbound: 978-1-58549-338-8
Clothbound: 978-0-7884-9043-9

INTRODUCTION

This book has been compiled for the purpose of serving as a research tool for locating the men and women of Montgomery County, Maryland, who served in the military, rendered material aid to the army or navy, took the Oath of Allegiance and Fidelity, served in an office or on a committee at the town, county or state level, or in some fashion contributed and supported the fight for freedom by the American colonies from the rule of Great Britain during the Revolutionary War, 1775-1783.

Information has been gleaned from many primary and secondary sources, making this book far more than just a listing of names and ranks. Most of the approximately 5,000 persons named herein also have genealogical data included with their respective entries, such as places of residence and dates of birth, death, and marriage, names of wives, husbands, children and other relatives, physical descriptions, occupations, and information gleaned from military, pension, probate, and other court records. It is hoped that this source book, which is the seventh in a series on the Revolutionary Patriots of Maryland, will encourage interested persons to become members of patriotic organizations such as The Sons of the American Revolution, The Daughters of the American Revolution, The Sons of the Revolution, and The Society of the Cincinnati.

Each entry in this book has been documented and a key to that documentation has been implemented within the text to enable the reader to review the cited source. A letter followed by a number is the code used for a source and the page within that source. For example, "Ref: D-555" indicates that the information can be found in "Archives of Maryland, Volume 18, page 555." Coded sources cited in this book are as follows:

A = *Archives of Maryland, Volume XI*. "Journal of the Maryland Convention, July 26, 1775 - August 14, 1775, and Journal and Correspondence of the Maryland Council of Safety, August 29, 1775 -July 6, 1776" (Baltimore: Maryland Historical Society, 1892)

B = *Archives of Maryland, Volume XII*. "Journal and Correspondence of the Maryland Council of Safety, July 7, 1776 - December 31, 1776" (Baltimore: Maryland Historical Society, 1893)

C = *Archives of Maryland, Volume XVI*. "Journal and Correspondence of the Council of Safety, January 1, 1777 - March 20, 1777" and "Journal and

Correspondence of the State Council, March 20, 1777 - March 28, 1778" (Baltimore: Maryland Historical Society, 1897)

D = *Archives of Maryland, Volume XVIII.* "Muster Rolls and Other Records of Service of Maryland Troops in the American Revolution, 1775-1783" (Baltimore: Maryland Historical Society, 1900)

DAR = *DAR Patriot Index, Volume I* (Washington, D. C.: National Society of the Daughters of the American Revolution, 1966)

E = *Archives of Maryland, Volume XXI.* "Journal and Correspondence of the Council of Maryland, April 1, 1778 - October 26, 1779" (Baltimore: Maryland Historical Society, 1901)

F = *Archives of Maryland, Volume XLIII.* "Journal and Correspondence of the State Council of Maryland, 1779-1780" (Baltimore: Maryland Historical Society, 1924)

G = *Archives of Maryland, Volume XLV.* "Journal and Correspondence of the State Council of Maryland, 1780-1781" (Baltimore: Maryland Historical Society, 1927)

H = *Archives of Maryland, Volume XLVII.* "Journal and Correspondence of the State Council of Maryland, 1781" (Baltimore: Maryland Historical Society, 1930)

I = *Archives of Maryland, Volume XLVIII.* "Journal and Correspondence of the State Council of Maryland, 1781-1784" (Baltimore: Maryland Historical Society, 1931)

J = *Maryland Pension Rolls of 1835: Report from the Secretary of War in Relation to the Pension Establishment of the United States* (Baltimore: Genealogical Publishing Company, 1968, reprint of the 1835 government report).

K = Brumbaugh, Gaius M. *Maryland Records: Colonial, Revolutionary, County and Church From Original Sources* (Baltimore: Genealogical Publishing Company, 1985, reprint, 2 volumes)

L = Carothers, Bettie. *9000 Men Who Took the Oath of Allegiance and Fidelity to Maryland During the Revolution* (Lutherville, Maryland:

Privately Compiled by the Author, 1978, 2 volumes)

M = Clements, S. Eugene and Wright, F. Edward. *The Maryland Militia in the Revolutionary War* (Silver Spring, Maryland: Family Line Publications, 1987)

N = Papenfuse, Edward, et al. *A Biographical Dictionary of the Maryland Legislature, 1635-1789* (Baltimore: Johns Hopkins Press, 1979)

O = Papenfuse, Edward, et al. *An Inventory of Maryland State Papers, Volume I*, "The Era of the American Revolution, 1775-1789" (Annapolis: Hall of Records Commission, 1977)

P = White, Virgil D. *Genealogical Abstracts of Revolutionary War Pension Files* (Waynesboro, TN: National Historical Publishing Company, 1990, 4 volumes)

Q = Meyer, Mary K., ed. *Westward of Fort Cumberland: Military Lots Set Off for Maryland's Revolutionary Soldiers*. With an Appended List of Revolutionary Soldiers Granted Pensions by the State of Maryland. (Finksburg, Maryland: Pipe Creek Publications, 1993)

R = *Maryland Genealogical Society Bulletin* (MGSB) articles:
R-6 = "Obituaries of Revolutionary Soldiers," by Robert W. Barnes (MGSB, Volume 6, No. 1, pp. 6-7; No. 2, pp. 14-15; No. 3, pp. 52-53, No. 4; pp. 96-98 (1965); R-10 = Volume 10, No. 2, p. 57 (1969)

R-27 = "Some Little Known Data Regarding Maryland Signers of the Oath of Fidelity," by Richard B. Miller (MGSB, Volume 27, No. 1, pp. 101-124, Winter, 1986)

R-28 = "Revolutionary and Military Service Pensioners Living in Maryland, Delaware, and the District of Columbia at the Time of the 1840 Census," by Elba Anthony Dardeau, Jr. (MGSB, Volume 28, No. 4, pp. 440-444, Fall, 1987)

R-31 = "1777 Tax List of Montgomery County," by Eleanor M. V. Cook (MGSB, Volume 31, No. 1, pp. 3-18, Winter, 1990)

R-33 = "A List of 20 Recruits Raised in Montgomery County Pursuant to the Act of Assembly Entitled An Act to Procure Recruits Anno 1781," by

Eleanor M. V. Cook (MGSB, Volume 33, No. 1, pp. 155-157, Winter, 1992)

S = *Records of the Sons of the American Revolution*. The Maryland Society Membership Applications, 1930-1990 (Baltimore: University of Baltimore Langsdale Library (filed by Maryland Society number), and The National Society's Graves Registration Project (S-1993).

T = Hodges, Margaret. *Unpublished Revolutionary Records of Maryland, Volumes 3 and 5* (Baltimore: Privately Compiled by the Author, 1939-1941)

U = "Abstracts of Revolutionary War Pension Applications" cited in the *National Genealogical Society Quarterly*: Volume 5, No. (1929); Volume 17, No. 4 (1929); Volume 20, No. 2 (1932); Volume 22, No. 3 (1934); Volume 23, No. 2 and No. 3 (1935); Volume 30, No. 2 (1942); Volume 34, No. 2 (1939); Volume 35, No. 2 (1947); Volume 36, No. 4 (1948)

V = Malloy, Mary G., Sween, Jane C., and Manuel, Janet D. *Abstracts of Wills, Montgomery County, Maryland, 1776-1825* (Westminster, MD: Family Line Publications, 1989, reprint)

W = *Montgomery County Minute Books, 1779-1780, 1780-1781*. Original records at the Maryland State Archives (Accession No. MdHR 15597)

X = *Revolutionary War Military Collection, Manuscript MS.1146* (Baltimore: Maryland Historical Society, Manuscript Division)

Y = McGhee, Lucy K. *Maryland Pension Abstracts: Revolution, War of 1812, and Indian Wars* (Washington, D.C.: Privately Compiled by the Author, 1966)

Z = Burns, Annie W. *Maryland Soldiers of the Revolutionary War Who Settled in Kentucky* (Baltimore: Compiled by the Author, 1939)

It should also be noted that an entry indicating that someone had "deserted" or was "missing" should not necessarily reflect in an adverse light. The rather lax military discipline of the day did allow individuals to leave the service unannounced, return home to handle personal business, and oftentimes to return to service in a short time. Naturally, many did "desert," but seeing this entry on the muster roll did not always mean they "went to the other side."

Likewise, the taking of the Oath of Allegiance and Fidelity in 1777-1783 did not always mean that the person who took the oath was all that patriotic. Many men (who were age 18 and over) took the oath out of fear for their lives, to avoid a treble tax, to avoid losing their land, or perhaps to avoid the social stigma of being labelled a coward. These people were considered non-enrollers and many others were Tories. Still, many Montgomery Countians were true and unfailing patriots and should be recognized for it. In fact, of the 3,441 persons (3,404 men and 37 women) listed in the 1777 tax list of Montgomery County, which taxed free white males and slaves over the age of 16 (taxables), not including clergy and persons who owned no property, 3,372 of them either served in the military or rendered other patriotic service, i. e., an amazing 98% "supported" the American cause against Great Britain between 1775 and 1783, whether it was voluntary or otherwise. Only 2% (just 69 persons) did not render aid or serve in the military in Montgomery County. Obviously, this statistic could change as younger men not listed in the 1777 tax list "came of age" during the war and served, or not.

It must also be noted that it is not possible to know who all of the patriots and soldiers were who served in or from Montgomery County during the Revolutionary War. This is especially true for those who joined the Maryland Line and served in the Continental Army. Due to the constant reorganization of Maryland troops during the war, it is not easily determined which soldier served from which county. Therefore, for the men who were listed in the 1776 tax list and the 1777 levy list for Montgomery County, I cross-referenced against available military rolls in order to determine which soldiers served from Montgomery County in the regular army. Apparently, most served in the 3rd and 7th Maryland Regiments.

Furthermore, since Montgomery County was not created until 1776, soldiers who began their service either in Frederick County or Prince George's County could appear later in Montgomery County rolls. It is possible that some may have been inadvertently omitted from this book. Therefore, one should compare the information in this book against my *Revolutionary Patriots of Frederick County, Maryland, 1775-1783*, as well as the *Archives of Maryland, Volume 18*, for additional names.

Henry C. Peden, Jr.
Bel Air, MD 21014
June 1, 1996

HUNDREDS OF MONTGOMERY COUNTY CIRCA 1777
Prepared by Henry C. Peden, Jr., 1996

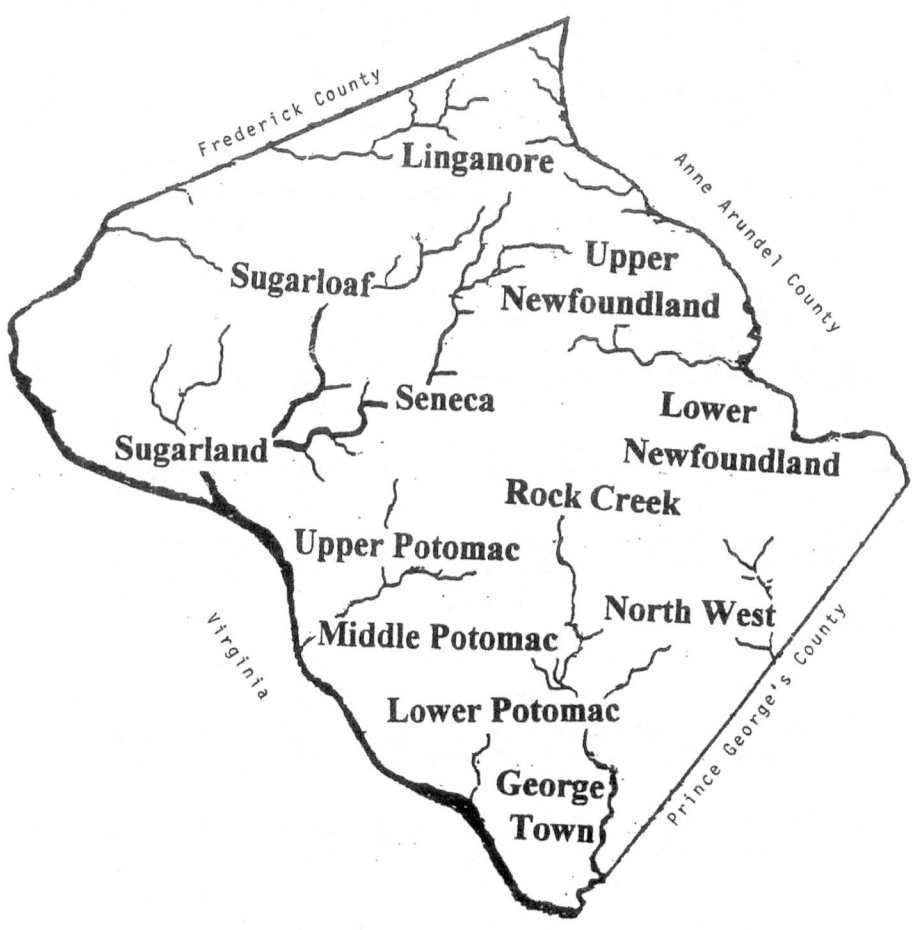

Based on information contained in Eleanor M. V. Cook's
Guide to the Records of Montgomery County, Maryland (1989)

REVOLUTIONARY PATRIOTS OF MONTGOMERY COUNTY, MARYLAND, 1776-1783

ABARRY (AVERY), Richard. "Richard Abarry" lived in Sugarland Hd. (one taxable) in 1777 [Ref: R-31:11]. "Richard Avery" was a private, 8th Co., Upper Bn., Militia, Aug. 30, 1777 [Ref: M-195].

ABINGTON (ABBINGTON), Bole or Boules (b. 1761). Son of John Abington of North West Hd., in 1776 [Ref: K-1:227]. "Boules Abbington" was a private, 8th Co., Lower Bn., Militia, Sep., 1777 [Ref: M-200, T-5:51].

ABINGTON (ABBINGTON), John (b. 1736). "John Abbington" was a private, 8th Co., Lower Bn., Militia, Sep., 1777 [Ref: M-200, T-5:51]. "John Abington" took the Oath of Allegiance before the Hon. Samuel W. Magruder in 1778 [Ref: T-3:72, L-1:37]. "John Abington" lived in North West Hd. in 1776 and had four taxables in 1777 [Ref: K-1:227, R-31:16].

ACORD, Joseph. Took the Oath of Allegiance in 1778 [Ref: L-2:27].

ADAIR (IDAIRE), William. Took the Oath of Allegiance before the Hon. William Deakins, Jr. before March 3, 1778 [Ref: T-3:68, L-1:37]. "William Idaire" was a private in the 3rd Co., Middle Bn., Militia, Sep., 1777 [Ref: M-196, T-5:38]. "William Adair" rendered aid by providing wheat for use of the military in 1781 [Ref: O-358].

ADAMS, Alexander. Private, 5th Co., Middle Bn., Militia, Sep., 1777 [Ref: M-197, T-5:40], and Second Corporal, 1st Co., Middle Bn., July 15, 1780 [Ref: M-201]. One Alexander Adams took the Oath of Allegiance before the Hon. Joseph Wilson on Feb. 28, 1778, and another took the Oath of Allegiance before the Hon. Samuel W. Magruder [Ref: T-3:67, T-3:73, L-1:37]. One Alexander Adams was born in 1746 [Ref: K-1:181].

ADAMS, Edward (b. 1743). Private, 5th Co., Lower Bn., Militia, Aug., 1777 [Ref: M-199, T-5:48]. Private, 2nd Co., Lower Bn., Militia, July 15, 1780 [Ref: M-204]. Took the Oath of Allegiance before the Hon. Samuel W. Magruder in 1778 [Ref: T-3:72, L-1:37]. Lived in Lower Potomac Hd. (one taxable) in 1776-1777 [Ref: R-31:4, K-1:181].

ADAMS, Jacob. Private, Capt. Thomas Beall's Co., Maryland Line, 1780 [Ref: D-351].

ADAMS, Jesse (b. 1758). Private, 7th Co., Upper Bn., Militia, Aug. 30, 1777 [Ref: M-194]. Took the Oath of Allegiance before the Hon. Aneas Campbell on March 2, 1778 [Ref: T-3:78, L-1:37]. Lived in Sugarland Hd. in 1776 [Ref: K-1:220].

ADAMS, Thomas (b. 1743). Lived in Sugarland Hd. in 1776 [Ref: K-1:214]. Private, Flying Camp, enlisted on July 20, 1776. Private, 3rd Maryland Line, enlisted on April 23, 1778 [Ref: D-46, D-79].

ADAMSON, Alexander. Served as a Drummer, 4th Maryland Line, and was reported missing on Aug. 16, 1780, at the Battle of Camden. He was listed as a "defective" in Oct., 1780 [Ref: D-80, D-414].

ADAMSON, Basil (1728-1785). Lived in Seneca Hd. (two taxables) in 1777 [Ref: R-31:7]. Private, 1st Co., Middle Bn., Militia, Aug. 30, 1777 [Ref:

M-195]. Took the Oath of Allegiance before the Hon. Gerrard Briscoe on March 2, 1778. Basil Adamson married Nancy Spiers and died on Nov. 17, 1785 [Ref: T-3:56, L-1:37, DAR-I:5].

ADAMSON, John. Private, 1st Co., Middle Bn., Militia, Aug. 30, 1777 [Ref: M-195]. Ensign, Middle Bn., Militia, April 8, 1780 [Ref: M-47, F-248]. Ensign, 5th Co., Middle Bn., Militia, July 15, 1780 [Ref: M-202]. Took the Oath of Allegiance before the Hon. Gerrard Briscoe on March 2, 1778 [Ref: T-3:56, L-1:37]. Rendered aid by providing wheat for use of the military in 1781 [Ref: O-380].

ADAMSON, Kensey. Private, 1st Co., Middle Bn., Militia, Aug. 30, 1777 [Ref: M-195]. Private, 5th Co., Middle Bn., July 15, 1780 [Ref: M-203].

ADAMSON, Ruth. See "Thomas Ricketts," q.v.

ADGATE, Elias. Private, 7th Co., Middle Bn., Militia, July 15, 1780 [Ref: M-203].

ADKINS, Joseph. Private, 1st Co., Lower Bn., Militia, July 15, 1780 [Ref: M-204]. Lived in Lower Potomac Hd. (two taxables) in 1777 [Ref: R-31:4].

ADLUM, John. Rendered aid by providing beef for use of the military in 1781 [Ref: O-396].

AHAIR (ADAIR?), John. Private who was recruited to serve in the Extra Regiment, Continental Army, in 1780 [Ref: D-342].

AITZIL, Jacob. Private, Capt. Thomas Beall's Co., Maryland Line, 1780 [Ref: D-350].

ALBERY (ALLBERRY, ABERRY, AUBREY), William (b. 1736). "William Albery" took the Oath of Allegiance before the Hon. Samuel W. Magruder in 1778 [Ref: T-3:73, L-1:37]. Private, 5th Co., Lower Bn., Militia, Aug., 1777 [Ref: M-200, T-5:48]. "William Aberry" was a private, 4th Co., Lower Bn., Militia, Aug., 1777 [Ref: M-199, T-5:47]. "William Allberry" lived in Lower Potomac Hd. (one taxable) in 1776-1777 [Ref: R-31:4, K-1:181].

ALBY, Joseph (b. 1746). Lived in North West Hd. (wife named Cassandra, aged 24) in 1776 [Ref: K-1:227]. Private, 8th Co., Lower Bn., Militia, Sep., 1777 [Ref: M-200, T-5:51].

ALDRIDGE, James. Private, 4th Co., Upper Bn., Militia, Aug. 30, 1777 [Ref: M-194]. Lived in Sugarland Hd. (one taxable) in 1777 [Ref: R-31:11].

ALDRIDGE, John (died 1799). Private, 1st Co., Lower Bn., Militia, Sep., 1777 [Ref: M-198, T-5:44]. Private, 7th Co., Lower Bn., Militia, July 15, 1780 [Ref: M-207]. Took the Oath of Allegiance before the Hon. Edward Burgess on Feb. 28, 1778 [Ref: T-3:62, L-1:37]. Lived in the Lower Part of Newfoundland Hd. (four taxables) in 1777 [Ref: R-31:5]. Died testate in Montgomery County in 1799 [Ref: V-1].

ALDRIDGE, Nathan. Private, 5th Class, 3rd Co., Middle Bn., Militia, July 15, 1780 [Ref: M-202]. Private, 2nd Maryland Line, 1782-1783 [Ref: D-447, D-498].

ALDRIDGE, Thomas. Private, 6th Co., Middle Bn., Militia, Aug., 1777 [Ref: M-197, T-5:41]. Took the Oath of Allegiance before the Hon. Edward Burgess on Feb. 28, 1778 [Ref: T-3:59, L-1:37]. Lived in Linganore Hd. (three taxables) in 1777 [Ref: R-31:8].

ALDRIDGE, Zachariah. Private, Capt. Edward Burgess' Co., Lower District of Frederick (now Montgomery) County, Militia, July, 1776 [Ref: D-42].

ALL (OLL), Adam. Took the Oath of Allegiance in 1778 [Ref: L-2:28].

ALL, John. Private, 1st or 32nd Bn., Militia (no date was given; possibly June, 1777). [Ref: T-5:1].

ALLCOCK (ELCOCK), Robert. "Robert Allcock" was a private, 7th Co., Middle Bn., Militia, Sep., 1777 [Ref: M-197, T-5:42]. "Robert Elcock" lived in Seneca Hd. (one taxable) in 1777 [Ref: R-31:7]. "Robert Elock" [sic] took the Oath of Allegiance before the Hon. Joseph Wilson on Feb. 28, 1778 [Ref: T-3:64, L-1:40].

ALLEN, Alexander. Private, 3rd Co., Lower Bn., Militia, July 15, 1780 [Ref: M-205].

ALLEN (ALLIN), Archibald (1741-1783). "Archibald Allin" was a private, 8th Co., Upper Bn., on Aug. 30, 1777 [Ref: M-195]. "Archibald Allen" was a captain, 16th Bn., Militia, on Dec. 9, 1777 [Ref: M-48, C-373]. Lived in Sugarland Hd. in 1776 and had three taxables in 1777 [Ref: K-1:211, R-31:11]. Died testate in Montgomery County in 1783 [Ref: V-1].

ALLEN, Thomas. Private, Capt. Price's Co., 3rd Maryland Line, 1781-1782 [Ref: D-453].

ALLEY, Basil. Private, 6th Co., Lower Bn., Militia, July 15, 1780 [Ref: M-206].

ALLEY, Samuel. Private, 7th Co., Lower Bn., Militia, July 15, 1780 [Ref: M-207].

ALLISON, Benjamin (died 1795). Private, 5th Co., Middle Bn., Militia, Sep., 1777 [Ref: M-197, T-5:40]. Took the Oath of Allegiance (made his "B" mark) before the Hon. Joseph Wilson on Feb. 28, 1778 [Ref: T-3:65, L-1:37]. Served as a grand juror in Aug., 1777 [Ref: R-31:17]. Lived in the Upper Part of Potomac Hd. (two taxables) in 1777 [Ref: R-31:13]. Died testate in Montgomery County in 1795 [Ref: V-1].

ALLISON, Burch (b. Feb. 24, 1765). Private, 2nd Class, 1st Co., Middle Bn., Militia, July 15, 1780 [Ref: M-201]. Born in (now) Montgomery County, where he enlisted in the war, and afterwards moved to Loudoun County, Virginia and then to Burke County, North Carolina in 1799. Applied for pension (S6493) on July 30, 1834, aged 70, and mentioned his sister Mrs. Jarrett Smith and brother Posey Allison, aged 83, in Burke County [Ref: P-45].

ALLISON, Charles. Private, 1st Co., Upper Bn., Militia, Aug. 30, 1777 [Ref: M-193]. Took the Oath of Allegiance (made his "P" mark) before the Hon. Joseph Wilson on Feb. 28, 1778 [Ref: T-3:66, L-1:37]. Rendered aid by providing wheat for use of the military in 1780 and

1781 [Ref: O-308, O-393]. One "Charles Allison, aged 25" lived in Sugarland Hd. in 1776-1777 [Ref: K-1:205, R-31:11], and another lived in the Upper Part of Potomac Hd. (one taxable) in 1777 [Ref: R-31:13].

ALLISON, Elisha (died 1798). Private, 3rd Class, 1st Co., Middle Bn., Militia, July 15, 1780 [Ref: M-201]. Died testate (wife named Ann) in Montgomery County in 1798 [Ref: V-1].

ALLISON, Elizabeth. Rendered aid by providing wheat for use of the military in 1781 [Ref: O-400]. See "David Walter," q.v.

ALLISON, Ellian. See "Robert Ricketts," q.v.

ALLISON, Henry or Hendery (b. 1720). "Hendrey Allison" took the Oath of Allegiance before the Hon. Aneas Campbell on March 2, 1778 [Ref: T-3:77, L-1:37]. "Hendery or Henry Allison" lived in Sugarland Hd. in 1776 and had four taxables in 1777, including a son Henry or Hendery, aged 18, in 1776 [Ref: K-1:220, R-31:11].

ALLISON, Henry (Hendery), Jr. (b. 1758). "Henry Allison" was a private, 7th Co., Upper Bn., Militia, Aug., 1777 [Ref: M-195, T-5:58]. Private, 5th Co., Middle Bn., Militia, Sep., 1777 [Ref: M-197, T-5:40]. "Hendery Allison, aged 18" lived in Sugarland Hd. in 1776 [Ref: K-1:220].

ALLISON, Hezekiah. Took the Oath of Allegiance before the Hon. Samuel W. Magruder in 1778 [Ref: T-3:72, L-1:37].

ALLISON, James. Private, 3rd Co., Middle Bn., Militia, Sep., 1777 [Ref: T-5:38]. Private, 1st Class, 2nd Co., Middle Bn., Militia, July 15, 1780 [Ref: M-201]. Took the Oath of Allegiance before the Hon. William Deakins, Jr. before March 3, 1778 [Ref: T-3:68, L-1:37]. Lived in the Upper Part of Potomac Hd. (one taxable) in 1777 [Ref: R-31:13].

ALLISON, John (1740-1793). Took the Oath of Allegiance (made his "X" mark) before the Hon. Joseph Wilson on Feb. 28, 1778 [Ref: T-3:66, L-1:37]. Rendered aid by providing wheat for use of the military in 1780 [Ref: O-321, O-331]. "John Allison, aged 36" lived in Sugarland Hd. in 1776 and he or another John Allison lived in the Upper Part of Potomac Hd. (four taxables) in 1777 [Ref: K-1:210, R-31:13]. John Allison (wife named Elizabeth) died testate in Montgomery County in 1793 [Ref: V-2].

ALLISON, Jonathan. Private, 5th Co., Middle Bn., Militia, Sep., 1777 [Ref: M-197, T-5:40], and First Corporal, 1st Co., Middle Bn., Militia, July 15, 1780 [Ref: M-201]. Took the Oath of Allegiance (made his "X" mark) before the Hon. Joseph Wilson on Feb. 28, 1778 [Ref: T-3:65, L-1:37]. Rendered aid by providing wheat for use of the military in 1781 [Ref: O-398]. Lived in Lower Potomac Hd. (one taxable) in 1777 [Ref: R-31:4].

ALLISON (ALESON), Posey or Pacey (b. 1751). Brother of "Burch Allison," q.v. "Pacey Allison" took the Oath of Allegiance before the Hon. Gerrard Briscoe on March 2, 1778 [Ref: T-3:57, L-1:37]. "Posey Aleson" lived in Sugar Loaf Hd. (one taxable) in 1777 [Ref: R-31:9]. He moved to Burke County, North Carolina with his brother. See "Burch Allison," q.v.

ALLISON (ALLESON), Richard Jr. Private, 5th Co., Middle Bn., Militia, Sep., 1777 [Ref: M-197, T-5:40]. One Richard Allison took the Oath of Allegiance before the Hon. Joseph Wilson on Feb. 28, 1778 [Ref: T-3:66, L-1:37]. "Richard Alleson, Jr." lived in Seneca Hd. (one taxable) in 1777 [Ref: R-31:7].

ALLISON (ALLESON), Richard Sr. Private, 5th Co., Middle Bn., Militia, Sep., 1777 [Ref: M-197, T-5:40]. Richard Allison took the Oath of Allegiance (made his "X" mark) before the Hon. Joseph Wilson on Feb. 28, 1778 [Ref: T-3:67, L-1:37]. Rendered aid by providing wheat for use of the military in 1780 [Ref: O-303]. "Richard Alleson" lived in Seneca Hd. (two taxables) in 1777 [Ref: R-31:7].

ALLISON, Ruth. See "Zachariah Prather," q.v.

ALLISON, Thomas. Private, 1st Co., Upper Bn., Militia, Aug. 30, 1777 [Ref: M-193]. Took the Oath of Allegiance before the Hon. Joseph Wilson on Feb. 28, 1778 [Ref: T-3:65, L-1:37]. Thomas Allison married Elizabeth Baxter in Montgomery County on Sep. 14, 1780 [Ref: K-2:517]. It was noted by the Council of Maryland on Sep. 5, 1781, that Thomas Allison, among other soldiers of the Maryland Line, "returned from captivity in South Carolina in a distressed situation" and it was ordered that he be paid five pounds on account [Ref: G-598].

ALLNUTT, Daniel. See "James Allnut," q.v.

ALLNUTT (ALNUTT), James (1713-1786). Lived in Sugarland Hd. (four taxables) in 1777 [Ref: R-31:11]. Took the Oath of Allegiance before the Hon. Elisha Williams on March 2, 1778 [Ref: T-3:81, L-1:37]. James Allnut, Sr. married (1) Sarah Lawrence and (2) Jane Coberth [Ref: DAR-I:12]. Died testate in Aug., 1786, naming wife Jane, sons Jesse, John, Lawrence, James, Talbert, and Daniel Allnutt, and daughters Ann Coats (wife of Charles Coats), Sarah Price (wife of William Price, deceased); Mary Peck (wife of Richard Peck), Susanna Allnutt, and Rebecca Allnutt [Ref: V-2, and "William Allnutt and wife Sarah (Mears) Talbott, widow of John Talbott, of Calvert County, Maryland: The Progenitors of the American Colonial Family of Allnutt With One Line of Their Descendants in Montgomery County, Maryland," by Ernest C. Allnutt, Jr., Lt. Col., AUS (Ret), *Maryland Genealogical Society Bulletin*, Volume 33, No. 4 (1992), pp. 712-766. This well-documented family history contains much more Allnutt information].

ALLNUTT (ALNUTT), James Jr. (1751-1838). Private, 3rd Co., Upper Bn., Militia, Aug. 30, 1777 [Ref: M-193]. Took the Oath of Allegiance before the Hon. Elisha Williams on March 2, 1778 [Ref: T-3:81, L-1:37]. "James Allnutt, aged 25" lived in Sugarland Hd. in 1776 and "James Alnutt, Jr." lived there (one taxable) in 1777. He married Verlinda Hawkins Dawson and died Feb. 21, 1838 [Ref: K-1:202, R-31:11, DAR-I:12]. See "James Allnutt," q.v.

ALLNUTT (ALNUTT), Jesse (1745-1815). Private, 6th Co., Upper Bn., Militia, Aug. 30, 1777 [Ref: M-194].Took the Oath of Allegiance before the Hon. Elisha Williams on March 2, 1778 [Ref: T-3:81, L-1:37]. "Jesse Allnutt, aged 31" and "Jesse Allnutt, aged 63" both lived in Sugarland Hd. in 1776-1777 [Ref: K-1:202, R-31:11]. Jesse Allnutt, Jr. married Anne Newton Chiswell and died Aug. 7, 1845 [Ref: DAR-I:12]. See "James Allnutt," q.v.

ALLNUTT, John (b. 1760). Private, 3rd Co., Upper Bn., Militia, Aug. 30, 1777 [Ref: M-193]. Took the Oath of Allegiance before the Hon. Elisha Williams on March 2, 1778 [Ref: T-3:81, L-1:37]. Lived in Sugarland Hd. in 1776 [Ref: K-1:202]. See "James Allnutt," q.v.

ALLNUTT (ALNUTT), Lawrence (1750-1825). Private, 3rd Co., Upper Bn., Militia, Aug. 30, 1777, and Ensign, Upper Bn., Militia, March 25, 1780 [Ref: M-48, M-193, F-120]. Lived in Sugarland Hd. (one taxable) in 1776-1777 [Ref: K-1:202, R-31:11], and died testate (wife named Eleanor Dawson) in Montgomery County in 1825 [Ref: V-2, DAR-I:12]. See "James Allnutt," q.v.

ALLNUT, Rebecca. See "James Allnutt," q.v.

ALLNUT, Sarah. See "Nicholas Hocker," q.v.

ALLNUT, Susanna and Talbert. See "James Allnut," q.v.

ALLNUTT, William. Private, 3rd Co., Upper Bn., Militia, Aug. 30, 1777 [Ref: M-193]. Private, 2nd Co., Lower Bn., Militia, July 15, 1780 [Ref: M-204]. "William Alnut" married Mary Riley in Montgomery County on Feb. 12, 1778 [Ref: K-2:516]. "William Allnut, aged 20" lived in Sugarland Hd. in 1776 [Ref: K-1:202]. See "James Allnutt," q.v.

ALLNUTT, William (1711-c1779). Took the Oath of Allegiance before the Hon. Elisha Williams on March 2, 1778 [Ref: T-3:81, L-1:37]. William Alnutt married Mary Talbot and died after 1779 [Ref: DAR-I:12].

ALLPHIN (ALPHIN), Edward. Private, 3rd Co., Middle Bn., Militia, Sep., 1777 [Ref: M-196, T-5:38]. "Edward Allphin" took the Oath of Allegiance before the Hon. William Deakins, Jr. before March 3, 1778 [Ref: T-3:68, L-1:37]. Lived in the Upper Part of Potomac Hd. (one taxable) in 1777 [Ref: R-31:13].

AMBROSE, Henry. Took the Oath of Allegiance in 1778 [Ref: L-2:27].

AMLEY, James. Private who was recruited to serve in the Continental Army in 1780 [Ref: D-341].

ANCRUM, Jacob Jr. Took the Oath of Allegiance in 1778 [Ref: L-2:27].

ANCRUM, Richard Jr. Took the Oath of Allegiance in 1778 [Ref: L-2:27].

ANCRUM, Richard Sr. Took the Oath of Allegiance in 1778 [Ref: L-2:27].

ANDERS, Edward. Took the Oath of Allegiance on Sep. 1, 1780, under the Act of May 12, 1780, having neglected to do so previously "due to ignorance of the duty owed the country." [Ref: R-27:104].

ANDERS, Richard. Took the Oath of Allegiance on Sep. 1, 1780, under the Act of May 12, 1780, having neglected to do so previously "due to ignorance of the duty owed the country." [Ref: R-27:104].

ANDERSON, Catherine. See "Greenberry Gaither," q.v.

ANDERSON, Charles. Rendered aid by providing wheat for use of the military in 1781 [Ref: O-423].

ANDERSON, James. (1) Private, 8th Co., Lower Bn., Militia, July 15, 1780 [Ref: M-207]. (2) Private, 1st Co., Middle Bn., Militia, Aug. 30, 1777 [Ref: M-195]. Third Sergeant, 5th Co., Middle Bn., Militia, July 15, 1780 [Ref: M-202]. (3) Took the Oath of Allegiance before the Hon. Gerrard Briscoe on March 2, 1778 [Ref: T-3:56, L-1:37].

ANDERSON, John (died 1815). Private, 1st Co., Middle Bn., Militia, Aug. 30, 1777 [Ref: M-195]. Private, 5th Co., Middle Bn., Militia, July 15, 1780 [Ref: M-203]. Took the Oath of Allegiance before the Hon. Joseph Wilson on Feb. 28, 1778 [Ref: T-3:67, L-1:37]. Lived in Seneca Hd. (three taxables) in 1777 [Ref: R-31:7]. John Anderson (wife named Mary) died testate in Montgomery County in 1815 [Ref: V-3].

ANDERSON, Richard. Served as a Second Lieutenant, Lower District, Frederick County (now Montgomery), Militia, July 20, 1776 [Ref: D-42]. Lived in Seneca Hd. (four taxables) in 1777 [Ref: R-31:7]. "Richard Anderson, planter" (wife named Priscilla) died testate in Montgomery County in 1778 [Ref: V-3]. See "James White," q.v.

ANDISON, Anne. See "Greenbury Gaither," q.v.

ANDREWS (ANDREW), Charles Jr. "Charles Andrews" was a private, 5th Co., Upper Bn., Militia, Aug. 30, 1777 [Ref: M-194]. "Charles Andrew, Jr." took the Oath of Allegiance on Sep. 1, 1780, under the Act of May 12, 1780, having neglected to do so previously "due to ignorance of the duty owed the country." [Ref: R-27:104]. Lived in Sugar Loaf Hd. (one taxable) in 1777 [Ref: R-31:9].

ANDREWS (ANDREW), Charles Sr. (died 1816). "Charles Andrews" lived in Sugar Loaf Hd. (three taxables) in 1777 [Ref: R-31:9]. "Charles Andrew" took the Oath of Allegiance on Sep. 1, 1780, under the Act of May 12, 1780, having neglected to do so previously "due to ignorance of the duty owed the country." [Ref: R-27:104]. Died testate (wife named Elizabeth) in Montgomery County in 1816 [Ref: V-3].

ANDREWS, Edward (died 1815). Private, 5th Co., Upper Bn., Militia, Aug. 30, 1777 [Ref: M-194]. Edward Andrews (wife named Ann) died testate in Montgomery County in 1815 [Ref: V-3].

ANDREWS, Richard. Private, 5th Co., Upper Bn., Militia, Aug. 30, 1777 [Ref: M-194].

ANGLE, Jacob. Took the Oath of Allegiance in 1778 [Ref: L-2:27].

ANKMAN (AUKMAN), John. Private, 3rd Co., Lower Bn., Militia, Sep., 1777 [Ref: T-5:46 and M-199, which latter source questions if name could be "Anthman"].

APPLE, John. Took the Oath of Allegiance in 1778 [Ref: L-2:27].

APPLE, Peter. Took the Oath of Allegiance in 1778 [Ref: L-2:27].

APPLEBY, John. Private, 3rd Maryland Line, 1778 [Ref: D-79].

APPLEBY, Thomas. Private, 6th Co., Middle Bn., Militia, Aug., 1777 [Ref: M-197, T-5:41]. Took the Oath of Allegiance before the Hon. Edward Burgess on Feb. 28, 1778 [Ref: L-1:37, T-3:59, which listed the name as "Applepe"]. Private, 6th Co., Middle Bn., Militia, July 15, 1780 [Ref: M-203]. Lived in Linganore Hd. (one taxable) in 1777 [Ref: R-31:8].

APPLEBY, William. Private, 3rd Maryland Line, 1778 [Ref: D-79].

ARMSE, Robert. Took the Oath of Allegiance in 1778 [Ref: L-2:27].

ARMSTRONG, John 2nd. Private, Capt. Price's Co., 3rd Maryland Line, 1781-1782 [Ref: D-452].

ARNOLD, Aeda. See "William Collier," q.v.

ARNOLD, George. Took the Oath of Allegiance in 1778 [Ref: L-2:27].

ARNOLD, Joseph or Josephus (b. 1743). "Joseph Arnold" was a private, 1st Co., Upper Bn., Militia, Aug. 30, 1777 [Ref: M-193]. "Josephus Arnold" took the Oath of Allegiance before the Hon. William Deakins, Jr. before March 3, 1778 [Ref: T-3:68, L-1:37]. "Joseph or Josephus Arnold" lived in Sugarland Hd. (two taxables) in 1776-1777 [Ref: K-1:200, R-31:11].

ARNOLD, William (b. 1741). Private, 1st Co., Upper Bn., Militia, Aug. 30, 1777 [Ref: M-193]. Served as a Drummer, 2nd Maryland Regiment, enlisted Jan. 1, 1780 [Ref: D-78]. Lived in Sugarland Hd. (two taxables) in 1776-1777 [Ref: K-1:206, R-31:11].

ARTIS, James. Private, Flying Camp, Frederick (now Montgomery) County, enlisted by Greenbury Gaither on July 29, 1776 [Ref: D-44].

ASHFORD, Sarah. See "William Mitchell," q.v.

ASKEY, Zachariah. Private, 7th Co., Upper Bn., Militia, Aug. 30, 1777 [Ref: M-194]. Took the Oath of Allegiance before the Hon. Aneas Campbell on March 2, 1778 [Ref: T-3:77, L-1:37].

ATCHISON (ATCHESON), Henry. Private who enrolled into a company of militia for the service of the Flying Camp on Aug. 5, 1776 and apparently again on Oct. 15, 1776 [Ref: D-44, B-352]. Private, 3rd Co., Upper Bn., Militia, Aug. 30, 1777 [Ref: M-193]. "Henry Atcheson" lived in the Upper Part of Potomac Hd. (two taxables) in 1777 [Ref: R-31:13].

ATCHISON, Jeremiah. Private, 1st Maryland Regiment, from May 30, 1777 until Sep. 23, 1778, when reported dead [Ref: D-78].

ATCHISON (ATCHINSON), William. Private, 3rd Co., Upper Bn., Militia, Aug. 30, 1777 [Ref: M-193]. "William Atchinson" took the Oath of Allegiance before the Hon. Edward Burgess on Feb. 28, 1778 [Ref: T-3:63, L-1:37, which listed the name only as "William Athins"]. "William Atchison, say Hutchinson" [sic] was a private, 1st Maryland Regiment, May 31, 1779 [Ref: D-78].

ATHERTON, Elijah C. See "Thomas Pender," q.v.

ATKINS (ATHINS), John. Took the Oath of Allegiance before the Hon. Gerrard Briscoe on March 2, 1778 [Ref: T-3:56].

ATKINS, Joseph (b. 1736). Private, 6th Co., Lower Bn., Militia, Aug., 1777 [Ref: M-200, T-5:49, K-1:181].

ATKINS (ATHINS), William. See "William Atchison," q.v.

AUCHTERLONY (OUCHTERLONY), Patrick. "Patrick Auchterlony" lived in Seneca Hd. (one taxable) in 1777 [Ref: R-31:7]. "Patrick Ouchterlony" was a private, 1st Co., Middle Bn., Militia, Aug. 30, 1777 [Ref: M-195].

AUSTIN (AUSTON), Alexander (b. 1757). Private, 5th Co., Lower Bn., Militia, Aug., 1777 [Ref: M-200, T-5:48]. "Alexander Auston" took the Oath of Allegiance (made his "/" mark) before the Hon. Samuel W. Magruder in 1778 [Ref: T-3:73, L-1:37, K-1:181].

AUSTIN (AUSTON), John (1739-1823). Private, 5th Co., Middle Bn., Militia, Sep., 1777 [Ref: M-197, T-5:40]. "John Auston" took the Oath of Allegiance before the Hon. Samuel W. Magruder in 1778 [Ref: T-3:72, L-1:37]. Rendered aid by providing wheat for use of the military in 1780 [Ref: O-302, O-309]. Lived in Lower Potomac Hd. (three taxables) in 1777 [Ref: R-31:4]. "John Austin, Sr." died testate in Montgomery County in 1823 [Ref: V-4, K-1:181].

AUSTIN, Joseph. Private, Capt. Price's Co., 3rd Maryland Line, 1781-1782 [Ref: D-452].

AUSTIN, Thomas (b. 1760 or 1761). Private, 4th Co., Lower Bn., Militia, Aug., 1777 [Ref: M-199, T-5:47]. Private, 2nd Co., Lower Bn., Militia, July 15, 1780 [Ref: M-204, K-1:181].

AUSTIN, Zachariah (b. 1762 or 1763). Private, 2nd Co., Lower Bn., Militia, July 15, 1780 [Ref: M-204, K-1:181].

AVERY, Richard. See "Richard Abarry," q.v.

AVES, Matthew. Private, 7th Co., Middle Bn., Militia, Sep., 1777 [Ref: M-197, T-5:42]. Lived in Seneca Hd. (one taxable) in 1777 [Ref: R-31:7].

BAGGERLY, David. See "David Beggarly," q.v.

BAILEY, Basil. Private, 4th Class, 1st Co., Middle Bn., Militia, July 15, 1780 [Ref: M-201].

BAILEY (BAYLEY), George. "George Bayley" took the Oath of Allegiance in 1778 [Ref: L-2:27].

BAILEY, John. Took the Oath of Allegiance (made his "X" mark) before the Hon. Joseph Wilson on Feb. 28, 1778 [Ref: T-3:65, L-1:37]. Lived in the Upper Part of Potomac Hd. (three taxables) in 1777 [Ref: R-31:13]. "John Bailey, Sr." rendered aid by providing wheat for use of the military in 1780 and 1781 [Ref: O-317, O-384].

BAILEY, John Jr. Private, 5th Co., Middle Bn., Militia, Sep., 1777 [Ref: M-197, T-5:40]. Private, 3rd Class, 1st Co., Middle Bn., Militia, July 15, 1780 [Ref: M-201]. Took the Oath of Allegiance before the Hon. Joseph Wilson on Feb. 28, 1778 [Ref: T-3:66, L-1:37].

BAILEY (BAYLEY), Ludwick. "Ludwick Bayley" [Bayrley?] took the Oath of Allegiance in 1778 [Ref: L-2:27].

BAILEY (BAYLY), Mountjoy (b. 1755). Adjutant in Col. Murdock's Co., 1776 [Ref: K-1:181, B-113, and *Revolutionary Patriots of Frederick County, Maryland, 1775-1783*, by Henry C. Peden, Jr., 1995]. Also see "Robert Green," q.v.

BAILEY, Nicholas (Nickols). Private, 5th Co., Middle Bn., Militia, Sep., 1777 [Ref: M-196, T-5:40]. "Nicholas Bailey" took the Oath of Allegiance before the Hon. Joseph Wilson on Feb. 28, 1778 [Ref: T-3:65, L-1:37]. "Nickols Bailey" rendered aid by providing wheat for use of the military in 1781 [Ref: O-384].

BAILEY, Ruth. See "John Taylor," q.v.

BAILEY (BAYLY), William (1746-1824). Son of William Bayly (1715-1782) of Fairfax County, Virginia, and Mary Hampton, daughter of Wade Hampton, of South Carolina. Married Susannah Fraser Hawkins on June 25, 1769, and had 8 children: Robert, Samuel, William, Rebecca, Anisia Mariah, Priscilla, Sarah, and Mary. Represented Frederick County at the Convention of 1776, on the Committee of Observation and Committee of Correspondence from 1775 to 1777, served in the Lower House of Montgomery County from 1777-1782, and was a justice of Prince George's County in 1799. Served as a Captain, 4th Co., Lower (29th) Bn., Militia, on Aug. 29, 1777, and Captain, 1st Co., Lower Bn., on July 15, 1780 [Ref: M-199, M-204, T-5:47]. Took the Oath of Allegiance before the Hon. Charles Jones on Jan. 10, 1778 [Ref: L-1:37, T-3:71, which had listed the name as "Bagly"]. "Capt. William Bayly" recruited George Campbell in April, 1781 [Ref: R-33:156, X-1146]. "William Bailey" rendered aid by providing wheat for use of the military in 1780 [Ref: O-329]. "Capt. William Bayly" lived in Lower Potomac Hd. (nine taxables) in 1776-1777 [Ref: R-31:4, K-1:181]. Died near Bladensburg, Prince George's County, on March 9, 1824 [Ref: N-119, N-120].

BAKELL, Jacob. Took the Oath of Allegiance in 1778 [Ref: L-2:27].

BAKER, Charity. See "James Johnson," q.v.

BAKER, Bartain, Baston, or Boston (b. 1755). "Bartain [Bastain?] Baker" lived in Sugarland Hd. in 1776 [Ref: K-1:205]. "Boston [Baston?, Barton?] Baker" was a private, 7th Maryland Line, from June 2, 1778 to April 1, 1779, when discharged [Ref: D-190].

BAKER, John. (1) Private, 4th Co., Middle Bn., Militia, Sep., 1777 [Ref: M-196, T-5:39]. (2) Private, 2nd Co., Lower Bn., Militia, Sep., 1777 [Ref: M-198, T-5:45]. (3) Private, 5th Class, 4th Co., Middle Bn., Militia, on July 15, 1780 [Ref: M-202]. One John Baker took the Oath of Allegiance before the Hon. Edward Burgess on Feb. 28, 1778 [Ref: T-3:58, L-1:37], and another took the Oath of Allegiance (made his "X" mark) before the Hon. Samuel W. Magruder in 1778 [Ref: T-3:72, L-1:37]. One "John Baker, aged 31" lived in Sugarland Hd. in 1776, another lived in the Upper Part of Newfoundland Hd. (one taxable) in 1777, and another lived in Rock Creek Hd. (five taxables) in 1777 [Ref: K-1:214, R-31:6, R-31:15].

BAKER, Joshua. "Born in the State of New York, 27 years of age, about 5 feet 5 or 6 inches high, fresh complexion, brown hair and well made, recruited by Edward Magruder [in Montgomery County] on March 12,

1781; sent to Annapolis under the care of Lt. William Murdock on April 29, 1781." [Ref: R-33:155, R-33:157, X-1146].

BAKER, Margaret. See "Gerrard Briscoe," q.v.

BAKER, Martha. See "Barton Duley," q.v.

BAKER, William (b. 1749). Took the Oath of Allegiance before the Hon. Richard Thompson in 1778 and was also a Justice of the Peace in 1778 [Ref: T-3:75, L-1:37, C-529]. "Doctor W. Baker" was a private, 3rd Co., Lower Bn., Militia, Sep., 1777 [Ref: M-199, T-5:46]. "Dr. William Baker" lived in George Town Hd. (four taxables) in 1777 [Ref: R-31:3], and "William Baker" owned a working plantation ("quarter") in Rock Creek Hd. in 1777 [Ref: R-31:16].

BALCH, Stephen Rev. See "Benjamin Greentree" and "Elisha Williams," q.v.

BALDWIN (BALDING), Thomas. "Thomas Baldwin" was a private, 6th Co., Middle Bn., Militia, Aug., 1777 [Ref: M-197, T-5:41]. "Thomas Balding" lived in Linganore Hd. (one taxable) in 1777 [Ref: R-31:9].

BALL, Elinor. See "Laurence O'Neal," q.v.

BALL, Henry. Private, 4th Co., Middle Bn., Militia, Sep., 1777 [Ref: M-196, T-5:39]. Private, 3rd Class, 4th Co., Middle Bn., Militia, July 15, 1780 [Ref: M-202]. Took the Oath of Allegiance before the Hon. Edward Burgess on Feb. 28, 1778 [Ref: T-3:60, L-1:37]. Lived in the Upper Part of Newfoundland Hd. (one taxable) in 1777 [Ref: R-31:6].

BALL, James. Private, 5th Co., Middle Bn., Militia, Sep., 1777 [Ref: M-197, T-5:40]. Private, 2nd Co., Lower Bn., Militia, July 15, 1780 [Ref: M-204]. Took the Oath of Allegiance before the Hon. Samuel W. Magruder in 1778 [Ref: T-3:72, L-1:37]. Lived in the Upper Part of Potomac Hd. (John Ball, security) in 1777 [Ref: R-31:13]. Jams Ball married Cassandra Ellis in Montgomery County on Nov. 11, 1779 [Ref: K-2:513].

BALL, John. Private, 5th Co., Middle Bn., Militia, Sep., 1777 [Ref: M-197, T-5:40]. Took the Oath of Allegiance before the Hon. Samuel W. Magruder in 1778 [Ref: T-3:72, L-1:37]. Lived in the Upper Part of Potomac Hd. (one taxable) in 1777 [Ref: R-31:14]. See "James Ball," q.v.

BALL, John Sr. Took the Oath of Allegiance before the Hon. Samuel W. Magruder in 1778 [Ref: T-3:72, L-1:37].

BALL, Thomas. See "Laurence O'Neal," q.v.

BALLARD (BALLAD), John. Took the Oath of Allegiance before the Hon. Edward Burgess on Feb. 28, 1778 [Ref: T-3:63, L-1:37].

BALLARD (BALLAD), Richard. "Richard Ballad" took the Oath of Allegiance before the Hon. Edward Burgess on Feb. 28, 1778 [Ref: T-3:63, L-1:37]. "Richard Ballard" lived in the Lower Part of Newfoundland Hd. (one taxable) in 1777 [Ref: R-31:5].

BALLOTT (BALLETT), John. Private, 1st Co., Lower Bn., Militia, Sep., 1777 [Ref: M-198, T-5:44]. "John Ballett" was recruited to serve in the Continental Army in 1780 [Ref: D-342].

BALSER, John. Rendered aid by providing beef for use of the military in 1780 [Ref: O-344, O-352].

BANFIELD, Nancy. See "Jeremiah Plummer," q.v.

BARBER, John (Jr.). Private, 6th Co., Middle Bn., Militia, Aug., 1777 [Ref: M-197, T-5:41]. Private, 1st Co., Lower Bn., Militia, July 15, 1780 [Ref: M-204]. Took the Oath of Allegiance before the Hon. Samuel W. Magruder in 1778 [Ref: T-3:72, L-1:37]. "John Barber, Jr." took the Oath of Allegiance before the Hon. Edward Burgess on Feb. 28, 1778 [Ref: T-3:61, L-1:37].

BARBER, John Sr. Took the Oath of Allegiance before the Hon. Edward Burgess on Feb. 28, 1778 [Ref: T-3:61, L-1:37]. Rendered aid by providing wheat for use of the military in 1781 [Ref: O-379]. "John Barber" lived in Lower Potomac Hd. (one taxable) in 1777 [Ref: R-31:4]. "John Barber, Sr." lived in the Upper Part of Newfoundland Hd. (two taxables) and "John Barber" lived in Linganore Hd. (two taxables) in 1777 [Ref: R-31:6, R-31:8]. "John Barber, Sr." died testate in Montgomery County in 1812 [Ref: V-5]. One John Barber was born in 1716 [Ref: K-1:181].

BARBER, Samuel. Private, 6th Co., Middle Bn., Militia, Aug., 1777 [Ref: M-197, T-5:41]. Private, 6th Co., Middle Bn., Militia, July 15, 1780 [Ref: M-203]. Took the Oath of Allegiance (made his "X" mark) before the Hon. Joseph Wilson on Feb. 28, 1778 [Ref: T-3:66, L-1:37]. Lived in Linganore Hd. (one taxable) in 1777 [Ref: R-31:8].

BARBER, Thomas (1751-1782). Lived in George Town Hd. in 1776 [Ref: K-1:193]. Private, Marbury's Artillery, 1778 [Ref: D-575], and private, Maryland Line, enlisted May 20, 1782 [Ref: D-418]. Thomas Barber was a sergeant whose name appeared on a list of men in Brown's Maryland Artillery and he was noted as having "died in Virginia" (exact date not given). [Ref: D-584].

BARD, Erwin. Rendered aid by providing wheat for use of the military in 1781 [Ref: O-386].

BARGER, Peter. Took the Oath of Allegiance in 1778 [Ref: L-2:27].

BARKER, Annenias (Ananias). Private, 3rd Co., Middle Bn., Militia, Sep., 1777 [Ref: M-196, T-5:38]. Private, 1st Class, 2nd Co., Middle Bn., Militia, July 15, 1780 [Ref: M-201]. "Ananias Barker" rendered aid by providing wheat for use of the military in 1781 [Ref: O-393].

BARKER, Cornelius. Private, 3rd Class, 2nd Co., Middle Bn., Militia, July 15, 1780 [Ref: M-201].

BARKER, John. Private, 3rd Co., Lower Bn., Militia, July 15, 1780 [Ref: M-205].

BARKLEY, Charles. Lived in Sugarland Hd. (two taxables) in 1777 [Ref: R-31:11]. Private, 4th Co., Upper Bn., Militia, Aug. 30, 1777 [Ref: M-194, which source listed the name as "Charles Burkley"]. Took the Oath of Allegiance before the Hon. Aneas Campbell on March 2, 1778 [Ref: T-3:77, L-1:37].

BARKSHIRE, Henry. Took the Oath of Allegiance in 1778 [Ref: L-2:27].
BARLOW, Zachariah (b. 1750). Private, 4th Co., Upper Bn., Militia, Aug. 30, 1777 [Ref: M-194]. Zachariah Barlow, aged 66, lived in Sugarland Hd. in 1776. Zacheriah Barlow (one taxable) and Zacheriah Barlow, Jr. (two taxables) both lived in Sugarland Hd. in 1777 [Ref: K-1:208, R-31:11].
BARN, Clementia. See "Mark Chilton," q.v.
BARNES, Adam. Private, 1st or 32nd Bn., Militia (no date was given; possibly June, 1777). [Ref: T-5:1].
BARNES, Alexander. Private, 1st or 32nd Bn., Militia (no date was given; possibly June, 1777). [Ref: T-5:1].
BARNES, Brice. Private, 1st or 32nd Bn., Militia (no date was given; possibly June, 1777). [Ref: T-5:1].
BARNES, Elijah. Private, 1st or 32nd Bn., Militia (no date was given; possibly June, 1777). [Ref: T-5:1].
BARNES, George, of James. Served as Ensign, 1st or 32nd Bn., Militia (no date was given; possibly June, 1777). [Ref: T-5:1].
BARNES, John. Private, 1st Co., Lower Bn., Militia, Sep., 1777 [Ref: M-198, T-5:44]. Private, 3rd Class, 2nd Co., Middle Bn., Militia, July 15, 1780 [Ref: M-201]. Took the Oath of Allegiance before the Hon. William Deakins, Jr. before March 3, 1778 [Ref: T-3:68, L-1:37]. Rendered aid by providing wheat for use of the military in 1781 [Ref: O-417].
BARNES, Joseph. Private, 3rd Co., Middle Bn., Militia, Sep., 1777 [Ref: T-5:38 and M-196, which latter source questions if the name was "Barns" or "Bains"]. "Joseph Barnes" was an Ensign, 2nd Co., Middle Bn., Militia, July 15, 1780 [Ref: M-201]. Took the Oath of Allegiance before the Hon. William Deakins, Jr. before March 3, 1778 [Ref: T-3:68, L-1:38]. Rendered aid by providing wheat for use of the military in 1780 and 1781 [Ref: O-303, O-393], and served as a grand juror in 1781 [Ref: W-2]. Lived in the Upper Part of Potomac Hd. (two taxables) in 1777 [Ref: R-31:14].
BARNES, Josiah or Josias. "Josiah Barnes" took the Oath of Allegiance before the Hon. Charles Jones on Jan. 10, 1778 [Ref: T-3:71, L-1:38]. "Josias Barnes" married Elizabeth Trammel in Montgomery County on Aug. 1, 1780 [Ref: K-2:513].
BARNES, Philip. Private, 7th Co., Lower Bn., Militia, July 15, 1780 [Ref: M-207]. Took the Oath of Allegiance on Sep. 1, 1780, under the Act of May 12, 1780, having neglected to do so previously "due to ignorance of the duty owed the country." [Ref: R-27:105].
BARNES, Priscilla. See "Thomas Clark," q.v.
BARNES, Resin. Private, 1st or 32nd Bn., Militia (no date was given; possibly June, 1777). [Ref: T-5:1].
BARNES, Richard (Colonel). See "John Taylor," q.v.
BARNES, Richard Weavour. Private, Capt. Edward Burgess' Co., Lower District of Frederick (now Montgomery) County, Militia, July, 1776 [Ref:

D-42]. Took the Oath of Allegiance before the Hon. Edward Burgess on Feb. 28, 1778 [Ref: T-3:59, L-1:38].

BARNES, Sarah. See "Charles Gartrell," q.v.

BARNES, Thomas. (1) Private, 7th Co., Lower Bn., Militia, July 15, 1780 [Ref: M-206]. (2) Private, 1st Co., Lower Bn., Militia, Sep., 1777 [Ref: M-198, T-5:44].

BARNES, Weaver (Weavour, Wever). Private, 1st Co., Lower Bn., Militia, Sep., 1777 [Ref: M-198, T-5:44]. Took the Oath of Allegiance before the Hon. Edward Burgess on Feb. 28, 1778 [Ref: T-3:61, L-1:38]. "Wever Barnes" married Eliza Pigman in Montgomery County on May 13, 1779 [Ref: K-2:517]. "Weaver Barnes, Sr." lived in the Lower Part of Newfoundland Hd. (twelve taxables) in 1777 [Ref: R-31:5]. "Weavour Barnes" (wife named Elizabeth) died testate in Montgomery County in 1785 [Ref: V-5].

BARNES, William. Private, 1st or 32nd Bn., Militia (no date was given; possibly June, 1777). [Ref: T-5:1].

BARNES, Zachariah. Private, 1st or 32nd Bn., Militia (no date was given; possibly June, 1777). [Ref: T-5:1].

BARNETT (BARNET), Jacob. Private, 1st Co., Middle Bn., Militia, Aug. 30, 1777 [Ref: M-195]. Private, 5th Co., Middle Bn., Militia, July 15, 1780 [Ref: M-203]. Lived in Seneca Hd. (one taxable) in 1777 [Ref: R-31:7].

BARNOSER (BARNOVER?), Daniel. Took the Oath of Allegiance in 1778 [Ref: L-2:27].

BARR (BARRE, BARRS, BEAR), John (died 1817). "John Barre" lived in the Upper Part of Potomac Hd. (one taxable) in 1777 [Ref: R-31:15]. "John Barr" took the Oath of Allegiance in 1778 [Ref: L-2:27]. "John Barrs" was a private, 3rd Co., Middle Bn., Militia, Sep., 1777 [Ref: M-196, T-5:38]. "John Bear" died testate in Montgomery County in 1817 [Ref: V-11].

BARRANCE, Mary. See "Joshua Collins," q.v.

BARRETT (BARRATT, BARROTT), Alexander (c1758-c1790). Private, Capt. Edward Burgess' Co., Lower District of Frederick (now Montgomery) County, Militia, July, 1776 [Ref: D-42]. Private, 6th Co., Lower Bn., Militia, July 15, 1780 [Ref: M-206]. "Alexander Barrott" married Eleanor Caecil or Cecil in Montgomery County on Jan. 19, 1779 and died after 1790 [Ref: K-2:514, DAR-I:39].

BARRETT, Benjamin. Took the Oath of Allegiance before the Hon. Charles Jones on Jan. 10, 1778 [Ref: T-3:71, L-1:38].

BARRETT (BARRET), John (b. 1757). Private, 6th Co., Lower Bn., Militia, July 15, 1780 [Ref: M-206]. Took the Oath of Allegiance before the Hon. Charles Jones on Jan. 10, 1778 [Ref: T-3:71, L-1:38]. Lived in North West Hd. in 1776-1777 [Ref: K-1:232, R-31:17]. John Barrett married Mary Price in Montgomery County on Dec. 16, 1778 [Ref: K-2:514].

BARRETT (BARRATT), Ninian (1751-1806/7). "Ninian Barratt" lived in North West Hd. in 1776 [Ref: K-1:227]. Private, 8th Co., Lower Bn., Militia, Sep., 1777 [Ref: M-200, T-5:51]. "Ninian Barrett" took the Oath of Allegiance before the Hon. Charles Jones on Jan. 10, 1778 [Ref: T-3:71, L-1:38]. "Ning Barrett" rendered aid by providing wheat for use of the military in 1781 [Ref: O-453]. He married Mary James [Ref: DAR-I:39].

BARRETT, Richard (b. 1762). Private, 6th Co., Lower Bn., Militia, July 15, 1780 [Ref: M-206]. Promoted to corporal and then sergeant. His pension application (S12058) was made in Montgomery County on March 27, 1833, aged 70 years and 8 months, stating he was drafted and served as a corporal under Capt. Robert Beall in 1779. He marched that same year to George Town (now in the District of Columbia) for its protection, as the inhabitants were under dread apprehension of an attack by the vessel "Roebuck" commanded by Lord Dunmore. He continued on service there between 30 and 32 days when he was permitted to return home. In 1780 he was again called into active service under Capt. Aaron Harris and on May 1, 1780, marched from his place of residence near Bladensburg to Frederick Town in Frederick County to guard the prisoners of war. On June 1, 1780, Capt. James White appointed him Orderly Sergeant. He remained in service until discharged on Nov. 25, 1780. He was born in July, 1762, and lived at the place of his birth when drafted into service. After the war he lived in the District of Columbia and since 1822 in Montgomery County, five miles from George Town [Ref: J-49, P-168, Y-19].

BARRETT, Thomas (b. 1743). Lived in George Town Hd. in 1776 [Ref: K-1:193]. Took the Oath of Allegiance before the Hon. Richard Thompson in 1778 [Ref: T-3:75, L-1:38].

BARRICK, John. Rendered aid by providing hay for use of the military in 1781 [Ref: O-355].

BARROW, James. Private who was recruited to serve in the Extra Regiment, Continental Army, in 1780 [Ref: D-342].

BARRUCK, Alexander. Private, 7th Co., Upper Bn., Militia, Aug. 30, 1777 [Ref: M-195].

BARTH (BURTH), Andrew. "Andrew Barth" rendered aid by providing wheat for use of the military in 1781 [Ref: O-391]. "Andrew Butch(?)" [Burth, Burtle?] lived in Sugarland Hd. (two taxables) in 1777 [Ref: R-31:11]. Perhaps this is "Andrew Burtle," q.v.

BARTLE, Andrew. See "Andrew Burtle," q.v.

BASTAIN, Michael. Took the Oath of Allegiance in 1778 [Ref: L-2:27].

BATEMAN, John. Private, 7th Co., Lower Bn., Militia, Aug., 1777 [Ref: M-200, T-5:51]. Took the Oath of Allegiance before the Hon. Edward Burgess on Feb. 28, 1778 [Ref: T-3:59, L-1:38]. Lived in the Lower Part of Newfoundland Hd. (two taxables) in 1777 [Ref: R-31:5].

BATEMAN (BATMAN), Thomas (1755-1835). Private, 6th Maryland Line, 1776-1779, under Capt. Adamson Tannehill in Col. Rawlings' Regiment. Applied for pension (S35182) on Nov. 9, 1825, aged 70, while residing in Jefferson County, Kentucky. His wife (not named) was aged 67 and they had two sons "who left him about ten years ago and are laboring for themselves" and four daughters who have married, namely Polly Jeter (aged 43), Sally Shaw (aged 39), Hannah Gibbons (aged 37), John Batman (aged 35), Rachel Dunagin (aged 33), and Thomas Batman (aged 26). Thomas is buried in Jefferson County, Kentucky [Ref: P-187, Z-51, S-1993].

BATES, John. Private, 7th Co., Lower Bn., Militia, Aug., 1777 [Ref: M-200, T-5:50]. Private, 6th Co., Lower Bn., Militia, July 15, 1780 [Ref: M-206]. Lived in the Lower Part of Newfoundland Hd. (one taxable) in 1777 [Ref: R-31:5].

BATESON (BATSON), William. Private, Flying Camp, Frederick (now Montgomery) County, enlisted by Greenbury Gaither on July 29, 1776 [Ref: D-44]. Took the Oath of Allegiance (made his "V" mark) before the Hon. Edward Burgess on Feb. 28, 1778 [Ref: T-3:58, L-1:38]. "William Batteson" was a private, 1st Co., Middle Bn., Militia, Aug. 30, 1777 [Ref: M-195]. "William Batson" was a Private, 5th Co., Middle Bn., Militia, July 15, 1780 [Ref: M-203]. Lived in Sugar Loaf Hd. (one taxable) in 1777 [Ref: R-31:9].

BATHE, Theophilus. Took the Oath of Allegiance before the Hon. Gerrard Briscoe on March 2, 1778 [Ref: T-3:57, L-1:38].

BATMAN, John and Thomas. See "Thomas Bateman (Batman)," q.v.

BATTEN, William. Served as a Sergeant, Capt. Thomas Beall's Co., Maryland Line, 1780 [Ref: D-350].

BAUM, Jacob. Took the Oath of Allegiance in 1778 [Ref: L-2:27].

BAXTER, Elizabeth. See "Thomas Allison," q.v.

BAXTER, Gabriel (1746-1779). Private, 4th Co., Upper Bn., Militia, Aug. 30, 1777 [Ref: M-194]. Took the Oath of Allegiance before the Hon. Edward Burgess on Feb. 28, 1778 [Ref: T-3:63, L-1:38]. Lived in Sugarland Hd. in 1776 and had four taxables in 1777 [Ref: R-31:11, K-1:209, which latter source spelled the name "Backster"]. Died testate (wife named Elizabeth) in Montgomery County in 1779 [Ref: V-6].

BAYER, Jacob. Took the Oath of Allegiance in 1778 [Ref: L-2:27].

BAYLY, William. See "William Bailey," q.v.

BAYNE, Balter [sic]. Took the Oath of Allegiance before the Hon. Joseph Wilson on Feb. 28, 1778 [Ref: T-3:64, L-1:38].

BEACHGOOD, James. Private, 1st or 32nd Bn., Militia (no date was given; possibly June, 1777). [Ref: T-5:1].

BEACHGOOD, Michael. Private, 1st or 32nd Bn., Militia (no date was given; possibly June, 1777). [Ref: T-5:1].

BEADEN, John and Thomas. See "John and Thomas Beeding," q.v.

BEALL, Alexander. (1) Private, 4th Co., Lower Bn., Militia, Aug., 1777 [Ref: M-199, T-5:47]. Private, 8th Class, 2nd Co., Middle Bn., Militia, July 15, 1780 [Ref: M-201]. (2) Private, 6th Co., Middle Bn., Militia, July 15, 1780 [Ref: M-203]. One Alexander Beall took the Oath of Allegiance before the Hon. William Deakins, Jr. before March 3, 1778 [Ref: T-3:68, L-1:38], and another took the Oath of Allegiance on Sep. 1, 1780, under the Act of May 12, 1780, having neglected to do so previously "due to ignorance of the duty owed the country." [Ref: R-27:105]. Rendered aid by providing wheat for use of the military in 1781 [Ref: O-386]. "Alexander Beal" lived in Linganore Hd. (one taxable) in 1777 [Ref: R-31:9].

BEALL, Alexander Edmonston. Private, Capt. Edward Burgess' Co., Lower District of Frederick (now Montgomery) County, Militia, July, 1776 [Ref: D-42]. Private, 5th Co., Middle Bn., Militia, Sep., 1777 [Ref: M-197, T-5:40]. Took the Oath of Allegiance before the Hon. Edward Burgess on Feb. 28, 1778 [Ref: T-3:60, L-1:38].

BEALL, Alexander Robert (b. 1757). "Alexander Robt. Beall" lived in North West Hd. in 1776, a son of Samuel and Jane Beall [Ref: K-1:227]. "Alexander Robert Beall" was a private, Capt. Edward Burgess' Co., Lower District of Frederick (now Montgomery) County, Militia, July, 1776 [Ref: D-42]. "Robert Alexander Beall" was a private, 1st Co., Lower Bn., Militia, Sep., 1777 [Ref: M-198, T-5:44].

BEALL, Ann. See "Zadock Wilson," q.v.

BEALL, Archibald (died 1791). Took the Oath of Allegiance before the Hon. Edward Burgess on Feb. 28, 1778 [Ref: T-3:60, L-1:38]. Lived in Rock Creek Hd. (four taxables) in 1777 [Ref: R-31:15]. Died testate (wife Jane, daughter of James Edmonston) in Montgomery County in 1791 [Ref: V-6].

BEALL, Ariana. See "Basil Beall," q.v.

BEALL, Basil (1751-c1819). Private, 6th Co., Lower Bn., Militia, Aug., 1777 [Ref: T-5:49 and M-200, which latter source listed the name as ".... Beall"]. First Corporal, 3rd Co., Lower Bn., July 15, 1780 [Ref: M-205]. "Bazil Beall" took the Oath of Allegiance before the Hon. Joseph Offutt on March 2, 1778 [Ref: T-3:70, L-1:38]. "Basil Beall" rendered aid by providing beef and hay for use of the military in 1780 [Ref: O-336, O-344]. He married Arianna Beall in Montgomery County on Oct. 24, 1780 [Ref: K-2:513]. It should be noted that the *DAR Patriot Index*, Vol. I, pp. 45-46, lists three men named Basil Beall in Maryland: one (1725-1818) had a wife named Harriet and served as a lieutenant; another (1754-1824) had a wife named Anne Jourdan and rendered patriotic service; and the above Basil Beall (b. March 19, 1751), wife named Ariana.

BEALL, Brooke (1742-1798). Private, 3rd Co., Middle Bn., Militia, Sep., 1777 [Ref: M-196, T-5:38]. Clerk of the Court, 1777-1779, and was appointed "Purchaser of Cloathing" for Montgomery County on June 5,

1781 [Ref: R-31:18, W-1, G-462, DAR-I:46]. One Brooke Beall lived in Sugarland Hd. (one taxable) in 1777 and another lived in the Upper Part of Potomac Hd. (five taxables) in 1777 [Ref: R-3:11, R-31:13].

BEALL, Charles (c1750-1789). Private, married Tabitha Beall, and rendered aid by providing beef for use of the military in 1780 [Ref: O-343, DAR-I:46].

BEALL, Christiana. See "Ninian Beall," q.v.

BEALL, Clement (1734-c1790). Private, 4th Co., Lower Bn., Militia, Aug., 1777 [Ref: M-199, T-5:47]. Private, 1st Co., Lower Bn., Militia, July 15, 1780 [Ref: M-204]. Took the Oath of Allegiance before the Hon. Joseph Wilson on Feb. 28, 1778 [Ref: T-3:64, L-1:38]. County Sheriff, 1777-1779 [Ref: R-31:18, W-1]. "Clem or Clemt. Beall" lived in North West Hd. in 1776 and had four taxables in 1777 [Ref: K-1:227, R-31:17]. He married Priscilla Perry, rendered patriotic and civil service, and died after 1790 [Ref: DAR-I:46].

BEALL, Daniel. Private, 2nd Co., Lower Bn., Militia, Sep., 1777 [Ref: M-198, T-5:45]. Took the Oath of Allegiance before the Hon. Edward Burgess on Feb. 28, 1778 [Ref: T-3:60, L-1:38].

BEALL, David. Private, 7th Co., Lower Bn., Militia, Aug., 1777 [Ref: M-200, T-5:50]. Took the Oath of Allegiance before the Hon. Edward Burgess on Feb. 28, 1778 [Ref: T-3:59, L-1:38]. Lived in the Lower Part of Newfoundland Hd. (one taxable) in 1777 [Ref: R-31:5].

BEALL, Edward (1743-1798). Private, 2nd Co., Lower Bn., Militia, Sep., 1777 [Ref: M-198, T-5:45]. Private, 5th Co., Lower Bn., Militia, July 15, 1780 [Ref: M-205]. Took the Oath of Allegiance before the Hon. Edward Burgess on Feb. 28, 1778 [Ref: T-3:60, L-1:38]. Served as a grand juror in Nov., 1777 [Ref: R-31:18]. Lived in Rock Creek Hd. (four taxables) in 1777 [Ref: R-31:15]. Edward Beall, Sr. was born on Oct. 25, 1743, married Rachel Edmonston, and died testate in Montgomery County on Dec. 7, 1797 [Ref: V-6, DAR-I:46].

BEALL, Elisha (1745-1837). Served as a Lieutenant and subsequently a Captain in the Flying Camp, 1776-1777. He was born Jan. 4, 1745, married Jane Perry, and died Dec. 17, 1837 [Ref: D-44, D-45, DAR-I:46].

BEALL, Elizabeth. See "Thomas Beall, of George" and "Benjamin Greentree" and "George Beall" and "Ninian Beall," q.v.

BEALL, George. (1) First Major, 29th Bn., Militia, June 21, 1777. Major, Upper Bn., Militia, Sep. 21, 1777 [Ref: M-51, M-198, C-296, C-373, T-5:44]. (2) Private, 8th Co., Upper Bn., Militia, Aug. 30, 1777 [Ref: M-195]. Took the Oath of Allegiance before the Hon. Richard Thompson in 1778 [Ref: T-3:75, L-1:38]. One George Beall was a Justice of the County Court in 1781 [Ref: W-2]. One George Beall married Elizabeth Beall in Montgomery County on Dec. 22, 1779 [Ref: K-2:513]. Major George Beall lived in Lower Potomac Hd. (seven taxables) and Col. George Beall lived in George Town Hd. (nine taxables) in 1777 [Ref: R-31:3, R-31:4]. One George Beall died testate in Montgomery County in

1780 and another "George Beall, of Washington Co. State of Columbia" (wife named Elizabeth) died testate in Montgomery County in 1807 [Ref: V-7]. "Col. George Beall" was aged 81 in 1776 [Ref: K-1:181]. Born in 1695, he married Elizabeth Brooke Dent, rendered patriotic service, and died in 1780 [Ref: DAR-I:46]. See "Thomas Beall, of George," q.v.

BEALL, George Jr. Private, 5th Class, 2nd Co., Middle Bn., Militia, July 15, 1780 [Ref: M-201]. Took the Oath of Allegiance before the Hon. Richard Thompson in 1778 [Ref: T-3:75, L-1:38]. Lived in Sugarland Hd. (four taxables) in 1777 [Ref: R-31:11]. George Beall, Jr., of Lower Potomac Hd., was aged 46 in 1776 [Ref: K-1:181].

BEALL, George 3rd. Took the Oath of Allegiance before the Hon. Samuel W. Magruder in 1778 [Ref: T-3:73].

BEALL, Harriet. See "Thomas Beall, of George," q.v.

BEALL, Henrietta. See "Lawson Beall," q.v.

BEALL, James. Took the Oath of Allegiance (made his "B" mark) before the Hon. Edward Burgess on Feb. 28, 1778 [Ref: T-3:62, L-1:38]. Two men named James Beall lived in Rock Creek Hd. (one with eight taxables and the other with six taxables) in 1777 [Ref: R-31:15, R-31:16].

BEALL, James, of James (1728-1804). Lived in Seneca Hd. (three taxables) in 1777 [Ref: R-31:7]. Took the Oath of Allegiance before the Hon. Edward Burgess on Feb. 28, 1778 [Ref: T-3:60, L-1:38]. Died testate in Montgomery County in Feb., 1804. His wife was Mary Elizabeth Edmonston [Ref: V-8, DAR-I:46].

BEALL, James, of Ninian (died 1780). Took the Oath of Allegiance before the Hon. Joseph Wilson on Feb. 21, 1778 [Ref: T-3:64, L-1:38]. James Beall, of Ninian, died testate in Montgomery County in 1780 (wife named Ann). [Ref: V-8]. See "Ninian Beall," q.v.

BEALL, James, of Roger (or Robert?). "James Beall, of Roger" was a private, Capt. Edward Burgess' Co., Lower District of Frederick (now Montgomery) County, Militia, July, 1776 [Ref: D-42]. "James Beall, of Robert" died testate in Montgomery County in 1783 [Ref: V-8].

BEALL, Jane. See "Thaddeus Beall" and "Samuel Beall" and "Alexander Robert Beall," q.v.

BEALL, Jeremiah. (1) Private, Capt. Edward Burgess' Co., Lower District of Frederick (now Montgomery) County, Militia, July, 1776 [Ref: D-42]. Private, 2nd Co., Lower Bn., Militia, Sep., 1777 [Ref: M-198, T-5:45]. Private, 7th Co., Lower Bn., Militia, July 15, 1780 [Ref: M-206]. Took the Oath of Allegiance before the Hon. Edward Burgess on Feb. 28, 1778 [Ref: T-3:58, L-1:38]. (2) Private, 1st Co., Lower Bn., Militia, Sep., 1777 [Ref: M-198, T-5:44]. Private, 5th Co., Lower Bn., Militia, July 15, 1780 [Ref: M-206]. Took the Oath of Allegiance (made his "X" mark) before the Hon. Edward Burgess on Feb. 28, 1778 [Ref: T-3:58, L-1:38]. One Jeremiah Beall lived in Rock Creek Hd. (four taxables) in 1777

[Ref: R-31:15]. One Jeremiah Beall (wife named Sabrina) died testate in Montgomery County in 1802 [Ref: V-9]. Also see "Ninian Beall," q.v.

BEALL (BEAL), John. (1) Private, 1st Co., Lower Bn., Militia, Sep., 1777 [Ref: M-198, T-5:44]. Private, 4th Co., Lower Bn., Militia, July 15, 1780 [Ref: M-205]. (2) "John Beale" was a private, 6th Co., Middle Bn., Militia, Aug., 1777 [Ref: M-197, T-5:41]. "John Beall" was a private, 6th Co., Middle Bn., Militia, July 15, 1780 [Ref: M-203]. (3) Private, 7th Co., Lower Bn., Militia, July 15, 1780 [Ref: M-207]. Three men named John Beall took the Oath of Allegiance: one before the Hon. Edward Burgess on Feb. 28, 1778 [Ref: T-3:58, L-1:38]; another before the Hon. Richard Thompson in 1778 [Ref: T-3:75]; and another took the Oath of Allegiance on Sep. 1, 1780, under the Act of May 12, 1780, having neglected to do so previously "due to ignorance of the duty owed the country." [Ref: R-27:105]. One rendered aid by providing wheat for use of the military in 1780 and 1781 [Ref: O-330, O-386, O-443]. "John Beall" (b. 1728) lived in George Town Hd. (three taxables), "John Beal" lived in Linganore Hd. (one taxable), and "John Beall" lived in Rock Creek Hd. (one taxable) in 1777 [Ref: K-1:193, R-31:3, R-31:9, R-31:16]. One John Beall (wife named Margaret) died testate in Montgomery County in 1817 [Ref: V-9]. See "Ninian Beall" and "Charles Tracy," q.v.

BEALL, John, of Lawson. Private, 7th Co., Lower Bn., Militia, Aug., 1777 [Ref: M-200, T-5:50].

BEALL, Joseph. Took the Oath of Allegiance (made his "X" mark) before the Hon. Edward Burgess on Feb. 28, 1778 [Ref: T-3:59, L-1:38]. "Joseph Beall" rendered aid by providing wheat for use of the military in 1780 [Ref: O-320]. "Joseph Beall, Sr." lived in the Lower Part of Newfoundland Hd. (eight taxables) in 1777 [Ref: R-31:5], and "Joseph Beall" lived in North West Hd. (one taxable) in 1777 [Ref: R-31:17]. "Joseph Beall, Sr." died testate in Montgomery County in 1801 [Ref: V-9]. See "Ninian Beall," q.v.

BEALL, Joseph Belt. Took the Oath of Allegiance before the Hon. Charles Jones on Jan. 10, 1778 [Ref: T-3:71, L-1:38]. "Joseph B. Beall" was a private, 4th Co., Lower Bn., Militia, Aug., 1777 [Ref: M-199, T-5:47].

BEALL, Josephus. Private, 2nd Co., Lower Bn., Militia, Sep., 1777 [Ref: M-199, T-5:45]. Private, 5th Co., Lower Bn., Militia, July 15, 1780 [Ref: M-206].

BEALL, Josiah (b. 1758). Took the Oath of Allegiance before the Hon. Richard Thompson in 1778 [Ref: T-3:76, L-1:38, K-1:181]. See "Samuel Beall (of Richard)," q.v.

BEALL, Kinsey. Private, 3rd Co., Lower Bn., Militia, July 15, 1780 [Ref: M-205].

BEALL, Lawson (1758-1826). Lived in the Lower Part of Newfoundland Hd. (two taxables) in 1777 [Ref: R-31:5]. Private, 7th Co., Lower Bn., Militia, Aug., 1777 [Ref: M-200, T-5:50]. Took the Oath of Allegiance (made his "X" mark) before the Hon. Edward Burgess on Feb. 28, 1778 [Ref: T-3:62, L-1:38]. Lawson Beall (Beal or Bell) applied for pension on Oct. 18, 1820, in Washington, D. C., aged 62, with wife Henrietta and three children: William (aged 11), Thomas (aged 9), and Mary Ann (aged 7). Lawson died on Aug. 5, 1826, and his widow applied for pension (W23575) on March 18, 1843, aged 82, in Washington, D. C., stating her maiden name was Harris and she was married in Montgomery County by Rev. Mr. Plunkett, a Catholic. She applied for bounty land warrant #36517-160-55 on Sep. 8, 1855, aged about 93, and son William Beall signed an affidavit in 1855 [Ref: P-197].

BEALL, Leaven or Levin. (1) Private, 2nd Class, 2nd Co., Middle Bn., Militia, July 15, 1780 [Ref: M-201]. (2) Private, Capt. Edward Burgess' Co., Lower District of Frederick (now Montgomery) County, Militia, July, 1776 [Ref: D-42]. Private, 4th Co., Lower Bn., Militia, July 15, 1780 [Ref: M-205]. (3) "Leven Beall" took the Oath of Allegiance before the Hon. William Deakins, Jr. before March 3, 1778 [Ref: T-3:68, L-1:38]. (4) "Levin Beall" was a private, 3rd Co., Middle Bn., Militia, Aug., 1777 [Ref: M-196, T-5:38], and an Ensign, Middle Bn., Militia, Sep. 12, 1777 [Ref: M-51, C-373]. "Leven Beall" married Esther Campbell in Montgomery County on July 14, 1779 [Ref: K-2:513]. One Levin Beall lived in the Upper Part of Potomac Hd. (five taxables) in 1777 [Ref: R-31:13].

BEALL, Lloyd (1756-1817). Served as a Lieutenant, Captain and/or Captain Lieutenant in the 7th Maryland Line, and as a Recruiting Officer. The Collector of Tax for Montgomery County was ordered by the Council of Maryland to pay "Capt. Lieut. Wm. Lloyd Beall of the 7th Maryland Regiment" money to be expended for recruiting services in 1780. He married Elizabeth Jones [Ref: F-54, G-237, DAR-I:46]. See "James Current," q.v.

BEALL, Lucy. See "Zephaniah Offutt" and Samuel Wade Magruder," q.v.

BEALL, Margaret. See "Ninian Beall," q.v.

BEALL, Menum or Mannim (1738-c1814). "Mannim Beall" lived in the Lower Part of Newfoundland Hd. (one taxable) in 1777 [Ref: R-31:5]. "Marrum Beall" was a private, 7th Co., Lower Bn., Militia, Aug., 1777 [Ref: T-5:50 and M-200, which latter source listed the name as ".... Beall"]. "Menum Beall" took the Oath of Allegiance (made his "X" mark) before the Hon. Edward Burgess on Feb. 28, 1778 [Ref: T-3:59, L-1:38]. He married Frances Lewis [Ref: DAR-I:46].

BEALL, Mary. See "Lawson Beall" and "George Suter," q.v.

BEALL, Ninian (1761-1836). Lived in Seneca Hd. (four taxables) in 1777 [Ref: R-31:7]. Took the Oath of Allegiance before the Hon. William Deakins, Jr. before March 3, 1778 [Ref: T-3:68, L-1:38, L-2:27]. Stated that he served as a private, Maryland Line, when he applied for a pension on May 5, 1818, in Frederick County, Maryland, aged 57. In 1820 he was living in Butler County, Ohio, a resident of St. Clair

Township, with wife Christiana (aged 47) and children: John (aged 15), Joseph (aged 12), Margaret (aged 10), James (aged 8), and Sarah (aged 5). He died on June 13, 1836, and his widow applied for pension (W9722) on Nov. 12, 1839, in Ripley County, Indiana, aged 66. She stated her maiden name was Stull and she married Ninian on July 25, 1790, in Frederick County (another record indicated Aug., 1790), by Rev. William Runkle, Pastor, Frederick City Charge and neighboring congregations. She also referred to her husband as "Ning Beall." Their son Ninian was born on Oct. 27, 1792, and son Zephaniah was born on April 10, 1795. The family Bible was lost in a fire at son Zephaniah's home. Also mentioned was a "Zeremiah" Beall, of Dearborn County, Indiana, in 1835 and a Mrs. Elizabeth Beall, of Montgomery County, Indiana, in 1842, but no relationships were given [Ref: P-197, but is not listed in *Archives of Maryland, Volume 18*]. There was also a Ninian Beall who died testate in Montgomery County in 1790 [Ref: V-9, V-10]. Also see "Ningel Bell," q.v.

BEALL, Ninian, of Ninian. Served as a grand juror in 1779 [Ref: W-1].

BEALL, Ninian Edmonston. Private, 2nd Co., Lower Bn., Militia, Sep., 1777 [Ref: M-198, T-5:45]. "Ninian E. Beal" was a Private, 5th Co., Lower Bn., Militia, July 15, 1780 [Ref: M-206]. "Ninian Edmonston Beall" took the Oath of Allegiance before the Hon. Edward Burgess on Feb. 28, 1778 [Ref: T-3:58, L-1:38].

BEALL, Richard (b. 1722). Took the Oath of Allegiance before the Hon. Charles Jones on Jan. 10, 1778 [Ref: T-3:71, L-1:38]. Lived in North West Hd. (wife named Elener) in 1776 and had two taxables in 1777 [Ref: K-1:227, R-31:17].

BEALL, Richard, of Samuel (1738-1778). Served as an Ensign, 7th Co., 29th (Lower) Bn., Militia, Sep. 12, 1777 [Ref: M-51, M-200, T-5:50 C-373]. Lived in North West Hd. in 1776 and had twelve taxables in 1777 [Ref: K-1:227, R-31:17]. Died testate in Montgomery County (wife named Sarah) in 1778 [Ref: V-10].

BEALL, Robert. Served as a Captain, 8th Co., Lower Bn., Militia, Sep., 1777 [Ref: M-200, T-5:51]. Two men with this name took the Oath of Allegiance before the Hon. Edward Burgess on Feb. 28, 1778 [Ref: T-3:58, L-1:38, T-3:59, L-1:38], and a third took the Oath of Allegiance before the Hon. Charles Jones on Jan. 10, 1778 [Ref: T-3:71, L-1:38]. Rendered aid by providing wheat for use of the military in 1780 and 1781 [Ref: O-341, O-398]. One Robert Beall lived in the Lower Part of Newfoundland Hd. (one taxable), [Ref: R-31:5], another lived in the Upper Part of Potomac Hd. (four taxables), another lived in Rock Creek Hd. (one taxable), and another lived in North West Hd. (two taxables) in 1777 [Ref: R-31:5, R-31:13, R-31:16, R-31:17]. One Robert Beall died testate in Montgomery County in 1788 [Ref: V-10].

BEALL, Robert, of James (b. 1722). Performed civil service by enumerating the 1776 "census" in North West Hd. [Ref: K-1:223, K-1:230]. See "Robert Beall," q.v.

BEALL, Robert, of Ninian. Took the Oath of Allegiance before the Hon. Joseph Offutt on March 2, 1778 [Ref: T-3:70, L-1:38].

BEALL, Robert Alexander. See "Alexander Robert Beall," q.v.

BEALL, Robert Asa. Took the Oath of Allegiance before the Hon. Edward Burgess on Feb. 28, 1778 [Ref: T-3:60, L-1:38]. Served as private, 7th Co., Lower Bn., Militia, July 15, 1780 [Ref: M-206].

BEALL, Robert Edmn. Private, 7th Co., Middle Bn., Militia, Sep., 1777 [Ref: M-197, T-5:42].

BEALL, Robert L. Soldier in the Maryland Line who applied for a pension (S12164) on Feb. 26, 1833, in Washington, D. C., aged 68. He was born in 1764 or 1765 in Montgomery County and enlisted there. Tyson Bell or Beall, of Montgomery County, made an affidavit in 1833, but no relationship was given [Ref: P-197, but not listed in *Archives of Maryland, Volume 18*].

BEALL, Samuel (died 1825). Private, 2nd Co., Lower Bn., Militia, Sep., 1777 [Ref: M-198, T-5:45]. Lived in Rock Creek Hd. (two taxables) in 1777 [Ref: R-31:15]. Samuel Beall (wife not named) died testate in Montgomery County in 1825 [Ref: V-10].

BEALL, Samuel Brook (b. 1762). On June 27, 1781, Josa. Beall, Lieut. of Prince George's County, wrote to Thomas Simm Lee, Governor of Maryland, stating, in part, "At the request of Samuel Beall, son of Richard, late of Montgomery County, I have taken the liberty of recommending him as a lieutenant or ensign in the two battalions that are now to be raised." [Ref: H-320]. "Samuel Brook Beall, aged 14," was a son of Richard Beall (of Samuel) of North West Hd. in 1776 [Ref: K-1:227].

BEALL, Samuel Jr. "Samuel Beall, Jr." took the Oath of Allegiance before the Hon. Charles Jones on Jan. 10, 1778 [Ref: T-3:71, L-1:38]. "Samuel Beall (of Samuel)" was a First Lieutenant, 5th Co., Lower Bn., Militia, March 23, 1780 [Ref: M-51, M-205, F-120].

BEALL, Samuel Sr. (1706-1780). Took the Oath of Allegiance before the Hon. Edward Burgess on Feb. 28, 1778 [Ref: T-3:60, L-1:38]. Rendered aid by providing wheat for use of the military in 1780 [Ref: O-305]. Lived in North West Hd. (wife named Jane, aged 61) in 1776 and had four taxables in 1777 [Ref: K-1:227, R-31:16]. Samuel Beall, Sr. (wife named Jane) died testate in Montgomery County in Dec., 1780 [Ref: V-11].

BEALL, Sarah. See "Ninian Beall," q.v.

BEALL (BEALE), Seybert. "Seybert Beale" was a private, 3rd Co., Lower Bn., Militia, Sep., 1777 [Ref: M-199, T-5:46]. "S. Sebert Beall" lived in George Town Hd. in 1776, aged 14, and was apparently a son of "John Beall," q.v., aged 48 [Ref: K-1:193].

BEALL, Tabitha. See "Charles Beall," q.v.
BEALL, Thaddeus (1747-1815). Lived in the Lower Part of Newfoundland Hd. (ten taxables) in 1777 [Ref: R-31:5]. Served as a Second Lieutenant, Lower District, Frederick County (now Montgomery), Militia, July 20, 1776, First Lieutenant, 29th Bn., Militia, June 21, 1777, and Captain, 7th Co., Lower Bn., Sep. 12, 1777, and Brigade Major [Ref: D-42, M-51, M-200, T-5:50, C-373]. Took the Oath of Allegiance before the Hon. Charles Jones on Jan. 10, 1778 [Ref: T-3:71, L-1:38]. Thaddeus Beall married Jane Beall [Ref: DAR-I:46].
BEALL, Thomas. (1) First Lieutenant, Middle Bn., Militia, Sep., 1777. Served as Captain Commandant of the Maryland part of Col. Rawlings' Regiment in the service of the United States from May, 1779, perhaps as early as July 25, 1776, to at least Aug. 16, 1780 [Ref: M-196, D-90, D-350, F-83]. Captain Thomas Beall lived in Lower Potomac Hd. (four taxables) in 1777 [Ref: R-31:4]. (2) Private, Capt. Edward Burgess' Co., Lower District of Frederick (now Montgomery) County, Militia, July, 1776 [Ref: D-42]. Private, 8th Co., Lower Bn., Militia, Sep., 1777 [Ref: M-200, T-5:51]. Ensign, 6th Co., Lower Bn., Militia, July 15, 1780 [Ref: M-51, M-206, F-248]. One Thomas Beall took the Oath of Allegiance before the Hon. Charles Jones on Jan. 10, 1778 [Ref: T-3:71, L-1:38], and another took the Oath of Allegiance before the Hon. Joseph Offutt on March 2, 1778 [Ref: T-3:70, L-1:38]. One Thomas Beall was a Justice of the County Court in 1781 [Ref: W-2]. One Thomas Beall was born in July, 1761, in Maryland, and applied for pension (S45270) on June 26, 1818, in Preble County, Ohio [Ref: P-197]. Thomas Beall married Catherine Brown in Montgomery County on Jan. 14, 1779 [Ref: K-2:515]. One Thomas Beall lived in the Upper Part of Potomac Hd. (three taxables) in 1777 [Ref: R-31:13]. Also see "Lawson Beall" and "John Ford" and "Charles Tracy," q.v.
BEALL, Thomas Brook (b. 1763). Son of Richard Beall, of Samuel, of North West Hd., in 1776 [Ref: K-1:227]. Served as Third Corporal, 6th Co., Lower Bn., Militia, July 15, 1780 [Ref: M-206]. A "Thomas B. Beall" was Bailiff for the County Court in 1781 [Ref: W-2].
BEALL, Thomas E. Private, 5th Co., Middle Bn., Militia, Sep., 1777 [Ref: M-197, T-5:40]. Private, 7th Class, 1st Co., Middle Bn., Militia, July 15, 1780 [Ref: M-201].
BEALL, Thomas, of Allen. Private, 4th Co., Lower Bn., Militia, July 15, 1780 [Ref: M-204]. Thomas Allen Beall (1762-c1826) served as a private during the war [Ref: DAR-I:46].
BEALL, Thomas, of George (1734-1819). Son of Col. George Beall (1695-1780) and wife Elizabeth Brooke (1699-1748). Married Nancy, granddaughter of John Orme, and had two daughters, Elizabeth and Harriet Ann (twins). Took the Oath of Allegiance before the Hon. William Deakins, Jr. before March 3, 1778. Private, 8th Co., Lower Bn., Militia, July 15, 1780, and Justice of Montgomery County, 1780-1785

[Ref: N-125, M-207, T-3:68, L-1:38]. He was appointed "Auctioner" of Montgomery County on March 2, 1781 [Ref: G-3343], and recruited William Veale Stewart in April, 1781 [Ref: R-33:156, X-1146].

BEALL, Tyson (Tison). Private, 7th Co., Lower Bn., Militia, Aug., 1777, and First Corporal, 4th Co., July 15, 1780 [Ref: M-200, M-205, T-5:50]. "Tison Beall" lived in the Lower Part of Newfoundland Hd. (one taxable) in 1777 [Ref: R-31:5]. See "Robert L. Beall," q.v.

BEALL, Walter. Lived in the Lower Part of Newfoundland Hd. (nine taxables) in 1777 [Ref: R-31:5]. Took the Oath of Allegiance before the Hon. Edward Burgess on Feb. 28, 1778 [Ref: T-3:59, L-1:38]. Justice of the Peace in 1778 and Justice of the County Court in 1779-1781 [Ref: C-529, W-1, W-2].

BEALL, William. See "Lawson Beall" and "Lloyd Beall," q.v.

BEALL, Zachariah (1742-1817). Private, 8th Co., Lower Bn., Militia, Sep., 1777 [Ref: M-200, T-5:51]. Private, 6th Co., Lower Bn., Militia, July 15, 1780 [Ref: M-206]. Took the Oath of Allegiance before the Hon. Samuel W. Magruder in 1778 [Ref: T-3:73]. Rendered aid by providing wheat for use of the military in 1780 [Ref: O-306]. Lived in North West Hd. (one taxable) in 1776-1777 [Ref: K-1:230, R-31:17]. Zachariah Beall (1742-1817) married Rebecca Tyson and another Zachariah Beall (1761-1826) married Nancy Evans. Both served as privates [Ref: DAR-I:46].

BEALL, Zephaniah. (1) Ensign, 16th (Middle) Bn., Militia, June 25, 1776, and Lieutenant, 3rd Co., Middle Bn., Sep. 4, 1777, Second Lieutenant, 1st Co., 29th (Lower) Bn., Militia, Sep. 12, 1777, and Captain, Middle Bn., from April 21, 1779, to at least March 25, 1780. He was born on Feb. 15, 1753 and died on June 15, 1809; wife named Anne [Ref: D-42, M-52, C-373, E-357, F-120, M-196, M-198, T-5:44, DAR-I:46]. (2) Private, 2nd Co., Lower Bn., Militia, Sep., 1777 [Ref: M-198, T-5:45]. Private, 7th Co., Lower Bn., Militia, July 15, 1780 [Ref: M-207]. Two men with this name took the Oath of Allegiance before the Hon. Edward Burgess on Feb. 28, 1778 [Ref: T-3:58, T-3:60, L-1:38], and another took the Oath of Allegiance before the Hon. William Deakins, Jr. before March 3, 1778 [Ref: T-3:68]. One Zephaniah Beall lived in the Upper Part of Potomac Hd. (two taxables) and another lived in Rock Creek Hd. (two taxables) in 1777 [Ref: R-31:13, R-31:16]. Zephaniah Beall (1753-1809) married Ann Gattrell in Montgomery County on Feb. 5, 1778 [Ref: K-2:516]. Also see "Ninian Beall," q.v.

BEALL, Zephaniah, of James. Private, 5th Co., Lower Bn., Militia, July 15, 1780 [Ref: M-206].

BEALL, Zeremiah (Jeremiah?). See "Ninian Beall," q.v.

BEAMER, Henry. Took the Oath of Allegiance in 1778 [Ref: L-2:27].

BEAN, Benjamin. Private, 3rd Co., Lower Bn., Militia, July 15, 1780 [Ref: M-205]. "Benjamin Beane" rendered aid by providing wheat for use of the military in 1781 [Ref: O-419].

BEAN, Christopher. Private, 8th Co., Middle Bn., Militia, Sep., 1777 [Ref: M-198, T-5:43]. Private, 6th Co., Lower Bn., Militia, July 15, 1780 [Ref: M-206]. "Christopher Beans" took the Oath of Allegiance before the Hon. Joseph Wilson on Feb. 28, 1778 [Ref: T-3:64, L-1:38].

BEAN, Josiah. (1) Private, 8th Co., Middle Bn., Militia, Sep., 1777. Private, 8th Class, 1st Co., Middle Bn., Militia, July 15, 1780 [Ref: M-198, M-201, T-5:43]. (2) Private, 6th Co., Lower Bn., Militia, July 15, 1780 [Ref: M-206]. "Josiah Beanes" died testate in Montgomery County in 1822 [Ref: V-11].

BEAN (BEEN), Thomas (b. 1758). Private, 11th Bn., Prince George's County, Aug. 21, 1776 [Ref: D-38]. Lived in George Town Hd. (now Montgomery County) on Aug. 22, 1776 [Ref: K-1:193].

BEAR, Jean. See "Joseph White," q.v.

BEARDEN (BOARDON), John. Took the Oath of Allegiance before the Hon. Charles Jones on Jan. 10, 1778 [Ref: T-3:71].

BEARDSLEY, D. D. See "William Byall," q.v.

BEASLEY (BEEZLEY), Moses (b. 1716). Took the Oath of Allegiance before the Hon. Charles Jones on Jan. 10, 1778 [Ref: T-3:71, L-1:38, K-1:181].

BEATTY, Charles (c1736-1804). Resided in Georgetown, Montgomery County, by 1783. Revolutionary War service rendered in Frederick County [Ref: N-126]. "Charles Beatty, of Frederick County," died testate in Montgomery County in 1804 (wife named Martha). [Ref: V-11. See *Revolutionary Patriots of Frederick County, 1775-1783*, by Henry C. Peden, Jr. (1995) for more information].

BEATTY, John. Private, 8th Co., Lower Bn., Militia, July 15, 1780 [Ref: M-207].

BEATTY, Thomas, of Thomas. Private, 8th Co., Lower Bn., Militia, July 15, 1780 [Ref: M-207].

BEATTY, William. Private, Capt. Thomas Beall's Co., Maryland Line, 1780 [Ref: D-351]. Took the Oath of Allegiance in 1778 [Ref: L-2:27].

BECKENBAUGH, Leonard and Michael. See "Leonard Peckinbaugh," q.v.

BECKETT, James. Took the Oath of Allegiance in 1778 [Ref: L-2:27].

BECKETT, William. Took the Oath of Allegiance in 1778 [Ref: L-2:27].

BECKWITH, Ann (Anna, Leannah). See "George Beckwith," q.v.

BECKWITH, Basil (1703-1780). Took the Oath of Allegiance before the Hon. Joseph Wilson on Feb. 28, 1778 [Ref: T-3:66, L-1:38]. Lived in Seneca Hd. (three taxables) in 1777, and married Volinda Clagett [Ref: R-31:7, DAR-I:49]. See "Volinda (Beckworth) Beckwith," q.v.

BECKWITH, Elizabeth. See "George Beckwith," q.v.

BECKWITH, George. There were two men with this name: one was a Captain and the other a Sergeant, Maryland Militia. The latter pensioned in Montgomery County and was paid in the District of Columbia in 1835. Applied for pension on March 25, 1833, stating he was born near Fredericktown, Frederick County, Maryland, on Nov. 16,

1760, and entered the Revolutionary War in July, 1776 under Capt. George Beckwith and Lt. John Lilly. They marched from Frederick to George Town to guard that town against the depredation of Governor Dunmore and returned home after two weeks, at which time his father removed him from service, with the consent of his captain, because he was under age 18 and had volunteered against the wishes of his father. In 1778 he again volunteered and served six months under the same captain and was stationed at Frederick Town to guard the Hessians who were kept prisoners of war in the old barracks there. He served under Colonel Bailey and the adjutant was Peter Minn(?), a Dutchman with one eye. Affidavits in support of his service were given by Charles Saffell (drummer), James B. Higgins, and Capt. George Beckwith (no relation was stated). On Dec. 16, 1858, Martha Beckwith, daughter of George, granted power of attorney to John O. Harry, of Washington, D. C., to ask for a pension for her father's service. In 1855 Leannah Beckwith, widow of George, applied for bounty land warrant #91507-160-55. Van Swearingen stated in April 4, 1851, that he had known George Beckwith for 60 years and George married Ann Clarkson (Classon?) in 1790 and died in Montgomery County in 1850. George R. Braddock also stated he knew George Beckwith about 60 years and he died in 1849. Ann or Leannah Beckwith applied for pension (W9355) on Sep. 17, 1850, in Montgomery County, aged 77 or 78, stating she had married George in Oct., 1781, and they lived in Prince George's County for a short time after the war and then moved to Montgomery County. George died on Dec. 13, 1849, and she lived in Washington, D. C. in 1855, aged about 80 [Ref: P-209, Y-20, Y-21, J-49]. Elizabeth Beckwith, daughter of George and Leean, was born Jan. 31, 1793. William Beckwith, son of George and Anna, was born Jan. 22, 1796. Ann Beckwith, son of George and Leean, was born March 24, 1798. Oratio Beckwith, son of George and Lean [sic], was born Jan. 18, 1801 [Ref: K-2:543, K-2:544, K-2:546, K-2:553].

BECKWITH, John. Private, 1st Co., Middle Bn., Militia, Aug. 30, 1777 [Ref: M-195]. Private, 5th Co., Middle Bn., Militia, July 15, 1780 [Ref: M-203]. Took the Oath of Allegiance before the Hon. Joseph Wilson on Feb. 28, 1778 [Ref: T-3:66, L-1:38]. Rendered aid by providing wheat for use of the military in 1781 [Ref: O-444]. Lived in Seneca Hd. (one taxable) in 1777 [Ref: R-31:7].

BECKWITH, Martha and Oratio. See "George Beckwith," q.v.

BECKWITH (BECKWORTH), Volinda. Widow of "Basil Beckwith," q.v. Rendered aid by providing wheat for use of the military in 1780 [Ref: O-305].

BECKWITH, William. Private, 2nd Co., Lower Bn., Militia, Sep., 1777 [Ref: M-198, T-5:45]. Took the Oath of Allegiance before the Hon. Joseph Wilson on Feb. 28, 1778 [Ref: T-3:66, L-1:38]. Served as a petit juror in Nov., 1777 [Ref: R-31:18]. Lived in Rock Creek Hd. (four taxables) in 1777 [Ref: R-31:15]. See "George Beckwith," q.v.

BECKWORTH, John. Rendered aid by providing wheat for use of the military in 1780 [Ref: O-305]. See "John Beckwith," q.v.

BECRAFT, Benjamin Jr. (1741-1806). Private, 3rd Co., Lower Bn., Militia, Sep., 1777 [Ref: M-199, T-5:46], and Private, 8th Co., Lower Bn., Militia, July 15, 1780 [Ref: M-207]. "Benjamin Becraft, Jr." took the Oath of Allegiance before the Hon. Richard Thompson in 1778 [Ref: T-3:75, L-1:38]. "Benjamin Becraft, Jr., aged 35" lived in George Town Hd. in 1776 [Ref: K-1:193], and "Benjamin Becraft" lived in George Town Hd. (one taxable) in 1777 [Ref: R-31:3]. "Benjamin Becraft, aged 67" lived in North West Hd. in 1776 and had seven taxables in 1777 [Ref: K-1:227 which listed the name as "Benjaman Bocraft," and Ref: R-31:17 which mistakenly listed the name as "Benjamin Mecraft"]. "Benjamin Becraft" died testate in Montgomery County in 1806 and mentioned his brother Peter Becraft in his will [Ref: V-11]. Benjamin Becraft (1710-1800) served as a private and also rendered patriotic service [Ref: DAR-I:49].

BECRAFT, Luraner. See "James Higgins," q.v.

BECRAFT, Peter (1740-1811). Private, 1st Co., Lower Bn., Militia, July 15, 1780 [Ref: M-204]. Took the Oath of Allegiance before the Hon. Samuel W. Magruder in 1778 [Ref: T-3:73, L-1:38, which latter source mistakenly listed the name as "Peter Beirait"]. "Peter Becraft" rendered aid by providing wheat for use of the military in 1780 [Ref: O-307]. "Charles Peter Becraft" rendered aid by providing wheat for use of the military in 1780 [Ref: O-325]. "Peter Becraft" lived in North West Hd. in 1776 (wife named Mary, aged 25) and had five taxables in 1777 [Ref: K-1:227, which listed the name as "Petter Bocraft," and Ref: R-31:17 mistakenly listed the name as "Peter Mecraft"]. He was born on Nov. 5, 1740, married Martha Nixon, and died on Nov. 5, 1811 [Ref: DAR-I:49]. See "Benjamin Becraft," q.v.

BEDDO, Absolom (c1754-1807). Lived in the Lower Part of Newfoundland Hd. (six taxables) in 1777 [Ref: R-31:5]. Private, 7th Co., Lower Bn., Militia, Aug., 1777 [Ref: M-200, T-5:50, which misspelled the name as "Bedds"], and Private, 4th Co., Lower Bn., Militia, July 15, 1780 [Ref: M-205]. Took the Oath of Allegiance before the Hon. Edward Burgess on Feb. 28, 1778 [Ref: T-3:62, L-1:38, which misspelled the name as "Bedds"]. "Absolem or Absolum Beddo" (wife named Mary) died testate in Montgomery County in 1807 [Ref: V-12, DAR-I:49].

BEDDO, James. Took the Oath of Allegiance before the Hon. Edward Burgess on Feb. 28, 1778 [Ref: T-3:62, L-1:38, which source misspelled the name as "Bedds"].

BEEDING, Edward (b. 1741). Private, 4th Co., Upper Bn., Militia, Aug. 30, 1777 [Ref: M-194]. Lived in Sugarland Hd. (one taxable) in 1776-1777 [Ref: K-1:206, R-31:11].

BEEDING, Henry (b. 1749). Private, 4th Co., Upper Bn., Militia, Aug. 30, 1777 [Ref: M-194]. "Henary Beegding" lived in Sugarland Hd. in 1776 [Ref: K-1:204].
BEEDING (BEADEN, BEEDON, BETON), John. "John Beton" was a private, 8th Co., Lower Bn., Militia, Sep., 1777 [Ref: M-200, T-5:51]. "John Beedon" was a wagoner for the military who carried arms and accoutrements to George Town in June, 1781 [Ref: H-304]. "John Beaden" was a private, Capt. Edward Burgess' Co., Lower District of Frederick (now Montgomery) County, Militia, July, 1776 [Ref: D-42]. Private, 6th Co., Lower Bn., Militia, July 15, 1780 [Ref: M-206].
BEEDING, Joseph (b. 1751). Private, 4th Co., Upper Bn., Militia, Aug. 30, 1777 [Ref: M-194]. Lived in Sugarland Hd. (one taxable) in 1776-1777 [Ref: K-1:206, R-31:11].
BEEDING, Thomas (b. 1739). "Thomas Beeding" was a private, 4th Co., Upper Bn., Militia, Aug. 30, 1777 [Ref: M-194]. "Thomas Beaden" took the Oath of Allegiance before the Hon. Edward Burgess on March 10, 1778 [Ref: T-3:63, L-1:38]. "Thomas Beeding" lived in Sugarland Hd. in 1776 and had three taxables in 1777 [Ref: K-1:213, R-31:11].
BEGGARLY, Benjamin. Private, 2nd Co., Lower Bn., Militia, Sep., 1777 [Ref: M-198, T-5:45]. Private, 5th Co., Lower Bn., Militia, July 15, 1780 [Ref: M-206]. Took the Oath of Allegiance before the Hon. Edward Burgess on Feb. 28, 1778 [Ref: T-3:58, L-1:38]. Rendered aid by providing wheat for use of the military in 1780 [Ref: O-323, O-332].
BEGGARLY (BAGGERLY, BEGERLY), David (1761-1817). Private, 8th Co., Middle Bn., Militia, Sep., 1777. Private, 5th Co., Lower Bn., Militia, July 15, 1780 [Ref: M-198, M-206, T-5:43]. "David Beggarly, a draught from Montgomery County" was discharged from the Maryland Line on Dec. 8, 1781 [Ref: I-17, D-406]. "David Baggerly" was born on Jan. 19, 1761, and married Rebecca Belt (b. on Jan. 5, 1761, daughter of Thomas Belt) on May 19, 1782, at her father's house in Montgomery County. Their children were: Thomas (b. March 22, 1783); Benjamin (b. Feb. 23, 1785); Rebecca (b. Aug. 19, 1787); David (b. Aug. 16, 1790); Selah (b. May 22, 1792); Daughter (name not stated, born April 27, 1795); David Belt (b. Sep. 4, 1797); and, Ethiel (b. Oct. 29, 1800, and married on Oct. 7, 1819, to Archibald McKee who was born May 27, 1791). "Captain David Baggarly" died Dec. 18, 1817, in Iredell County, North Carolina. His widow applied for bounty land warrant #29860-160-55 on Sep. 1, 1855, in Lincoln County, Tennessee, and also received a pension (W8120) for his service in the Maryland Line [Ref: P-111 and K-2:515, which latter source states they were married on May 20, 1782, by Rev. James Hunt]. "David Begerly" lived in Rock Creek Hd. (one taxable) in 1777 [Ref: R-31:16].
BEGGARLY (BEGARLY), Henry (b. 1746). Private, 8th Co., Lower Bn., Militia, Sep., 1777 [Ref: M-200, T-5:51]. Private, 6th Co., Lower Bn.,

Militia, July 15, 1780 [Ref: M-206]. Lived in North West Hd. (wife named Elizabeth, aged 26) in 1776 [Ref: K-1:227].

BELL, John. Private, 5th Co., Lower Bn., Militia, Aug., 1777 [Ref: M-199, T-5:48].

BELL, Ningel. Rendered aid by providing wheat for use of the military in 1781 [Ref: O-395]. See "Ninian Beall," q.v.

BELL, Rebecca and Thomas. See "David Beggarly," q.v.

BELSER, Peter. Took the Oath of Allegiance in 1778 [Ref: L-2:27].

BELT, Carlton (1744-1802). Private, 8th Co., Upper Bn., Militia, Aug. 30, 1777, and Ensign, 16th Bn., Militia, Sep. 12, 1777 [Ref: M-52, M-195, C-373]. Took the Oath of Allegiance before the Hon. Aneas Campbell on March 2, 1778 [Ref: T-3:77, L-1:38]. Lived in Sugarland Hd. in 1776 (wife named Mary) and had six taxables in 1777 [Ref: K-1:214, R-31:11]. "Carlton Belt, Sr." (wife named Ann) died testate in Montgomery County in 1802 [Ref: V-13].

BELT, Elizabeth. See "Thomas Sprigg" and "Aneas Campbell," q.v.

BELT, Esther. See "Walter Smith," q.v.

BELT, Greenbury or Greenberry. Private, 8th Co., Middle Bn., Militia, Sep., 1777 [Ref: M-198, T-5:43]. Private, 7th Co., Middle Bn., Militia, July 15, 1780 [Ref: M-203]. "Greenberry Belt" took the Oath of Allegiance on Sep. 1, 1780, under the Act of May 12, 1780, having neglected to do so previously "due to ignorance of the duty owed the country." [Ref: R-27:105]. "Greenbury Bell" [Belt] lived in Seneca Hd. (one taxable) in 1777 [Ref: R-31:7].

BELT (BEALT, BETTS), Higginson. Took the Oath of Allegiance before the Hon. Elisha Williams on March 2, 1778 [Ref: T-3:81, L-1:38]. A "Higginson Betts" [sic] took the Oath of Allegiance before the Hon. Gerrard Briscoe on March 2, 1778 [Ref: T-3:57]. "Higason Bealt" rendered aid by providing wheat for use of the military in 1781 [Ref: O-388, O-391]. "Higginson Bell" [sic] lived in Seneca Hd. (six taxables) in 1777 [Ref: R-31:7], and "Higinson or Higginson Belt, aged 31" lived in Sugarland Hd. in 1776 and had four taxables in 1777 [Ref: R-31:11]. One Higginson Belt (wife named Sarah) died testate in Montgomery County in 1788 [Ref: V-13]. See "Leonard Belt," q.v.

BELT, John (c1743-1814). Private, 3rd Co., Upper Bn., Militia, Aug. 30, 1777 [Ref: M-193]. Took the Oath of Allegiance before the Hon. Gerrard Briscoe on March 2, 1778 [Ref: T-3:56, L-1:38]. Lived in Sugar Loaf Hd. (four taxables) in 1777 [Ref: R-31:9]. Died testate in Montgomery County in 1814 [Ref: V-13].

BELT, Joseph (1716-1793). Took the Oath of Allegiance before the Hon. Richard Thompson in 1778 [Ref: T-3:75, L-1:38]. Lived in George Town Hd. (two taxables) in 1776-1777 and also had a working plantation ("quarter") in Lower Potomac Hd. [Ref: K-1:193, R-31:3, R-31:4]. There was a "Joseph Belt, Quaker" in Lower Potomac Hd. (one taxable) in

1777 [Ref: R-31:4]. One Joseph Belt married Mary Smith and died on June 16, 1793 [Ref: DAR-I:52]. See "Leonard Belt," q.v.

BELT, Joseph Sprigg. Private, 4th Co., Lower Bn., Militia, Aug., 1777 [Ref: M-199, T-5:47]. Private, 1st Co., Lower Bn., Militia, July 15, 1780 [Ref: M-204]. Lived in Lower Potomac Hd. (ten taxables) in 1777 [Ref: R-31:4].

BELT, Keziah. See "Joshua Lazenby," q.v.

BELT, Leonard (1727-1793). Lived in Lower Potomac Hd. (two taxables) in 1776-1777 [Ref: R-31:4, K-1:181]. Rendered aid by providing wheat for use of the military in 1780 [Ref: O-307, O-317]. Died testate in Montgomery County in 1793 and mentioned his brothers Joseph Belt and Higginson Belt in his will [Ref: V-13].

BELT, Middleton (1747-1807). Private, 8th Co., Lower Bn., Militia, July 15, 1780 [Ref: M-207. He married Mary Ann Dyer and served in a civil capacity [Ref: DAR-1:52].

BELT, Rebecca. See "David Beggarly," q.v.

BELT, Thomas. Private, 2nd Co., Lower Bn., Militia, Sep., 1777 [Ref: T-5:45]. Private, 5th Co., Lower Bn., Militia, July 15, 1780 [Ref: M-206]. Took the Oath of Allegiance before the Hon. Edward Burgess on Feb. 28, 1778 [Ref: T-3:60, L-1:38]. Rendered aid by providing wheat for use of the military in 1780 [Ref: O-341]. Lived in Rock Creek Hd. (four taxables) in 1777 [Ref: R-31:16]. Moved to Iredell County, North Carolina in 1786 and circa 1802 helped found the New Hope Baptist Church. For a more detailed family history, see Mary E. Lazenby's *Thomas Belt of Montgomery County, Maryland and Iredell County, North Carolina* (1960). Also see "David Beggarly," q.v.

BENJAMIN, Abraham (Abram). Private, 5th Co., Middle Bn., Militia, Sep., 1777 [Ref: M-197, T-5:40]. "Abram Benjamin" took the Oath of Allegiance (made his "A" mark) before the Hon. Joseph Wilson on Feb. 24, 1778 [Ref: T-3:64, L-1:38]. "Abraham Benjamin" lived in the Upper Part of Potomac Hd. (one taxable) in 1777 [Ref: R-31:14].

BENNETT, John. (1) Private, 8th Co., Lower Bn., Militia, Sep., 1777 [Ref: M-200, T-5:51]. (2) Private, 2nd Co., Upper Bn., Militia, Aug. 30, 1777 [Ref: M-193]. One John Bennett was a private who enrolled into a company of militia for the service of the Flying Camp on Oct. 15, 1776 [Ref: B-352]. "John Bennet" lived in Sugar Loaf Hd. (three taxables) in 1777 [Ref: R-31:9].

BENSON, John. Private, 4th Co., Lower Bn., Militia, July 15, 1780 [Ref: M-205].

BENSON, Thomas. Private, 4th Co., Lower Bn., Militia, July 15, 1780 [Ref: M-205].

BENSON, William. Private, 2nd Co., Middle Bn., Militia, Sep. 4, 1777 [Ref: M-196, T-5:37], and Fourth Sergeant, 3rd Co., Middle Bn., Militia, July 15, 1780 [Ref: M-202]. Took the Oath of Allegiance before the Hon. Gerrard Briscoe on March 2, 1778 [Ref: T-3:56, L-1:38]. Served as a grand juror in Aug., 1777 [Ref: R-31:17]. Rendered aid by providing corn for use of the military in 1780 [Ref: O-298]. One William Benson lived in Linganore Hd. (one taxable) in 1777 and another lived in Sugar Loaf Hd. (three taxables) in 1777 [Ref: R-31:8, R-31:9].

BENSON, William Thomas. Rendered aid by providing wheat for use of the military in 1781 [Ref: O-380]. Lived in the Upper Part of Newfoundland Hd. (three taxables) in 1777 [Ref: R-31:6].

BENTON, Benjamin Smith. Private, 5th Co., Lower Bn., Militia, Aug., 1777, and Second Corporal 2nd Co., Lower Bn., July 15, 1780 [Ref: M-199, M-204, T-5:48]. "Benjamin S. Benton" took the Oath of Allegiance before the Hon. Samuel W. Magruder in 1778 [Ref: T-3:73]. "Benjamin Benton" was born in 1760 [Ref: K-1:181].

BENTON, Joseph. Private, 2nd Co., Lower Bn., Militia, Sep., 1777 [Ref: M-198, T-5:45]. Took the Oath of Allegiance (made his "B" mark) before the Hon. Samuel W. Magruder in 1778 [Ref: T-3:73, L-1:38]. Rendered aid by providing wheat for use of the military in 1780 [Ref: O-313]. "Joseph Benton" lived in Lower Potomac Hd. (five taxables) in 1777 [Ref: R-31:4], and "Joseph Bonton" lived in Rock Creek Hd. (three taxables) in 1777 [Ref: R-31:16]. One Joseph Benton (wife named Rachel) died testate in Montgomery County in 1807 and another Joseph Benton (wife named Ann) died testate in Montgomery County in 1815 [Ref: V-14, V-15]. One Joseph Benton was born in 1724 [Ref: K-1:181].

BENTON, Nathan (b. 1763 or 1764). Private, 2nd Co., Lower Bn., Militia, July 15, 1780 [Ref: M-204, K-1:181].

BENTON, Thomas. Private, 2nd Co., Middle Bn., Militia, Sep. 4, 1777 [Ref: M-196, T-5:37].

BENTON, William. Private, 5th Co., Lower Bn., Militia, Aug., 1777 [Ref: M-199, T-5:48]. Private, 2nd Co., Lower Bn., Militia, July 15, 1780 [Ref: M-204]. Took the Oath of Allegiance before the Hon. Samuel W. Magruder in 1778 [Ref: T-3:73]. Rendered aid by providing wheat for use of the military in 1780 [Ref: O-313].

BERGER, John. Took the Oath of Allegiance in 1778 [Ref: L-2:27].

BERNARD, Jacob. Took the Oath of Allegiance before the Hon. Gerrard Briscoe on March 2, 1778 [Ref: T-3:56, L-1:38].

BERNOND, Burdit Gray. Took the Oath of Allegiance before the Hon. Gerrard Briscoe on March 2, 1778 [Ref: L-1:38, T-1:37, which latter source listed the name as "Brudit Gray Brnond(?)"].

BERRY, Jeremiah. Private, 1st Co., Lower Bn., Militia, Sep., 1777 [Ref: M-198, T-5:44]. Private, 4th Co., Lower Bn., Militia, July 15, 1780 [Ref: M-205]. Took the Oath of Allegiance before the Hon. Edward Burgess on Feb. 28, 1778 [Ref: T-3:59, L-1:38]. Lived in the Lower Part of Newfoundland Hd. (two taxables) in 1777 [Ref: R-31:5].

BERRY, John (died 1786). Took the Oath of Allegiance before the Hon. Edward Burgess on Feb. 28, 1778 [Ref: T-3:59, L-1:38]. Rendered aid by providing wheat for use of the military in 1780 [Ref: O-306]. Lived in

the Lower Part of Newfoundland Hd. (five taxables) in 1777 [Ref: R-31:5]. John Berry (wife named Eleanor) died testate in Montgomery County in 1786 [Ref: V-14].
BERRY, Nicholas. Private, 2nd Co., Lower Bn., Militia, Sep., 1777 [Ref: M-199, T-5:45]. Took the Oath of Allegiance before the Hon. Edward Burgess on Feb. 28, 1778 [Ref: T-3:58, L-1:38].
BERRY, Richard (died 1819). Private, 5th Co., Upper Bn., Militia, Aug. 30, 1777 [Ref: M-194]. Took the Oath of Allegiance before the Hon. Edward Burgess on Feb. 28, 1778 [Ref: T-3:58, L-1:38]. Rendered aid by providing wheat for use of the military in 1780 [Ref: O-318]. Lived in the Lower Part of Newfoundland Hd. (eight taxables) in 1777 [Ref: R-31:5]. Died testate in Montgomery County in 1819 [Ref: V-15].
BERRY, Ruth. See "Samuel Griffith," q.v.
BERRY, William W. See "Samuel Wade Magruder," q.v.
BERRY, Zachariah. Private, Capt. Thomas Beall's Co., Maryland Line, 1780 [Ref: D-351].
BETON, John. See "John Beeding (Beedon)," q.v.
BETTS, Higginson. See "Higginson Belt," q.v.
BEVER, Mary. See "John Payne," q.v.
BIGGS, John. Private, 8th Co., Middle Bn., Militia, Sep., 1777 [Ref: M-198, T-5:43]. Private, 5th Co., Lower Bn., Militia, July 15, 1780 [Ref: M-206]. Took the Oath of Allegiance before the Hon. Edward Burgess on Feb. 28, 1778 [Ref: T-3:60, L-1:38]. "John Biggs, an Englishman born, about 32 years of age, about 5 feet 6 inches high, black hair, fair complexion, recruited by Robert Owen on Jan. 31, 1781." [Ref: R-33:155, X-1146]. "John Bigg" and "John Biggs" rendered aid by providing wheat for use of the military in 1780 [Ref: O-316, O-320].
BIGGS, Samuel (1730-1782). Served as a petit juror in Nov., 1777 [Ref: R-31:18]. Took the Oath of Allegiance before the Hon. Aneas Campbell on March 2, 1778 [Ref: T-3:77, L-1:38]. Lived in Sugarland Hd. in 1776 (wife named Hannrator) and had three taxables in 1777 [Ref: K-1:214, R-31:11]. "Samuel Biggs, of Frederick County, innholder" (wife named Hennerita) died testate in Montgomery County in 1782 [Ref: V-16].
BIGGS, Sarah. See "Robert Housley (Howsley)," q.v.
BIGNAL (BIGNELL), Robert. Private, 3rd Co., Lower Bn., Militia, Sep., 1777 [Ref: M-199, T-5:46]. Private, 8th Co., Lower Bn., Militia, July 15, 1780 [Ref: M-207, which source misspelled the name as "Robert Rignall"]. "Robert Bignell" took the Oath of Allegiance before the Hon. Richard Thompson in 1778 [Ref: T-3:75, L-1:38]. "Robert Bignal" lived in George Town Hd. (one taxable) in 1777 [Ref: R-31:3].
BIGWOOD, James. Private who was recruited to serve in the Extra Regiment, Continental Army, in 1780 [Ref: D-342].
BIRDWHISTLE (BURDWHISTLE, BIRDWHISTELL), Thomas (died 1803). "Thomas Birdwhistle" took the Oath of Allegiance before the Hon. Gerrard Briscoe on March 2, 1778 [Ref: T-3:56, L-1:38]. "Thomas

Burdwhistle" lived in Sugar Loaf Hd. (five taxables) in 1777 [Ref: R-31:9]. "Thomas Birdwhistell" (wife named Susannah) died testate in Montgomery County in 1803 [Ref: V-16].

BISBIN (BISBIND), James (b. 1723). Took the Oath of Allegiance before the Hon. Richard Thompson in 1778 [Ref: T-3:75, L-1:38]. "James Bisbin or Bisbind" lived in George Town Hd. (one taxable) in 1776-1777 [Ref: K-1:193, R-31:3].

BLACKBURN, William. Private, Capt. Edward Burgess' Co., Lower District of Frederick (now Montgomery) County, Militia, July, 1776 [Ref: D-42].

BLACKLOCK, Edward. Private, 2nd Maryland Line, enlisted on Feb. 10, 1776 [Ref: D-8].

BLACKLOCK, Richard (b. 1750). Private, 5th Co., Lower Bn., Militia, Aug., 1777, and Ensign, July 15,, 1780 [Ref: M-53, M-199, M-204, T-5:48, F-248]. Took the Oath of Allegiance before the Hon. Samuel W. Magruder in 1778 [Ref: T-3:73, L-1:38, which source listed the name as "Richard Blocklock"]. Served as a grand juror in 1781 [Ref: W-2]. Lived in Lower Potomac Hd. (two taxables) in 1776-1777 [Ref: R-31:4, K-1:181].

BLACKMORE, Elizabeth. See "Thomas Fletchall," q.v.

BLACKMORE, Samuel (b. 1736). Private, 1st Co., Upper Bn., Militia, Aug. 30, 1777 [Ref: M-193], Second Lieutenant, 16th Bn., Militia, Sep. 12, 1777, and First Lieutenant, Upper Bn., Militia, Aug. 4, 1780 [Ref: M-53, C-373, F-120]. Took the Oath of Allegiance before the Hon. Aneas Campbell on March 2, 1778 [Ref: T-3:77, L-1:38, which source mistakenly spelled the name "Samuel Beackmore"]. Lived in Sugarland Hd. (four taxables) in 1776-1777 and served as a grand juror in 1779 [Ref: K-1:205, R-31:11, W-1].

BLACKMORE, William (b. 1745). Served as Captain, 16th Bn., Militia, Sep. 12, 1777 [Ref: M-53, M-195, C-373, C-392]. Took the Oath of Allegiance before the Hon. William Deakins, Jr. before March 3, 1778 [Ref: T-3:68, L-1:38]. Rendered aid by providing corn for use of the military in 1780 [Ref: O-301]. Lived in Sugarland Hd. in 1776 and had four taxables in 1777 [Ref: K-1:221, R-31:11].

BLACKWOOD, William. Took the Oath of Allegiance before the Hon. Edward Burgess on Feb. 28, 1778 [Ref: T-3:62, L-1:38]. Lived in the Lower Part of Newfoundland Hd. (two taxables) in 1777 [Ref: R-31:5].

BLAIR, John. Private who was recruited to serve in the Continental Army in 1780 [Ref: D-341]. Invalid (disability) pension commenced June 10, 1783 and he was still on the rolls as of Nov. 1, 1789 [Ref: D-632].

BLESSATT, George. Private, 6th Co., Upper Bn., Militia, Aug. 30, 1777 [Ref: M-194].

BLOIS (BLOYCE, BLOYS), Charles (b. 1761). "Charls Bloys" [sic] was a son of William Bloys, Sr., of North West Hd., in 1776 [Ref: K-1:229]. "Charles Blois" was a private, 8th Co., Lower Bn., Militia, Sep., 1777

[Ref: M-200, T-5:51]. "Charles Bloyce" was a private, 6th Co., Lower Bn., Militia, July 15, 1780 [Ref: M-206].

BLOIS (BLOICE, BLAISE, BLOWIS, BLOYCE, BLOYS), David. There were two men with this name in 1776. "David Bloyce, aged 24" lived in Lower Potomac Hd. in 1776 and "David Bloys or Blowis, aged 26" lived in North West Hd. (one taxable) in 1776-1777 [Ref: R-31:17, K-1:181. K-1:229]. "David Blois" was a private, 8th Co., Lower Bn., Militia, Sep., 1777 [Ref: M-200, T-5:51]. "David Bloice" was a private, 6th Co., Lower Bn., Militia, July 15, 1780 [Ref: M-206]. "David Bloyss" took the Oath of Allegiance before the Hon. Charles Jones on Jan. 10, 1778 [Ref: T-3:71, L-1:38]. "David Blaise" [sic] rendered aid by providing wheat for use of the military in 1781 [Ref: O-384].

BLOIS (BLOYS, BLAISE, BLOWIS), William. "William Bloys, Sr." lived in North West Hd. (wife named Sarah, aged 50) in 1776, and "William Blowis" lived there (two taxables) in 1777 [Ref: K-1:229, R-31:17]. "William Blaise" [sic] rendered aid by providing wheat for use of the military in 1781 [Ref: O-384].

BLOWER, James. Private who was recruited to serve in the Continental Army in 1780 [Ref: D-342].

BLOWERS, Benjamin. Private, 4th Co., Middle Bn., Militia, Sep., 1777 [Ref: M-196, T-5:39]. Private, 8th Class, 4th Co., Middle Bn., Militia, July 15, 1780 [Ref: M-202]. Took the Oath of Allegiance before the Hon. Edward Burgess on Feb. 28, 1778 [Ref: T-3:60, L-1:38].

BLUEBAUG, Jacob. Took the Oath of Allegiance in 1778 [Ref: L-2:27].

BOCKES, John. Took the Oath of Allegiance in 1778 [Ref: L-2:27].

BOERSHAVE, Simon. Took the Oath of Allegiance before the Hon. Richard Thompson in 1778 [Ref: T-3:76, L-1:38]. "Simon Bowshave" was a private, 3rd Co., Lower Bn., Militia, Sep., 1777 [Ref: M-199, T-5:46].

BOERSHAVE, Valentine. Took the Oath of Allegiance before the Hon. Richard Thompson in 1778 [Ref: T-3:75, L-1:38].

BOFFUTT, Mordecai. See "Mordecai B. Offutt," q.v.

BOGLER (BOGLOR, BOGLE), John. "John Boglor" lived in the Upper Part of Potomac Hd. (one taxable) in 1777 [Ref: R-31:13]. "John Bogle" was a private, 6th Co., Lower Bn., Militia, Aug., 1777 [Ref: T-5:49]. "John Bogler" was a Private, 3rd Co., Lower Bn., Militia, July 15, 1780 [Ref: M-205]. "John Bogler" took the Oath of Allegiance before the Hon. Joseph Offutt on March 2, 1778 [Ref: T-3:70, L-1:38].

BOLSOM, Thomas. Took the Oath of Allegiance before the Hon. Edward Burgess on Feb. 28, 1778 [Ref: T-3:63, L-1:38].

BOND, Richard. Private who was recruited to serve in the Continental Army in 1780 [Ref: D-341].

BONNEY, Alexander. "An Irishman born, 42 years of age, about 5 feet 3 or 4 inches high, dark hair, brown complexion, and grey eyes, recruited by Thomas Reed and Mr. John Carroll on Feb. 1, 1781." [Ref: R-33:155, X-1146].

BONNIFIELD (BONIFANT), Samuel. "Samuel Bonnifield" was a private, 5th Co., Lower Bn., Militia, July 15, 1780 [Ref: M-206]. "Samuel Bonifant" is buried in Colesville, Montgomery County, Maryland [Ref: S-1993].

BOOGHER, Andro. Took the Oath of Allegiance in 1778 [Ref: L-2:27].

BOONE, Abram. Took the Oath of Allegiance in 1778 [Ref: L-2:27].

BOONE, Arnold. Private, 5th Co., Middle Bn., Militia, Sep., 1777 [Ref: M-197, T-5:40]. Lived in the Upper Part of Potomac Hd. (two taxables) in 1777 [Ref: R-31:13]. "Arnold Boone, Quaker" (wife named Mary) died testate in Montgomery County in 1782 [Ref: V-17].

BOONE (BOONS), Josiah. "Josiah Boone" was a private, 5th Co., Middle Bn., Militia, Sep., 1777 [Ref: M-197, T-5:40]. "Josiah Boons" lived in Rock Creek Hd. (two taxables) in 1777 [Ref: R-31:16].

BORAM (BORING), Thomas. "Thomas Boram" was a private, 1st Co., Lower Bn., Militia, Sep., 1777 [Ref: M-198, T-5:44]. This name is not listed in the 1777 tax (levy) list in Montgomery County, but a "Thomas Boring" lived in the Lower Part of Newfoundland Hd. (one taxable) in 1777 [Ref: R-31:5].

BORASE, Felter. Private, 3rd Co., Lower Bn., Militia, Sep., 1777 [Ref: M-199, T-5:46].

BOREHAM, Vallentine. Private, 3rd Co., Lower Bn., Militia, Sep., 1777 [Ref: M-199, T-5:46].

BOREMAN, George. Took the Oath of Allegiance (made his "X" mark) before the Hon. Edward Burgess on Feb. 28, 1778 [Ref: T-3:60, L-1:38].

BOREMAN (BORMAN), Jacob. Took the Oath of Allegiance before the Hon. Edward Burgess on Feb. 28, 1778 [Ref: T-3:63, L-1:38].

BORING, Thomas. See "Thomas Boram," q.v.

BOSWELL, James. Private, 4th Co., Middle Bn., Militia, Sep., 1777 [Ref: M-196, T-5:39]. Private, 2nd Class, 4th Co., Middle Bn., Militia, July 15, 1780 [Ref: M-202]. "James Bosswell" took the Oath of Allegiance (made his "X" mark) before the Hon. Edward Burgess on Feb. 28, 1778 [Ref: T-3:60, L-1:38]. "James Boswell" lived in the Upper Part of Newfoundland Hd. (two taxables) in 1777 [Ref: R-31:6].

BOSWELL, Nicholas. Private, 4th Co., Middle Bn., Militia, Sep., 1777 [Ref: M-196, T-5:39]. Private, 2nd Class, 4th Co., Middle Bn., Militia, July 15, 1780 [Ref: M-202]. "Nicholas Bosswell" took the Oath of Allegiance before the Hon. Edward Burgess on Feb. 28, 1778 [Ref: T-3:60, L-1:38]. "Nicholas Boswell" lived in the Upper Part of Newfoundland Hd. (one taxable) in 1777 [Ref: R-31:6].

BOUNDS, Thomas. Took the Oath of Allegiance in 1778 [Ref: L-2:27]. "Thomas Bounds, a recruit from Montgomery County, enlisted by Basil Roberts, is discharged on his returning the 60 dollars bounty and paying 10 pounds for the clothes he received into the hands of Col. Griffith, who is requested to receive it and give credit to the public, June 22,

1778." [Ref: E-144, but was not listed in *Archives of Maryland, Volume 18*].

BOURGEY, Thomas. See "Thomas Burgee," q.v.

BOWEN, George. Private, 7th Co., Upper Bn., Militia, Aug. 30, 1777 [Ref: M-194].

BOWEN (BOWAN), John (b. 1747). Served as a private when enrolled into a company of militia for the service of the Flying Camp on Oct. 15, 1776 [Ref: B-353]. Private, 7th Co., Upper Bn., Militia, Aug. 30, 1777 [Ref: M-195]. Took the Oath of Allegiance (made his "X" mark) before the Hon. Aneas Campbell on March 2, 1778 [Ref: T-3:77, L-1:38]. "John Bowan" lived in Sugarland Hd. in 1776 [Ref: K-1:213].

BOWIE, Allen (1737-1803). Son of John Bowie, Jr. (1708-1753) and Elizabeth Pottinger, of Prince George's County, who married his stepsister Ruth Cramphin, daughter of Thomas Cramphin, in 1766, and had children: Thomas, John, Washington, Allen, Richard, Elizabeth, Mary, and Hannah. Served as a First Lieutenant, 2nd Co., 29th Bn., Militia, May 14, 1776, and Colonel, 1780. Justice of Montgomery County in 1777, Tax Commissioner in 1785, Levy Court in 1799 [Ref: M-55, M-198, T-5:45, A-424, C-373, N-149, N-150]. Took the Oath of Allegiance before the Hon. Charles Jones on Jan. 10, 1778 [Ref: T-3:71, L-1:38]. Lived in Rock Creek Hd. (ten taxables) in 1777 [Ref: R-31:16]. Recruited Joseph Carroll in Feb., 1781 [Ref: R-33:155, X-1146], and rendered aid by providing wheat for use of the military in 1780 [Ref: O-311]. Died testate (wife named Ruth) in Montgomery County in 1803 [Ref: V-18].

BOWIE, Eleanor. See "George Frazer Magruder," q.v.

BOWIE, John Jr. See "Allen Bowie," q.v.

BOWIE, Mary. See "James Magruder," q.v.

BOWIE, Rachel. See "Zadock Magruder," q.v.

BOWIE, Susannah. See "Jeffrey Magruder," q.v.

BOWMAN, Ann. See "Henry Coontz," q.v.

BOWMAN, George. Private, 4th Co., Middle Bn., Militia, Sep., 1777 [Ref: M-196, T-5:39]. Fourth Corporal, 4th Co., Middle Bn., Militia, July 15, 1780 [Ref: M-202]. Lived in the Upper Part of Newfoundland Hd. (one taxable) in 1777 [Ref: R-31:6]. George Bowman married Margaret Gue in Montgomery County on Feb. 3, 1779 [Ref: K-2:517].

BOWMAN, Jacob (died 1821). Lived in the Upper Part of Newfoundland Hd. (two taxables) in 1777 [Ref: R-31:6]. Private, 4th Co., Middle Bn., Militia, Sep., 1777 [Ref: M-196, T-5:39]. Private, 5th Class, 4th Co., Middle Bn., Militia, July 15, 1780 [Ref: M-202]. Jacob Bowman married Mary Chambers in Montgomery County on July 6, 1778 [Ref: K-2:516]. "Jacob Boman" [sic] rendered aid by providing wheat for use of the military in 1781 [Ref: O-399]. Died testate in Montgomery County in 1821 [Ref: V-18].

BOWMAN, John. Took the Oath of Allegiance in 1778 [Ref: L-2:27].

BOYALL, William. See "William Byall," q.v.
BOYD (BOYED), Abraham. Private, 8th Co., Middle Bn., Militia, Sep., 1777 [Ref: M-198, T-5:43]. Private, 7th Co., Middle Bn., Militia, July 15, 1780 [Ref: M-203]. Took the Oath of Allegiance before the Hon. Joseph Wilson on Feb. 28, 1778 [Ref: T-3:67, L-1:38]. "Abraham Boyd" rendered aid by providing wheat for use of the military in 1780 [Ref: O-309, O-332, O-343]. "Abraham Boyed" lived in Rock Creek Hd. (two taxables) in 1777 [Ref: R-31:15].
BOYD, Benjamin. Private, 8th Co., Lower Bn., Militia, July 15, 1780 [Ref: M-207]. Rendered aid by providing wheat for use of the military in 1780 [Ref: O-314].
BOYD (BOYED), John. Private, 2nd Co., Lower Bn., Militia, Sep., 1777 [Ref: M-198, T-5:45]. Private, 7th Co., Middle Bn., Militia, July 15, 1780 [Ref: M-203]. Took the Oath of Allegiance before the Hon. Joseph Wilson on Feb. 28, 1778 [Ref: T-3:67, L-1:38]. "John Boyd" served as a petit juror in Nov., 1777 [Ref: R-31:18]. "John Boyed" lived in Rock Creek Hd. (two taxables) in 1777 [Ref: R-31:16].
BOYD (BOYED), William. Private, 2nd Co., Lower Bn., Militia, Sep., 1777 [Ref: M-198, T-5:45]. Private, 7th Co., Middle Bn., Militia, July 15, 1780 [Ref: M-203]. "William Boyd" took the Oath of Allegiance before the Hon. Joseph Wilson on Feb. 28, 1778 [Ref: T-3:67, L-1:38], and served as a petit juror in Nov., 1777 [Ref: R-31:18]. "William Boyed" lived in Rock Creek Hd. (one taxable) in 1777 [Ref: R-31:16]. Rendered aid by providing wheat for use of the military in 1780 [Ref: O-313].
BOYL, Richard. Took the Oath of Allegiance before the Hon. Richard Thompson in 1778 [Ref: T-3:75, L-1:38].
BRADDOCK, Joseph. "Joseph Braddock" was a private, 3rd Co., Middle Bn., Militia, Sep., 1777 [Ref: M-196, T-5:38]. "Joseph Broadack" took the Oath of Allegiance before the Hon. William Deakins, Jr. before March 3, 1778 [Ref: T-3:68, L-1:38].
BRADISH, John. Private, 8th Co., Lower Bn., Militia, July 15, 1780 [Ref: M-207].
BRAGG, William (died 1782). Took the Oath of Allegiance before the Hon. William Deakins, Jr. before March 3, 1778 [Ref: T-3:68, L-1:38]. William Bragg (wife named Mary) died testate in Montgomery County in 1782 [Ref: V-19].
BRANNAN, George (b. 1757). Lived in George Town Hd. in 1776 [Ref: K-1:193]. Private, Maryland Line, Rawlings' Regiment, 1776 to Aug. 9, 1779, when discharged [Ref: D-90].
BRANNAN (BRANAN), Lawrence (b. 1755). Lived in Sugarland Hd. in 1776 [Ref: K-1:200]. Private, 7th Maryland Line, April 22, 1778, and corporal, June 18, 1778, and sergeant, Jan. 1, 1780, and served in the Battle of Camden on Aug. 16, 1780, when reported missing [Ref: D-190, D-312, D-435]. The Council of Maryland noted on Sep. 5, 1781, that Lawrence Branan, among other soldiers of the Maryland Line, "returned

from captivity in South Carolina in a distressed situation" and it was ordered that he be paid five pounds on account [Ref: G-598, D-616].

BRANNAN (BRANEN, BRANNUM), Thomas (b. 1730). "Thomas Brannan" was constable in George Town Hd., 1780-1781 [Ref: W-2]. "Thomas Brannum" was a private, 3rd Co., Lower Bn., Militia, Sep., 1777 [Ref: M-199, T-5:46]. "Thomas Brannan or Branen" lived in George Town Hd. in 1776-1777 and he apparently had a son Thomas (b. 1761), among others [Ref: K-1:193, R-31:3].

BRANNAN (BRENAN), Timothy. Private, 7th Co., Middle Bn., Militia, July 15, 1780 [Ref: M-203], and private, 6th Maryland Line, who was listed as an invalid on June 19, 1781 [Ref: D-623].

BRANDIS, Thomas. Private, 3rd Co., Lower Bn., Militia, Sep., 1777 [Ref: M-199, T-5:46]. "Thomas Brandish" took the Oath of Allegiance before the Hon. Richard Thompson in 1778 [Ref: T-3:75, L-1:38].

BRASHEARS, Morris. Private, Capt. Edward Burgess' Co., Lower District of Frederick (now Montgomery) County, Militia, July, 1776 [Ref: D-42]. Private, 7th Co., Lower Bn., Militia, Aug., 1777, and Third Sergeant, 4th Co., July 15, 1780 [Ref: M-200, M-205, T-5:50]. Took the Oath of Allegiance before the Hon. Edward Burgess on Feb. 28, 1778 [Ref: T-3:59, L-1:38]. Lived in the Lower Part of Newfoundland Hd. (three taxables) in 1777 [Ref: R-31:5].

BRASHEARS, Morris Jr. Took the Oath of Allegiance before the Hon. Edward Burgess on Feb. 28, 1778 [Ref: T-3:59, L-1:38].

BRAUDSABURGH, Samuel. Took the Oath of Allegiance in 1778 [Ref: L-2:27].

BRIAN, Dennis. Private, 6th Co., Middle Bn., Militia, July 15, 1780 [Ref: M-203].

BRIGGS, William (b. 1740). Private, 6th Co., Upper Bn., Militia, Aug. 30, 1777 [Ref: M-194]. Lived in Sugarland Hd. in 1776-1777 [Ref: K-1:199, R-31:11].

BRISCOE, Gerrard (1737-c1790). Served as Captain, 1st Co., Middle Bn., Militia, June 20, 1777, and Major, Sep. 12, 1777 [Ref: M-56, M-195, C-373]. Justice of the Peace who administered the Oath of Allegiance in 1778 [Ref: C-529, T-3:56, L-1:38]. Lived in Seneca Hd. (twelve taxables) in 1777 [Ref: R-31:7]. He was born on Aug. 17, 1737, married (1) Ruth McMillan and (2) Margaret Baker, served as a Lieutenant Colonel, and died after 1790 [Ref: DAR-I:86].

BRISCOE, Robert (died 1798). Took the Oath of Allegiance before the Hon. Gerrard Briscoe on March 2, 1778 [Ref: T-3:57, L-1:38]. Rendered aid by providing wheat for use of the military in 1781 [Ref: O-445]. Lived in Seneca Hd. (five taxables) in 1777 [Ref: R-31:7]. Robert Briscoe (wife named Sarah) died testate in Montgomery County in 1798 [Ref: V-19].

BROADBACK, Henry. Took the Oath of Allegiance in 1778 [Ref: L-2:27].

BROADHEAD, Thomas. Private, 2nd Co., Middle Bn., Militia, Sep. 4, 1777 [Ref: M-196, T-5:37]. Private, 7th Class, 3rd Co., Middle Bn., Militia, July 15, 1780 [Ref: M-202]. Took the Oath of Allegiance before the Hon. William Deakins, Jr. before March 3, 1778 [Ref: T-3:68, L-1:38]. Lived in Sugar Loaf Hd. (one taxable) in 1777 [Ref: R-31:9].

BROCKHART, George. Rendered aid by providing beef for use of the military in 1780 [Ref: O-344].

BROMER (BROOMER), Henry. Took the Oath of Allegiance in 1778 [Ref: L-2:27].

BROMER, Peter. Took the Oath of Allegiance in 1778 [Ref: L-2:27].

BROMER, Stephen. Took the Oath of Allegiance in 1778 [Ref: L-2:27].

BROOKE, Basil (died 1794). Private, 8th Co., Middle Bn., Militia, Sep., 1777 [Ref: M-197]. Private, 4th Class, 4th Co., Middle Bn., Militia, July 15, 1780 [Ref: M-202]. Lived in the Upper Part of Newfoundland Hd. (five taxables) in 1777 [Ref: R-31:6]. Basil Brooke (wife named Elizabeth) died testate in Montgomery County in 1794 [Ref: V-19]. See "Thomas Brooke," q.v.

BROOKE, Charles. Private who was recruited to serve in the Continental Army in 1780 [Ref: D-341].

BROOKE, Clement. Rendered aid by providing wheat for use of the military in 1780 [Ref: O-317].

BROOKE, Elizabeth. See "Thomas Beall, of George," q.v.

BROOKE (BROOK, BROOKES), Henry. Took the Oath of Allegiance in 1778 [Ref: L-2:27]. Rendered aid by providing wheat for use of the military in 1781 [Ref: O-398]. "Henry Brooke" (wife not named) died testate in Montgomery County in 1813 and "Henry Brookes" (wife named Martha) died testate in Montgomery County in 1807 [Ref: V-20, V-21].

BROOKE (BROOK, BROOKS), Isaac. Private, 4th Co., Lower Bn., Militia, Aug., 1777 [Ref: M-199, T-5:47], and Second Sergeant, 1st Co., Lower Bn., July 15, 1780 [Ref: M-204]. "Isaac Brook" took the Oath of Allegiance before the Hon. Samuel W. Magruder in 1778 [Ref: T-3:73, L-1:38], and served as a grand juror in 1779 [Ref: W-1]. "Isaac Brooke" lived in Lower Potomac Hd. (four taxables) in 1777 [Ref: R-31:4]. "Isaac Brooks" rendered aid by providing wheat for use of the military in 1780 [Ref: O-331].

BROOKE, James (died 1784). Took the Oath of Allegiance before the Hon. Edward Burgess on Feb. 28, 1778 [Ref: T-3:64, L-1:38]. Lived in the Upper Part of Newfoundland Hd. (eleven taxables) in 1777 [Ref: R-31:6]. "James Brooke, of Frederick County" died testate in Montgomery County in 1784 [Ref: V-20].

BROOKE, Richard (died 1788). Served as Captain, 8th Co., Middle Bn., Militia, and First Major, 29th Bn., and Colonel, Middle Bn., 1776-1778 [Ref: C-373, M-56, M-197]. Took the Oath of Allegiance before the Hon. Joseph Wilson on Feb. 28, 1778 [Ref: T-3:64, L-1:38]. Lived in the

Upper Part of Newfoundland Hd. (five taxables) in 1777 [Ref: R-31:6]. Died testate in Montgomery County in 1788 [Ref: V-20, V-21].

BROOKE, Roger. (1) Captain, Middle Bn., Militia, Sep. 12, 1777 [Ref: M-56, C-373]. (2) Private, 8th Co., Middle Bn., Militia, Sep., 1777 [Ref: M-198, T-5:43]. Private, 7th Co., Middle Bn., Militia, July 15, 1780 [Ref: M-203]. Took the Oath of Allegiance before the Hon. Edward Burgess on Feb. 28, 1778 [Ref: T-3:64, L-1:38, L-2:27, which latter source spelled the name "Roger Brook"]. One Roger Brooke lived in the Upper Part of Newfoundland Hd. (four taxables) in 1777 [Ref: R-31:6]. See "Thomas Brooke," q.v.

BROOKE, Samuel. Private, 8th Co., Middle Bn., Militia, Sep., 1777 [Ref: M-198, T-5:43]. Took the Oath of Allegiance before the Hon. Edward Burgess on Feb. 28, 1778 [Ref: T-3:64, L-1:38].

BROOKE (BROOKS), Thomas. Private, 8th Co., Middle Bn., Militia, Sep., 1777 [Ref: M-198, T-5:43]. Private, 3rd Class, 4th Co., Middle Bn., Militia, July 15, 1780 [Ref: M-202]. Took the Oath of Allegiance before the Hon. Edward Burgess on Feb. 28, 1778 [Ref: T-3:64, L-1:38]. "Thomas Brook" rendered aid by providing wheat for use of the military in 1781 [Ref: O-391]. "Thomas Brookes" took the Oath of Allegiance before the Hon. Edward Burgess on Feb. 28, 1778 [Ref: T-3:63, L-1:38]. One Thomas Brooks (b. 1746) lived in George Town Hd. in 1776, another Thomas Brookes lived in the Upper Part of Newfoundland Hd. (three taxables) in 1777, and another lived in Seneca Hd. (one taxable) in 1777 [Ref: K-1:193, R-31:6, R-31:7]. "Thomas Brooke" died testate in Montgomery County in 1789 and mentioned his brothers Roger and Basil [Ref: V-21].

BROOME (BROME), John. Took the Oath of Allegiance before the Hon. Joseph Wilson on Feb. 28, 1778 [Ref: T-3:64, L-1:38].

BROOME (BROME), Peter. Took the Oath of Allegiance (made his mark) before the Hon. Joseph Wilson on Feb. 28, 1778 [Ref: T-3:64, L-1:38].

BROWN, Anne. See "Leonard Green," q.v.

BROWN, Catherine. See "Thomas Beall," q.v.

BROWN, Colin (Coaly). "Colin Brown" was a sailor (able seaman) aboard the ship "Defence" in Sep., 1776 [Ref: D-606, D-654]. "Coaly Brown" married Elizabeth Holly in Montgomery County on Aug. 20, 1779 [Ref: K-2:513].

BROWN, Edward. Took the Oath of Allegiance (made his "U" mark) before the Hon. Edward Burgess on Feb. 28, 1778 [Ref: T-3:62, L-1:38]. Took the Oath of Allegiance before the Hon. William Deakins, Jr. before March 3, 1778 [Ref: T-3:68, L-1:38].

BROWN, George. Took the Oath of Allegiance in 1778 [Ref: L-2:27].

BROWN, John. Private, 5th Co., Middle Bn., Militia, Sep., 1777 [Ref: M-196, T-5:40], Corporal, Capt. Thomas Beall's Co., Maryland Line, 1780 [Ref: D-350], and Third Sergeant, 1st Co., Middle Bn., Militia, July 15, 1780 [Ref: M-201]. Took the Oath of Allegiance before the Hon. Joseph

Offutt on March 2, 1778 [Ref: T-3:70, L-1:38, L-2:27]. Rendered aid by providing wheat for use of the military in 1780 [Ref: O-317]. Lived in the Upper Part of Potomac Hd. (one taxable) in 1777 [Ref: R-31:14]. John Brown married Alice Noding on Montgomery County on Oct. 1, 1778 [Ref: K-2:517].

BROWN, John 2nd. Private, Capt. Price's Co., 3rd Maryland Line, 1781-1782 [Ref: D-453].

BROWN, Peter. Rendered aid by providing wheat for use of the military in 1780 [Ref: O-304, O-313]. Lived in the Upper Part of Potomac Hd. (three taxables) in 1777 [Ref: R-31:14].

BROWN, Thomas. Took the Oath of Allegiance in 1778 [Ref: L-2:27].

BROWN, William. Private, 6th Class, 2nd Co., Middle Bn., Militia, July 15, 1780 [Ref: M-201]. Took the Oath of Allegiance before the Hon. William Deakins, Jr. before March 3, 1778 [Ref: T-3:68, L-1:38]. "William Brown" lived in Rock Creek Hd. (one taxable) in 1777 [Ref: R-31:16]. "William Browen" [sic] was a private, 6th Co., Lower Bn., Militia, July 15, 1780 [Ref: M-206]. "William Brown" died testate in Montgomery County in 1782 [Ref: V-22].

BROWNING, Archibald. Lived in Linganore Hd. (one taxable) in 1777 [Ref: R-31:8]. Private, 6th Co., Middle Bn., Militia, Aug., 1777 [Ref: M-197, T-5:41]. Private, 6th Co., Middle Bn., Militia, July 15, 1780 [Ref: M-203]. Took the Oath of Allegiance on Sep. 1, 1780, under the Act of May 12, 1780, having neglected to do so previously "due to ignorance of the duty owed the country." [Ref: R-27:106].

BROWNING, Benjamin. Private, 6th Co., Middle Bn., Militia, Aug., 1777 [Ref: M-197, T-5:41]. Lived in Linganore Hd. (one taxable) in 1777 [Ref: R-31:8].

BROWNING, Edward. Private, 1st Co., Lower Bn., Militia, Sep., 1777, and Third Corporal, 7th Co., Lower Bn., July 15, 1780 [Ref: M-198, M-206, T-5:44]. Took the Oath of Allegiance (made his "B" mark) before the Hon. Edward Burgess on Feb. 28, 1778 [Ref: T-3:62, L-1:38]. This or perhaps another Edward Browning took the Oath of Allegiance on Sep. 1, 1780, under the Act of May 12, 1780, having neglected to do so previously "due to ignorance of the duty owed the country." [Ref: R-27:106]. Rendered aid by providing wheat for use of the military in 1781 [Ref: O-398]. "Edward Browning, Sr." lived in the Lower Part of Newfoundland Hd. (three taxables) in 1777 [Ref: R-31:5]. "Edward Browning, Sr., of Frederick County" (wife not named) died testate in Montgomery County in 1788, and "Edward Browning, Sr., planter" (wife named Rebecca) died testate in Montgomery County in 1800 [Ref: V-22]. Also see "Edward Browning, Jr.," q.v.

BROWNING, Edward Jr. "Edward Browning, Jr." took the Oath of Allegiance before the Hon. Edward Burgess on Feb. 28, 1778 [Ref: T-3:61, L-1:38]. "Edward Browning" lived in Linganore Hd. (one taxable) in 1777 [Ref: R-31:8].

BROWNING, Elias. Private, 4th Co., Lower Bn., Militia, July 15, 1780 [Ref: M-205]. Also see "John Smith," q.v.

BROWNING, Jeremiah. Private, 1st Co., Lower Bn., Militia, Sep., 1777 [Ref: M-198, T-5:44]. Private, 7th Co., Lower Bn., Militia, July 15, 1780 [Ref: M-207].

BROWNING, Jonathan Jr. Private, 6th Co., Middle Bn., Militia, Aug., 1777 [Ref: M-197, T-5:41]. Took the Oath of Allegiance on Sep. 1, 1780, under the Act of May 12, 1780, having neglected to do so previously "due to ignorance of the duty owed the country." [Ref: R-27:106]. See "Jonathan Browning," q.v.

BROWNING, Jonathan Sr. Took the Oath of Allegiance on Sep. 1, 1780, under the Act of May 12, 1780, having neglected to do so previously "due to ignorance of the duty owed the country." [Ref: R-27:106]. "Jonathan Browning" was a private, 6th Co., Middle Bn., Militia, July 15, 1780 [Ref: M-203]. Rendered aid by providing wheat for use of the military in 1781 [Ref: O-398]. Two men named Jonathan Browning (one with one taxable and the other with two taxables) lived in Linganore Hd. in 1777; perhaps one was "Sr." and one was "Jr." [Ref: R-31:8]. "Jonathan Browning" (wife named Elizabeth) died testate in Montgomery County in 1805 [Ref: V-22].

BROWNING, Joseph. Private, 1st Co., Lower Bn., Militia, Sep., 1777 [Ref: M-198, T-5:44]. Private, 7th Co., Lower Bn., Militia, July 15, 1780 [Ref: M-206]. Took the Oath of Allegiance before the Hon. Edward Burgess on Feb. 28, 1778 [Ref: T-3:63, L-1:38]. Lived in the Lower Part of Newfoundland Hd. (one taxable) in 1777 [Ref: R-31:5].

BROWNING, Nathan (Nathaniel) Jr. "Nathaniel Browning, Jr." was a private, 6th Co., Middle Bn., Militia, Aug., 1777 [Ref: M-197, T-5:41]. "Nathan Browning, Jr." was a private, 6th Co., Middle Bn., Militia, July 15, 1780 [Ref: M-203].

BROWNING, Nathan (Nathaniel) Sr. "Nathaniel Browning" was a private, 6th Co., Middle Bn., Militia, Aug., 1777 [Ref: M-197, T-5:41]. "Nathan Browning, Sr." was a private, 6th Co., Middle Bn., Militia, July 15, 1780 [Ref: M-203]. "Nathan Browning" took the Oath of Allegiance on Sep. 1, 1780, under the Act of May 12, 1780, having neglected to do so previously "due to ignorance of the duty owed the country." [Ref: R-27:106]. Rendered aid by providing wheat for use of the military in 1781 [Ref: O-398]. Lived in Linganore Hd. (one taxable) in 1777 [Ref: R-31:8].

BROWNING, Susanna. See "John Smith," q.v.

BROWNING, Verlinda. See "Nathan Harrison," q.v.

BROWNING, Zephaniah. Private, Capt. Edward Burgess' Co., Lower District of Frederick (now Montgomery) County, Militia, July, 1776 [Ref: D-42], and private, 1st Co., Lower Bn., Militia, Sep., 1777 [Ref: M-198, T-5:44]. Lived in the Lower Part of Newfoundland Hd. (one taxable) in 1777 [Ref: R-31:5].

BRUCE, Charles. Private, 1st Co., Middle Bn., Militia, Aug. 30, 1777 [Ref: T-5:36 and M-195, which latter source questions if the name could be "Bause"]. Ensign, Middle Bn., Militia, Sep. 12, 1777, and Captain, April 21, 1779 [Ref: M-57, C-373, E-357]. Took the Oath of Allegiance before the Hon. Gerrard Briscoe on March 2, 1778 [Ref: T-3:57, L-1:38]. Lived in Seneca Hd. (five taxables) in 1777 [Ref: R-31:7].

BRUCE, John. Served as Second Lieutenant, 16th Bn., Militia, Aug. 30, 1777, and as Captain, 7th Co., Middle Bn., Militia, from Sep. 12, 1777, to at least March 25, 1780 [Ref: M-57, M-197, C-350, C-373, F-120, T-5:41]. Took the Oath of Allegiance before the Hon. Gerrard Briscoe on March 2, 1778 [Ref: T-3:56, L-1:38]. Lived in Seneca Hd. (three taxables) in 1777 [Ref: R-31:7].

BRUEBACK, Rudolph. Took the Oath of Allegiance in 1778 [Ref: L-2:27].

BRYAN, Dennis (Denis). Took the Oath of Allegiance on Sep. 1, 1780, under the Act of May 12, 1780, having neglected to do so previously "due to ignorance of the duty owed the country." [Ref: R-27:106].

BRYAN, Gilbert. Private, Capt. Edward Burgess' Co., Lower District of Frederick (now Montgomery) County, Militia, July, 1776 [Ref: D-42].

BRYAN, Richard. Took the Oath of Allegiance before the Hon. Edward Burgess on Feb. 28, 1778 [Ref: T-3:63, L-1:38].

BUCEY, John, and others. See "John Busey" and others, q.v.

BUCEY, Rebecca. See "Samuel Davis," q.v.

BUCKLAND, John. Private, 3rd Co., Middle Bn., Militia, Sep., 1777 [Ref: M-196, T-5:38]. Took the Oath of Allegiance before the Hon. William Deakins, Jr. before March 3, 1778 [Ref: T-3:68, L-1:38].

BUCKLEY (BUCKLER), John (b. 1736). "John Buckley" took the Oath of Allegiance before the Hon. Charles Jones on Jan. 10, 1778 [Ref: T-3:71, L-1:38]. "John Buckler, aged 40" lived in North West Hd. in 1776, and "John Buckler" lived in the Upper Part of Potomac Hd. (three taxables) in 1777 [Ref: K-1:232, R-31:14].

BULGAR, Daniel. Private, 8th Co., Lower Bn., Militia, July 15, 1780 [Ref: M-207], and was recruited to serve in the Extra Regiment, Continental Army, in 1780 [Ref: D-342].

BULLER, John. Private who was recruited to serve in the Extra Regiment, Continental Army, in 1780 [Ref: D-342]. John Buller married Catherine Smith in Montgomery County in July 27, 1780 [Ref: K-2:517].

BURCH, Benjamin (c1755-1830). Served as a Sergeant, Capt. Thomas Beall's Co., Maryland Line, 1780 [Ref: D-350]. It was noted by the Council of Maryland on Sep. 5, 1781, that Benjamin Burch, and other soldiers of the Maryland Line, "returned from captivity in South Carolina in a distressed situation," and it was ordered that he be paid five pounds on account [Ref: G-598]. Applied for pension on Sep. 27, 1828, in Ohio County, Kentucky, stating he was married to Chloe ---- in late 1809 about two miles from Washington, D. C., by Rev. Joseph Messenger, of Prince George's County, an Episcopalian Minister.

Benjamin died on Dec. 17, 1830. In 1855 Chloe Burch was aged 84 and received bounty land warrant #108-160-55, as well as pension W4137 [Ref: P-464, and *Marylanders to Kentucky, 1775-1825*, by Henry C. Peden, Jr. (1991), p. 21].

BURCH, Chloe. See "Benjamin Burch," q.v.

BURCH (BIRCH), Thomas. Private, 7th Co., Middle Bn., Militia, July 15, 1780 [Ref: M-203], and was recruited to serve in the Continental Army in 1780 [Ref: D-342].

BURCH (BIRCH), Zephaniah. Private, 3rd Co., Middle Bn., Militia, Sep., 1777 [Ref: M-196, T-5:38], and as Fourth Corporal, 1st Co., Lower Bn., July 15, 1780 [Ref: M-204].

BURDETT (BURDITT), Benjamin. "Benjamin Burdett" was a private, 2nd Co., Middle Bn., Militia, Sep. 4, 1777 [Ref: M-196, T-5:37]. "Benjamin Burditt" was a private, 4th Class, 3rd Co., Middle Bn., Militia, July 15, 1780 [Ref: M-202]. Took the Oath of Allegiance before the Hon. Gerrard Briscoe on March 2, 1778 [Ref: T-3:57, L-1:38]. Another Benjamin Burdett took the Oath of Allegiance on Sep. 1, 1780, under the Act of May 12, 1780, having neglected to do so previously "due to ignorance of the duty owed the country." [Ref: R-27:106]. Rendered aid by providing wheat for use of the military in 1781 [Ref: O-426, O-445]. "Benjamin Burditt" lived in Linganore Hd. (three taxables) in 1777 [Ref: R-31:8].

BURDETT (BURDIT), Nathan. "Nathan Burdett" was a private, 5th Co., Upper Bn., Militia, Aug. 30, 1777 [Ref: M-194]. "Nathan Burdit" took the Oath of Allegiance before the Hon. Elisha Williams on March 2, 1778 [Ref: T-3:80, L-1:38]. Lived in Sugar Loaf Hd. (one taxable) in 1777 [Ref: R-31:9].

BURDETT, William. Private, 5th Co., Upper Bn., Militia, Aug. 30, 1777 [Ref: M-194]. Took the Oath of Allegiance on Sep. 1, 1780, under the Act of May 12, 1780, having neglected to do so previously "due to ignorance of the duty owed the country." [Ref: R-27:106].

BURGEE (BOURGEY), Thomas. "Thomas Burgee" was a private, 6th Co., Middle Bn., Militia, Aug., 1777 [Ref: M-197, T-5:41]. "Thomas Bourgey" lived in Linganore Hd. (two taxables) in 1777 [Ref: R-31:9].

BURGESS, Benjamin. Private, Capt. Edward Burgess' Co., Lower District of Frederick (now Montgomery) County, Militia, July, 1776 [Ref: D-42].

BURGESS, Charles. Private, 7th Co., Middle Bn., Militia, July 15, 1780 [Ref: M-203].

BURGESS, Edward. (1) Son of John Burgess (1696-1774), of Anne Arundel County, and Jane Mackelfresh (MacElfresh). Served as a Captain, 7th Co., 29th Bn., Militia, from June 26, 1776, to at least May 12, 1781 [Ref: D-42, M-58, M-206, A-522, R-33:156, X-1146]. Served as a Justice of the Orphans Court in 1778 and a Justice of the Peace who administered the Oath of Allegiance in 1778 [Ref: T-3:58, L-1:38, C-529]. He married by 1767 to Mary Davis and had children: Edward, John, Ephraim, Thomas, Elizabeth, Ann (Nancy), Jane, Margaret, Sally

(Sarah), and Mary. Served in the Lower House of Montgomery County, 1777-1779, Tax Commissioner, 1779-1795 (various dates), Justice of Orphans' Court, 1777-1790, Justice of Frederick County, 1773-1775, and Montgomery County, 1776-1792. Died in Dec., 1809 [Ref: N-181, N-182, W-2]. (2) Private, 1st Co., Lower Bn., Militia, Sep., 1777 [Ref: M-198, T-5:44]. One Edward Burgess lived in Linganore Hd. (three taxables) in 1777 [Ref: R-31:9].

BURGESS, Elias. Private, 6th Co., Lower Bn., Militia, July 15, 1780 [Ref: M-206].

BURGESS, James. Private, Capt. Edward Burgess' Co., Lower District of Frederick (now Montgomery) County, Militia, July, 1776 [Ref: D-42]. Private, 8th Co., Middle Bn., Militia, Sep., 1777 [Ref: M-198, T-5:43]. Private, 6th Co., Lower Bn., Militia, July 15, 1780 [Ref: M-206]. Took the Oath of Allegiance in 1778 [Ref: L-2:27]. Lived in Rock Creek Hd. (one taxable) in 1777 [Ref: R-31:16].

BURGESS, John. Private, enrolled into a company of militia for the service of the Flying Camp, Oct. 15, 1776 [Ref: B-353]. See "Edward Burgess," q.v.

BURGESS, Josiah or Josias (1758-1834). Private, 8th Co., Lower Bn., Militia, Sep., 1777 [Ref: M-200, T-5:51]. Applied for pension (S31589) on Oct. 26, 1832, aged 74, in Jasper County, Georgia, stating he enlisted from Montgomery County, Maryland, on April 20, 1778, for three years, and was a private in the 7th Maryland Regiment. He participated in the battles of Monmouth, Camden (wounded), and Cowpens, and was taken prisoner and later released [Ref: U-17:63, P-469]. Josiah Burgess married Virlinda Bean in Montgomery County on Nov. 18, 1783 [Ref: K-2:521, DAR-I:101].

BURGESS, Richard. Private, Capt. Edward Burgess' Co., Lower District of Frederick (now Montgomery) County, Militia, July, 1776 [Ref: D-42].

BURK (BURKE), John (b. 1746). "John Burk" lived in Sugarland Hd. in 1776 [Ref: K-1:200]. "John Burke" was a private, 7th Co., Upper Bn., Militia, Aug. 30, 1777 [Ref: M-194]. "John Burk" was a private, Capt. Thomas Beall's Co., Maryland Line, 1780 [Ref: D-351].

BURKLEY, Charles. See "Charles Barkley," q.v.

BURN (BURNS), Adam (b. 1736). "Adam Burn" was a private, 8th Co., Upper Bn., Militia, Aug. 30, 1777 [Ref: M-195]. Took the Oath of Allegiance before the Hon. Aneas Campbell on March 2, 1778 [Ref: T-3:78, L-1:38]. "Adom Burn or Adam Burns" lived in Sugarland Hd. in 1776 and had six taxables in 1777 [Ref: K-1:212, R-31:11]. "Adam Burn" married Mary McCrea in Montgomery County on April 3, 1781 [Ref: K-2:517].

BURNS, Catherine. See "James Chilton," q.v.

BURN, Charles. See "Charles Byrn," q.v.

BURN (BURNS, BURNES), James. "James Burns" rendered aid by providing wheat for use of the military in 1780 [Ref: O-306]. "James

Burnes" was a private, 6th Co., Lower Bn., Militia, July 15, 1780 [Ref: M-206].

BURN (BURNS), John. Rendered aid by providing wheat for use of the military in 1781 [Ref: O-375].

BURN (BURNS, BYRN), Matthias (b. 1743). "Mathias Burn" was a private, 8th Co., Upper Bn., Militia, Aug. 30, 1777 [Ref: M-195]. Took the Oath of Allegiance before the Hon. Aneas Campbell on March 2, 1778 [Ref: T-3:77, L-1:38]. "Matthias Byrn" lived in Sugarland Hd. in 1776 and "Mathias Burns" lived there (two taxables) in 1777 [Ref: K-1:206, R-31:11].

BURN (BURNS), William. "William Burns" was a private, 8th Co., Upper Bn., Militia, Aug. 30, 1777 [Ref: M-195]. "William Burn" married Mary Wilson in Montgomery County on Feb. 27, 1781 [Ref: K-2:517].

BURNSIDES (BURNSIDE), James. Private, 5th Co., Middle Bn., Militia, Sep., 1777 [Ref: M-197, T-5:40]. "James Burnsides" was a private, 7th Class, 1st Co., Middle Bn., Militia, July 15, 1780 [Ref: M-201]. "James Burnside" lived in the Upper Part of Potomac Hd. (one taxable) in 1777 [Ref: R-31:13].

BURRISS (BURROWS, BURRACE), Charles. Private, 8th Co., Middle Bn., Militia, Sep., 1777 [Ref: M-198, T-5:43]. "Charles Burrace" was a private, 3rd Class, 4th Co., Middle Bn., Militia, July 15, 1780 [Ref: M-202]. "Charles Burriss" and "Charles Burress" took the Oath of Allegiance before the Hon. Edward Burgess on Feb. 28, 1778 [Ref: T-3:60, T-3:62, L-1:38]. One "Charles Burress" married Anne Morgan in Montgomery County on April 4, 1779 [Ref: K-2:517]. "Charles Burrows, Sr." lived in the Upper Part of Newfoundland Hd. (one taxable) in 1777 [Ref: R-31:6], and "Charles Burriss" lived in Rock Creek Hd. (one taxable) in 1777 [Ref: R-31:16].

BURRISS (BURROWS), Henry. Private, 4th Co., Middle Bn., Militia, Sep., 1777 [Ref: M-196, T-5:39]. First Sergeant, 4th Co., Middle Bn., Militia, July 15, 1780 [Ref: M-202]. "Henry Burrers" took the Oath of Allegiance (made his "X" mark) before the Hon. Edward Burgess on Feb. 28, 1778 [Ref: T-3:60, L-1:38]. "Henry Burrows" lived in the Upper Part of Newfoundland Hd. (one taxable) in 1777 [Ref: R-31:6]. Also see "Henry Burriss, Jr.," q.v.

BURRISS (BURRIS), Henry Jr. "Henry Burriss, Jr." took the Oath of Allegiance before the Hon. Edward Burgess on Feb. 28, 1778 [Ref: T-3:62, L-1:38]. "Henry Burris" married Frances Davis in Montgomery County on Jan. 22, 1778 [Ref: K-2:516].

BURRISS, Thomas. Private, 5th Co., Lower Bn., Militia, July 15, 1780 [Ref: M-206].

BURRISS (BURRIS), William. "William Burriss" was a private, 5th Class, 4th Co., Middle Bn., Militia, July 15, 1780 [Ref: M-202]. "William Burris" married Lucy Redman in Montgomery County on Dec. 28, 1780 [Ref: K-2:517].

BURTLE (BARTLE), Andrew (b. 1743). "Andrew Burtler" lived in Sugarland Hd. in 1776 [Ref: K-1:203]. "Andrew Burtle or Bartle" was a private, 3rd Co., Upper Bn., Militia, Aug. 30, 1777 [Ref: M-193]. Also see "Andrew Barth (Burth)," q.v.
BURTLE (BARTLE), Benjamin. Private, 4th Class, 2nd Co., Middle Bn., Militia, July 15, 1780 [Ref: M-201].
BURTON, Allen Basil. See "Basil Burton," q.v.
BURTON, Allie May Moxley. See "Nehemiah Moxley," q.v.
BURTON, Basil. Private, 1st Co., Lower Bn., Militia, Sep., 1777 [Ref: M-198, T-5:44]. Private, 7th Co., Lower Bn., Militia, July 15, 1780 [Ref: M-207]. "Basil Burton" took the Oath of Allegiance before the Hon. Edward Burgess on Feb. 28, 1778 [Ref: T-3:63, L-1:38]. "Allen Basil Burton" lived in the Lower Part of Newfoundland Hd. (one taxable) in 1777 [Ref: R-31:5].
BURTON, Henry. Took the Oath of Allegiance in 1778 [Ref: L-2:27].
BURTON, Jacob. Private, 7th Co., Lower Bn., Militia, July 15, 1780 [Ref: M-207]. Jacob Burton married Sarah Tucker in Montgomery County on Nov. 19, 1779 [Ref: K-2:515].
BURTON, Joseph. Private, 5th Co., Upper Bn., Militia, Aug. 30, 1777 [Ref: M-194]. There appears to have been two Joseph Burton's who took the Oath of Allegiance: one before the Hon. Edward Burgess on Feb. 28, 1778 and one before the Hon. Joseph Wilson on Feb. 28, 1778 [Ref: T-3:60, T-3:64, L-1:38]. A "Joseph Watker Burton" lived in Sugar Loaf Hd. (three taxables) in 1777 [Ref: R-31:9].
BURTON, William. Private, 1st Co., Middle Bn., Militia, Aug. 30, 1777 [Ref: M-195]. Private, 5th Co., Middle Bn., Militia, July 15, 1780 [Ref: M-203]. "William Burton Sr." took the Oath of Allegiance before the Hon. Gerrard Briscoe on March 2, 1778 [Ref: T-3:56, L-1:38]. Lived in Seneca Hd. (two taxables) in 1777 [Ref: R-31:7].
BURTON, William. Jr. Took the Oath of Allegiance before the Hon. Gerrard Briscoe on March 2, 1778 [Ref: T-3:56, L-1:38].
BUSBY (BUZBY), Christopher. Took the Oath of Allegiance before the Hon. Edward Burgess on Feb. 28, 1778 [Ref: T-3:61, L-1:38]. "Christopher Buzby" was a private in the 8th Co., Middle Bn., Militia, in Sep., 1777 [Ref: M-198, T-5:43]. Christopher Busby was married to Sarah Byall on June 1, 1778, by Rev. Thomas Reed in Montgomery County [Ref: K-2:516]. See "William Byall," q.v.
BUSEY, Benjamin. Private, 5th Co., Upper Bn., Militia, Aug. 30, 1777 [Ref: M-194].
BUSEY (BEWSEY), Charles. Served as Second Lieutenant, 5th Co., 16th Bn., Militia, Sep. 12, 1777, and First Lieutenant, Upper Bn., Militia, April 21, 1779 [Ref: M-58, M-194, C-373, E-357]. Took the Oath of Allegiance (made his "X" mark) before the Hon. Joseph Wilson on Feb. 28, 1778 [Ref: T-3:66, L-1:38]. "Charles Bussey" rendered aid by

providing wheat for use of the military in 1781 [Ref: O-446]. "Charles Bewsey" lived in Linganore Hd. (one taxable) in 1777 [Ref: R-31:9].
BUSEY, Edward. Private, 5th Co., Upper Bn., Militia, Aug. 30, 1777 [Ref: M-194]. Took the Oath of Allegiance before the Hon. Joseph Wilson on Feb. 28, 1778 [Ref: T-3:64, L-1:38]. "Edward Busey, Jr." lived in Sugar Loaf Hd. (one taxable) in 1777 [Ref: R-31:9].
BUSEY, Henry. Private, 5th Co., Upper Bn., Militia, Aug. 30, 1777 [Ref: M-194].
BUSEY (BUCEY), John (1751-1807). Private, 4th Co., Lower Bn., Militia, Aug., 1777, and First Sergeant, 1st Co., Lower Bn., July 15, 1780 [Ref: M-199, M-204, T-5:47]. "John Bucey" served as a petit juror in Nov., 1777 [Ref: R-31:18]. "John Busey" took the Oath of Allegiance before the Hon. Charles Jones on Jan. 10, 1778 [Ref: T-3:71, L-1:38]. "John Bussey" rendered aid by providing wheat for use of the military in 1780 and 1781 [Ref: O-303, O-445]. "John Bucey" lived in Lower Potomac Hd. in 1776-1777 and was a constable in 1779 [Ref: W-1, R-31:4, K-1:181]. "John Busey" married ---- Lansdale and died on June 24, 1807 [Ref: DAR-I:105].
BUSEY (BUCEY), Joshua (1711-c1786/90). Took the Oath of Allegiance before the Hon. Charles Jones on Jan. 10, 1778 [Ref: T-3:71, L-1:38]. Lived in Lower Potomac Hd. (four taxables) in 1776-1777 [Ref: R-31:4, K-1:181]. He married Eleanor ---- and rendered patriotic service [Ref: DAR-I:105].
BUSEY (BEWSEY), Paul. Took the Oath of Allegiance (made his "P B" mark) before the Hon. Joseph Wilson on Feb. 28, 1778 [Ref: T-3:64, L-1:38]. "Paul Bewsey" lived in Linganore Hd. (one taxable) in 1777 [Ref: R-31:9].
BUSEY (BUCEY), Rebecca. See "Samuel Davis," q.v.
BUSEY, Samuel (b. 1756). Private, 1st Co., Lower Bn., Militia, July 15, 1780 [Ref: M-204]. Took the Oath of Allegiance before the Hon. Charles Jones on Jan. 10, 1778 [Ref: T-3:71, L-1:38]. "Samuel Bussey" rendered aid by providing wheat for use of the military in 1780 [Ref: O-302]. "Samuel Bussey of Montgomery County" was a substitute who was discharged from the Maryland Line on Dec. 3, 1781 [Ref: I-11, D-406].
BUSHNELL, George. See "Zadock Wilson," q.v.
BUTCHER, John. Private who was recruited to serve in the Continental Army in 1780 [Ref: D-342].
BUTLER, Ann. See "Edward Harding," q.v.
BUTLER, James. Private, 6th Co., Middle Bn., Militia, Aug., 1777 [Ref: M-197, T-5:41]. Private, 6th Co., Middle Bn., Militia, July 15, 1780 [Ref: M-203]. Rendered aid by providing wheat for use of the military in 1781 [Ref: O-383].
BUTLER, Margaret. See "Zephaniah Offutt," q.v.
BUTLER, Tobias. Private, 3rd Co., Middle Bn., Militia, Sep., 1777 [Ref: M-196, T-5:38]. Private, 2nd Class, 2nd Co., Middle Bn., Militia, July 15,

1780 [Ref: M-201]. Took the Oath of Allegiance before the Hon. William Deakins, Jr. before March 3, 1778 [Ref: T-3:68, L-1:38]. Lived in the Upper Part of Potomac Hd. (one taxable) in 1777 [Ref: R-31:15]. Tobias Butler married Sarah Tool in Montgomery County on April 5, 1782 [Ref: K-2:515].

BUTT, Archibald. Applied for pension (S39252) in Greenbriar County, Virginia in 1819, aged 54 (64?), stating he had enlisted in 1777 at Georgetown in Prince George's County, Maryland, and served until the surrender of the British at Yorktown in 1781 [Ref: P-501, D-394, D-449]. See "Zachariah Butt," q.v.

BUTT, Azel. (1) Private, 8th Co., Middle Bn., Militia, Sep., 1777, and Second Corporal, 5th Co., Lower Bn., July 15, 1780 [Ref: M-198, M-205, T-5:43]. (2) Private, 5th Co., Lower Bn., Militia, July 15, 1780 [Ref: M-206].

BUTT, Barruck (Baruch, Barrock). Private, 2nd Maryland Line, 1778-1783 [Ref: D-84, D-523]. He moved to Virginia. See "Zachariah Butt," q.v.

BUTT (BUTTS), Edward. Served as a fifer and private, 2nd Maryland Line, 1778-1780, and was killed on March 15, 1781 [Ref: D-84, D-523]. See "Zachariah Butt," q.v.

BUTT, Richard. Private, 2nd Co., Lower Bn., Militia, Sep., 1777 [Ref: M-198, T-5:45]. Private, 5th Co., Lower Bn., Militia, July 15, 1780 [Ref: M-206]. Took the Oath of Allegiance (made his "R" mark) before the Hon. Joseph Wilson on Feb. 28, 1778 [Ref: T-3:66, L-1:38]. Lived in Rock Creek Hd. (one taxable) in 1777 [Ref: R-31:16].

BUTT, Rignal (died 1822). Private, 2nd Co., Lower Bn., Militia, Sep., 1777 [Ref: T-5:45]. Private, 5th Co., Lower Bn., Militia, July 15, 1780 [Ref: M-206]. "Rignuld Butt" took the Oath of Allegiance (made his "X" mark) before the Hon. Joseph Wilson on Feb. 28, 1778 [Ref: T-3:64, L-1:38]. Lived in Rock Creek Hd. (one taxable) in 1777 [Ref: R-31:15]. Rignal Butt (wife not named) died testate in Montgomery County in 1822 [Ref: V-24].

BUTT, Samuel (died 1786). Took the Oath of Allegiance before the Hon. Edward Burgess on Feb. 28, 1778 [Ref: T-3:60, L-1:38]. "Samuel Butt" lived in Rock Creek Hd. (four taxables) in 1777 [Ref: R-31:15]. "Samuel Butt, planter" (wife named Elizabeth) died testate in Montgomery County in 1786 [Ref: V-24].

BUTT, Swearingen (Swerringe). "Swearingen Butt" was a private, 2nd Co., Lower Bn., Militia, Sep., 1777 [Ref: M-198, T-5:45], and private, 5th Co., Lower Bn., Militia, July 15, 1780 [Ref: M-206]. "Swerringe Butt" took the Oath of Allegiance (made his "X" mark) before the Hon. Edward Burgess on Feb. 28, 1778 [Ref: T-3:60, L-1:38]. "Swewaringen Butt" lived in Rock Creek Hd. (two taxables) in 1777 [Ref: R-31:16].

BUTT (BUTTS), Thomas (1763-1833). Served as a drummer and private, 2nd Maryland Line, 1778-1783 [Ref: D-84, D-523]. Applied for a pension in Greenbriar County, Virginia on May 25, 1829, and died on March 1, 1833. He had married Mary Taylor in 1809. She applied for a pension (W8232) in 1854 in Henry County, Illinois, and lived near Lancaster, Missouri, in 1856. Thomas Butt was born Sep. 18, 1763 [Ref: P-501, DAR-I:107]. See "Zachariah Butt," q.v.

BUTT, Zachariah. Private, 8th Co., Middle Bn., Militia, Sep., 1777 [Ref: M-198, T-5:43], and private, 2nd Maryland Line, enlisted March 28, 1778 and reported missing (killed) on Aug. 16, 1780, at the Battle of Camden on Aug. 16, 1780. He served in the same company with Edward Butt, fifer, who was killed on March 15, 1781. They were brothers and served in the 2nd Maryland Line, both having enlisted on March 28, 1778. On Oct. 15, 1823, a Thomas Butt of Greenbriar County, Virginia, was an heir of Zachariah and Edward Butt, and also mentioned was a Barruck Butt, of Berkeley, Virginia, but no relationships were stated. "Archibald Butt," q.v., also received a pension in Greenbriar County, Virginia [Ref: P-501, U-5:119, U-20:56, D-84].

BUXTON, John. Private, 2nd Co., Middle Bn., Militia, Sep. 4, 1777 [Ref: T-5:37, and M-196 which questions if the name could have been "Burton"]. Private, 6th Class, 3rd Co., Middle Bn., Militia, July 15, 1780 [Ref: M-202]. "John Buxtor" took the Oath of Allegiance before the Hon. Gerrard Briscoe on March 2, 1778 [Ref: T-3:56, L-1:38]. "John Buxton" rendered aid by providing wheat for use of the military in 1780 and 1781 [Ref: O-317, O-407]. Lived in Sugar Loaf Hd. (four taxables) in 1777 [Ref: R-31:9].

BUXTON, Thomas. Private, 1st Class, 3rd Co., Middle Bn., Militia, July 15, 1780 [Ref: M-202]. Rendered aid by providing wheat for use of the military in 1781 [Ref: O-444]. Lived in Sugar Loaf Hd. (one taxable) in 1777 [Ref: R-31:9].

BUXTON (BUCKSTON), William. Served as private, 2nd Co., Middle Bn., Militia, Sep. 4, 1777 [Ref: T-5:37, M-196, which questions if the name could have been "Burton"]. Third Corporal, 3rd Co., Middle Bn., Militia, July 15, 1780 [Ref: M-202]. Took the Oath of Allegiance before the Hon. Gerrard Briscoe on March 2, 1778 [Ref: T-3:56, L-1:38]. Lived in Sugar Loaf Hd. (one taxable) in 1777 [Ref: R-31:9]. William Buxton married Sarah McCoy in Montgomery County on Nov. 12, 1780 [Ref: K-2:517]. One "William Buckston" (wife Eleanor) died testate in Montgomery County in 1822 [Ref: V-23].

BYALL (BOYALL), Peter (died 1782). "Peter Byall" was a soldier in the 1st Maryland Line by March, 1781 [Ref: G-332]. "Peter Boyall" was a corporal, Capt. Price's Co., 3rd Maryland Line, 1781, and died Jan. 15, 1782 [Ref: D-452].

BYALL, Sarah. See "Christopher Busby," q.v.

BYALL (BYAL, BOYALL), William. "William Byall" was a private, 6th Co., Middle Bn., Militia, Aug., 1777 [Ref: M-197, T-5:41]. "William Boyall" took the Oath of Allegiance (made his "X" mark) before the Hon.

Edward Burgess on Feb. 28, 1778 [Ref: T-3:61, L-1:38]. "William Byall" lived in the Upper Part of Newfoundland Hd. (one taxable) in 1777 [Ref: R-31:6]. Some notes on the Byall family: "John Byal, one of the pioneers of that [Liberty] township, was born in the city of Baltimore, Maryland, on the 25th day of July, 1791, and was the second son of William Byal, who died in Findley [Ohio] in 1840. The Byal family removed from Maryland to Pennsylvania, first to Huntington, and afterwards to Westmoreland County. In 1809 the family came to Ohio, settling first in Stark County, and here [Hancock County] in 1816." [Ref: *History of Hancock County, Ohio*, by D. B. Beardsley (1881), pp. 261-262]. One "William Byall" married Elizabeth Stafford on Aug. 8, 1782 and had these children: James, John, Martha, Charles, William J., Elizabeth, Sarah, Peter, Ann, Deliah, Henrietta, Henry, Hores, Absalom, Amy Catherine, William W., Sarah Jane, and Samuel Adam. This family settled in Stark County, Ohio in the early 1800's [Ref: *DAR Maryland Genealogical Records, Volume 35* (1967), pp. 24-26]. There was a "William Buyall, weaver" in Frederick County, Maryland by 1766 and, after Montgomery County was created out of Frederick County in 1776, William Byall appeared on the 1777 tax list. Court records in 1780 indicate that one "William Byall" was accused of stealing livestock, as also was "Christopher Busby," q.v. William failed to appear in court and no further records have been located in Montgomery County after 1780 with respect to him. He may have gone to Baltimore County or, most likely, migrated westward [Ref: R-31:6; *Frederick County Land Records, Liber K*, p. 838, Nov. 3, 1766; *Montgomery County Court Proceedings, March Court, 1780*, pp. 375-378; *Frederick County Land Records, Liber WR #3*, pp. 474-476, July 31, 1782]. It remains to be determined whether or not the William Byall in Montgomery County and the William Byle (Byles, Byler) in Baltimore County was the same person. Extensive research has failed thus far to make the distinction, but it should also be noted that the William Byall in Frederick County was a weaver by trade while the William Byle (Byles or Byler?) in Baltimore County was a cordwainer. No marriage records have yet been found in Maryland records for either man [Ref: Research files of Ronald B. Myers, of San Francisco, California, and Henry C. Peden, Jr., of Bel Air, Maryland].

BYER, John. Private, 6th Co., Middle Bn., Militia, Aug., 1777 [Ref: M-197, T-5:41]. Private, 4th Class, 4th Co., Middle Bn., Militia, July 15, 1780 [Ref: M-202].

BYFIELD, Robert. Took the Oath of Allegiance in 1778 [Ref: L-2:27].

BYRN (BYRNE, BURN), Charles (1747-1780). "Charles Byrn" lived in Sugarland Hd. in 1776 [Ref: K-1:204]. "Charles Byrn (Burn)" was a private, Flying Camp, who enlisted on July 18, 1776 [Ref: D-49]. "Charles Byrne" was a private, 2nd Maryland Regiment, who enlisted on

July 28, 1780, and was killed on Aug. 16, 1780 at the Battle of Camden [Ref: D-84, D-360].

BYRN, Matthias. See "Matthias Burn (Burns, Byrn)," q.v.

CADWELL, Ezekiel. Private, 4th Class, 4th Co., Middle Bn., Militia, July 15, 1780 [Ref: M-202].

CAHILL, Dennis. Private, 7th Co., Middle Bn., Militia, Sep., 1777 [Ref: M-197, T-5:42]. Took the Oath of Allegiance before the Hon. Gerrard Briscoe on March 2, 1778 [Ref: T-3:57, L-1:38]. Lived in Seneca Hd. (one taxable) in 1777 [Ref: R-31:7].

CAHILL (CAYHILL, CAHELL), William (died 1782). "William Cahill" lived in Seneca Hd. (two taxables) in 1777 [Ref: R-31:7]. "William Cayhill" took the Oath of Allegiance before the Hon. Edward Burgess on Feb. 28, 1778 [Ref: T-3:63, L-1:38]. "William Cahell" (wife named Jane) died testate in Montgomery County in 1782 [Ref: V-25].

CAHOE, Roger. Private, 6th Co., Lower Bn., Militia, July 15, 1780 [Ref: M-206]. Private, 8th Co., Lower Bn., Militia, Sep., 1777 [Ref: M-200, T-5:51].

CAHOE (CAHO, CAHOWE), William. "William Cahoe" was a private, 7th Co., Middle Bn., Militia, Sep., 1777 [Ref: M-197, T-5:42]. "William Caho" was a Private, 7th Co., Middle Bn., Militia, July 15, 1780 [Ref: M-203]. "William Cahowe" lived in the Upper Part of Newfoundland Hd. (one taxable) in 1777 [Ref: R-31:6].

CALBART, Simon. Private, 7th Maryland Line, 1780 [Ref: D-197].

CALLAHAN, Richard. Private, 5th Co., Lower Bn., Militia, July 15, 1780 [Ref: M-206]. "Richard Callehan" was a private, 8th Co., Middle Bn., Militia, Sep., 1777 [Ref: M-198, T-5:43]. "Richard Callihan" took the Oath of Allegiance (made his "X" mark) before the Hon. Joseph Wilson on Feb. 28, 1778 [Ref: T-3:67, L-1:38].

CALLICO, Basil. Private, 2nd Class, 2nd Co., Middle Bn., Militia, July 15, 1780 [Ref: M-201].

CALLICO, Ignatius. Private, 7th Class, 2nd Co., Middle Bn., Militia, July 15, 1780 [Ref: M-201].

CALVERT, Emma and George. See "Josiah Hoskinson, Jr.," q.v.

CAMBRON, Henry. Private, 6th Co., Lower Bn., Militia, July 15, 1780 [Ref: M-206].

CAMBRON, Milborn. Private, 6th Co., Lower Bn., Militia, July 15, 1780 [Ref: M-206].

CAMBURN, Thomas. Rendered aid by providing wheat for use of the military in 1781 [Ref: O-386].

CAMP, John. Took the Oath of Allegiance in 1778 [Ref: L-2:27].

CAMPBELL, Alexander. Private, 8th Class, 2nd Co., Middle Bn., Militia, July 15, 1780 [Ref: M-201]. Rendered aid by providing wheat for use of the military in 1781 [Ref: O-394]. Alexander Campbell married Mary Sparrow in Montgomery County on Dec. 12, 1779 [Ref: K-2:517].

CAMPBELL, Aneas or Eneas (1730-1812). Served as a Major, 16th Bn., Militia, Sep. 12, 1777, and Colonel, Oct. 7, 1777 [Ref: M-59, C-373, C-392]. Justice of the Peace who administered the Oath of Allegiance in 1777 and 1778 [Ref: T-3:77, L-1:38, R-31:18]. Justice of the Orphans Court in 1781 and Justice of the County Court in 1779-1781 [Ref: C-529, W-1, W-2]. "Aeneas or Eneas Campbell, Sr." lived in Sugarland Hd. (six taxables) in 1776-1777 [Ref: K-1:206, R-31:11]. Died testate in Montgomery County (wife named Henrietta) in 1812 [Ref: V-25].

CAMPBELL, Aneas (Eneas) Jr. (1757-1828). Son of Aneas and Henrietta Campbell [Ref: V-25, K-1:206]. "Aeneas or Eneas Campbell, Jr." lived in Sugarland Hd. in 1776 and had two taxables in 1777 [Ref: K-1:206, R-31:11]. Private, 8th Co., Upper Bn., Militia, on Aug. 30, 1777 [Ref: M-195, which source misspelled the name as "Ereas"]. Served as a Second Lieutenant, 16th Bn., Militia, on Sep. 12, 1777 [Ref: M-59, C-373]. "Ens. Campbell" took the Oath of Allegiance in 1778 [Ref: L-1:39, T-3:78]. He was born on Oct. 3, 1757 and married Elizabeth Ann Belt (b. Feb. 20, 1767) on Feb. 25, 1791 (his second wife; name of first wife not stated). Their children were: Thomas (b. April 10, 1793); Elijah (b. Jan. 17, 1795); Umprey (b. Feb. 18, 1797); Esther (b. Jan. 3, 1799); Asa (b. March 28, 1801); Rutha (b. May 27, 1803); Belt (b. Sep. 9, 1805); Elizabeth C. (b. Sep. 23, 1807); and, David C. (b. Feb. 26, 1810). "Enos Campbell" died on Oct. 15, 1828, and his widow died on Jan. 3, 1853. Their son David applied for any pension due his father or mother on Aug. 6, 1855, in Wilkes County, Georgia, but was rejected (R1627). [Ref: P-522, DAR-I:111].

CAMPBELL, Anne. See "Thomas Dowden," q.v.

CAMPBELL (CAMBLE), Daniel (b. 1756). "David Camble" was a servant of Aaron Harris in North West Hd. in 1776 [Ref: K-1:230, which source mistakenly spelled the name as "Camblo"]. "David Campbell" was a private in the Maryland Line, enlisted April 27, 1782 [Ref: D-424, D-474].

CAMPBELL, George (1738-1804?). Lived in Sugarland Hd. (one taxable) in 1777 [Ref: R-31:11]. Private, 7th Co., Upper Bn., Militia, Aug. 30, 1777 [Ref: M-195]. Private, 2nd Class, 1st Co., Middle Bn., Militia, July 15, 1780 [Ref: M-201]. "George Cambell" took the Oath of Allegiance before the Hon. Edward Burgess on Feb. 28, 1778 [Ref: T-3:63, L-1:39]. "George Campbell, a Welshman, 43 years of age, 5 feet 6 inches high, dark hair, pretty much pitted with the smallpox, recruited by Capt. William Bayly on April 28, 1781." [Ref: R-33:156, X-1146]. "George Campbell, gentleman" died testate in Montgomery County (wife named Sarah) in 1804 [Ref: V-25].

CAMPBELL, James. (1) Son of Aneas and Henrietta Campbell [Ref: V-25]. Private, 8th Co., Upper Bn., Militia, Aug. 30, 1777 [Ref: M-195]. Took the Oath of Allegiance before the Hon. Aneas Campbell on March 2, 1778 [Ref: T-3:78, L-1:39]. Also, a private who was recruited to serve in the Continental Army in 1780 [Ref: D-342]. (2) Private, Virginia Line, who pensioned in 1818, aged 71, while living in Montgomery County, Maryland, and died on Sep. 14, 1827 [Ref: J-38].

CAMPBELL, John. Took the Oath of Allegiance before the Hon. William Deakins, Jr. before March 3, 1778 [Ref: T-3:68, L-1:39, L-2:28]. "John Campbell" rendered aid by providing wheat for use of the military in 1781 [Ref: O-383]. "John Camel" lived in the Upper Part of Potomac Hd. (two taxables) in 1777 [Ref: R-31:14]. "John Campbell" died testate in Montgomery County (wife named Mary) in 1819 and "John R. Campbell" died testate in Montgomery County (wife named Mary) in 1815 [Ref: V-25, V-26].

CAMPBELL, John Jr. Took the Oath of Allegiance before the Hon. Aneas Campbell on March 2, 1778 [Ref: T-3:77, L-1:39].

CAMPBELL, Joseph. Private, 4th Co., Lower Bn., Militia, July 15, 1780 [Ref: M-205].

CAMPBELL, Robert. Private, Capt. Price's Co., 3rd Maryland Line, 1781-1782 [Ref: D-453].

CANADY, Judith. See "Robert Sutton," q.v.

CANDLER, Daniel (died 1810). Private, 1st Co., Middle Bn., Militia, Aug. 30, 1777 [Ref: M-195]. Took the Oath of Allegiance before the Hon. Gerrard Briscoe on March 2, 1778 [Ref: T-3:56, L-1:39]. Acted in roll of commissary at Benson's Mill in 1781 [Ref: O-378, O-379]. Lived in Seneca Hd. (two taxables) in 1777 [Ref: R-31:7]. Died testate in Montgomery County (wife named Rosetta) in 1810 [Ref: V-26].

CANDLER, James. Private, 5th Co., Middle Bn., Militia, July 15, 1780 [Ref: M-203]. Took the Oath of Allegiance before the Hon. Gerrard Briscoe on March 2, 1778 [Ref: T-3:57, L-1:39].

CAPELL, Peter. Took the Oath of Allegiance in 1778 [Ref: L-2:27].

CARBURY, Peter. Private, Capt. Grayson's Co., 1780, and Capt. Price's Co., 3rd Maryland Line, 1781-1782 [Ref: D-453, D-603].

CARLILE, David. Private, 6th Co., Upper Bn., Militia, Aug. 30, 1777 [Ref: M-194]. Lived in Sugar Loaf Hd. (one taxable) in 1777 [Ref: R-31:9].

CARMACK, Effie B. See "Kid Marquess," q.v.

CARMAN, Thomas. Private, 8th Co., Lower Bn., Militia, July 15, 1780 [Ref: M-207]. Took the Oath of Allegiance before the Hon. Richard Thompson in 1778 [Ref: T-3:75, L-1:39].

CARMICHEL, John. Took the Oath of Allegiance in 1778 [Ref: L-2:27].

CARNOLE, Samuel. Took the Oath of Allegiance before the Hon. Joseph Wilson on Feb. 28, 1778 [Ref: T-3:67, L-1:39]. Cryer, County Court, 1777 [Ref: R-31:18].

CARNY, Patrick. Private, 1st or 32nd Bn., Militia (no date was given; possibly June, 1777). [Ref: T-5:2].

CARPENTER, Umphrey. Private who was recruited to serve in the Continental Army in 1780 [Ref: D-341].

CARR (KARR), Stephen (b. 1754). "Stephen Carr" was a private, 7th Maryland Regiment, 1780 [Ref: D-197, D-341]. "Stephen Karr" lived in Lower Potomac Hd. in 1776 [Ref: K-1:183].
CARRENT, James. See "James Current," q.v.
CARRICO, Thomas Ignatius. Took the Oath of Allegiance before the Hon. Edward Burgess on Feb. 28, 1778 [Ref: T-3:64, L-1:39]. He may have been the "Ignatius Caricoe" who rendered aid by providing wheat for use of the military in 1781 [Ref: O-390]. Vincent Carrico, son of Thomas Ignatius Carrico and Elizabeth Kirby, was born in Montgomery County, Maryland, circa 1773 and married Mary Elder in Nelson County, Kentucky on Jan. 27, 1807 [Ref: *Filson Club Quarterly*, Vol. XXV (1951), pp. 217-252].
CARROLL, Daniel (1730-1796). "Daniel Carroll" was a private, 8th Co., Lower Bn., Militia, Sep., 1777 [Ref: M-200, T-5:51]. "Daniel Carroll, aged 46" lived in North West Hd. in 1776 and "Daniel Carroll, Sr." lived there (ten taxables) in 1777 [Ref: K-1:231, R-31:16]. Died testate in Montgomery County in 1796 and mentioned his deceased son Daniel Carroll and brother John Carroll [Ref: V-26]. Also see "Daniel Carroll, Jr.," q.v.
CARROLL, Daniel Jr. (b. 1753). Private, 3rd Co., Lower Bn., Militia, Sep., 1777 [Ref: M-199, T-5:46]. Took the Oath of Allegiance before the Hon. Charles Jones on Jan. 10, 1778 [Ref: T-3:71, L-1:39]. Lived in North West Hd. in 1776 and had five taxables in 1777 [Ref: K-1:232, R-31:17, which source mistakenly listed the name as "Carroll Daniel, Jr."]. See "Daniel Carroll," q.v.
CARROLL, Eleanor (died 1796). Lived in North West Hd. (head of household) in 1777 [Ref: R-31:16]. "Elinor Carroll" rendered aid by providing wheat for use of the military in 1780 [Ref: O-327]. "Elleanor Carroll" died testate in Montgomery County in 1796 [Ref: V-27].
CARROLL, John (Catholic Bishop). "Rev. J. Carroll" took the Oath of Allegiance before the Hon. Charles Jones on Jan. 10, 1778 [Ref: T-3:71, L-1:39]. "Mr. John Carroll" recruited Alexander Bonney for the military in Feb., 1781 [Ref: R-33:155, X-1146]. There was also a John Carroll, private, who enrolled in a company of militia for the service of the Flying Camp on Oct. 15, 1776 [Ref: B-353]. "John Carroll, aged 40" lived in North West Hd. in 1776 [Ref: K-1:231]. See "Leonard Green" and "Ralph Knott" and Richard Nicholson" and "Daniel Carroll," q.v.
CARROLL, Joseph. "An American born, 20 years of age, 5 feet 7 or 8 inches high, smooth faced, brown hair and well made, recruited by Allen Bowie on Feb. 19, 1781." [Ref: R-33:155, X-1146].
CARTER, George. Private, 6th Co., Upper Bn., Militia, Aug. 30, 1777 [Ref: M-194]. Took the Oath of Allegiance before the Hon. Edward Burgess on Feb. 28, 1778 [Ref: T-3:63, L-1:39].
CARTER, James. Private, Capt. Edward Burgess' Co., Lower District of Frederick (now Montgomery) County, Militia, July, 1776 [Ref: D-42].

CARTER, Lanslott. Private, 4th Co., Lower Bn., Militia, Aug., 1777 [Ref: T-5:47].

CARTER, Rebecca. See "Daniel McCarty," q.v.

CARTER, Samuel. Private, Capt. Edward Burgess' Co., Lower District of Frederick (now Montgomery) County, Militia, July, 1776 [Ref: D-42]. Private, 7th Co., Middle Bn., Militia, Sep., 1777 [Ref: M-197, T-5:42]. Private, 7th Co., Middle Bn., Militia, July 15, 1780 [Ref: M-203]. Lived in Seneca Hd. (one taxable) in 1777 [Ref: R-31:7].

CARTER, William (b. 1752). Served as an Ensign, 3rd Co., 29th (Lower) Bn., Militia, Sep. 12, 1777, and Captain, Lower (29th) Bn., Militia, Aug. 4, 1780. Served as a Recruiting Officer in Montgomery County and was paid for services in Jan., 1780 [Ref: M-60, M-199, T-5:46, C-373, F-54, F-248]. Took the Oath of Allegiance before the Hon. Richard Thompson in 1778 [Ref: T-3:75, L-1:39]. Lived in George Town Hd. (one taxable) in 1776-1777 [Ref: K-1:193, R-31:3].

CARTHEW, Edmond (b. 1756). Private, 3rd Maryland Regiment, from April 25, 1778 until Feb. 3, 1780, when reported "deserted" [Ref: D-96, D-297]. "Edmund Carthew, Srt." [servant] lived in North West Hd. in 1776 [Ref: K-1:226].

CARTWRIGHT, John. Served as Captain, 7th Co., Upper Bn., Militia, Aug. 30, 1777 [Ref: M-194].

CARTWRIGHT, Samuel (b. 1734). Private, 7th Co., Upper Bn., Militia, Aug. 30, 1777 [Ref: M-195]. Took the Oath of Allegiance before the Hon. Aneas Campbell on March 2, 1778 [Ref: T-3:77, L-1:39]. Lived in Sugarland Hd. (one taxable) in 1776-1777 [Ref: K-1:204, R-31:11].

CARTWRIGHT, Thomas (1726-1779). Private, 8th Co., Upper Bn., Militia, Aug. 30, 1777 [Ref: M-195]. Took the Oath of Allegiance before the Hon. Aneas Campbell on March 2, 1778 [Ref: T-3:77, L-1:39]. Lived in Sugarland Hd. in 1776 and had three taxables in 1777 [Ref: K-1:211, R-31:11]. Died testate in Montgomery County (wife named Barbara) in 1779 [Ref: V-27].

CARTY, Dennis. Private, Capt. Thomas Beall's Co., Maryland Line, 1780 [Ref: D-350].

CARTY, Patrick. Private, 1st or 32nd Bn., Militia (no date was given; possibly June, 1777). [Ref: T-5:2].

CARVILL, John. Took the Oath of Allegiance in 1778 [Ref: L-2:27].

CARY, Benjamin. Private, 6th Co., Lower Bn., Militia, July 15, 1780 [Ref: M-206].

CARY, James. Private, 1st Co., Middle Bn., Militia, Aug. 30, 1777 [Ref: M-195]. Private, 5th Co., Middle Bn., Militia, July 15, 1780 [Ref: M-203]. Lived in Seneca Hd. (one taxable) in 1777 [Ref: R-31:7].

CASE, Brock. Private, 2nd Co., Middle Bn., Militia, Sep. 4, 1777 [Ref: M-196, T-5:37]. Private, 5th Class, 3rd Co., Middle Bn., Militia, July 15, 1780 [Ref: M-202]. Took the Oath of Allegiance before the Hon. Gerrard

Briscoe on March 2, 1778 [Ref: T-3:57, L-1:39]. Lived in Sugar Loaf Hd. (one taxable) in 1777 [Ref: R-31:9].

CASE, Charles. Private, 7th Co., Lower Bn., Militia, Aug., 1777 [Ref: M-200, T-5:50]. Private, 4th Co., Lower Bn., Militia, July 15, 1780 [Ref: M-205]. Took the Oath of Allegiance before the Hon. Edward Burgess on Feb. 28, 1778 [Ref: T-3:63, L-1:39]. Lived in the Lower Part of Newfoundland Hd. (one taxable) in 1777 [Ref: R-31:5].

CASE, Israel (b. 1749). Private, 6th Co., Upper Bn., Militia, Aug. 30, 1777 [Ref: M-194]. Private, 2nd Class, 3rd Co., Middle Bn., Militia, July 15, 1780 [Ref: M-202]. Took the Oath of Allegiance on Sep. 1, 1780, under the Act of May 12, 1780, having neglected to do so previously "due to ignorance of the duty owed the country." [Ref: R-27:107]. Lived in Sugarland Hd. (one taxable) in 1777 [Ref: K-1:200, R-31:11].

CASE, James. Private, 2nd Co., Middle Bn., Militia, Sep. 4, 1777 [Ref: M-196, T-5:37]. Private, 5th Class, 3rd Co., Middle Bn., Militia, July 15, 1780 [Ref: M-202]. Took the Oath of Allegiance before the Hon. Gerrard Briscoe on March 2, 1778 [Ref: T-3:57, L-1:39].

CASE, Shadrach (Shadrick). Private, 1st Co., Lower Bn., Militia, Sep., 1777 [Ref: M-198, T-5:44]. Private, 5th Co., Middle Bn., Militia, July 15, 1780 [Ref: M-203]. Took the Oath of Allegiance before the Hon. Edward Burgess on Feb. 28, 1778 [Ref: T-3:59, L-1:39]. Lived in the Lower Part of Newfoundland Hd. (two taxables) in 1777 [Ref: R-31:5].

CASE, Thomas. Private, 2nd Co., Middle Bn., Militia, Sep. 4, 1777 [Ref: M-196, T-5:37]. Private, 6th Class, 3rd Co., Middle Bn., Militia, July 15, 1780 [Ref: M-202]. Took the Oath of Allegiance before the Hon. Gerrard Briscoe on March 2, 1778 [Ref: T-3:56, L-1:39]. Lived in Sugar Loaf Hd. (one taxable) in 1777 [Ref: R-31:9].

CASEY, Archibald. "Archibald Casey, born in Maryland, between 17 and 18 years of age, about 5 feet 4 or 5 inches high, brown hair, slender made and a little pitted with the smallpox, recruited by Dr. Thomas Sprigg Wootton on May 4, 1781." [Ref: R-33:156, X-1146].

CASEY, Daniel (b. 1752). Private, 6th Class, 2nd Co., Middle Bn., Militia, July 15, 1780 [Ref: M-201]. Took the Oath of Allegiance before the Hon. Edward Burgess on Feb. 28, 1778 [Ref: T-3:63, L-1:39]. "Daniel Carsey or Casey" lived in Sugarland Hd. (one taxable) in 1776-1777 [Ref: K-1:207, R-31:11].

CASEY, James (b. 1754). Private, Maryland Line, 1780-1783 [Ref: D-528]. Lived in Sugarland Hd. in 1776 [Ref: K-1:220].

CASEY, Levin. Private, 7th Co., Middle Bn., Militia, Sep., 1777 [Ref: M-197, T-5:42]. "Leven Casey" took the Oath of Allegiance before the Hon. Joseph Wilson on Feb. 28, 1778 [Ref: T-3:64, L-1:39].

CASEY, Peter. Private, 7th Maryland Line, March 28, 1777, and Corporal, Oct. 19, 1778, until Aug. 16, 1780, when reported missing at the Battle of Camden [Ref: D-196].

CASEY, Philip (died 1787). Served as Third Corporal, 1st Co., Middle Bn., Militia, July 15, 1780 [Ref: M-201]. Took the Oath of Allegiance before the Hon. Joseph Wilson on Feb. 28, 1778 [Ref: T-3:64, L-1:39]. He recruited William Medley in March, 1781 [Ref: R-33:155, X-1146]. "Philip Ceasy" rendered aid by providing wheat for use of the military in 1780 [Ref: O-307]. "Philip Casey, planter" died testate in Montgomery County (wife not named) in 1787 [Ref: V-28].

CASH, Caleb (b. 1735). Private, 5th Co., Upper Bn., Militia, Aug. 30, 1777 [Ref: M-194]. Private, 6th Co., Lower Bn., Militia, July 15, 1780 [Ref: M-206]. "Calab Cash, aged 41" lived in North West Hd. in 1776 [Ref: K-1:228].

CASH, Dawson (died 1795). Took the Oath of Allegiance before the Hon. Gerrard Briscoe on March 2, 1778 [Ref: T-3:57, L-1:39]. Lived in Sugar Loaf Hd. (one taxable) in 1777 [Ref: R-31:9]. Died testate in Montgomery County (no wife or children) in 1795 and mentioned his brother John Cash [Ref: V-28].

CASH, John. Private, 6th Co., Upper Bn., Militia, Aug. 30, 1777 [Ref: M-194]. This name appeared twice on the list of those who took the Oath of Allegiance before the Hon. Gerrard Briscoe on March 2, 1778 [Ref: T-3:57, L-1:39]. One lived in Sugar Loaf Hd. (three taxables) in 1777 [Ref: R-31:9]. A John Cash died testate in Montgomery County (wife named Ann) in 1794 and mentioned a son John, among others [Ref: V-28]. See "Dawson Cash," q.v.

CASH, Mary. See "Benjamin Greentree," q.v.

CASH, William. Took the Oath of Allegiance before the Hon. Gerrard Briscoe on March 2, 1778 [Ref: T-3:57, L-1:39].

CASHELL (GASHELL), Thomas. Took the Oath of Allegiance before the Hon. Edward Burgess on Feb. 28, 1778 [Ref: T-3:62, L-1:39, which indicated the name may have been "Gashell"].

CASHELL (CASHIRE), George. Private, 2nd Co., Lower Bn., Militia, Sep., 1777 [Ref: M-198, T-5:45]. Private, 5th Co., Lower Bn., Militia, July 15, 1780 [Ref: M-206]. "George Cashell" took the Oath of Allegiance before the Hon. Edward Burgess on Feb. 28, 1778 [Ref: T-3:60, L-1:39]. "George Chashire" lived in Seneca Hd. (one taxable) in 1777 [Ref: R-31:7].

CASNER, Michael (b. 1759). Lived in George Town Hd. in 1776 [Ref: K-1:193]. Private, 3rd Co., Lower Bn., Militia, Sep., 1777 [Ref: M-199, T-5:46].

CASPER, C. J. Took the Oath of Allegiance in 1778 [Ref: L-2:27].

CASTER, Jacob. Took the Oath of Allegiance in 1778 [Ref: L-2:27].

CASTER (CASTOR, CATER), James. Rendered aid by providing wheat for use of the military in 1780 [Ref: O-318]. "James Castor" was a private, 6th Co., Lower Bn., Militia, July 15, 1780 [Ref: M-206]. "James Cater" took the Oath of Allegiance in 1778 [Ref: L-2:27]. "James Castor" lived in North West Hd. (one taxable) in 1777 [Ref: R-31:17].

CASTER, John. Rendered aid by providing wheat for use of the military in 1780 [Ref: O-316].

CATLETT (CATTILIT), Alexander. "Alexander Catlett" was a private, 7th Class, 3rd Co., Middle Bn., Militia, July 15, 1780 [Ref: M-202]. "Alexander Cattilit" rendered aid by providing wheat for use of the military in 1781 [Ref: O-398].

CATOE (CATO), William. "William Catoe" was a private, 8th Co., Upper Bn., Militia, Aug. 30, 1777 [Ref: M-195]. Took the Oath of Allegiance before the Hon. Aneas Campbell on March 2, 1778 [Ref: T-3:77, L-1:39, which source listed the name as "William Catol"]. "William Cato" lived in Sugarland Hd. (one taxable) in 1777 [Ref: R-31:11].

CATON, Charles. Private, 3rd Co., Upper Bn., Militia, Aug. 30, 1777 [Ref: M-193]. Took the Oath of Allegiance on Sep. 1, 1780, under the Act of May 12, 1780, having neglected to do so previously "due to ignorance of the duty owed the country." [Ref: R-27:107]. Rendered aid by providing wheat for use of the military in 1780 [Ref: O-316]. Lived in Sugar Loaf Hd. (two taxables) in 1777 [Ref: R-31:9].

CATON, John. Private, 3rd Co., Upper Bn., Militia, Aug. 30, 1777 [Ref: M-193].

CATON (CAYTON), Joshua. "Joshua Caton" was a private, 7th Co., Upper Bn., Militia, Aug. 30, 1777 [Ref: M-195]. "Joshua Cayton" lived in Sugarland Hd. (one taxable) in 1777 [Ref: R-31:11].

CATON, Stephen. Private, 2nd Co., Upper Bn., Militia, Aug. 30, 1777 [Ref: M-193, T-5:54]. Took the Oath of Allegiance on Sep. 1, 1780, under the Act of May 12, 1780, having neglected to do so previously "due to ignorance of the duty owed the country." [Ref: R-27:107].

CATON, William. Private, 8th Co., Upper Bn., Militia, Aug. 30, 1777 [Ref: M-195], and was recruited to serve in the Continental Army in 1780 [Ref: D-341].

CATREL, James. Private, 8th Co., Lower Bn., Militia, Sep., 1777 [Ref: T-5:51 and M-200, which latter source listed the name as "Jas. Castree(?)"].

CAVENOUGH, Patrick. Private who was recruited to serve in the Extra Regiment, Continental Army in 1780 [Ref: D-342]. Patrick Cavenough married Mary Eustice in Montgomery County on June 1, 1780 [Ref: K-2:517].

CAVIN, Thomas. Private, 3rd Co., Lower Bn., Militia, Sep., 1777 [Ref: M-199, T-5:46].

CAWOOD (CAWARD), Stephen (died 1802). "Stephen Cawood" was a private, 3rd Co., Upper Bn., Militia, Aug. 30, 1777 [Ref: M-193]. Took the Oath of Allegiance before the Hon. Elisha Williams on March 2, 1778 [Ref: T-3:81, L-1:39]. "Stephen Caward" lived in Sugarland Hd. (one taxable) in 1777 [Ref: R-31:11]. "Stephen Cawood" died testate in Montgomery County (wife named Priscilla) in 1802 [Ref: V-29].

CECIL (SCISSELL), Archibald. Private, 5th Co., Upper Bn., Militia, Aug. 30, 1777 [Ref: M-194].
CECIL, Eleanor. See "Alexander Barrett," q.v.
CECIL, Elizabeth. See "Bennett Woodard (Woodward)," q.v.
CECIL (SCISSELL, SCISSILL), James (b. 1761). Son of Sabrit Cecil, of North West Hd. in 1776 [Ref: K-1:229]. "James Scissill" was a private, 8th Co., Lower Bn., Militia, Sep., 1777 [Ref: M-200, T-5:51]. "James Scissell" was a private, 6th Co., Lower Bn., Militia, July 15, 1780 [Ref: M-206].
CECIL (SCISSELL), John (b. 1758). Son of Sabrit Cecil, of North West Hd. in 1776 [Ref: K-1:229]. "John Scissell" was a private, 8th Co., Lower Bn., Militia, Sep., 1777, and Second Corporal, 6th Co., Lower Bn., on July 15, 1780 [Ref: M-200, M-206, T-5:51]. "John Cecil" took the Oath of Allegiance before the Hon. Richard Thompson in 1778 [Ref: T-3:75, L-1:39].
CECIL (SCISSELL, SCISSILL, SISSEL), Joshua. "Joshua Scissill" was a private, 6th Co., Middle Bn., Militia, Aug., 1777 [Ref: M-197, T-5:41]. "Joshua Scissell" was a private, 6th Co., Middle Bn., Militia, July 15, 1780 [Ref: M-203]. "Joshua Sissel" lived in Linganore Hd. (one taxable) in 1777 [Ref: R-31:9].
CECIL, Philip. Took the Oath of Allegiance in 1778 [Ref: L-2:27].
CECIL (CICIL), Sabrit (1723-1810). "Sabrat Cecil" took the Oath of Allegiance before the Hon. Richard Thompson in 1778 [Ref: T-3:75, L-1:39]. "Sabiet Cecil or Sabrot Cicil" lived in North West Hd. (wife named Mary, aged 46) in 1776 and had four taxables in 1777 [Ref: K-1:229, R-31:17]. "Sabrit Cecil" died testate in Montgomery County (wife named Mary) in 1810 [Ref: V-29].
CECIL, Samuel (b. 1753). Son of Sabrit Cecil, of North West Hd., in 1776 [Ref: K-1:229]. "Samuel Scissill" was a private, 8th Co., Lower Bn., Militia, Sep., 1777 [Ref: M-200, T-5:51]. "Samuel Cecil" took the Oath of Allegiance before the Hon. Richard Thompson in 1778 [Ref: T-3:75, L-1:39]. Rendered aid by providing wheat for use of the military in 1781 [Ref: O-386, O-447].
CECIL (SCISSILL), Thomas. Private, 5th Co., Upper Bn., Militia, Aug. 30, 1777 [Ref: M-194].
CECIL (SCISSILL, SISSEL, SISSILE, CECILL), William. "William Scissill" was a private, 5th Co., Upper Bn., Militia, Aug. 30, 1777 [Ref: M-194]. "William Sissel" lived in Sugar Loaf Hd. (four taxables) in 1777 [Ref: R-31:11]. "William Sissile" took the Oath of Allegiance on Sep. 1, 1780, under the Act of May 12, 1780, having neglected to do so previously "due to ignorance of the duty owed the country." [Ref: R-27:120]. "William Cecill, Sr." died testate in Montgomery County (wife not named) in 1807 [Ref: V-29]. Descendants can be found in the records of Rowan and Davidson Counties, North Carolina, and Johnson

County, Missouri [Ref: Elise Greenup Jourdan's *Early Families of Southern Maryland*, Vol. I (1992), pp. 43-44].
CHAMBERLAIN, Jeremiah. Took the Oath of Allegiance in 1778 [Ref: L-2:27].
CHAMBERLAIN, John. Took the Oath of Allegiance in 1778 [Ref: L-2:27].
CHAMBERS, Amos. Private, 1st or 32nd Bn., Militia (no date was given; possibly June, 1777). [Ref: T-5:1].
CHAMBERS, Clement. Rendered aid by providing wheat for use of the military in 1781 [Ref: O-385].
CHAMBERS, Edward. Private, 4th Co., Middle Bn., Militia, Sep., 1777 [Ref: M-196, T-5:39]. Took the Oath of Allegiance before the Hon. Edward Burgess on Feb. 28, 1778 [Ref: T-3:58, L-1:39]. Lived in the Upper Part of Newfoundland Hd. (one taxable) in 1777 [Ref: R-31:6].
CHAMBERS, Eliza. See "Jacob Cramlet (Cramblit)," q.v.
CHAMBERS, Henry. Private, 2nd Class, 2nd Co., Middle Bn., Militia, July 15, 1780 [Ref: M-201]. Took the Oath of Allegiance before the Hon. William Deakins, Jr. before March 3, 1778 [Ref: T-3:68, L-1:39]. Lived in the Upper Part of Potomac Hd. (two taxables) in 1777 [Ref: R-31:14].
CHAMBERS, James. Private, 3rd Co., Middle Bn., Militia, Sep., 1777 [Ref: M-196, T-5:38]. Took the Oath of Allegiance before the Hon. William Deakins, Jr. before March 3, 1778 [Ref: T-3:68, L-1:39].
CHAMBERS, John. (1) Private, 3rd Co., Middle Bn., Militia, Sep., 1777 [Ref: M-196, T-5:38]. (2) Private, 4th Co., Middle Bn., Militia, Sep., 1777 [Ref: M-196, T-5:39]. One John Chambers was a private, 8th Class, 4th Co., Middle Bn., Militia, on July 15, 1780 [Ref: M-202]. Two men with this name took the Oath of Allegiance before the Hon. Edward Burgess on Feb. 28, 1778 [Ref: T-3:60, L-1:39, T-3:63, L-1:39]. Rendered aid by providing wheat for use of the military in 1781 [Ref: O-391]. One John Chambers married Rebeccah Winsor in Montgomery County in March 5, 1780 [Ref: K-2:517]. One John Chambers lived in the Upper Part of Newfoundland Hd. (one taxable) in 1777 [Ref: R-31:6].
CHAMBERS, John, of Henry. Private, 5th Class, 2nd Co., Middle Bn., Militia, July 15, 1780 [Ref: M-201].
CHAMBERS, John, of William. Private, 5th Class, 2nd Co., Middle Bn., Militia, July 15, 1780 [Ref: M-201].
CHAMBERS, Joshua. Took the Oath of Allegiance (made his "X" mark) before the Hon. Edward Burgess on Feb. 28, 1778 [Ref: T-3:60, L-1:39].
CHAMBERS, Josiah (Josias). "Josiah Chambers" took the Oath of Allegiance (made his "X" mark) before the Hon. Edward Burgess on Feb. 28, 1778 [Ref: T-3:60, L-1:39]. Lived in the Upper Part of Newfoundland Hd. (one taxable) in 1777 [Ref: R-31:6]. "Josias Chambers" was a private, 4th Co., Middle Bn., Militia, Sep., 1777 [Ref: M-196, T-5:39].
CHAMBERS, Mary. See "Jacob Bowman," q.v.

CHAMBERS, William (died 1780). Took the Oath of Allegiance before the Hon. William Deakins, Jr. before March 3, 1778 [Ref: T-3:68, L-1:39]. Lived in the Upper Part of Potomac Hd. (two taxables) in 1777 [Ref: R-31:14]. Died testate in Montgomery County (wife not named) in 1780 and mentioned a son William, among other children [Ref: V-30].

CHAMBERS, William T. Private, 5th Co., Lower Bn., Militia, Aug., 1777 [Ref: T-5:48]. Private, 2nd Co., Lower Bn., Militia, July 15, 1780 [Ref: M-204]. Took the Oath of Allegiance before the Hon. Samuel W. Magruder in 1778 [Ref: T-3:73].

CHANDLER, William. See "Leonard Hays," q.v.

CHANEY (CHENEY), Charles. Took the Oath of Allegiance before the Hon. Edward Burgess on Feb. 28, 1778 [Ref: T-3:62, L-1:39]. "Charles Chainey" was a private, 7th Co., Lower Bn., Militia, Aug., 1777 [Ref: M-200, T-5:50]. "Charles Cheney" lived in the Lower Part of Newfoundland Hd. (four taxables) in 1777 [Ref: R-31:5].

CHANEY (CHEYNEY), Edward. Private, 5th Co., Upper Bn., Militia, Aug. 30, 1777 [Ref: M-194].

CHANEY, Hezekiah. Private, 8th Co., Lower Bn., Militia, July 15, 1780 [Ref: M-207]. Rendered aid by providing wheat for use of the military in 1780 [Ref: O-326].

CHANEY (CHENEY), Richard (died 1786). "Richard Chaney" took the Oath of Allegiance before the Hon. Edward Burgess on Feb. 28, 1778 [Ref: T-3:63, L-1:39]. "Richard Cheney" died testate in Montgomery County (no wife or children) in 1786 [Ref: V-30].

CHAPMAN, William. Served as an Ensign, 5th Co., Upper Bn., Militia, Aug. 30, 1777 [Ref: M-194]. Took the Oath of Allegiance before the Hon. Joseph Wilson on Feb. 28, 1778 [Ref: T-3:64, L-1:39]. "William Chapmon" lived in Sugar Loaf Hd. (one taxable) in 1777 [Ref: R-31:9].

CHAPPLE (CHAPPEL), Archibald. "Archibald Chapple" was a private, 5th Co., Upper Bn., Militia, Aug. 30, 1777 [Ref: M-194]. Rendered aid by providing wheat for use of the military in 1781 [Ref: O-398]. "Archibald Chappel" lived in Sugar Loaf Hd. (one taxable) in 1777 [Ref: R-31:9].

CHAPPLE, George (b. 1760). Private, 1st Co., Lower Bn., Militia, July 15, 1780 [Ref: M-204, K-1:182].

CHAPPLE (CHAPPEL, CHAPPELL), Henry. Private, 2nd Co., Lower Bn., Militia, Sep., 1777 [Ref: T-5:45]. Private, 5th Co., Lower Bn., Militia, July 15, 1780 [Ref: M-206]. "Henry Chappell" took the Oath of Allegiance before the Hon. Edward Burgess on Feb. 28, 1778 [Ref: T-3:62, L-1:39]. "Henry Chappel, Sr." (b. 1716) lived in Lower Potomac Hd. (two taxables) in 1776-1777 [Ref: R-31:4, K-1:182], and "Henry Chapel" lived in Rock Creek Hd. (one taxable) in 1777 [Ref: R-31:16].

CHAPPLE, James. Private, 7th Class, 1st Co., Middle Bn., Militia, July 15, 1780 [Ref: M-201].

CHAPPLE (CHAPPEL, CHAPPELL), John (b. 1746). Private, 1st Co., Lower Bn., Militia, July 15, 1780 [Ref: M-204]. "John Chappell" took the

Oath of Allegiance before the Hon. Richard Thompson in 1778 [Ref: T-3:75, L-1:39]. "John Chappel or Chapple" lived in Lower Potomac Hd. (two taxables) in 1776-1777 [Ref: R-31:4, K-1:182].

CHAPPLE (CHAPPELL), Thomas (b. 1755). Private, 4th Co., Lower Bn., Militia, Aug., 1777, and First Corporal, 1st Co., Lower Bn., July 15, 1780 [Ref: M-199, M-204, T-5:47]. "Thomas Chappell" took the Oath of Allegiance before the Hon. Charles Jones on Jan. 10, 1778 [Ref: T-3:71, L-1:39, K-1:182].

CHATTLE (CHATTLE), Thomas. Served as a private in the Flying Camp, Frederick (now Montgomery) County, enlisted by Greenbury Gaither on July 29, 1776 [Ref: D-44]. Private, 1st Co., Middle Bn., Militia, Aug. 30, 1777, and private, 5th Co., July 15, 1780 [Ref: M-195, M-203]. Took the Oath of Allegiance before the Hon. Gerrard Briscoe on March 2, 1778 [Ref: T-3:57, L-1:39]. Lived in Seneca Hd. (one taxable) in 1777 [Ref: R-31:7].

CHENEY, Richard. See "Richard Chaney," q.v.

CHESHIRE, Burch. Son of John Cheshire [Ref: V-30]. Took the Oath of Allegiance before the Hon. Samuel W. Magruder in 1778 [Ref: T-3:73, L-1:39]. "Berch Cheshire" was a private, 5th Co., Lower Bn., Militia, Aug., 1777, and Fourth Sergeant, 2nd Co., Lower Bn., July 15, 1780 [Ref: M-199, M-204, T-5:48].

CHESHIRE (CASHIRE), George. See "George Cashell (Cashire)," q.v.

CHESHIRE, John (1753-1792). Private, 5th Co., Lower Bn., Militia, Aug., 1777 [Ref: M-200, T-5:48]. "John Cheshese" [sic] took the Oath of Allegiance before the Hon. Samuel W. Magruder in 1778 [Ref: T-3:73, L-1:39]. "John Cheshire" died testate in Montgomery County (wife not named) in 1792 and mentioned his only son "Birch Cheshire," q.v. [Ref: V-30, K-1:182].

CHESHIRE, John Baptist. Private, 8th Class, 1st Co., Middle Bn., Militia, July 15, 1780 [Ref: M-201].

CHESHIRE (CHESHER), John Nicholls. Private, 5th Co., Lower Bn., Militia, Aug., 1777 [Ref: M-199, T-5:48]. Took the Oath of Allegiance before the Hon. Joseph Wilson on Feb. 28, 1778 [Ref: T-3:64, L-1:39].

CHEW, Joseph. Private, 6th Co., Upper Bn., Militia, Aug. 30, 1777 [Ref: M-194]. Took the Oath of Allegiance before the Hon. Joseph Wilson on Feb. 28, 1778 [Ref: T-3:64, L-1:39].

CHEW, Samuel L. "Samuel L. Chew" took the Oath of Allegiance before the Hon. Edward Burgess on Feb. 28, 1778 [Ref: T-3:62, L-1:39]. "Samuel Chewe" lived in Linganore Hd. (six taxables) in 1777 and "Samuel Chew" owned a working plantation ("quarter") in the Lower Part of Newfoundland Hd. in 1777 [Ref: R-31:5, R-31:9].

CHEYNEY, Edward. See "Edward Chaney," q.v.

CHILDS, Benjamin. Took the Oath of Allegiance (made his "B" mark) before the Hon. Edward Burgess on Feb. 28, 1778 [Ref: T-3:62, L-1:39].

CHILDS (CHILD), Henry. Private, 6th Co., Lower Bn., Militia, Aug., 1777 [Ref: M-200, T-5:49]. Private, 3rd Co., Lower Bn., Militia, July 15, 1780 [Ref: M-205]. Took the Oath of Allegiance before the Hon. Joseph Offutt on March 2, 1778 [Ref: T-3:70, L-1:39]. Lived in the Upper Part of Potomac Hd. (two taxables) in 1777 [Ref: R-31:14].

CHILDS, John. Private, 3rd Co., Lower Bn., Militia, July 15, 1780 [Ref: M-205].

CHILTON, James. Took the Oath of Allegiance before the Hon. Aneas Campbell on March 2, 1778 [Ref: T-3:77, L-1:39]. "James Chilton, aged 36" lived in Sugarland Hd. in 1776 (wife Ann and several young children) and had four taxables in 1777 [Ref: R-31:11, K-1:210]. A James Chilton married Catherine Burns in Montgomery County on June 25, 1778 [Ref: K-2:517].

CHILTON (CHELTON), Mark (b. 1754). Lived in Sugarland Hd. in 1776 [Ref: K-1:206]. Private, Flying Camp, enlisted July 18, 1776 [Ref: D-49]. Private, 8th Co., Upper Bn., Militia, Aug. 30, 1777 [Ref: M-195]. "Marke Chilton" took the Oath of Allegiance (made his "X" mark) before the Hon. Aneas Campbell on March 2, 1778 [Ref: T-3:78, L-1:39]. "Mark Chelton" married Clementia Barn [Barns or Burn?] in Montgomery County on June 17, 1779 [Ref: K-2:513].

CHILTON, Stearman. Private, 3rd Co., Upper Bn., Militia, Aug. 30, 1777 [Ref: M-193]. "Sturman Chilton" took the Oath of Allegiance before the Hon. William Deakins, Jr. before March 3, 1778 [Ref: T-3:68, L-1:39]. "Stearman Chilton" lived in Sugarland Hd. (two taxables) in 1777 [Ref: R-31:11].

CHILTON, Thomas (b. 1752). Served as an Ensign, 7th Co., 16th Bn., Militia, by Sep. 12, 1777, and Second Lieutenant, Upper Bn., Militia, Aug. 4, 1780 [Ref: M-62, M-194, C-373, F-248]. Took the Oath of Allegiance before the Hon. Aneas Campbell on March 2, 1778 [Ref: T-3:78, L-1:39]. "Thomas Chitton or Chilton" lived in Sugarland Hd. in 1776 and had three taxables in 1777 [Ref: K-1:211, R-31:11].

CHILTON (CHILITEN), William (b. 1752). "William Chiliten" lived in Sugarland Hd. in 1776 [Ref: K-1:214]. "William Chilton" was a private, 5th Maryland Regiment, from July 13, 1777 to Nov. 4, 1777 [Ref: D-276].

CHINN, Edward. Rendered aid by providing wheat for use of the military in 1781 [Ref: O-393].

CHISWELL, Anne Newton. See "Jesse Allnutt," q.v.

CHISWELL (CHISSELL), Joseph Newton (1747-1837). Son of Stephen Newton Chiswell [Ref: V-31]. Lived in Sugar Loaf Hd. (two taxables) in 1777 [Ref: R-31:9]. Private, 6th Co., Upper Bn., Militia, Aug. 30, 1777 [Ref: M-194]. "Joseph N. Chiswell" took the Oath of Allegiance before the Hon. Elisha Williams on March 2, 1778 [Ref: T-3:80, L-1:39]. "Joseph Newton Chissell" married Eleanor White in Montgomery County on Nov. 11, 1779 [Ref: K-2:517]. Rendered aid by providing wheat for use of the military in 1781 [Ref: O-427]. For more details see the well-documented history entitled "A Chiswell Family From Leicestershire, England to Maryland: Six Generations," by Ernest C. Allnutt, Jr., *Maryland Genealogical Society Bulletin*, Vol. 32, No. 4 (1991), pp. 496-531.

CHISWELL, Sarah Newton. See "Stephen Newton Chiswell" and "Robert Doyne Dawson," q.v.

CHISWELL, Stephen Newton (1721-1805). Lived in Sugar Loaf Hd. (three taxables) in 1777 [Ref: R-31:9]. Took the Oath of Allegiance before the Hon. Elisha Williams on March 2, 1778 [Ref: T-3:80, L-1:39]. He was the "Newton Chiswell" who rendered aid by providing corn for use of the military in 1780 [Ref: O-299]. Died testate in Montgomery County (wife not named) and his will was probated in 1805 [Ref: V-31]. The *DAR Patriot Index* (Volume I, p. 130) states he was born in 1715, married Sarah Newton, and died in 1800, but this is incorrect. Stephen Newton Chiswell, son of William Chiswell and Mary Newton, was baptized at the Borough of Leicestershire, England, on July 10, 1721 and died near present day Poolesville, Montgomery County, Maryland in 1805. He married his first cousin Sarah Newton, oldest daughter of his uncle Joseph Newton and wife Ann Odell. The known children of Stephen Newton Chiswell were: Joseph Newton Chiswell (b. 1747), Ann Newton Chiswell (b. 1750), Sarah Newton Chiswell (b. 1754), Margaret Presbury Chiswell, Margaret Presbury Chiswell, Frances Elizabeth Chiswell, Rebecca Odell Chiswell, and Rachel Newton Chiswell. For more details see the well-documented history entitled "A Chiswell Family From Leicestershire, England to Maryland: Six Generations," by Ernest C. Allnutt, Jr., *Maryland Genealogical Society Bulletin*, Vol. 32, No. 4 (1991), pp. 496-531.

CHRISMAN, Margaret. See "William Hocker," q.v.

CLABAUGH, Charles. Took the Oath of Allegiance in 1778 [Ref: L-2:27].

CLAGETT, Alexander (1745-1821). Served as a First Lieutenant, Middle Bn., Sep. 12, 1777 [Ref: M-62, C-373, M-196]. Served as a grand juror in Aug., 1777 [Ref: R-31:17], and as a petit juror in Nov., 1777 [Ref: R-31:18]. Took the Oath of Allegiance before the Hon. William Deakins, Jr. before March 3, 1778 [Ref: T-3:68, L-1:39]. Lived in the Upper Part of Potomac Hd. (six taxables) in 1777 [Ref: R-31:14].

CLAGETT, Ann. See "John Summers," q.v.

CLAGETT, Asa. See "Thomas Pennifield," q.v.

CLAGETT, Charles (1729-1791). Lived in Sugar Loaf Hd. (three taxables) in 1777 [Ref: R-31:9]. Took the Oath of Allegiance before the Hon. Elisha Williams on March 2, 1778 [Ref: T-3:80, L-1:39, and DAR-I:132, which stated his wife was named Mary].

CLAGETT, Elizabeth. See "Jesse Willcoxen," q.v.

CLAGETT, Henry (1730-1778). Private who enrolled into a company of militia for the service of the Flying Camp on Oct. 15, 1776 [Ref: B-352]. Private, 2nd Co., Upper Bn., Militia, Aug. 30, 1777 [Ref: M-193]. Took the Oath of Allegiance before the Hon. Elisha Williams on March 2, 1778 [Ref: T-3:80, L-1:39]. Lived in Sugar Loaf Hd. (one taxable) in 1777 [Ref: R-31:9]. Died testate in Montgomery County (wife named Ann Magruder) in Jan., 1778 [Ref: V-32, and DAR-I:132, which also indicated that there was another Henry Clagett (1755-1823) who married Elizabeth Hayse [sic], served as a soldier, and rendered patriotic service in Maryland].

CLAGETT, Hezekiah. Private, 3rd Co., Lower Bn., Militia, July 15, 1780 [Ref: M-205]. Rendered aid by providing wheat for use of the military in 1780 [Ref: O-328].

CLAGETT, John. (1) Private, 2nd Co., Upper Bn., Militia, Aug. 30, 1777 [Ref: M-193]. (2) Private, 3rd Co., Middle Bn., Militia, Sep., 1777 [Ref: M-196, T-5:38]. (3) Private, 5th Co., Lower Bn., Militia, Aug., 1777 [Ref: M-199, T-5:48]. Private, 2nd Co., Lower Bn., Militia, July 15, 1780 [Ref: M-204]. One John Clagett took the Oath of Allegiance before the Hon. Elisha Williams on March 2, 1778 [Ref: T-3:80, L-1:39], and another took the Oath of Allegiance before the Hon. Samuel W. Magruder in 1778 [Ref: T-3:73]. One rendered aid by providing wheat for use of the military in 1780 [Ref: O-320, O-340]. One John Clagett lived in the Upper Part of Potomac Hd. (two taxables) in 1777 and "John Clagett, of Thomas" (b. 1744) lived in Lower Potomac Hd. (three taxables) in 1776-1777 [Ref: R-31:4, R-31:14, K-1:182]. One John Clagett died testate in Montgomery County (wife named Mary) in 1815 [Ref: V-32]. Also see "John Clagett, Sr.," q.v.

CLAGETT, John Jr. (b. 1754). Took the Oath of Allegiance before the Hon. William Deakins, Jr. before March 3, 1778 [Ref: T-3:68, L-1:39].

CLAGETT, John Sr. (1713-1790). Took the Oath of Allegiance before the Hon. Richard Thompson in 1778 [Ref: T-3:75, L-1:39]. He recruited Benjamin Smith in May, 1781 [Ref: R-33:156, X-1146]. Lived in Lower Potomac Hd. (seven taxables) in 1776-1777 [Ref: R-31:4, K-1:182]. Died testate in Montgomery County (wife not named) in 1790 [Ref: V-32]. Also see "John Clagett," q.v.

CLAGETT, Joseph. Private, 6th Co., Lower Bn., Militia, Aug., 1777, and Fourth Sergeant, 3rd Co., July 15, 1780 [Ref: M-200, M-205, T-5:49]. Took the Oath of Allegiance before the Hon. Samuel W. Magruder in 1778 [Ref: T-3:73]. Rendered aid by providing wheat for use of the military in 1780 and 1781 [Ref: O-304, O-356].

CLAGETT, Nathan (b. 1756). Private, 5th Co., Lower Bn., Militia, Aug., 1777 [Ref: M-199, T-5:48]. Private, 2nd Co., Lower Bn., Militia, July 15, 1780 [Ref: M-204]. Took the Oath of Allegiance before the Hon. Samuel W. Magruder in 1778 [Ref: T-3:73, L-1:39]. Served as a grand juror in 1779 [Ref: W-1]. Rendered aid by providing wheat for use of the military in 1780 [Ref: O-307, O-312, O-335]. Lived in Lower Potomac Hd. by 1776 and served as a constable in 1781 [Ref: W-2, K-1:182].

CLAGETT, Ninian (1750-1805). Private, 1st Co., Upper Bn., Militia, Aug. 30, 1777 [Ref: M-193]. Took the Oath of Allegiance before the Hon. Elisha Williams on March 2, 1778 [Ref: T-3:80, L-1:39]. "Nin'n. Cleckett" lived in Sugarland Hd. in 1776 and "Ninian Clagett" lived there (one taxable) in 1777 [Ref: K-1:201, R-31:11].

CLAGETT, Richard Keene or Cain (b. 1746). "Richard Keene Clagett" was a private, 4th Co., Lower Bn., Militia, Aug., 1777 [Ref: M-199, T-5:47]. Took the Oath of Allegiance before the Hon. Richard Thompson in 1778 [Ref: T-3:75, L-1:39]. "Richard Cain Clagett" rendered aid by providing wheat for use of the military in 1780 [Ref: O-309]. "Richard C. Clagett" was a private, 1st Co., Lower Bn., Militia, July 15, 1780 [Ref: M-204]. Richard Keen (or Keene) Clagett lived in Lower Potomac Hd. (seven taxables) in 1776-1777 [Ref: R-31:4, K-1:182].

CLAGETT, Samuel. Private, 6th Co., Lower Bn., Militia, Aug., 1777, and Third Sergeant, 3rd Co., July 15, 1780 [Ref: M-200, M-205, T-5:49]. Took the Oath of Allegiance before the Hon. Joseph Offutt on Feb. 13, 1778 [Ref: T-3:70, L-1:39. Source DAR-I:132 also indicates that there was a Samuel Clagett (c1750-1821) who married Annie Jane Ramey and served as a Surgeon's Mate].

CLAGETT, Volinda. See "Basil Beckwith," w.v.

CLAGETT, Walter (b. 1763 or 1764). Private, 1st Co., Lower Bn., Militia, July 15, 1780 [Ref: M-204, K-1:182].

CLAGETT, Zachariah. Private, 6th Co., Lower Bn., Militia, Aug., 1777, and Third Corporal, 3rd Co., July 15, 1780 [Ref: M-200, M-204, T-5:49]. Rendered aid by providing wheat for use of the military in 1781 [Ref: O-356].

CLANCEY, Edward. Private who was recruited to serve in the Continental Army in 1780 [Ref: D-341].

CLANCY, Margaret. See "James Ruglass (Ruggles)," q.v.

CLANCY, Michael. Private, enrolled into a company of militia for the service of the Flying Camp, Oct. 15, 1776 [Ref: B-353].

CLAPSADDLE, George. Took the Oath of Allegiance in 1778 [Ref: L-2:27].

CLAPSADDLE, John. Took the Oath of Allegiance in 1778 [Ref: L-2:27].

CLAPSADDLE, Michael. Took the Oath of Allegiance in 1778 [Ref: L-2:27].

CLARK, Aaron. Private, 7th Co., Upper Bn., Militia, Aug. 30, 1777 [Ref: M-195].

CLARK, Ann. See "Zadock Wilson," q.v.

CLARK (CLARKE), Benedict (b. 1753). "Benedict Clarke" was a private, 1st Co., Lower Bn., Militia, July 15, 1780 [Ref: M-204]. "Benedict Clark" lived in Lower Potomac Hd. (one taxable) in 1776-1777 [Ref: R-31:4, K-1:182].

CLARK, Clement. Private, 3rd Co., Middle Bn., Militia, Sep., 1777 [Ref: M-196, T-5:38]. Took the Oath of Allegiance before the Hon. William

Deakins, Jr. before March 3, 1778 [Ref: T-3:68, L-1:39]. Lived in the Upper Part of Potomac Hd. (one taxable) in 1777 [Ref: R-31:14].

CLARK, Edward. (1) Private, 3rd Co., Upper Bn., Militia, Aug. 30, 1777 [Ref: M-193]. (2) Private, 8th Co., Middle Bn., Militia, Sep., 1777 [Ref: M-198, T-5:43]. "Edward Clark, born in Maryland, 38 years of age, about 5 feet 8 or 9 inches high, yellow visage, and thin dark coloured hair, recruited by Zachariah Dowden [in Montgomery County] on April 5, 1781, and sent to Annapolis under the care of Lt. William Murdock on April 29, 1781." [Ref: R-33:156, X-1156]. One Edward Clark lived in Sugarland Hd. (one taxable) in 1777 [Ref: R-31:11], and another lived in Rock Creek Hd. (one taxable) in 1777 [Ref: R-31:16].

CLARK (CLARKE), Elijah. "Elijah Clarke" was recruited to serve in the Continental Army in 1780 [Ref: D-342]. "Elijah Clark" married Mary Graves in Montgomery County on July 28, 1780 [Ref: K-2:517].

CLARK (CLARKE), George. "George Clarke" was a private who was recruited to serve in the Extra Regiment, Continental Army, in 1780 [Ref: D-342].

CLARK, Harmon or Herman (b. 1729). "Herman Clark" took the Oath of Allegiance before the Hon. Richard Thompson in 1778 [Ref: T-3:75, L-1:39]. "Harmon Clark" lived in Lower Potomac Hd. in 1776-1777 [Ref: R-31:4, K-1:182].

CLARK (CLARKE), Henry (1734-1807). Lived in North West Hd. (wife named Nancy, aged 42) in 1776 and had three taxables in 1777 [Ref: K-1:229, R-31:17]. Served as a private in Capt. Edward Burgess' Co., Lower District of Frederick (now Montgomery) County, Militia, July, 1776 [Ref: D-42]. Took the Oath of Allegiance before the Hon. Richard Thompson in 1778 [Ref: T-3:75, L-1:39]. Private, Capt. Price's Co., 3rd Maryland Line, 1781-1782 [Ref: D-454]. "Henry Clarke" was a private, 4th Co., Lower Bn., Militia, July 15, 1780 [Ref: M-205]. Served as a grand juror in Aug., 1777, and again in 1781 [Ref: R-31:17, W-2]. "Henry Clark, Sr." died testate in Montgomery County (wife named Ann) in 1807 [Ref: V-33].

CLARK, James. Private, 3rd Maryland Regiment, 1778, and he may have enlisted in Anne Arundel County in 1777 [Ref: D-275, D-313]. Lived in Rock Creek Hd. (one taxable) in 1777 [Ref: R-31:16].

CLARK (CLARKE), John (died 1803). "John Clarke" was a private, 3rd Co., Lower Bn., Militia, July 15, 1780 [Ref: M-205]. "John Clark" died testate in Montgomery County (wife named Ann) in 1803 [Ref: V-34].

CLARK (CLARKE), Leonard. "Leonard Clarke" was a private, 3rd Co., Lower Bn., Militia, July 15, 1780 [Ref: M-205].

CLARK, Richard. Private, 3rd Co., Middle Bn., Militia, Sep., 1777 [Ref: M-196, T-5:38]. Took the Oath of Allegiance before the Hon. William Deakins, Jr. before March 3, 1778 [Ref: T-3:68, L-1:39]. Lived in the Upper Part of Potomac Hd. (one taxable) in 1777 [Ref: R-31:14].

CLARK (CLARKE), Thomas. *Records with the name spelled "Thomas Clark"*: (1) Private, 2nd Co., Lower Bn., Militia, Sep., 1777 [Ref: M-198, T-5:45]. (2) Private, 6th Co., Lower Bn., Militia, Aug., 1777 [Ref: M-200, T-5:49]. Private, Capt. Price's Co., 3rd Maryland Line, 1781-1782 [Ref: D-452]. One Thomas Clark married Priscilla Barnes (Barns) in Montgomery County on Feb. 11, 1779 [Ref: K-2:515]. One Thomas Clark (aged 30) lived in Lower Potomac Hd. (one taxable) and another lived in Seneca Hd. (two taxables) in 1777 [Ref: R-31:4, R-31:7, K-1:182]. *Records with the name spelled "Thomas Clarke"*: (1) Private, 8th Co., Lower Bn., Militia, July 15, 1780 [Ref: M-207]. (2) Private, 1st Co., Lower Bn., Militia, July 15, 1780 [Ref: M-204]. (3) Private, 7th Co., Middle Bn., Militia, July 15, 1780 [Ref: M-203]. (4) Private, 3rd Co., Lower Bn., Militia, July 15, 1780 [Ref: M-205]. One rendered aid by providing wheat for use of the military in 1781 [Ref: O-447]. A Thomas Clarke lived in the Upper Part of Potomac Hd. (one taxable) in 1777 [Ref: R-31:14].

CLARK (CLARKE), Walter (b. 1764). "Walter Clark, aged 12" was a son of Henry and Nancy Clark who lived in North West Hd. in 1776 [Ref: K-1:230]. "Walter Clarke" was a private, 6th Co., Lower Bn., Militia, July 15, 1780 [Ref: M-206].

CLARK (CLARKE), William. *Records with the name spelled "William Clark"*: (1) Private, 8th Co., Lower Bn., Militia, Sep., 1777 [Ref: M-200, T-5:51]. (2) Two men with this name took the Oath of Allegiance before the Hon. Edward Burgess on Feb. 28, 1778 [Ref: T-3:62, L-1:39, T-3:63, L-1:39]. One William Clark lived in North West Hd. (one taxable) in 1777 [Ref: R-31:17, which source mistakenly listed the name as "Clark William"]. "William Clark, aged 26" lived in North West Hd. in 1776 [Ref: K-1:230]. *Records with the name spelled "William Clarke"*: (1) Private, 7th Co., Middle Bn., Militia, July 15, 1780 [Ref: M-203]. (2) Took the Oath of Allegiance before the Hon. Joseph Wilson on Feb. 28, 1778 [Ref: T-3:64, L-1:39]. One William Clarke was Bailiff of the Montgomery County Court in 1779 [Ref: W-1].

CLARKSON, Notley (died 1804). Rendered aid by providing wheat for use of the military in 1780 [Ref: O-306]. Died testate in Montgomery County (wife named Vilettee) in 1804 [Ref: V-34].

CLAVELY (CLEVELY), Henry. "Henry Clavely" was a private, 3rd Co., Lower Bn., Militia, Sep., 1777 [Ref: M-199, T-5:46]. "Henry Clevely" took the Oath of Allegiance before the Hon. Richard Thompson in 1778 [Ref: T-3:75, L-1:39].

CLAYTON, John. Private who was recruited to serve in the Continental Army in 1780 [Ref: D-342]. John Clayton married Virlinda Riggs in Montgomery County on Nov. 13, 1781 [Ref: K-2:517].

CLEMENTS, Catherine. See "Richard Roberts," q.v.

CLEMENTS, Charles. Private, Capt. Price's Co., 3rd Maryland Line, 1781-1782 [Ref: D-453].

CLEMENTS, Francis (died 1793). Rendered aid by providing wheat for use of the military in 1780 [Ref: O-307]. Died testate in Montgomery County (wife named Elizabeth) in 1793 [Ref: V-34].
CLEMENTS, Mary. See "Nicholas Hocker," q.v.
CLEMENTS, Oswald. Rendered aid by providing wheat for use of the military in 1781 [Ref: O-394].
CLEMENTS (CLEMONS), William. Private, 5th Co., Lower Bn., Militia, Aug., 1777, and First Sergeant, 2nd Co., Lower Bn., July 15, 1780 [Ref: M-199, M-204, T-5:48]. Took the Oath of Allegiance before the Hon. Samuel W. Magruder in 1778 [Ref: T-3:73], and served as a grand juror in 1781 [Ref: W-2]. "William Clements" (one taxable) and "William Clemons" (two taxables) both lived in the Upper Part of Potomac Hd. in 1777 [Ref: R-31:14].
CLEMENTS, William Wallace. Private, 7th Class, 1st Co., Middle Bn., Militia, July 15, 1780 [Ref: M-201].
CLEWLEY (CLULEY), Joseph. Private, Maryland Line, from April 5, 1782 until discharged Nov. 29, 1783. He received a pension from the State of Maryland in 1815. On Feb. 2, 1830, the Treasurer of the Western Shore was directed to pay to Henry Harding for the use of Mary Whelan, legal heir of Joseph Clewley, the balance due said Joseph Clewley, late a pensioner [Ref: K-2:329, Q-100, D-468, D-530].
CLIFFORD, Hugh. Took the Oath of Allegiance before the Hon. William Deakins, Jr. before March 3, 1778 [Ref: T-3:68, L-1:39]. Lived in the Upper Part of Potomac Hd. (three taxables) in 1777 [Ref: R-31:14].
CLINE, Daniel. Took the Oath of Allegiance in 1778 [Ref: L-2:27].
CLINE, Jacob. Took the Oath of Allegiance in 1778 [Ref: L-2:27].
COALE, Michael. Private who was recruited to serve in the Continental Army in 1780 [Ref: D-341].
COATS, Ann. See "James Allnutt," q.v.
COATS (COARTS), Charles (b. 1715). Took the Oath of Allegiance before the Hon. Elisha Williams on March 2, 1778 [Ref: T-3:80, L-1:39]. "Charles Coats or Coarts" lived in Sugarland Hd. in 1776 and had four taxables in 1777 [Ref: K-1:221, R-31:11]. See "James Allnutt," q.v.
COATS (COARTS), Notley (b. 1755). Private, 8th Co., Upper Bn., Militia, Aug. 30, 1777 [Ref: M-195]. "Notly Coats" took the Oath of Allegiance before the Hon. Elisha Williams on March 2, 1778 [Ref: T-3:80, L-1:39]. "Notley Coarts" lived in Sugarland Hd. in 1776 [Ref: K-1:221].
COATS, Richard. Private, 3rd Co., Lower Bn., Militia, Sep., 1777 [Ref: M-199, T-5:46].
COBERT (COBETH), Aaron. "Aaron Cobert" took the Oath of Allegiance before the Hon. Gerrard Briscoe on March 2, 1778 [Ref: T-3:56, L-1:39]. "Aaron Cobeth" was a private, 7th Co., Middle Bn., Militia, July 15, 1780 [Ref: M-203].
COBERTH, Jane. See "James Allnutt, Sr.," q.v.

COCHANTOFER (COCHANTOPHER, COCHENTOFFER, COFFENTERVER, COCENDOFER), Christopher Jr. (b. 1752). Private, 4th Co., Lower Bn., Militia, Aug., 1777 [Ref: M-199, T-5:47]. Private, 1st Co., Lower Bn., Militia, July 15, 1780 [Ref: M-204]. "Christopher Coffenterver or Cocendofer" lived in Lower Potomac Hd. (two taxables) in 1776-1777 [Ref: R-31:4, K-1:182].
COCHANTOFER (COCHANTOPHER, COCHENTOFFER, COCENDOFER, KOGENDERFER), Frederick (b. 1754). "Frederick Cochantofer" was a private, 3rd Co., Lower Bn., Militia, Sep., 1777 [Ref: M-199, T-5:46]. Private, 8th Co., Lower Bn., Militia, July 15, 1780 [Ref: M-207]. "Frederick Kogenderfer" took the Oath of Allegiance before the Hon. Richard Thompson in 1778 [Ref: T-3:75, L-1:39]. "Frederick Kokendoffer" married Susanna Yonst [Youst?] in Montgomery County on Dec. 29, 1779 [Ref: K-2:514]. "Frederick Kodenderfer or Cokendofer" lived in George Town Hd. (one taxable) in 1776-1777 [Ref: K-1:193, R-31:3].
COCHANTOFER (COCHANTOPHER, COCHENTOFFER, KODENDERFER, KOGENDERFOR), Leonard. "Leonard Cochantofer" was a private, 4th Co., Lower Bn., Militia, Aug., 1777 [Ref: M-199, T-5:47]. Private, 8th Co., Lower Bn., Militia, July 15, 1780 [Ref: M-207]. "Leonard Kogenderfer" took the Oath of Allegiance before the Hon. Richard Thompson in 1778 [Ref: T-3:76, L-1:39]. "Leonard Kogenderfor" married Susannah Crons in Montgomery County on Sep. 18, 1780 [Ref: K-2:514].
COCHANTOFER (COCHANTOPHER, COCHENTOFFER, COCENDOFER, COOKONTOFFT), Michael (b. 1751). "Michael Cochantofer" was a private, 4th Co., Lower Bn., Militia, Aug., 1777 [Ref: M-199, T-5:47]. Private, 1st Co., Lower Bn., Militia, July 15, 1780 [Ref: M-204]. "Michael Cookontofft" took the Oath of Allegiance before the Hon. Charles Jones in Jan., 1778 [Ref: T-3:71, L-1:39]. Michael Coffenterfer or Cocendofer" lived in Lower Potomac Hd. (one taxable) in 1776-1777 [Ref: R-31:4, K-1:182]. Michael Cookendorfer was a fifer in the Maryland Militia and applied for and received a pension (S30337) in 1831 (aged 84 in 1835) in Pendleton County, Kentucky [Ref: *Marylanders to Kentucky, 1775-1825*, by Henry C. Peden, Jr. (1991), p. 31].
COCHANTOFER (COCHANTOPHER, COCHENTOFFER, COCENDOFER, COOKONTOFFT), Stophel. "Stofol Cookontofft" took the Oath of Allegiance before the Hon. Charles Jones in Jan., 1778 [Ref: T-3:71, L-1:39].
COCHRAN, John. Private, 7th Maryland Line, 1780 [Ref: D-197].
COCKINDALL, Elisha. Served as a Corporal, Capt. Thomas Beall's Co., Maryland Line, 1780 [Ref: D-350].
COFFEE, Cloe. See "Hezekiah Roberts," q.v.
COLGAN (COLAGIN, COLEGON), Michael. Private, 7th Co., Middle Bn., Militia, Sep., 1777 [Ref: M-197, T-5:42]. Private, 7th Co., Middle Bn., Militia, July 15, 1780 [Ref: M-203]. Took the Oath of Allegiance before

the Hon. Joseph Wilson on Feb. 28, 1778 [Ref: T-3:66, L-1:39]. "Michael Colagin" rendered aid by providing wheat for use of the military in 1781 [Ref: O-446]. "Michael Colegon" lived in Seneca Hd. (one taxable) in 1777 [Ref: R-31:7].

COLLIER, Sarah. See "John Pool," q.v.

COLLIER (COLLIAR, COLYAR, COLLYAR), William. (1) Private, 1st Co., Upper Bn., Militia, Aug. 30, 1777 [Ref: M-193]. (2) Private, 5th Co., Lower Bn., Militia, Aug., 1777 [Ref: M-199, T-5:48]. Private, 2nd Co., Lower Bn., Militia, July 15, 1780 [Ref: M-204]. Took the Oath of Allegiance before the Hon. Aneas Campbell on March 2, 1778 [Ref: T-3:78, L-1:39]. "William Collyar, Jr." took the Oath of Allegiance before the Hon. Samuel W. Magruder in 1778 [Ref: T-3:73], and "William Collyar, Sr." also took the Oath of Allegiance before the Hon. Samuel W. Magruder in 1778 [Ref: T-3:73, L-1:39]. "William Colliar" rendered aid by providing wheat for use of the military in 1780 [Ref: O-313]. "William Collier" rendered aid by providing wheat for use of the military in 1780 [Ref: O-321, O-335]. One William Collier married Aeda Arnold in Montgomery County on June 22, 1779 [Ref: K-2:517]. One William Collier lived in Lower Potomac Hd. (five taxables) in 1777 and another lived in Sugarland Hd. (one taxable) in 1777 [Ref: R-31:4, R-31:11]. "William Collyar, Sr." died testate in Montgomery County (wife named Sarah) in 1794 and mentioned a son William, among other children. "Sarah Collyar, widow of William" died testate in Montgomery County in 1801 [Ref: V-35]. "William Colyar" (b. 1732) and "William Colyar, Jr." (b. 1759) lived together (with others) in Lower Potomac Hd. in 1776 [Ref: K-1:182]. "William Colliar, aged 31" lived in Sugarland Hd. in 1776 [Ref: K-1:218].

COLLINS, Edmond. Private, 2nd Co., Middle Bn., Militia, Sep. 4, 1777 [Ref: M-196, T-5:37].

COLLINS, Edward. Took the Oath of Allegiance before the Hon. Gerrard Briscoe on March 2, 1778 [Ref: T-3:56, L-1:39].

COLLINS (COLLINGS), George. "George Collins" was a private, 2nd Co., Upper Bn., Militia, Aug. 30, 1777 [Ref: M-193]. "George Collings" lived in Sugar Loaf Hd. (three taxables) in 1777 [Ref: R-31:9].

COLLINS (COLLINGS), James. (1) Private, 1st Co., Lower Bn., Militia, July 15, 1780 [Ref: M-204]. (2) Private, 4th Co., Middle Bn., Militia, Sep., 1777 [Ref: M-196, T-5:39]. Private, 6th Class, 4th Co., Middle Bn., Militia, July 15, 1780 [Ref: M-202]. Took the Oath of Allegiance (made his "X" mark) before the Hon. Edward Burgess on Feb. 28, 1778 [Ref: T-3:60, L-1:39]. One James Collins or Collings (b. 1743) lived in Lower Potomac Hd. (one taxable) in 1776-1777 [Ref: R-31:4, K-1:182], and another lived in Rock Creek Hd. (one taxable) in 1777 [Ref: R-31:16].

COLLINS (COLLINGS), John. Served as a private in the Flying Camp, Frederick (now Montgomery) County, enlisted by Greenbury Gaither on July 29, 1776 [Ref: D-44]. Private, 8th Co., Lower Bn., Militia, Sep.,

1777 [Ref: M-200, T-5:51]. Private, 6th Co., Lower Bn., Militia, July 15, 1780 [Ref: M-206]. Took the Oath of Allegiance before the Hon. Edward Burgess on Feb. 28, 1778 [Ref: T-3:63, L-1:39]. One John Collins (b. 1716) lived in Lower Potomac Hd. (two taxables) in 1776-1777 [Ref: K-1:182 and R-31:4, which latter source misspelled the name as "Cottins"], another John Collins lived in North West Hd. (one taxable) in 1777 [Ref: R-31:17], and "John Collings, aged 24" lived in Sugarland Hd. in 1776 [Ref: K-1:217]. "John Collens, aged 34" lived in Northwest Hd. (wife named Sarah, aged 30) in 1776 [Ref: K-1:224].

COLLINS (COLLINGS), Joshua (b. 1759). Private, 4th Co., Lower Bn., Militia, Aug., 1777 [Ref: M-199, T-5:47]. Private, 6th Co., Lower Bn., Militia, on July 15, 1780 [Ref: M-206]. Joshua Collins or Collings lived in Lower Potomac Hd. in 1776 and married Mary Barrance on May 15, 1779 [Ref: K-1:182, K-2:515].

COLLINS (COLLINGS), Nathan (b. 1754). Private, 1st Co., Lower Bn., Militia, July 15, 1780 [Ref: M-204]. Took the Oath of Allegiance before the Hon. Edward Burgess on Feb. 28, 1778 [Ref: T-3:63, L-1:39]. Nathan Collins or Collings married Ann Maddin on Feb. 11, 1779 [Ref: K-1:182, K-2:515].

COLLINS, Richard. (1) Private, 3rd Co., Middle Bn., Militia, Sep., 1777 [Ref: M-196, T-5:38]. (2) Private, 2nd Co., Upper Bn., Militia, Aug. 30, 1777 [Ref: M-193].

COLLINS (COLLINGS), Robert. Private, 3rd Co., Lower Bn., Militia, Sep., 1777 [Ref: M-199, T-5:46]. "Robert Collings" lived in George Town Hd. (one taxable) in 1777 [Ref: R-31:4].

COLLINS (COLLINGS), Thomas. (1) Private, 4th Co., Middle Bn., Militia, Sep., 1777 [Ref: M-196, T-5:39]. Private, 2nd Class, 4th Co., Middle Bn., Militia, July 15, 1780 [Ref: M-202]. (2) Private, 6th Co., Lower Bn., Militia, July 15, 1780 [Ref: M-206]. Took the Oath of Allegiance before the Hon. Edward Burgess on Feb. 28, 1778 [Ref: T-3:63, L-1:39]. One Thomas Collins or Collings was born in 1762 or 1763 [Ref: K-1:182].

COLYER, Stephen Rev. See "Zachariah Evans," q.v.

COMBERS, Ann. Rendered aid by providing wheat for use of the military in 1781 [Ref: O-387].

COMBS, Leonard. Private, 6th Co., Lower Bn., Militia, July 15, 1780 [Ref: M-206].

COMPTON (CUMPTON, CRUMPTON), Ignatius. "Ignatius Compton" was a private, 7th Maryland Line, 1780 [Ref: D-197]. "Ignatius Crumpton" was a private who was recruited to serve in the Continental Army in 1780 [Ref: D-341]. "Igns. Cumpton" was a private in the 1st Maryland Regiment and served in the Southern Army of the United States in the summer of 1781 [Ref: D-389].

CONES, Richard. Rendered aid by providing wheat for use of the military in 1781 [Ref: O-447].

CONN, Jane. Rendered aid by providing wheat for use of the military in 1780 [Ref: O-322].
CONN, William Young. Private, Capt. Edward Burgess' Co., Lower District of Frederick (now Montgomery) County, Militia, July, 1776 [Ref: D-42].
CONNER, Ann. See "Nathan Musgrove," q.v.
CONNER (CONNOR), James. Private, 5th Maryland Line, and was transferred to Col. Nicola's Invalids Corps on July 24, 1780 [Ref: D-623]. Lived in the Lower Part of Newfoundland Hd. (one taxable) in 1777 [Ref: R-31:5].
CONNER, Richard. Private, 6th Co., Middle Bn., Militia, Aug., 1777 [Ref: M-197, T-5:41]. Took the Oath of Allegiance before the Hon. Edward Burgess on Feb. 28, 1778 [Ref: T-3:61, L-1:39]. Private, 6th Co., Middle Bn., Militia, July 15, 1780 [Ref: M-203]. Lived in Linganore Hd. (five taxables) in 1777 [Ref: R-31:9].
CONNER, Thomas. (1) Ensign, 16th Bn., Militia, May 20, 1776. Ensign, Middle Bn., Militia, Sep. 12, 1777, and First Lieutenant, Upper Bn., Militia, April 21, 1779, and Captain, 6th Co., Middle Bn., Militia, March 25, 1780 [Ref: M-64, M-203, A-432, C-373, F-120]. (2) Private, 6th Co., Middle Bn., Militia, Aug., 1777 [Ref: M-197, T-5:41]. Took the Oath of Allegiance before the Hon. Edward Burgess on Feb. 28, 1778 [Ref: T-3:61, L-1:39]. One Thomas Conner lived in Linganore Hd. (two taxables) in 1777 [Ref: R-31:9].
CONNER (CONNOR), Zadock. Private, 1st Co., Lower Bn., Militia, Sep., 1777 [Ref: M-198, T-5:44].
CONNOLLY (CONELY), John. Private, 8th Co., Middle Bn., Militia, Sep., 1777 [Ref: M-198, T-5:43]. Private, 5th Co., Lower Bn., Militia, July 15, 1780 [Ref: M-205]. "John Connolly" took the Oath of Allegiance before the Hon. Charles Jones on Jan. 10, 1778 [Ref: T-3:71, L-1:39]. "John Conely" lived in Rock Creek Hd. (one taxable) in 1777 [Ref: R-31:16].
CONNOLLY (CONELY), Michael. Private, 8th Co., Middle Bn., Militia, Sep., 1777 [Ref: M-198, T-5:43]. Private, 5th Co., Lower Bn., Militia, July 15, 1780 [Ref: M-205]. "Michael Connolly" took the Oath of Allegiance before the Hon. Charles Jones on Jan. 10, 1778 [Ref: T-3:71, L-1:39]. "Michael Conely" lived in Rock Creek Hd. (one taxable) in 1777 [Ref: R-31:16].
CONNOLLY (CONELY), Thomas. Private, 8th Co., Middle Bn., Militia, Sep., 1777 [Ref: M-198, T-5:43]. Private, 6th Co., Lower Bn., Militia, July 15, 1780 [Ref: M-206]. Took the Oath of Allegiance before the Hon. Charles Jones on Jan. 10, 1778 [Ref: T-3:71, L-1:39]. "Thomas Connolly" rendered aid by providing wheat for use of the military in 1780 [Ref: O-317]. "Thomas Conely" lived in Rock Creek Hd. (one taxable) in 1777 [Ref: R-31:16].
CONSTABLE, Robert (died 1779). Took the Oath of Allegiance before the Hon. Edward Burgess on Feb. 28, 1778 [Ref: T-3:63, L-1:39]. Lived in

Sugar Loaf Hd. (two taxables) in 1777 [Ref: R-31:9]. Died testate in Montgomery County (wife named Susanna) in 1779 [Ref: V-35].

CONSTABLE (CARNSTABLE), Samuel. Son of Robert and Susanna Constable [Ref: V-35]. "Samuel Constable" took the Oath of Allegiance on Sep. 1, 1780, under the Act of May 12, 1780, having neglected to do so previously "due to ignorance of the duty owed the country." [Ref: R-27:108]. "Samuel Carnstable" was a private, 5th Co., Upper Bn., Militia, Aug. 30, 1777 [Ref: M-194]. It appears he moved to Illinois. See "James Wilson," q.v.

CONTEE, Alexander. Private, 3rd Co., Lower Bn., Militia, Sep., 1777 [Ref: M-199, T-5:46].

CONTEE, Benjamin. Attorney at law, 1779 [Ref: W-1]. Private, 8th Co., Lower Bn., Militia, July 15, 1780 [Ref: M-207].

CONTEE, Elijah. See "Elijah Cooke," q.v.

CONWAY, Sarah. See "James Ruglass (Ruggles)," q.v.

COOK, Caleb. Private, 1st or 32nd Bn., Militia (no date was given; possibly June, 1777). [Ref: T-5:2].

COOK (COOKE), Elijah. "Elijah Cooke" was a private, 6th Co., Lower Bn., Militia, Aug., 1777 [Ref: T-5:49 and M-200, which latter source questions if the name could have been "Elijah Contee"]. "Elijah Cook" married Jean McNeer in Montgomery County on May 12, 1778 [Ref: K-2:521, which mistakenly listed the first name as "Elizab" rather than "Elijah"].

COOK (COOKE), George. "George Cooke" was a private, 6th Co., Lower Bn., Militia, Aug., 1777 [Ref: M-200, T-5:49]. "George Cooke, Jr." lived in the Upper Part of Potomac Hd. (three taxables) in 1777 [Ref: R-31:14].

COOK (COOKE), John. (1) "John Cook" was a Second Lieutenant, Middle Bn., Militia, Sep. 12, 1777 [Ref: M-64, C-373]. (2) "John Cooke" was a private, 7th Co., Middle Bn., Militia, Sep., 1777 [Ref: M-197, T-5:42]. "John Cooke" lived in Seneca Hd. (one taxable) in 1777 [Ref: R-31:7]. Died testate in Montgomery County (wife not named) in 1778 [Ref: V-36].

COOK (COOKE), Richard. Private, Flying Camp, enlisted by Greenbury Gaither on July 29, 1776 [Ref: D-44]. "Richard Cooke" was a private, 3rd Co., Middle Bn., Militia, Sep., 1777 [Ref: M-196, T-5:38]. "Richard Cook" took the Oath of Allegiance before the Hon. William Deakins, Jr. before March 3, 1778 [Ref: T-3:68, L-1:39]. "Richard Cooke" lived in the Upper Part of Potomac Hd. (one taxable) in 1777 [Ref: R-31:14].

COOK, Sarah. See "Zadock Dickinson," q.v.

COOK, Thomas. Private, 1st or 32nd Bn., Militia (no date was given; possibly June, 1777). [Ref: T-5:1].

COOK (COOKE), William. Private, 3rd Maryland Regiment, discharged from the invalids corps on Dec. 7, 1778, and may have been the William Cooke in Capt. John Sprigg Belt's Co., Aug., 1780 to Jan., 1781 [Ref: D-97, D-353]. One "William Cooke" lived in the Upper Part of Potomac Hd.

(one taxable) in 1777 [Ref: R-31:14], and "William Cooke, aged 45" lived in North West Hd. in 1776-1777 [Ref: K-1:227, R-31:17, which latter source spelled the name "Cuck"].
COOLEY, Joseph. Private, Capt. Price's Co., 3rd Maryland Line, 1781-1782 [Ref: D-453].
COOLEY (CULEY), Thomas. Private, 5th Co., Middle Bn., Militia, July 15, 1780 [Ref: M-203].
COONE, Philip. Took the Oath of Allegiance in 1778 [Ref: L-2:27].
COONTZ (KOONTZ), George. "George Koontz" rendered aid by providing beef for use of the military in 1780 [Ref: O-343].
COONTZ (COUNCE, COONS, COUNTZ, KOONTZ, KUHNES), Henry. "Henry Counce" was a private, 3rd Co., Middle Bn., Militia, Sep., 1777 [Ref: M-196, T-5:38]. "Henry Countz" took the Oath of Allegiance before the Hon. William Deakins, Jr. before March 3, 1778 [Ref: L-2:27, T-3:68, L-1:39]. "Henry Koontz" rendered aid by providing flour for use of the military in 1781 [Ref: O-351]. "Henry Countz" married Ann Bowman in Montgomery County on Aug. 4, 1778 [Ref: K-2:518]. "Henry Kuhnes" was a private who enrolled into a company of militia for the service of the Flying Camp on Oct. 15, 1776 [Ref: B-353]. "Henry Coons" lived in the Upper Part of Potomac Hd. (two taxables) in 1777 [Ref: R-31:14].
COONTZ, Martin. Took the Oath of Allegiance in 1778 [Ref: L-2:27].
COONTZ (CONSE), Patrick. "Patrick Conse" took the Oath of Allegiance in 1778 [Ref: L-2:27].
COOPER, John 1st. Private, Capt. Price's Co., 3rd Maryland Line, 1781-1782 [Ref: D-452].
COSGROVE, Edward. Private, Capt. Price's Co., 3rd Maryland Line, 1781-1782 [Ref: D-454].
COTTINS, John. See "John Collins," q.v.
COURTS, Richard Henley. Surgeon's Mate in the Continental Army. Took the Oath of Allegiance before the Hon. Richard Thompson on Feb. 23, 1778 [Ref: X-1146].
COVENTRY, Charles. Private, 6th Co., Lower Bn., Militia, Aug., 1777 [Ref: M-200, T-5:49]. Private, 3rd Co., Lower Bn., Militia, July 15, 1780 [Ref: M-205]. Took the Oath of Allegiance before the Hon. Samuel W. Magruder in 1778 [Ref: T-3:73]. Rendered aid by providing wheat for use of the military in 1781 [Ref: O-386].
COVER, Artheart. Took the Oath of Allegiance in 1778 [Ref: L-2:27].
COVER, Yost. Took the Oath of Allegiance in 1778 [Ref: L-2:27].
COWMAN, Richard. Private, 1st Co., Lower Bn., Militia, Sep., 1777 [Ref: M-198, T-5:44]. Took the Oath of Allegiance before the Hon. Edward Burgess on Feb. 28, 1778 [Ref: T-3:64, L-1:39]. Lived in the Lower Part of Newfoundland Hd. (seven taxables) in 1777 [Ref: R-31:5].
COX, Benjamin. Private, 8th Co., Lower Bn., Militia, July 15, 1780 [Ref: M-207].

COX, John. Private, 6th Co., Middle Bn., Militia, Aug., 1777 [Ref: M-197, T-5:41]. Private, 6th Co., Middle Bn., Militia, July 15, 1780 [Ref: M-203]. Rendered aid by providing wheat for use of the military in 1780 [Ref: O-315]. Lived in the Upper Part of Newfoundland Hd. (one taxable) in 1777 [Ref: R-31:6].

COX, William. Private who was recruited to serve in the Extra Regiment, Continental Army, in 1780 [Ref: D-342].

COY, Charles. Took the Oath of Allegiance (made his "X" mark) before the Hon. Joseph Wilson on Feb. 28, 1778 [Ref: T-3:66, L-1:39, which source listed the name as "Charles Coyl"].

COY, Christopher. Private, 4th Co., Middle Bn., Militia, Sep., 1777 [Ref: M-196, T-5:39].

COY (COYE), Samuel. Private, 8th Co., Middle Bn., Militia, Sep., 1777 [Ref: M-198, T-5:43]. "Samuel Coye" took the Oath of Allegiance before the Hon. Joseph Wilson on Feb. 28, 1778 [Ref: T-3:66, L-1:39, which source listed the name as "Samuel Coyl"].

COY (KOYE), William. Private, 4th Co., Middle Bn., Militia, Sep., 1777 [Ref: M-196, T-5:39]. Third Corporal, 5th Co., Middle Bn., Militia, July 15, 1780 [Ref: M-202]. "William Koye" took the Oath of Allegiance before the Hon. Edward Burgess on Feb. 28, 1778 [Ref: T-3:63, L-1:39]. "William Coy" lived in Rock Creek Hd. (three taxables). He married Mary Ann Dennis in Montgomery County on Nov. 25, 1779 [Ref: K-2:518].

CRABB, Charles Henry, and others. See "Jeremiah Crabb," q.v.

CRABB, Henry Wright. See "Jeremiah and Richard Crabb," q.v.

CRABB, Jeremiah (1760 - Feb. 10, 1800). Son of Henry Wright Crabb and Ann Snowden, and the brother of "Richard Crabb," q.v. Service rendered in Frederick County, Lieutenant, 4th Maryland Regiment, 1776-1778, and as Brigadier General, Maryland Militia, 1794-1800. Served in the Lower House of Montgomery County, 1788-1793, and was an Associate Judge, 5th District Court, 1791-1792. Jeremiah Crabb married Elizabeth Ridgely Griffith (1764-1828), daughter of "Charles Greenbury Griffith," q.v., and had these children: Charles Henry, Richard, Elizabeth Ridgely, Sarah Griffith, Ann Snowden, Matilda, Emeline, and Lydia Ridgely. Jeremiah and Elizabeth are buried in the Crabb family cemetery on Route 355 near Rockville, Maryland [Ref: N-240, S-1993, and *Historic Graves of Maryland and the District of Columbia*, by Helen W. Ridgely (1908), p. 177]. Also see "Charles Greenbury Griffith," q.v.

CRABB, John. Private, 5th Co., Middle Bn., Militia, Sep., 1777 [Ref: M-197, T-5:40]. Took the Oath of Allegiance before the Hon. Thomas Sprigg Wootton on March 3, 1778 [Ref: T-3:79, L-1:39].

CRABB, Richard. (1) Son of Henry Wright Crabb (1722-1764) and Ann Snowden. Never married. Served as Second Major, 16th Bn., Militia, June 1, 1776. He served in the Lower House of Montgomery County, 1777-1779, and died in 1780 [Ref: M-65, N-241]. Lived in Seneca Hd.

(ten taxables) in 1777 [Ref: R-31:7]. Took the Oath of Allegiance before the Hon. Joseph Wilson on Feb. 28, 1778 [Ref: T-3:64, L-1:39]. (2) Private, 5th Co., Middle Bn., Militia, Sep., 1777 [Ref: M-197, T-5:40]. See "Jeremiah Crabb," q.v.

CRADDOCK, Mary. See "James Murphy," q.v.

CRADOCK, Charles. Private, 3rd Co., Lower Bn., Militia, July 15, 1780 [Ref: M-205].

CRAFT, Edward North. See "Edward Northcraft," q.v.

CRAGER, Laurence (Lawrence). Took the Oath of Allegiance before the Hon. Elisha Williams on March 2, 1778 [Ref: T-3:80, L-1:39]. Lived in Sugarland Hd. (one taxable) in 1777 [Ref: R-31:11].

CRAGUE, John. Private who was recruited to serve in the Continental Army in 1780 [Ref: D-341].

CRAIG, Laurence. Private, 8th Co., Upper Bn., Militia, Aug. 30, 1777 [Ref: M-195].

CRAIG, Robert. Private, 3rd Co., Lower Bn., Militia, Sep., 1777 [Ref: M-199, T-5:46]. "Robert Craigg" lived in George Town Hd. (one taxable) in 1777 [Ref: R-31:4].

CRAIG, Thomas. Private, Capt. Thomas Beall's Co., Maryland Line, 1780 [Ref: D-351].

CRALL, Jeremiah. Private, 6th Class, 1st Co., Middle Bn., Militia, July 15, 1780 [Ref: M-201].

CRAMLET (CRAMBLIT), Jacob. "Jacob Cramlet" married Eliza Chambers in Montgomery County on March 18, 1779 [Ref: K-2:518]. "Jacob Cramblit" rendered aid by providing wheat for use of the military in 1781 [Ref: O-424].

CRAMPHIN, Ruth. See "Allen Bowie," q.v.

CRAMPHIN, Thomas Jr. (1740-1830). Lived in Rock Creek Hd. (eleven taxables) in 1777 [Ref: R-31:16]. Son of Thomas Cramphin, Sr. (1715-1783) and Mary Jackson. Never married. Represented Frederick County at the Conventions of 1774 and 1775, and served in the Lower House of Montgomery County, 1778-1788 (various dates). He held many civil offices during and after the Revolutionary War, including Committee of Observation, Committee of Correspondence, Court Justice, and Tax Commissioner. He took the Oath of Allegiance before the Hon. Joseph Wilson on Feb. 28, 1778 [Ref: T-3:64, L-1:39, N-242]. "Thomas Cramphin" was a private, 2nd Co., Lower Bn., Militia, in Sep., 1777 [Ref: M-198, T-5:45]. Helen W. Ridgely's *Historic Graves of Maryland the District of Columbia* (page 263) states that "Thomas Gramphin" died July 29, 1783, aged 68, and is buried in Rock Creek Cemetery. "Thomas Cramphin, aged 90 years and 10 months, died in Montgomery County in Dec., 1830." [Ref: F. Edward Wright's *Marriages and Deaths in the Newspapers of Frederick and Montgomery Counties, Maryland, 1820-1830*, p. 81]. See "Allen Bowie," q.v.

CRANE, Henry. Private who was recruited to serve in the Extra Regiment, Continental Army, in 1780 [Ref: D-342].
CRAVER, Philip. Private, 8th Co., Lower Bn., Militia, July 15, 1780 [Ref: M-207]. Lived in George Town Hd. (one taxable) in 1777 [Ref: R-31:3].
CRAWFORD (CRAFFORD), Alexander. Son of Nathaniel and Rachel "Crafford" [Ref: V-37]. Private, 6th Class, 1st Co., Middle Bn., Militia, July 15, 1780 [Ref: M-201].
CRAWFORD, John. Private, 6th Class, 1st Co., Middle Bn., Militia, July 15, 1780 [Ref: M-201]. Lived in Seneca Hd. (two taxables) in 1777 [Ref: R-31:7].
CRAWFORD (CRAFFORD), John Sutton (died 1814). "John S. Crawford" was a private, 5th Co., Middle Bn., Militia, Sep., 1777 [Ref: M-197, T-5:40]. "John Sutton Crafford" took the Oath of Allegiance before the Hon. Joseph Wilson on Feb. 28, 1778 [Ref: T-3:67, L-1:39]. "John Sutton Crawford" died testate in Montgomery County (wife named Elizabeth) in 1814 [Ref: V-37].
CRAWFORD (CRAFFORD), Nathaniel (died 1783). Served as a Second Lieutenant, Middle Bn., Militia, Sep. 12, 1777, and First Lieutenant, April 21, 1779 [Ref: M-66, M-196, T-5:40, C-373, E-357]. Served as a petit juror in Aug., 1777 [Ref: R-31:17]. "Nathaniel Crafford" took the Oath of Allegiance before the Hon. Joseph Wilson on Feb. 28, 1778 [Ref: T-3:66, L-1:39]. "Nat Crafford" lived in the Upper Part of Potomac Hd. (three taxables) in 1777 [Ref: R-31:14]. "Nathaniel Crafford" died testate in Montgomery County (wife named Rachel) in 1783 [Ref: V-37].
CRAWFORD, Rachel. See "Caleb Summers," q.v.
CRAWFORD (CRAFFORD), Robert Beall. "Robert Crawford" was a private, 7th Co., Middle Bn., Militia, Sep., 1777 [Ref: M-197, T-5:42]. Private, 1st Class, 1st Co., Middle Bn., Militia, July 15, 1780 [Ref: M-201]. "Robert Beall Crafford" took the Oath of Allegiance before the Hon. Joseph Wilson on Feb. 28, 1778 [Ref: T-3:66, L-1:39]. "Robert Beall Crawford" married Eleanor Owen in Montgomery County on April 11, 1780 [Ref: K-2:518].
CRAWFORD, Thomas. Private, 6th Co., Lower Bn., Militia, Aug., 1777 [Ref: M-200, T-5:49]. Private, 8th Co., Lower Bn., Militia, July 15, 1780 [Ref: M-207]. Took the Oath of Allegiance before the Hon. Richard Thompson in 1778 [Ref: T-3:75, L-1:39]. Lived in the Upper Part of Potomac Hd. (one taxable) in 1777 [Ref: R-31:14].
CREIGHTON, James. "James Creighton, an Englishman, a blacksmith by trade, 40 years of age, about 5 feet 2 or 3 inches high and wears his own short, dark coloured hair, recruited by John Young on April 13, 1781." [Ref: R-33:156, X-1146].
CROMPTON, Ignatius. See "Ignatius Compton (Cumpton)," q.v.
CRONS, Susannah. See "Leonard Cochantofer," q.v.
CROOK, John. Private, Capt. Edward Burgess' Co., Lower District of Frederick (now Montgomery) County, Militia, July, 1776 [Ref: D-42].

CROSS, Benjamin. Took the Oath of Allegiance (made his "A" mark) before the Hon. Edward Burgess on Feb. 28, 1778 [Ref: T-3:61, L-1:39]. Lived in the Lower Part of Newfoundland Hd. (two taxables) in 1777 [Ref: R-31:5].
CROSS, Friday (Fryday). Private, 1st Co., Middle Bn., Militia, Aug. 30, 1777 [Ref: M-195]. Private, 5th Class, 2nd Co., Middle Bn., Militia, July 15, 1780 [Ref: M-201]. Took the Oath of Allegiance before the Hon. Gerrard Briscoe on March 2, 1778 [Ref: T-3:56, L-1:39, which latter source mistakenly listed the name as "Friday Crysp"].
CROSS, Gabriel. Private, 4th Co., Lower Bn., Militia, July 15, 1780 [Ref: M-205].
CROSS, George. Took the Oath of Allegiance in 1778 [Ref: L-2:27].
CROSS, John. Private, 4th Co., Lower Bn., Militia, July 15, 1780 [Ref: M-205].
CROSS, Thomas. (1) Private, 1st Co., Lower Bn., Militia, Sep., 1777 [Ref: T-5:44]. (2) Private, 1st Co., Lower Bn., Militia, Sep., 1777 [Ref: M-198, T-5:44]. Private, 7th Co., Lower Bn., Militia, July 15, 1780 [Ref: M-207].
CROUTZ, Theodorus. See "Theodorus Kraus," q.v.
CROW, Edward Jr. (died 1790). Served as a First Lieutenant, 16th Bn., Militia, May 20, 1776, and First Lieutenant, Middle Bn., Militia, Sep. 20, 1777 [Ref: M-66, M-197, A-432, C-373, T-5:41]. "Edward Crow, Jr." rendered aid by providing wheat for use of the military in 1781 [Ref: O-375]. "Edward Crowe, Jr." rendered aid by providing wheat for use of the military in 1781 [Ref: O-394, O-442, which source mistakenly listed the name as "Crewe"]. "Edward Crow, Sr." lived in the Upper Part of Newfoundland Hd. in 1777 [Ref: R-31:6, which source listed the name twice, one with five taxables and the other with nine taxables; apparently, one of them was Edward Crow, Jr.]. "Edward Crow, Sr." died testate in Montgomery County (wife not named) in 1790 [Ref: V-37].
CROW, Joshua. Son of Edward Crow, Sr. [Ref: V-37]. Private, 6th Co., Middle Bn., Militia, Aug., 1777 [Ref: M-197, T-5:41]. Private, 6th Co., Middle Bn., Militia, July 15, 1780 [Ref: M-203].
CROW, Samuel. Son of Edward Crow, Sr. [Ref: V-37]. Private, 6th Co., Middle Bn., Militia, Aug., 1777 [Ref: M-197, T-5:41], and Second Lieutenant, Middle Bn., Militia, April 24, 1779, and First Lieutenant, 6th Co., March 25, 1780 [Ref: M-66, M-203, E-357, F-120]. Served as a Constable in Upper Newfoundland Hd. in 1781 [Ref: W-2].
CROW, William. Private, Capt. Edward Burgess' Co., Lower District of Frederick (now Montgomery) County, Militia, July, 1776 [Ref: D-42].
CROWN, Lancelot (b. 1750). Private, 1st Co., Lower Bn., Militia, July 15, 1780 [Ref: M-204]. Took the Oath of Allegiance before the Hon. Richard Thompson in 1778 [Ref: T-3:75, L-1:39]. "Lance or Lancelot Crown" lived in Lower Potomac Hd. (one taxable) in 1776-1777 [Ref: R-31:4, K-1:182].
CROXALL, Frederick. Took the Oath of Allegiance in 1778 [Ref: L-2:27].
CRYDER, John. Took the Oath of Allegiance in 1778 [Ref: L-2:27].

CULLOM (CULLUM), Francis. Private, 2nd Co., Middle Bn., Militia, Sep. 4, 1777 [Ref: M-196, T-5:37]. Private, 5th Class, 3rd Co., Middle Bn., Militia, July 15, 1780 [Ref: M-202]. Took the Oath of Allegiance before the Hon. Edward Burgess on Feb. 28, 1778 [Ref: T-3:63, L-1:39]. "Francis Cullum" lived in Linganore Hd. (three taxables) in 1777 [Ref: R-31:9].

CULLOM (CULLUM), George. Served as a First Lieutenant, Middle Bn., Militia, March 26, 1776, annd First Lieutenant, 2nd Co., 16th Bn., Sep. 4, 1777, and Captain, Middle Bn., Militia, April 21, 1779, and Captain, Upper Bn., Militia, March 25, 1780 [Ref: M-66, M-67, M-195, A-287, C-362, C-373, E-357, F-120]. Took the Oath of Allegiance before the Hon. Edward Burgess on Feb. 28, 1778 [Ref: T-3:59, L-1:39]. "George Cullum" lived in Linganore Hd. (four taxables) in 1777 [Ref: R-31:9]. "George Cullam" was a Justice of the Peace in 1778 [Ref: C-529].

CULP (CULPH), George Jr. "George Culp" was a private, 6th Co., Lower Bn., Militia, Aug., 1777 [Ref: T-5:49]. "George Culph, Jr." was a private, 3rd Co., Lower Bn., Militia, July 15, 1780 [Ref: M-205]. "George Culph, Jr." took the Oath of Allegiance before the Hon. Joseph Offutt on March 2, 1778 [Ref: T-3:70, L-1:39]. "George Collop, aged 20" lived in Sugarland Hd. in 1776 and "George Culp" lived in the Upper Part of Potomac Hd. (two taxables) in 1777 [Ref: K-1:210, R-31:14]. "George Culp, Sr." died testate in Montgomery County (wife not named) in 1811 and mentioned a son George, among other children [Ref: V-38].

CULVER, Henry. Took the Oath of Allegiance before the Hon. Edward Burgess on Feb. 28, 1778 [Ref: T-3:59, L-1:39]. Rendered aid by providing wheat for use of the military in 1780 [Ref: O-306]. Lived in Rock Creek Hd. (six taxables) in 1777 [Ref: R-31:16].

CULVER, Susy. See "Richard Jones," q.v.

CULVER, Thomas. Private, Capt. Edward Burgess' Co., Lower District of Frederick (now Montgomery) County, Militia, July, 1776 [Ref: D-42].

CULVER, William. Private, 7th Co., Lower Bn., Militia, Aug., 1777, and Third Corporal, 4th Co., July 15, 1780 [Ref: M-200, M-205, T-5:50]. Took the Oath of Allegiance before the Hon. Edward Burgess on Feb. 28, 1778 [Ref: T-3:62, L-1:39].

CUMMING, Robert. His death notice appeared in the *Maryland Journal* (Rockville) on May 2, 1826: "Another Rev Hero Gone! Died at his residence in Liberty-Town, Monday evening, Nov. 14th last, Major General Robert Cumming, commander of the first division of Maryland Militia, in the 72nd year of his age. Address delivered by Rev. Caleb Reynolds." [Ref: F. Edward Wright's *Marriages and Deaths in the Newspapers of Frederick and Montgomery Counties, Maryland, 1820-1830*, p. 75, Family Line Publications, 1987].

CUNNINGHAM, James. Private, Capt. Thomas Beall's Co., Maryland Line, 1780 [Ref: D-350].

CURD, John. Private, 1st Co., Middle Bn., Militia, Aug. 30, 1777 [Ref: M-195].
CURRENT (CARRENT), James (1752-1822). Private, 2nd Maryland Line, from May 25, 1778 until he reportedly "deserted" on Dec. 26, 1778; however, he reenlisted to serve in the 7th Maryland Line, Continental Army, on Feb. 8, 1780, and was discharged Nov. 1, 1780 [Ref: D-94, D-197]. He served under Capt. Lloyd Beall [in the 7th Maryland Line] and was in the battles of Guilford and Camden (Aug. 16, 1780), where he was wounded three times and lost two fingers of his left hand. His invalid (disability) pension commenced March 4, 1789, and he reapplied Nov. 11, 1818, in Montgomery County, aged 66 (S34724). In 1820 he lived in Frederick County, aged 68, but had no family. Died on Sep. 4, 1822 [Ref: D-341, D-391, D-632, J-16, K-2:327, which sources listed the name as "Carrent," and Ref: D-94, P-845, Y-26, which sources listed the name as "Currin" or "Current"].
CURRENTON (CURRINGTON), John (b. 1734). "John Currenton" lived in Sugarland Hd. in 1776 [Ref: K-1:203]. "John Currington" was a private, Flying Camp, who enlisted on July 29, 1778 [Ref: D-43].
CURTIN, William. Private who was recruited to serve in the Extra Regiment, Continental Army, in 1780 [Ref: D-342].
CUSTER, Christian. Took the Oath of Allegiance before the Hon. Elisha Williams on March 2, 1778 [Ref: T-3:80, L-1:39].
CUTMORE, Joshua. Private, 4th Co., Middle Bn., Militia, Sep., 1777 [Ref: M-196, T-5:39]. Private, 7th Class, 4th Co., Middle Bn., Militia, July 15, 1780 [Ref: M-202].
CUTSINGER, Alcy. See "Josiah Hoskinson," q.v.
CYPHERT, Hugh. Rendered aid by providing wheat for use of the military in 1781 [Ref: O-393].
CYPRUSS, William. Private, 7th Co., Lower Bn., Militia, July 15, 1780 [Ref: M-206].
DADE (DODE), Daniel. Took the Oath of Allegiance (made his "D" mark) before the Hon. Aneas Campbell on March 2, 1778 [Ref: T-3:77, L-1:40].
DAILEY, Mary. See "Richard Sillings (Stillings)," q.v.
DALEY (DAILEY), John (b. 1750). Served as a grand juror in Aug., 1777 [Ref: R-31:17]. Took the Oath of Allegiance before the Hon. Richard Thompson in 1778 [Ref: T-3:75, L-1:39]. "John Dailey or Daley" lived in George Town Hd. (two taxables) in 1776-1777 [Ref: K-1:193, R-31:3].
DARBY, Anne. See "Asa Darby," q.v.
DARBY, Asa (1756-1833). Lived in Sugarland Hd. (two taxables) in 1777 [Ref: R-31:12]. Born in Anne Arundel County, Maryland on April 13, 1756, he served in the war from Montgomery County, Maryland. He married Dorcas Goore or Goar (b. May 3, 1759) in Craven County, South Carolina on Nov. 30, 1779, and died in Chester County on Dec. 30, 1833. Their children were: Nancy (b. Sep. 15, 1780, married Edward Sealy); George (b. April 11, 1783, married ---- Clark); Anne (b. April 5,

1785, married Thomas Sanders); Lydia (b. July 9, 1788, married John Sanders); John (b. Feb. 28, 1792, married Mary Ann Smith, Leonora Foote, and Mary Kidd); Elizabeth (b. July 3, 1796, married Thomas Estes); James (b. Jan. 29, 1799, married Elizabeth Estes); Mary (b. Aug. 9, 1801, married a Humphries); William Jefferson (b. Sep. 22, 1804, never married); and, Thomas (birth date illegible, married, and died by 1833, leaving two minor sons). "Asa Darby was a Revolutionary War soldier in 6th Bn. of Upper Maryland Troops. He was the son of George and Anne Darby of Maryland." [Ref: *Old Southern Bible Records*, by Memory Aldridge Lester (1974), pp. 97-98]. It should be noted that he is not named in his father's will in 1788. However, the final account of his mother's will ("Ann Darby, of Ann Arundel County" died testate in Montgomery County in 1818) does include him as one of her sons in 1822 [Ref: V-38]. Asa Darby was a private, 6th Co., Upper Bn., Militia, on Aug. 30, 1777, and took the Oath of Allegiance before the Hon. William Deakins, Jr., on March 3, 1778 [Ref: M-194, T-3:68, L-1:39, DAR-I:175].

DARBY, Basil. Son of George and Anne Darby [Ref: V-38]. Private, 4th Co., Middle Bn., Militia, Sep., 1777 [Ref: M-196, T-5:39]. Took the Oath of Allegiance before the Hon. Edward Burgess on Feb. 28, 1778 [Ref: T-3:60, L-1:39].

DARBY, Benjamin. Served as a First Lieutenant, 3rd Co., Upper Bn., Militia, Aug. 30, 1777 [Ref: M-193]. "Benjamin Darby" took the Oath of Allegiance before the Hon. Elisha Williams on March 2, 1778 [Ref: T-3:81, L-1:39]. "Benjamin Darbey" lived in Sugar Loaf Hd. (three taxables) in 1777 [Ref: R-31:9].

DARBY, Caleb (March 17, 1762 - March, 1802). Son of George and Anne Darby [Ref: V-38]. Served as Third Corporal, 4th Co., Middle Bn., Militia, July 15, 1780. Caleb Darby married twice: (1) Elizabeth Ray, and (2) Sarah Gartrell [Ref: M-202, DAR-I:175].

DARBY, Dorcas and Elizabeth. See "Asa Darby," q.v.

DARBY, George (June 12, 1726 - March 29, 1788). Took the Oath of Allegiance before the Hon. Edward Burgess on Feb. 28, 1778 [Ref: T-3:60, L-1:39]. Rendered aid by providing wheat for use of the military in 1781 [Ref: O-387]. Lived in the Upper Part of Newfoundland Hd. (five taxables) in 1777 [Ref: R-31:6]. Died testate in Montgomery County (wife named Ann or Anna) in 1788 [Ref: V-38, DAR-I:175]. See "Asa Darby," q.v.

DARBY, James and John. See "Asa Darby," q.v.

DARBY, Josiah or Josias (c1734-c1820). "Josiah Darby" took the Oath of Allegiance before the Hon. Gerrard Briscoe on March 2, 1778 [Ref: T-3:56, L-1:39]. "Josias Darby" was a private, 3rd Co., Upper Bn., Militia, Aug. 30, 1777 [Ref: M-193]. "Josiah Darby" is listed twice in the 1777 tax list (with one taxable each) in Sugar Loaf Hd. [Ref: R-31:9].

DARBY, Lydia and Nancy. See "Asa Darby," q.v.

DARBY, Mary. See "Robert Doyne Dawson" and "Asa Darby," q.v.
DARBY, Samuel (1760-1822). Son of George and Anne Darby [Ref: V-38]. Private, 4th Co., Middle Bn., Militia, Sep., 1777 [Ref: M-196, T-5:39], and Third Sergeant, 4th Co., Middle Bn., Militia, July 15, 1780 [Ref: M-202].
DARBY, Thomas and William Jefferson. See "Asa Darby," q.v.
DARLING, Lott. Private, 8th Co., Lower Bn., Militia, July 15, 1780 [Ref: M-207].
DARNAL (DARNALL), Isaac. "Isaac Darnal" was a private, 3rd Co., Upper Bn., Militia, Aug. 30, 1777 [Ref: M-193]. "Isaac Darnall" took the Oath of Allegiance before the Hon. Edward Burgess on Feb. 28, 1778 [Ref: T-3:64, L-1:39].
DARNAL (DARNALL, DARNOLD), John (b. 1736). "John Darnal" took the Oath of Allegiance before the Hon. Elisha Williams on March 2, 1778 [Ref: T-3:81, L-1:39]. "John Darnall or Darnold" lived in Sugarland Hd. (two taxables) in 1776-1777 and had a large family [Ref: K-1:202, R-31:12].
DARNEAL, Elizabeth. See "Clement Dowden," q.v.
DAVENPORT (DEVENPORT), William. Private, 2nd Class, 2nd Co., Middle Bn., Militia, July 15, 1780 [Ref: M-201].
DAVIDSON (DAVERSON), Henry. "Henry Davidson" rendered aid by providing wheat for use of the military in 1780 [Ref: O-312]. "Henry Daverson" lived in Rock Creek Hd. (four taxables) in 1777 [Ref: R-31:16].
DAVIES, John. Private, enrolled into a company of militia for the service of the Flying Camp, Oct. 15, 1776 [Ref: B-352]. Also see "John Davis," q.v.
DAVIS, Amos. See "Lodowick Davis," q.v.
DAVIS, Baxley (b. 1754). "Baxley or Bexly Davis" lived in Sugarland Hd. (one taxable) in 1776-1777 [Ref: K-1:198, R-31:12]. "Benley Davis" [sic] was a private, 7th Co., Upper Bn., Militia, Aug. 30, 1777 [Ref: M-194]. "Baxley Davis" took the Oath of Allegiance before the Hon. Aneas Campbell on March 2, 1778 [Ref: T-3:78, L-1:39].
DAVIS, Betsy. Rendered aid by providing wheat for use of the military in 1781 [Ref: O-391].
DAVIS, Blanford. Private, 2nd Co., Middle Bn., Militia, Sep. 4, 1777 [Ref: M-195].
DAVIS, Charles. Private, 1st Co., Middle Bn., Militia, Aug. 30, 1777 [Ref: M-195]. Lived in Seneca Hd. (four taxables) in 1777 [Ref: R-31:7].
DAVIS, Charles, of Griffith. "Charles Davis" lived in Seneca Hd. (one taxable) in 1777 [Ref: R-31:7]. "Charles Davis, of Griffith" took the Oath of Allegiance before the Hon. Gerrard Briscoe on March 2, 1778 [Ref: T-3:56, L-1:39].
DAVIS, David. Private, 4th Co., Upper Bn., Militia, Aug. 30, 1777 [Ref: M-194].

DAVIS, Dicky and Dolly Ann. See "Lodowick Davis," q.v.
DAVIS, Ephraim (b. 1735). Private, 8th Co., Upper Bn., Militia, Aug. 30, 1777 [Ref: M-195]. Took the Oath of Allegiance (made his "E" mark) before the Hon. Aneas Campbell on March 2, 1778 [Ref: T-3:78, L-1:39]. "Efrom Davis" lived in Sugarland Hd. in 1776 [Ref: K-1:208].
DAVIS, Forrest (b. 1761). Private, 6th Co., Middle Bn., Militia, Aug., 1777 [Ref: M-197, T-5:41]. He applied for pension (S30369) in Hardin County, Kentucky, on Oct. 15, 1832, "aged 70 last Dec.," stating he was born in Dec., 1761, lived in Montgomery County, Maryland, enlisted in 1780 at Fort Frederick, Maryland, and served in the Maryland Line for 3 years. Benjamin Gray, of Warrick County, Indiana, stated on Sep. 10, 1832, that he resided in Montgomery County, Maryland in 1780 and could verify the service of Forrest Davis. "Lodowick Davis," q.v., of Spencer County, Indiana, aged 70 in 1834, also verified his service [Ref: Y-13, Z-43, P-894].
DAVIS, Frances. See "Henry Burriss, Jr.," q.v.
DAVIS, Griffith. Private, 1st Co., Middle Bn., Militia, Aug. 30, 1777, and Ensign, Upper Bn., Militia, April 21, 1779, and First Lieutenant, 5th Co., Middle Bn., Militia, July 15, 1780 [Ref: M-68. M-195, M-202, E-145, E-357]. Took the Oath of Allegiance before the Hon. Gerrard Briscoe on March 2, 1778 [Ref: T-3:57, L-1:39]. Lived in Seneca Hd. (two taxables) in 1777 (Ref: R-31:7], served as a Constable in 1779 [Ref: W-1], and rendered aid by providing wheat for use of the military in 1781 [Ref: O-379].
DAVIS, Harper. See "Lodowick Davis," q.v.
DAVIS, Henry. Private, 7th Co., Lower Bn., Militia, Aug., 1777 [Ref: M-200, T-5:50]. Lived in the Lower Part of Newfoundland Hd. (two taxables) in 1777 [Ref: R-31:5].
DAVIS, Henry Culver. Took the Oath of Allegiance before the Hon. Edward Burgess on Feb. 28, 1778 [Ref: T-3:59, L-1:39].
DAVIS, Hezekiah. See "Lodowick Davis," q.v.
DAVIS, Isaiah (died 1793). Took the Oath of Allegiance (made his "T" mark) before the Hon. Aneas Campbell on March 2, 1778 [Ref: T-3:78, L-1:39]. Lived in Sugarland Hd. (one taxable) in 1777 [Ref: R-31:12]. Died testate in Montgomery County (no wife or children) in 1793 [Ref: V-40].
DAVIS, Jemima. See "Lodowick Davis," q.v.
DAVIS, John. (1) Private, 8th Co., Middle Bn., Militia, Sep., 1777 [Ref: M-198, T-5:43]. (2) Private, 1st Co., Middle Bn., Militia, Aug. 30, 1777 [Ref: M-195]. One John Davis was recruited to serve in the Continental Army in 1780 [Ref: D-341]. One John Davis married Ann Legg in Montgomery County on July 3, 1778 [Ref: K-2:516]. Also see "John Davies," q.v.
DAVIS, Joseph (b. 1751). Lived in Sugarland Hd. in 1776 [Ref: K-1:208]. Private, Maryland Line, Rawlings' Regiment, 1776-1779 [Ref: D-105].
DAVIS, Joshua. See "Lodowick Davis," q.v.

DAVIS, Josias. Private, 7th Co., Upper Bn., Militia, Aug. 30, 1777 [Ref: M-194].
DAVIS, Leonard. Son of William Davis, Sr. [Ref: V-39]. Private, 5th Co., Middle Bn., Militia, Sep., 1777 [Ref: M-197, T-5:40]. Took the Oath of Allegiance before the Hon. Joseph Wilson on Feb. 28, 1778 [Ref: T-3:64, L-1:39]. Assisted in finding a house to hold the courts and a prison for the reception of prisoners in 1777 [Ref: R-31:18]. Rendered aid by providing wheat for use of the military in 1780 [Ref: O-304, O-314], and also served as a grand juror in 1781 [Ref: W-2]. "Loanhart Davis" rendered aid by providing wheat for use of the military in 1781 [Ref: O-399]. "Leonard Davis" lived in Seneca Hd. (three taxables) in 1777 [Ref: R-31:7], and owned a working plantation ("quarter") in Rock Creek Hd. (four taxables) in 1777 [Ref: R-31:16].
DAVIS, Leroy. See "Lodowick Davis," q.v.
DAVIS, Levy. Private, Capt. Thomas Beall's Co., Maryland Line, 1780 [Ref: D-351].
DAVIS, Lodowick or Lodwick. (1) Private, 1st Co., Middle Bn., Militia, Aug. 30, 1777 [Ref: M-195]. Fourth Corporal, 3rd Co., Middle Bn., Militia, July 15, 1780 [Ref: M-202]. (2) Second Lieutenant, Middle Bn., Militia, April 21, 1779 [Ref: M-68, E-357]. One Lodowick Davis lived in the Upper Part of Newfoundland Hd. (four taxables) and another lived in Seneca Hd. (one taxable) in 1777 [Ref: R-31:6, R-31:7]. One took the Oath of Allegiance before the Hon. Gerrard Briscoe on March 2, 1778 [Ref: T-3:56, L-1:39]. One Lodowick Davis applied for pension (R2713) on Nov. 4, 1833, in Spencer County, Indiana, stating he was born in Feb., 1764, in Montgomery County, Maryland, and lived there during the war. He married Dolly Ann ---- on Jan. 12, 1790, in Montgomery County, and moved to Ohio County, Kentucky, in 1801. Children: Hezekiah (b. Nov. 29, 1790); Sally (b. June 29, 1792, and died in Aug., 1794); Lucey (b. Jan. 15, 1794); Polly (b. Jan. 15, 1796); Amos (b. Sep. 25, 1797); Jemima (b. June 2, 1799); Joshua (b. March 7, 1801, and died in May, 1801); Dicky (b. April 3, 1802); Leroy (b. Aug. 7, 1804); Forrest (b. March 19, 1807); Harper (b. Dec. 18, 1808); and, Miranda (b. Oct. 13, 1810, married ---- McCool, and was living in Warrick County, Indiana, in 1843). Also mentioned was a Forrest Davis, aged about 71, in Hardin County, Kentucky, in 1833. Lodowick Davis had moved to Warrick County, Indiana, in Oct., 1831, and died on Aug. 13, 1841 [Ref: P-904]. One "Lodowick Davis" married Margaret Jones in Montgomery County, Maryland, on Feb. 7, 1779 [Ref: K-2:518]. One "Lodowick Davis, planter" died testate in Montgomery County (wife named Eleanor) in 1778 [Ref: V-39]. See "Forrest Davis," q.v.
DAVIS, Lucey. See "Lodowick Davis," q.v.
DAVIS, Luke. Private, 6th Co., Middle Bn., Militia, Aug., 1777 [Ref: M-197, T-5:41]. Took the Oath of Allegiance before the Hon. Edward Burgess on Feb. 28, 1778 [Ref: T-3:61, L-1:39].

DAVIS, Mary. See "Edward Burgess," q.v.
DAVIS, Miranda and Polly. See "Lodowick Davis," q.v.
DAVIS, Richard. Private, 7th Co., Middle Bn., Militia, July 15, 1780 [Ref: M-203]. Private, 1st Co., Middle Bn., Militia, Aug. 30, 1777 [Ref: M-195]. Took the Oath of Allegiance before the Hon. Gerrard Briscoe on March 2, 1778 [Ref: T-3:57, L-1:39]. Rendered aid by providing wheat for use of the military in 1780 [Ref: O-313]. Lived in Seneca Hd. (one taxable) in 1777 [Ref: R-31:7].
DAVIS, Sally. See "Lodowick Davis," q.v.
DAVIS, Samuel. Private, 7th Co., Upper Bn., Militia, Aug. 30, 1777 [Ref: M-195]. Lived in Sugarland Hd. (four taxables) in 1777 [Ref: R-31:12]. Samuel Davis married Rebecca Bucey in Montgomery County on April 21, 1778 [Ref: K-2:518].
DAVIS, Vachel. Private, 2nd Co., Middle Bn., Militia, Sep. 4, 1777 [Ref: M-195].
DAVIS, William. (1) Private, 7th Co., Upper Bn., Militia, Aug. 30, 1777 [Ref: M-195]. (2) Private, 6th Co., Lower Bn., Militia, Aug., 1777 [Ref: M-200, T-5:49]. Private, 3rd Co., Lower Bn., Militia, July 15, 1780 [Ref: M-205]. (3) Fourth Corporal, 5th Co., Middle Bn., Militia, July 15, 1780 [Ref: M-202]. One William Davis was constable in Middle Potomac Hd. in 1779 [Ref: W-1]. One "William Davis, aged 30" and a "William Davis, aged 22" both lived in Sugarland Hd. in 1776-1777 [Ref: K-1:204, K-1:211, R-31:11], and another lived in the Upper Part of Potomac Hd. (four taxables) in 1777 [Ref: R-31:14]. "William Davis, Sr., of Frederick County" died testate in Montgomery County (wife not named) in 1779 and mentioned sons William and Leonard, among other children [Ref: V-39].
DAVIS, William L. Private, 3rd Co., Lower Bn., Militia, July 15, 1780 [Ref: M-205].
DAVISON, Henry. Took the Oath of Allegiance before the Hon. Edward Burgess on Feb. 28, 1778 [Ref: T-3:63, L-1:39].
DAW, Edward. Private who was recruited to serve in the Extra Regiment, Continental Army, in 1780 [Ref: D-342].
DAW (DAWE), Robert. "Robert Daw" rendered aid by providing wheat for use of the military in 1781 [Ref: O-383]. "Robert Dawe" lived in Seneca Hd. (one taxable) in 1777 [Ref: R-31:7].
DAWSON, Benjamin. Took the Oath of Allegiance in 1778 [Ref: L-2:27].
DAWSON, Benoni. Son of Thomas and Elizabeth Dawson [Ref: V-40]. Private, 2nd Co., Middle Bn., Militia, Sep. 4, 1777 [Ref: M-195]. Took the Oath of Allegiance before the Hon. Elisha Williams on March 2, 1778 [Ref: T-3:81, L-1:39]. Rendered aid by providing corn for use of the military in 1780 [Ref: O-288]. Lived in Sugar Loaf Hd. (three taxables) in 1777 [Ref: R-31:9].
DAWSON, Eleanor. See "Lawrence Allnut," q.v.

DAWSON, John. Took the Oath of Allegiance (made his "X" mark) before the Hon. Joseph Wilson on Feb. 28, 1778 [Ref: T-3:66, L-1:39]. "John Dawson or Davison" was a private in the 7th Maryland Line who was reported missing on Aug. 16, 1780, at the Battle of Camden [Ref: D-202].

DAWSON, Nicholas. Son of Thomas and Elizabeth Dawson [Ref: V-40]. Private, 3rd Co., Upper Bn., Militia, Aug. 30, 1777 [Ref: M-193]. Took the Oath of Allegiance before the Hon. Elisha Williams on March 2, 1778 [Ref: T-3:81, L-1:39]. Lived in Sugar Loaf Hd. (two taxables) in 1777 [Ref: R-31:9].

DAWSON, Robert Doyne (July 10, 1758 - Aug. 13, 1824). Son of Thomas and Elizabeth Dawson [Ref: V-40]. "Robert Doyne Dawson" took the Oath of Allegiance before the Hon. Elisha Williams on March 2, 1778 [Ref: T-3:81, L-1:39]. "Robert Den Dawson" was a private, 3rd Co., Upper Bn., Militia, Aug. 30, 1777 [Ref: M-193]. "Robert Doyne Dawson" married Sarah Newton Chiswell in Montgomery County on Oct. 25, 1782 [Ref: K-2:518]. He is buried in Monocacy Cemetery [Ref: *Historic Graves of Maryland and the District of Columbia*, by Helen W. Ridgely (1908), p. 172]. William C. Dawson (1791-1845), son of Robert, married Mary Darby and moved to Logan County, Kentucky in 1810, where their son George C. Dawson was born on April 6, 1815 [Ref: Thomas Westerfield's *Kentucky Biography and Genealogy*, Volume 4, p. 187].

DAWSON, Thomas (died 1800). Private, 7th Co., Lower Bn., Militia, July 15, 1780 [Ref: M-207]. Took the Oath of Allegiance before the Hon. Elisha Williams on March 2, 1778 [Ref: T-3:81, L-1:39]. Lived in Sugar Loaf Hd. (six taxables) in 1777 [Ref: R-31:9]. Died testate in Montgomery County (wife named Elizabeth) in 1800 [Ref: V-40].

DAWSON, Verlinda Hawkins. See "James Allnutt, Sr.," q.v.

DAWSON, William C. See "Robert Doyne Dawson," q.v.

DAY, Daniel. Private, 4th Co., Middle Bn., Militia, Sep., 1777 [Ref: M-196, T-5:39]. Private, 8th Class, 4th Co., Middle Bn., Militia, July 15, 1780 [Ref: M-202]. Took the Oath of Allegiance before the Hon. Edward Burgess on Feb. 28, 1778 [Ref: T-3:60, L-1:39]. Lived in the Upper Part of Newfoundland Hd. (one taxable) in 1777 [Ref: R-31:6].

DAY, James. Private, 8th Class, 1st Co., Middle Bn., Militia, July 15, 1780 [Ref: M-201]. See "Vachel Harding," q.v.

DAY, Leonard (b. 1736). Private, 8th Co., Lower Bn., Militia, Sep., 1777 [Ref: M-200, T-5:51]. Took the Oath of Allegiance before the Hon. Richard Thompson in 1778 [Ref: T-3:75, L-1:39]. "Lenerd or Leonard Day" lived in North West Hd. in 1776 and had two taxables in 1777 [Ref: K-1:226, R-31:17].

DAY, Samuel (b. 1761 or 1762). Son of Leonard Day, of North West Hd., in 1776 [Ref: K-1:226]. Private, 8th Co., Lower Bn., Militia, Sep., 1777 [Ref: M-200, T-5:51].

DAY, William. Private, 1st or 32nd Bn., Militia (no date was given; possibly June, 1777). [Ref: T-5:1].

DAYLEY, John. Private, 3rd Co., Lower Bn., Militia, Sep., 1777 [Ref: M-199, T-5:46].

DEACON, Pierce. Private, Capt. Thomas Beall's Co., Maryland Line, 1780 [Ref: D-351].

DEAKINS, Francis. Served as Captain and First Major, 16th Bn., Militia, Jan. 6, 1776, and Lieutenant Colonel, Aug. 30, 1777, and Colonel, Oct. 7, 1777 [Ref: M-68, M-193, C-373, C-393]. "Francis Deakins, Esq." was appointed the Examiner General in Montgomery County under the Act to appropriate lands to the use of officers and soldiers of Maryland and for the sale of vacant land in 1782 [Ref: I-78, I-95]. Lived in Sugar Loaf Hd. (three taxables) in 1777 [Ref: R-31:9].

DEAKINS, Leonard. Served as Captain, Lower District, Frederick County (now Montgomery), Militia, July 20, 1776 [Ref: D-42].

DEAKINS, William Jr. (died 1798). Served as a Second Major, 29th Bn., Militia, Jan. 6, 1776, Lieutenant Colonel on June 21, 1777, and Colonel to at least May, 1782 [Ref: M-68, M-198, T-5:44, C-296, C-373, R-33:156, X-1146, O-133]. Was a Justice of the Orphans Court in 1778 and Justice of the Peace who administered the Oath of Allegiance in 1778 [Ref: C-529, T-3:68, T-3:69, L-1:39]. "William Deakins" lived in the Upper Part of Potomac Hd. (seven taxables) in 1777 [Ref: R-31:14]. "William Deakins, Jr. of Georgetown, merchant" died testate in Montgomery County (wife named Jane) in 1798 [Ref: V-40].

DEBOY, Joseph. Took the Oath of Allegiance in 1778 [Ref: L-2:27].

DELANY, John. Private, 7th Maryland Line, from Feb. 7, 1779 until June 2, 1780, when he reportedly deserted [Ref: D-202].

DENBACK (DOMBACK, DANBACK, DONBOCH), Frederick (b. 1726). Took the Oath of Allegiance before the Hon. Richard Thompson in 1778 [Ref: T-3:75, L-1:39]. "Frederick Danback or Donboch" lived in George Town Hd. (one taxable) in 1776-1777 [Ref: K-1:193, R-31:2].

DENBACK (DONBACK, DONBOCH), Michael (b. 1763). Lived in George Town Hd. in 1776 and apparently a son of "Frederick Donboch," q.v. [Ref: K-1:193]. Private, 8th Co., Lower Bn., Militia, July 15, 1780 [Ref: M-207].

DEMOREY, John. Took the Oath of Allegiance in 1778 [Ref: L-2:27].

DENNIS, Ann. See "William Coy," q.v.

DENNIS, Henry. Private, Capt. Thomas Beall's Co., Maryland Line, 1780 [Ref: D-350].

DENNIS, John. Private, 1st Co., Lower Bn., Militia, Sep., 1777 [Ref: M-198, T-5:44]. Took the Oath of Allegiance before the Hon. Edward Burgess on Feb. 28, 1778 [Ref: T-3:62, L-1:39].

DENNIS, William (1736-1807). Private, 4th Co., Upper Bn., Militia, Aug. 30, 1777 [Ref: M-194]. Took the Oath of Allegiance before the Hon. William Deakins, Jr. before March 3, 1778 [Ref: T-3:68, L-1:39].

Rendered aid by providing wheat for use of the military in 1781 [Ref: O-396]. William Dennis died testate in Montgomery County in 1807 (wife not named, but he was apparently married twice). [Ref: V-40]. He may have been the "William Dennair" [Dennais?], aged 40, in Sugarland Hd. in 1776 and, if so, his wife at that time was named Mary, who was aged 39 [Ref: K-1:203].

DENNISTON, James. Private, Capt. Thomas Beall's Co., Maryland Line, 1780 [Ref: D-350].

DENT, John. Private, 6th Co., Lower Bn., Militia, Aug., 1777 [Ref: M-200, T-5:49]. Took the Oath of Allegiance before the Hon. Joseph Offutt on March 2, 1778 [Ref: T-3:70, L-1:39]. Rendered aid by providing wheat for use of the military in 1781 [Ref: O-403]. Lived in the Upper Part of Potomac Hd. (one taxable) in 1777 [Ref: R-31:14].

DESELM (DEZELM, DESALAM), Moses. "Moses Deselm" was a private, 2nd Co., Lower Bn., Militia, on July 15, 1780 [Ref: M-204]. "Moses Dezelm" took the Oath of Allegiance (made his "M" mark) before the Hon. Samuel W. Magruder in 1778 [Ref: T-3:73]. "Moses Desalam" lived in the Upper Part of Potomac Hd. (one taxable) in 1777 [Ref: R-31:14].

DEVINE, Daniel. Private who was recruited to serve in the Continental Army in 1780 [Ref: D-341].

DEVONSHIRE (DEVENISH), George. "George Devonshire" was a private who was recruited to serve in the Continental Army in 1780 [Ref: D-341]. "George Devenish" was a private in the 7th Maryland Line who was reported missing on Aug. 16, 1780, at the Battle of Camden [Ref: D-202].

DEWIST (DUIS), Francis (b. 1743). "Francis Dewist" was a private, Capt. Thomas Beall's Co., Maryland Line, 1780 [Ref: D-351]. "Francis Duis" lived in Lower Potomac Hd. in 1776 [Ref: K-1:182].

DICKERSON, Hannah. See "Serratt Dickerson," q.v.

DICKERSON (DICKASON, DICKESON), Serratt (Serrett). Took the Oath of Allegiance before the Hon. Edward Burgess on Feb. 28, 1778 [Ref: T-3:60, L-1:39]. "Serret Dickeson" rendered aid by providing wheat for use of the military in 1780 [Ref: O-306]. "Serratt Dickason" rendered aid by providing wheat for use of the military in 1781 [Ref: O-383]. "Serratt Dickerson" lived in Rock Creek Hd. (two taxables) in 1777 [Ref: R-31:16]. When Hannah Dickerson died testate in Montgomery County in 1820 (will written in 1816) she mentioned her son "Surratt Dickerson, lately of Kentucky, deceased." [Ref: V-41].

DICKERSON (DICKENSON, DICKASON), Solomon (b. 1754). Private, Capt. Edward Burgess' Co., Lower District of Frederick (now Montgomery) County, July, 1776 [Ref: D-42]. Took the Oath of Allegiance before the Hon. Edward Burgess on Feb. 28, 1778 [Ref: T-3:60, L-1:39]. "Solomon Dickason" rendered aid by providing wheat for use of the military in 1781 [Ref: O-379]. "Solomon Dickerson" applied for a pension (S30990) in Monroe County, Kentucky, on Sep. 3, 1832, aged

78, stating he was born in Maryland in Sep., 1754, and enlisted in Montgomery County in 1777, serving four months. After the war he moved to Berkeley County, Virginia, then on to Surry County, North Carolina, and Washington County, Virginia, and Bourbon County, Green County, and Monroe County, Kentucky [Ref: P-969, Y-15]. He is buried in the Old Mulkey Meetinghouse Cemetery in Monroe County [Ref: *Monroe County, Kentucky, Cemetery Records, Volume 2*, by Eva Coe Peden (1975), p. 51. There were no dates given, but it is noted that he served as a private in Griffin's Maryland Regiment]. It should also be noted that a "Solomon Peckinson" (Dickenson?) married Mary Reily in Montgomery County, Maryland, on July 8, 1779 [Ref: K-2:515].

DICKINSON (DICKERSON), John. Served as an Ensign, Middle Bn., Militia, Sep. 12, 1777, First Lieutenant, April 21, 1779, and Captain, March 25, 1780 [Ref: M-69, M-70, M-196, C-373, E-357, F-120]. "John Dickerson" took the Oath of Allegiance before the Hon. Edward Burgess on Feb. 28, 1778 [Ref: T-3:60, L-1:39]. Lived in Rock Creek Hd. (two taxables) in 1777 [Ref: R-31:16].

DICKINSON, William. Rendered aid by providing wheat for use of the military in 1781 [Ref: O-392].

DICKINSON (DICKERSON, DICKESON), Zadock. Private, 4th Co., Middle Bn., Militia, Sep., 1777, and Ensign, March 25, 1780 [Ref: M-70, M-196, F-120]. "Zadock Dickinson" was a Second Lieutenant, 4th Co., Middle Bn., Militia, July 15, 1780 [Ref: M-202]. "Zadock Dickerson" took the Oath of Allegiance before the Hon. Edward Burgess on Feb. 28, 1778 [Ref: T-3:60, L-1:39]. "Zadock Dickerson" lived in Rock Creek Hd. (one taxable) in 1777 [Ref: R-31:16]. "Zadock Dickason" was constable in Seneca Hd. in 1781 [Ref: W-2]. "Zadock Dickeson" married Sarah Cook in Montgomery County on Feb. 4, 1779 [Ref: K-2:518].

DIFFENDALLER, Mike. Took the Oath of Allegiance in 1778 [Ref: L-2:27].

DIXON (DICKSON), John (b. 1759). Private, 4th Co., Upper Bn., Militia, Aug. 30, 1777 [Ref: M-194]. "John Dickson, aged 52" and "John Dickson, aged 17" lived in Sugarland Hd. in 1776-1777 [Ref: K-1:208, R-31:12].

DIXON (DICKSON), Richard. "Richard Dixon, an Englishman, about 42 or 43 years of age, 5 feet 4 or 5 inches high, is partly grey and he has already served, as he says, between 3 and 4 years in the Army, was recruited by Capt. Aaron Harris on April 7, 1781." [Ref: R-33:156, X-1146]. "Richard Dickson" was a private, Capt. Price's Co., 3rd Maryland Line, 1781, and was reported dead Dec. 27, 1782 [Ref: D-453]. "Richard Dixon, aged 45" lived in North West Hd. in 1776 [Ref: K-1:231].

DIXON, William. (1) Private, 3rd Co., Lower Bn., Militia, Sep., 1777 [Ref: M-199, T-5:46]. (2) Private, 4th Co., Upper Bn., Militia, Aug. 30, 1777 [Ref: M-194]. Letter from John Murdock to the Governor and Council of Maryland, April 7, 1781, in part: "William Dixon, late an inhabitant of George Town, and subject of this State, took the Oath of Fidelity before

Mr. Thompson on June 22, 1778, having been absent at the time limited by law for taking that Oath. Master Dixon was this day committed by Mr. Thompson to our County Goal [Montgomery County Jail] on strong suspicions of treason, i. e., by his having adhered to persons bearing arms and employed in the service of Great Britain... [and] ...I request your orders in what manner to dispose of him [and three other British prisoners]." [Ref: H-169]. "William Dixon, aged 23" lived in George Town Hd. (one taxable) in 1776-1777 [Ref: K-1:193, R-31:3], and "William Dixon, aged 19" lived in Sugarland Hd. in 1776 [Ref: K-1:208].

DOBBS (DOBS), Thomas. Took the Oath of Allegiance before the Hon. Gerrard Briscoe on March 2, 1778 [Ref: T-3:56, L-1:40]. "Thomas Dobs" lived in Sugar Loaf Hd. (one taxable) in 1777 [Ref: R-31:9].

DOD, James. Took the Oath of Allegiance before the Hon. Joseph Wilson on Feb. 28, 1778 [Ref: T-3:64, L-1:40].

DODSON, Thomas. Took the Oath of Allegiance in 1778 [Ref: L-2:27].

DODSWORTH, James. Private, 5th Class, 2nd Co., Middle Bn., Militia, July 15, 1780 [Ref: M-201].

DOFLER, Peter. Took the Oath of Allegiance in 1778 [Ref: L-2:27].

DOHERTY, John and Nicholas. See "John and Nicholas Dougherty," q.v.

DONALDSON, Alexander. Took the Oath of Allegiance before the Hon. Aneas Campbell on March 2, 1778 [Ref: T-3:77, L-1:40].

DONCASTER (DUNCASTER), James. "James Doncaster" was recruited to serve in the Continental Army in 1780 [Ref: D-342]. "James Donkester" took the Oath of Allegiance before the Hon. Edward Burgess on Feb. 28, 1778 [Ref: T-3:61, L-1:40]. "James Duncaster" lived in the Lower Part of Newfoundland Hd. (two taxables) in 1777 [Ref: R-31:5].

DOOINBAUGH(?), John. Took the Oath of Allegiance in 1778 [Ref: L-2:27].

DORAN (DORIN), Edward. "Edward Doran" took the Oath of Allegiance (made his "V" mark) before the Hon. Edward Burgess on Feb. 28, 1778 [Ref: T-3:58, L-1:40]. "Edward Dorin" lived in the Lower Part of Newfoundland Hd. (one taxable) in 1777 [Ref: R-31:5].

DORAN (DORON, DORIN), John. "John Doran" was a private, 3rd Co., Middle Bn., Militia, Sep., 1777 [Ref: M-196, T-5:38]. Private, 5th Co., Lower Bn., Militia, July 15, 1780 [Ref: M-206]. "John Doron" took the Oath of Allegiance before the Hon. William Deakins, Jr. before March 3, 1778 [Ref: T-3:68, L-1:40]. "John Dorin" lived in the Upper Part of Potomac Hd. (one taxable) in 1777 [Ref: R-31:14].

DORSEN, Benoni. Served as an Ensign, Upper Bn., Militia, March 23, 1780 [Ref: M-70, F-120], and Ensign, 3rd Co., Middle Bn., Militia, July 15, 1780 [Ref: M-202].

DORSEY, Amelia. See "Samuel Riggs," q.v.

DORSEY, Elizabeth. See "Joseph Warfield" and "Henry Griffith," q.v.

DORSEY, Greenberry. Took the Oath of Allegiance before the Hon. Samuel W. Magruder in 1778 [Ref: T-3:73, L-1:40]. Lived in Lower Potomac Hd. (one taxable) in 1777 [Ref: R-31:4].
DORSEY, John. Private, 1st or 32nd Bn., Militia (no date was given; possibly June, 1777). [Ref: T-5:1].
DORSEY, Joseph. Rendered aid by providing wheat for use of the military in 1781 [Ref: O-406].
DORSEY, Joshua. Private, 3rd Maryland Regiment, July, 1779 [Ref: D-103]. One Joshua Dorsey owned a working plantation ("quarter") in the Upper Part of Newfoundland Hd. in 1777 [Ref: R-31:6].
DORSEY, Nicholas. Rendered aid by providing wheat for use of the military in 1781 [Ref: O-393]. Lived in Seneca Hd. (seven taxables) in 1777 [Ref: R-31:7]. See "Joseph Warfield," q.v.
DORUS(?), Philip. Private, 7th Co., Middle Bn., Militia, July 15, 1780 [Ref: M-203].
DOUCH, William. See "William Dutch (Douch, Dorch)," q.v.
DOUGHERTY (DOHERTY, DOHITY), John. (1) Private, 3rd Co., Middle Bn., Militia, Sep., 1777 [Ref: M-196, T-5:38]. (2) Private, 3rd Co., Upper Bn., Militia, Aug. 30, 1777 [Ref: M-193]. One John Dougherty took the Oath of Allegiance before the Hon. Gerrard Briscoe on March 2, 1778 [Ref: T-3:57, L-1:40], and another took the Oath of Allegiance before the Hon. William Deakins, Jr. before March 3, 1778 [Ref: T-3:68, L-1:40]. "John Dougherty" rendered aid by providing wheat for use of the military in 1781 [Ref: O-444]. "John Doherty" rendered aid by providing wheat for use of the military in 1781 [Ref: O-379]. "John Dohity" lived in Sugar Loaf Hd. (two taxables) in 1777 [Ref: R-31:9], and "John Doherty" lived in the Upper Part of Potomac Hd. (one taxable) in 1777 [Ref: R-31:14].
DOUGHERTY, Neill. Private, 2nd Co., Middle Bn., Militia, Sep. 4, 1777 [Ref: M-196, T-5:37]. "Neal Dougherty" took the Oath of Allegiance before the Hon. Gerrard Briscoe on March 2, 1778 [Ref: T-3:56, L-1:40]. "Neil Doherty" was a private, 3rd Class, 3rd Co., Middle Bn., Militia, July 15, 1780 [Ref: M-202].
DOUGHERTY (DOHERTY), Nicholas. "Nicholas Doherty" was a private, 6th Class, 3rd Co., Middle Bn., Militia, July 15, 1780 [Ref: M-202].
DOUGHERTY (DOHERTY), Philip. "Philip Dougherty" was a private, 2nd Co., Middle Bn., Militia, Sep. 4, 1777 [Ref: M-196, T-5:37]. Took the Oath of Allegiance before the Hon. Gerrard Briscoe on March 2, 1778 [Ref: T-3:56, L-1:40]. "Philip Doherty" was a private, 3rd Class, 3rd Co., Middle Bn., Militia, July 15, 1780 [Ref: M-202].
DOUGHERTY, William. Private, 3rd Co., Upper Bn., Militia, Aug. 30, 1777 [Ref: M-193].
DOUGHTY, Ruben. Rendered aid by providing beef and pork for use of the military in 1781 [Ref: O-378].

DOUGLASS, Hugh. Son of Samuel and Susannah Douglass [Ref: V-41]. Rendered aid by providing pork for use of the military in 1781 [Ref: O-378].
DOUGLASS (DOUGLAS), Samuel. "Samuel Douglas" was a private, 1st Co., Upper Bn., Militia, Aug. 30, 1777 [Ref: M-193]. "Samuel Douglass" took the Oath of Allegiance before the Hon. Elisha Williams on March 2, 1778 [Ref: T-3:82]. "Samuel Duglace, aged 33" lived in Sugarland Hd. (wife named Rebecca) in 1776 [Ref: K-1:213], and "Samuel Douglass" lived in Sugarland Hd. (one taxable) in 1777 [Ref: R-31:12]. One died testate in Montgomery County (wife named Susannah) in 1803 and mentioned sons Hugh and Samuel, among other children [Ref: V-41].
DOUGLASS, William (b. 1739). Private, 4th Co., Upper Bn., Militia, Aug. 30, 1777 [Ref: M-194]. Took the Oath of Allegiance before the Hon. Edward Burgess on Feb. 28, 1778 [Ref: T-3:63, L-1:40]. "William Duglace or Douglass" lived in Sugarland Hd. in 1776-1777 [Ref: K-1:208, R-31:12]. William Douglass married Elizabeth Gentle in Montgomery County on April 26, 1778 [Ref: K-2:518].
DOVE, Benjamin. Private, 3rd Co., Middle Bn., Militia, Sep., 1777 [Ref: M-196, T-5:38]. Private, 2nd Class, 2nd Co., Middle Bn., Militia, July 15, 1780 [Ref: M-201]. Took the Oath of Allegiance before the Hon. William Deakins, Jr. before March 3, 1778 [Ref: T-3:68, L-1:40]. Lived in the Upper Part of Potomac Hd. (one taxable) in 1777 [Ref: R-31:14].
DOVE, William (Jr.). "William Dove" lived in the Upper Part of Potomac Hd. (one taxable) in 1777 [Ref: R-31:14]. "William Dove, Jr." was a private in Capt. Edward Tillard's Co. in 1776 and appears to have enlisted in Anne Arundel County [Ref: D-39].
DOVER, George. Took the Oath of Allegiance in 1778 [Ref: L-2:27].
DOWDEN, Clementius (1762-c1836). Private, 6th Class, 2nd Co., Middle Bn., Militia, July 15, 1780 [Ref: M-201]. "Clementius Doudon" applied for a pension (S30995) in Bourbon County, Kentucky (where he had lived four years) on Dec. 3, 1832, aged 70, stating he was born on Jan. 11, 1762, in Prince George's County, Maryland. He had been drafted in 1779 or 1780 in Montgomery County, Maryland, and served under Capt. Thomas Bell [Beall] for one month, and then volunteered and served another month. In the fall of 1780 he moved to Washington County, Pennsylvania, and in 1781 he volunteered and served another month under Capt. Edward Richardson. In 1782 he was drafted and served one month under Col. George Vanlandingham. He volunteered again in 1782, served as an Orderly Sergeant under Col. John Marshall, and also served four months in 1783 in keeping refugees and Indians from stealing horses in Washington County. Elizabeth Darneal, of Washington County, Pennsylvania, verified that she and Clementius Douden resided at the same house in the fall of 1780 and she assisted in fitting him out with clothing and provisions for his journey at every time he served. In 1833 Robert M. Johnson wrote the Commissioner of Pensions that "my

particular friend Clematius Dowden asks that the case be put through as expeditiously as possible as Mr. Dowden wishes to go to Illinois." His pension certificate, dated May 14, 1833, listed "Clematius Douden" as being of the State of Tennessee and it was never shown if he ever lived in Illinois [Ref: P-1015, Y-3, Z-9, DAR-I:200].

DOWDEN, James. Private, Capt. Thomas Beall's Co., Maryland Line, 1780 [Ref: D-351].

DOWDEN, John (b. 1741). Private, 1st Co., Upper Bn., Militia, Aug. 30, 1777, Second Lieutenant, April 21, 1779, and First Lieutenant, March 25, 1780 [Ref: M-71, M-193, E-356, F-120]. Took the Oath of Allegiance before the Hon. Elisha Williams on March 2, 1778 [Ref: T-3:80, L-1:40]. Served as a petit juror in Aug., 1777 [Ref: R-31:17]. Lived in Sugarland Hd. in 1776-1777 [Ref: K-1:217, R-31:12].

DOWDEN, Michael (b. 1737). Private, 1st Co., Upper Bn., Militia, Aug. 30, 1777 [Ref: M-193]. Took the Oath of Allegiance before the Hon. William Deakins, Jr. before March 3, 1778 [Ref: T-3:68, L-1:40, which source misspelled the name as "Michael Wowden"]. Served as a petit juror in Aug., 1777 [Ref: R-31:17]. Rendered aid by providing corn for use of the military in 1780 [Ref: O-285, O-298]. "Michael Downden" lived in Sugarland Hd. in 1776 and "Michael Ashford Dowden" lived there in 1777 (two taxables). [Ref: K-1:204, R-31:12].

DOWDEN, Thomas. Private, 4th Class, 2nd Co., Middle Bn., Militia, July 15, 1780 [Ref: M-201]. Private, 1st Co., Upper Bn., Militia, Aug. 30, 1777 [Ref: M-193]. Took the Oath of Allegiance before the Hon. Elisha Williams on March 2, 1778 [Ref: T-3:80, L-1:40]. Rendered aid by providing wheat and corn for use of the military in 1780 [Ref: O-283, O-313]. One Thomas Dowden (b. 1745) lived in Sugarland Hd. (one taxable) in 1776-1777 [Ref: K-1:198, R-31:12], and another lived in the Upper Part of Potomac Hd. (two taxables) in 1777 [Ref: R-31:14]. Also see "Thomas Dowden, Jr.," q.v.

DOWDEN, Thomas Jr. "Thomas Dowden, Jr." took the Oath of Allegiance before the Hon. William Deakins, Jr. before March 3, 1778 [Ref: T-3:68, L-1:40]. Private, 3rd Co., Middle Bn., Militia, Sep., 1777 [Ref: M-196, T-5:38]. "Thomas Dowden" married Anne Campbell in Montgomery County on Jan. 27, 1780 [Ref: K-2:518].

DOWDEN, Zachariah (died 1821). Private, 3rd Co., Middle Bn., Militia, Sep., 1777 [Ref: M-196, T-5:38]. Private, 2nd Class, 2nd Co., Middle Bn., Militia, July 15, 1780 [Ref: M-201]. Took the Oath of Allegiance before the Hon. William Deakins, Jr. before March 3, 1778 [Ref: T-3:68, L-1:40]. Recruited Edward Clark in April, 1781 [Ref: R-33:156, X-1146]. Rendered aid by providing wheat for use of the military in 1781 [Ref: O-390]. "Zachy. Dowden" lived in the Upper Part of Potomac Hd. (one taxable) in 1777 [Ref: R-31:14]. Zachariah Dowden died testate in Montgomery County (wife named Sarah) in 1821 [Ref: V-41].

DOWDEN, Zephaniah. Private, 3rd Co., Middle Bn., Militia, Sep., 1777 [Ref: M-196, T-5:38]. Private, 3rd Class, 2nd Co., Middle Bn., Militia, July 15, 1780 [Ref: M-201]. Took the Oath of Allegiance before the Hon. William Deakins, Jr. before March 3, 1778 [Ref: T-3:68, L-1:40]. Lived in the Upper Part of Potomac Hd. (two taxables) in 1777 [Ref: R-31:14].
DOWELL (DOULL), James. Took the Oath of Allegiance before the Hon. Richard Thompson in 1778 [Ref: T-3:75, L-1:40]. "James Doull" lived in the Upper Part of Potomac Hd. (nine taxables) in 1777 [Ref: R-31:14].
DOWELL (DOWEL), John (b. 1751). Private, 8th Co., Upper Bn., Militia, Aug. 30, 1777 [Ref: M-195]. Took the Oath of Allegiance before the Hon. Elisha Williams on March 2, 1778 [Ref: T-3:82]. "John Dowel or Dowell" lived in Sugarland Hd. in 1776-1777 [Ref: K-1:220, R-31:12].
DOWELL (DOWEL), Peter Jr. (b. 1749). Private, 8th Co., Upper Bn., Militia, Aug. 30, 1777 [Ref: M-195]. "Peter Dowel, Jr." lived in Sugarland Hd. in 1776-1777 [Ref: K-1:220, R-31:12].
DOWELL, Peter Sr. (b. 1719). Took the Oath of Allegiance before the Hon. Elisha Williams on March 2, 1778 [Ref: T-3:81, L-1:40]. "Peter Dowel, Sr." lived in Sugarland Hd. (two taxables) in 1776-1777 [Ref: K-1:220, R-31:12].
DOWELL (DOWEL), Philip. Private, 8th Co., Upper Bn., Militia, Aug. 30, 1777 [Ref: M-195]. Took the Oath of Allegiance before the Hon. Elisha Williams on March 2, 1778 [Ref: T-3:82]. "Philip Dowel" lived in Sugarland Hd. (one taxable) in 1777 [Ref: R-31:12].
DOWELL (DOWEL), Richard. Private, 8th Co., Upper Bn., Militia, Aug. 30, 1777 [Ref: M-195]. Took the Oath of Allegiance before the Hon. Elisha Williams on March 2, 1778 [Ref: T-3:81, L-1:40]. "Richard Dowel" lived in Sugarland Hd. (one taxable) in 1777 [Ref: R-31:12].
DOWELL (DOWL, DOWE), Robert. Took the Oath of Allegiance before the Hon. Joseph Wilson on Feb. 28, 1778 [Ref: T-3:66, L-1:40].
DOWELL (DOWL, DOWLES), Samuel. "Samuel Dowl" lived in Linganore Hd. (one taxable) in 1777 [Ref: R-31:9]. "Samuel Dowles" was a private, 6th Co., Middle Bn., Militia, Aug., 1777 [Ref: M-197, T-5:41].
DOWELL (DOWEL), William (b. 1761). Private, 8th Co., Upper Bn., Militia, Aug. 30, 1777 [Ref: M-195]. "William Dowel or Dowell" lived in Sugarland Hd. in 1776-1777 [Ref: K-1:220, R-31:12].
DOWLEN, James. Private, 6th Co., Lower Bn., Militia, July 15, 1780 [Ref: M-206].
DOWLEY, Thomas. See "Thomas Duley (Douly)," q.v.
DOWNING, Francis (1746-1834). Private, 3rd Co., Lower Bn., Militia, July 15, 1780 [Ref: M-205]. Private, 3rd Co., Middle Bn., Militia, Sep., 1777 [Ref: M-196, T-5:38]. "Francis Downing" took the Oath of Allegiance before the Hon. William Deakins, Jr. before March 3, 1778 [Ref: T-3:68, L-1:40]. "Francis Dowon" [sic] lived in the Upper Part of Potomac Hd. (one taxable) in 1777 [Ref: R-31:14]. Francis Downing was born on Jan. 1, 1746 in Yorkshire, England and came to America in

1768. He married Henrietta ---- and had six children, but only John (b. Oct. 10, 1773 or 1775) was named. Francis applied for pension in Scott County, Kentucky on Aug. 29, 1832 and died there on Sep. 2, 1834. His widow also applied for and received a pension (W8674) in Scott County on Nov. 22, 1836, aged 88 [Ref: P-1017].

DOWNS (DOWNES), Henry. Private, 3rd Co., Lower Bn., Militia, July 15, 1780 [Ref: M-205].

DOWNS, Margaret. See "Michael Downs," q.v.

DOWNS (DOWNES), Michael (c1760-1789). Private, Capt. Price's Co., 3rd Maryland Line, 1781-1782 [Ref: D-394, D-448, D-453]. On Sep. 11, 1838, Margaret McCaw, aged 75, former widow of Michael Downs, applied for a pension (R6614) in Gallatin County, Kentucky, stating they had been married in Montgomery County, Maryland, in Jan., 1781, by Rev. Threlkeld. Michael Downs died in March, 1789, and Margaret married John McCaw, who died on Jan. 31, 1805. Polly Downs, Matthew Gorman, and Luticia Gorman stated that they were acquainted with Michael Downs and his widow. In Harrison County, Kentucky, on Dec. 24, 1833, James Remington and Alexander Lewis said they had known the pensioner in Montgomery County, Maryland, and knew that Michael Downs married Margaret Lewis in 1781 [Ref: Z-40, P-1019].

DOWNS, Polly. See "Michael Downs," q.v.

DOWNS, Richard. Private who was recruited to serve in the Extra Regiment of the Continental Army in 1780 [Ref: D-341, D-342].

DOWNS (DOWNES), Zachariah (c1784-c1826). Private, 1st Co., Lower Bn., Militia, Sep., 1777 [Ref: M-198, T-5:44]. Took the Oath of Allegiance before the Hon. Edward Burgess on Feb. 28, 1778 [Ref: T-3:62, L-1:40]. Private, 7th Co., Lower Bn., Militia, July 15, 1780 [Ref: M-206]. Lived in the Lower Part of Newfoundland Hd. (one taxable) in 1777. Zachariah Downs married Elizabeth Ann Mason [Ref: R-31:5, DAR-I:201].

DRAKE, Robert. Private, 3rd Co., Middle Bn., Militia, Sep., 1777 [Ref: M-196, T-5:38]. Took the Oath of Allegiance before the Hon. William Deakins, Jr. before March 3, 1778 [Ref: T-3:68, L-1:40]. Lived in the Upper Part of Potomac Hd. (one taxable) in 1777 [Ref: R-31:14].

DRANE (DRAIN), Thomas (died 1823). "Thomas Drane" was a private, 6th Co., Lower Bn., Militia, Aug., 1777 [Ref: M-200, T-5:49]. "Thomas Drain" was a private, 3rd Co., Lower Bn., Militia, July 15, 1780 [Ref: M-205]. Rendered aid by providing wheat for use of the military in 1780 and 1781 [Ref: O-305, O-402]. Thomas Drane died testate in Montgomery County (wife and children not named) in 1823 [Ref: V-42].

DRANE (DRAINE), Walter. Private, 3rd Co., Lower Bn., Militia, July 15, 1780 [Ref: M-205].

DRAPER, John (b. 1714). Lived in Sugarland Hd. in 1776 [Ref: K-1:213]. Took the Oath of Allegiance before the Hon. Elisha Williams on March 2, 1778 [Ref: T-3:81, L-1:40].

DRAPER, William (b. 1754). Private, 1st Co., Upper Bn., Militia, Aug. 30, 1777 [Ref: M-193]. Lived in Sugarland Hd. (one taxable) in 1776-1777 [Ref: K-1:206, R-31:12].

DROGULA, Fred W. See "Kid Marquess," q.v.

DRUMBO, Conrad. Took the Oath of Allegiance in 1778 [Ref: L-2:27].

DUCKER, Jeremiah. Served as a Second Lieutenant, 29th Bn., Militia, June 21, 1777, and First Lieutenant, 1st Co., Lower Bn., Sep. 12, 1777 [Ref: M-72, M-198, T-5:44, C-296, C-373]. Took the Oath of Allegiance before the Hon. Edward Burgess on Feb. 28, 1778 [Ref: T-3:58, L-1:40]. Rendered aid by providing wheat for use of the military in 1780 [Ref: O-306]. Lived in the Lower Part of Newfoundland Hd. (eight taxables) in 1777 [Ref: R-31:5].

DUCKER, Nathaniel. Private, 6th Class, 3rd Co., Middle Bn., Militia, July 15, 1780 [Ref: M-202]. Took the Oath of Allegiance before the Hon. Gerrard Briscoe on March 2, 1778 [Ref: T-3:56, L-1:40]. Rendered aid by providing wheat for use of the military in 1781 [Ref: O-443]. Nathaniel Ducker married Sarah Segar in Montgomery County in Nov. 25, 1779 [Ref: K-2:518].

DUCKETT, Isaac. Private, 2nd Co., Lower Bn., Militia, Sep., 1777 [Ref: M-198, T-5:45]. Took the Oath of Allegiance (made his "X" mark) before the Hon. Joseph Wilson on Feb. 28, 1778 [Ref: T-3:67, L-1:40]. Lived in Seneca Hd. (one taxable) in 1777 [Ref: R-31:7].

DUCKETT, Samuel (b. 1751). Private, 2nd Co., Lower Bn., Militia, July 15, 1780 [Ref: M-204]. Private, 5th Co., Lower Bn., Militia, Aug., 1777 [Ref: M-199, T-5:48]. Took the Oath of Allegiance before the Hon. Samuel W. Magruder in 1778 [Ref: T-3:73]. Lived in Lower Potomac Hd. (two taxables) in 1776-1777 [Ref: R-31:4, K-1:182].

DUKE, William. Private, 2nd Co., Lower Bn., Militia, Sep., 1777 [Ref: M-198, T-5:45]. Took the Oath of Allegiance (make his "X" mark) before the Hon. Edward Burgess on Feb. 28, 1778 [Ref: T-3:58, L-1:40]. Private, 5th Co., Lower Bn., Militia, July 15, 1780 [Ref: M-206]. Lived in Rock Creek Hd. (one taxable) in 1777 [Ref: R-31:16].

DULEY (DOULY), Barton. Private, 6th Co., Lower Bn., Militia, Aug., 1777 [Ref: M-200, T-5:49]. Private, 3rd Co., Lower Bn., Militia, July 15, 1780 [Ref: M-205]. "Barton Duley" lived in the Upper Part of Potomac Hd. (two taxables) in 1777 [Ref: R-31:14]. Barton Duley married Martha Baker in Montgomery County on March 3, 1778 [Ref: K-2:521].

DULEY (DOULY), James. Private, 6th Co., Lower Bn., Militia, Aug., 1777 [Ref: M-200, T-5:49]. Private, 3rd Co., Lower Bn., Militia, July 15, 1780 [Ref: M-205]. Two men with this name took the Oath of Allegiance before the Hon. Samuel W. Magruder in 1778. One made his "I X" mark [Ref: T-3:73, L-1:40], and the other made his "X" mark [Ref: T-3:73]. "James Duley, Sr." (two taxables) and "James Duley, Jr." (one taxable) both lived in the Upper Part of Potomac Hd. in 1777 [Ref: R-31:14].

DULEY (DOULY), John. Private, 6th Co., Lower Bn., Militia, Aug., 1777 [Ref: M-200, T-5:49]. Private, 6th Co., Lower Bn., Militia, July 15, 1780 [Ref: M-206]. Lived in the Upper Part of Potomac Hd. (one taxable) in 1777 [Ref: R-31:14].

DULEY (DOULY, DOWLEY), Thomas. Private, 6th Co., Lower Bn., Militia, Aug., 1777 [Ref: M-200, T-5:49]. "Thomas Douly" took the Oath of Allegiance (made his "X" mark) before the Hon. Samuel W. Magruder in 1778 [Ref: T-3:73]. Thomas Dowley or Duley (b. 1740) lived in Lower Potomac Hd. (four taxables) in 1776-1777 [Ref: R-31:4, K-1:182].

DULEY, William. Rendered aid by providing wheat for use of the military in 1780 [Ref: O-332].

DUNAGIN, Rachel. See "Thomas Bateman (Batman)," q.v.

DUNCASTER, James. See "James Doncaster (Duncaster)," q.v.

DUNN, Auguston. Served as Fourth Sergeant, 4th Co., Lower Bn., Militia, July 15, 1780 [Ref: M-205]. Took the Oath of Allegiance before the Hon. Edward Burgess on Feb. 28, 1778 [Ref: T-3:62, L-1:40].

DUNN, Hugh Smith. Private, 2nd Co., Lower Bn., Militia, Sep., 1777 [Ref: M-198, T-5:45]. Took the Oath of Allegiance before the Hon. Edward Burgess on Feb. 28, 1778 [Ref: T-3:60, L-1:40].

DUNN, Margaret. See "Nicholas Hocker," q.v.

DUNN, Osburn. Private, 7th Co., Lower Bn., Militia, Aug., 1777 [Ref: M-200, T-5:50].

DUNN, Thomas. Took the Oath of Allegiance (made his "X" mark) before the Hon. Joseph Wilson on Feb. 28, 1778 [Ref: T-3:66, L-1:40].

DUNN, William. Private, 7th Co., Lower Bn., Militia, Aug., 1777 [Ref: M-200, T-5:50]. Took the Oath of Allegiance before the Hon. Edward Burgess on Feb. 28, 1778 [Ref: T-3:62, L-1:40]. Rendered aid by providing wheat for use of the military in 1780 [Ref: O-307]. Lived in the Lower Part of Newfoundland Hd. (two taxables) in 1777 [Ref: R-31:5].

DUNN, William Jr. Took the Oath of Allegiance before the Hon. Edward Burgess on Feb. 28, 1778 [Ref: T-3:62, L-1:40].

DURANT, John. Private, Capt. Price's Co., 3rd Maryland Line, 1781-1782 [Ref: D-453].

DURHAM (DERHAM), Patrick. Private, 2nd Co., Middle Bn., Militia, Sep. 4, 1777 [Ref: M-195]. "Patrick Derham" took the Oath of Allegiance before the Hon. Gerrard Briscoe on March 2, 1778 [Ref: T-3:57, L-1:40]. "Patrick Durham" lived in Sugar Loaf Hd. (one taxable) in 1777 [Ref: R-31:9].

DUSTMAN, Martin. Took the Oath of Allegiance in 1778 [Ref: L-2:27].

DUTCH (DOUCH, DYCH, DORTCH, DORCH), William. "William Dutch" lived in the Lower Part of Newfoundland Hd. (one taxable) in 1777 [Ref: R-31:5]. "William Douch" was a private in the 4th Maryland Regiment from March 28, 1777 to April 12, 1777, when reported "deserted" [Ref: D-277]. "William Dortch" was a private in the 1st Maryland Regiment who enlisted June 25, 1780 [Ref: D-101]. "William Dych" was a private in 1781 and an artificer in 1782 in Capt. Price's Co. in the 3rd Maryland Line [Ref: D-454]. "William Doaik?" [Dorch?] took the Oath of Allegiance before the Hon. Edward Burgess on Feb. 28, 1778 [Ref: T-3:59].

DUVALL, Aquilla. Private, 6th Co., Middle Bn., Militia, Aug., 1777 [Ref: M-197, T-5:41]. Took the Oath of Allegiance before the Hon. Edward Burgess on Feb. 28, 1778 [Ref: T-3:61, L-1:40]. Lived in the Upper Part of Newfoundland Hd. (four taxables) in 1777 [Ref: R-31:6]. Died testate in Montgomery County (wife not named) in 1783 and mentioned a son Aquilla, among other children [Ref: V-42].

DUVALL, Charity. See "John McDougal," q.v.

DUVALL, Joseph. On Feb. 20, 1820, the Treasurer of the Western Shore was directed to pay to Joseph Duvall, of Montgomery County, an old soldier, for life, half pay of a private, for his services during the Revolutionary War [Ref: K-2:338, Q-106, P-1058].

DUVALL, Levy. Private, 6th Co., Middle Bn., Militia, Aug., 1777 [Ref: M-197, T-5:41]. "Levey Duvall" took the Oath of Allegiance (made his "X" mark) before the Hon. Edward Burgess on Feb. 28, 1778 [Ref: T-3:61, L-1:40]. "Levi Duvall" was a private, 6th Co., Middle Bn., Militia, July 15, 1780 [Ref: M-203].

DUVALL, Lewis. Brother of "Aquilla Duvall," q.v. [Ref: V-42, V-43]. Private, 6th Co., Middle Bn., Militia, Aug., 1777 [Ref: M-197, T-5:41]. Took the Oath of Allegiance before the Hon. Edward Burgess on Feb. 28, 1778 [Ref: T-3:59, L-1:40]. Lived in Linganore Hd. (two taxables) in 1777, and served as a Constable in 1780-1781 [Ref: R-31:9, W-2].

DUVALL, Mareen (1726-1807). "Mareen Duvall" took the Oath of Allegiance before the Hon. Richard Thompson in 1778 [Ref: T-3:75, L-1:40]. "Nerreen [?] Duvall" [sic] lived in Rock Creek Hd. (four taxables) in 1777 [Ref: R-31:16, which noted that "This is not Maureen," i. e., Maureen Duvall, of Anne Arundel County]. "Mareen Duvall" died testate in Montgomery County in 1807 and his wife was Mrs. Sarah Miles [Ref: V-43, DAR-I:209].

DUVALL, Mary. See "John Prather," q.v.

DUVALL, Zadock. Son of Aquilla Duvall [Ref: V-42]. Private, 6th Co., Middle Bn., Militia, July 15, 1780 [Ref: M-203].

DYAN, Philip. Took the Oath of Allegiance before the Hon. Edward Burgess on Feb. 28, 1778 [Ref: T-3:63, L-1:40].

DYCH, William. See "William Dutch," q.v.

DYER, Mary Ann. See "Middleton Belt," q.v.

DYER (DYAR), Samuel. "Samuel Dyar" was a private, 2nd Co., Lower Bn., Militia, July 15, 1780 [Ref: M-204]. "Samuel Dyer" took the Oath of Allegiance before the Hon. Joseph Wilson on Feb. 28, 1778 [Ref: T-3:66, L-1:40]. "Samuel Dyer" lived in the Upper Part of Potomac Hd. (one taxable) in 1777 [Ref: R-31:14]. Samuel Dyer married Elizabeth Griffith in Montgomery County on Oct. 19, 1779 [Ref: K-2:518].

DYER (DYAR), Thomas. "Thomas Dyer" was a private, 2nd Maryland Regiment, on Jan. 22, 1777, a sergeant on May 1, 1778, and served to Jan., 1780 [Ref: D-101]. "Thomas Dyar" took the Oath of Allegiance before the Hon. Joseph Wilson on Feb. 28, 1778 [Ref: T-3:64, L-1:40]. "Thomas Dyer" rendered aid by providing wheat for use of the military in 1780 [Ref: O-316].

DYSON, Barton (b. 1751). Private, 1st Co., Upper Bn., Militia, Aug. 30, 1777 [Ref: M-193]. Took the Oath of Allegiance before the Hon. Elisha Williams on March 2, 1778 [Ref: T-3:80, L-1:40]. Lived in Sugarland Hd. in 1776-1777 [Ref: K-1:217, R-31:12].

DYSON, Basil (b. 1749). Private, 3rd Co., Upper Bn., Militia, Aug. 30, 1777 [Ref: M-193]. Took the Oath of Allegiance before the Hon. Edward Burgess on Feb. 28, 1778 [Ref: T-3:63, L-1:40]. Lived in Sugarland Hd. in 1776 and had two taxables in 1777 [Ref: K-1:214, R-31:12].

DYSON, Maddox (b. 1744). Private, 3rd Co., Upper Bn., Militia, Aug. 30, 1777 [Ref: M-193]. Took the Oath of Allegiance before the Hon. William Deakins, Jr. before March 3, 1778 [Ref: T-3:68, L-1:40]. "Matdox or Maddox Dyson" lived in Sugarland Hd. (one taxable) in 1776-1777 [Ref: K-1:201, R-31:12].

DYSON, Mary. Rendered aid by providing wheat for use of the military in 1781 [Ref: O-396]. Lived in Sugarland Hd. (one taxable) in 1777 [Ref: R-31:12].

DYSON, Philip (b. 1746). Lived in Sugarland Hd. in 1776 [Ref: K-1:200]. Private, 3rd Co., Upper Bn., Militia, Aug. 30, 1777 [Ref: M-193].

DYSON, Rosewell (Roswell). "Rosewell Dyson" was a private, 7th Co., Upper Bn., Militia, Aug. 30, 1777 [Ref: M-194]. "Oswell [Roswell?] Dyson" took the Oath of Allegiance before the Hon. Edward Burgess on Feb. 28, 1778 [Ref: T-3:63, L-1:40].

DYSON, Samuel. Private, 5th Co., Lower Bn., Militia, 1777 [Ref: M-199, T-5:48], Ensign, 3rd Co., Upper Bn., Aug. 30, 1777, and Second Lieutenant, March 25, 1780 [Ref: M-72, M-193, F-120]. Took the Oath of Allegiance before the Hon. Edward Burgess on Feb. 28, 1778 [Ref: T-3:63, L-1:40]. Served as a grand juror in 1779 [Ref: W-1]. Rendered aid by providing wheat for use of the military in 1781 [Ref: O-387, O-396]. Lived in Sugarland Hd. (two taxables) in 1777 [Ref: R-31:12].

DYSON, Zephaniah (b. 1750). Private, 3rd Co., Upper Bn., Militia, Aug. 30, 1777 [Ref: M-193]. Took the Oath of Allegiance before the Hon. Elisha Williams on March 2, 1778 [Ref: T-3:81, L-1:40]. Lived in Sugarland Hd. (one taxable) in 1776-1777 [Ref: K-1:202, R-31:12].

EAB, Christian. Took the Oath of Allegiance in 1778 [Ref: L-2:27].

EADS (EEDS), Charles. "Charles Eeds" was a private, 3rd Co., Lower Bn., Militia, July 15, 1780 [Ref: M-205].

EADS (EADES, EDES), Edward. "Edward Eads" took the Oath of Allegiance before the Hon. Joseph Offutt on March 2, 1778 [Ref: T-3:70, L-1:40]. "Edward Eades" was a private, 6th Co., Lower Bn., Militia, Aug.,

1777 [Ref: M-200, T-5:49]. "Edward Edes" was a private in the 3rd Maryland Regiment in 1781 [Ref: D-396]. "Edward Eades" lived in the Upper Part of Potomac Hd. (one taxable) in 1777 [Ref: R-31:14].
EADS (EDES), James. Private, Capt. Munson's Co., 2nd Canadian or Hazen's Regiment, by 1783 [Ref: D-598].
EADS, Rebecca. See "King English," q.v.
EADS, Samuel. Took the Oath of Allegiance before the Hon. Gerrard Briscoe on March 2, 1778 [Ref: T-3:57, L-1:40]. Lived in Sugar Loaf Hd. (one taxable) in 1777 [Ref: R-31:9].
EARLY, Benjamin (b. 1733). Private, 4th Co., Lower Bn., Militia, Aug., 1777 [Ref: M-199, T-5:47]. Private, 1st Co., Lower Bn., Militia, July 15, 1780 [Ref: M-204]. Took the Oath of Allegiance before the Hon. Samuel W. Magruder in 1778 [Ref: T-3:73, L-1:40]. Benjamin Early or Earley lived in Lower Potomac Hd. (one taxable) in 1776-1777 [Ref: R-31:4, K-1:182].
EARP, Josiah (1761-1844). Applied for pension (S31004) in Pulaski County, Kentucky, on Nov. 18, 1833, "where he had lived for 16 years." He stated he was born on March 10, 1761 in (now) Montgomery County, Maryland, and lived there at the time of his enlistment. After the war he moved to North Carolina for 4 or 5 years and then on to Kentucky. Died on Nov. 25, 1844, leaving no widow, and his children applied for his pension on Aug. 27, 1853, in Pulaski County, Kentucky, namely Singleton Earp, Allin Earp, Eleanor Randol, and Jemima Randol [Ref: P-1067, DAR-I:211, but he is not listed in *Archives of Maryland, Volume 18*].
EASTON, Benjamin. See "Giles Easton," q.v.
EASTON, Giles (1762-1842). Private, 4th Class, 1st Co., Middle Bn., Militia, July 15, 1780 [Ref: M-201]. Applied for pension (S10633) on March 25, 1833, in Montgomery County, stating he was born on Sep. 30, 1762, in Prince George's County and removed from there while very young. He has lived in Montgomery County since the Revolutionary War. He enlisted in March, 1778 and served nine months under Capt. John Nicholls in the Maryland Line. He also guarded prisoners at Frederick Town. Giles Easton died in April 14, 1842. He had seven children, but only Jeffrey Easton, of Montgomery County in 1852, and Benjamin Easton were named [Ref: Y-27, P-1071]. Giles Easton was a pensioner in 1840, aged 80 [sic], living in the household of Lewis Easton in Montgomery County, 1st Division [Ref: R-28:442, J-49].
EASTON, Jeffrey. See "Giles Easton," q.v.
EASTON (EASTEN), John. Private, 7th Co., Middle Bn., Militia, Sep., 1777 [Ref: M-197, T-5:42]. Took the Oath of Allegiance before the Hon. Edward Burgess on Feb. 8, 1778 [Ref: T-3:60, L-1:40]. "John Easter" [Easten] lived in Seneca Hd. (one taxable) in 1777 [Ref: R-31:7].
EBERT, Adam. Rendered aid by providing beef for use of the military in 1781 [Ref: O-352].

EDELIN, Bartholomew (b. 1748). Lived in Sugarland Hd. in 1776 [Ref: K-1:213]. Private, Flying Camp, enlisted on July 13, 1776 [Ref: D-43].
EDELIN, Barton. Private, 7th Co., Upper Bn., Militia, Aug. 30, 1777 [Ref: M-195].
EDELIN, Thomas (b. 1750). Private, 7th Co., Upper Bn., Militia, Aug. 30, 1777 [Ref: M-194]. Lived in Sugarland Hd. in 1776 and had one taxable in 1777 [Ref: K-1:213, R-31:12].
EDMONSTON, Archibald (died 1779). Took the Oath of Allegiance before the Hon. Edward Burgess on Feb. 28, 1778 [Ref: T-3:63, L-1:40]. Lived in the Lower Part of Newfoundland Hd. (two taxables) in 1777 [Ref: R-31:5]. Died testate in Montgomery County (wife named Dorrithy) in 1779 [Ref: V-44].
EDMONSTON, Jane and James. See "Archibald Beall," q.v.
EDMONSTON (EDMONDSON), Maccubin (Mac). "Maccubin Edmonston" took the Oath of Allegiance before the Hon. Joseph Offutt on March 2, 1778 [Ref: T-3:70, L-1:40]. "Mac. Edmonston" was a private, 6th Co., Lower Bn., Militia, Aug., 1777 [Ref: M-200, T-5:49]. "Maccalon Edmonston" was a private, 3rd Co., Lower Bn., Militia, July 15, 1780 [Ref: M-205]. "Masien [Macun?] Edmondson" lived in the Upper Part of Potomac Hd. (one taxable) in 1777 [Ref: R-31:14].
EDMONSTON, Mary Elizabeth. See "James Beall," q.v.
EDMONSTON, Priscilla. See "Robert Orme," q.v.
EDMONSTON, Rachel. See "Edward Beall," q.v.
EDMONSTON (EDMONDSON), Thomas. (1) Ensign and First Lieutenant, Lower District, Frederick County (now Montgomery), July, 1776, First Lieutenant, 7th Co., 29th (Lower) Bn., Montgomery County, Militia, Sep. 12, 1777, and Captain, 4th Co., Lower Bn., from July 15, 1780, to at least June 19, 1781 [Ref: D-42, M-73, M-200, M-205, T-5:50, C-373, H-304, R-33:156, X-1146]. Took the Oath of Allegiance before the Hon. Edward Burgess on Feb. 28, 1778 [Ref: T-3:61, L-1:40]. (2) Private, 6th Co., Lower Bn., Militia, Aug., 1777 [Ref: M-200, T-5:49]. Took the Oath of Allegiance before the Hon. Samuel W. Magruder in 1778 [Ref: T-3:73]. One Thomas Edmonston lived in Lower Potomac Hd. (two taxables) and another lived in the Lower Part of Newfoundland Hd. (two taxables) in 1777 [Ref: R-31:4, R-31:5]. One Thomas Edmonston was a son of "Archibald Edmonston," q.v. [Ref: V-44]. "Thomas Edmonston, Sr." died testate in Montgomery County (wife named Mary) in 1805 and mentioned a son Thomas, among others [Ref: V-44. V-45].
EDWARDS, Benjamin. Represented Montgomery County in the House of Delegates, 1782-1783 [Ref: N-87].
EDWARDS, John. (1) Private, 7th Co., Middle Bn., Militia, Sep., 1777 [Ref: M-197, T-5:42]. Private, 7th Co., Middle Bn., Militia, July 15, 1780 [Ref: M-203]. (2) Private, 3rd Co., Upper Bn., Militia, Aug. 30, 1777 [Ref: M-193].

One John Edwards took the Oath of Allegiance in 1778 [Ref: L-2:27]. One John Edwards married Mary Leach in Montgomery County on Aug. 22, 1778 [Ref: K-2:521]. Two men named John Edwards lived in Seneca Hd. (one had one taxable and the other had two taxables) in 1777 [Ref: R-31:7], and another lived in the Upper Part of Potomac Hd. (one taxable) in 1777 [Ref: R-31:14].

EDWARDS, John Bridget. Took the Oath of Allegiance before the Hon. Gerrard Briscoe on March 2, 1778 [Ref: T-3:56, L-1:40].

EDWARDS, Robert. Private, 6th Co., Lower Bn., Militia, July 15, 1780 [Ref: M-206]. Took the Oath of Allegiance in 1778 [Ref: L-2:27].

ELEANER, Mary. See "John Riggs," q.v.

ELCOCK, Robert. See "Robert Allcock," q.v.

ELDER, Guy. Took the Oath of Allegiance in 1778 [Ref: L-2:27].

ELDER, Hugh. Private, 5th Co., Lower Bn., Militia, Aug., 1777 [Ref: M-199, T-5:48]. Took the Oath of Allegiance before the Hon. Samuel W. Magruder in 1778 [Ref: T-3:73]. Private, 2nd Co., Lower Bn., Militia, July 15, 1780 [Ref: M-204]. Rendered aid by providing wheat for use of the military in 1780 [Ref: O-335]. Lived in Lower Potomac Hd. (three taxables) in 1777 [Ref: R-31:4].

ELDER, Mary. See "Thomas Ignatius Carrico," q.v.

ELKINS, William. Private, Capt. Price's Co., 3rd Maryland Line, 1781-1782 [Ref: D-452].

ELLIOTT, Benjamin (b. 1756). Son of March Ellett (Mark Elliott) of Sugarland Hd. [Ref: K-1:203]. Private, 4th Co., Upper Bn., Militia, Aug. 30, 1777 [Ref: M-194].

ELLIOTT, Jacob. Private, 7th Co., Middle Bn., Militia, Sep., 1777 [Ref: M-197, T-5:42]. Second Lieutenant, 7th Co., Middle Bn., Militia, July 15, 1780 [Ref: M-73, M-203, F-248]. Took the Oath of Allegiance before the Hon. Edward Burgess on Feb. 28, 1778 [Ref: T-3:60, L-1:40].

ELLIOTT, Joseph (b. 1758). Son of March Ellett (Mark Elliott) of Sugarland Hd., 1776 [Ref: K-1:203]. Private, 4th Co., Upper Bn., Militia, Aug. 30, 1777 [Ref: M-194].

ELLIOTT (ELLETT), March or Mark (b. 1726). Took the Oath of Allegiance before the Hon. William Deakins, Jr. before March 3, 1778 [Ref: T-3:68, L-1:40]. Served as a petit juror in Aug., 1777 [Ref: R-31:17]. "March Ellett" lived in Sugarland Hd. in 1776 and "Mark Elliot" lived there (four taxables) in 1777 with son Mark, among others [Ref: K-1:203, R-31:12].

ELLIOTT (ELLIOT), Mark (b. 1760 or 1761). Son of March Ellett (Mark Elliott) of Sugarland Hd. [Ref: K-1:203]. Private, 4th Co., Upper Bn., Militia, Aug. 30, 1777 [Ref: M-194]. "Mark Elliott" married Sarah Walter in Montgomery County on July 29, 1781 [Ref: K-2:518].

ELLIOTT, Samuel. Private, 3rd Co., Lower Bn., Militia, July 15, 1780 [Ref: M-205].

ELLIS, Cassandra. See "James Ball" and "Humphrey Tomlinson," q.v.

ELLIS (ELLESS), John. (1) Private, 7th Co., Upper Bn., Militia, Aug. 30, 1777 [Ref: M-195]. (2) Private, 6th Co., Middle Bn., Militia, Aug., 1777 [Ref: M-197, T-5:41]. One "John Elles, aged 24" lived in Sugarland Hd. in 1776 [Ref: K-1:211], and "John Ellis" lived in Linganore Hd. (one taxable) in 1777 [Ref: R-31:9]. "John Elless" rendered aid by providing wheat for use of the military in 1781 [Ref: O-388]. "John Ellis, planter" died testate in Montgomery County (wife not named) in 1805 and mentioned a son John, among others [Ref: V-45]. See "William Ellis," q.v.

ELLIS, Joshua. Private, 1st Co., Upper Bn., Militia, Aug. 30, 1777 [Ref: M-193]. Took the Oath of Allegiance before the Hon. Elisha Williams on March 2, 1778 [Ref: T-3:82]. Joshua Ellis lived in Sugar Loaf Hd. (one taxable) in 1777 [Ref: R-31:9].

ELLIS, Nancy. See "William Lewis," q.v.

ELLIS, Samuel. (1) Took the Oath of Allegiance before the Hon. Elisha Williams on March 2, 1778 [Ref: T-3:81, L-1:40]. Samuel Ellis, aged 55, lived in Sugarland Hd. in 1776 and had two taxables in 1777 [Ref: K-1:218, R-31:12]. (2) Private, North Carolina Militia. Applied for pension (S30400) in Russell County, Kentucky, on Oct. 3, 1833, stating he was born on April 9, 1762, in Montgomery County, Maryland, and lived in Rowan County, North Carolina at the time of enlistment. About 3 years after the war he moved to Surry County, North Carolina, then back to Rowan County for a few years, and then to Buck County and Jefferson County, Tennessee until 1826 when he moved to Cumberland County, Kentucky. In 1832 he moved to Russell County and in 1834 to Adair County, Kentucky. Between Sep. 16, 1843 and March 5, 1845 he lived in Knoxville, Ray County, Missouri, during which time his wife died. He moved back to Kentucky and lived in Hart County with two daughters and a son (no names given). [Ref: Y-1, P-1106, Z-1, and *Marylanders to Carolina*, by Henry C. Peden, Jr. (1994), p. 51]. See "Humphrey Beckett Tomlinson," q.v.

ELLIS, Shadrick (b. 1755). "Shadrack Elles" lived in Sugarland Hd. in 1776 [Ref: K-1:211]. Private, 1st Co., Upper Bn., Militia, Aug. 30, 1777 [Ref: M-193]. "Shederick Ellis" took the Oath of Allegiance before the Hon. Aneas Campbell on March 2, 1778 [Ref: T-3:77, L-1:40].

ELLIS, Solomon (b. 1744). Lived in Sugarland Hd. in 1776 and had two taxables in 1777 [Ref: K-1:218, R-31:12]. Private, 1st Co., Upper Bn., Militia, Aug. 30, 1777 [Ref: M-193]. Took the Oath of Allegiance before the Hon. Elisha Williams on March 2, 1778 [Ref: T-3:82].

ELLIS, Thomas. Private who was recruited to serve in the Continental Army in 1780 [Ref: D-342].

ELLIS, William (b. 1759). Private, 7th Co., Upper Bn., Militia, Aug. 30, 1777 [Ref: M-195]. "Willilam Ellis or William Elles" [sic] lived in Sugarland Hd. in 1776 and John Ellis was his security in 1777 [Ref: K-1:211, R-31:12].

ELLIS, Zachariah (b. 1734). Lived in Sugarland Hd. in 1776 and had four taxables in 1777 [Ref: K-1:211, R-31:12]. Served as a Lieutenant, 1st Co., Upper Bn., Militia, June 20, 1777 [Ref: M-73, M-193]. Took the Oath of Allegiance before the Hon. Aneas Campbell on March 2, 1778 [Ref: T-3:77, L-1:40].

ELLIS, Zephaniah (b. 1755). Lived in Sugarland Hd. in 1776-1777 [Ref: K-1:218, R-31:12]. Private, 1st Co., Upper Bn., Militia, Aug. 30, 1777 [Ref: M-193]. Took the Oath of Allegiance before the Hon. Elisha Williams on March 2, 1778 [Ref: T-3:81, L-1:40].

ELWOOD, John. Private, Capt. Edward Burgess' Co., Lower District of Frederick (now Montgomery) County, Militia, July, 1776 [Ref: D-42].

ENGLAR, Jacob. Took the Oath of Allegiance in 1778 [Ref: L-2:27].

ENGLISH, King. Private, 3rd Co., Lower Bn., Militia, July 15, 1780 [Ref: M-205]. Took the Oath of Allegiance before the Hon. Joseph Offutt on March 2, 1778 [Ref: T-3:70, L-1:40]. Lived in the Upper Part of Potomac Hd. (one taxable) in 1777 [Ref: R-31:14]. King English married Rebecca Eades in Montgomery County on Aug. 24, 1779 [Ref: K-2:515].

ENNIS, John and Nicholas. See "John and Nicholas Hennis," q.v.

EPPRACHT, Jacob. Took the Oath of Allegiance before the Hon. Richard Thompson in 1778 [Ref: T-3:76, L-1:40].

ERVIN (ERVINE), James (1751-1827). Private, Maryland Line, who pensioned in 1818, aged 67, while living in Montgomery County, and died on June 28, 1827 [Ref: J-38, D-533].

ESTEP, Alexander. Son of Richard and Elizabeth Estep [Ref: V-46]. Served as a Second Lieutenant, Capt. Edward Burgess' Co., Lower District of Frederick (now Montgomery) County, Militia, July, 1776 [Ref: D-42], and Lieutenant, 6th Maryland Line, from Feb. 20, 1777 until Oct. 13, 1777, when he resigned [Ref: D-203]. First Lieutenant, 7th Co., Lower Bn., Militia, July 15, 1780 [Ref: M-206]. Took the Oath of Allegiance before the Hon. Edward Burgess on Feb. 28, 1778 [Ref: T-3:62, L-1:40]. Lived in the Lower Part of Newfoundland Hd. (one taxable) in 1777 [Ref: R-31:5].

ESTEP (EASTEP), Joseph. Private, Capt. Edward Burgess' Co., Lower District of Frederick (now Montgomery) County, Militia, July, 1776 [Ref: D-42]. Private, 1st Co., Lower Bn., Militia, Sep., 1777, and Third Sergeant, 7th Co., Lower Bn., July 15, 1780 [Ref: M-198, M-206, T-5:44]. Took the Oath of Allegiance before the Hon. Edward Burgess on Feb. 28, 1778 [Ref: T-3:63, L-1:40]. "Joseph Estep" was a constable in Lower Newfoundland Hd. in 1781 [Ref: W-2]. "Joseph Eastep" married Lucy Prather in Montgomery County on Jan. 28, 1779 [Ref: K-2:515].

ESTEP, Richard (died 1787). Took the Oath of Allegiance before the Hon. Edward Burgess on Feb. 28, 1778 [Ref: T-3:61, L-1:40]. Lived in the Lower Part of Newfoundland Hd. (three taxables) in 1777 [Ref: R-31:5]. Died testate in Montgomery County (wife named Elizabeth) in 1787 [Ref: V-46].

ESTES, Elizabeth and Thomas. See "Asa Darby," q.v.
EUSTICE, Mary. See "Patrick Cavenough," q.v.
EVANS, Elijah. Served as a Lieutenant in Capt. Thomas Beall's Co., Maryland Line, commissioned on Aug. 8, 1776 and still in service in 1780 [Ref: D-350].
EVANS, John (b. 1760). Private, 1st or 32nd Bn., Militia (no date was given; probably June, 1777). [Ref: K-1:182, T-5:1, and U-30:57, which latter source stated that John Evans served from Montgomery County with "Zachariah Evans," q.v., for 5 months and 9 days in 1777].
EVANS, Joseph. Took the Oath of Allegiance before the Hon. Joseph Offutt on March 2, 1778 [Ref: T-3:70, L-1:40].
EVANS (EVINS), Samuel. "Samuel Evans" took the Oath of Allegiance before the Hon. Richard Thompson in 1778 [Ref: T-3:75, L-1:40]. "Samuel Evins" lived in Lower Potomac Hd. (one taxable) in 1777 [Ref: R-31:4].
EVANS, Thomas. Private, 1st or 32nd Bn., Militia (no date was given; possibly June, 1777). [Ref: T-5:1].
EVANS, Walter. Private, 3rd Co., Lower Bn., Militia, July 15, 1780 [Ref: M-205].
EVANS, William (1724-1785). Private, 4th Co., Upper Bn., Militia, Aug. 30, 1777 [Ref: M-194]. Took the Oath of Allegiance before the Hon. William Deakins, Jr. before March 3, 1778 [Ref: T-3:68, L-1:40]. "William Evans" rendered aid by providing wheat for use of the military in 1781 [Ref: O-387, O-395]. "William Evins or Evens" lived in Sugarland Hd. in 1776 and had three taxables in 1777 [Ref: K-1:208, R-31:12]. "William Evans" died testate in Montgomery County (wife not named) in 1785 [Ref: V-46].
EVANS, Zachariah (b. 1755 or 1759). "Zechariah Evans" lived in Lower Potomac Hd. in 1776, aged 17, with John Evans, aged 16, and Samuel Evans, aged 51 [Ref: K-1:182]. Private, 1st Co., Lower Bn., Militia, July 15, 1780 [Ref: M-204]. Took the Oath of Allegiance before the Hon. Charles Jones on Jan. 10, 1778 [Ref: T-3:71, L-1:40]. Applied for a pension (S30403) on Oct. 27, 1834, in Rockcastle County, Kentucky, aged 79, stating he was born in 1755 in Prince George's County, Maryland, and enlisted in Montgomery County, Maryland, in 1776. He served as a private for 5 months and 9 days under Capt. Sparks [sic] in the Flying Camp, Maryland Line. He marched to Philadelphia and New York and fought in the Battle of White Plains. He returned home in Jan., 1777. He was called out again in 1778 and served two months in Georgetown as a guard to keep the British from landing. After the war he moved to Rowan County, North Carolina, and then to Pulaski County, Kentucky, where he lived in 1834. A John Evans verified that he knew of Zachariah's service in the war, and Rev. Stephen Colyer testified as to his character [Ref: U-30:57, P-1135, P-1136].

EVERITT, Elisha. A letter from the Council in Annapolis to the Attorney General of Maryland or the Prosecutor of Montgomery County Court, March 7, 1778, stated: "Information being received that one Elisha Everitt who was enlisted in the service of this State in the regiment commanded by Smallwood is a prisoner in Montgomery Jail charged with horse stealing, you are desired and authorized to stay any criminal prosecution against the said Elisha Everitt of or for the said offence and accordingly enter a *noli prosequi* in his favor on his enlisting into the first Maryland Continental Regiment now commanded by Col. Stone." [Ref: C-529].

EVERLY (EVELY), John. "John Everly" was a private, 4th Co., Middle Bn., Militia, Sep., 1777 [Ref: M-196, T-5:39]. "John Eveley" took the Oath of Allegiance before the Hon. Edward Burgess on Feb. 28, 1778 [Ref: T-3:62, L-1:40]. "John Evely" lived in the Upper Part of Newfoundland Hd. (one taxable) in 1777 [Ref: R-31:6].

FAIR, Nancy Ann. See "Hezekiah Gray," q.v.

FAIRBAIRN (FARBAIRN, FAIRBURN), William (1746-1782). Lived in George Town Hd. in 1776 [Ref: K-1:193]. Private, 3rd Maryland Regiment, Sep., 1776 to Aug. 16, 1780, when captured at the Battle of Camden; exchanged prisoner on Aug. 1, 1781; reported dead on March 16, 1782 [Ref: D-109, D-296, D-460, D-617].

FANNING, Thomas (b. 1739). Lived in Sugarland Hd. in 1776 [Ref: K-1:213]. Private who enrolled into a company of militia for the service of the Flying Camp on Oct. 15, 1776 [Ref: B-353].

FARDO (FARADO, FARDOWE), Absolom. "Absolam Farado" was a private, 7th Maryland Line, 1777-1780 [Ref: D-207]. "Absolum Farlowe" [Fardowe?] was a private, 5th Co., Lower Bn., Militia, Aug., 1777 [Ref: M-199, T-5:48].

FARDO, John Lewis. Took the Oath of Allegiance before the Hon. Samuel W. Magruder in 1778 [Ref: T-3:73].

FARELONG, Bridget. See "Richard Nicholson," q.v.

FARIS, John. Took the Oath of Allegiance in 1778 [Ref: L-2:27].

FARLOWE, Absolum. See "Absolam Fardo," q.v.

FARMER, John. Private, 2nd Co., Middle Bn., Militia, Sep. 4, 1777 [Ref: M-196, T-5:37]. Private, 4th Class, 3rd Co., Middle Bn., Militia, July 15, 1780 [Ref: M-202]. Took the Oath of Allegiance (made his "X" mark) before the Hon. Joseph Wilson on Feb. 28, 1778 [Ref: T-3:66, L-1:40]. Lived in Linganore Hd. (two taxables) in 1777 [Ref: R-31:9].

FARMER, Nathaniel. Served as a Sergeant, 3rd Maryland Line, 1777-1779 [Ref: D-109].

FARMER, Samuel. Served as an Ensign, 1777, and Lieutenant, 3rd Maryland Line, paid for recruiting services in Montgomery County in Jan., 1780. Wounded at Battle of Camden on Aug. 16, 1780 [Ref: D-109, F-54].

FARMER, William. Private, 6th Co., Middle Bn., Militia, Aug., 1777 [Ref: M-197, T-5:41]. Took the Oath of Allegiance before the Hon. Edward Burgess on Feb. 28, 1778 [Ref: T-3:59, L-1:40]. Lived in the Upper Part of Newfoundland Hd. (six taxables) in 1777 [Ref: R-31:6].
FARMWALD, L. Took the Oath of Allegiance in 1778 [Ref: L-2:27].
FAUCIT (FORSET), James. "James Faucit" lived in the Lower Part of Newfoundland Hd. (one taxables) in 1777 [Ref: R-31:5]. "James Forset" took the Oath of Allegiance (made his "X" mark) before the Hon. Edward Burgess on Feb. 28, 1778 [Ref: T-3:58, L-1:40].
FAUGHMAN, John. Took the Oath of Allegiance in 1778 [Ref: L-2:27].
FEE, William (died 1791). Lived in the Upper Part of Potomac Hd. (ten taxables) in 1777 [Ref: R-31:14]. Rendered aid by providing wheat for use of the military in 1780 [Ref: O-326]. Died testate in Montgomery County (wife and children not named) in 1791 [Ref: V-47].
FEILOS, John. Private, 6th Co., Lower Bn., Militia, Aug., 1777 [Ref: M-200, T-5:49, which questions if name could be "Feiler?"]. Rendered aid by providing wheat for use of the military in 1781 [Ref: O-387].
FELTIN, Henry. Rendered aid by providing beef for use of the military in 1781 [Ref: O-373].
FELTON, Thomas. Private, 6th Maryland Line, from March 3, 1777 until May 7, 1780, when discharged by Col. Forrest [Ref: D-206].
FENEMORE (FENNAMOE), William (b. 1711). "William Fennamoe" lived in Sugarland Hd. in 1776 [Ref: K-1:213]. "William Fenemore" took the Oath of Allegiance before the Hon. Aneas Campbell on March 2, 1778 [Ref: T-3:77, L-1:40].
FENNELL, Stephen. Private who was recruited to serve in the Continental Army in 1780 [Ref: D-342].
FERGUSON (FURGUSSON, FORGUSSON), Basil (b. 1755). "Basil Furgusson" was a private, 4th Co., Upper Bn., Militia, Aug. 30, 1777 [Ref: M-194]. "Basil Ferguson or Forgusson" lived in Sugarland Hd. (one taxable) in 1776-1777 [Ref: K-1:207, R-31:12].
FERGUSON (FURGUSSON, FORGUSSON, FARGUSON), Daniel (b. 1757). "Daniel Furgusson" was a private, 4th Co., Upper Bn., Militia, Aug. 30, 1777 [Ref: M-194]. "Daniel Farguson" lived in Sugarland Hd. in 1776 and "Daniel Forgusson" lived there (one taxable) in 1777 [Ref: R-31:12].
FERGUSON (FURGUSSON, FARGUSON), Elias (b. 1760). Lived in Sugarland Hd. in 1776 [Ref: K-1:204]. Private, 4th Co., Upper Bn., Militia, Aug. 30, 1777 [Ref: M-194].
FERGUSON (FURGUSSON, FORGUSSON, FARGUSON), John. "John Furguson" was a private, 4th Co., Upper Bn., Militia, Aug. 30, 1777 [Ref: M-194]. It was noted by the Council of Maryland on Sep. 5, 1781, that "John Ferguson," and other soldiers of the Maryland Line, "had returned from captivity in South Carolina in a distressed situation." It was ordered that he be paid 5 pounds on account [Ref: G-598]. "John

Farguson, aged 53" and "John Farguson, aged 26" lived in Sugarland Hd. in 1776 as did "John Forgusson" and John Forgusson, Sr." in 1777 [Ref: K-1:204, R-31:12].

FERGUSON (FURGUSSON, FORGUSSON), Joseph. "Joseph Furgusson" was a private, 4th Co., Upper Bn., Militia, Aug. 30, 1777 [Ref: M-194]. Took the Oath of Allegiance before the Hon. Aneas Campbell on March 2, 1778 [Ref: T-3:77, L-1:40]. "Joseph Forgusson" lived in Sugarland Hd. (one taxable) in 1777 [Ref: R-31:12].

FERGUSON (FURGUSSON, FARGUSON), Rezin (1762-1808). "Reson Farguson" lived in Sugarland Hd. in 1776 [Ref: K-1:204]. "Rezin Furgusson" was a private, 5th Class, 2nd Co., Middle Bn., Militia, July 15, 1780 [Ref: M-201]. "Rezin Ferguson" died testate in Montgomery County (wife named Elizabeth) in 1808 [Ref: V-47].

FERGUSON, Robert. "Robert Ferguson, formerly of George Town in Montgomery County, appeared before the Governor and Council and took and subscribed [to] the Oath of Support and Fidelity on Aug. 25, 1779." [Ref: E-503].

FERRELL (FARRAL), Henry. Private, 2nd Co., Lower Bn., Militia, Sep., 1777, and Third Sergeant, 5th Co., Lower Bn., July 15, 1780 [Ref: M-198, M-205, T-5:45]. "Henry Farral" took the Oath of Allegiance before the Hon. Edward Burgess on Feb. 28, 1778 [Ref: T-3:60, L-1:40]. "Henry Ferrell" rendered aid by providing wheat for use of the military in 1780 [Ref: O-329].

FERRELL (FEARELL, FARRALL), James. Took the Oath of Allegiance (made his "X" mark) before the Hon. Edward Burgess on Feb. 28, 1778 [Ref: T-3:60, L-1:40, which listed the name as "Janus Ferrell"]. "James Ferrell" was a private, 2nd Co., Lower Bn., Militia, Sep., 1777 [Ref: M-198, T-5:45]. "James Fearell" lived in Rock Creek Hd. (one taxable) in 1777 [Ref: R-31:16]. One "James Farrall, of Frederick County" died testate in Montgomery County (wife not named) by June, 1777. Many of his children were mentioned, but not all were named; perhaps the above James was one of his sons [Ref: V-46].

FERRELL, Jeremiah. Private, Capt. Edward Burgess' Co., Lower District of Frederick (now Montgomery) County, Militia, July, 1776 [Ref: D-42].

FERRELL (FERRILL, FARRALL, FEARELL), John. (1) "John Ferrill" was a private, 2nd Co., Lower Bn., Militia, July 15, 1780 [Ref: M-204]. (2) "John Ferrell" was a private, Capt. Edward Burgess' Co., Lower District of Frederick (now Montgomery) County, Militia, July, 1776 [Ref: D-42]. Private, 5th Co., Lower Bn., Militia, July 15, 1780 [Ref: M-206]. (3) Private, 8th Co., Middle Bn., Militia, Sep., 1777 [Ref: M-198, T-5:43]. "John Ferrell" took the Oath of Allegiance before the Hon. Edward Burgess on Feb. 28, 1778 [Ref: T-3:60, L-1:40]. "John Farrall" took the Oath of Allegiance before the Hon. Charles Jones on Jan. 10, 1778 [Ref: T-3:71, L-1:40]. "John Ferrell" rendered aid by providing wheat for use of the military in 1780 [Ref: O-331]. "John Fearell" lived in Rock Creek Hd. (four taxables) in 1777 [Ref: R-31:16].

FERRELL (PHERILL), Joseph. "Joseph Ferrell" lived in North West Hd. (one taxable) in 1777 [Ref: R-31:17]. "Joseph Pherill" was granted a pardon by the Council of Maryland on May 10, 1780, having been "convicted in Montgomery County Court for a rape, on condition that he forthwith enlist himself into some one of the regiments of the quota of this State in the Continental Army during the war and that he not desert therefrom." [Ref: F-170, F-171]. "Joseph Ferrell" was recruited by Col. Orme to serve in the Continental Army in 1780 [Ref: D-341]. "Joseph Ferrel, aged 60" lived in North West Hd. in 1776 [Ref: K-1:224].

FERRELL, Robert. Private who was recruited to serve in the Continental Army in 1780 [Ref: D-342].

FERVER, Philip. Took the Oath of Allegiance in 1778 [Ref: L-2:27].

FERVOR, Leonard. Took the Oath of Allegiance in 1778 [Ref: L-2:27].

FETHERKEYL (FEDERKICTEL), George Michael. "George Michael Fetherkeyl" took the Oath of Allegiance before the Hon. Richard Thompson in 1778 [Ref: T-3:76, L-1:40]. "George Federkictel" lived in George Town Hd. (one taxable) in 1777 [Ref: R-31:3].

FIEGLE, Charles. Took the Oath of Allegiance in 1778 [Ref: L-2:27].

FIELDS, Abraham. Private, 3rd Co., Middle Bn., Militia, Sep., 1777 [Ref: M-196, T-5:38]. Took the Oath of Allegiance before the Hon. Gerrard Briscoe on March 2, 1778 [Ref: T-3:56, L-1:40]. Lived in Seneca Hd. (one taxable) in 1777 [Ref: R-31:7]. Abraham Fields married Johan [sic] Peck in Montgomery County on March 19, 1778 [Ref: K-2:518].

FIELDS (FIELD), Edward. "Edward Fields" was a private, 4th Co., Middle Bn., Militia, Sep., 1777 [Ref: M-196, T-5:39]. "Edward Field" lived in the Upper Part of Newfoundland Hd. (one taxable) in 1777 [Ref: R-31:6].

FIELDS (FEALDS), George (b. 1744). "George Fealds, aged 32" lived in Sugarland Hd. in 1776 [Ref: K-1:214]. "George Fields" was a private in Capt. Price's Co., 3rd Maryland Line, April 20, 1778 and taken prisoner on March 23, 1780; sergeant, 1781 [Ref: D-452, D-110, D-297]. He pensioned in 1818, aged 80 [sic], and was still on the rolls in 1835 [Ref: J-38].

FIELDS (FEALDS), James (b. 1741). Private, 4th Co., Upper Bn., Militia, Aug. 30, 1777 [Ref: M-194]. Took the Oath of Allegiance on Sep. 1, 1780, under the Act of May 12, 1780, having neglected to do so previously "because of sickness or other unavoidable accident prevented him from doing so." [Ref: R-27:110]. "James Fealds or Fields" lived in Sugarland Hd. (one taxable) in 1776-1777 [Ref: K-1:207, R-31:12].

FIELDS (FIELD), John. Served as a petit juror in Nov., 1777 [Ref: R-31:18]. "John Fields" took the Oath of Allegiance before the Hon. William Deakins, Jr. before March 3, 1778 [Ref: T-3:68, L-1:40]. "John Field" lived in the Upper Part of Potomac Hd. (one taxable) in 1777 [Ref: R-31:14].

FIELDS (FEALDS), Joseph (b. 1743). Private, 4th Co., Upper Bn., Militia, Aug. 30, 1777 [Ref: M-194]. Took the Oath of Allegiance before the Hon. Edward Burgess on Feb. 28, 1778 [Ref: T-3:63, L-1:40]. "Joseph Fealds or Fields" lived in Sugarland Hd. (one taxable) in 1776-1777 [Ref: K-1:207, R-31:12].

FIELDS (FEALDS), Matthew (b. 1735). Private, 4th Co., Upper Bn., Militia, Aug. 30, 1777 [Ref: M-194]. Took the Oath of Allegiance before the Hon. Gerrard Briscoe on March 2, 1778 [Ref: T-3:57, L-1:40]. Rendered aid by providing wheat for use of the military in 1781 [Ref: O-448]. "Matthew Fealds or Fields" lived in Sugarland Hd. (one taxable) in 1776-1777 [Ref: R-31:12].

FIELDS, Rezin. Private, 6th Class, 1st Co., Middle Bn., Militia, July 15, 1780 [Ref: M-201].

FIELDS, Thomas. Private, 5th Class, 2nd Co., Middle Bn., Militia, July 15, 1780 [Ref: M-201].

FIFE, James, and others. See "James Fyffe" and others, q.v.

FIGHTMASTER, George. Private, 1st Co., Lower Bn., Militia, Sep., 1777 [Ref: M-198, T-5:44]. Private, 7th Co., Lower Bn., Militia, July 15, 1780 [Ref: M-206]. Took the Oath of Allegiance (made his "X" mark) before the Hon. Edward Burgess on Feb. 28, 1778 [Ref: T-3:62, L-1:40]. George Fightmaster lived in the Lower Part of Newfoundland Hd. (one taxable) in 1777 [Ref: R-31:5].

FIGHTMASTER, John. Took the Oath of Allegiance before the Hon. Edward Burgess on Feb. 28, 1778 [Ref: T-3:62, L-1:40]. John Fightmaster lived in the Lower Part of Newfoundland Hd. (one taxable) in 1777 [Ref: R-31:5].

FIGHTMASTER, Sarah. See "Lazarus Isaac," q.v.

FILLIPE, Charles. See "Charles Phillips," q.v.

FINNESEE, William. Took the Oath of Allegiance in 1778 [Ref: L-2:27].

FISH, Eleven and Mary. See "Benjamin Willett," q.v.

FISHER, Henry. One Henry Fisher was a private, 7th Maryland Regiment, July 24, 1777 to Feb., 1778, and another served in the German Regiment from April 1, 1778 until Aug. 1, 1780, when discharged. One or both appear to have originally been from Frederick County [Ref: D-207, D-208, D-262, D-320]. One Henry Fisher lived in Lower Potomac Hd. (one taxable) in 1777 [Ref: R-31:4].

FISHER, Jacob. Private, 1st or 32nd Bn., Militia (no date was given; possibly June, 1777). [Ref: T-5:1].

FISHER, Martin. Private, 5th Co., Middle Bn., Militia, Sep., 1777 [Ref: M-197, T-5:40]. Private, 5th Class, 1st Co., Middle Bn., Militia, July 15, 1780 [Ref: M-201]. Took the Oath of Allegiance before the Hon. Joseph Wilson on Feb. 28, 1778 [Ref: T-3:64, L-1:40]. Served as a grand juror in Nov., 1777 [Ref: R-31:17]. Rendered aid by providing wheat for use of the military in 1780 [Ref: O-309]. Lived in the Upper Part of Potomac Hd. (three taxables) in 1777 [Ref: R-31:14]. One Martin Fisher died testate in Montgomery County (wife not named) in 1815, and another died in 1821 (wife not named) and mentioned a son Martin, among others [Ref: V-47].

FITZGERALD, Benjamin (b. 1753). Private, Capt. Edward Burgess' Co., Lower District of Frederick (now Montgomery) County, Militia, July, 1776 [Ref: D-42]. Private, 7th Maryland Line, on Feb. 11, 1777, and corporal on Sep. 20, 1778, and sergeant on June 1, 1780 [Ref: D-207]. Applied for pension (S35931) in Mason County, Kentucky, on June 12, 1818, aged 65. He mentioned "a very old and lame wife" in 1820, but no name was given, and stated his property was only worth $25.00 [Ref: Z-64, P-1205, Y-15, and *Marylanders to Kentucky, 1775-1825*, by Henry C. Peden, Jr. (1991), p. 50].

FITZGERALD (FITZGARREL), Clement. Private, 5th Co., Upper Bn., Militia, Aug. 30, 1777 [Ref: M-194]. Took the Oath of Allegiance on Sep. 1, 1780, under the Act of May 12, 1780, having neglected to do so previously "due to ignorance of the duty owed the country." [Ref: R-27:110]. "Clemt. Fitzgarrel" lived in Linganore Hd. (one taxable) in 1777 [Ref: R-31:9].

FITZGERALD (FITZGARRALD), Edward. Private, 7th Co., Lower Bn., Militia, Aug., 1777 [Ref: M-200, T-5:50]. Took the Oath of Allegiance (made his "X" mark) before the Hon. Edward Burgess on Feb. 28, 1778 [Ref: T-3:59, L-1:40]. "Edward Fitzgarrald" lived in the Lower Part of Newfoundland Hd. (three taxables) in 1777 [Ref: R-31:5].

FITZGERALD (FITZGARRALD), John. Served as a private when enrolled into a company of militia for the service of the Flying Camp on Oct. 15, 1776 [Ref: B-353]. Private, 2nd Co., Lower Bn., Militia, Sep., 1777 [Ref: M-198, T-5:45]. Took the Oath of Allegiance (made his "I" mark) before the Hon. Edward Burgess on Feb. 28, 1778 [Ref: T-3:59, L-1:40, which source mistakenly listed the name as "John Litzgarreld" (sic)]. Private, 5th Co., Lower Bn., Militia, July 15, 1780 [Ref: M-206]. Rendered aid by providing wheat for use of the military in 1780 [Ref: O-323].

FITZGERALD, Matthew. Took the Oath of Allegiance before the Hon. Edward Burgess on Feb. 28, 1778 [Ref: T-3:59, L-1:40]. Private, 4th Co., Lower Bn., Militia, July 15, 1780 [Ref: M-205]. Matthew Fitzgerald married Sarah Wilson in Montgomery County on Jan. 7, 1779 [Ref: K-2:515].

FITZGERALD, Richard. Took the Oath of Allegiance (made his "R" mark) before the Hon. Edward Burgess on Feb. 28, 1778 [Ref: T-3:58, L-1:40].

FITZGERALD, Walter. Took the Oath of Allegiance before the Hon. Edward Burgess on Feb. 28, 1778 [Ref: T-3:62, L-1:40].

FITZGERALD (FITZGARRALD), William. Private, 1st Co., Lower Bn., Militia, Sep., 1777 [Ref: M-198, T-5:44]. Took the Oath of Allegiance (made his "X" mark) before the Hon. Edward Burgess on Feb. 28, 1778 [Ref: T-3:58, L-1:40]. Private, 7th Co., Lower Bn., Militia, July 15, 1780

[Ref: M-206]. "William Fitzgarrald" lived in the Lower Part of Newfoundland Hd. (two taxables) in 1777 [Ref: R-31:5].

FLANAGAN, John. Private, Capt. Price's Co., 3rd Maryland Line, 1781-1782 [Ref: D-453].

FLEMING, Catherine. See "Joseph Magruder," q.v.

FLEMING, James (died 1792). Private, 6th Co., Lower Bn., Militia, Aug., 1777 [Ref: M-200, T-5:49]. Private, 3rd Co., Lower Bn., Militia, July 15, 1780 [Ref: M-205]. Took the Oath of Allegiance before the Hon. Joseph Offutt on March 2, 1778 [Ref: T-3:70, L-1:40]. Lived in the Upper Part of Potomac Hd. (three taxables) in 1777 [Ref: R-31:14]. Died testate in Montgomery County (wife named Elizabeth) in 1792 [Ref: V-48].

FLEMING (FLEMMING), John. Private, 6th Co., Lower Bn., Militia, Aug., 1777 [Ref: M-200, T-5:49]. "John Fleming" took the Oath of Allegiance before the Hon. Joseph Offutt on March 2, 1778 [Ref: T-3:70, L-1:40]. "John Flemming" lived in the Upper Part of Potomac Hd. (two taxables) in 1777 [Ref: R-31:14]. One John Flemming married Anne Hopkins in Montgomery County on Nov. 20, 1777 [Ref: K-2:518]. Died testate in Montgomery County (wife named Ann) in 1797 [Ref: V-48]. Another John Fleming died testate in 1814, but no wife or children [Ref: V-48, V-49].

FLEMING (FLEMMING), John Jr. Took the Oath of Allegiance before the Hon. Joseph Offutt on March 2, 1778 [Ref: T-3:70, L-1:40]. Served as a grand juror in Nov., 1777 [Ref: R-31:17]. "John Flemming, Jr." lived in the Upper Part of Potomac Hd. (one taxable) in 1777 [Ref: R-31:14].

FLEMING, Thomas. Private, Capt. Thomas Beall's Co., Maryland Line, 1780 [Ref: D-351].

FLETCHALL, Abraham. See "Abraham Fletcher," q.v.

FLETCHALL, George. See "George Fletcher," q.v.

FLETCHALL, John (1727-1777). Lived in Sugarland Hd. (wife named Elizabeth) in 1776 [Ref: K-:221]. "John Fletchall" died testate in Montgomery County (wife named Betty) and his will was probated on June 14, 1777 [Ref: V-49]. He was probably the "Captain Fletchall" who was reported deceased by June 20, 1777 [Ref: M-75].

FLETCHALL, Thomas (1760-1819?). Son of John Fletchall, of Sugarland Hd., in 1776 [Ref: K-1:221]. Private, 4th Co., Upper Bn., Militia, Aug. 30, 1777 [Ref: M-194]. Rendered aid by providing wheat for use of the military in 1781 [Ref: O-396]. Lived in Sugarland Hd. (seven taxables) in 1777 [Ref: R-31:12]. Thomas Fletchall married Elizabeth Blackmore in Montgomery County on June 15, 1780 [Ref: K-2:518]. He may have been the Thomas Fletchall who died testate in Montgomery County in 1819, but his wife was named Sarah Newton (not Elizabeth) in his will [Ref: V-49, V-50]. See "Thomas Fletcher," q.v.

FLETCHER (FLETCHALL), Abraham (b. 1725). "Abraham Flether" [sic] lived in Sugarland Hd. in 1776 and "Abraham Fletchall" lived there (one taxable) in 1777 [Ref: K-1:207, R-31:12]. "Abraham Fletcher" was a private, 4th Co., Upper Bn., Militia, Aug. 30, 1777 [Ref: M-194].

FLETCHER (FLETCHALL), George (b. 1747). "George Flether" [sic] lived in Sugarland Hd. in 1776 and "George Fletchall" lived there (one taxable) in 1777 [Ref: R-31:12]. "George Fletcher" was a private, 4th Co., Upper Bn., Militia, Aug. 30, 1777 [Ref: M-194]. "George W. Fletchall" was a son of Thomas Fletchall who died testate in 1819 [Ref: V-49, V-50].

FLETCHER, Priscilla. See "Levy Walter," q.v.

FLETCHER, Thomas. Private, 3rd Co., Lower Bn., Militia, Sep., 1777 [Ref: M-199, T-5:46]. Took the Oath of Allegiance before the Hon. Aneas Campbell on March 2, 1778 [Ref: T-3:78, L-1:40]. Two new named Thomas Fletcher lived in George Town Hd. in 1777: one was a merchant (one taxable) and one was a carpenter (one taxable). [Ref: R-31:3]. Also see "Thomas Fletchall," q.v.

FLIGH, Nal. [sic]. Took the Oath of Allegiance in 1778 [Ref: L-2:27].

FLING, James (1759?-1836). Private, Virginia Line, who pensioned in Montgomery County, Maryland, in 1818, aged 73 [in 1832?], and was dropped from the rolls in 1820 [Ref: J-49]. He was born in Stafford County, Virginia, where he enlisted and served; applied for pension (S8489) on June 8, 1818, in Georgetown, D. C., aged 57 [sic]; resided in Montgomery County in 1832 [Ref: P-1215]. On Feb. 24, 1824, the Treasurer of Maryland was directed to pay James Fling, quarterly, the half pay of a sergeant. On Jan. 23, 1837, the balance due was paid to Henry Harding for the use of James W. Fling, executor of James Fling. He is buried in Montgomery County, Maryland [Ref: Q-108, K-2:342, S-1993].

FLINN, Judith. See "James McDonack (McDonough)," q.v.

FLINT, Thomas (b. 1731). Private, 5th Co., Lower Bn., Militia, Aug., 1777 [Ref: M-199, T-5:48]. Private, 2nd Co., Lower Bn., Militia, July 15, 1780 [Ref: M-204]. Took the Oath of Allegiance before the Hon. Samuel W. Magruder in 1778 [Ref: T-3:73, L-1:40]. Thomas Flint lived in Lower Potomac Hd. (one taxable) in 1776-1777 [Ref: R-31:4, K-1:182].

FLINT, Thomas Jr. Private, 3rd Co., Lower Bn., Militia, July 15, 1780 [Ref: M-205].

FLOSKINSON, Hugh. See "Hugh Hoskinson," q.v.

FLOYD, Joseph. Private who was recruited to serve in the Extra Regiment, Continental Army, in 1780 [Ref: D-342].

FOEACH [sic], Daniel. Took the Oath of Allegiance in 1778 [Ref: L-2:27].

FOGLESONG, George. Took the Oath of Allegiance in 1778 [Ref: L-2:27].

FOOTE, Leonora. See "Asa Darby," q.v.

FORD, John (1754-1833). Sergeant, 4th Maryland Line, who applied for pension (S39532) in Monroe County, Virginia, on March 18, 1824, aged 70 in Sep., 1823, stating he had enlisted in Montgomery County, Maryland, on Aug. 3, 1776, and was at once appointed Sergeant in Capt.

Thomas Bell's Rifle Co. in Col. Rawlings' Regiment. On Nov. 16, 1776, he was taken prisoner at Fort Washington. After making his escape, he returned to Baltimore and there as a Sergeant he joined Capt. Calderwood's Co. in Col. Febecker's Regiment, Virginia Line, and served from 18 months to 2 years, after which he was attached to the 4th Maryland Line under Col. Josias Carvil Hall. He was sent to Pittsburgh and was again put under command of Thomas Bell, his former Captain then acting as Colonel. He served there until discharged by Capt. Tanneyhill. He also fought in the battles of Monmouth, Germantown, Brandywine, Cooch's Bridge, Paoli, and a number of smaller skirmishes. In 1824 his wife was aged 63 and they had 5 sons and 3 daughters all of age (no names were given). His administrator received the final pension payment in Jan., 1842, and was paid to Jan. 8, 1833 [Ref: U-20:59, P-1230].

FORD, Joseph. Private, 6th Class, 1st Co., Middle Bn., Militia, July 15, 1780 [Ref: M-201].

FORD, William (b. 1763). Private, Maryland Line, and applied for a pension (S31034) in Caldwell County, Kentucky, on Aug. 20, 1832, aged 69, stating that he was born in Montgomery County, Maryland, on March 5, 1763, and he volunteered under Capt. Nicholls in 1781 for 9 months service "to appease his master for leaving him when drafted for 2 months [when] he took the place of ---- Anderson and served under Capt. Hillary." [Ref: Y-7, P-1232, Z-23].

FORD, Zadock. Private, 7th Co., Middle Bn., Militia, Sep., 1777 [Ref: M-197, T-5:42]. Lived in Seneca Hd. (two taxables) in 1777 [Ref: R-31:7].

FORMAN, Jacob. Took the Oath of Allegiance in 1778 [Ref: L-2:27].

FORMAN, John. Took the Oath of Allegiance in 1778 [Ref: L-2:27].

FORSET, James. See "James Faucit," q.v.

FORTUNE, William. Private, 7th Maryland Line, 1778-1780 [Ref: D-207].

FORWHOALOR, Francis. Took the Oath of Allegiance before the Hon. Charles Jones on Jan. 10, 1778 [Ref: T-3:71, L-1:40].

FOWLER, Elisha (1734-1795). Private, 3rd Co., Lower Bn., Militia, Sep., 1777 [Ref: M-199, T-5:46]. Took the Oath of Allegiance before the Hon. Richard Thompson in 1778 [Ref: T-3:75, L-1:40]. Elisha Fowler, aged 42, lived in Lower Potomac Hd. in 1776 with Elisha Fowler, Jr., aged 8, and Thomas Fowler, aged 6 [Ref: K-1:182], and Elisha Fowler lived in George Town Hd. (one taxable) in 1777 [Ref: R-31:3]. "Elisha Fowler, Jr." died testate in Montgomery County (wife named Ann) in 1795 [Ref: V-50].

FOWLER, Ila E. See "Nicholas Hocker" and "Samuel Hocker," q.v.

FOWLER, Mary Ann. See "Hezekiah Gray," q.v.

FRANCIS (FRANCES), Joseph (b. 1742). "Joseph Francis" was a private, 8th Co., Lower Bn., Militia, Sep., 1777 [Ref: M-200, T-5:51], and private, 6th Co., Lower Bn., Militia, July 15, 1780 [Ref: M-206]. "Joseph Frances" rendered aid by providing wheat for use of the military in 1780 [Ref: O-

315]. "Joseph Francis or Frances" lived in North West Hd. (wife named Elizabeth, aged 28) in 1776-1777 [Ref: K-1:230, R-31:17].
FRANKLIN, William (b. 1757). Lived in Sugarland Hd. in 1776 [Ref: K-1:210]. Private, Flying Camp, enlisted on July 18, 1776 [Ref: D-49].
FRAZER, Jonathan. Took the Oath of Allegiance in 1778 [Ref: L-2:27].
FRAZER, Thomas. Took the Oath of Allegiance in 1778 [Ref: L-2:27].
FREDERICK, Henry. Private, 6th Class, 2nd Co., Middle Bn., Militia, July 15, 1780 [Ref: M-201].
FREEMAN, Aaron. Private, 8th Co., Middle Bn., Militia, Sep., 1777 [Ref: M-198, T-5:43]. Private, 5th Co., Middle Bn., Militia, July 15, 1780 [Ref: M-203]. "Aaron Freeman" rendered aid by providing wheat for use of the military in 1781 [Ref: O-393]. "Aaron Freman" [sic] lived in Rock Creek Hd. (one taxable) in 1777 [Ref: R-31:16].
FREEMAN, John. Private who was recruited to serve in the Continental Army in 1780 [Ref: D-342].
FREEMAN, Richard. Took the Oath of Allegiance before the Hon. William Deakins, Jr. before March 3, 1778 [Ref: T-3:68, L-1:40]. Private, 3rd Maryland Line, enlisted on June 8, 1778, reenlisted on April 17, 1779, and discharged Jan. 12, 1782 [Ref: D-110, D-467, E-351].
FREEMAN, Thomas. Private, Capt. Edward Burgess' Co., Lower District of Frederick (now Montgomery) County, Militia, July, 1776 [Ref: D-42].
FRIDDLE, John. Took the Oath of Allegiance in 1778 [Ref: L-2:27].
FRYBACK, George. Private, Capt. Edward Burgess' Co., Lower District of Frederick (now Montgomery) County, Militia, July, 1776 [Ref: D-42]. George Fryback lived in the Lower Part of Newfoundland Hd. (one taxable) in 1777 [Ref: R-31:5].
FRYBACK, John. Private, Capt. Edward Burgess' Co., Lower District of Frederick (now Montgomery) County, Militia, July, 1776 [Ref: D-42].
FRYE, Abraham. Took the Oath of Allegiance in 1778 [Ref: L-2:27].
FRYE, Isaac. Took the Oath of Allegiance in 1778 [Ref: L-2:27].
FRYER, Frances. See "Osborn Trail," q.v.
FRYER, Richard. Son of John Fryer [Ref: V-51]. Private, 2nd Co., Middle Bn., Militia, Sep. 4, 1777 [Ref: M-196, T-5:37]. Took the Oath of Allegiance before the Hon. Gerrard Briscoe on March 2, 1778 [Ref: T-3:56, L-1:40]. Lived in Sugar Loaf Hd. (one taxable) in 1777 [Ref: R-31:9].
FRYER, Walter. Son of John Fryer [Ref: V-51]. Private, 2nd Co., Middle Bn., Militia, Sep. 4, 1777 [Ref: M-196, T-5:37], and First Corporal, 3rd Co., Middle Bn., Militia, July 15, 1780 [Ref: M-202]. Rendered aid by providing wheat for use of the military in 1780 and 1781 [Ref: O-315, O-444]. Walter Fryer married Margery Trail in Montgomery County on May 9, 1780 [Ref: K-2:518].
FULFORD, John. Private, Capt. Price's Co., 3rd Maryland Line, 1781-1782 [Ref: D-454].

FULKS, William. Private, 5th Co., Middle Bn., Militia, July 15, 1780 [Ref: M-203].
FULTON (FOULTON), Robert (b. 1721). Took the Oath of Allegiance (made his "R E" mark) before the Hon. Samuel W. Magruder in 1778 [Ref: T-3:73, L-1:40]. Robert Fulton lived in Lower Potomac Hd. (one taxable) in 1776-1777 [Ref: R-31:4, K-1:182].
FYFFE (FIFE), Abijah (b. 1746). Son of James and Sarah Fyffe, of Sugarland Hd., in 1776 [Ref: V-51, K-1:200]. Private, 1st Co., Upper Bn., Militia, Aug. 30, 1777, and private, 8th Class, 1st Co., Middle Bn., Militia, July 15, 1780 [Ref: M-193, M-201]. Took the Oath of Allegiance before the Hon. William Deakins, Jr. before March 3, 1778 [Ref: T-3:68, L-1:40].
FYFFE (FIFE), Jacob. Rendered aid by providing corn for use of the military in 1780 [Ref: O-288].
FYFFE (FIFFE, FIFE), James Jr. (b. 1753). Son of James and Sarah Fyffe, of Sugarland Hd., in 1776 [Ref: V-51]. "James Fyffe" took the Oath of Allegiance before the Hon. Elisha Williams on March 2, 1778 [Ref: T-3:81, L-1:40]. A "James Fifer" married Rebeckah Perry in Montgomery County on Jan. 23, 1780 [Ref: K-2:518]. "Jas. Fyfe, Jr." was a private, 1st Co., Upper Bn., Militia, Aug. 30, 1777 [Ref: M-193].
FYFFE (FIFE), James Sr. (1713-1791). "James Fyffe, Sr." took the Oath of Allegiance before the Hon. Elisha Williams on March 2, 1778 [Ref: T-3:81, L-1:40]. "James Fyfe" recruited John Predix in Feb., 1781 [Ref: R-33:155, X-1146]. "James Fyffe" rendered aid by providing wheat for use of the military in 1781 [Ref: O-396]. "James Fiffe or Fyffe" lived in Sugarland Hd. (one taxable) in 1776-1777 [Ref: K-1:200, R-31:12]. "James Fyffe" died testate in Montgomery County (wife named Sarah Watson) in 1791 [Ref: V-51, DAR-I:235].
FYFFE (FIFE), John (b. 1761). Son of James and Sarah Fyffe, of Sugarland Hd., in 1776 [Ref: K-1:200, V-51]. Private, 1st Co., Upper Bn., Militia, Aug. 30, 1777 [Ref: M-193].
FYFFE (FIFE), Jonathan (1755-c1820). Son of James and Sarah Fyffe, of Sugarland Hd., in 1776 [Ref: K-1:200, V-51]. "Jonathan Fyffe" was a private, 1st Co., Upper Bn., Militia, Aug. 30, 1777 [Ref: M-193]. Took the Oath of Allegiance before the Hon. Elisha Williams on March 2, 1778 [Ref: T-3:81, L-1:40, DAR-I:235].
FYFFE (FIFFE, FIFE), Joseph (b. 1751). Son of James and Sarah Fyffe, of Sugarland Hd., in 1776 [Ref: V-51]. "Joseph Fyffe" was a private, 1st Co., Upper Bn., Militia, Aug. 30, 1777 [Ref: M-193]. Took the Oath of Allegiance before the Hon. Elisha Williams on March 2, 1778 [Ref: T-3:81, L-1:40]. Lived in Sugarland Hd. (three taxables) in 1776-1777 [Ref: K-1:200, R-31:12].
FYRTH, Robert. Private, Capt. Thomas Beall's Co., Maryland Line, 1780 [Ref: D-351].

GAITHER, Basil (c1751-1803). Served as Captain, 16th Bn., Militia, Aug. 30, 1777 [Ref: M-77, M-195, C-350, C-373]. Took the Oath of Allegiance before the Hon. Gerrard Briscoe on March 2, 1778 [Ref: T-3:56, L-1:40]. Lived in Seneca Hd. (three taxables) in 1777 [Ref: R-31:7]. He married Margaret Watkins and had seven children: Walter, Nathan, Basil, Gassaway, Eleanor, Betsy, and Nicholas. Basil Gaither settled in Rowan County, North Carolina circa 1780 and died there testate in 1803 [Ref: DAR-I:257, and Henry C. Peden's *Marylanders to Carolina* (1994), p. 58, and Harry Wright Newman's *Anne Arundel Gentry*, Vol. I (1980), p. 111].

GAITHER, Benjamin. (1) First Lieutenant, 29th Bn., Militia, May 14, 1776. Captain, Middle Bn., Militia, from April 21, 1779, to at least March 25, 1780 [Ref: M-77, M-196, C-373, E-357, F-120]. (2) Private, 6th Co., Upper Bn., Militia, Aug. 30, 1777 [Ref: M-194]. Took the Oath of Allegiance before the Hon. Edward Burgess on Feb. 28, 1778 [Ref: T-3:63, L-1:40]. "Benjamin Gaither, born in Maryland, about 19 years of age, 5 feet 2 or 3 inches high, full faced, dark brown hair and slow in speech, has not had the smallpox; recruited by Capt. Edward Burgess on May 7, 1781." [Ref: R-33:156, X-1146]. "Benjamin Gaither" lived in the Upper Part of Newfoundland Hd. (three taxables) and "Benjamin Gater" lived in Sugar Loaf Hd. (one taxable) in 1777 [Ref: R-31:10].

GAITHER, Burgess (1753/57-1820). Private, 7th Co., Middle Bn., Militia, 1777 [Ref: M-197, T-5:42], and Ensign, Middle Bn., Militia, Sep. 12, 1777 [Ref: M-77, C-373]. Took the Oath of Allegiance before the Hon. Joseph Wilson on Feb. 28, 1778 [Ref: T-3:64, L-1:40]. By May 12, 1784 he had settled in Rowan County, North Carolina where he had purchased a tract on Little Dutchman's Creek. He was married to Amelia Martin by 1792 and had ten children: Alfred, Martin, Sarah, Elvira, Forrest, Lemira, Milly Maria, Burgess, Eleanora, and Charles Cotesworth Pinkney. Burgess became a prominent figure in post-Revolutionary politics in western North Carolina and represented Iredell County in the State Legislature in 1792 and from 1795 to 1801 [Ref: Harry Wright Newman's *Anne Arundel Gentry*, Vol. I (1980), p. 112, and DAR-I:257].

GAITHER, Ephraim. Private, 4th Co., Middle Bn., Militia, Sep., 1777 [Ref: M-196, T-5:39]. Took the Oath of Allegiance before the Hon. Edward Burgess on Feb. 28, 1778 [Ref: T-3:60, L-1:40].

GAITHER, Gerrard (died 1816). Served as First Corporal, 4th Co., Middle Bn., Militia, July 15, 1780 [Ref: M-202]. Died testate in Montgomery County (wife named Agnes) in 1816 [Ref: V-52].

GAITHER, Greenbury or Greenberry (b. 1754 - died after 1781). Lived in Seneca Hd. (23 taxables) in 1777 [Ref: R-31:7]. Brother of "Johnsey Gaither," q.v. [Ref: V-53]. Served as First Lieutenant, Lower District, Frederick County (now Montgomery), July 20, 1776, Quartermaster, 16th Bn., Militia, Aug. 30, 1777, and First Lieutenant, 7th Co., Middle Bn., Militia, Sep. 12, 1777 [Ref: D-42, M-77, M-197, C-350, C-373, T-

5:41]. Served as a grand juror in Aug., 1777 [Ref: R-31:17]. Took the Oath of Allegiance before the Hon. Gerrard Briscoe on March 2, 1778 [Ref: T-3:57, L-1:40]. Paid for his recruiting services by the Collector of the Tax in Montgomery County in 1780 [Ref: F-54]. He married Anne Andison (or Catherine Anderson) in Montgomery County on April 13, 1779 [Ref: K-2:518, DAR-I:257].

GAITHER, Henry. Took the Oath of Allegiance before the Hon. Edward Burgess on Feb. 28, 1778 [Ref: T-3:58, L-1:40]. Justice of the Peace in 1778 and Justice of the County Court in 1779 [Ref: C-529, W-1]. There was also a Henry Gaither who was an ensign in the 2nd Maryland Line in 1776 and a captain in the 4th Maryland Line in 1781 [Ref: D-7, G-604]. "Henry Chew Gaither" was a captain in the 1st Maryland Line and was paid for recruiting services by the Collector of the Tax in Montgomery County in 1780 [Ref: F-54]. One Henry Gaither lived in the Upper Part of Newfoundland Hd. (five taxables) in 1777 [Ref: R-31:6]. "Henry Gaither, planter" died testate in Montgomery County (wife named Martha) in 1783, and "Henry Gaither, Colonel, of Carenot" died in 1811 (no wife or children named) and mentioned Henry Chew Gaither in his will [Ref: V-52].

GAITHER, John (c1741-1809). Served as a First Lieutenant, Lower District of Frederick County (now Montgomery), July 20, 1776, and Captain, 1st Co., 29th Bn., Militia, from June 21, 1777, through at least Aug. 11, 1779 [Ref: D-42, M-77, M-198, T-5:44, C-296, DAR-I:257]. Took the Oath of Allegiance before the Hon. Edward Burgess on Feb. 28, 1778 [Ref: T-3:59, L-1:40]. "John Gaither, Jr." lived in the Lower Part of Newfoundland Hd. (two taxables) in 1777 [Ref: R-31:5].

GAITHER, Johnsey (c1760-1797). Private, 7th Co., Middle Bn., Militia, Sep., 1777 [Ref: M-197, T-5:42]. Died testate in Montgomery County (wife Mary "who is pregnant") in Dec., 1797 [Ref: V-53, DAR-I:257].

GAITHER, Nicholas. Private, Flying Camp, Frederick (now Montgomery) County, enlisted by Greenbury Gaither on July 29, 1776 [Ref: D-44]. Took the Oath of Allegiance before the Hon. Gerrard Briscoe on March 2, 1778 [Ref: T-3:57, L-1:40]. Private, 7th Co., Middle Bn., Militia, Sep., 1777 [Ref: M-197, T-5:42]. Nicholas married Eleanor Greenfield in Montgomery County on Oct. 26, 1779 [Ref: K-2:518].

GAITHER, Seth. "Seth Gaither" was a private, 2nd Co., Upper Bn., Militia, Aug. 30, 1777 [Ref: M-193]. "Seth Gater" lived in Sugar Loaf Hd. (one taxable) in 1777 [Ref: R-31:10].

GAITHER, William. Served as an Ensign, 29th Bn., Militia, May 14, 1776, and Second Lieutenant, Middle Bn., Militia, Sep. 12, 1777 [Ref: M-77, M-196, A-424, C-373]. Took the Oath of Allegiance before the Hon. Edward Burgess on Feb. 28, 1778 [Ref: T-3:58, L-1:40]. Lived in the Upper Part of Newfoundland Hd. (three taxables) in 1777 [Ref: R-31:6].

GALWORTH, Gabriel (b. 1757). Private, 2nd Maryland Line, from Dec. 24, 1776, until discharged on Jan. 10, 1780 [Ref: D-113]. In 1816 the

Treasurer of Maryland was directed to pay him, quarterly, half pay of a private [Ref: K-2:345]. Applied for pension (S8549) on Nov. 10, 1818, and again on March 14, 1834, aged 77, in Montgomery County, stating he had enlisted at Bladensburg and continued in service four years until discharged on Jan. 8, 1780, in Baltimore (same source indicated he was discharged at Morris Town). He fought in the Battle of Staten Island in Aug., 1777, where he was taken prisoner, held captive for 12 months. He was exchanged in Aug., 1778, and also fought in the Battle of White Plains [Ref: J-49, P-1302, Q-109, Y-29].

GALWORTH (GALLWORTH), Peter. Private, 2nd Maryland Line, enlisted in Jan. 31, 1776 [Ref: D-7].

GANT, John. Private, 8th Co., Lower Bn., Militia, July 15, 1780 [Ref: M-207].

GARDNER, Thomas. Rendered aid by providing wheat for use of the military in 1781 [Ref: O-423].

GARLICK, Joseph. Private, 8th Co., Lower Bn., Militia, July 15, 1780 [Ref: M-207]. Took the Oath of Allegiance before the Hon. Richard Thompson in 1778 [Ref: T-3:75, L-1:40].

GARNER, Eleanor and John. See "John Miller," q.v.

GARNER, Paul. Took the Oath of Allegiance before the Hon. Richard Thompson in 1778 [Ref: T-3:75, L-1:40].

GARRETT (GARROTT), Allen. Private, 2nd Co., Lower Bn., Militia, Sep., 1777 [Ref: M-198, T-5:45].

GARRETT, Barton. Brother of "Edward Garrett," q.v. [Ref: V-53]. Took the Oath of Allegiance in 1778 [Ref: L-2:27].

GARRETT (GARROTT, GARROT), Edward (died 1785). Private, 2nd Co., Lower Bn., Militia, Sep., 1777 [Ref: M-198, T-5:45], and private, 5th Co., Lower Bn., Militia, July 15, 1780 [Ref: M-206]. Constable in Rock Creek Hd., 1780-1781 [Ref: W-2]. "Edward Garrot" lived in Rock Creek Hd. (eight taxables) in 1777 [Ref: R-31:16]. "Edward Garrett" died testate in Montgomery County (no wife or children) in 1785 [Ref: V-53].

GARRETT (GARROT), John. Brother of "Edward Garrett," q.v. [Ref: V-53]. Took the Oath of Allegiance in 1778 [Ref: L-2:27]. "John Garrot" lived in Rock Creek Hd. (one taxable) in 1777 [Ref: R-31:16].

GARRETT (GARROT), William. "William Garrot" lived in Sugar Loaf Hd. (two taxables) in 1777 [Ref: R-31:10]. "William Garrett" was a corporal, 5th Maryland Line, 1778 [Ref: D-209].

GARTEN, William. See "William Gatton," q.v.

GARTRELL (GAITHRIL), Aaron (died 1802). "Aaron Gartrell" was a private, 4th Co., Middle Bn., Militia, Sep., 1777 [Ref: M-196, T-5:39]. Took the Oath of Allegiance (made his "A" mark) before the Hon. Edward Burgess on Feb. 28, 1778 [Ref: T-3:60, L-1:40]. "Aaron Gaithril" lived in the Upper Part of Newfoundland Hd. (four taxables) in 1777 [Ref: R-31:6]. "Aaron Gartrell" died testate in Montgomery County (wife not named) in 1802 [Ref: V-53].

GARTRELL (GATTRELL), Ann. See "Zephaniah Beall," q.v.
GARTRELL (GARTRILL), Charles. Private, Capt. Edward Burgess' Co., Lower District of Frederick (now Montgomery) County, Militia, July, 1776 [Ref: D-42]. Private, 1st Co., Lower Bn., Militia, Sep., 1777 [Ref: M-198, T-5:44]. Private, 7th Co., Lower Bn., Militia, July 15, 1780 [Ref: M-207]. Took the Oath of Allegiance before the Hon. Edward Burgess on Feb. 28, 1778 [Ref: T-3:59, L-1:40]. "Charles Gartrill" lived in the Lower Part of Newfoundland Hd. (three taxables) in 1777 [Ref: R-31:5]. "Charles Gartrell" married Sarah Barnes in Montgomery County on Dec. 7, 1777 [Ref: K-2:516].
GARTRELL, Felter. Private, 1st Co., Lower Bn., Militia, Sep., 1777 [Ref: M-198, T-5:44].
GARTRELL (GATHRIL), Francis. Private, 1st Co., Lower Bn., Militia, Sep., 1777 [Ref: M-198, T-5:44]. Two men with this name took the Oath of Allegiance before the Hon. Edward Burgess on Feb. 28, 1778 [Ref: T-3:61, T-3:58, L-1:40, which latter source listed the name once as "Gastrell"]. "Francis Rawlings Gartrell" married Rachel Hamilton in Montgomery County on March 19, 1778 [Ref: K-2:516]. "Francis Gartrell" lived in the Lower Part of Newfoundland Hd. (three taxables) in 1777 [Ref: R-31:5]. "Francis Gathril" lived in the Upper Part of Newfoundland Hd. (one taxable) in 1777 [Ref: R-31:6].
GARTRELL, Jehoshaphat. Took the Oath of Allegiance before the Hon. Edward Burgess on Feb. 28, 1778 [Ref: T-3:60, L-1:40].
GARTRELL, John. (1) Private, 1st Co., Lower Bn., Militia, Sep., 1777 [Ref: M-198, T-5:44]. Private, 7th Co., Lower Bn., Militia, July 15, 1780 [Ref: M-206]. (2) Private, 7th Class, 4th Co., Middle Bn., Militia, July 15, 1780 [Ref: M-202]. Took the Oath of Allegiance before the Hon. Edward Burgess on Feb. 28, 1778 [Ref: T-3:58, L-1:40, which source listed the name as "Gastrell"].
GARTRELL (GARTRILL), Joseph. Private, Capt. Edward Burgess' Co., Lower District of Frederick (now Montgomery) County, Militia, July, 1776 [Ref: D-42]. Private, 7th Co., Lower Bn., Militia, July 15, 1780 [Ref: M-207]. Took the Oath of Allegiance before the Hon. Edward Burgess on Feb. 28, 1778 [Ref: T-3:58, L-1:40]. "Joseph Gartrill" lived in the Lower Part of Newfoundland Hd. (one taxable) in 1777 [Ref: R-31:5].
GARTRELL (GARTRILL), Richard. Took the Oath of Allegiance (made his "R" mark) before the Hon. Edward Burgess on Feb. 28, 1778 [Ref: T-3:58, L-1:40]. "Richard Gartrill" lived in the Lower Part of Newfoundland Hd. (three taxables) in 1777 [Ref: R-31:5]. "Richard Gattrel" lived in Linganore Hd. (four taxables) in 1777 [Ref: R-31:9].
GARTRELL, Sarah. See "Caleb Darby," q.v.
GARTRELL, Stephen. Private, Capt. Edward Burgess' Co., Lower District of Frederick (now Montgomery) County, Militia, July, 1776 [Ref: D-42].

GASSAWAY, Charles. (1) First Lieutenant, 16th Bn., Militia, Sep. 12, 1777. Captain, Upper Bn., Militia, March 25, 1780 [Ref: C-373, F-120, M-78, and which latter source mistakenly listed his name as "George" Gassaway]. (2) Private, 3rd Co., Upper Bn., Militia, Aug. 30, 1777 [Ref: M-193]. Served as a petit juror in Aug. and Nov., 1777 [Ref: R-31:17, R-31:18], and a grand juror in 1781 [Ref: W-2]. Took the Oath of Allegiance before the Hon. William Deakins, Jr. before March 3, 1778 [Ref: T-3:68, L-1:40, which listed the name as "Charles Gazaway"]. Rendered aid by providing corn for use of the military in 1780 [Ref: O-287]. One Charles Gassaway lived in the Upper Part of Potomac Hd. (three taxables) in 1777 [Ref: R-31:14]. One Charles Gassaway died testate in Montgomery County (wife named Ruth) in 1816 and mentioned a son Charles [Ref: V-54].

GASTLER (GASSLER, GOSSLER, GUSLER, GUSSALER), Anthony (b. 1736). "Anthony Gastler" was a private, 3rd Co., Lower Bn., Militia, Sep., 1777 [Ref: M-199, T-5:46]. "Anthony Gassler" took the Oath of Allegiance before the Hon. Richard Thompson in 1778 [Ref: T-3:75, L-1:40]. "Anthony Gossler or Gussaler" lived in George Town Hd. (one taxable) in 1776-1777 [Ref: K-1:193, R-31:3]." Anthony Gusler" was a private, 8th Co., Lower Bn., Militia, July 15, 1780 [Ref: M-207].

GATES (GATTS), Edward. "Edward Gates" was a private, 2nd Co., Lower Bn., Militia, Sep., 1777 [Ref: M-198, T-5:45]. Took the Oath of Allegiance (made his "X" mark) before the Hon. Edward Burgess on Feb. 28, 1778 [Ref: T-3:60, L-1:40]. "Edward Gatts" was a private, 5th Co., Lower Bn., Militia, July 15, 1780 [Ref: M-206]. "Edward Gates" lived in Rock Creek Hd. (two taxables) in 1777 [Ref: R-31:16].

GATES (GEATS), James (b. 1742). Took the Oath of Allegiance before the Hon. Aneas Campbell on March 2, 1778 [Ref: T-3:78, L-1:40]. "James Geats, aged 34" lived in Sugarland Hd. in 1776 [Ref: K-1:217].

GATTON, Azariah (b. 1762). Son of James Gatton [Ref: K-1:209]. Substitute from Montgomery County who was discharged from the Maryland Line on Dec. 11, 1781 [Ref: I-18].

GATTON (GATTEN, GIRTEN), Benjamin (1734-1779). Private, 4th Co., Upper Bn., Militia, Aug. 30, 1777 [Ref: M-194]. "Benjamin Gatton" took the Oath of Allegiance before the Hon. Aneas Campbell on March 2, 1778 [Ref: T-3:78, L-1:40]. "Benjamin Gatten or Girten" lived in Sugarland Hd. in 1776 and had four taxables in 1777 [Ref: K-1:219, R-31:12]. "Benjamin Gatton" died testate in Montgomery County (wife named Elizabeth) in 1779 [Ref: V-55].

GATTON, Hezekiah. Private, 4th Co., Upper Bn., Militia, Aug. 30, 1777 [Ref: M-194].

GATTON (GATTEN), James. Private, 8th Co., Upper Bn., Militia, Aug. 30, 1777 [Ref: M-195]. Took the Oath of Allegiance before the Hon. Aneas Campbell on March 2, 1778 [Ref: T-3:77, L-1:40]. Rendered aid by providing wheat for use of the military in 1780 [Ref: O-316]. One

"James Gatten, aged 38" lived in Sugarland Hd. in 1776 (wife named Mary) and had five taxables in 1777 [Ref: K-1:209, R-31:12]. Died testate in Montgomery County (wife named Mary) in 1778. Another James Gatten, also aged 38, lived in Sugarland Hd. in 1776 (wife named Elizabeth) and had a large family. Died testate in 1807 [Ref: V-55].

GATTON, John. Son of James Gatton [Ref: V-55]. Private, 4th Co., Upper Bn., Militia, Aug. 30, 1777 [Ref: M-194].

GATTON (GIRTON), Mary. See "Zephaniah McCray," q.v.

GATTON (GARTAIN, GETTON), Richard. (1) Private, 5th Co., Lower Bn., Militia, Aug., 1777 [Ref: T-5:48]. Private, 2nd Co., Lower Bn., Militia, July 15, 1780 [Ref: M-204]. (2) Private, 4th Co., Upper Bn., Militia, Aug. 30, 1777 [Ref: M-194]. Took the Oath of Allegiance before the Hon. Joseph Wilson on Feb. 28, 1778 [Ref: T-3:67, L-1:40]. "Richard Gatton" rendered aid by providing wheat for use of the military in 1781 [Ref: O-393]. "Richard Gartain" rendered aid by providing wheat for use of the military in 1780 [Ref: O-313]. "Richard Getton" lived in the Upper Part of Potomac Hd. (two taxables) in 1777 [Ref: R-31:14].

GATTON, Silvester. Private, 1st Maryland Regiment, enlisted Oct. 4, 1778; captured (no date given) and exchanged on Oct. 1, 1781 [Ref: D-112, D-617. Ed. Note: It is possible he may have been from Charles County, but he has been included here because of the number of other men named Gatton who served from Montgomery County].

GATTON (GARTEN), William (c1756-1816). Private, 6th Co., Lower Bn., Militia, Aug., 1777 [Ref: M-200, T-5:49]. Took the Oath of Allegiance before the Hon. Joseph Wilson on Feb. 28, 1778 [Ref: T-3:67, L-1:40]. Private, 3rd Co., Lower Bn., Militia, July 15, 1780 [Ref: M-205]. Rendered aid by providing wheat for use of the military in 1781 [Ref: O-423]. "William Garten" was a private, Capt. Edward Burgess' Co., Lower District of Frederick (now Montgomery) County, Militia, July, 1776 [Ref: D-42]. "William Gatton" married Sarah Murphy in Montgomery County on May 6, 1781 [Ref: K-2:518, DAR-I:262].

GATTON, Zachariah. Private, 5th Co., Lower Bn., Militia, Aug., 1777 [Ref: M-199, T-5:48]. Took the Oath of Allegiance before the Hon. Joseph Wilson on Feb. 28, 1778 [Ref: T-3:67, L-1:40]. Rendered aid by providing wheat for use of the military in 1781 [Ref: O-393]. "Zachy. Gatton" lived in the Upper Part of Potomac Hd. (six taxables) in 1777 [Ref: R-31:14].

GAUNOR, Paul. Private, 3rd Co., Lower Bn., Militia, Sep., 1777 [Ref: M-199, T-5:46].

GEBHART (KIPHART), John Jr. (1760/64-1845). "John Kiphart, aged 16" lived in George Town Hd. in 1776 with "John Kiphart, aged 38" [Ref: K-1:193]. "John Gebhart" served as a private, 8th Co., Lower Bn., Militia, July 15, 1780 [Ref: M-207. According to the *DAR Patriot Index* (Vol. I, p. 263), "John Gebhart" was born on Aug. 15, 1760, served as a drummer in Maryland, married Phebe Vansickle, and died on Sep. 23, 1845].

GEBHART (GIBHART, KIPHART), John Sr. (b. 1738). "John Gebhart, Sr." was a private, 8th Co., Lower Bn., Militia, on July 15, 1780 [Ref: M-207]. "John Gibhart" took the Oath of Allegiance before the Hon. Richard Thompson in 1778 [Ref: T-3:75, L-1:40]. "John Gibhart or Kiphart, aged 38" lived in George Town Hd. in 1776-1777 [Ref: K-1:193, R-31:3].

GEE, David. Private, 4th Co., Middle Bn., Militia, Sep., 1777 [Ref: M-196, T-5:39]. Took the Oath of Allegiance before the Hon. Edward Burgess on Feb. 28, 1778 [Ref: T-3:62, L-1:40]. Private, 2nd Class, 4th Co., Middle Bn., Militia, July 15, 1780 [Ref: M-202]. "David Ghee" lived in the Upper Part of Newfoundland Hd. (two taxables) in 1777 [Ref: R-31:6].

GEE, John. Private, 7th Co., Middle Bn., Militia, Sep., 1777 [Ref: M-197, T-5:42]. John Gee lived in Seneca Hd. (one taxable) in 1777 [Ref: R-31:8].

GEE, John Baptist. Took the Oath of Allegiance (made his "V" mark) before the Hon. Edward Burgess on Feb. 28, 1778 [Ref: T-3:60, L-1:40, which listed the name as "Gel"].

GEEHAN (GUHAN?), John. Private, Capt. Edward Burgess' Co., Lower District of Frederick (now Montgomery) County, Militia, July, 1776 [Ref: D-42].

GENTLE, Eleanor. See "Shadrick Locker," q.v.

GENTLE, Elizabeth. See "William Douglass," q.v.

GENTLE, George. (1) Private, 1st Co., Upper Bn., Militia, Aug. 30, 1777 [Ref: M-193, D-49]. (2) Private, 7th Co., Upper Bn., Militia, Aug. 30, 1777 [Ref: M-194]. Took the Oath of Allegiance before the Hon. Edward Burgess on Feb. 28, 1778 [Ref: T-3:63, L-1:40]. "George Gentle" and "George Gentle, of Stephen" (both born in 1753) lived in Sugarland Hd. in 1776-1777 [Ref: K-1:199, K-1:204, R-31:12]. One George Gentle married Virlinda Locker in Montgomery County on April 21, 1778 [Ref: K-2:518].

GENTLE (GENTILS), John (b. 1761). "John Gentile, aged 15" lived in Sugarland Hd. in 1776 and was apparently a son of Stephen Gentile, aged 66 [Ref: K-1:199]. "James Gentils" was a private, 4th Maryland Regiment, from Feb. 5, 1778 until July 3, 1778, when he reportedly "deserted" [Ref: D-115].

GENTLE, Stephen (b. 1755). Private, 1st Co., Upper Bn., Militia, Aug. 30, 1777 [Ref: M-193, D-49]. Stephen Gentle, aged 66, and family (including Sary Gentle, aged 52, Stephen Gentle, aged 21, George Gentle, aged 23, and John Gentle, age 15) lived in Sugarland Hd. (two taxables) in 1776-1777 [Ref: K-1:199, R-31:12]. Stephen Gentle died testate in Montgomery County (wife named Sarah) in 1795 and mentioned several grandchildren in his will [Ref: V-56].

GIBBONS, Hannah. See "Thomas Bateman (Batman)," q.v.

GIBBONS, William. On Feb. 6, 1781, John Murdock and Richard Thompson, Esquires of Montgomery County, informed the Maryland Council that William Gibbons, William O'Brien, and Matthew Griffen, of Georgia, "were driven from that State by the enemy and have settled in this State, that they have taken the Oath of Allegiance to the State of Georgia and have done everything that good citizens could do in support of their country. They have the approbation of the Board to settle in this State." [Ref: G-311].

GIBNEY, Hugh. Private, 3rd Co., Lower Bn., Militia, Sep., 1777 [Ref: M-199, T-5:46].

GIBSON, John (b. 1758). Lived in Sugarland Hd. in 1776 [Ref: K-1:218]. Served as a private when enrolled into a company of militia for the service of the Flying Camp on Oct. 15, 1776, and private, 8th Co., Upper Bn., Militia, on Aug. 30, 1777 [Ref: B-353, M-195]. Took the Oath of Allegiance before the Hon. Elisha Williams on March 2, 1778 [Ref: T-3:82]. John Gibson applied for pension (S38729) in Wilson County, Tennessee, on Sep. 25, 1818, aged 60, stating he had enlisted on April 20, 1778, in Montgomery County, Maryland, and served 3 years in the 3rd Maryland Line. He was taken prisoner at the Battle of Monmouth and also took part in the battles of Camden, Cowpens, and Guilford. He was discharged in Camden, South Carolina on April 17, 1779 [sic]. In 1818 he had a wife and daughter (aged 26), but no names were given [Ref: P-1340, U-23:54].

GILBERT, Amos. See "Norman Bruce Magruder," q.v.

GILKEY, Samuel. Private, 3rd Co., Middle Bn., Militia, Sep., 1777 [Ref: M-196, T-5:38]. Private, 1st Class, 2nd Co., Middle Bn., Militia, July 15, 1780 [Ref: M-201]. Took the Oath of Allegiance before the Hon. William Deakins, Jr. before March 3, 1778 [Ref: T-3:68, L-1:41].

GILL, Anne. See "Thomas Wilmot," q.v.

GILL, John (b. 1761 or 1762). Private, 2nd Co., Lower Bn., Militia, July 15, 1780 [Ref: M-204, K-1:183].

GILL, Joseph (b. 1727). Private, 5th Co., Lower Bn., Militia, Aug., 1777 [Ref: M-199, T-5:48]. Rendered aid by providing wheat for use of the military in 1780 [Ref: O-311]. Joseph Gill lived in Lower Potomac Hd. (five taxables) in 1776-1777 [Ref: R-31:4, K-1:183].

GILLAM (GILLHAM, GILLOM), John (b. 1753). Private, 4th Co., Upper Bn., Militia, Aug. 30, 1777 [Ref: M-194]. "John Gillham" took the Oath of Allegiance before the Hon. Edward Burgess on Feb. 28, 1778 [Ref: T-3:63, L-1:41]. "John Gillam or Gillom" lived in Sugarland Hd. (one taxable) in 1776-1777 [Ref: K-1:204, R-31:12].

GILLAM (GILLUM, GILLHAM), Thomas. Private, 4th Co., Upper Bn., Militia, Aug. 30, 1777 [Ref: M-194]. "Thomas Gillham" took the Oath of Allegiance before the Hon. Richard Thompson in 1778 [Ref: T-3:75, L-1:41]. "Thomas Gillham, aged 42" lived in Lower Potomac Hd. in 1776 and "Thomas Gillum, aged 23" lived in Sugarland Hd. in 1776 [Ref: K-1:183, K-1:206].

GILLIGAN, John (b. 1746). Lived in North West Hd. in 1776 [Ref: K-1:232]. Private, 7th Maryland Line, from April 6, 1778 until Aug. 16, 1780, when reported missing at the Battle of Camden [Ref: D-211].

GINGLE (GRINGUL), George (b. 1744). "George Gingle" was a private, 2nd Co., Lower Bn., Militia, July 15, 1780 [Ref: M-204]. "George Gringul" lived in Lower Potomac Hd. in 1776 [Ref: K-1:182].

GITTINGS (GETTINGS, GIDDINS, GIDINGS), Basil. "Basil Gittings" was a private, 8th Co., Middle Bn., Militia, Sep., 1777 [Ref: M-198, T-5:43]. Private, 5th Co., Lower Bn., Militia, July 15, 1780 [Ref: M-205]. Took the Oath of Allegiance before the Hon. Charles Jones on Jan. 10, 1778 [Ref: T-3:71, L-1:41]. Rendered aid by providing wheat for use of the military in 1780 [Ref: O-329]. "Basil Gidings" lived in Rock Creek Hd. (one taxable) in 1777 [Ref: R-31:16].

GITTINGS (GETTINGS, GIDDINS, GEDDIN), Benjamin (1736-1781). "Benjamin Gittings" was a private, 5th Co., Lower Bn., Militia, Aug., 1777 [Ref: M-199, T-5:48]. Private, 2nd Co., Lower Bn., Militia, July 15, 1780 [Ref: M-204]. Took the Oath of Allegiance before the Hon. Samuel W. Magruder in 1778 [Ref: T-3:73]. Rendered aid by providing wheat for use of the military in 1780 [Ref: O-309]. "Benjamin Geddin" was a private, 8th Co., Lower Bn., Militia, Sep., 1777 [Ref: T-5:51 and M-200, which latter source listed the name as "Ben: Gedilin(?)"]. Benjamin Gettings or Gittings lived in Lower Potomac Hd. (three taxables) in 1776-1777 [Ref: R-31:4, K-1:182]. Died testate in Montgomery County (wife named Ann) in 1781 [Ref: V-56].

GITTINGS (GIDEN, GIDDONS), Henry. "Henry Gittings" was a private, 8th Co., Lower Bn., Militia, Sep., 1777 [Ref: M-200, T-5:51]. Took the Oath of Allegiance before the Hon. Gerrard Briscoe on March 2, 1778 [Ref: T-3:57, L-1:41]. "Henry Giden" rendered aid by providing wheat for use of the military in 1780 [Ref: O-314]. "Henry Gittings, aged 46" lived in North West Hd. in 1776 and "Henry Giddons" lived there (three taxables) in 1777 [Ref: K-1:226, R-31:17].

GITTINGS (GETTINGS), Ninian. Took the Oath of Allegiance before the Hon. Charles Jones on Jan. 10, 1778 [Ref: T-3:71].

GITTINGS (GETTINGS, GIDDINS, GIDINGS), Thomas. Private, Capt. Edward Burgess' Co., Lower District of Frederick (now Montgomery) County, Militia, July, 1776 [Ref: D-42]. "Thomas Gittings" was a private, 8th Co., Middle Bn., Militia, Sep., 1777 [Ref: M-198, T-5:43]. Private, 6th Co., Lower Bn., Militia, July 15, 1780 [Ref: M-206]. Took the Oath of Allegiance before the Hon. Charles Jones on Jan. 10, 1778 [Ref: T-3:71, L-1:40]. Rendered aid by providing wheat for use of the military in 1780 [Ref: O-312]. "Thomas Gidings" lived in Rock Creek Hd. (one taxable) in 1777 [Ref: R-31:16].

GLAZE, Basil. Private, 2nd Co., Lower Bn., Militia, Sep., 1777 [Ref: M-198, T-5:45]. Letter from the Council in Annapolis to the Sheriff of Montgomery County, Feb. 19, 1778: "There has been a representation of the circumstances of Basil Glaze whose effects are distrainable for substitute money, and his father Samuel Glaze and his family, in so strong and favourable a light by several gentleman of Montgomery County that, we have no doubt the Assembly will stop the levying the money. We therefore request you to stay the execution 'til we have an opportunity of laying the matter before the Assembly." [Ref: C-508]. Basil Glaze took the Oath of Allegiance before the Hon. Edward Burgess on Feb. 28, 1778 [Ref: T-3:62, L-1:41]. Private, 5th Co., Lower Bn., Militia, on July 15, 1780 [Ref: M-206].
GLAZE, Jonathan. Private, 5th Co., Lower Bn., Militia, July 15, 1780 [Ref: M-206]. Private, 2nd Co., Lower Bn., Militia, Sep., 1777 [Ref: M-198, T-5:45].
GLAZE (GLASE), Joseph (b. 1712). Took the Oath of Allegiance before the Hon. Samuel W. Magruder in 1778 [Ref: T-3:73, L-1:41]. Rendered aid by providing wheat for use of the military in 1780 [Ref: O-302, O-313]. Joseph Glaze lived in Lower Potomac Hd. (three taxables) in 1776-1777 [Ref: R-31:4, K-1:182].
GLAZE, Nathan. Private, 2nd Co., Lower Bn., Militia, Sep., 1777 [Ref: M-198, T-5:45]. Took the Oath of Allegiance before the Hon. Edward Burgess on Feb. 28, 1778 [Ref: T-3:63, L-1:41]. Rendered aid by providing wheat for use of the military in 1780 [Ref: O-327]. Nathan Glaze lived in Rock Creek Hd. (one taxable) in 1777 [Ref: R-31:16].
GLAZE, Nathaniel. Took the Oath of Allegiance before the Hon. Edward Burgess on Feb. 28, 1778 [Ref: T-3:60, L-1:41]. "Natt. Glaze" was a private, 2nd Co., Lower Bn., Militia, Sep., 1777 [Ref: M-198, T-5:45].
GLAZE, Samuel. Took the Oath of Allegiance before the Hon. Edward Burgess on Feb. 28, 1778 [Ref: T-3:60, L-1:41]. Rendered aid by providing wheat for use of the military in 1780 [Ref: O-307]. Samuel Glaze lived in Rock Creek Hd. (five taxables) in 1777 [Ref: R-31:16]. See "Basil Glaze," q.v.
GLAZE (GLAYS), William (1753-c1806). Took the Oath of Allegiance before the Hon. Charles Jones on Jan. 10, 1778 [Ref: T-3:71, L-1:41, K-1:182, DAR-I:271, which latter source states that his wife was Mary O. ----].
GLOVER, John. Rendered aid by providing wheat for use of the military in 1780 [Ref: O-314].
GLOVER, William. Private who was recruited to serve in the Continental Army in 1780 [Ref: D-341].
GODMAN (GOODMAN), Humphrey. Private, 7th Co., Upper Bn., Militia, Aug. 30, 1777 [Ref: M-195]. Took the Oath of Allegiance before the Hon. Elisha Williams on March 2, 1778 [Ref: T-3:80, L-1:41]. Rendered aid by providing corn for use of the military in 1780 [Ref: O-288, O-295].

"Humphry Goodman, aged 40" lived in North West Hd. in 1776 and "Humphrey Godman" lived in Sugarland Hd. (three taxables) in 1777 [Ref: K-1:225, R-31:12].

GODMAN, Samuel Israel. Took the Oath of Allegiance before the Hon. Edward Burgess on Feb. 28, 1778 [Ref: T-3:58, L-1:41]. Private, 1st Co., Lower Bn., Militia, Sep., 1777. Private, 7th Co., Lower Bn., July 15, 1780 [Ref: T-5:44, M-198, M-207, which listed the name as "Samuel J. Godman"]. "Samuel Godman" lived in the Lower Part of Newfoundland Hd. (four taxables) in 1777 [Ref: R-31:5].

GOISTE, Allen. Took the Oath of Allegiance in 1778 [Ref: L-2:27].

GOLDEN, John. Private, 5th Co., Middle Bn., Militia, July 15, 1780 [Ref: M-203].

GOLDEN (GOULDEN, GOULDY) Samuel. Private, 5th Co., Middle Bn., Militia, July 15, 1780 [Ref: M-203]. Took the Oath of Allegiance before the Hon. Gerrard Briscoe on March 2, 1778 [Ref: T-3:57, L-1:41]. "Samuel Golden" rendered aid by providing wheat for use of the military in 1781 [Ref: O-396]. "Samuel Goulden" lived in Seneca Hd. (one taxable) in 1777 [Ref: R-31:8]. "Samuel Gouldy" was a private, 1st Co., Middle Bn., Militia, Aug. 30, 1777 [Ref: M-195].

GOODRICK (GUDRICK), Benjamin (b. 1746). Private, 1st Co., Lower Bn., Militia, July 15, 1780 [Ref: M-204]. Took the Oath of Allegiance before the Hon. Charles Jones on Jan. 10, 1778 [Ref: T-3:71, L-1:41]. "Benjamin Gudrick or Goodrick)" lived in North West Hd. in 1776-1777 [Ref: K-1:224, R-31:17].

GOORE, Dorcas. See "Asa Darby," q.v.

GORDON, John. Private, 1st Co., Middle Bn., Militia, Aug. 30, 1777 [Ref: M-195]. Private, Capt. Thomas Beall's Co., Maryland Line, 1780 [Ref: D-351]. See "John Jordan," q.v.

GORDON, Joseph (b. 1753). Lived in North West Hd. in 1776 [Ref: K-1:226]. Took the Oath of Allegiance before the Hon. Gerrard Briscoe on March 2, 1778 [Ref: T-3:56, L-1:41]. Private, 7th Maryland Regiment, from April 20, 1778 until Aug. 16, 1780, when reported missing at the Battle of Camden [Ref: D-211].

GORDON, Thomas. "Thomas Gordon, an Englishman, about 25 years of age, 5 feet 2 inches high, light coloured hair and beard, slender made and a little pitted with the smallpox, recruited by Col. Nathaniel Pigman on May 14, 1781." [Ref: R-33:157, X-1146].

GORMAN, Luticia and Matthew. See "Michael Downs," q.v.

GOTARD, Valentine. Took the Oath of Allegiance in 1778 [Ref: L-2:27].

GOVER, Daniel. Took the Oath of Allegiance in 1778 [Ref: L-2:27].

GRABBER (GRABER, GRAVER), Philip (b. 1749). "Philip Graver" lived in George Town Hd. in 1776 [Ref: K-1:193]. "Philip Grabber" took the Oath of Allegiance before the Hon. Richard Thompson in 1778 [Ref: T-3:75, L-1:41].

GRACE, Jesse. Private, 8th Co., Upper Bn., Militia, Aug. 30, 1777 [Ref: M-195].

GRAFT, George. Private, 1st Co., Upper Bn., Militia, Aug. 30, 1777 [Ref: M-193]. George Graft lived in Sugarland Hd. (two taxables) in 1777 [Ref: R-31:12].

GRAMMER, Jacob. Took the Oath of Allegiance in 1778 [Ref: L-2:27].

GRANT, William. Private, 6th Co., Lower Bn., Militia, Aug., 1777 [Ref: M-200, T-5:49]. Took the Oath of Allegiance before the Hon. Joseph Offutt on March 2, 1778 [Ref: T-3:70, L-1:41].

GRAVER, Philip. See "Philip Grabber (Graber)," q.v.

GRATSINGER, John. Private, Capt. Thomas Beall's Co., Maryland Line, 1780 [Ref: D-351].

GRAVES (GREAVES), Isaac. "Isaac Greaves" was a private, 6th Maryland Line, 1778-1780 [Ref: D-210].

GRAVES, John (b. 1759 or 1760). Private, 4th Co., Lower Bn., Militia, Aug., 1777 [Ref: M-199, T-5:47]. Private, 1st Co., Lower Bn., Militia, July 15, 1780 [Ref: M-204]. Lived in Lower Potomac Hd. in 1776 [Ref: K-1:183].

GRAVES, Mary. See "Elijah Clark," q.v.

GRAVES, Perry or Peregrine (b. 1750). Private, 4th Co., Lower Bn., Militia, Aug., 1777 [Ref: M-199, T-5:47]. Took the Oath of Allegiance before the Hon. Charles Jones on Jan. 10, 1778 [Ref: T-3:71, L-1:41]. Lived in Lower Potomac Hd. in 1776 [Ref: K-1:183].

GRAVES (GREAVES), Thomas (b. 1729). Private, 4th Co., Lower Bn., Militia, Aug., 1777 [Ref: M-199, T-5:47]. "Thomas Graves" lived in Lower Potomac Hd. (three taxables) in 1776-1777 [Ref: R-31:4, K-1:183], and served as a petit juror in Aug., 1777 [Ref: R-31:17]. "Thomas Greaves" took the Oath of Allegiance before the Hon. Charles Jones on Jan. 10, 1778 [Ref: T-3:71, L-1:41].

GRAVES, William. Rendered aid by providing pork for use of the military in 1781 [Ref: O-380].

GRAY, Adin. Private, 7th Co., Middle Bn., Militia, Sep., 1777, and Fourth Corporal, July 15, 1780 [Ref: M-197, M-203, T-5:42]. Took the Oath of Allegiance before the Hon. Edward Burgess on Feb. 28, 1778 [Ref: T-3:63, L-1:41]. Adin Gray lived in Sugar Loaf Hd. (one taxable) in 1777 [Ref: R-31:10].

GRAY, Benjamin. Private, 7th Co., Middle Bn., Militia, Sep., 1777, Ensign, April 21, 1779, Second Lieutenant, March 25, 1780, and First Lieutenant, 7th Co., July 15, 1780 [Ref: M-80, M-197, M-203, T-5:42, A-444, F-120, F-248]. Took the Oath of Allegiance before the Hon. Edward Burgess on Feb. 28, 1778 [Ref: T-3:63, L-1:41]. Rendered aid by providing wheat for use of the military in 1780 [Ref: O-307]. Benjamin Gray lived in Seneca Hd. (one taxable) in 1777 [Ref: R-31:7]. See "Forrest Davis," q.v.

GRAY, Hezekiah. Private, 1st Co., Middle Bn., Militia, Aug. 30, 1777 [Ref: M-195]. Born in Frederick County, Maryland, he married Nancy Ann Fair in Prince George's County, Maryland, on Jan. 2, 1782. Their son Hezekiah was born Aug. 30, 1799, in Forestville, Maryland, married Mary Ann Fowler (died in 1861), and both are buried in Howard County, Maryland [Ref: S-3027].

GRAY, Jeremiah. Private, 7th Co., Middle Bn., Militia, Sep., 1777 [Ref: M-197, T-5:42]. Private, 7th Co., Middle Bn., Militia, July 15, 1780 [Ref: M-203]. Took the Oath of Allegiance before the Hon. Edward Burgess on Feb. 28, 1778 [Ref: T-3:63, L-1:41]. Jeremiah Gray lived in Sugar Loaf Hd. (one taxable) in 1777 [Ref: R-31:10].

GRAY, Mathias. Private, 7th Co., Middle Bn., Militia, July 15, 1780 [Ref: M-203].

GRAY, William. Private, 1st or 32nd Bn., Militia (no date was given; possibly June, 1777). [Ref: T-5:1]. Private, 7th Co., Middle Bn., Militia, Sep., 1777 [Ref: M-197, T-5:42]. Took the Oath of Allegiance before the Hon. Edward Burgess on Feb. 28, 1778 [Ref: T-3:63, L-1:41]. "William Gray" and "William H. Gray" both lived in Seneca Hd. (one taxable each) in 1777 [Ref: R-31:7].

GREAVES, Thomas. See "Thomas Graves (Greaves)," q.v.

GREEN, Allen. See "Richard Green," q.v.

GREEN, Ann, and others. See "Robert Green," q.v.

GREEN, Benedict or Benedick (b. 1742)). "Benedict Green" lived in Sugarland Hd. in 1776-1777 [Ref: K-1:212, R-31:12]. "Benedick Green" took the Oath of Allegiance before the Hon. Aneas Campbell on March 2, 1778 [Ref: T-3:77, L-1:41]. "Benedict Green" served as a petit juror in Nov., 1777 [Ref: R-31:18]. Francis Green died testate in Montgomery County (no wife or children) in 1818 and mentioned his father Benedict Green when he wrote his will in 1814 [Ref: V-57].

GREEN, Bennett. Private, 8th Co., Upper Bn., Militia, Aug. 30, 1777 [Ref: M-195]. Rendered aid by providing wheat for use of the military in 1781 [Ref: O-404, O-435].

GREEN, Clement. Private, 7th Co., Middle Bn., Militia, Sep., 1777, and 4th Sergeant, July 15, 1780 [Ref: M-197, M-203, T-5:42].

GREEN, David. Served as an Ensign, 7th Maryland Line, Jan. 26, 1780, and the Collector of the Tax in Montgomery County was directed to pay him for recruiting services on Feb. 16, 1780 [Ref: D-211, D-341, F-86, which latter source listed him in the 1st Maryland Brigade and 7th Maryland Regiment on the same day, Feb. 16, 1780]. He was the brother of "Robert Green," q.v.

GREEN, Dudley. Private, 8th Co., Lower Bn., Militia, Sep., 1777 [Ref: M-200, T-5:51]. Lived in North West Hd. (one taxable) in 1777 [Ref: R-31:17].

GREEN, Elizabeth, and others. See "Robert Green," q.v.

GREEN, Francis. See "Benedict Green," q.v.

GREEN, Henry. Took the Oath of Allegiance in 1778 [Ref: L-2:27].
GREEN, Ignatius. Private, 7th Co., Middle Bn., Militia, Sep., 1777 [Ref: M-197, T-5:42]. Private, 7th Co., Middle Bn., Militia, July 15, 1780 [Ref: M-203]. Took the Oath of Allegiance before the Hon. Edward Burgess on Feb. 28, 1778 [Ref: T-3:58, L-1:41]. "Ignatious Green" lived in Seneca Hd. (two taxables) in 1777 [Ref: R-31:8].
GREEN, Isaac (b. 1755). Lived in Sugarland Hd. in 1776 [Ref: K-1:210]. Private, 4th Co., Upper Bn., Militia, Aug. 30, 1777 [Ref: M-194]. Took the Oath of Allegiance before the Hon. Aneas Campbell on March 2, 1778 [Ref: T-3:78, L-1:41].
GREEN, John. Private, 7th Co., Middle Bn., Militia, July 15, 1780 [Ref: M-203]. Took the Oath of Allegiance (made his mark) before the Hon. Aneas Campbell on March 2, 1778 [Ref: T-3:78, L-1:41]. "John Green, aged 50" lived in Sugarland Hd. in 1776-1777 [Ref: K-1:210, R-31:12].
GREEN, Joshua. Private, 6th Co., Upper Bn., Militia, Aug. 30, 1777 [Ref: M-194].
GREEN, Leonard. Private, 5th Co., Lower Bn., Militia, Aug., 1777 [Ref: M-199, T-5:48]. Private, 3rd Class, 2nd Co., Middle Bn., Militia, July 15, 1780 [Ref: M-201]. "Lanhart Green" rendered aid by providing wheat for use of the military in 1781 [Ref: O-394]. "Leonard Green" and Anne Brown were married by Bishop John Carroll (Roman Catholic) in Montgomery County on Jan. 29, 1778 [Ref: K-2:514]. Leonard Green lived in the Upper Part of Potomac Hd. (one taxable) in 1777 [Ref: R-31:14].
GREEN, Nacey. Private, 7th Co., Middle Bn., Militia, July 15, 1780 [Ref: M-203].
GREEN, Philip (b. 1754). Private, 1st Co., Upper Bn., Militia, Aug. 30, 1777 [Ref: M-193]. Took the Oath of Allegiance before the Hon. Aneas Campbell on March 2, 1778 [Ref: T-3:77, L-1:41]. Lived in Sugarland Hd. in 1776 and had two taxables in 1777 [Ref: K-1:211, R-31:12].
GREEN, Raphel. Took the Oath of Allegiance before the Hon. Elisha Williams on March 2, 1778 [Ref: T-3:80, L-1:41]. "Reph. Gren" [sic] was a private, 6th Co., Upper Bn., Militia, Aug. 30, 1777 [Ref: M-194]. "Raphel Green" lived in Sugar Loaf Hd. (one taxable) in 1777 [Ref: R-31:10].
GREEN, Richard (1741-1818). Took the Oath of Allegiance before the Hon. Edward Burgess on Feb. 28, 1778 [Ref: T-3:59, L-1:41]. Lived in the Upper Part of Newfoundland Hd. (six taxables) in 1777 [Ref: R-31:6]. Died testate in Montgomery County (wife not named) on July 30, 1818 and mentioned his son Allen Green in Cincinnati, Ohio [Ref: V-57, V-58]. "Sarah Green, wife of Major Richard Green, died on March 21, 1815, aged 77" and they are buried in the Laytonsville District of Montgomery County [Ref: *Historic Graves of Maryland and the District of Columbia*, by Helen W. Ridgely (1908), p. 176].

GREEN, Robert (1755-1833). Served as a Sergeant, 7th Maryland Line, Jan. 8, 1777 to Jan. 4, 1780. Applied for pension in Byrd Township, Cape Girardeau County, Missouri, on Aug. 14, 1832, aged 77, stating he had enlisted in Montgomery County, Maryland, in 1776 or 1777, and with David Green served 3 years in the 7th Maryland Regiment under Capt. Montgomery Bailey [Mountjoy Bayley]. He fought in the battles of Brandywine, Germantown, Monmouth, and Gates' defeat in South Carolina. Benjamin Reeder, of near Staunton, Henrico County, Virginia, declared on March 18, 1839, that he was a brother of Elizabeth Reeder who married Robert Green on March 11, 1781. They moved to Upper Louisiana about 1790 or 1791 while it was still under Spanish dominion and he died in 1833, in what was then Cape Girardeau County, Missouri. Elizabeth Green applied for pension (W10065) from Cape Girardeau County on March 18, 1840, aged 79, as the widow of Robert Green who died on Dec. 16, 1833, and she repeated the declaration made by Benjamin Reeder. On Feb. 21, 1839, David Green, of Jackson, Cape Girardeau County, Missouri, aged 55, declared that he was a son of Robert and Elizabeth Green, and submitted the following family record of their children: Jane (b. April 13, 1782); Lyrein? (David Green?, 1st son, born July 29, 1783); Jane (2nd child with this name, born Feb. 17, 1785); Margaret (b. Dec. --, 1787); Sarah (b. April 24, 1788 [sic]); Richard Robert Reeder (2nd son, born June 6, 1789, and died May 20, 1811); Mary (b. Feb. 15, 1791); Elizabeth (b. May 29, 1793); 7th daughter (died without name, Oct. 18, 1794); Ann (b. Nov. 3, 1795); Elenlu (b. March 12, 1797); Robert (third son, born Sep. 5, 1798); 10th daughter (died without name, April 8, 1800); Ann (2nd daughter with this name, and 11th daughter born, April 5, 1801); Ann (12th daughter, born Dec. 15, 1802); Sarah (b. Dec. 5, 1805); and Lulu (Sula?), born Nov. 24, 1806 [Ref: P-1424, U-35:61]. Robert Green is listed as a sergeant, 7th Maryland Regiment, from Jan. 8, 1777 until Jan. 4, 1780, when discharged; yet, Robert Green and "David Green," q.v., were both listed as ensigns in the 1st Maryland Brigade in Feb., 1780 [Ref: F-86, D-211, D-341].

GREEN, Samuel. Private, 2nd Co., Middle Bn., Militia, Sep. 4, 1777 [Ref: M-195]. Took the Oath of Allegiance before the Hon. Elisha Williams on March 2, 1778 [Ref: T-3:80, L-1:41]. Served as a grand juror in 1781 [Ref: W-2]. Samuel Green lived in Sugar Loaf Hd. (four taxables) in 1777 [Ref: R-31:10].

GREEN, Thomas (died 1823). Private, 8th Co., Upper Bn., Militia, Aug. 30, 1777 [Ref: M-195]. Lived in Sugarland Hd. (two taxables) in 1777 [Ref: R-31:12]. Died testate in Montgomery County (wife named Margaret) in 1823 [Ref: V-58].

GREEN, William. Private, 8th Co., Lower Bn., Militia, July 15, 1780 [Ref: M-207]. Took the Oath of Allegiance (made his mark) before the Hon. Joseph Wilson on Feb. 28, 1778 [Ref: T-3:67, L-1:41].

GREENFIELD, Charles (b. 1760 or 1761). Private, 2nd Co., Lower Bn., Militia, July 15, 1780 [Ref: M-204]. Private, 5th Co., Lower Bn., Militia, Aug., 1777 [Ref: M-199, M-200, T-5:48]. Lived in Lower Potomac Hd. in 1776 [Ref: K-1:183].
GREENFIELD, Eleanor. See "Nicholas Gaither," q.v.
GREENFIELD, Thomas (b. 1762 or 1763). Private, 1st Co., Lower Bn., Militia, July 15, 1780 [Ref: M-204]. Lived in Lower Potomac Hd. in 1776 [Ref: K-1:183].
GREENFIELD, Walter Smith (b. 1731). "Walter Smith Greenfield" took the Oath of Allegiance before the Hon. Samuel W. Magruder in 1778 [Ref: T-3:73, L-1:41], and served as a petit juror in Aug., 1777 [Ref: R-31:17]. "Walter Greenfield" rendered aid by providing wheat for use of the military in 1780 [Ref: O-308]. Lived in Lower Potomac Hd. (five taxables) in 1776-1777 [Ref: R-31:4, K-1:183].
GREENTREE, Benjamin, alias Benjamin Marshall (May 16, 1760 - March 29, 1839). Private, 6th Co., Lower Bn., Militia, July 15, 1780 [Ref: M-206]. Benjamin Greentree applied for pension on Nov. 13, 1818, in Montgomery County, stating he was born on May 16, 1760, at sea on passage from England to America. When an infant he was adopted by a family named Marshall. He was given this name and was enlisted and pensioned as Benjamin Marshall. He enlisted on March 10, 1777, at Bladensburg and served 3 years and 1 month as a private under Capt. Benjamin Stoddard in Col. Thomas Hartley's Regiment, Pennsylvania Troops. He was in the Battle of Brandywine, the battle with the Indians on the North Fork of Susquehannah River, and the Battle of Brunswick, New Jersey. On Feb. 12, 1820, the Treasurer of Maryland was directed to pay Benjamin Greentree, quarterly, the half pay of a private, in Montgomery County. On March 3, 1840, the balance due was paid to Mary Greentree, of Frederick County, widow of Benjamin. Mary Greentree, widow of Benjamin Greentree, alias Marshall, applied for pension (W4020) on March 21, 1843, from Frederick County, Maryland, stating that he had died near New Market, Maryland, on March 29, 1839. She was married to Benjamin by Rev. Stephen B. Balch in Georgetown, Montgomery County, on Oct. 8, 1786. Her maiden name was Mary Cash and she was born on April 15, 1760. Their children were: Eleanor (b. June 22, 1787, married John Wesley Ward on Jan. 13, 1807); Margaret (b. Nov. 5, 1788); James C. (b. Aug. 24, 1790); Elizabeth (b. Aug. 11, 1792); Mary (b. June 4, 1794); John D. (b. Aug. 27, 1796); Ezra (b. Oct. 14, 1798); and, Asa (b. Feb. 7, 1801). On Jan. 26, 1848, any pension balance due to the late Mary Greentree was ordered paid to Elizabeth Beall [Ref: K-2:348, Q-111, U-22:80-81, P-1430, P-2195]. One "Benjamin Greentre" [sic] married Sarah Roberts in Montgomery County on May 19, 1782 [Ref: K-2:515]. It should be noted that a "Benjm. Greetree, aged 14" lived in North West Hd. in 1776 [Ref: K-1:223, which source mistakenly listed the name as "Grootroo"].

GREENWELL, Bennett. Private, 3rd Co., Middle Bn., Militia, Sep., 1777 [Ref: M-196, T-5:38]. Served as an Ensign, Middle Bn., Militia, April 21, 1779, and Second Lieutenant, 2nd Co., Middle Bn., Militia, July 15, 1780 [Ref: M-80, M-201, E-357, F-248]. Took the Oath of Allegiance before the Hon. William Deakins, Jr. before March 3, 1778 [Ref: T-3:68, L-1:41]. Bennett Greenwell lived in the Upper Part of Potomac Hd. (one taxable) in 1777 [Ref: R-31:14, which source listed the name as "Bennet Greewell"].

GREGG (GRAGG), Joshua (b. 1734). Private, 5th Co., Lower Bn., Militia, Aug., 1777 [Ref: M-199, T-5:48]. Rendered aid by providing wheat for use of the military, as well as acting in the roll of a commissary, 1780-1781 [Ref: O-299, O-306, O-307]. Joshua Gregg or Gragg lived in Lower Potomac Hd. (four taxables) in 1776-1777 [Ref: R-31:4, K-1:182].

GRIFFIN, Ann Nancy. See "George Silver," q.v.

GRIFFIN, George. Rendered aid by providing wheat for use of the military in 1781 [Ref: O-394]. George Griffin lived in the Upper Part of Potomac Hd. (one taxable) in 1777 [Ref: R-31:14].

GRIFFIN (GRIFFEN), Matthew. See "William Gibbons," q.v.

GRIFFITH, Alfred. See "Samuel Griffith," q.v.

GRIFFITH, Benjamin. Private, 4th Co., Middle Bn., Militia, Sep., 1777 [Ref: M-196, T-5:39]. Private, 8th Class, 4th Co., Middle Bn., Militia, July 15, 1780 [Ref: M-202]. Took the Oath of Allegiance before the Hon. Edward Burgess on Feb. 28, 1778 [Ref: T-3:59, L-1:41]. Lived in the Upper Part of Newfoundland Hd. (four taxables) in 1777 [Ref: R-31:6].

GRIFFITH, Benjamin, of James. Private, 8th Co., Middle Bn., Militia, Sep., 1777 [Ref: M-198, T-5:43]. Lived in the Upper Part of Newfoundland Hd. (one taxable) in 1777 [Ref: R-31:6].

GRIFFITH, Caleb. Private, 2nd Co., Middle Bn., Militia, Sep. 4, 1777 [Ref: M-196, T-5:37].

GRIFFITH, Charles. Private, 8th Co., Middle Bn., Militia, Sep., 1777 [Ref: M-198, T-5:43]. Lived in Sugar Loaf Hd. (four taxables) in 1777 [Ref: R-31:10].

GRIFFITH, Charles, of Harry. Took the Oath of Allegiance before the Hon. Aneas Campbell on March 2, 1778 [Ref: T-3:77, L-1:41].

GRIFFITH, Charles Greenbury (1744-1792). Son of Orlando Griffith (1688-1757) and Katherine Howard. He married Sarah Ridgely and had a daughter Elizabeth who married "Jeremiah Crabb," q.v. Charles Griffith served in many capacities, including: County Lieutenant of Frederick County, 1777; Committee of Observation; Court Justice of Montgomery County, 1777; Subscription Officer, Continental Loan Office, 1779; Colonel, 16th Bn., Militia, Jan. 6, 1776. County Lieutenant from July 1, 1777 until he resigned Feb. 27, 1781 [Ref: N-377, M-80, A-304, G-334, R-33:155, H-90, which latter source had listed the name as "Charles G. Griffin"]. "Charles G. Griffith" lived in Linganore Hd. (ten taxables) in 1777 [Ref: R-31:9]. "Charles Grey. [sic] Griffith" took the

Oath of Allegiance before the Hon. Joseph Wilson on Feb. 28, 1778 [Ref: T-3:64, L-1:41]. See "Jeremiah Crabb" and "Samuel Griffith," q.v.
GRIFFITH, Chisholm. Took the Oath of Allegiance in 1778 [Ref: L-2:27].
GRIFFITH, Dennis. Served as an Ensign, Lower District, Frederick County (now Montgomery), Militia, Oct. 2, 1776 [Ref: D-42].
GRIFFITH, Elisha. Private, 4th Co., Middle Bn., Militia, Sep., 1777 [Ref: M-196, T-5:39].
GRIFFITH, Elizabeth. See "Jeremiah Crabb" and "Samuel Dyer," q.v.
GRIFFITH, George. Lived in the Upper Part of Potomac Hd. (one taxable) in 1777 [Ref: R-31:14]. Private, 3rd Co., Middle Bn., Militia, Sep., 1777 [Ref: M-196, T-5:38]. Took the Oath of Allegiance before the Hon. Joseph Wilson on Feb. 28, 1778 [Ref: T-3:67, L-1:41].
GRIFFITH, Greenbury or Greenberry (1761-1831). Lived in Linganore Hd. (one taxable) in 1777 [Ref: R-31:9]. Private, 2nd Co., Middle Bn., Militia, Sep. 4, 1777 [Ref: M-196, T-5:37]. Private, 2nd Class, 3rd Co., Middle Bn., Militia, July 15, 1780 [Ref: M-202]. "Died on the Lord's Day last, Greenburg [sic] Griffith, aged 70 years, and 3 days." *Maryland Journal and True American*, Aug. 3, 1831 [Ref: L. Tilden Moore's *Abstracts of Marriages and Deaths in the Newspapers of Frederick and Montgomery Counties, Maryland, 1831-1840*, (1991), p. 333].
GRIFFITH, Henry Jr. Served as First Lieutenant, 8th Co., Middle Bn., Militia, Aug. 28, 1777 [Ref: M-81, M-197, A-346]. Took the Oath of Allegiance before the Hon. Edward Burgess on Feb. 28, 1778 [Ref: T-3:62, L-1:41]. Lived in the Upper Part of Newfoundland Hd. (six taxables) in 1777 [Ref: R-31:6]. See "Henry Griffith, Sr," q.v.
GRIFFITH, Henry Sr. (1720-1794). Born on Feb. 14, 1720, a son of Orlando Griffith and Katherine Howard, and brother of "Charles Greenbury Griffith," q.v. Served as Lieutenant Colonel, Middle Bn., Militia, Sep. 12, 1777 [Ref: M-81, C-373] and held numerous public offices in Frederick County, Anne Arundel County, and Montgomery County before and during the Revolutionary War, including commissioner for the formation of Montgomery County in 1776. Henry married (1) Elizabeth Dorsey and (2) Ruth Hammond and his children were Henry, Samuel, John Hammond, Philemon, Joshua, Sarah, Ruth, Rachel, Ann, Eleanor, Elizabeth, and Ruth [Ref: N-378, which source does not indicate military service during the Revolutionary War, but states he was a captain by 1768]. Also rendered aid by providing wheat for use of the military in 1781 [Ref: O-443]. Lived in the Upper Part of Newfoundland Hd. (17 taxables) in 1777, and owned a working plantation ("quarter") in the Lower Part of Newfoundland Hd. [Ref: R-31:5, R-31:6]. He died testate on Sep. 28, 1794 in Montgomery County and is buried in Laytonsville Cemetery [Ref: V-58, DAR-I:286, S-1993].
GRIFFITH, Hezekiah (1752-1825). Lived in Linganore Hd. (three taxables) in 1777 [Ref: R-31:9]. Private, 2nd Co., Middle Bn., Militia, Aug., 1777, First Lieutenant, Middle Bn., Militia, Sep. 12, 1777, and

Captain, March 25, 1780 [Ref: M-81, M-196, T-5:37, C-373, F-120, F-248]. Took the Oath of Allegiance before the Hon. Joseph Wilson on Feb. 28, 1778 [Ref: T-3:64, L-1:41]. Hezekiah Griffith married Catherine Warfield [Ref: DAR-I:286].

GRIFFITH, Horatio, Israel, and Jefferson. See "Samuel Griffith," q.v.

GRIFFITH, Howard. Private, 2nd Co., Middle Bn., Militia, Sep. 4, 1777 [Ref: M-196, T-5:37]. Private, 1st Class, 3rd Co., Middle Bn., Militia, July 15, 1780 [Ref: M-202].

GRIFFITH, John. (1) Ensign, Middle Bn., Militia, Sep. 12, 1777 [Ref: M-81, C-373, D-42]. (2) Private, 8th Co., Middle Bn., Militia, Sep., 1777 [Ref: M-198, T-5:43]. Private, 3rd Class, 4th Co., Middle Bn., Militia, July 15, 1780 [Ref: M-202].

GRIFFITH, Michael. See "Samuel Griffith," q.v.

GRIFFITH, Orlando. See "Charles Greenbury Griffith," q.v., and "Henry Griffith," q.v.

GRIFFITH, Philemon, of Henry (Aug. 29, 1756 - April 29, 1838). Captain of Rifles at Fort Washington; taken prisoner Nov. 16, 1776; commissioned a major on Dec. 10, 1776. He married Elinor Jacobs and is buried in the Laytonsville Cemetery [Ref: DAR-I:287, and *Historic Graves of Maryland and the District of Columbia*, by Helen W. Ridgely (1908), p. 180].

GRIFFITH, Richard. See "Samuel Griffith" and "Henry Griffith," q.v.

GRIFFITH, Ruth. See "Samuel Griffith" and "Henry Griffith, Sr." and "Samuel Riggs," q.v.

GRIFFITH, Samuel, of Henry (1752-1833). Served as Captain, 3rd Maryland Line, Dec. 10, 1776, and resigned on Aug. 12, 1778 [Ref: D-114]. He pensioned in 1818 in Montgomery County and was dropped in 1820, but restored in 1831 [Ref: J-49]. He had applied for pension on June 3, 1818, in Montgomery County, stating he was born on May 7, 1752, entered the service in June, 1776, and served as Quartermaster for over 5 months in Col. Charles G. Griffith's Maryland Regiment. He also served as Captain from Dec. 5, 1776 to Aug. 12, 1778, under Col. Mordecai Gist. Samuel married Ruth Berry on April 1, 1779. She applied for pension (W4214) on Aug. 14, 1838, aged 76, and stated that Samuel had died on May 12, 1833. Amelia Thomas, widow aged 69, declared on Aug. 8, 1836, that she was a sister of Ruth Griffith, widow of Samuel, and she was present at their wedding. Ruth died on May 23, 1846, leaving these children: Ruth H. Griffith, Sarah Lyon or Logan, Betsy Matthews, Jefferson Griffith, Richard Griffith, Alfred Griffith (b. March 16, 1783), Horatio Griffith, Israel Griffith, Philemon Griffith, and Michael H. Griffith [Ref: P-1442, K-2:348, K-2:349, K-2:518, Q-112, Y-32, Y-33, Y-34, U-23:54]. Samuel Griffith owned a working plantation ("quarter") in the Upper Part of Newfoundland Hd. in 1777 [Ref: R-31:6]. "Capt. Samuel Griffith, of H." is buried in the Laytonsville

Cemetery [Ref: *Historic Graves of Maryland and the District of Columbia*, by Helen W. Ridgely (1908), p. 180].

GRINGUL, George. See "George Gingle (Gringul)," q.v.

GRIST, Jacob. Rendered aid by providing whiskey for use of the military in 1781 [Ref: O-373].

GRIST, Michael. Rendered aid by providing hay for use of the military in 1780 [Ref: O-343].

GROOM (GROOME), James. Private, 7th Co., Middle Bn., Militia, July 15, 1780 [Ref: M-203]. "James Groome" was a private, 7th Co., Middle Bn., Militia, Sep., 1777 [Ref: M-197, T-5:42]. "James Groom" lived in Seneca Hd. (one taxable) in 1777 [Ref: R-31:8].

GROSEMAN (GROSMON), Benedick (Benedict). "Benedick Groseman" was a private, 2nd Co., Middle Bn., Militia, Sep. 4, 1777 [Ref: M-196, T-5:37]. "Benedict Grosmon" lived in Sugar Loaf Hd. (one taxable) in 1777 [Ref: R-31:10].

GROVES, William. Private who was recruited to serve in the Continental Army in 1780 [Ref: D-342].

GUE, Elizabeth. See "George Bowman," q.v.

GUE (GEW), George. Private, 4th Co., Middle Bn., Militia, Sep., 1777 [Ref: M-196, T-5:39]. Private, 1st Class, 4th Co., Middle Bn., Militia, July 15, 1780 [Ref: M-202]. Took the Oath of Allegiance before the Hon. Edward Burgess on Feb. 28, 1778 [Ref: T-3:62, L-1:41].

GUE (GEW), Henry. Private, 4th Co., Middle Bn., Militia, Sep., 1777 [Ref: M-196, T-5:39]. Took the Oath of Allegiance before the Hon. Edward Burgess on Feb. 28, 1778 [Ref: T-3:58, L-1:41]. Henry Gue married Sarah Scribner in Montgomery County on Feb. 23, 1779 [Ref: K-2:518]. Henry Gue lived in the Upper Part of Newfoundland Hd. (two taxables) in 1777 [Ref: R-31:6].

GUE, Hezekiah. Rendered aid by providing wheat for use of the military in 1781 [Ref: O-395].

GUE (GEW), Joseph. Private, 4th Co., Middle Bn., Militia, Sep., 1777 [Ref: M-196, T-5:39]. Private, 3rd Class, 4th Co., Middle Bn., Militia, July 15, 1780 [Ref: M-202]. Took the Oath of Allegiance (made his "I" mark) before the Hon. Edward Burgess on Feb. 28, 1778 [Ref: T-3:59, L-1:41].

GUTHRIE, Laurence B. See "James Veatch," q.v.

HADEEN, Robert J. See "Kid Marquess," q.v.

HADLEY, James. Private, 2nd Class, 2nd Co., Middle Bn., Militia, July 15, 1780 [Ref: M-201]. Took the Oath of Allegiance before the Hon. Joseph Wilson on Feb. 28, 1778 [Ref: T-3:66, L-1:41].

HADON, William. Took the Oath of Allegiance in 1778 [Ref: L-2:27].

HAGAN, Alexander Jr. Took the Oath of Allegiance in 1778 [Ref: L-2:27].

HAGAN, Alexander Sr. Took the Oath of Allegiance in 1778 [Ref: L-2:27].

HAGAN (HAGIN), Bennett. Took the Oath of Allegiance before the Hon. Edward Burgess on Feb. 28, 1778 [Ref: T-3:63, L-1:41]. Private, 2nd Co.,

Upper Bn., Militia, Aug. 30, 1777 [Ref: M-193]. "Bennett Hagin" lived in Sugar Loaf Hd. (two taxables) in 1777 [Ref: R-31:10].

HAGAN, Leonard. Private, 2nd Co., Upper Bn., Militia, Aug. 30, 1777 [Ref: M-193]. Took the Oath of Allegiance before the Hon. Elisha Williams on March 2, 1778 [Ref: T-3:81, L-1:41]. Private, 7th Maryland Regiment, Continental Army, from Jan. 1, 1780 to Oct. 1, 1780 [Ref: D-217, D-341, F-86].

HAGAN, Michael. Took the Oath of Allegiance (made his "X" mark) before the Hon. Aneas Campbell on March 2, 1778 [Ref: T-3:78, L-1:41].

HAGAN, Walter. Private who was recruited to serve in the Continental Army in 1780 [Ref: D-341].

HAGARTY (HAGARTHY, HEAGERTY), James. "James Heagerty" took the Oath of Allegiance before the Hon. Aneas Campbell on March 2, 1778 [Ref: T-3:77, L-1:41]. "James Hagarthy" lived in Sugarland Hd. (one taxable) in 1777 [Ref: R-31:12].

HAGMAN, George. Took the Oath of Allegiance in 1778 [Ref: L-2:27].

HAISLIP, James. Private, 6th Co., Lower Bn., Militia, Aug., 1777 [Ref: M-200, T-5:49]. Served as a grand juror in Nov., 1777 [Ref: R-31:18]. Took the Oath of Allegiance before the Hon. Joseph Offutt on March 2, 1778 [Ref: T-3:70, L-1:41]. James Haislip lived in the Upper Part of Potomac Hd. (one taxable) in 1777 [Ref: R-31:14].

HALFPENNY, Thomas. Private, 6th Co., Upper Bn., Militia, Aug. 30, 1777 [Ref: M-194]. "Thomas Halfpenny" took the Oath of Allegiance in 1778 [Ref: L-2:27]. "Thomas Harfpenny" lived in Sugar Loaf Hd. (one taxable) in 1777 [Ref: R-31:10].

HALL, Alexander. Took the Oath of Allegiance before the Hon. Elisha Williams on March 2, 1778 [Ref: T-3:80, L-1:41].

HALL, Andrew Jr. Took the Oath of Allegiance in 1778 [Ref: L-2:27].

HALL, Ann. See "Thomas Wood," q.v.

HALL, Joseph. (Doctor). Private, 2nd Co., Lower Bn., Militia, Sep., 1777 [Ref: M-199, T-5:45]. Private, 6th Co., Middle Bn., Militia, July 15, 1780 [Ref: M-203]. Private, 6th Co., Middle Bn., Militia, Aug., 1777 [Ref: M-197, T-5:41]. Surgeon, 29th Bn., Militia, Sep. 4, 1777 [Ref: M-82, C-362]. Took the Oath of Allegiance before the Hon. Edward Burgess on Jan. 29, 1778 [Ref: T-3:58, L-1:41]. Joseph Hall lived in Linganore Hd. (two taxables) in 1777 [Ref: R-31:9].

HALL, Josias Carvil. See "John Ford," q.v.

HALL, Richard (b. 1758). Lived in Sugarland Hd. in 1776 [Ref: K-1:210]. Private, 3rd Maryland Line, 1778-1780 [Ref: D-121].

HALL, William. Private, 8th Co., Lower Bn., Militia, Sep., 1777 [Ref: M-200, T-5:51]. Private, 1st Class, 2nd Co., Middle Bn., Militia, July 15, 1780 [Ref: M-201].

HAM, George. Private, 4th Co., Middle Bn., Militia, Sep., 1777 [Ref: M-196, T-5:39]. Private, 4th Class, 4th Co., Middle Bn., Militia, July 15,

1780 [Ref: M-202]. Took the Oath of Allegiance before the Hon. Edward Burgess on Feb. 28, 1778 [Ref: T-3:62, L-1:41].

HAMILTON, David. Took the Oath of Allegiance before the Hon. Joseph Offutt on March 2, 1778 [Ref: T-3:70, L-1:41]. David Hamilton lived in the Upper Part of Potomac Hd. (one taxable) in 1777 [Ref: R-31:14].

HAMILTON, George. Served as a Corporal, Capt. Price's Co., 3rd Maryland Line, 1781-1782 [Ref: D-452].

HAMILTON, John. Took the Oath of Allegiance in 1778 [Ref: L-2:27].

HAMILTON, Rachel. See "Francis Gartrell," q.v.

HAMILTON, Richard. Rendered aid by providing corn for use of the military in 1781 [Ref: O-351].

HAMMOND, Charles, of Charles. Private, 1st or 32nd Bn., Militia (no date was given; possibly June, 1777). [Ref: T-5:1].

HAMMOND, Ruth. See "Henry Griffith," q.v.

HAMOTT, James. Took the Oath of Allegiance in 1778 [Ref: L-2:27].

HAMPTON, Mary and Wade. See "William Bailey," q.v.

HANCE, Kinsey (b. 1752). Private, Capt. Edward Burgess' Co., Lower District of Frederick (now Montgomery) County, Militia, July, 1776 [Ref: D-42, which listed the name as "Hanee"]. Lived in Lower Potomac Hd. in 1776 [Ref: K-1:183].

HANCOCK, Stephen. "An Englishman born, 21 years of age, about 5 feet 7 or 8 inches high, brown hair, fair complexion, grey eyes, and has his little finger off the left hand, recruited by Thomas Nicholls on Feb. 9, 1781." [Ref: R-33:155, X-1146].

HANNON, John. Served as a Fifer in Capt. Price's Co., 3rd Maryland Line, 1781-1782 [Ref: D-452].

HANSKINS (HAUSKINS), George. Served as an Ensign, 1st Co., 16th Bn., Militia, Aug. 30, 1777 [Ref: M-83, M-193, C-350].

HARBIN, Elias (died 1801). Son of James and Eleanor Harbin [Ref: V-59]. Private, 8th Co., Upper Bn., Militia, Aug. 30, 1777 [Ref: M-195]. Died testate in Montgomery County (wife named Dorcas) in 1801 [Ref: V-58].

HARBIN, Gerrard. Son of James and Eleanor Harbin [Ref: V-59]. Rendered aid by providing corn for use of the military in 1780 [Ref: O-287].

HARBIN, James (1726-1778). Lived in Sugarland Hd. in 1776 [Ref: K-1:203]. Served as a grand juror in Aug., 1777 [Ref: R-31:17]. Died testate in Montgomery County (wife named Eleanor) in 1778 [Ref: V-58, V-59]. Another James Harbin (possibly a son of the aforementioned James Harbin, although not named in his will) was a private, 8th Co., Upper Bn., Militia, Aug. 30, 1777, and a private, 7th Class, 2nd Co., Middle Bn., Militia, July 15, 1780 [Ref: M-195, M-201]. Rendered aid by providing corn for use of the military in 1780 [Ref: O-297].

HARBIN (HARVIN), Joshua. Private, Flying Camp, enlisted July 25, 1776 [Ref: D-49]. Private, 1st Co., Upper Bn., Militia, Aug. 30, 1777 [Ref: M-

193]. Served as a petit juror in Aug., 1777 [Ref: R-31:17]. One Joshua Harbin took the Oath of Allegiance before the Hon. Joseph Wilson on Feb. 28, 1778 [Ref: T-3:66, L-1:41], and another one took the Oath of Allegiance before the Hon. Elisha Williams on March 2, 1778 [Ref: T-3:81, L-1:41]. One rendered aid by providing corn for use of the military in 1780 [Ref: O-283, O-286]. One "Joshua Harbin" married Ruth Hoskinson in Montgomery County on July 23, 1778 [Ref: K-2:518]. One "Joshua Harvin" [sic] lived in Sugar Loaf Hd. (one taxable) in 1777 [Ref: R-31:10], and another "Joshua Harvin" lived in the Upper Part of Potomac Hd. (five taxables) in 1777 [Ref: R-31:14]. One "Joshua Harbin, aged 21" was a son of "James Harbin," q.v., of Sugarland Hd. in 1776 [Ref: K-1:203, V-59].

HARDESTY (HARDISTY), George. Private, 2nd Co., Upper Bn., Militia, Aug. 30, 1777 [Ref: M-193]. Private, 5th Co., Middle Bn., Militia, July 15, 1780 [Ref: M-203]. George Hardesty lived in Sugar Loaf Hd. (one taxable) in 1777 [Ref: R-31:10].

HARDESTY (HARDISTY, HARDAYSTAY), Samuel. Private, 1st Co., Middle Bn., Militia, Aug. 30, 1777 [Ref: M-195]. Took the Oath of Allegiance before the Hon. Gerrard Briscoe on March 2, 1778 [Ref: T-3:57, L-1:41]. Served as a grand juror in 1779 [Ref: W-1]. "Samuel Hardaystay" rendered aid by providing wheat for use of the military in 1781 [Ref: O-399, O-401]. "Samuel Hardesty" lived in Seneca Hd. (five taxables) in 1777 [Ref: R-31:8].

HARDING (HARDEN), Basil. Private, 2nd Co., Lower Bn., Militia, Sep., 1777, and Third Corporal, 5th Co., Lower Bn., July 15, 1780 [Ref: M-198, M-204, T-5:45]. Took the Oath of Allegiance before the Hon. Edward Burgess on Feb. 28, 1778 [Ref: T-3:60, L-1:41].

HARDING, Charles. Took the Oath of Allegiance before the Hon. Edward Burgess on Feb. 28, 1778 [Ref: T-3:60, L-1:41]. Lived in Rock Creek Hd. (four taxables) in 1777 [Ref: R-31:16]. One Charles Harding died testate in Montgomery County (wife named Eleanor) in 1792 and mentioned a son Charles, among others, in his will [Ref: V-59].

HARDING, Clement. Son of "Charles Harding," q.v. [Ref: V-59]. Took the Oath of Allegiance before the Hon. Joseph Wilson on Feb. 28, 1778 [Ref: T-3:64, L-1:41].

HARDING (HARDEN), Edward. Private, Capt. Edward Burgess' Co., Lower District of Frederick (now Montgomery) County, Militia, July, 1776 [Ref: D-42]. Private, 5th Co., Lower Bn., Militia, July 15, 1780 [Ref: M-206]. Private, 2nd Co., Lower Bn., Militia, Sep., 1777 [Ref: M-198, T-5:45]. Took the Oath of Allegiance before the Hon. Edward Burgess on Feb. 28, 1778 [Ref: T-3:60, L-1:41]. Rendered aid by providing wheat for use of the military in 1780 [Ref: O-310]. Served as a grand juror in 1779 and 1781 [Ref: W-1, W-2]. Lived in Rock Creek Hd. (one taxable) in 1777 [Ref: R-31:16]. Edward Harding married Ann Butler in Montgomery County on May 12, 1778 [Ref: K-2:518].

HARDING (HARDEN), Elias (1727-1799). Served as a Captain, 2nd Co., 29th Bn., Militia, from May 14, 1776, to at least Aug. 11, 1779 [Ref: M-84, M-198, T-5:45, A-424, C-373]. Served as a grand juror in Nov., 1777 [Ref: R-31:17]. Took the Oath of Allegiance before the Hon. Edward Burgess on Feb. 28, 1778 [Ref: T-3:60, L-1:41]. Rendered aid by providing wheat for use of the military in 1780 [Ref: O-305]. Lived in Rock Creek Hd. (six taxables) in 1777 [Ref: R-31:16]. Died testate in Montgomery County (wife named Elizabeth Beall) and his will was probated in 1800, naming children and grandchildren, including a grandson Elias [Ref: V-59, DAR-I:303].

HARDING, Elias Jr. Private, 2nd Co., Lower Bn., Militia, Sep., 1777 [Ref: M-199, T-5:45].

HARDING, Elizabeth. See "Erasmus Perry," q.v.

HARDING, Henry. See "Joseph Clewley" and "James Fling" and "James White," q.v.

HARDING (HARDEN), John. Son of Charles and Eleanor Harding [Ref: V-59]. Private, Capt. Edward Burgess' Co., Lower District of Frederick (now Montgomery) County, Militia, July, 1776 [Ref: D-42]. Private, 2nd Co., Lower Bn., Militia, Sep., 1777 [Ref: M-198, T-5:45]. Took the Oath of Allegiance before the Hon. Edward Burgess on Feb. 28, 1778 [Ref: T-3:60, L-1:41]. Private, 6th Co., Middle Bn., Militia, July 15, 1780 [Ref: M-203].

HARDING (HARDEN), Josiah. Son of Elias and Elizabeth Harding [Ref: V-59]. Private, Capt. Edward Burgess' Co., Lower District of Frederick (now Montgomery) County, Militia, July, 1776 [Ref: D-42]. Private, 2nd Co., Lower Bn., Militia, Sep., 1777 [Ref: M-199, T-5:45]. Took the Oath of Allegiance before the Hon. Edward Burgess on Feb. 28, 1778 [Ref: T-3:60, L-1:41].

HARDING, Vachel (1762-1837). Son of Charles and Eleanor Harding [Ref: V-59]. Private, 5th Co., Lower Bn., Militia, July 15, 1780 [Ref: M-206]. Applied for a pension in Jefferson County, Kentucky, on April 5, 1834, aged 76, stating he was born in 1762 and lived in Montgomery County, Maryland when he enlisted in March, 1778, and was stationed at Georgetown. On July 9, 1850, Mary Harding, widow of Vachel Harding, applied for pension (W1601) at Louisville, Kentucky, aged 68, stating that her maiden name was Mary Parker and she was married to Vachel Harding on March 18, 1798, in Frederick County, Maryland, by a Presbyterian minister. Vachel died on May 11, 1837, in Jefferson County, Kentucky. Their children were mentioned, but none were named. Sarah Hurley, an acquaintance in Jefferson County, aged 64, stated on July 20, 1850, that she was present at their wedding in Frederick County, Maryland in 1798. James Day, of Montgomery County, Maryland, in 1834, aged 71, stated that he had served in the war with Vachel Harding [Ref: P-1517, Y-14, Z-51].

HARDING (HARDEN), Walter (1754-1782). Lived in Sugarland Hd. in 1776 and had three taxables in 1777 [Ref: K-1:212, R-31:12]. Private, 1st Co., Upper Bn., Militia, Aug. 30, 1777, and Ensign, April 21, 1779, and Second Lieutenant, March 25, 1780 [Ref: M-84, M-193, E-256, F-120]. Served as a petit juror in Aug., 1777 [Ref: R-31:17]. Took the Oath of Allegiance before the Hon. Elisha Williams on March 2, 1778 [Ref: T-3:81, L-1:41]. Rendered aid by providing corn for use of the military in 1780 [Ref: O-288]. Died testate in Montgomery County (wife named Mary) in 1782 [Ref: V-59].

HARDING (HARDIN), William. Two men with this name were privates in the 2nd Co., Lower Bn., Militia, Sep., 1777 [Ref: M-198, M-199, T-5:45]. One took the Oath of Allegiance before the Hon. Edward Burgess on Feb. 28, 1778 [Ref: T-3:60, L-1:41]. One "William Hardin" lived in the Upper Part of Potomac Hd. (two taxables) in 1777 [Ref: R-31:14]. One "William Harding" was a son of "Charles Harding," q.v., who died in 1792 [Ref: V-59].

HARDMAN, Henry. Served as a Captain, 7th Maryland Line, Dec. 10, 1776, and Major, June 1, 1779. Took the Oath of Allegiance in 1778 [Ref: D-217, L-2:27].

HARDY, Ann. See "Greenbury Riggs," q.v.

HARDY, Baptist. Rendered aid by providing wheat for use of the military in 1780 [Ref: O-314].

HARDY, Eleanor. See "Leonard Hays," q.v.

HARDY, Elias (b. 1761). Private, 3rd Maryland Line, Smallwood's Regiment, from April 25, 1778 to April 25, 1781, when discharged [Ref: D-121, D-359]. Son of Fielder Hardy whose family lived in Sugarland Hd. in 1776 [Ref: K-1:212].

HARDY, Fielder. See "Elias Hardy" and "Kinsey Hardy," q.v.

HARDY, George (b. 1761). Private, 1st Co., Upper Bn., Militia, Aug. 30, 1777 [Ref: M-193]. Private, 1st Maryland Line, discharged April 17, 1779 [Ref: E-351]. Lived in Sugarland Hd. in 1776 [Ref: K-1:220].

HARDY, John (b. 1730). Private, 7th Co., Upper Bn., Militia, Aug. 30, 1777 [Ref: M-194]. Took the Oath of Allegiance before the Hon. Elisha Williams on March 2, 1778 [Ref: T-3:80, L-1:41]. Lived in Sugarland Hd. in 1776 and had three taxables in 1777 [Ref: K-1:220, R-31:12].

HARDY, Kinsey or Kenzey (b. 1761 or 1762). Son of Fielder Hardy whose family lived in Sugarland Hd. in 1776 [Ref: K-1:212]. Served as a substitute from Montgomery County and was discharged from the Maryland line on Dec. 3, 1781 [Ref: I-11, D-408].

HARDY, Mary Gore. See "Hazel Williams," q.v.

HARDY, Sarah. See "Lawrence Owen," q.v.

HARDY, William. Took the Oath of Allegiance in 1778 [Ref: L-2:27].

HARDY, Zadock (b. 1739). Private, 8th Co., Upper Bn., Militia, Aug. 30, 1777 [Ref: M-195]. Took the Oath of Allegiance before the Hon. Elisha Williams on March 2, 1778 [Ref: T-3:81, L-1:41]. Zadock Hardy or

Hardey lived in Sugarland Hd. (one taxable) in 1776-1777 [Ref: K-1:205, R-31:12].

HARLIN, James. Took the Oath of Allegiance in 1778 [Ref: L-2:27].

HARLYNTIS, Naly. Rendered aid by providing wheat for use of the military in 1781 [Ref: O-396].

HARNICKER, Isaac. Took the Oath of Allegiance in 1778 [Ref: L-2:27].

HARP, Josiah (b. 1762). Private, 3rd Co., Lower Bn., Militia, July 15, 1780 [Ref: M-205]. Lived in Lower Potomac Hd. in 1776 [Ref: K-1:183]

HARP, Philip (b. 1755). Private, 6th Co., Lower Bn., Militia, Aug., 1777 [Ref: M-200, T-5:49]. Private, 3rd Co., Lower Bn., Militia, July 15, 1780 [Ref: M-205]. Lived in the Upper Part of Potomac Hd. (one taxable) in 1776-1777 [Ref: R-31:14, K-1:183].

HARP, William. Private, 6th Co., Lower Bn., Militia, Aug., 1777 [Ref: T-5:49 and M-200, which latter source questions if the name could be "Will: Hays?"]. Took the Oath of Allegiance before the Hon. Joseph Offutt on March 2, 1778 [Ref: T-3:70, L-1:41]. Private, 4th Class, 2nd Co., Middle Bn., Militia, July 15, 1780 [Ref: M-201]. William Harp (b. 1729) and William Harp (b. 1759) lived together in Lower Potomac Hd. in 1776-1777 [Ref: R-31:4, K-1:183], and another lived in the Upper Part of Potomac Hd. (one taxable) in 1777 [Ref: R-31:14].

HARPER, Francis. Private, 3rd Class, 2nd Co., Middle Bn., Militia, July 15, 1780 [Ref: M-201]. Took the Oath of Allegiance before the Hon. William Deakins, Jr. before March 3, 1778 [Ref: T-3:68, L-1:41]. Francis Harper lived in Seneca Hd. (two taxables) in 1777 [Ref: R-31:8].

HARPER, Francis Jr. Took the Oath of Allegiance before the Hon. William Deakins, Jr. before March 3, 1778 [Ref: T-3:68, L-1:41]. Private, 3rd Co., Middle Bn., Militia, Sep., 1777 [Ref: M-196, T-5:38].

HARPER, Mary. See "Thomas Malone," q.v.

HARPER, William. Private, 8th Class, 2nd Co., Middle Bn., Militia, July 15, 1780 [Ref: M-201].

HARRARD, John. Served as a petit juror in Nov., 1777 [Ref: R-31:18].

HARRIS, Aaron. Served as First Lieutenant, 29th Bn., Militia, Sep. 12, 1777, and Captain, 6th Co., Lower Bn., Militia, July 15, 1780 [Ref: M-84, M-200, M-206, T-5:51, C-373, F-248]. Served as a petit juror in Nov., 1777 [Ref: R-31:18]. Took the Oath of Allegiance before the Hon. Charles Jones on Jan. 10, 1778 [Ref: T-3:71, L-1:41]. Lived in North West Hd. (wife named Mary) in 1776 and had seven taxables in 1777 [Ref: K-1:230, R-31:17]. Captain Aaron Harris recruited Richard Dixon in April, 1781 [Ref: R-33:156, X-1146], and served as a constable in 1780-1781 [Ref: W-2]. See "Richard Dixon" and "Daniel Campbell," q.v.

HARRIS, Barton. Son of Joseph Harris [Ref: V-61]. "Barton B. Harris" took the Oath of Allegiance before the Hon. Samuel W. Magruder in 1778 [Ref: T-3:73]. "Barton Harris" died testate in Montgomery County (wife Elizabeth) in 1825 and he had a son Barton, among other children [Ref: V-60].

HARRIS (HARRISS), Benjamin (b. 1742). Took the Oath of Allegiance before the Hon. Samuel W. Magruder in 1778 [Ref: T-3:73]. "Benjamin Harriss" lived in Lower Potomac Hd. (four taxables) in 1776-1777 [Ref: R-31:4, K-1:183]. "Benjamin Harris, Jr." served as a grand juror in Aug., 1777 [Ref: R-31:17].

HARRIS, Eleanor. See "Levi Hays," q.v.

HARRIS, Ezekiel (b. 1740). Private who enrolled into a company of militia for the service of the Flying Camp on Oct. 15, 1776 [Ref: B-353]. "Ezekel Harres, aged 36" lived in North West Hd. in 1776 [Ref: K-1:227].

HARRIS, George (b. 1749). Private, 4th Co., Lower Bn., Militia, Aug., 1777 [Ref: M-199, T-5:47]. Private, 1st Co., Lower Bn., Militia, July 15, 1780 [Ref: M-204]. Took the Oath of Allegiance before the Hon. Samuel W. Magruder in 1778 [Ref: T-3:73]. Lived in Lower Potomac Hd. in 1776 [Ref: K-1:183].

HARRIS, Henrietta. See "Lawson Beall," q.v.

HARRIS, James (b. 1758). Lived in Sugarland Hd. in 1776 [Ref: K-1:221]. Private, 2nd Maryland Regiment, 1780-1781 [Ref: D-120, D-357].

HARRIS, Jesse. Son of Joseph Harris [Ref: V-61]. Served as a private when he enrolled into a company of militia for the service of the Flying Camp, Oct. 15, 1776 [Ref: B-352]. Private, 6th Co., Upper Bn., Militia, Aug. 30, 1777 [Ref: M-194]. Took the Oath of Allegiance before the Hon. Elisha Williams on March 2, 1778 [Ref: T-3:80, L-1:41].

HARRIS (HARRISS), John. Served as a private when enrolled into a company of militia for the service of the Flying Camp on Oct. 15, 1776 [Ref: B-353], and Ensign, 6th Co., 16th Bn., Militia, by Sep. 12, 1777, and Second Lieutenant, Upper Bn., April 21, 1779 [Ref: M-84, M-194, C-373, E-256]. Took the Oath of Allegiance before the Hon. Elisha Williams on March 2, 1778 [Ref: T-3:80, L-1:41]. John Harris married Darcus Weyman in Montgomery County on Feb. 18, 1781 [Ref: K-2:518]. "John Haris" [sic], aged 23, lived in Sugarland Hd. in 1776 and "John Harriss" lived in Sugar Loaf Hd. (one taxable) in 1777 [Ref: R-31:10].

HARRIS (HARRISS), Joseph. Took the Oath of Allegiance before the Hon. Elisha Williams on March 2, 1778 [Ref: T-3:80, L-1:41]. "Joseph Harriss" lived in Sugar Loaf Hd. (five taxables) in 1777 [Ref: R-31:10]. "Joseph Harriss" died testate in Montgomery County (wife not named) in 1797 and mentioned a son Joseph, among others [Ref: V-60, V-61].

HARRIS, Kinsey. Private, 7th Co., Middle Bn., Militia, July 15, 1780 [Ref: M-203].

HARRIS, Mary. See "William Waters," q.v.

HARRIS (HARRISS), Nathan. Private, 6th Co., Upper Bn., Militia, Aug. 30, 1777 [Ref: M-194]. Private, 8th Class, 1st Co., Middle Bn., Militia, July 15, 1780 [Ref: M-201]. Three men with this name took the Oath of Allegiance: one before the Hon. Joseph Wilson on Feb. 28, 1778 [Ref: T-3:66, L-1:41], one before the Hon. Elisha Williams on March 2, 1778

[Ref: T-3:80, L-1:41], and one before the Hon. Samuel W. Magruder in 1778 [Ref: T-3:73, L-1:41]. One "Nathan Harriss" lived in Sugar Loaf Hd. (one taxable) in 1777 [Ref: R-31:10], and another "Nathan Harris" lived in the Upper Part of Potomac Hd. (two taxables) in 1777 [Ref: R-31:14]. "Joseph Harriss" died testate in 1797 and mentioned a son Nathan, among others [Ref: V-6), V-61].

HARRIS (HARRISS), Nathaniel. Private, 1st Co., Middle Bn., Militia, Aug. 30, 1777 [Ref: M-195]. Took the Oath of Allegiance before the Hon. Gerrard Briscoe on March 2, 1778 [Ref: T-3:57, L-1:41]. "Nathaniel Harriss" lived in Seneca Hd. (four taxables) in 1777 [Ref: R-31:8].

HARRIS, Norris. Private, 6th Co., Upper Bn., Militia, Aug. 30, 1777 [Ref: M-194]. Took the Oath of Allegiance before the Hon. Elisha Williams on March 2, 1778 [Ref: T-3:80, L-1:41].

HARRIS, Samuel (died 1826). Matross in the Continental Army who was pensioned in Montgomery County in 1810 and died on Sep. 19, 1826 [Ref: J-16, K-2:351].

HARRIS, William. Private, 3rd Co., Lower Bn., Militia, July 15, 1780 [Ref: M-205].

HARRIS, Zadock (b. 1750). Served as a Second Lieutenant, 29th Bn., Militia, Sep. 12, 1777, and First Lieutenant, 6th Co., Lower Bn., July 15, 1780 [Ref: M-85, M-200, T-5:51, C-373, F-248]. Took the Oath of Allegiance before the Hon. Charles Jones on Jan. 10, 1778 [Ref: T-3:71, L-1:41]. Rendered aid by providing wheat for use of the military in 1780 and 1781 [Ref: O-303, O-312, O-449, O-453]. Lived in North West Hd. in 1776 (wife named Sarah) and had two taxables in 1777 [Ref: K-1:229, R-31:17].

HARRIS (HARRISS), Zephaniah. Private, 5th Co., Upper Bn., Militia, Aug. 30, 1777 [Ref: M-194]. Took the Oath of Allegiance on Sep. 1, 1780, under the Act of May 12, 1780, having neglected to do so previously "due to ignorance of the duty owed the country." [Ref: R-27:112]. Rendered aid by providing wheat for use of the military in 1781 [Ref: O-445]. "Zepheniah Harriss" lived in Sugar Loaf Hd. (one taxable) in 1777 [Ref: R-31:10].

HARRISON, Benjamin. Served as a Fifer, Maryland Line (no exact dates were given, but the listing indicated he served between Aug. 1, 1780 and Nov. 15, 1783). [Ref: D-541]. Lived in Seneca Hd. (one taxable) in 1777 [Ref: R-31:8].

HARRISON, Elisha. Private, 6th Co., Lower Bn., Militia, Aug., 1777 [Ref: M-200, T-5:49]. Lived in the Upper Part of Potomac Hd. (one taxable) in 1777 [Ref: R-31:14].

HARRISON, Greenbury or Greenberry. Son of Josias Harrison [Ref: V-60]. Private, 6th Co., Middle Bn., Militia, Aug., 1777, and private, 6th Co., Middle Bn., Militia, July 15, 1780 [Ref: M-197, M-203, T-5:41]. "Greenbury Harrison" took the Oath of Allegiance on Sep. 1, 1780, under the Act of May 12, 1780, having neglected to do so previously

"due to ignorance of the duty owed the country." [Ref: R-27:112].
"Greenberry Harrison" lived in Linganore Hd. (one taxable) in 1777 [Ref: R-31:10].

HARRISON, James. Took the Oath of Allegiance before the Hon. Charles Jones on Jan. 10, 1778 [Ref: T-3:71, L-1:41].

HARRISON, John. Took the Oath of Allegiance in 1778 [Ref: L-2:27].

HARRISON, Joshua. Son of Josias Harrison [Ref: V-60]. Private, 6th Co., Middle Bn., Militia, Aug., 1777 [Ref: M-197, T-5:41]. Took the Oath of Allegiance on Sep. 1, 1780, under the Act of May 12, 1780, having neglected to do so previously "due to ignorance of the duty owed the country." [Ref: R-27:112].

HARRISON, Josias or Josiah (died 1803). "Josias Harrison" rendered aid by providing wheat for use of the military in 1781 [Ref: O-379]. "Josiah Harrison" lived in Linganore Hd. (two taxables) in 1777 [Ref: R-31:9]. "Josias Harrison" died testate in Montgomery County (wife named Elizabeth) in 1803 [Ref: V-60]. Also see "Nathan Harrison," q.v.

HARRISON, Moses. Private, 1st Class, 5th Co., Middle Bn., Militia, July 15, 1780 [Ref: M-202].

HARRISON, Nathan. Private, 6th Co., Middle Bn., Militia, Aug., 1777 [Ref: M-197, T-5:41]. Private, 6th Co., Middle Bn., Militia, July 15, 1780 [Ref: M-203]. Took the Oath of Allegiance on Sep. 1, 1780, under the Act of May 12, 1780, having neglected to do so previously "due to ignorance of the duty owed the country." [Ref: R-27:112]. Nathan Harrison lived in Linganore Hd. (one taxable) in 1777 [Ref: R-31:9]. He married Verlinda Browning in Montgomery County on Nov. 3, 1779 [Ref: K-2:515]. "Josias Harrison," q.v., wrote his will in 1803 and mentioned his children, including a son Nathan, deceased [Ref: V-60].

HARRISON, Shadrack. Private, 1st Class, 5th Co., Middle Bn., Militia, July 15, 1780 [Ref: M-202].

HARRY, Allan. Private, 6th Co., Middle Bn., Militia, July 15, 1780 [Ref: M-203]. Also see "Allen Harvey (Harway)," q.v.

HARRY, Charles. Private, 6th Co., Middle Bn., Militia, July 15, 1780 [Ref: M-203]. Also see "Charles Harvey (Harway)," q.v.

HARRY (HURRY), David. "David Harry" was a private, 5th Co., Middle Bn., Militia, Sep., 1777 [Ref: M-197, T-5:40]. "David Hurry" was a private, 8th Co., Lower Bn., Militia, July 15, 1780 [Ref: M-207].

HARRY, John O. See "George Beckwith," q.v.

HARRY, Richard (c1758-1828). Private, 6th Class, 1st Co., Middle Bn., Militia, July 15, 1780 [Ref: M-201]. Rendered aid by providing wheat for use of the military in 1780 [Ref: O-317]. "Richard Harvy or Harry" was a substitute who was discharged from the Maryland Line on Dec. 3, 1781 [Ref: I-11, D-408]. He died in Montgomery County in Sep., 1828, aged about 70 [Ref: F. Edward Wright's *Marriages and Deaths in the Newspapers of Frederick and Montgomery Counties, Maryland*, p. 79].

HARRY, William. Private, 6th Co., Middle Bn., Militia, July 15, 1780 [Ref: M-203]. Also see "William Harvey (Harway)," q.v.

HART, Christopher. Took the Oath of Allegiance in 1778 [Ref: L-2:27].

HART, William. Private, Capt. Thomas Beall's Co., Maryland Line, 1780 [Ref: D-350].

HARTLEY (HORTLEY), John (b. 1747). "John Hartley" was a private, 5th Maryland Regiment, 1778 [Ref: D-213]. "John Hortley" lived in Sugarland Hd. in 1776 [Ref: K-1:206].

HARTMAN, William. "William Hartman, an Englishman, about 20 years of age, 5 feet 8 or 9 inches high, fair complexion and pitted with the smallpox, recruited by Col. William Deakins [in Montgomery County] on April 26, 1781, and sent to Annapolis under the care of Lt. William Murdock on April 29, 1781." [Ref: R-33:156, R-33:157, X-1146].

HARVEY (HARWAY), Allen. "Allen Harvey" was a private, 6th Co., Middle Bn., Militia, Aug., 1777 [Ref: M-197, T-5:41]. "Allen Harway" lived in Linganore Hd. (one taxable) in 1777 [Ref: R-31:9].

HARVEY (HARWAY), Charles. "Charles Harvey" took the Oath of Allegiance on Sep. 1, 1780, under the Act of May 12, 1780, having neglected to do so previously "due to ignorance of the duty owed the country." [Ref: R-27:112]. "Charles Harway" lived in Linganore Hd. (one taxable) in 1777 [Ref: R-31:9]. Also see "Charles Harry," q.v.

HARVEY, James. Private, Capt. Edward Burgess' Co., Lower District of Frederick (now Montgomery) County, Militia, July, 1776 [Ref: D-42].

HARVEY, John. Private who was recruited to serve in the Extra Regiment, Continental Army, in 1780 [Ref: D-342].

HARVEY, Nathaniel. Substitute from Montgomery County who was discharged from the Maryland Line on Dec. 3, 1781 [Ref: I-11].

HARVEY, Richard. See "Richard Harry," q.v.

HARVEY (HARWAY, HERVEY), William (Jr.). Private, 6th Co., Middle Bn., Militia, Aug., 1777 [Ref: M-197, T-5:41]. Rendered aid by providing wheat for use of the military in 1781 [Ref: O-443]. "William Harway, Jr." lived in Linganore Hd. (one taxable) in 1777 [Ref: R-31:9]. "William Hervey, Jr." took the Oath of Allegiance on Sep. 1, 1780, under the Act of May 12, 1780, having neglected to do so previously "due to ignorance of the duty owed the country." [Ref: R-27:113].

HARVEY (HARWAY, HERVEY), William Sr. "William Harvey, Sr." rendered aid by providing wheat for use of the military in 1781 [Ref: O-386]. "William Harway" lived in Linganore Hd. (one taxable) in 1777 [Ref: R-31:9]. "William Hervey, Sr." took the Oath of Allegiance on Sep. 1, 1780, under the Act of May 12, 1780, having neglected to do so previously "due to ignorance of the duty owed the country." [Ref: R-27:113].

HARVIN, Joshua. See "Joshua Harbin," q.v.

HARWOOD, John (1744-1823). Served as a Second Lieutenant, 1st Co., 16th Bn., Militia, on Aug. 30, 1777, and Captain, 8th Co., Upper Bn., by

Sep. 12, 1777 [Ref: M-85, M-193, M-195, C-350, C-373]. Took the Oath of Allegiance before the Hon. Aneas Campbell on March 2, 1778 [Ref: T-3:77, L-1:41]. Lived in Sugarland Hd. in 1776 and had six taxables in 1777 [Ref: K-1:211, R-31:12]. Died testate in Montgomery County (wife named Mary) in 1823 [Ref: V-61].

HARWOOD, Samuel (b. 1747). Took the Oath of Allegiance before the Hon. Charles Jones on Jan. 10, 1778 [Ref: T-3:71, L-1:41]. Lived in North West Hd. in 1776 (wife named Mary Elizabeth) and had nine taxables in 1777 [Ref: K-1:230, R-31:17].

HASE, James. Took the Oath of Allegiance on Sep. 1, 1780, under the Act of May 12, 1780, having neglected to do so previously "due to ignorance of the duty owed the country." [Ref: R-27:112].

HASS, Philip. Private, 8th Co., Lower Bn., Militia, July 15, 1780 [Ref: M-207].

HAWES (HAWS), Michael. "Michael Haws" was a private, 1st Co., Middle Bn., Militia, Aug. 30, 1777 [Ref: M-195]. Private, 5th Co., Middle Bn., Militia, July 15, 1780 [Ref: M-203]. "Michael Hawes" took the Oath of Allegiance before the Hon. Edward Burgess on Feb. 28, 1778 [Ref: T-3:63, L-1:41].

HAWKER, Ambrose, and others. See "Ambrose Hocker" and others, q.v.

HAWKINS, Dorothy (died 1814). Lived in the Upper Part of Potomac Hd. (head of house with five taxables) in 1777 [Ref: R-31:14]. Rendered aid by providing wheat for use of the military in 1781 [Ref: O-397]. She died testate in Montgomery County in 1814 and mentioned many grandchildren [Ref: V-62]. See "John Hawkins," q.v.

HAWKINS, John. (1) Private, 4th Co., Lower Bn., Militia, Aug., 1777 [Ref: M-199, T-5:47]. Private, 1st Co., Lower Bn., Militia, July 15, 1780 [Ref: M-204]. (2) Private, 3rd Co., Lower Bn., Militia, July 15, 1780 [Ref: M-205]. One served as a petit juror in Aug., 1777 [Ref: R-31:17], and one took the Oath of Allegiance before the Hon. Samuel W. Magruder in 1778 [Ref: T-3:73, L-1:41]. Served as a grand juror in 1779 [Ref: W-1]. One John Hawkins (aged 38) lived in Lower Potomac Hd. (six taxables) in 1776-1777 [Ref: R-31:4, K-1:183]. When "Dorothy Hawkins," q.v., died in 1814 she mentioned her deceased son John, among others, in her will [Ref: V-62].

HAWKINS, Susannah Fraser. See "William Bailey," q.v.

HAWN, George. Took the Oath of Allegiance in 1778 [Ref: L-2:27].

HAWN, Michael. Took the Oath of Allegiance in 1778 [Ref: L-2:27].

HAYLEY, George. Rendered aid by providing pork for use of the military in 1781 [Ref: O-384].

HAYMON, George. Private, 6th Co., Middle Bn., Militia, Aug., 1777 [Ref: M-197, T-5:41].

HAYMON, Owen. Private, Capt. Edward Burgess' Co., Lower District of Frederick (now Montgomery) County, Militia, July, 1776 [Ref: D-42].

HAYS, Abigail and Abraham. See "Leonard Hays," q.v.

HAYS, Basil. Private, 2nd Co., Upper Bn., Militia, Aug. 30, 1777 [Ref: M-193]. Took the Oath of Allegiance before the Hon. Elisha Williams on March 2, 1778 [Ref: T-3:80, L-1:41].
HAYS, Charles Jr. Private, 2nd Co., Upper Bn., Militia, Aug. 30, 1777 [Ref: M-193]. "Charles Hays" took the Oath of Allegiance before the Hon. Elisha Williams on March 2, 1778 [Ref: T-3:80, L-1:41]. "Charles Hays, Jr." lived in Sugar Loaf Hd. (three taxables) in 1777 [Ref: R-31:10].
HAYS, Charles Sr. Took the Oath of Allegiance before the Hon. Elisha Williams on March 2, 1778 [Ref: T-3:80, L-1:41]. Charles Hays, Sr. lived in Sugar Loaf Hd. (four taxables) in 1777 [Ref: R-31:10]. "Charles Hays, planter" died testate in Montgomery County (wife named Elizabeth) in 1787 and mentioned sons Charles and Thomas [Ref: V-62].
HAYS, Eleanor. See "Leonard Hays," q.v.
HAYS, George. Private, 2nd Co., Upper Bn., Militia, Aug. 30, 1777 [Ref: M-193]. Took the Oath of Allegiance before the Hon. Elisha Williams on March 2, 1778 [Ref: T-3:80, L-1:41]. "George Hays" lived in Sugar Loaf Hd. (two taxables) in 1777 [Ref: R-31:10]. When "Jeremiah Hayes" wrote his will in Sep., 1783, he mentioned his sons, including "George, if he shall return." [Ref: V-62]. "George B. Hays" died testate in Montgomery County (wife named Elizabeth) in 1823. He was a son of William Hays who died testate in 1791 [Ref: V-62, V-63].
HAYS, James. Took the Oath of Allegiance (made his "X" mark) before the Hon. Edward Burgess on Feb. 28, 1778 [Ref: T-3:62, L-1:41].
HAYS, Jeremiah Jr. Son of Jeremiah Hays [Ref: V-62]. Took the Oath of Allegiance before the Hon. Elisha Williams on March 2, 1778 [Ref: T-3:81, L-1:41]. Jeremiah Hays, Jr. lived in Sugar Loaf Hd. (one taxable) in 1777 [Ref: R-31:10].
HAYS, Jeremiah Sr. (died 1783). Took the Oath of Allegiance before the Hon. Elisha Williams on March 2, 1778 [Ref: T-3:81, L-1:41]. Rendered aid by providing wheat for use of the military in 1781 [Ref: O-392]. "Jeremiah Hays, Sr." lived in Sugar Loaf Hd. (two taxables) in 1777 [Ref: R-31:10]. "Jeremiah Hayes" died testate in Montgomery County (wife not named) in 1783 and mentioned numerous children [Ref: V-62].
HAYS, Leonard (c1759-1822). Private, 2nd Co., Upper Bn., Militia, Aug. 30, 1777 [Ref: M-193]. Leonard Hays, of Barnesville, was born circa 1759, probably the son of William and Mary Hays. He married Eleanor Simmons in Frederick County in 1782 and died testate on Sep. 14, 1822. His children were: Abraham S. (b. on June 12, 1783, married Elizabeth Tillard, and died in Lafayette County, Missouri, in 1861); Sarah (b. July 17, 1785, married William Chandler); Samuel S. (b. April 1, 1787, married Anna Rawlings, and died Sep. 5, 1857); Abigail (b. June 5, 1789, married William Trail, and died May 10, 1857); Eleanor (b. July 13, 1791, married Elisha Howard, and died Feb. 8, 1873); Leonard, Jr. (b. July 30, 1793, married Eliza Sprigg Poole, and died April 25, 1864); and,

William S. (b. May 9, 1797, married Eleanor Hardy, and died Oct. 24, 1842). [Ref: V-63, and "Hays Family Bible Records," by R. G. Smith, *Western Maryland Families*, edited by Raymond B. Clark, Jr. (1987), p. 67].

HAYS (HAYES), Leven (Levin). Son of Jeremiah Hays [Ref: V-62]. "Levin Hayes" was a private who enrolled into a company of militia for the service of the Flying Camp, Oct. 15, 1776 [Ref: B-352]. "Leven Hays" was a private, 2nd Co., Upper Bn., Militia, Aug. 30, 1777 [Ref: M-193]. "Leaven Hays" took the Oath of Allegiance before the Hon. Elisha Williams on March 2, 1778 [Ref: T-3:81, L-1:41]. "Leven Hays" lived in Sugar Loaf Hd. (one taxable) in 1777 [Ref: R-31:10].

HAYS (HAYES), Levi (Levy). "Levi Hayes" was a private, enrolled into a company of militia for the service of the Flying Camp, Oct. 15, 1776 [Ref: B-352]. "Levy Hays" was a private, 2nd Co., Upper Bn., Militia, Aug. 30, 1777 [Ref: M-193]. "Levi Hays" married Eleanor Harris in Montgomery County on Dec. 9, 1779 [Ref: K-2:519].

HAYS, Notley. Son of William Hays [Ref: V-63]. Private, 2nd Co., Upper Bn., Militia, Aug. 30, 1777 [Ref: M-193].

HAYS, Samuel. Private, 2nd Co., Upper Bn., Militia, Aug. 30, 1777 [Ref: M-193]. See "Leonard Hays," q.v.

HAYS, Sarah. See "Leonard Hays," q.v.

HAYS (HAYES), Thomas. (1) Ensign, Militia, March 26, 1776, and First Lieutenant, 2nd Co., 16th Bn., Militia, Sep. 12, 1777. "Thomas Hayes" was a Lieutenant, enrolled into a company of militia for the service of the Flying Camp, Oct. 15, 1776 [Ref: B-352]. "Thomas Hays" was a Captain, Upper Bn., from April 21, 1779, to at least March 25, 1780 [Ref: M-86, M-193, A-287, C-373, E-356, F-120]. (2) Private, enrolled into a company of militia for the service of the Flying Camp, Oct. 15, 1776 [Ref: B-353]. One served as a petit juror in Aug., 1777 [Ref: R-31:17], and one took the Oath of Allegiance before the Hon. Elisha Williams on March 2, 1778 [Ref: T-3:80, L-1:41]. Thomas Hays lived in Sugar Loaf Hd. (one taxable) in 1777 [Ref: R-31:10]. On Nov. 9, 1833, in Bourbon County, Kentucky, one Thomas Hays, aged 79, applied for pension (S31110), stating he was born in Montgomery County, Maryland, on May 10, 1762, and served in 1775 (two months) under Capt. Richard Smith, again in 1777 (one and a half months) under Capt. Thomas Sprigg, and again in 1778 (nine months) under Capt. Enos Campbell. In 1801 he moved to Kentucky. On April 30, 1832, "Benjamin Willett," q.v., of Montgomery County, Maryland, stated that he served as a private with Thomas Hays in Capt. Thomas Sprigg's Co. [Ref: Z-10, Y-4, P-1580]. One Thomas Hayes was a son of "Jeremiah Hays," q.v. [Ref: V-62]. Also see "Thomas Hayes," q.v.

HAYS, Thomas Jr. Private, 2nd Co., Upper Bn., Militia, Aug. 30, 1777 [Ref: M-193].

HAYS (HAES), William (1751-1791?). "William Haes" [sic] lived in Sugarland Hd. in 1776 [Ref: K-1:214]. "William Hays" took the Oath of Allegiance before the Hon. Elisha Williams on March 2, 1778 [Ref: T-3:80, L-1:41]. One William Hays died testate in Montgomery County (wife not named) in 1791 and mentioned sons William, Notley, and George B. [Ref: V-63]. See "Leonard Hays," q.v.

HEAD, William (b. 1750). Private, 3rd Maryland Line, Smallwood's Regiment, from May 3, 1777 until April, 1778 [Ref: D-120]. Lived in Sugarland Hd. in 1776 [Ref: K-1:214].

HEARD (HERD, HURD), Bennett (b. 1751). Lived in Sugarland Hd. in 1776 [Ref: K-1:201]. Private, Flying Camp, enlisted on July 29, 1776 [Ref: D-44]. He also enlisted and served in the Continental Army in 1781 [Ref: D-408, D-428].

HEATER (HEETER, HEITER), George (b. 1751). Private, 1st Co., Middle Bn., Militia, Aug. 30, 1777 [Ref: M-195, T-5:36]. Private, 5th Co., Middle Bn., Militia, July 15, 1780 [Ref: M-203]. Took the Oath of Allegiance before the Hon. Gerrard Briscoe on March 2, 1778 [Ref: T-3:56, L-1:41]. "George Heiter" lived in Seneca Hd. (one taxable) in 1777 [Ref: R-31:8]. "George Heater" married Catherine Space in Montgomery County, Maryland, on Jan. 21, 1779 [Ref: K-2:519]. On Oct. 13, 1832, in Allen County, Kentucky, "George Heeter," aged 80, applied for pension (S16410), stating he enlisted in Frederick County, Maryland in 1776, served in the Flying Camp and fought in the Battle of White Plains. He was born in Frederick County in 1751, lived in Montgomery County after the war, and migrated to Allen County, Kentucky in 1810 [Ref: Z-5, Y-1, P-1595, which latter source mistakenly stated he moved to Allen County, Ohio].

HEATHMAN (HETHMAN), George (b. 1749). Private, 2nd Co., Middle Bn., Militia, Sep. 4, 1777 [Ref: M-196, T-5:37]. Private, 7th Class, 3rd Co., Middle Bn., Militia, July 15, 1780 [Ref: M-202]. Lived in Sugar Loaf Hd. (one taxable) in 1777 [Ref: R-31:10]. Took the Oath of Allegiance before the Hon. Gerrard Briscoe on March 2, 1778 [Ref: T-3:57, L-1:41]. The pension application (S1255) of "John Smith," q.v., in Clark County, Kentucky, indicated he served with George Heathman and they fought in the Battle of Germantown. In 1832, George Heathman, aged 83, whose wife was named Lydia, stated he had known John Smith since he was aged 12 or 15 in Montgomery County, Maryland [Ref: Y-8, and not found in Source P-1592].

HEATHMAN (HETHMAN), John. Private, 2nd Co., Middle Bn., Militia, Sep. 4, 1777 [Ref: T-5:37], and Second Sergeant, 3rd Co., Middle Bn., Militia, July 15, 1780 [Ref: M-202]. Took the Oath of Allegiance before the Hon. Gerrard Briscoe on March 2, 1778 [Ref: T-3:56, L-1:41]. Lived in Sugar Loaf Hd. (one taxable) in 1777 [Ref: R-31:10].

HEATHMAN (HETHMAN), Jonathan. Private, 2nd Co., Middle Bn., Militia, Sep. 4, 1777 [Ref: M-196, T-5:37]. Lived in Seneca Hd. (three taxables) in 1777 [Ref: R-31:8].

HEATHMAN, Lydia. See "George Heathman (Hethman)," q.v.

HECKATHORN, Jacob. Took the Oath of Allegiance in 1778 [Ref: L-2:27].

HEDGCOCK, Robert E. See "Humphrey Beckett Tomlinson," q.v.

HEDLY (HEDLEY, HADLAY), Jacob (b. 1751). Took the Oath of Allegiance before the Hon. Joseph Offutt on March 2, 1778 [Ref: T-3:70, L-1:41]. Rendered aid by providing wheat for use of the military in 1781 [Ref: O-394]. Jacob Hadlay or Hedley lived in Lower Potomac Hd. (one taxable) in 1776-1777 [Ref: R-31:4, K-1:183].

HEFFNER, James. Took the Oath of Allegiance in 1778 [Ref: L-2:27].

HEFFNER, Michael. Rendered aid by providing beef for use of the military in 1781 [Ref: O-373].

HEMPSTON, Charity. See "Mathias Hempston" and "Jeremiah Plummer," q.v.

HEMPSTON (HEMSTONE), Christopher. Private, 6th Co., Upper Bn., Militia, on Aug. 30, 1777 [Ref: M-194]. This appears to be the "Christian Hemsear" (or Hemsean?) who took the Oath of Allegiance before the Hon. Elisha Williams in 1778 [Ref: T-3:80, L-1:41].

HEMPSTON, Eleanor and Mary. See "Mathias Hempston," q.v.

HEMPSTON (HEMSTONE, HAMPSTONE), Mathias. Served as a private and enrolled into a company of militia for the service of the Flying Camp on Oct. 15, 1776 [Ref: B-352]. Private, 6th Co., Upper Bn., Militia, on Aug. 30, 1777 [Ref: M-194]. "Mathias Hampstone" lived in Sugar Loaf Hd. (three taxables) in 1777 [Ref: R-31:10]. This appears to be the "Mathias Hemsear" (Hemsean?) who took the Oath of Allegiance before the Hon. Elisha Williams in 1778 [Ref: T-3:80, L-1:41]. "Mathias Hempstone" was born circa 1740, married Mary ----(?), and had the following children: Christian, William, Charity (married Zephaniah Plummer, a Quaker, on Jan. 15, 1791, and he died on Sep. 28, 1846, Frederick County, and their daughter Mahala Plummer, born on April 21, 1800, married Henry Rhine), Eleanor (married ---- Spaulding), and Mary (married ---- McCubbin). [Ref: Research files of Margaret V. Williams, of Baltimore, Maryland, and Henry C. Peden, Jr., of Bel Air, Maryland].

HEMPSTON, Nathan T. See "William Hempston," q.v.

HEMPSTON (HEMSTONE, HEMPSTONE), William. Private who was recruited and served in the 7th Maryland Regiment, Continental Army, from Jan. 31, 1780, to Nov. 1, 1780 [Ref: D-217, D-341, which source listed the name as "Wm. Hamston" and "William Hampton"]. On Feb. 19, 1819, the Treasurer of Maryland was directed to pay him, an old soldier, the half pay of a private. On March 7, 1834, the balance due William Hempston, deceased, was ordered paid to his son Nathan T. Hempston, of Montgomery County [Ref: K-2:353, Q-115]. "William Hempstone, a soldier of the Revolution, known as Major Hempstone, is buried on a farm [in Montgomery County] belonging of late years [circa 1908] to William Griffith, and before the Revolution to the Hempstone family, but there is no stone to mark the spot. There are two stones in memory of William Hempstone (1793-1825) and Mary Hempstone (1823-1827)." [Ref: *Historic Graves of Maryland and the District of Columbia*, by Helen W. Ridgely (1908), p. 181]. See "Mathias Hempston," q.v.

HENLEY, James (b. 1736). Private, 4th Co., Upper Bn., Militia, Aug. 30, 1777 [Ref: M-194]. Took the Oath of Allegiance before the Hon. Aneas Campbell on March 2, 1778 [Ref: T-3:78, L-1:41]. Lived in Sugarland Hd. in 1776-1777 [Ref: K-1:219, R-31:12].

HENLEY (HENLY), John. "John Henley" rendered aid by providing wheat for use of the military in 1780 [Ref: O-331]. "John Henly" lived in Rock Creek Hd. (three taxables) in 1777 [Ref: R-31:16].

HENLEY (HENLY, HENDLEY), William. "William Henly" was a private, 2nd Co., Lower Bn., Militia, Sep., 1777 [Ref: M-198, T-5:45]. "William Hendley" was a private, 5th Co., Lower Bn., Militia, July 15, 1780 [Ref: M-206]. "William Henley" took the Oath of Allegiance before the Hon. Edward Burgess on Feb. 28, 1778 [Ref: T-3:62, L-1:41].

HENNIS (HENNES), Benjamin (b. 1760). "Benjamin Hennes" lived in Lower Potomac Hd. in 1776 with David Hennes (aged 49 and head of household), John Hennes (aged 17), and Henry Hennes (aged 14). [Ref: K-1:183]. On July 20, 1818, in Fleming County, Kentucky, "Benjamin Hennis," aged 58, applied for pension (S35402), stating he entered the service in Montgomery County, Maryland, on April 1, 1777, and served for 3 years. He also fought at the Battles of Brandywine and Monmouth with the 7th Maryland Line and was discharged on March 31, 1780. In 1820, aged 60, he stated his property was valued at $151.25 and had a wife (no name given) aged upwards of 57 years and "who was entirely helpless." His daughters were Dorcas (aged 25), Sarah (aged 18), Charity (aged 14), and Angelina (aged 10). [Ref: P-1605, Z-10, Z-34, Z-35, Y-4].

HENNIS, David, Dorcas, and others. See "Benjamin Hennis," q.v.

HENNIS (HENNES, ENNIS), John (b. 1759). "John Hennis" was a private who enrolled into a company of militia for the service of the Flying Camp, Oct. 15, 1776 [Ref: B-353]. "John Ennis" was a private, 6th Co., Upper Bn., Militia, Aug. 30, 1777 [Ref: M-194]. Took the Oath of Allegiance before the Hon. Elisha Williams on March 2, 1778 [Ref: T-3:80, L-1:40]. John Hennes lived in Lower Potomac Hd. in 1776 with David Hennes (aged 49 and head of household), and John Ennis lived in Sugar Loaf Hd. (one taxable) in 1777 [Ref: R-31:9, K-1:183]. See "Benjamin Hennis," q.v.

HENNIS (ENNIS), Nicholas. Took the Oath of Allegiance before the Hon. Gerrard Briscoe on March 2, 1778 [Ref: T-3:57, L-1:40]. Private, 8th Class, 3rd Co., Middle Bn., Militia, July 15, 1780 [Ref: M-202].

HENRY, Daniel (b. 1755). Private, 6th Co., Upper Bn., Militia, Aug. 30, 1777 [Ref: M-194]. Served as a grand juror in Aug., 1777, and a petit juror in Nov., 1777 [Ref: R-31:17, R-31:18]. Took the Oath of Allegiance before the Hon. Elisha Williams on March 2, 1778 [Ref: T-3:81, L-1:41]. Lived in Sugarland Hd. (five taxables) in 1776-1777 [Ref: K-1:201, R-31:12].

HENRY (HENNARY), John (b. 1749). "John Hennary" lived in Sugarland Hd. in 1776 [Ref: K-1:204]. "John Henry" was a private, Flying Camp, who enlisted on July 18, 1776 [Ref: D-49].

HEPBURN (HEBORN), Samuel. Rendered aid by providing wheat for use of the military in 1780 [Ref: O-314]. "Samuel Hepburn" lived in Sugar Loaf Hd. (five taxables) in 1777 [Ref: R-31:10], and "Samuel Heborn" owned a working plantation ("quarter") in Rock Creek Hd. (ten taxables) in 1777 [Ref: R-31:16].

HERD, Bennett. Private, Flying Camp, Frederick (now Montgomery) County, enlisted by Greenbury Gaither on July 29, 1776 [Ref: D-44].

HERRING (HERRON), John. "John Herron" was a private, 5th Co., Lower Bn., Militia, Aug., 1777 [Ref: M-199, T-5:48]. "John Herring" took the Oath of Allegiance before the Hon. Samuel W. Magruder in 1778 [Ref: T-3:73, L-1:41]. "John Herring" was a private, 2nd Co., Lower Bn., Militia, July 15, 1780 [Ref: M-204]. "John Herring" married Mary Strahan in Montgomery County on Oct. 2, 1777 [Ref: K-2:519].

HERVEY, William. See "William Harvey (Harway)," q.v.

HESS (HESSE), Jacob (b. 1740). "Jacob Hesse" was a private who enrolled into a company of militia for the service of the Flying Camp, Oct. 15, 1776 [Ref: B-353]. "Jacob Hess" lived in George Town Hd. (one taxable) in 1776-1777 [Ref: K-1:193, R-31:3]. Private, 4th Co., Lower Bn., Militia, Aug., 1777 [Ref: M-199, T-5:47]. Took the Oath of Allegiance before the Hon. Richard Thompson in 1778 [Ref: T-3:75, L-1:41].

HESSONG, Balser. Took the Oath of Allegiance in 1778 [Ref: L-2:27].

HEUGH (HUGHES), Andrew (1727-1789). "Andrew Heugh" lived in Lower Potomac Hd. (twelve taxables) in 1776-1777 [Ref: R-31:4, K-1:183]. "Andrew Hughes" was a private who enrolled into a company of militia for the service of the Flying Camp on Oct. 15, 1776 [Ref: B-352]. "Andrew Heugh" took the Oath of Allegiance before the Hon. Richard Thompson in 1778 [Ref: T-3:75, L-1:41]. "Andrew Hughes" rendered aid by providing wheat for use of the military in 1780 [Ref: O-321, O-334]. "Andrew Heugh" died testate in Montgomery County (wife named Sarah) in 1789 [Ref: V-64].

HEWLETT, John. Private, Capt. Price's Co., 3rd Maryland Line, 1781-1782 [Ref: D-454].

HICKE (HICKEY), William. Private, Capt. Edward Burgess' Co., Lower District of Frederick (now Montgomery) County, Militia, July, 1776 [Ref: D-42].

HICKMAN, Arthur (b. 1713). Took the Oath of Allegiance before the Hon. Aneas Campbell on March 2, 1778 [Ref: T-3:77, L-1:41]. Arthur Hickman lived in Sugarland Hd. (five taxables) in 1776-1777 [Ref: K-1:198, R-31:12].

HICKMAN, Elihu (Elihue, Elihia). "Elihu Hickman" was a private, 8th Co., Upper Bn., Militia, Aug. 30, 1777 [Ref: M-195]. "Elitrue [sic] Hickman" took the Oath of Allegiance before the Hon. Aneas Campbell on March 2, 1778 [Ref: T-3:77, L-1:41]. "Elihu Hickman, aged 15" lived in Sugarland Hd. in 1776 and "Elihia Hickman" lived there and had two taxables in 1777 [Ref: K-1:210, R-31:12].

HICKMAN, Joshua (1762-1818). Son of Solomon Hickman, of Sugarland Hd., in 1776 [Ref: K-1:217]. Substitute from Montgomery County who was discharged from the Maryland Line on Dec. 3, 1781 [Ref: I-11, D-408]. A Joshua Hickman died testate in Montgomery County (wife named Mary) in 1818 and mentioned his son Joshua [Ref: V-64].

HICKMAN, Solomon (b. 1736). Lived in Sugarland Hd. in 1776 and had three taxables in 1777 [Ref: K-1:217, R-31:12]. Private, 4th Co., Upper Bn., Militia, Aug. 30, 1777 [Ref: M-194].

HICKMAN, William. Private, 4th Co., Upper Bn., Militia, Aug. 30, 1777 [Ref: M-194], and Second Lieutenant, Upper Bn., Militia, March 25, 1780 [Ref: M-87, F-120]. Took the Oath of Allegiance before the Hon. Aneas Campbell on March 2, 1778 [Ref: T-3:78, L-1:41]. "William Hickman, aged 30" and "William Hickman, aged 21" both lived in Sugarland Hd. in 1776 [Ref: K-1:198, K-1:206]. A William Hickman married Ann Lucas in Montgomery County on July 29, 1781 [Ref: K-2:519]. One William Hickman died testate in Montgomery County (wife named Nancy) in 1808 [Ref: V-65]. See "William Hickman, Jr.," q.v.

HICKMAN, William Jr. Took the Oath of Allegiance before the Hon. Aneas Campbell on March 2, 1778 [Ref: T-3:78, L-1:41]. William Hickman, Jr. (two taxables) and William Hickman, Jr. [sic] (three taxables) both lived in Sugarland Hd. in 1777 [Ref: R-31:12. It appears that perhaps one may have been "Sr." instead of "Jr."]. See "William Hickman," q.v.

HIGDON, Benjamin. Private, 1st Co., Middle Bn., Militia, Aug. 30, 1777 [Ref: M-195]. Private, 5th Co., Middle Bn., Militia, July 15, 1780 [Ref: M-203]. Took the Oath of Allegiance before the Hon. Gerrard Briscoe on March 2, 1778 [Ref: T-3:56, L-1:41]. Lived in Seneca Hd. (one taxable) in 1777 [Ref: R-31:8].

HIGDON, John. Private, 7th Co., Upper Bn., Militia, Aug. 30, 1777 [Ref: M-195]. Took the Oath of Allegiance before the Hon. Elisha Williams on March 2, 1778 [Ref: T-3:81, L-1:41]. One John Higdon (aged 60) lived in Lower Potomac Hd. in 1776 and a John Higdon in Sugarland Hd. (two taxables) in 1777 [Ref: R-31:12, K-1:183].

HIGDON, John Jr. (b. 1756). Private, 7th Co., Upper Bn., Militia, Aug. 30, 1777 [Ref: M-195]. Lived in Lower Potomac Hd. in 1776 [Ref: K-1:183].

HIGDON, Joseph (1759-1836). Private, 7th Co., Upper Bn., Militia, Aug. 30, 1777 [Ref: M-195]. Lived in Lower Potomac Hd. in 1776 with John Higdon (aged 60 and head of household). [Ref: K-1:183]. Took the Oath of Allegiance before the Hon. Elisha Williams on March 2, 1778 [Ref: T-3:81, L-1:41]. Joseph Higdon applied for pension on Oct. 16, 1832, in Barren County, Kentucky, stating he was born on July 18, 1759, in Charles County, Maryland, and entered the service in June, 1781, in Montgomery County, Maryland, where he was living at the time. In 1784 he moved to North Carolina for 13 years and then on to Tennessee. Joseph Higdon married Margaret Holbrook (b. Feb. 17, 1766) on April 5, 1786, and their children were: Gabriel (b. Feb. 5, 1787, and living in Barren County, Kentucky in 1840); John (b. Aug. 8, 1788); Mary (b. Feb. 12, 1790); Susannah (b. Oct. 11, 1791); Jane (b. Aug. 30, 1793); Hays (b. June 22, 1795); Rebecca (b. March 17, 1797); Ishmale (b. Dec. 14, 1798); Joseph (b. Oct. 10, 1800, and living in Barren County, Kentucky, in 1839); Margaret (b. Sep. 23, 1802); Thomas (b. Aug. 4, 1804); Enoch E. (b. May 3, 1806); and Sarah (b. March 13, 1810, who apparently married a Davis). Also shown was a William Holbrook (b. March 11, 1784, but no relation was stated). In Dec., 1801, Joseph and family moved to Barren County, Kentucky, where he died on Feb. 6, 1836. His widow applied for and received a pension (W8935) on April 12, 1839 [Ref: P-1627, Z-6, Z-7, Y-2, DAR-I:327].

HIGDON, Mary. See "Leonard Watkins," q.v.

HIGDON, Thomas (b. 1751). Lived in North West Hd. in 1776 [Ref: K-1:224]. Private, 4th Co., Lower Bn., Militia, Aug., 1777 [Ref: M-199, T-5:47]. Thomas J. Higdon (or Rigdon?) took the Oath of Allegiance before the Hon. Samuel W. Magruder in 1778 [Ref: T-3:73].

HIGGINS, Ann. See "Walter Prather," q.v.

HIGGINS, James (1732-1816). Private, 5th Co., Lower Bn., Militia, Aug., 1777 [Ref: T-5:48], and private, 2nd Co., Lower Bn., Militia, July 15, 1780 [Ref: M-204]. Served as a grand juror in Aug., 1777 and 1779 [Ref: R-31:17, W-1]. Took the Oath of Allegiance before the Hon. Charles Jones on Jan. 10, 1778 [Ref: T-3:71, L-1:41]. Died testate in Montgomery County (wife not named) in 1816 [Ref: V-65, DAR-I:327, which latter source states he died on Jan. 18, 1816, and his wife was Luraner Becraft]. See "George Beckwith," q.v.

HIGGINS, John (died 1808). Private, 5th Co., Upper Bn., Militia, Aug. 30, 1777 [Ref: M-194]. Private, Extra Regiment, Continental Army, 1780 [Ref: D-342]. Lived in Sugar Loaf Hd. (two taxables) in 1777 [Ref: R-31:10]. Died testate in Montgomery County (wife named Jamima) in 1808 [Ref: V-65, V-66].

HILAND, Hugh. See "Hugh Hyland," q.v.

HILDEBRIDLE, Jacob. Took the Oath of Allegiance in 1778 [Ref: L-2:27].
HILL, Ann. See "George Frazer Magruder," q.v.
HILL, Henry. Private who was recruited to serve in the Continental Army in 1780 [Ref: D-341].
HILL, Isaac. Served as a Fifer, Capt. Price's Co., 3rd Maryland Line, 1781-1782 [Ref: D-452].
HILL, John. Private, 8th Co., Lower Bn., Militia, July 15, 1780 [Ref: M-207]. Private, 3rd Co., Lower Bn., Militia, Sep., 1777 [Ref: M-199, T-5:46]. Two men with this name took the Oath of Allegiance: one before the Hon. Edward Burgess on Feb. 28, 1778 [Ref: T-3:63, L-1:41], and another before the Hon. Richard Thompson [Ref: T-3:75, L-1:41]. One "John Hill, aged 36" lived in North West Hd. in 1776 (wife named Kesiah) and another lived in George Town Hd. (one taxable) in 1777 [Ref: R-31:3]. One John Hill married Elizabeth Richards in Montgomery County on July 14, 1778 [Ref: K-2:516].
HILL, Joseph Jr. Took the Oath of Allegiance in 1778 [Ref: L-2:27].
HILL, Joseph Sr. Took the Oath of Allegiance in 1778 [Ref: L-2:27].
HILL, Leah. See "Thomas Smith," q.v.
HILL, Thomas. Private, Capt. Thomas Beall's Co., Maryland Line, 1780 [Ref: D-351]. Took the Oath of Allegiance in 1778 [Ref: L-2:27, which source indicates Montgomery County].
HILLARD, Thomas. Private, 6th Co., Middle Bn., Militia, July 15, 1780 [Ref: M-203]. Took the Oath of Allegiance before the Hon. Edward Burgess on Feb. 28, 1778 [Ref: T-3:61, L-1:41].
HILLARY (HILLEARY, HILLERY), Henry. (1) "Henry Hilleary" was a private, 1st Co., Middle Bn., Militia, Aug. 30, 1777 [Ref: M-195]. Took the Oath of Allegiance before the Hon. Gerrard Briscoe on March 2, 1778 [Ref: T-3:57, L-1:41]. "Henry Hillery" was a private, 5th Co., Middle Bn., Militia, July 15, 1780 [Ref: M-203]. (2) "Henry Hillary" was a First Lieutenant, Middle Bn., Militia, April 21, 1779 [Ref: M-87, E-357]. One "Henry Hilleary" died testate in Montgomery County (wife named Elizabeth) in 1792 and mentioned only siblings and nieces and nephews [Ref: V-66]. "McHenry Hilleary departed this life July 19, 1792, in the 54th year of his age" and is buried in Rockville Cemetery [Ref: *Historic Graves of Maryland and the District of Columbia*, by Helen W. Ridgely (1908), p. 173].
HILLARY (HILLEARY, HILLERY), John. "John Hilleary" was a private, 1st Co., Middle Bn., Militia, Aug. 30, 1777 [Ref: M-195]. Took the Oath of Allegiance before the Hon. Gerrard Briscoe on March 2, 1778 [Ref: T-3:57, L-1:41]. "John Hillery" was a private, 5th Co., Middle Bn., Militia, July 15, 1780 [Ref: M-203]. "John Hillary" rendered aid by providing wheat for use of the military in 1780 [Ref: O-305]. "John Hilleary" lived in Seneca Hd. (five taxables) in 1777 [Ref: R-31:8].
HILTON, Freeman. Took the Oath of Allegiance in 1778 [Ref: L-2:27].
HILTON, James. Took the Oath of Allegiance in 1778 [Ref: L-2:27].

HILTON, James Sr. Took the Oath of Allegiance in 1778 [Ref: L-2:27].
HILTON, John. Took the Oath of Allegiance in 1778 [Ref: L-2:27].
HILTON, William (died 1822). Rendered aid by providing wheat for use of the military in 1781 [Ref: O-435]. Died testate in Montgomery County (wife named Elizabeth) in 1822 [Ref: V-66].
HINES (HEINS), Jacob. Private, 8th Co., Middle Bn., Militia, Sep., 1777 [Ref: M-198, T-5:43]. "Jacob Hines" lived in the Upper Part of Newfoundland Hd. (one taxable) in 1777 [Ref: R-31:6]. "Jacob Heins" took the Oath of Allegiance in 1778 [Ref: L-2:27].
HINTON (HENTON), John. "John Hinton" was a private who enrolled in a company of militia for the service of the Flying Camp, Oct. 15, 1776. Private, 5th Co., Upper Bn., Militia, Aug. 30, 1777 [Ref: B-352, M-194]. "John Henton" was Second Lieutenant, Upper Bn., Militia, on April 21, 1779 [Ref: M-87, E-257]. "John Hinton" took the Oath of Allegiance (made his "I" mark) before the Hon. Joseph Wilson on Feb. 26, 1778 [Ref: T-3:64, L-1:41]. John Hinton lived in Sugar Loaf Hd. (three taxables) in 1777 [Ref: R-31:10].
HINTON, Michael. Son of Thomas Hinton [Ref: V-66]. Private, 5th Co., Upper Bn., Militia, Aug. 30, 1777 [Ref: M-194].
HINTON, Phillip. Son of Thomas Hinton [Ref: V-66]. Private, 5th Co., Upper Bn., Militia, Aug. 30, 1777 [Ref: M-194].
HINTON, Richard. Private, 5th Co., Upper Bn., Militia, Aug. 30, 1777 [Ref: M-194]. Took the Oath of Allegiance in 1778 [Ref: L-2:27].
HINTON, Thomas (died 1792). Private, 5th Co., Upper Bn., Militia, Aug. 30, 1777 [Ref: M-194]. Took the Oath of Allegiance on Sep. 1, 1780, under the Act of May 12, 1780, having neglected to do so previously "due to ignorance of the duty owed the country." [Ref: R-27:113]. Lived in Sugar Loaf Hd. (two taxables) in 1777 [Ref: R-31:10]. Died testate in Montgomery County (wife named Rebeckah) in 1792 [Ref: V-66].
HINTON, Thomas Jr. Son of Thomas Hinton [Ref: V-66]. Private, 5th Co., Upper Bn., Militia, Aug. 30, 1777 [Ref: M-194]. Lived in Sugar Loaf Hd. (one taxable) in 1777 [Ref: R-31:10].
HIPSLEY, Jonathan. Private, 1st or 32nd Bn., Militia (no date was given; possibly June, 1777). [Ref: T-5:1].
HITCH, John. Private, 6th Co., Lower Bn., Militia, Aug., 1777 [Ref: M-200, T-5:49]. Took the Oath of Allegiance before the Hon. Joseph Offutt on March 2, 1778 [Ref: T-3:70, L-1:41]. "John Hetch" was a private, 3rd Co., Lower Bn., Militia, July 15, 1780 [Ref: M-205].
HOBBS, Amos. Private, 1st or 32nd Bn., Militia (no date was given; possibly June, 1777). [Ref: T-5:1].
HOBBS, Charles. Private, 6th Co., Middle Bn., Militia, Aug., 1777, to at least July 15, 1780 [Ref: M-197, M-203, T-5:41]. Took the Oath of Allegiance on Sep. 1, 1780, under the Act of May 12, 1780, having neglected to do so previously "due to ignorance of the duty owed the country." [Ref: R-27:113].

HOBBS, George. Private, 1st or 32nd Bn., Militia (no date was given; possibly June, 1777). [Ref: T-5:1].
HOBBS, Greenbury or Greenberry. Private, 6th Co., Middle Bn., Militia, Aug., 1777 [Ref: M-197, T-5:41]. Lived in Linganore Hd. (one taxable) in 1777 [Ref: R-31:9].
HOBBS, Joshua. Private, 1st or 32nd Bn., Militia (no date was given; possibly June, 1777). [Ref: T-5:1].
HOBBS, Ninian. Private, 1st or 32nd Bn., Militia (no date was given; possibly June, 1777). [Ref: T-5:1].
HOBBS, Samuel. (1) Private, 5th Co., Upper Bn., Militia, Aug. 30, 1777 [Ref: M-194]. (2) Private, 1st Co., Lower Bn., Militia, Sep., 1777 [Ref: M-198, which source questions if name could be "Wells," but Source T-5:44 states the name is "Hobbs"]. Second Sergeant, 7th Co., Lower Bn., July 15, 1780 [Ref: M-206]. Served as a petit juror in Nov., 1777 [Ref: R-31:18]. Rendered aid by providing wheat for use of the military in 1781 [Ref: O-379]. One Samuel Hobbs lived in the Lower Part of Newfoundland Hd. (five taxables) in 1777 and one lived in Linganore Hd. (two taxables) in 1777 [Ref: R-31:5, R-31:9]. One Samuel Hobbs died testate in Montgomery County (wife not named) in 1806 and mentioned a son Samuel, among others [Ref: V-66].
HOBBS, Samuel, of Samuel. Took the Oath of Allegiance on Sep. 1, 1780, under the Act of May 12, 1780, having neglected to do so previously "due to ignorance of the duty owed the country." [Ref: R-27:113].
HOBBS, Thomas. Private, 1st or 32nd Bn., Militia (no date was given; possibly June, 1777). [Ref: T-5:1].
HOCKER (HAWKER), Ambrose (Amberos). "Ambrose Hawker" took the Oath of Allegiance (made his "X" mark) before the Hon. Joseph Wilson on Feb. 28, 1778 [Ref: T-3:66, L-1:41]. "Amberos Hawker" was a private, 5th Co., Lower Bn., Militia, July 15, 1780 [Ref: M-206]. "Ambrus Hawker" lived in Rock Creek Hd. (one taxable) in 1777 [Ref: R-31:16].
HOCKER (HAWKER), Andrew. "Andrew Hawker" was a private, 2nd Co., Lower Bn., Militia, Sep., 1777 [Ref: T-5:45].
HOCKER, Larkin. See "William Hocker," q.v.
HOCKER (HAWKER), Nicholas (1752-1813). "Nicholas Hocker" took the Oath of Allegiance before the Hon. Edward Burgess on Feb. 28, 1778 [Ref: T-3:58, L-1:41]. Rendered aid by providing wheat for use of the military in 1780 [Ref: O-308]. "Nicholas Hawker" was a private, 1st Co., Lower Bn., Militia, Sep., 1777, and Ensign, 7th Co., Lower Bn., July 15, 1780 [Ref: M-198, M-206, T-5:44]. Died testate in March, 1813, in Lincoln County, Kentucky, naming wife Sarah (whose maiden name was Barnes) and children Philip Hocker, Alfred Hocker, Nicholas Hocker, George Hocker, Margaret Dunn, Mary Clements, and Dorcas Hocker [Ref: Ila E. Fowler's *Kentucky Pioneers and Their Descendants* (1967), p. 240, and DAR-I:334].

HOCKER (HAWKER), Philip (1750-c1820). Lived in Sugar Loaf Hd. (two taxables) in 1777 [Ref: R-31:10]. "Philip Hocker" served as a private, 2nd Co., Middle Bn., Militia, Sep. 4, 1777 [Ref: M-195]. "Philip Hawker" was a private, 2nd Class, 3rd Co., Middle Bn., Militia, July 15, 1780 [Ref: M-202]. "Philip Hawker" took the Oath of Allegiance before the Hon. Gerrard Briscoe on March 2, 1778 [Ref: T-3:56, L-1:41]. Wife named Dorcas [Ref: DAR-I:334].

HOCKER (HAWKER), Samuel. "Samuel Hocker" was a private, 2nd Co., Middle Bn., Militia, Sep. 4, 1777 [Ref: M-195]. "Samuel Hoker" [sic] took the Oath of Allegiance before the Hon. Elisha Williams on March 2, 1778 [Ref: T-3:81, L-1:41]. "Samuel Hawker" was Second Corporal, 3rd Co., Middle Bn., Militia, July 15, 1780 [Ref: M-202]. Rendered aid by providing wheat for use of the military in 1780 [Ref: O-308]. "Samuel Hocker" lived in Sugar Loaf Hd. (two taxables) in 1777 [Ref: R-31:10]. A Samuel Hocker died testate in 1815 in Lincoln County, Kentucky, naming his wife Nancy and children Joseph, John, Richard Weaver, Philip, Jacob (deceased), Polly, Nancy, and Betsy Helen [Ref: Ila E. Fowler's *Kentucky Pioneers and Their Descendants* (1967), p. 204].

HOCKER (HAWKER), William (1752-1823). "William Hocker, aged 24" lived in Sugarland Hd. in 1776 and in Sugar Loaf Hd. (one taxable) in 1777 [Ref: R-31:10, K-1:213]. "William Hawker" was a private, 1st Co., Upper Bn., Militia, Aug. 30, 1777 [Ref: M-193, which mistakenly listed the name as "Hawkes"]. One William Hocker married Sarah Allnutt in Maryland and migrated to Lincoln County, Kentucky by 1811. Their son Larkin Hocker was born there on Nov. 20, 1811, and a son William Hocker was born on Sep. 8, 1814. They were in Missouri by 1824 [Ref: Stuart Seely Sprague's *Kentuckians in Missouri* (1984), p. 98. However, the *DAR Patriot Index* (Vol. I, p. 34) indicates William Hocker married Margaret Chrisman].

HOCKER (HAWKER), William Sr. (1721-1800). "William Hocker, Sr., aged 55" lived in Sugarland Hd. in 1776 and had three taxables in 1777 [Ref: K-1:213, R-31:12]. "William Hawker" took the Oath of Allegiance before the Hon. Gerrard Briscoe on March 2, 1778 [Ref: T-3:57, L-1:41]. Died testate in Montgomery County (wife named Susannah) in 1800 and had a son William (aged 24 in 1776), among other children [Ref: V-62].

HOCKMAN, John. Took the Oath of Allegiance in 1778 [Ref: L-2:27].

HOFFMAN, Martin. Took the Oath of Allegiance before the Hon. Richard Thompson in 1778 [Ref: T-3:75, L-1:41].

HOFFMAN, Peter. Took the Oath of Allegiance in 1778 [Ref: L-2:27].

HOGAN, Roger. Private, 6th Co., Lower Bn., Militia, July 15, 1780 [Ref: M-206].

HOGGINS (HUGGINS), John (died 1805). "John Huggins" rendered aid by providing wheat for use of the military in 1780 [Ref: O-337]. "John Hoggins" died testate in Montgomery County (wife named Tamer) in 1805 and mentioned a son John, among other children [Ref: V-67].

HOGGINS (HUGGINS), Peter (died 1798). "Peter Huggins" rendered aid by providing corn for use of the military in 1780 [Ref: O-288]. "Peter Hoggins" died testate in Montgomery County (wife named Catherine) in 1798 [Ref: V-67].

HOGGINS, Richard (died 1815). Private, 2nd Co., Upper Bn., Militia, Aug. 30, 1777 [Ref: M-193]. Private, Capt. Thomas Beall's Co., Maryland Line, 1780 [Ref: D-351]. Rendered aid by providing wheat for use of the military in 1781 [Ref: O-380]. Lived in Sugar Loaf Hd. (two taxables) in 1777 [Ref: R-31:10]. Died testate in Montgomery County (wife named Ann) in 1815 and mentioned his son Richard, among other children [Ref: V-67].

HOLBROOK, Margaret and William. See "Joseph Higdon," q.v.

HOLDEN, Charles. Private, 1st or 32nd Bn., Militia (no date was given; possibly June, 1777). [Ref: T-5:1].

HOLDER, John. Private, Capt. Price's Co., 3rd Maryland Line, 1781-1782 [Ref: D-453].

HOLLAND, Abraham. Took the Oath of Allegiance before the Hon. Gerrard Briscoe on March 2, 1778 [Ref: T-3:57, L-1:41]. Lived in Seneca Hd. (three taxables) in 1777 [Ref: R-31:8]. Abraham Holland married Asenath Spiers [Ref: DAR-I:337].

HOLLAND, Archibald. Private, 2nd Co., Middle Bn., Militia, Sep. 4, 1777 [Ref: M-196, T-5:37]. Took the Oath of Allegiance before the Hon. Gerrard Briscoe on March 2, 1778 [Ref: T-3:56, L-1:41]. Private, 6th Class, 2nd Co., Middle Bn., Militia, July 15, 1780 [Ref: M-201]. Lived in Sugar Loaf Hd. (one taxable) in 1777 [Ref: R-31:10]. See "Thomas Holland," q.v.

HOLLAND, Arnold. Son of William Holland [Ref: V-69]. Took the Oath of Allegiance before the Hon. Edward Burgess on Feb. 28, 1778 [Ref: T-3:60, L-1:41]. See "Nathan Holland," q.v.

HOLLAND, Benjamin (died 1810). Took the Oath of Allegiance before the Hon. Edward Burgess on Feb. 28, 1778 [Ref: T-3:63, L-1:41]. Rendered aid by providing wheat for use of the military in 1781 [Ref: O-394, O-445]. "Benjamin Holland" lived in Seneca Hd. (two taxables) in 1777 [Ref: R-31:8]. "Benjamin Holland, Sr." died testate in Montgomery County in 1810 and only named his grandson Zadok Holland [Ref: V-68]. Also see "Thomas Holland," q.v.

HOLLAND, Benjamin Jr. Private, 8th Co., Middle Bn., Militia, Sep., 1777 [Ref: M-197, T-5:43]. Took the Oath of Allegiance before the Hon. Gerrard Briscoe on March 2, 1778 [Ref: T-3:57, L-1:41]. Private, 5th Co., Middle Bn., Militia, July 15, 1780 [Ref: M-203]. Lived in the Upper Part of Newfoundland Hd. (one taxable) in 1777 [Ref: R-31:6].

HOLLAND, Capel. "Capel Holland" took the Oath of Allegiance before the Hon. Edward Burgess on Feb. 28, 1778 [Ref: T-3:60, L-1:41]. "Capil Holland" was a private, 7th Co., Lower Bn., Militia, July 15, 1780 [Ref: M-207]. "Capril Holland" was a private, 1st Co., Lower Bn., Militia, Sep.,

1777 [Ref: M-198, T-5:44]. "Capal Holland" lived in the Lower Part of Newfoundland Hd. (two taxables) in 1777 [Ref: R-31:5].

HOLLAND (HALLON), Edward. Two men with this name served at the same time: "Edward Holland" was a private, 4th Co., Lower Bn., Militia, July 15, 1780 [Ref: M-205]. "Edward Hallon" was a private, 6th Co., Middle Bn., Militia, July 15, 1780 [Ref: M-203].

HOLLAND, Jacob (1754-1838). Private, 2nd Maryland Line, enlisted on Feb. 29, 1776 [Ref: D-8]. He applied for pension (R5141) on July 23, 1832, in Monongalia County, Virginia, stating that he was born in March, 1754 and lived at Unity in Montgomery County, Maryland at the time of his enlistment. In 1790 he moved to Washington County, Maryland, in 1796 to Berkeley County, Virginia, and in 1801 to Monongalia County, Virginia. Jacob died on Sep. 17, 1838, while on a visit to a son in Harrison County. His widow Mary (maiden name Smith) died on April 12, 1840. Their children in 1851 were Allen (b. June 14, 1787), Elizabeth (aged 62), Daniel (aged 57), William (aged 54), Richard (aged 52), and Solomon (aged 47). A son Isaac Holland had pre-deceased his parents [Ref: P-83, DAR-I:337].

HOLLAND (HALAND, HOLLON), Joel (b. 1749). Private, 2nd Co., Middle Bn., Militia, Sep. 4, 1777 [Ref: M-196, T-5:37]. Private, 8th Class, 3rd Co., Middle Bn., Militia, July 15, 1780 [Ref: M-202]. "Joel Haland" took the Oath of Allegiance on Sep. 1, 1780, under the Act of May 12, 1780, having neglected to do so previously "due to ignorance of the duty owed the country." [Ref: R-27:112]. "Joel Hollon or Holland" lived in Sugar Loaf Hd. (one taxable) in 1776-1777 [Ref: K-1:204, R-31:10].

HOLLAND, John Jr. Private, 4th Co., Middle Bn., Militia, Sep., 1777 [Ref: M-196, T-5:39]. Took the Oath of Allegiance before the Hon. Edward Burgess on Feb. 28, 1778 [Ref: T-3:61, L-1:41]. Private, 5th Class, 4th Co., Middle Bn., Militia, July 15, 1780 [Ref: M-202].

HOLLAND (HALAND), John Sr. (died 1816). Private, 4th Co., Middle Bn., Militia, Sep., 1777 [Ref: M-196, T-5:39]. Private, 1st Class, 4th Co., Middle Bn., Militia, July 15, 1780 [Ref: M-202]. "John Haland" took the Oath of Allegiance on Sep. 1, 1780, under the Act of May 12, 1780, having neglected to do so previously "due to ignorance of the duty owed the country." [Ref: R-27:112]. "John Holland" lived in the Upper Part of Newfoundland Hd. (four taxables) in 1777 [Ref: R-31:6]. Died testate in Montgomery County (wife not named) in 1816 and mentioned his deceased sons Stephen and John, among other children then still living [Ref: V-68].

HOLLAND, Joseph. Private, 4th Co., Middle Bn., Militia, Sep., 1777 [Ref: M-196, T-5:39]. Took the Oath of Allegiance before the Hon. Edward Burgess on Feb. 28, 1778 [Ref: T-3:59, L-1:41].

HOLLAND, Nathan. Private, 2nd Co., Lower Bn., Militia, Sep., 1777 [Ref: M-198, T-5:45]. Took the Oath of Allegiance before the Hon. Edward Burgess on Feb. 28, 1778 [Ref: T-3:60, L-1:41]. Rendered aid by providing wheat for use of the military in 1780 [Ref: O-308]. Nathan Holland lived in Rock Creek Hd. (four taxables) in 1777 [Ref: R-31:16]. "Nathan Holland, Sr." died testate in Montgomery County (wife not named) in 1803 and mentioned son Nathan Holland, Jr., among others [Ref: V-68]. Also, William Holland died testate in 1781 and mentioned sons Nathan and Arnold [Ref: V-69].

HOLLAND (HALAND, HOLLON), Nehemiah. "Nehemiah Haland" took the Oath of Allegiance on Sep. 1, 1780, under the Act of May 12, 1780, having neglected to do so previously "due to ignorance of the duty owed the country." [Ref: R-27:112]. "Nehemiah Hollon" lived in Sugar Loaf Hd. (one taxable) in 1777 [Ref: R-31:10].

HOLLAND (HALAND), Otho. "Otho Holland" was a private, 4th Class, 4th Co., Middle Bn., Militia, July 15, 1780 [Ref: M-202]. Private, 4th Co., Middle Bn., Militia, Sep., 1777 [Ref: M-196, T-5:39]. "Otho Haland" took the Oath of Allegiance on Sep. 1, 1780, under the Act of May 12, 1780, having neglected to do so previously "due to ignorance of the duty owed the country." [Ref: R-27:112].

HOLLAND (HALAND), Richard. "Richard Haland" took the Oath of Allegiance on Sep. 1, 1780, under the Act of May 12, 1780, having neglected to do so previously "due to ignorance of the duty owed the country." [Ref: R-27:112].

HOLLAND, Rezin. Private, Capt. Edward Burgess' Co., Lower District of Frederick (now Montgomery) County, Militia, July, 1776 [Ref: D-42, which listed the name as "Reson Hollon"]. Private, 5th Co., Middle Bn., Militia, July 15, 1780 [Ref: M-203].

HOLLAND, Sollaman. Son of Nathan Holland, Sr. [Ref: V-68]. Private, 2nd Co., Lower Bn., Militia, Sep., 1777 [Ref: M-198, T-5:45]. "Solomon Holland" took the Oath of Allegiance before the Hon. Edward Burgess on Feb. 28, 1778 [Ref: T-3:60, L-1:41].

HOLLAND, Stephen. Private, 4th Co., Middle Bn., Militia, Sep., 1777 [Ref: M-196, T-5:39], and Ensign, Middle Bn., Militia, April 21, 1779, and Second Lieutenant, March 25, 1780 [Ref: M-88, E-357, F-120], and First Lieutenant, 4th Co., Middle Bn., Militia, July 15, 1780 [Ref: M-202]. Took the Oath of Allegiance before the Hon. Edward Burgess on Feb. 28, 1778 [Ref: T-3:61, L-1:41]. See "John Holland," q.v.

HOLLAND, Thomas. (1) Private, 7th Co., Middle Bn., Militia, Sep., 1777 [Ref: M-197, T-5:42]. Private, 7th Co., Middle Bn., Militia, July 15, 1780 [Ref: M-203]. (2) First Corporal, 5th Co., Middle Bn., Militia, July 15, 1780 [Ref: M-202]. Took the Oath of Allegiance (made his mark) before the Hon. Joseph Wilson on Feb. 28, 1778 [Ref: T-3:67, L-1:41]. One Thomas Holland lived in Seneca Hd. (one taxable) in 1777 [Ref: R-31:8]. "Thomas Holland, of Benjamin" died testate in Montgomery County (no wife or children) in 1787 and mentioned his father Benjamin and mother (not named) and brothers Archibald and Benjamin [Ref: V-69].

HOLLAND, William Jr. "William Holland, Jr." was a private, 5th Co., Upper Bn., Militia, Aug. 30, 1777 [Ref: M-194]. One "William Holland" married Ann Weyman in Montgomery County on Feb. 26, 1781 [Ref: K-2:519]. "William Holland, Jr." lived in Linganore Hd. (three taxables) in 1777 [Ref: R-31:9].

HOLLAND, William Sr. "William Holland, Sr." was a private, 5th Co., Upper Bn., Militia, Aug. 30, 1777 [Ref: M-194]. "William Holland" took the Oath of Allegiance (made his "H" mark) before the Hon. Edward Burgess on Feb. 28, 1778 [Ref: T-3:60, L-1:41]. William Holland lived in the Upper Part of Newfoundland Hd. (six taxables) in 1777 [Ref: R-31:6]. "William Holland" lived in Linganore Hd. (three taxables) in 1777 [Ref: R-31:9]. "William Holland, of Frederick County" died testate in Montgomery County (wife named Susanna) in 1781 and mentioned sons Nathan and Arnold. "William Holland, of Cassy(?)" died in 1794 (wife named Sary) and mentioned children, but none were named except son Nathan [Ref: V-69]. See Source DAR-I:337, and also "William Holland, Jr.," q.v.

HOLLAND, William, of Nathan. Constable in Linganore Hd. in 1779 [Ref: W-1]. Also see "William Holland, Jr.," q.v.

HOLLAND, Zadok. See "Benjamin Holland," q.v.

HOLLY, Elizabeth. See "Colin (Coaly) Brown," q.v.

HOLMEAD (HOLMED, HOLMAN), Anthony (b. 1724). "Antony Holmod or Anthony Holmed" lived in North West Hd. in 1776 and "Anthony Holman" lived there (three taxables) in 1777 [Ref: K-1:225, R-31:17]. "Anthony Holmead" took the Oath of Allegiance before the Hon. Richard Thompson in 1778 [Ref: T-3:75, L-1:41].

HOLMES, Harriet. See "Samuel Wade Magruder," q.v.

HOLMES, John. Took the Oath of Allegiance before the Hon. William Deakins, Jr. before March 3, 1778 [Ref: T-3:68, L-1:41]. Justice of the County Court in 1781 [Ref: W-2]. "John Holms" married Mary Turner in Montgomery County on Dec. 16, 1779 [Ref: K-2:514]. One John Holmes lived in the Lower Part of Newfoundland Hd. (six taxables) in 1777 and another lived in the Upper Part of Newfoundland Hd. (three taxables) in 1777 [Ref: R-31:5, R-31:6]. One John Holmes died testate in Montgomery County (wife named Isabella) in 1778 and mentioned his sons John and Josiah, among others. Another John Holmes died testate in 1797 (wife named Mary), leaving minor children, but no names were given [Ref: V-69].

HOLMES, Josias (Josiah). Son of John Holmes [Ref: V-69]. "Josias Holmes" was a private, 1st Co., Lower Bn., Militia, Sep., 1777 [Ref: M-198, T-5:44]. "Josiah Holmes" was a private, 7th Co., Lower Bn., Militia, July 15, 1780 [Ref: M-207].

HOLT (HOULT), Laurence. "Laurence Holt" was a private, 5th Co., Middle Bn., Militia, Sep., 1777 [Ref: M-197, T-5:40]. "Lawrence Owen

Hoult" was a son of Ralph Hoult "of Frederick County alias Montgomery County" who died testate in May, 1777 [Ref: V-70, V-71].

HOLT (HOULT), Ralph. See "Laurence and William Holt," q.v.

HOLT (HOULT), Thomas. "Thomas Hoult" was a private, 7th Co., Middle Bn., Militia, Sep., 1777 [Ref: M-197, T-5:42]. "Thomas Holt" was a private, 7th Co., Middle Bn., Militia, July 15, 1780 [Ref: M-204]. Took the Oath of Allegiance before the Hon. Gerrard Briscoe on March 2, 1778 [Ref: T-3:56, L-1:41]. Lived in Seneca Hd. (one taxable) in 1777 [Ref: R-31:8].

HOLT (HOULT), William. Son of Ralph Hoult who died testate in 1777 [Ref: V-70, V-71]. Private, 4th Class, 1st Co., Middle Bn., Militia, July 15, 1780 [Ref: M-201].

HOOD, John, of John. Private, 1st or 32nd Bn., Militia (no date was given; possibly June, 1777). [Ref: T-5:2].

HOOD, Thomas, of John. Served as a Captain, 1st or 32nd Bn., Militia (no date was given; possibly June, 1777). [Ref: T-5:1, T-5:2, which source indicated Montgomery County, but it actually may have been Anne Arundel or Frederick County].

HOOK, James. Took the Oath of Allegiance before the Hon. Edward Burgess on Feb. 28, 1778 [Ref: T-3:63, L-1:41].

HOPKINS, Anne. See "John Fleming," q.v.

HOPKINS, John. Private, 3rd Co., Middle Bn., Militia, Sep., 1777 [Ref: M-196, T-5:38]. Lived in the Upper Part of Potomac Hd. (eight taxables) in 1777 [Ref: R-31:14].

HOPKINS, John Jr. Took the Oath of Allegiance before the Hon. Richard Thompson in 1778 [Ref: T-3:75, L-1:41].

HOPKINS, Philip. Private, 4th Class, 1st Co., Middle Bn., Militia, July 15, 1780 [Ref: M-201].

HOPKINS, Richard. Private, 5th Co., Middle Bn., Militia, Sep., 1777 [Ref: M-196, T-5:40]. Served as a grand juror in Aug., 1777 [Ref: R-31:17], and as a petit juror in Nov., 1777 [Ref: R-31:18]. Took the Oath of Allegiance before the Hon. Joseph Offutt on March 2, 1778 [Ref: T-3:70, L-1:41]. Lived in the Upper Part of Potomac Hd. (one taxable) in 1777 [Ref: R-31:14].

HOPKINS, William. Private, Capt. Edward Burgess' Co., Lower District of Frederick (now Montgomery) County, Militia, July, 1776 [Ref: D-42].

HOPWOOD, John. Private, 6th Co., Middle Bn., Militia, Aug., 1777 [Ref: M-197, T-5:41]. Private, 6th Co., Middle Bn., Militia, July 15, 1780 [Ref: M-203]. Lived in Linganore Hd. (one taxable) in 1777 [Ref: R-31:9].

HORSFIELD, Thomas. Served as a Corporal, Capt. Thomas Beall's Co., Maryland Line, 1780 [Ref: D-350].

HOSKINS, Charles. See "Charles Hoskinson," q.v.

HOSKINS, Hugh. See "Hugh Hoskinson," q.v.

HOSKINS, Randolph. Private, Capt. Price's Co., 3rd Maryland Line, 1781-1782 [Ref: D-453].

HOSKINSON, Archibald. Private, Capt. Edward Burgess' Co., Lower District of Frederick (now Montgomery) County, Militia, July, 1776 [Ref: D-42].

HOSKINSON, Charles (b. 1749). Private, 1st Co., Upper Bn., Militia, Aug. 30, 1777 [Ref: M-193]. Took the Oath of Allegiance before the Hon. Elisha Williams on March 2, 1778 [Ref: T-3:82]. On Nov. 19, 1832, he applied for pension (S30493) in Breckenridge County, Kentucky, aged 73, stating that he lived in Frederick County, Maryland, at the time of his enlistment, and served in the Maryland Line. Rev. David Hoskinson was a witness to his statement [Ref: P-1714, Z-15]. "Charles Hoskinson" lived in Sugarland Hd. (one taxable) in 1777 [Ref: R-31:12]. "Charles Hoskins" [sic] married Eleanor Standiford in Montgomery County, Maryland, on Aug. 10, 1779 [Ref: K-2:515].

HOSKINSON, David Rev. See "Charles Hoskinson," q.v.

HOSKINSON, Elisha. Private, 7th Co., Lower Bn., Militia, Aug., 1777 [Ref: M-200, T-5:50]. Private, 4th Co., Lower Bn., Militia, July 15, 1780 [Ref: M-205]. Served as a grand juror in 1781 [Ref: W-2]. This name appeared twice on the list of men who took the Oath of Allegiance before the Hon. Edward Burgess on Feb. 28, 1778 [Ref: T-3:59, T-3:60, L-1:41]. Lived in the Lower Part of Newfoundland Hd. (three taxables) in 1777 [Ref: R-31:5].

HOSKINSON, Emma. See "Josiah Hoskinson, Jr.," q.v.

HOSKINSON, George (1751-1815). Private, 1st Co., Upper Bn., Militia, Aug. 30, 1777, and Ensign, 16th Bn., Sep. 12, 1777, and First Lieutenant, Upper Bn., April 21, 1779, and Captain, March 25, 1780 [Ref: M-89, M-193, E-356, F-120, and C-373, which latter source listed the name as "Horskins"]. Took the Oath of Allegiance before the Hon. Aneas Campbell on March 2, 1778 [Ref: T-3:77, L-1:41]. "George Hoskinson" lived in Sugarland Hd. (one taxable) in 1776-1777 [Ref: K-1:205, R-31:12]. Died testate in Montgomery County (wife not named) in 1815 [Ref: V-70]. Also see "George Hanskins," q.v.

HOSKINSON, Granville H. See "Josiah Hoskinson, Jr.," q.v.

HOSKINSON, Hugh (b. 1755). Served as an Ensign, Upper Bn., Militia, March 25, 1780 [Ref: M-89, F-120]. Took the Oath of Allegiance before the Hon. Elisha Williams on March 2, 1778 [Ref: T-3:80, L-1:40, which sources mistakenly listed the name as "Hugh Floskinson"]. "Heugh Hoskinson" lived in Sugarland Hd. in 1776 and "Hugh Hoskins" [sic] lived in Sugar Loaf Hd. (one taxable) in 1777 [Ref: K-1:218, R-31:10].

HOSKINSON, Jean. See "John Summers," q.v.

HOSKINSON, John (died 1795). Took the Oath of Allegiance before the Hon. Edward Burgess on Feb. 28, 1778 [Ref: T-3:62, L-1:41]. Served as a grand juror in 1781 [Ref: W-2]. Lived in the Lower Part of Newfoundland Hd. (one taxable) in 1777 [Ref: R-31:5]. Died testate in Montgomery County (wife not named) in 1795 [Ref: V-70]. See "Josiah Hoskinson, Jr.," q.v.

HOSKINSON (HOSKENSON), Josiah. Took the Oath of Allegiance before the Hon. Edward Burgess on Feb. 28, 1778 [Ref: T-3:63, L-1:41]. "Josiah Hoskenson" lived in the Upper Part of Newfoundland Hd. (one taxable) in 1777 [Ref: R-31:6], and "Josiah Hoskinson" lived in Rock Creek Hd. (one taxable) in 1777 [Ref: R-31:16. It must be noted that the *DAR Patriot Index* lists both Josiah Hoskinson (1756-1836, wife named Margaret Summers) and Josiah Hoskinson (1759-1836, second wife named Alcy Cutsinger) as sergeants from Maryland]. Also see "Josiah Hoskinson, Jr.," q.v.

HOSKINSON, Josiah Jr. (1756-1836). Private, 8th Co., Middle Bn., Militia, Sep., 1777, and Third Sergeant, 6th Co., Lower Bn., Militia, July 15, 1780 [Ref: M-198, M-206, T-5:43]. "Josiah Hoskinson, Jr." took the Oath of Allegiance before the Hon. Edward Burgess on Feb. 28, 1778 [Ref: T-3:62, L-1:41]. "Josiah Hoskinson" applied for pension (S41649) in Scioto County, Ohio, on June 27, 1818, and in 1820 stated he was aged 64 with a wife (not named) aged about 50 and these children: Polly (aged 31); John H. (aged 15); Granville H. (aged 13); Julia Chelia (aged 7); and Emma Dent (aged 7) [sic]. Josiah died on Feb. 12, 1836 in Scioto County, Ohio, and his widow Margaret died on Jan. 1, 1847, in Clinton County, Ohio, leaving these children: Emma Calvert, wife of George Calvert, of Scioto County, Ohio; Iorasa or Jorasa Oard, of Scioto County, Ohio; Ann Wilcoxon, wife of George Wilcoxon, of Illinois; and, John Hoskinson, of Iowa [Ref: P-1714].

HOSKINSON, Julia and Margaret. See "Josiah Hoskinson, Jr.," q.v.

HOSKINSON, Ninian. Fourth Corporal, 4th Co., Lower Bn., Militia, July 15, 1780 [Ref: M-205].

HOSKINSON, Polly. See "Josiah Hoskinson, Jr.," q.v.

HOSKINSON, Ruth. See "Joshua Harbin," q.v.

HOUCK, John. Took the Oath of Allegiance in 1778 [Ref: L-2:27].

HOUSE, Alexander. Private, 1st Co., Middle Bn., Militia, Aug. 30, 1777 [Ref: M-195].

HOUSE (HOWES), Edward. "Edward House" was a private, 8th Class, 3rd Co., Middle Bn., Militia, July 15, 1780 [Ref: M-202]. "Edward Hower" [Howes] rendered aid by providing wheat for use of the military in 1781 [Ref: O-424]. "Capt. Edward Howes, aged about 68, died Friday, Feb. 1, 1828, at Middlebrook Mills, long an inhabitant of this county." [Ref: F. Edward Wright's *Marriages and Deaths in the Newspapers of Frederick and Montgomery County, 1820-1830*, p. 77, Family Line Publications, 1987].

HOUSE (HOWES), John. Private, 1st Co., Middle Bn., Militia, Aug. 30, 1777 [Ref: M-195]. "John Howes" took the Oath of Allegiance before the Hon. Richard Thompson in 1778 [Ref: T-3:76, L-1:41]. Rendered aid by providing wheat for use of the military in 1781 [Ref: O-424]. "John House" (b. 1713) lived in George Town Hd. (one taxable) in 1776-1777 and "John Howes" lived in Seneca Hd. (one taxable) in 1777 [Ref: K-

1:193, R-31:8]. [Ref: R-31:3, R-31:7]. "John Hows" died testate in Montgomery County (wife named Mary) in 1809 and mentioned a son John, among others [Ref: V-71].

HOUSE (HOWES), William. Private, 1st Co., Middle Bn., Militia, Aug. 30, 1777 [Ref: M-195]. "William House" took the Oath of Allegiance before the Hon. Gerrard Briscoe on March 2, 1778 [Ref: T-3:56, L-1:41]. "William Howes" lived in Seneca Hd. (one taxable) in 1777 [Ref: R-31:8].

HOUSER (HOWSER), Martin (died 1812). Private, 3rd Co., Middle Bn., Militia, Sep., 1777 [Ref: M-196, T-5:38]. "Martin Houser or Howser" took the Oath of Allegiance before the Hon. Edward Burgess on Feb. 28, 1778 [Ref: T-3:63, L-1:41]. "Martin Houssen" [sic] rendered aid by providing wheat for use of the military in 1781 [Ref: O-412]. "Martin Howser" died testate in 1812 in Montgomery County; his wife Mary had died testate in 1807 [Ref: V-72].

HOUSER (HOWZER), Phillip. Youngest son of "Martin Howser," q.v. [Ref: V-72]. Private, 3rd Co., Middle Bn., Militia, Sep., 1777 [Ref: M-196, T-5:38]. Private, 4th Class, 2nd Co., Middle Bn., Militia, July 15, 1780 [Ref: M-201]. "Philip Houser" rendered aid by providing wheat for use of the military in 1781 [Ref: O-392]. "Philip Howzer" lived in the Upper Part of Potomac Hd. (four taxables) in 1777 [Ref: R-31:14].

HOUSLEY (HOWSLEY), Robert (c1710-1794). Took the Oath of Allegiance before the Hon. Charles Jones on Jan. 10, 1778 [Ref: T-3:71, L-1:41]. "Robert Housle, aged 56" [66?] lived in North West Hd. in 1776 and "Robert Housely" lived there in 1777 with a large family [Ref: K-1:223, R-31:17]. "Robert Howsley was born in London, England in 1710 and married Sarah Biggs in Maryland in 1735. Died in 1794. Robert Howsley, Jr. (b. 1762) married Catherine McNear in 1786 and migrated to Bardstown, Nelson County, Kentucky, in 1793." [Ref: Research files of Curtis Smith, of Santa Ana, California, 1967].

HOUSLEY (HOWSLEY), Robert Jr. (b. 1761 or 1762). Private, 8th Co., Lower Bn., Militia, Sep., 1777 [Ref: M-200, T-5:51]. Private, 7th Co., Middle Bn., Militia, July 15, 1780 [Ref: M-203]. Moved to Kentucky. See "Robert Housley" above.

HOUSLEY, William. "William Housley" was a private, Flying Camp, enlisted on July 18, 1776 [Ref: D-49]. "William Howley, aged 22" lived in Sugarland Hd. in 1776 [Ref: K-1:209].

HOUSTATTER, Francis. Took the Oath of Allegiance in 1778 [Ref: L-2:27].

HOWARD, Elisha. See "Leonard Hays," q.v.

HOWARD, George. Son of Thomas Howard [Ref: V-71]. Private, 3rd Co., Upper Bn., Militia, Aug. 30, 1777 [Ref: M-193]. Lived in Sugar Loaf Hd. (two taxables) in 1777 [Ref: R-31:10].

HOWARD, Henry. See "John Howard," q.v.

HOWARD, Jacob. Son of Thomas Howard [Ref: V-71]. Private, 3rd Co., Upper Bn., Militia, Aug. 30, 1777 [Ref: M-193]. Rendered aid by providing wheat, rye, corn, and flour for use of the military in 1780 and 1781 [Ref: O-295, O-306, O-341, O-379]. Lived in Sugar Loaf Hd. (two taxables) in 1777 [Ref: R-31:10].

HOWARD, John (c1760-1835). Private, 4th Co., Upper Bn., Militia, Aug. 30, 1777 [Ref: M-194], and private, Capt. Gray's Co., Maryland Line, 1780 [Ref: D-603]. Applied for pension in Mason County, Kentucky, on May 22, 1818, stating he had enlisted on Feb. 25, 1778, in Frederick County, Maryland, served in the 2nd Maryland Line, and moved to Montgomery County, Maryland after the war. In 1821 his wife, Margaret Stallions, was aged 61. In 1853, Henry Howard, son of John, stated his father died on Jan. 18, 1835, and that his mother Margaret Stallions had married his father in Montgomery County, Maryland in 1784. She died in Mason County, Kentucky, on Dec. 24, 1848, leaving these surviving children: Henry Howard (who was aged 62 in 1853), John Howard, Richard Howard, Maxie Johnson, Cynthia Reed (b. about 1790 before her parents moved to Kentucky), and Howard Howard [sic]. Some of the soldier's children lived in Kentucky and some in Ohio. A grandson, John Howard, son of Henry, lived in Mason County, Kentucky, in 1853 [Ref: K-2:357, P-1727, Y-16, Z-64, which latter two sources listed Howard Howard as a son of John Howard, but Ref: P-1727 did not].

HOWARD, Katherine. See "Charles Greenbury Griffith" and "Henry Griffith," q.v.

HOWARD, Margaret. See "John Howard," q.v.

HOWARD, Mary. See "Abraham Umstattd," q.v.

HOWARD, Rebecca. See "Thomas Pender," q.v.

HOWARD, Richard. See "John Howard," q.v.

HOWARD, Sarah. See "John Summers," q.v.

HOWARD, Thomas. Private, 3rd Co., Upper Bn., Militia, Aug. 30, 1777 [Ref: M-193]. Took the Oath of Allegiance before the Hon. Elisha Williams on March 2, 1778 [Ref: T-3:80, L-1:41]. Thomas Howard (four taxables) and Thomas Howard, Jr. (one taxable) lived in Sugar Loaf Hd. in 1777 [Ref: R-31:10]. "Thomas Howard, Sr., planter, of Frederick County" died testate in Montgomery County (wife named Susanna) in 1786 and mentioned his son Thomas, among others [Ref: V-71].

HOWARD, William. Son of "Thomas Howard," q.v. [Ref: V-71]. Private, 8th Co., Middle Bn., Militia, Sep., 1777 [Ref: M-198, T-5:43]. Private, 3rd Co., Upper Bn., Militia, Aug. 30, 1777 [Ref: M-193]. Private, 1st Class, 1st Co., Middle Bn., Militia, July 15, 1780 [Ref: M-201]. Took the Oath of Allegiance before the Hon. Elisha Williams on March 2, 1778 [Ref: T-3:81, L-1:41]. Lived in Sugar Loaf Hd. (one taxable) in 1777 [Ref: R-31:10].

HOWE, Daniel. Served as a musician (drum & fife) in Capt. Thomas Beall's Co., Maryland Line, 1780 [Ref: D-350].

HOWE, Paul. Took the Oath of Allegiance before the Hon. Joseph Wilson on Feb. 28, 1778 [Ref: T-3:64, L-1:41].

HOWELL, Joseph (b. 1743). Lived in Sugarland Hd. in 1776 [Ref: K-1:203]. It is not clear whether or nor he was the Joseph Howell, Jr. who was paymaster general in 1783-1785. Additional research is necessary before such a determination can be made, but he is included here just in case [Ref: D-268, D-272, D-477].

HOWES, John and William. See "John and William House," q.v.

HOY (HOYE), Paul (1736-1816). Lived in Linganore Hd. (two taxables) in 1777 [Ref: R-31:9]. Served as First Lieutenant, 8th Co., Middle Bn., Militia, Sep. 12, 1777 [Ref: M-90, M-197, C-373]. Rendered aid by providing wheat for use of the military in 1780 [Ref: O-337]. He was born on March 26, 1736, married Mariam Waller, and died on Oct. 13, 1816 [Ref: DAR-I:349].

HOY (HOYE), Thomas (1760-c1793). Private, 7th Maryland Line, 1778-1780. He married Agnes Scott [Ref: D-217, DAR-I:349].

HOYLE, Frederick. Took the Oath of Allegiance in 1778 [Ref: L-2:27].

HUFF, Jacob. Took the Oath of Allegiance in 1778 [Ref: L-2:27].

HUFF, Philip. Took the Oath of Allegiance in 1778 [Ref: L-2:27].

HUFFAN, David. Took the Oath of Allegiance in 1778 [Ref: L-2:28].

HUGGINS, John and Peter. See "John and Peter Hoggins," q.v.

HUGH (HUGHES), Andrew. See "Andrew Heugh," q.v.

HUGH, Thomas. Private, 4th Co., Lower Bn., Militia, Aug., 1777 [Ref: M-199, T-5:47].

HUGHES, Ann. See "Hezekiah Speaks," q.v.

HUGHES (HEUGHS), Edward. Private, 5th Co., Lower Bn., Militia, Aug., 1777 [Ref: M-199, T-5:48]. Private, 2nd Co., Lower Bn., Militia, July 15, 1780 [Ref: M-204]. "Edward Heughs" took the Oath of Allegiance before the Hon. Samuel W. Magruder in 1778 [Ref: T-3:74, L-1:41]. "Edward Hughes" lived in Lower Potomac Hd. (one taxable) in 1777 [Ref: R-31:4].

HUGHES, Henry. Private who was recruited to serve in the Continental Army in 1780 [Ref: D-341]. Private, Capt. Price's Co., 3rd Maryland Line, 1781-1782 [Ref: D-452].

HUGHES, John. (1) Private, 2nd Co., Middle Bn., Militia, Sep. 4, 1777 [Ref: M-196, T-5:37]. (2) Private, 7th Co., Middle Bn., Militia, Sep., 1777 [Ref: M-197, T-5:42]. "John Heughes, aged 34" lived in Sugarland Hd. in 1776 [Ref: K-1:205], and "John Hughs" lived in the Upper Part of Newfoundland Hd. (one taxable) in 1777 [Ref: R-31:6].

HUGHES, Kinsey. Served as a Second Corporal, 7th Co., Middle Bn., Militia, July 15, 1780 [Ref: M-203].

HUGHES (HEWS), Nathaniel. Private, 5th Co., Middle Bn., Militia, Sep., 1777 [Ref: M-197, T-5:40]. Private, 3rd Class, 1st Co., Middle Bn., Militia, July 15, 1780 [Ref: M-201]. "Nathaniel Hews" took the Oath of Allegiance (made his "X" mark) before the Hon. Joseph Wilson on Feb. 28, 1778 [Ref: T-3:67, L-1:41].

HULL, Anthony W. Took the Oath of Allegiance in 1778 [Ref: L-2:28].
HULL, John. Took the Oath of Allegiance in 1778 [Ref: L-2:28].
HUMPHRIES, Mary. See "Asa Darby," q.v.
HUNGERFORD, Charles. Private, 1st Co., Upper Bn., Militia, Aug. 30, 1777 [Ref: M-193]. Took the Oath of Allegiance before the Hon. Elisha Williams on March 2, 1778 [Ref: T-3:81, L-1:42]. Justice of Montgomery County who represented that county in the House of Delegates, 1780-1781 [Ref: N-84, H-467]. "Charles Hungarford" lived in Sugarland Hd. (eight taxables) in 1777 [Ref: R-31:12].
HUNTER, Henry (died 1781). Private, 2nd Co., Upper Bn., Militia, Aug. 30, 1777 [Ref: M-193]. Took the Oath of Allegiance before the Hon. Elisha Williams on March 2, 1778 [Ref: T-3:80, L-1:42]. Lived in Sugar Loaf Hd. (one taxable) in 1777 [Ref: R-31:10]. Died testate in Montgomery County (wife named Susannah) in 1781 [Ref: V-72].
HUNTER, Joshua (b. 1750). Private, 8th Co., Upper Bn., Militia, Aug. 30, 1777 [Ref: M-195]. Took the Oath of Allegiance (made his "X" mark) before the Hon. Aneas Campbell on March 2, 1778 [Ref: T-3:78, L-1:42]. Lived in Sugarland Hd. in 1776 and had three taxables in 1777 [Ref: K-1:210, R-31:12].
HURDLE, Lawrence (1758-1848). Private, Capt. Edward Burgess' Co., Lower District of Frederick (now Montgomery) County, Militia, July, 1776 [Ref: D-42]. Private, 6th Co., Lower Bn., Militia, Aug., 1777 [Ref: M-200, T-5:49]. Private, 7th Maryland Line, from May 11, 1778 to Nov. 1, 1780 [Ref: D-216]. Took the Oath of Allegiance before the Hon. Joseph Wilson on Feb. 28, 1778 [Ref: T-3:64, L-1:42]. Lawrence Hurdle or Hurdell applied for pension in Montgomery County on July 21, 1818, aged 60, and in 1820 he had a wife Nancy (aged 45), two daughters (aged 12 and 8), and three sons (aged 10, 5, and 3). In Alexandria County, Virginia on Aug. 30, 1849, his widow Nancy, aged 77, applied for pension (W2157) and stated she was a daughter of Leonard Wheeler and had married Lawrence Hurdle in Georgetown, D. C. on Oct. 20, 1790 or 1793 at the home of Leonard Hurdle, the uncle of Noble Hurdle. In 1855, Noble Hurdle of Washington, D. C. stated that Lawrence and wife had twelve children, but nine died before their father. Lawrence Hurdle died Dec. 1, 1848, and his three surviving children were Levi, Thomas and Ann Hurdle [Ref: P-1781].
HURDLE, Nancy and Noble. See "Lawrence Hurdle," q.v.
HURDLE, Richard (b. 1741). Lived in Lower Potomac Hd. in 1776 [Ref: K-1:183]. Private, 5th Class, 1st Co., Middle Bn., Militia, July 15, 1780 [Ref: M-201]. Took the Oath of Allegiance before the Hon. Edward Burgess on Feb. 28, 1778 [Ref: T-3:63, L-1:42].
HURDLE, Robert (1759-1840). Private, 6th Maryland Line, from June 9, 1777 until March 13, 1778, when "discharged by the Governor of Maryland." Applied for pension on May 17, 1818, aged 59, in Montgomery County, stating he had enlisted at Georgetown, Maryland

and married Susan Riggs on Jan. 29, 1809. In 1822 he referred to two children aged 12 and 10, but no names were given. Sarah W. Smith stated she was "one of the family of Robert Hurdle" and a James Smith stated he married into the family. Robert died on Feb. 3 or 5, 1840, in Montgomery County, and his widow applied for a pension (W7845) on Feb. 26, 1853, aged 82 [Ref: D-282, J-38, P-1781].

HURDLY, Hezekiah. Private, 6th Co., Lower Bn., Militia, Aug., 1777 [Ref: M-200, T-5:49].

HURLEY, Josiah (died 1778). Lived in Lower Potomac Hd. (one taxable) in 1777 [Ref: R-31:4]. Private, 5th Maryland Regiment, from June 6, 1778 until it was noted in Feb., 1779, that he had "died some months since." [Ref: D-213].

HURLEY, Sarah. See "Vachel Harding," q.v.

HURLEY, Thomas. Private, 5th Co., Upper Bn., Militia, Aug. 30, 1777 [Ref: M-194]. Lived in Sugar Loaf Hd. (one taxable) in 1777 [Ref: R-31:10].

HURLEY, William (b. 1760). Lived in Lower Potomac Hd. in 1776 [Ref: K-1:183]. Served as a private in the 7th Maryland Regiment, Continental Army, in 1780 [Ref: D-217, D-341, F-114]. His invalid (disability) pension commenced on Dec. 14, 1784, and he was still on the rolls on Nov. 1, 1789 [Ref: D-632].

HURRY, David. Took the Oath of Allegiance before the Hon. Edward Burgess on Feb. 28, 1778 [Ref: T-3:63, L-1:42]. Also see "David Harry," q.v.

HUSTON, John. Private, 8th Class, 3rd Co., Middle Bn., Militia, July 15, 1780 [Ref: M-202].

HUSTON, Thomas. Took the Oath of Allegiance in 1778 [Ref: L-2:28].

HUTCHINSON, Francis (b. 1753). Private and invalid (disabled) pensioner in 1840, aged 87, living in the household of Samuel Thrift in Montgomery County, 3rd Division [Ref: R-28:443, J-16].

HUTCHINSON (HUCHINSON), John. "John Hutchinson" took the Oath of Allegiance before the Hon. Edward Burgess on Feb. 28, 1778 [Ref: T-3:63, L-1:42]. "John Huchinson" lived in Rock Creek Hd. (one taxable) in 1777 [Ref: R-31:16].

HUTH (HUTT?), Samuel (b. 1718). Took the Oath of Allegiance before the Hon. Richard Thompson in 1778 [Ref: T-3:75, L-1:42]. "Samuel Huth" lived in George Town Hd. (two taxables) in 1777 [Ref: R-31:3]. "Samuel Hatt" [Hutt?] lived there in 1776 [Ref: K-1:193].

HUTTON, Paul. "Recruit from Montgomery County who was retained in the service and sent on board the Galleys" in June 22, 1778 [Ref: E-144, but not listed in *Archives of Maryland, Volume 18*].

HUTTS, Andrew (b. 1740). Private, 1st Co., Upper Bn., Militia, Aug. 30, 1777 [Ref: M-193]. Took the Oath of Allegiance before the Hon. Aneas Campbell on March 2, 1778 [Ref: T-3:78, L-1:42]. "Andrew Huts or

Hutts" lived in Sugarland Hd. (one taxable) in 1776-1777 [Ref: K-1:204, R-31:12].
HUTTS, James. Took the Oath of Allegiance before the Hon. Aneas Campbell on March 2, 1778 [Ref: T-3:78, L-1:42].
HYETT, James. Private, 1st or 32nd Bn., Militia (no date was given; possibly June, 1777). [Ref: T-5:1].
HYLAND (HILAND), Hugh. "Hugh Hyland" was a private, 4th Co., Middle Bn., Militia, Sep., 1777 [Ref: M-196, T-5:39]. "Hugh Hiland" took the Oath of Allegiance before the Hon. Edward Burgess on Feb. 28, 1778 [Ref: T-3:59, L-1:42]. "Hugh Hilard" [Hiland] lived in the Upper Part of Newfoundland Hd. (two taxables) in 1777 [Ref: R-31:6].
HYNER, Nicholas. Private, Capt. Price's Co., 3rd Maryland Line, 1781-1782 [Ref: D-452].
IHENBURY, John. Took the Oath of Allegiance in 1778 [Ref: L-2:28].
INGRAM, Thomas (b. 1753). Private, 3rd Co., Lower Bn., Militia, Sep., 1777 [Ref: M-199, T-5:46]. Took the Oath of Allegiance before the Hon. Richard Thompson in 1778 [Ref: T-3:76, L-1:42]. Private, 8th Co., Lower Bn., Militia, July 15, 1780 [Ref: M-207]. "Thomas Jingrims" lived in George Town Hd. in 1776 [Ref: K-1:193].
INMAN (INGMAN), William. "William Inman" was a private, 6th Co., Middle Bn., Militia, Aug., 1777 [Ref: M-197, T-5:41]. "William Ingman" lived in Linganore Hd. (one taxable) in 1777 [Ref: R-31:0].
IRELAND, Alerd [sic]. Took the Oath of Allegiance in 1778 [Ref: L-2:28].
IRELAND, William. Private, 8th Co., Middle Bn., Militia, Sep., 1777 [Ref: M-198, T-5:43]. Private, 7th Co., Middle Bn., Militia, July 15, 1780 [Ref: M-203].
IRLAND (ISLAND?), Hugh. Private, 8th Class, 4th Co., Middle Bn., Militia, July 15, 1780 [Ref: M-202].
IRONBROAD, John Yost. Took the Oath of Allegiance in 1778 [Ref: L-2:28].
ISAAC (ISAACS), Lazarus. "Lasarus Isaac" was a private, 7th Co., Lower Bn., Militia, Aug., 1777 [Ref: M-200, T-5:50]. "Lazarus Isaacs" married Sarah Fightmaster in Montgomery County on Oct. 23, 1777 [Ref: K-2:522]. "Lazarus Isade" [Isaac?] took the Oath of Allegiance before the Hon. Edward Burgess on Feb. 28, 1778 [Ref: T-3:60, L-1:42].
JACKSON, Benjamin (a free mulatto). Took the Oath of Allegiance in Montgomery County on March 30, 1778 [Ref: C-559].
JACKSON, Bennett (b. 1728). Private, 2nd Co., Upper Bn., Militia, Aug. 30, 1777 [Ref: M-193]. Rendered aid by providing wheat for use of the military in 1780 [Ref: O-316]. Lived in Sugarland Hd. (one taxable) in 1776-1777 [Ref: K-1:198, R-31:12].
JACKSON, James (b. 1759). Lived in Lower Potomac Hd. in 1776 [Ref: K-1:183]. Rendered aid by providing wheat for use of the military in 1780 [Ref: O-328]. James Jackson married Charity Baker in Montgomery County on Jan. 6, 1780 [Ref: K-2:519].

JACKSON, John. Private, 5th Co., Lower Bn., Militia, Aug., 1777 [Ref: M-199, T-5:48]. One John Jackson, aged 20, lived in Lower Potomac Hd. (two taxables) in 1776-1777 [Ref: R-31:4, K-1:183], and another John Jackson, aged 18, lived in Sugarland Hd. in 1776 [Ref: K-1:198].
JACKSON, Margaret. See "Samuel Magruder," q.v.
JACKSON, Mary. See "Thomas Cramphin, Jr." and "Charles Jones" and "Joseph Magruder," q.v.
JACKSON, Nicholas. Took the Oath of Allegiance before the Hon. Edward Burgess on Feb. 28, 1778 [Ref: T-3:62, L-1:42]. Lived in the Lower Part of Newfoundland Hd. (six taxables) in 1777 [Ref: R-31:5].
JACKSON, William. Private, 1st Co., Lower Bn., Militia, Sep., 1777 [Ref: M-198, T-5:44]. Took the Oath of Allegiance before the Hon. Edward Burgess on Feb. 28, 1778 [Ref: T-3:62, L-1:42].
JACOBS, Edward (b. 1759). Son of Jeremiah Jacobs, of Sugarland Hd., in 1776 [Ref: K-1:218]. Private, 2nd Co., Upper Bn., Militia, Aug. 30, 1777 [Ref: M-193]. Edward Jacobs married Mary Summers in Montgomery County on Oct. 28, 1779 [Ref: K-2:519]. "Edward G. Jacobs" applied for a pension (S1540) on June 27, 1833 in Rutherford County, North Carolina, aged 73 (on Jan. 4, 1833), stating he was born in Jan., 1759, "in Montgomery or an adjoining county in Maryland." He lived in Montgomery County when he served in the war, married in 1779 [wife not named], and moved to North Carolina and enlisted again. He lived in Iredell County for 20 years, then moved to the Clinch River in East Tennessee for 5 years, and then he moved to Wilson County, Tennessee around 1803 [Ref: P-1816].
JACOBS, Elinor. See "Philemon Griffith," q.v.
JACOBS, Greenberry. See "Joseph Jacobs," q.v.
JACOBS, Jeremiah (b. 1718). Took the Oath of Allegiance before the Hon. Aneas Campbell on March 2, 1778 [Ref: T-3:77, L-1:42]. Lived in Sugarland Hd. in 1776 (wife named Rachel) and had six taxables in 1777 [Ref: K-1:218, R-31:12].
JACOBS, Jesse. It was noted by the Council of Maryland on Sep. 5, 1781, that Jesse Jacobs, among other soldiers of the Maryland Line, "returned from captivity in South Carolina in a distressed situation," and it was ordered that he be paid five pounds on account [Ref: G-598].
JACOBS (JACOB), Joseph (1750-1838). Private, 6th Co., Upper Bn., Militia, Aug. 30, 1777 [Ref: M-194]. "Joseph Jacob" took the Oath of Allegiance before the Hon. Elisha Williams on March 2, 1778 [Ref: T-3:80, L-1:42]. "Joseph Jacobs" lived in Sugar Loaf Hd. (one taxable) in 1777 [Ref: R-31:10]. One Joseph Jacobs applied for a pension in Bedford County, North Carolina, on Feb. 5, 1834, "aged 83 years, 8 months and some few days." He stated he was born in Maryland in 1750 and lived in Rowan County, North Carolina at the time of his enlistment. After the war he moved to Anderson County, Tennessee, then to Rutherford County, and then to Bedford County. His widow Lucy applied for

pension (W7875) on March 25, 1841, aged 90, stating Joseph had died on Dec. 9, 1838. A son Greenberry Jacobs made affidavit in Rutherford County in 1841 [Ref: P-1817].

JACOBS, Zachariah (b. 1753). Son of Jeremiah Jacobs, of Sugarland Hd., in 1776 [Ref: K-1:218]. Private, 2nd Co., Upper Bn., Militia, Aug. 30, 1777 [Ref: M-193]. Took the Oath of Allegiance before the Hon. Edward Burgess on Feb. 28, 1778 [Ref: T-3:63, L-1:42]. He married Dorkus Summers in Montgomery County on Aug. 5, 1779 [Ref: K-2:519].

JAMES, Edward. See "Edward Janes," q.v.

JAMES, Mary. See "Ninian Barrett," q.v.

JAMES, Thomas. Private, 8th Co., Lower Bn., Militia, Sep., 1777 [Ref: M-200, T-5:51]. Private, 6th Co., Lower Bn., Militia, July 15, 1780 [Ref: M-206]. Also see "Thomas Janes," q.v.

JAMISON, Samuel. Took the Oath of Allegiance in 1778 [Ref: L-2:28].

JAMLINE, Grove. Took the Oath of Allegiance (made his "X" mark) before the Hon. Aneas Campbell on March 2, 1778 [Ref: T-3:77, L-1:42].

JANES, Edward. Private, 7th Co., Lower Bn., Militia, Aug., 1777 [Ref: M-200, T-5:50]. "Edward Janes" took the Oath of Allegiance (made his "I" mark) before the Hon. Edward Burgess on Feb. 28, 1778 [Ref: T-3:62, L-1:42]. "Edward James" [sic] lived in the Lower Part of Newfoundland Hd. (two taxables) in 1777 [Ref: R-31:5].

JANES, Thomas. Private, 5th Co., Lower Bn., Militia, Aug., 1777 [Ref: M-199, T-5:48]. Also see "Thomas James," q.v.

JANES, William, and others. See "William Jeans" and others, q.v.

JARBOE (JARBO), Gerrard (Gerard). "Gerard Jarboe" took the Oath of Allegiance before the Hon. Edward Burgess on Feb. 28, 1778 [Ref: T-3:58, L-1:42]. "Garrard Jarbo" lived in the Lower Part of Newfoundland Hd. (two taxables) in 1777 [Ref: R-31:5].

JARBOE, Henry Barton. Took the Oath of Allegiance before the Hon. Edward Burgess on Feb. 28, 1778 [Ref: T-3:58, L-1:42].

JARBOE (JARBO), Stephen. Private, 6th Co., Lower Bn., Militia, Aug., 1777 [Ref: T-5:49]. Took the Oath of Allegiance before the Hon. Joseph Offutt on March 2, 1778 [Ref: T-3:70, L-1:42]. "Stephen Jarbo" was a private, 3rd Co., Lower Bn., Militia, July 15, 1780 [Ref: M-205]. "Stephen Jarboe" lived in the Upper Part of Potomac Hd. (one taxable) in 1777 [Ref: R-31:14].

JARMEY (JARMY), William. Private, Rawlings' Regiment, March 1, 1779, and Private, Capt. Thomas Beall's Co., Maryland Line, 1780 [Ref: D-128, D-351].

JARVIS, Elisha. Private, 1st Co., Middle Bn., Militia, Aug. 30, 1777 [Ref: M-195]. Took the Oath of Allegiance before the Hon. Gerrard Briscoe on March 2, 1778 [Ref: T-3:57, L-1:42]. Private, 1st Class, 5th Co., Middle Bn., Militia, July 15, 1780 [Ref: M-202].

JARVIS, Susannah. See "Lewis Mullikin," q.v.

JARVIS (JERVIS), Zadock. Private, 1st Co., Middle Bn., Militia, Aug. 30, 1777 [Ref: M-195]. Private, 1st Class, 5th Co., Middle Bn., Militia, July 15, 1780 [Ref: M-202]. "Zadock Jarvis" took the Oath of Allegiance before the Hon. Gerrard Briscoe on March 2, 1778 [Ref: T-3:57, L-1:42]. "Zadock Jervis" lived in Seneca Hd. (one taxable) in 1777 [Ref: R-31:8]. He was probably a son of "Jarrett Garvis" who died testate in 1804 [Ref: V-54].

JAVETT, William. Took the Oath of Allegiance before the Hon. Elisha Williams on March 2, 1778 [Ref: T-3:80, L-1:42].

JEANS, Henry (b. 1753). Lived in Lower Potomac Hd. in 1776 [Ref: K-1:183]. Servd as a private, 1st Co., Lower Bn., Militia, July 15, 1780 [Ref: M-204].

JEANS, Joseph. Private, and then Sergeant, in Rawlings Regiment, Maryland Line, on Oct. 1, 1779, and Sergeant, Capt. Thomas Beall's Co., Maryland Line, 1780 [Ref: D-128, D-350].

JEANS (JANES), William. "William Janes" was a private, 7th Co., Middle Bn., Militia, Sep., 1777 [Ref: M-197, T-5:42]. "William Jeans" lived in the Upper Part of Potomac Hd. (four taxables) in 1777 [Ref: R-31:14].

JEANS (JEAN), Zachariah. Private, 7th Co., Lower Bn., Militia, July 15, 1780 [Ref: M-207]. "Zachariah Jean" took the Oath of Allegiance (made his "Z" mark) before the Hon. Edward Burgess on Feb. 28, 1778 [Ref: T-3:58, L-1:42].

JEFFERY, Benjamin. Took the Oath of Allegiance before the Hon. Edward Burgess on Feb. 28, 1778 [Ref: T-3:62, L-1:42]. "Benjamin Jeffereys" lived in the Upper Part of Newfoundland Hd. (one taxable) in 1777 [Ref: R-31:6].

JENKINS, Edward (b. 1756). Substitute from Montgomery County who was discharged from the Maryland Line on Dec. 3, 1781 [Ref: I-11, D-409]. "Edward Ginkinks" lived in Sugarland Hd. in 1776 [Ref: K-1:219].

JENKINS, John. Private, 2nd Co., Middle Bn., Militia, Sep. 4, 1777 [Ref: M-195].

JENKINS, Philip. Private, 1st Maryland Line, from Dec. 10, 1776 until taken prisoner on Sep. 16, 1778; discharged Dec. 27, 1779 [Ref: D-125]. This or perhaps another Philip Jenkins was a Substitute from Montgomery County who was discharged on Nov. 29, 1781 [Ref: I-7].

JENNINGS, Elizabeth. See "Richard Stevens," q.v.

JENNINGS, John (b. 1720). "John Jennens" lived in North West Hd. in 1776 [Ref: K-1:224]. "John Jennings" took the Oath of Allegiance before the Hon. Charles Jones on Jan. 10, 1778 [Ref: T-3:71, L-1:42]. Rendered aid by providing wheat for use of the military in 1780 [Ref: O-315, O-333].

JENNINGS, Lucy. See "Thomas Rigdon," q.v.

JENNINGS (GENING), William. "William Gening (Jennings)" lived in North West Hd. (one taxable) in 1777 [Ref: R-31:17]. "William Jennings" was a private, 2nd Maryland Regiment, 1776-1778 [Ref: D-126, D-314].

JERRARD, William. Private, 2nd Co., Upper Bn., Militia, Aug. 30, 1777 [Ref: M-193].

JERRE, Alexander. Took the Oath of Allegiance before the Hon. Elisha Williams on March 2, 1778 [Ref: T-3:80, L-1:42].

JETER, Polly. See "Thomas Bateman (Batman)," q.v.

JEWELL, William (b. 1741). Private, 1st Co., Upper Bn., Militia, Aug. 30, 1777 [Ref: M-193]. Took the Oath of Allegiance before the Hon. Edward Burgess on Feb. 28, 1778 [Ref: T-3:63, L-1:42]. Lived in Sugarland Hd. (two taxables) in 1776-1777 [Ref: K-1:206, R-31:12].

JOHNS, Elizabeth. See "Archibald Orme," q.v.

JOHNS, Margaret A. See "Elisha Williams," q.v.

JOHNS, Richard. Private, 5th Class, 2nd Co., Middle Bn., Militia, July 15, 1780 [Ref: M-201]. "Capt. Richard Johns, of Montgomery County" is mentioned in a letter from Thomas Price, of Frederick County, to Governor Lee on Nov. 23, 1781, regarding his delivery of "cattle unfit for slaughter" and noting that the local farmers were not willing to incur the expense of maintaining them through the winter [Ref: H-555]. The wills of "Richard Johns, of Georgetown" and "Thomas Johns" (whose eldest son was named Richard) were both probated on July 25, 1794 [Ref: V-73].

JOHNS, Richard W. Private, 1st Co., Lower Bn., Militia, Sep., 1777 [Ref: M-198, T-5:44]. Private, 7th Co., Lower Bn., Militia, July 15, 1780 [Ref: M-206].

JOHNS (JOHN), Thomas. (1) Lieutenant Colonel, 29th Bn., Militia, Jan. 6, 1776 [Ref: M-92]. Took the Oath of Allegiance before the Hon. Charles Jones on Jan. 10, 1778 [Ref: T-3:71, L-1:42]. Register of Wills, appointed May 6, 1779 [Ref: O-220, E-380]. He resigned on May 19, 1779 [Ref: E-401]. (2) Private, 4th Co., Lower Bn., Militia, Aug., 1777 [Ref: M-199, T-5:47]. One "Thomas Johns" rendered aid by providing wheat for use of the military in 1780 [Ref: O-308]. One Thomas Johns (aged 39) lived in Lower Potomac Hd. in 1776 and had seven taxables in 1777 [Ref: R-31:4, K-1:183]. See "Richard Johns," q.v.

JOHNS, Weavour. Took the Oath of Allegiance before the Hon. Edward Burgess on Feb. 28, 1778 [Ref: T-3:62, L-1:42].

JOHNSON, Bartholomew (b. 1741). Private, 4th Co., Upper Bn., Militia, Aug. 30, 1777 [Ref: M-194]. Took the Oath of Allegiance before the Hon. Aneas Campbell on March 2, 1778 [Ref: T-3:77, L-1:42]. "Barthlomer or Batholomew Johnson" lived in Sugarland Hd. (two taxables) in 1776-1777 [Ref: K-1:205, R-31:12].

JOHNSON, Benjamin. Private, 5th Co., Upper Bn., Militia, Aug. 30, 1777 [Ref: M-194]. Took the Oath of Allegiance on Sep. 1, 1780, under the Act of May 12, 1780, having neglected to do so previously "due to ignorance of the duty owed the country." [Ref: R-27:114]. Rendered aid by providing wheat for use of the military in 1781 [Ref: O-395]. Benjamin Johnson, Sr. (four taxables) and Benjamin Johnson, Jr. (one taxable) lived in Sugar Loaf Hd. in 1777 [Ref: R-31:10]. One Benjamin Johnson died testate in Montgomery County (wife named Rachel) in 1795 and mentioned a son Benjamin, among others [Ref: V-73].

JOHNSON, Isaac (b. 1751 or 1752). Private, 1st Co., Upper Bn., Militia, Aug. 30, 1777 [Ref: M-193]. Took the Oath of Allegiance before the Hon. Elisha Williams on March 2, 1778 [Ref: T-3:81, L-1:42]. Lived in Sugarland Hd. in 1776-1777 [Ref: K-1:219, R-31:12].

JOHNSON, James. Private, 2nd Class, 1st Co., Middle Bn., Militia, July 15, 1780 [Ref: M-201].

JOHNSON, John. (1) Captain, 5th Co., Lower Bn., Militia, from Dec. 7, 1776, to at least Feb. 5, 1781 [Ref: M-92, M-199, T-5:48, B-464, B-511, R-33:155, X-1146]. "Capt. John Johnson" lived in Lower Potomac Hd. (three taxables) in 1777 [Ref: R-31:4]. (2) Private, 3rd Co., Upper Bn., Militia, Aug. 30, 1777 [Ref: M-193]. (3) Private, 4th Co., Middle Bn., Militia, Sep., 1777 [Ref: M-196, T-5:39]. Private, 2nd Co., Lower Bn., Militia, July 15, 1780 [Ref: M-204]. One John Johnson took the Oath of Allegiance before the Hon. Edward Burgess on Feb. 28, 1778 [Ref: T-3:58, L-1:42], and another took the Oath of Allegiance before the Hon. Samuel W. Magruder in 1778 [Ref: T-3:73, L-1:42]. Served as a grand juror in 1779 [Ref: W-1]. Rendered aid by providing wheat for use of the military in 1780 [Ref: O-306, O-312]. One John Johnson married Ann Kimey in Montgomery County on Jan. 4, 1781 [Ref: K-2:519]. One John Johnson lived in Sugar Loaf Hd. (one taxable) in 1777 [Ref: R-31:10].

JOHNSON, Jonathan. Private, 3rd Co., Upper Bn., Militia, Aug. 30, 1777 [Ref: M-193]. Jonathan Johnson married Mary Summers in Montgomery County on Oct. 10, 1779 [Ref: K-2:519].

JOHNSON, Joseph. Private, 4th Co., Middle Bn., Militia, Sep., 1777 [Ref: M-196, T-5:39]. Private, 3rd Class, 4th Co., Middle Bn., Militia, July 15, 1780 [Ref: M-202].

JOHNSON, Maxie. See "John Howard," q.v.

JOHNSON, Richard. Son of Thomas Johnson, Sr. [Ref: V-74]. Private, 6th Co., Middle Bn., Militia, Aug., 1777 [Ref: M-197, T-5:41]. Took the Oath of Allegiance before the Hon. Edward Burgess on Feb. 28, 1778 [Ref: T-3:61, L-1:42]. Private, 6th Co., Middle Bn., Militia, July 15, 1780 [Ref: M-203]. Lived in Linganore Hd. (one taxable) in 1777 [Ref: R-31:9].

JOHNSON, Robert M. See "Clement Dowden," q.v.

JOHNSON, Samuel. Private, 3rd Co., Upper Bn., Militia, Aug. 30, 1777 [Ref: M-193]. Samuel Johnson married Agnes Wilson in Montgomery County on Oct. 12, 1777 [Ref: K-2:516].

JOHNSON, Thomas. Private, 4th Co., Middle Bn., Militia, Sep., 1777 [Ref: M-196, T-5:39]. Private, 3rd Class, 4th Co., Middle Bn., Militia, July 15, 1780 [Ref:202].One Thomas Johnson took the Oath of Allegiance (made his "X" mark) before the Hon. Edward Burgess on Feb. 28, 1778 [Ref: T-3:59, L-1:42], and two took the Oath of Allegiance (made their "X" marks) before the Hon. Edward Burgess on Feb. 28, 1778 [Ref: T-3:58, T-3:60, L-1:42]. One Thomas Johnson married Mary Larure in Montgomery County on March 17, 1778 [Ref: K-2:516]. Thomas Johnson (one taxable) and Thomas Johnson, Sr. (three taxables) both lived in the Upper Part of Newfoundland Hd. in 1777 [Ref: R-31:6]. One Thomas Johnson died testate in Montgomery County (wife not named) in 1823 and mentioned a son Thomas, among others, and Thomas Johnson, Sr. died testate in Montgomery County (wife not named) in 1796 [Ref: V-74].

JOHNSON, William. (1) Captain, 29th Bn., Militia, Sep. 12, 1777, to at least Aug. 8, 1780 [Ref: M-93, C-373, F-248, K-2:360, K-2:408]. (2) Private, enrolled into a company of militia for the service of the Flying Camp, Oct. 15, 1776 [Ref: B-353].

JOHNSTON, Ann. See "James Wilson," q.v.

JOHNSTON, Archibald. Served as a Sergeant, Capt. Price's Co., 3rd Maryland Line, 1781-1782 [Ref: D-452].

JOHNSTON (JOHNSTONE), Henry. Took the Oath of Allegiance in 1778 [Ref: L-2:28].

JOHNSTON, Thomas. Served as a private and corporal, 6th Maryland Line, 1777-1780 [Ref: D-219].

JONES, Abraham (1754-1823). Private, 8th Co., Upper Bn., Militia, Aug. 30, 1777 [Ref: M-195]. Lived in North West Hd. in 1776 [Ref: K-1:228]. Died testate in Montgomery County (wife named Elizabeth Ann) in 1823, but named no children [Ref: V-74].

JONES, Charles. (1) Justice of the Orphans Court in 1778 and County Court, 1779-1781. Justice of the Peace who administered the Oath of Allegiance in 1778 [Ref: T-3:71, L-1:42, W-1, W-2, C-529]. (2) Private, 6th Co., Lower Bn., Militia, Aug., 1777 [Ref: M-200, T-5:49]. Served as a petit juror in Aug., 1777 [Ref: R-31:17]. One Charles Jones took the Oath of Allegiance before the Hon. Joseph Offutt on March 2, 1778 [Ref: T-3:70, L-1:42], and another took the Oath of Allegiance before the Hon. Charles Jones on Jan. 10, 1778 [Ref: T-3:71, L-1:42]. One rendered aid by providing wheat for use of the military in 1781 [Ref: O-403]. "Charles Jones (millwright)" was a private, 3rd Co., Lower Bn., Militia, July 15, 1780 [Ref: M-205]. One Charles Jones married Mary Jackson in Montgomery County on Feb. 24, 1782 [Ref: K-2:515]. Charles Jones (twelve taxables) and "Charles Jones (R. Creek)" both lived in Lower Potomac Hd. (seven taxables) in 1777 [Ref: R-31:4]. Also, Charles Jones (three taxables) and Charles Jones (one taxable) both lived in the Upper Part of Potomac Hd. in 1777 [Ref: R-31:14]. "Charles Jones, R C" was born in 1711 and died testate in Montgomery County (wife named Mary) in 1785, and "Charles Jones, of Clean Drinking Manor" was born in 1712 and died testate in Montgomery County (wife not named) in 1801 [Ref: V-75, K-1:183]. "Mary Jones, widow of the late Charles Jones of Rock Creek" died testate in 1791 [Ref: V-76].

JONES, Charles, of John. Took the Oath of Allegiance before the Hon. Samuel W. Magruder in 1778 [Ref: T-3:73, L-1:42].
JONES, Charles Courts (b. 1762 or 1763). "Charles Coats Jones" was a private, 1st Co., Lower Bn., Militia, July 15, 1780 [Ref: M-204]. "Charles Courts Jones" was a son of "Charles Jones, of Clean Drinking Manor" who died testate in 1801 [Ref: V-75]. They lived in Lower Potomac Hd. in 1776 [Ref: K-1:183].
JONES, Daniel (b. 1731). Took the Oath of Allegiance before the Hon. Aneas Campbell on March 2, 1778 [Ref: T-3:78, L-1:42]. Lived in Sugarland Hd. (one taxable) in 1776-1777 [Ref: K-1:210, R-31:12].
JONES, Edward. (1) Private, 6th Co., Middle Bn., Militia, Aug., 1777 [Ref: M-197, T-5:41]. Private, 6th Co., Middle Bn., Militia, July 15, 1780 [Ref: M-203]. Took the Oath of Allegiance before the Hon. Aneas Campbell on March 2, 1778 [Ref: T-3:77, L-1:42]. (2) Private, 1st Co., Upper Bn., Militia, Aug. 30, 1777 [Ref: M-193]. Took the Oath of Allegiance before the Hon. Edward Burgess on Feb. 28, 1778 [Ref: T-3:61, L-1:42]. One Edward Jones lived in Linganore Hd. (one taxable) in 1777 and another lived in Sugar Loaf Hd. (six taxables) in 1777 [Ref: R-31:9, R-31:10].
JONES, Elizabeth. See "Lloyd Beall" and Thomas Kelly," q.v.
JONES, Evan. Took the Oath of Allegiance before the Hon. Samuel W. Magruder in 1778 [Ref: T-3:73]. Rendered aid by providing wheat for use of the military in 1780 [Ref: O-313]. Evan Jones (one taxable) and Evan Jones, Sr. (one taxable) both lived in the Upper Part of Potomac Hd. in 1777 [Ref: R-31:14]. One Evans Jones died testate in Montgomery County (wife named Ann) in 1782 and mentioned sons Nathan and Evans, among other children [Ref: V-75].
JONES, Evan Jr. Private, 5th Co., Middle Bn., Militia, Sep., 1777 [Ref: M-197, T-5:40]. Private, 3rd Class, 1st Co., Middle Bn., Militia, July 15, 1780 [Ref: M-201]. Took the Oath of Allegiance (made his "X" mark) before the Hon. Samuel W. Magruder in 1778 [Ref: T-3:73].
JONES, Henry (1749-1797). Private, 4th Co., Lower Bn., Militia, Aug., 1777 [Ref: M-199, T-5:47]. Private, 1st Co., Lower Bn., Militia, July 15, 1780 [Ref: M-204]. Took the Oath of Allegiance before the Hon. Charles Jones on Jan. 10, 1778 [Ref: T-3:71, L-1:42]. Lived in Lower Potomac Hd. in 1776, with "Charles Jones, C. D." (aged 64) as head of house [Ref: K-1:183]. Died testate in Montgomery County in 1797 [Ref: V-76]. See "Charles Court Jones," q.v.
JONES, Hezekiah. Private, 3rd Co., Lower Bn., Militia, July 15, 1780 [Ref: M-205].
JONES, John. (1) Private, 2nd Co., Middle Bn., Militia, Sep. 4, 1777 [Ref: M-195]. Private, 5th Class, 3rd Co., Middle Bn., Militia, July 15, 1780 [Ref: M-202]. (2) Private, 7th Co., Lower Bn., Militia, July 15, 1780 [Ref: M-206]. Private who was recruited to serve in the Continental Army in 1780 [Ref: D-342]. Ensign, Select Militia, April 13, 1781 [Ref: M-93, G-

396]. One John Jones lived in Sugar Loaf Hd. (one taxable) in 1777 [Ref: R-31:10], and one lived in the Upper Part of Potomac Hd. (one taxable) in 1777 [Ref: R-31:14]. "John Johnjones" [sic], aged 20, lived in Sugarland Hd. in 1776 [Ref: K-1:208]. One John Johns took the Oath of Allegiance (made his mark) before the Hon. Joseph Wilson on Feb. 28, 1778 [Ref: T-3:67, L-1:42]. One rendered aid by providing wheat for use of the military in 1780 and 1781 [Ref: O-317, O-423].

JONES, John 2nd. Served as a Drummer, Capt. Price's Co., 3rd Maryland Line, 1781, and was reduced to a private on Feb. 1, 1782 [Ref: D-452].

JONES, John 3rd. Took the Oath of Allegiance before the Hon. Elisha Williams on March 2, 1778 [Ref: T-3:80, L-1:42]. Lived in Sugar Loaf Hd. (one taxable) in 1777 [Ref: R-31:10].

JONES, John Raymond. Rendered aid by providing corn for use of the military in 1781 [Ref: O-358].

JONES, Joseph. (1) Private, 1st Co., Upper Bn., Militia, Aug. 30, 1777 [Ref: M-193]. (2) Private, 4th Co., Upper Bn., Militia, Aug. 30, 1777 [Ref: M-194]. (3) Private, 6th Co., Lower Bn., Militia, Aug., 1777 [Ref: M-200, T-5:49]. One Joseph Jones took the Oath of Allegiance before the Hon. Elisha Williams on March 2, 1778 [Ref: T-3:82]. One "Joseph Jones, aged 40" and "Joseph Jones, aged 23" both lived in Sugarland Hd. in 1776-1777 [Ref: K-1:207, R-31:12].

JONES, Lewis (b. 1739). Lived in Sugarland Hd. in 1776 [Ref: K-1:209]. One Lewis Jones was a private, 2nd Maryland Regiment, 1779. Another Lewis Jones was a fifer, 3rd Maryland Regiment, from April 5, 1779 to Dec., 1779, when he died [Ref: D-126, D-127].

JONES, Leonard. Private, 4th Co., Upper Bn., Militia, Aug. 30, 1777 [Ref: M-194].

JONES, Margaret. See "Lodowick Davis," q.v.

JONES, Martha. See "Elias Lazenby," q.v.

JONES, Mary. See "Charles Jones," q.v.

JONES, Nathan (died 1812). Private, 5th Co., Middle Bn., Militia, Sep., 1777 [Ref: M-197, T-5:40]. Private, 3rd Class, 1st Co., Middle Bn., Militia, July 15, 1780 [Ref: M-201]. Lived in the Upper Part of Potomac Hd. (one taxable) in 1777 [Ref: R-31:14]. Died testate in Montgomery County (wife named Nancy) in 1812 [Ref: V-77].

JONES, Nathaniel. Took the Oath of Allegiance (made his mark) before the Hon. Samuel W. Magruder in 1778 [Ref: T-3:73].

JONES, Peter. Rendered aid by providing corn and meal for use of the military in 1780 and 1781 [Ref: O-299, O-376].

JONES, Philip (b. 1752). Private, 2nd Co., Upper Bn., Militia, Aug. 30, 1777 [Ref: M-193]. Private, 6th Co., Lower Bn., Militia, July 15, 1780 [Ref: T-5:27]. Took the Oath of Allegiance before the Hon. Aneas Campbell on March 2, 1778 [Ref: T-3:77, L-1:42]. Lived in Sugarland Hd. in 1776-1777 [Ref: K-1:212, R-31:12].

JONES, Priscilla. See "William Mackee," q.v.

JONES, Richard. Served as a Second Lieutenant, 4th Co., Lower Bn., Militia, July 15, 1780 [Ref: M-205]. Took the Oath of Allegiance before the Hon. Edward Burgess on Feb. 28, 1778 [Ref: T-3:59, L-1:42]. Richard Jones married Susy Culver in Montgomery County on March 17, 1778 [Ref: K-2:516].

JONES, Samuel. (1) Private, 3rd Co., Lower Bn., Militia, July 15, 1780 [Ref: M-205]. (2) Private, 4th Co., Lower Bn., Militia, July 15, 1780 [Ref: M-205]. One Samuel Jones married Rebecca Wood in Montgomery County on Feb. 12, 1782 [Ref: K-2:515].

JONES, Thomas. Private, 3rd Co., Upper Bn., Militia, Aug. 30, 1777 [Ref: M-193]. Took the Oath of Allegiance before the Hon. William Deakins, Jr. before March 3, 1778 [Ref: T-3:68, L-1:42]. "Thomas Jones from Montgomery County" was a substitute who was discharged from the Maryland Line on Nov. 30, 1781 [Ref: I-8]. "Thomas Jones, aged 25" lived in Sugarland Hd. (one taxable) in 1776-1777 [Ref: K-1:202, R-31:12], and another lived in the Upper Part of Potomac Hd. (one taxable) and also owned a working plantation ("quarter") in 1777 [Ref: R-31:14].

JONES, Thomas 3rd. Private, Capt. Price's Co., 3rd Maryland Line, 1781-1782 [Ref: D-453].

JONES, William. Private, 6th Co., Lower Bn., Militia, Aug., 1777 [Ref: M-200, T-5:49]. Private, 3rd Co., Lower Bn., Militia, July 15, 1780 [Ref: M-205]. Two men with this name took the Oath of Allegiance: one before the Hon. Samuel W. Magruder in 1778 [Ref: T-3:73, L-1:42], and another before the Hon. Richard Thompson in 1778 [Ref: T-3:75, L-1:42]. One William Jones lived in the Upper Part of Potomac Hd. (three taxables) in 1777 [Ref: R-31:14].

JONES, Zephaniah. Private, 1st Co., Lower Bn., Militia, Sep., 1777 [Ref: M-198, T-5:44].

JORDAN (JURDEN, JORDON, GORDON), James. Private who enrolled into a company of militia for the service of the Flying Camp on Oct. 15, 1776 [Ref: B-353]. "James Jurden" was a private, 7th Co., Middle Bn., Militia, Sep., 1777, and 3rd Corporal, July 15, 1780 [Ref: M-197, M-203, T-5:42]. "James Jordon" took the Oath of Allegiance before the Hon. Joseph Wilson on Feb. 28, 1778 [Ref: T-3:64, L-1:42]. "James Jordan" rendered aid by providing wheat for use of the military in 1781 [Ref: O-403]. "James Gordon" lived in Seneca Hd. (one taxable) in 1777 [Ref: R-31:8].

JORDAN (JORDON), John (b. 1741). Private, Rawlings Regiment, Maryland Line, May 3, 1779. He pensioned in 1818, aged 77, and was still on the pension rolls in 1835 [Ref: D-128, J-38]. "John Jordon" was a private, Capt. Thomas Beall's Co., Maryland Line, 1780 [Ref: D-350].

JORDAN (JORDON, JURDEN), Joshua. "Joshua Jordon" lived in Linganore Hd. (one taxable) in 1777 [Ref: R-31:9]. "Joshua Jurden" was a private, 5th Co., Upper Bn., Militia, Aug. 30, 1777 [Ref: M-194].

"Joshua Jordan" rendered aid by providing wheat for use of the military in 1780 [Ref: O-304].

JORDAN, Thomas. Private who was recruited to serve in the Continental Army in 1780 [Ref: D-341].

JOSEPH, Joseph. Private, 5th Co., Middle Bn., Militia, July 15, 1780 [Ref: M-203]. Rendered aid by providing wheat for use of the military in 1781 [Ref: O-398].

JOURDAN, Anne. See "Basil Beall," q.v.

JOURDAN, Elise G. See "Jeremiah Plummer" and "William Cecil," q.v.

JOY, Baptist. Private, 1st Co., Lower Bn., Militia, July 15, 1780 [Ref: M-204].

JUDSON (JADSON), John. Took the Oath of Allegiance before the Hon. Charles Jones on Jan. 10, 1778 [Ref: T-3:71, L-1:42].

JULIVAN, Sibusty [sic]. Private, 1st or 32nd Bn., Militia (no date was given; possibly June, 1777). [Ref: T-5:1].

JUNNAN(?), William. Took the Oath of Allegiance before the Hon. Edward Burgess on Feb. 28, 1778 [Ref: T-3:60, L-1:42].

JURY (JEWRY), Stephen. Private, 6th Co., Middle Bn., Militia, Aug., 1777 [Ref: M-197, T-5:41]. Private, 6th Co., Middle Bn., Militia, July 15, 1780 [Ref: M-203]. Lived in Linganore Hd. (one taxable) in 1777 [Ref: R-31:9].

KAVITY, George. Took the Oath of Allegiance in 1778 [Ref: L-2:28].

KEECH (KACH), John. "John Keech" was a private, Capt. Price's Co., 3rd Maryland Line, 1781-1782 [Ref: D-453]. "John Kach" was a private, Capt. Beall's Co., 6th Maryland Line, from July 16, 1777 until May 16, 1780, when discharged [Ref: D-221].

KEEMER, John. Private, Flying Camp, Frederick (now Montgomery) County, enlisted by Greenbury Gaither on July 29, 1776 [Ref: D-44].

KEEN (KEIN, KEENE), James. Took the Oath of Allegiance before the Hon. Edward Burgess on Feb. 28, 1778 [Ref: T-3:60, L-1:42]. "James Kein" was a private, 8th Co., Middle Bn., Militia, Sep., 1777 [Ref: M-198, T-5:43]. "James Keene" was a private, 8th Co., Lower Bn., Militia, July 15, 1780 [Ref: M-207].

KEER, Thomas. Private, 4th Co., Lower Bn., Militia, July 15, 1780 [Ref: M-205].

KEISER, John, and others. See "John Kiser," and others, q.v.

KEISEY, Henry. Took the Oath of Allegiance in 1778 [Ref: L-2:28].

KEITH (KEETH), James. "James Keith" was a private, 7th Co., Lower Bn., Militia, Aug., 1777 [Ref: M-200, T-5:50]. "James Keeth" lived in the Lower Part of Newfoundland Hd. (one taxable) in 1777 [Ref: R-31:5].

KEITH (KEATH), Andrew. "Andrew Keath" was a private who enrolled into a company of militia for the service of the Flying Camp on Oct. 15, 1776 [Ref: B-352].

KELLY (KELLEY), Benjamin. Took the Oath of Allegiance before the Hon. Gerrard Briscoe on March 2, 1778 [Ref: T-3:56, L-1:42], and served as a grand juror in 1779 [Ref: W-1]. "Benjamin Kelley" lived in Seneca Hd. (two taxables) in 1777 [Ref: R-31:8]. There was also a Benjamin Kelly who was a private in the 3rd Maryland Regiment in Jan., 1776 [Ref: D-9].

KELLY, James. Served as a Corporal, 7th Maryland Line, 1780 [Ref: D-222].

KELLY (KELLEY), John. "John Kelly" was a private, 1st Co., Middle Bn., Militia, Aug. 30, 1777 [Ref: M-195], and First Sergeant, 5th Co., Middle Bn., Militia, July 15, 1780 [Ref: M-202]. "John Kelley" lived in the Upper Part of Newfoundland Hd. (three taxables) in 1777 [Ref: R-31:6].

KELLY, Patrick. Private, Capt. Price's Co., 3rd Maryland Line, 1781-1782 [Ref: D-452].

KELLY (KELLEY), Thomas. Private, 1st Co., Middle Bn., Militia, Aug. 30, 1777 [Ref: M-195]. Took the Oath of Allegiance before the Hon. Gerrard Briscoe on March 2, 1778 [Ref: T-3:56, L-1:42]. Served as a grand juror in 1779 [Ref: W-1]. Thomas Kelly married Elizabeth Jones in Montgomery County on Feb. 7, 1781 [Ref: K-2:519]. "Thomas Kelley" lived in Seneca Hd. (three taxables) in 1777 [Ref: R-31:8]. "Thomas Kelly" died testate in Montgomery County (wife named Hannah) in 1804 and mentioned a son Thomas, among others [Ref: V-78]. There was also a "Tom Kelly, servant, aged 16" who lived in North West Hd. in 1776 [Ref: K-1:231].

KEMP, Jacob. Took the Oath of Allegiance in 1778 [Ref: L-2:28].

KENDALL, Aaron. Took the Oath of Allegiance in 1778 [Ref: L-2:28].

KENNEDY (KENEDY), Hugh. Private, 6th Co., Middle Bn., Militia, Aug., 1777 [Ref: M-197, T-5:41]. Lived in Linganore Hd. (one taxable) in 1777 [Ref: R-31:9].

KENNEDY (KENEDY), John. Soldier (Ensign?), 7th Co., Middle Bn., Militia, Sep., 1777 [Ref: M-197, T-5:41]. Took the Oath of Allegiance before the Hon. Edward Burgess on Feb. 28, 1778 [Ref: T-3:58, L-1:42]. Rendered aid by providing corn for use of the military in 1781 [Ref: O-356]. Lived in Seneca Hd. (three taxables) in 1777 [Ref: R-31:8].

KENNY, William. Private, 7th Maryland Line, 1780 [Ref: D-222].

KERSEY, Daniel. Private, 4th Co., Upper Bn., Militia, Aug. 30, 1777 [Ref: M-194].

KERSEY, Philip. Private, 5th Co., Middle Bn., Militia, Sep., 1777 [Ref: M-197, T-5:40].

KERSNER, Michael. Took the Oath of Allegiance before the Hon. Richard Thompson in 1778 [Ref: T-3:75, L-1:42].

KEYMER, Elizabeth. See "Thomas Peak," q.v.

KEYSER, Frederick. See "Frederick Kiser," q.v.

KIDD, Mary. See "Asa Darby," q.v.

KILLEHOCK(?), John. Private, 7th Co., Middle Bn., Militia, July 15, 1780 [Ref: M-204].

KILTEY (KITELY, KEETLEY), Francis (b. 1759). "Francis Kiltey" lived in Sugarland Hd. in 1776 and "Francis Kelley" [Keltey?] lived in Sugarland Hd. (one taxable) in 1777 [Ref: K-1:203, R-31:12]. "Francis Kitely" was a private, 4th Co., Upper Bn., Militia, Aug. 30, 1777 [Ref: M-184]. "Francis Keetley (or Kelley)" [sic] was a private in the Maryland Line who enlisted on June 30, 1778, for nine months [Ref: D-309]. "Francis Kitely" was a private, 7th Maryland Line, who reenlisted on April 17, 1779 [Ref: E-352]. Also see "Francis Kitely," q.v.

KILTY, James. Private, Capt. Thomas Beall's Co., Maryland Line, 1780 [Ref: D-350].

KIMBLE, Stephen. Private, Capt. Price's Co., 3rd Maryland Line, 1781-1782 [Ref: D-452].

KIMEY, Ann. See "John Johnson," q.v.

KING, Edward (b. 1740). Private, 4th Co., Lower Bn., Militia, Aug., 1777 [Ref: M-199, T-5:47]. Took the Oath of Allegiance before the Hon. Edward Burgess on Feb. 28, 1778 [Ref: T-3:64, L-1:42]. Private, 1st Co., Lower Bn., Militia, July 15, 1780 [Ref: M-204]. Lived in North West Hd. (wife named Rebeckah) in 1776-1777 [Ref: K-1:224, R-31:17].

KING, Elizabeth. See "Thomas Miles," q.v.

KING, John. Private, 1st Co., Lower Bn., Militia, Sep., 1777 [Ref: M-198, T-5:44]. Private, 7th Co., Lower Bn., Militia, July 15, 1780 [Ref: M-206]. Took the Oath of Allegiance before the Hon. Edward Burgess on Feb. 28, 1778 [Ref: T-3:63, L-1:42]. Lived in the Lower Part of Newfoundland Hd. (one taxable) in 1777 [Ref: R-31:5].

KING, Rebeckah. See "Edward King," q.v.

KING, Samuel (b. 1753). Served as a Third Corporal, 1st Co., Lower Bn., Militia, July 15, 1780 [Ref: M-204]. Took the Oath of Allegiance (made his "X" mark) before the Hon. Samuel W. Magruder in 1778 [Ref: T-3:73]. Lived in Lower Potomac Hd. in 1776 [Ref: K-1:184].

KING, William. Private, 7th Co., Lower Bn., Militia, July 15, 1780 [Ref: M-207].

KIPHART, John. See "John Gebhart," q.v.

KIRBY, Elizabeth. See "Thomas Ignatius Carrico," q.v.

KIRBY (KERBY), Enoch. Lived in the Upper Part of Potomac Hd. (one taxable) in 1777 [Ref: R-31:14]. "Enoch Kirby" took the Oath of Allegiance before the Hon. William Deakins, Jr. before March 3, 1778 [Ref: T-3:68, L-1:42]. "Eanock Kerby" was a private, 3rd Co., Middle Bn., Militia, Sep., 1777 [Ref: T-5:38, M-196].

KIRBY (KISBY?), Richard. Private who was recruited to serve in the Extra Regiment, Continental Army, in 1780 [Ref: D-342].

KIRK, Edward. Private, Capt. Thomas Beall's Co., Maryland Line, 1780 [Ref: D-350].

KIRK, George. Private, 5th Co., Upper Bn., Militia, Aug. 30, 1777 [Ref: M-194].

KIRK, Thomas. Served as a First Lieutenant, 5th Co., 16th Bn., Militia, 1777 [Ref: M-95, M-194, C-373]. Served as a petit juror in Aug., 1777 [Ref: R-31:17]. Took the Oath of Allegiance before the Hon. Joseph Wilson on Feb. 28, 1778 [Ref: T-3:64, L-1:42]. Lived in Sugar Loaf Hd. (three taxables) in 1777 [Ref: R-31:10].

KIRK, Thomas Jr. Private, 5th Co., Upper Bn., Militia, Aug. 30, 1777 [Ref: M-194].

KIRTZ, Christian. Private, 8th Co., Lower Bn., Militia, July 15, 1780 [Ref: M-207].

KIRTZ (KURTZ, KIRTZE), Nicholas (b. 1760). "Nicholas Kirtz" was a private, 3rd Co., Lower Bn., Militia, Sep., 1777 [Ref: M-199, T-5:46]. "Nicholas Kurtz" took the Oath of Allegiance before the Hon. Richard Thompson in 1778 [Ref: T-3:75, L-1:42]. "Nicholas Kurtz or Kirtze" lived in George Town Hd. (one taxable) in 1776-1777 [Ref: K-1:194, R-31:3].

KIRTZ (KURTZ, KIRTS, KIRTZE), Peter (b. 1750). Served as a Second Lieutenant, 3rd Co., 29th Bn., Militia, June 21, 1777 [Ref: M-96, M-199, C-296, C-373, T-5:46]. "Peter Kurtz or Kirtze" lived in George Town Hd. (one taxable) in 1776-1777 [Ref: K-1:194, R-31:3].

KISER (KEISER), Christian or Christopher. "Christopher Keiser" lived in Lower Potomac Hd. (one taxable) in 1777 [Ref: R-31:4]. "Christian Kiser" took the Oath of Allegiance before the Hon. Charles Jones on Jan. 10, 1778 [Ref: T-3:71, L-1:42].

KISER (KEYSER, KIZER, KISENER), Frederick (b. 1726). "Frederick Keyser" took the Oath of Allegiance before the Hon. Richard Thompson in 1778 [Ref: T-3:75, L-1:42]. "Frederick Kisener" was a private, 6th Co., Lower Bn., Militia, July 15, 1780 [Ref: M-206]. "Frederick Keyser or Kizer" lived in George Town Hd. in 1776-1777 [Ref: K-1:194, R-31:3].

KISER (KYSER, KEIZER), Jacob (b. 1760 or 1761). Private, 4th Co., Lower Bn., Militia, Aug., 1777 [Ref: M-199, T-5:47]. "Jacob Keizer" lived in Lower Potomac Hd. in 1776 [Ref: K-1:184].

KISER (KEISER, KEIZER), John (b. 1739). "John Kiser" was a private, 4th Co., Lower Bn., Militia, Aug., 1777 [Ref: M-199, T-5:47]. "John Keiser" took the Oath of Allegiance before the Hon. Charles Jones on Jan. 10, 1778 [Ref: T-3:71, L-1:42]. John Keizer lived in Lower Potomac Hd. (two taxables) in 1776-1777 [Ref: R-31:4, K-1:183].

KISER (KYSER), Martin (b. 1751). Private, 2nd Co., Upper Bn., Militia, Aug. 30, 1777 [Ref: M-193]. Took the Oath of Allegiance before the Hon. Aneas Campbell on March 2, 1778 [Ref: T-3:77, L-1:42]. "Martain Hyser" [Martin Kyser] lived in Sugarland Hd. in 1776 and "Martin Kiser" lived there (one taxable) in 1777 [Ref: K-1:205, R-31:12].

KISER (KEISER), Michael. "Michael Keiser" took the Oath of Allegiance before the Hon. Charles Jones on Jan. 10, 1778 [Ref: T-3:71, L-1:42].

KISER, Philip. Private, 1st Co., Lower Bn., Militia, July 15, 1780 [Ref: M-204].

KISER (KYZER, KEISER, KEIZER), Stophel (b. 1746). Served as a Second Lieutenant, 4th Co., Lower Bn., Militia, Aug., 1777, and Second Lieutenant, 1st Co., Lower Bn., July 15, 1780 [Ref: M-199, M-204, T-5:47]. "Stophel Kison" [sic] served as a petit juror in Aug., 1777 [Ref: R-31:17]. "Stofield Kyzer" rendered aid by providing wheat for use of the military in 1780 [Ref: O-320]. "Stophel Keizer" lived in Lower Potomac Hd. in 1776 [Ref: K-1:183].

KITELY (KILTEY, KEETLEY), Francis. See "Francis Kiltey," q.v.

KNEWSTEP, Robert and Thomason. See "Robert Newstep," q.v.

KNIGHT, John (b. 1746). Lived in North West Hd. in 1776 [Ref: K-1:230]. One John Knight served as a fifer in the 4th Maryland Regiment, 1778-1780, and another was a private, 1779-1780 [Ref: D-131].

KNIGHT (NIGHT), Peter. Private who enrolled into a company of militia for the service of the Flying Camp on Oct. 15, 1776 [Ref: B-352].

KNIGHT (NIGHT), William. Took the Oath of Allegiance in 1778 [Ref: L-2:28].

KNIGHTON (KNEIGHTON), William. "William Knighton" took the Oath of Allegiance before the Hon. Edward Burgess on Feb. 28, 1778 [Ref: T-3:62, L-1:42]. "William Kneighton" was a private, 4th Co., Lower Bn., Militia, July 15, 1780, and "William Knighters" was a private, 7th Co., Lower Bn., 1780 [Ref: M-200, M-205].

KNOTT, Basil. Private, 6th Co., Upper Bn., Militia, Aug. 30, 1777 [Ref: M-194]. Rendered aid by providing wheat for use of the military in 1781 [Ref: O-388]. Basil Knott lived in Sugar Loaf Hd. (one taxable) in 1777 [Ref: R-31:10].

KNOTT, James. Private, Capt. Price's Co., 3rd Maryland Line, 1781-1782 [Ref: D-452].

KNOTT, Jeremiah. Private, 7th Co., Lower Bn., Militia, Aug., 1777 [Ref: M-200, T-5:50].

KNOTT, Ralph. Private, 7th Co., Lower Bn., Militia, Aug., 1777 [Ref: M-200, T-5:50]. "Ralph Knott" rendered aid by providing wheat for use of the military in 1780 and 1781 [Ref: O-328, O-351]. One "Raphael Knott" and Catherine Pearce were married by Bishop John Carroll (Roman Catholic) in Montgomery County on June 16, 1778 [Ref: K-2:514].

KNOTT, Thomas. Private, 2nd Co., Upper Bn., Militia, Aug. 30, 1777 [Ref: M-193]. Took the Oath of Allegiance before the Hon. Edward Burgess on Feb. 28, 1778 [Ref: T-3:59, L-1:42, L-2:28, which latter source listed the name as "Thomas Knol"]. Rendered aid by providing wheat for use of the military in 1781 [Ref: O-388]. Lived in the Lower Part of Newfoundland Hd. (one taxable) in 1777 [Ref: R-31:5].

KNOTT, William. Private, 6th Co., Upper Bn., Militia, Aug. 30, 1777 [Ref: M-194]. William Knott lived in Sugar Loaf Hd. (four taxables) in 1777 [Ref: R-31:10]. One William Knott died testate in Montgomery County (wife named Mary) in 1802 and another William Knott died testate (wife also named Mary) in 1825 [Ref: V-79].

KNOTT (NOTT), Zachariah (died 1820). "Zachariah Knott" was a private, 6th Co., Upper Bn., Militia, Aug. 30, 1777 [Ref: M-194]. "Zachariah Nott" took the Oath of Allegiance before the Hon. Elisha Williams on March 2, 1778 [Ref: T-3:81, L-1:42]. Rendered aid by providing wheat for use of the military in 1781 [Ref: O-391, O-425]. Lived in Sugar Loaf Hd. (two taxables) in 1777 [Ref: R-31:10]. Died testate in Montgomery County (wife named Jane) in 1820 [Ref: V-79].

KNOX, John. Private, 1st or 32nd Bn., Militia (no date was given; possibly June, 1777). [Ref: T-5:1].

KNOX, William. Private, 7th Co., Middle Bn., Militia, Sep., 1777 [Ref: M-197, T-5:42]. Lived in Seneca Hd. (one taxable) in 1777 [Ref: R-31:8].

KOGENDERFER, Frederick. See "Frederick Cochantofer," q.v.

KOGENDERFOR, Leonard. See "Leonard Cochantofer," q.v.

KOMIG, Frederick. Took the Oath of Allegiance in 1778 [Ref: L-2:28].

KOMIG, Gilbert. Took the Oath of Allegiance in 1778 [Ref: L-2:28].

KOMIG, Lewis. Took the Oath of Allegiance in 1778 [Ref: L-2:28].

KOMIG, Peter Jr. Took the Oath of Allegiance in 1778 [Ref: L-2:28].

KOONTZ, Henry. See "Henry Coontz," q.v.

KRAUS (CROUTZ), Theodorus (b. 1737). Took the Oath of Allegiance before the Hon. Richard Thompson in 1778 [Ref: T-3:75, L-1:42]. "Theodorus or Theodoris Kraus" lived in George Town Hd. in 1776-1777 [Ref: K-1:194, R-31:3]. "Theodorous Croutz" was a private, 3rd Co., Lower Bn., Militia, Sep., 1777 [Ref: M-199, T-5:46].

KUHNES, Henry. See "Henry Coontz," q.v.

KYBER, Philip. Private, 3rd Co., Lower Bn., Militia, Sep., 1777 [Ref: M-199, T-5:46].

KYSER, Martin. See "Martin Kiser," q.v.

LACEY, Benjamin. Private, 8th Co., Lower Bn., Militia, July 15, 1780 [Ref: M-207].

LACKLAND, James (died 1814). Served as a Second Lieutenant, 2nd Co., 29th Bn., Militia, from May 14, 1776, to at least Sep. 12, 1777 [Ref: M-96, M-198, T-5:45, A-424, C-373]. Took the Oath of Allegiance before the Hon. Edward Burgess on Feb. 28, 1778 [Ref: T-3:60, L-1:42]. Died testate in Montgomery County (wife not named) in 1814 [Ref: V-80].

LACKLAND (LACKLAN), John. "John Lackland" served as a petit juror in Nov., 1777 [Ref: R-31:18]. "John Lacklan" took the Oath of Allegiance before the Hon. Edward Burgess on Feb. 28, 1778 [Ref: T-3:58, L-1:42]. "John Lackland" lived in Rock Creek Hd. (six taxables) in 1777 [Ref: R-31:16].

LACKLAND (LACKLIN), Zadock. "Zadock Lackland" was a private, 2nd Co., Lower Bn., Militia, Sep., 1777 [Ref: M-198, T-5:45]. "Zadock Lacklin" took the Oath of Allegiance before the Hon. Edward Burgess on Feb. 28, 1778 [Ref: T-3:60, L-1:42].

LAMAR, Susanna. See "Ignatius Pigman," q.v.

LAMBERT, Balson. Took the Oath of Allegiance in 1778 [Ref: L-2:28].

LAMBETH, Joseph. Private, 6th Co., Middle Bn., Militia, Aug., 1777 [Ref: M-197, T-5:41]. Took the Oath of Allegiance before the Hon. Edward Burgess on Feb. 28, 1778 [Ref: T-3:61, L-1:42].

LAMBETH, Samuel (b. 1743). Lived in North West Hd. in 1776 [Ref: K-1:226]. Private, 8th Co., Lower Bn., Militia, Sep., 1777 [Ref: M-200, T-5:51].

LAMPARD, Thomas. Rendered aid by providing wheat for use of the military in 1781 [Ref: O-384].

LANGE, John Peter. Private, 8th Co., Lower Bn., Militia, July 15, 1780 [Ref: M-207], and Ensign, 8th Co., Lower Bn., Militia, Aug. 4, 1780 [Ref: M-96, M-297, F-248]. "Peter Lange, aged 22" lived in George Town Hd. in 1776 [Ref: K-1:194].

LANGTON (LAUGTON), James (b. 1733). Lived in Lower Potomac Hd. in 1776 [Ref: K-1:184]. Took the Oath of Allegiance before the Hon. Richard Thompson in 1778 [Ref: T-3:75, L-1:42, which spelled the name "Laugton"].

LANHAM (LANNAM), Aaron (1731-1795). Private, 4th Co., Lower Bn., Militia, Aug., 1777 [Ref: M-199, T-5:47]. Private, 1st Co., Lower Bn., Militia, July 15, 1780 [Ref: M-204]. Took the Oath of Allegiance before the Hon. Charles Jones on Jan. 10, 1778 [Ref: T-3:71, L-1:42]. Served as a grand juror in Aug., 1777 [Ref: R-31:17]. Rendered aid by providing wheat for use of the military in 1780 [Ref: O-314, O-337]. Lived in Lower Potomac Hd. (five taxables) in 1776-1777 [Ref: R-31:4, K-1:184]. "Aaron Landhorn" [Landham?] rendered aid by providing wheat for use of the military in 1780 [Ref: O-313]. "Aaron Lanham" died testate in Montgomery County (wife named Elizabeth) in 1795 [Ref: V-81].

LANHAM (LANNAM), Hance. Private, 8th Co., Middle Bn., Militia, Sep., 1777 [Ref: M-198, T-5:43]. "Hanzy or Hauzy Lanham" was a private, 5th Co., Lower Bn., Militia, July 15, 1780 [Ref: M-206].

LANHAM, Henry (May 28, 1761 - Nov. 20, 1849). Private, 2nd Maryland Line, enlisted on Feb. 3, 1776; wife named Eleanor [Ref: D-8, DAR-I:401].

LANHAM, Hillery. Private, 6th Co., Lower Bn., Militia, July 15, 1780 [Ref: M-206].

LANHAM, John. Private, 1st Maryland Line, from Dec. 10, 1776 to Dec. 10, 1779 [Ref: D-131]. Took the Oath of Allegiance before the Hon. Elisha Williams on March 2, 1778 [Ref: T-3:81, L-1:42]. Lived in Sugarland Hd. (one taxable) in 1777 [Ref: R-31:12].

LANHAM, John D. Private, 2nd Maryland Line, enlisted Feb. 3, 1776 [Ref: D-8].

LANHAM (LANNAM), Lewis. Private, 7th Co., Lower Bn., Militia, Aug., 1777 [Ref: M-200, T-5:50].

LANHAM, Nathan. Private, 6th Co., Lower Bn., Militia, July 15, 1780 [Ref: M-206].

LANHAM, Nehemiah. Private, Capt. Thomas Beall's Co., Maryland Line, 1780 [Ref: D-351].

LANHAM, Notley. Rendered aid by providing wheat for use of the military in 1780 [Ref: O-327].

LANHAM (LENNHAM), Ralph. Took the Oath of Allegiance (made his "X" mark) before the Hon. Joseph Wilson on Feb. 28, 1778 [Ref: T-3:66, L-1:42]. "Ralph Lennham" lived in Seneca Hd. (one taxable) in 1777 [Ref: R-31:8].

LANHAM, Richard. Private, 6th Co., Middle Bn., Militia, Aug., 1777 [Ref: M-197, T-5:41]. Private, 1st Maryland Line, June 5, 1778 to at least April 5, 1779 [Ref: D-132, E-351]. Private, 5th Co., Lower Bn., Militia, July 15, 1780 [Ref: M-206]. Took the Oath of Allegiance before the Hon. Edward Burgess on Feb. 7, 1778 [Ref: T-3:59, L-1:42].

LANHAM (LANAM), Shadrick (1729-c1814). Rendered aid by providing wheat for use of the military in 1780 and 1781; wife named Sarah [Ref: O-321, O-453, DAR-I:401].

LANHAM (LANNAM), Stephen (1726-c1806). Lived in the Lower Part of Newfoundland Hd. (three taxables) in 1777 [Ref: R-31:5]. Private, 7th Co., Lower Bn., Militia, Aug., 1777 [Ref: M-200, T-5:50]. Took the Oath of Allegiance before the Hon. Edward Burgess on Feb. 28, 1778 [Ref: T-3:62, L-1:42]. Died testate in Montgomery County (wife named Susannah) in 1797 and mentioned a son Stephen, among others [Ref: V-81, DAR-I:401, which latter source states his first wife was named Leah]. It appears that their son Stephen moved to Madison County, Kentucky, and was living there in 1836. See "Thomas Lanham," q.v.

LANHAM, Thomas (1757-c1840). Soldier in the Maryland Line. Applied for pension (S30534) in Madison County, Kentucky, on June 8, 1836, stating he was born in 1757 and lived with his parents on a farm that laid in Price George's and Montgomery Counties, Maryland. In the spring of 1776 he enlisted near Bladensburg and served eleven months as a private under Capt. Rezin Beall. He was stationed at Port Tobacco on the Potomac River when taken sick with smallpox. He remained in the hospital until his parents came and took him home. After the war he moved to Wheeling, Virginia, and then to Madison County, Kentucky, where he has lived about 50 years. "Stephen Lanham," q.v., also of Madison County, stated that he was born in Prince George's County, Maryland, in 1760 and Thomas Lanham was his brother [Ref: U-23:97, U-23:98, P-2012].

LANHAM (LANNUM), William (b. 1753). Private, 2nd Co., Lower Bn., Militia, Sep., 1777 [Ref: M-198, T-5:45]. Private, 5th Co., Lower Bn., Militia, July 15, 1780 [Ref: M-206]. Took the Oath of Allegiance (made his "W" mark) before the Hon. Edward Burgess on Feb. 28, 1778 [Ref: T-3:58, L-1:42]. "William Lanham" lived in George Town Hd. in 1776 and

"William Lannum" lived in Rock Creek Hd. (one taxable) in 1777 [Ref: K-1:194, R-31:16].
LANSDALE, Thomas Lancaster. Private, 7th Co., Lower Bn., Militia, Aug., 1777 [Ref: T-5:50 and M-200, which latter source listed the name as "Thomas La..."]. "Thomas Lancaster Landsdale" took the Oath of Allegiance before the Hon. Edward Burgess on Feb. 28, 1778 [Ref: T-3:58, L-1:42]. "Thomas Lansdale" lived in the Lower Part of Newfoundland Hd. (seven taxables) in 1777 [Ref: R-31:5].
LANSLEY, Thomas. Rendered aid by providing wheat for use of the military in 1780 [Ref: O-305].
LARENBY, Isaac. See "Isaac Lazenby" and others, q.v.
LARROW, Frances. See "John Selby," q.v.
LARURE, Mary. See "Thomas Johnson," q.v.
LASHLEY, Cesiah and Lucy. See "Robert Lashley," q.v.
LASHLEY, George. Son of Robert Lashley [Ref: V-82]. Private, 2nd Co., Upper Bn., Militia, Aug. 30, 1777 [Ref: M-193]. Took the Oath of Allegiance before the Hon. Edward Burgess on Feb. 28, 1778 [Ref: T-3:63, L-1:42].
LASHLEY (LASHLEE), John (b. 1736). Son of Robert Lashley [Ref: V-82]. Private, 8th Co., Lower Bn., Militia, Sep., 1777 [Ref: M-200, T-5:51]. Private, 6th Co., Lower Bn., Militia, July 15, 1780 [Ref: M-206]. "John Lashlee" lived in North West Hd. in 1776 (wife named Rachel Lee, aged 46) and "John Lashley" lived there (two taxables) in 1777 [Ref: R-31:17, K-1:223, which latter source mistakenly listed the name as "Lashloo"].
LASHLEY, Robert (died 1780). Private, 6th Co., Upper Bn., Militia, Aug. 30, 1777 [Ref: M-194]. Lived in Sugar Loaf Hd. (three taxables) in 1777 [Ref: R-31:10]. "Robert Lashley, planter" died testate in Montgomery County (wife named Lucy) in 1780, naming sons John, William, Thomas and George, and daughter Cesiah [Kesiah] in his will [Ref: V-82].
LASHLEY (LASHLEE), Thomas (b. 1753). Son of Robert Lashley [Ref: V-82]. Private, 8th Co., Lower Bn., Militia, Sep., 1777 [Ref: M-200, T-5:51]. Thomas Lashlee or Lashley lived in North West Hd. (one taxable) in 1776-1777 [Ref: K-1:229, R-31:17].
LASHLEY (LASHLEE), William (b. 1746). Son of Robert Lashley [Ref: V-82]. Private, 8th Co., Lower Bn., Militia, Sep., 1777 [Ref: M-200, T-5:51]. "William Lashlee" lived in North West Hd. in 1776 (wife named Margry [sic], aged 25), and "William Lashley" lived there (one taxable) in 1777 [Ref: R-31:17, K-1:223, which latter source mistakenly listed the name as "Lashloo"].
LATON (LATEN), Ashwood (Asher). "Ashwood Laton" was a private, 5th Co., Upper Bn., Militia, Aug. 30, 1777 [Ref: M-194]. "Asher Laten" lived in Linganore Hd. (one taxable) in 1777 [Ref: R-31:9].

LATON (LUTON), Isaac. "Isaac Laton" was a private, 5th Co., Upper Bn., Militia, Aug. 30, 1777 [Ref: M-194]. "Isaac Luton" [sic] lived in Linganore Hd. (one taxable) in 1777 [Ref: R-31:9].

LATON (LEATON), Uriah. "Uriah Laton" was a private, 5th Co., Upper Bn., Militia, Aug. 30, 1777 [Ref: M-194]. "Uriah Laton" rendered aid by providing wheat for use of the military in 1781 [Ref: O-388]. "Hughriah Leaten" also rendered aid by providing wheat for use of the military in 1781 [Ref: O-399]. "Uriah Leaton" lived in Sugar Loaf Hd. (one taxable) in 1777 [Ref: R-31:10].

LAW, David. Rendered aid by providing wheat for use of the military in 1780 [Ref: O-320].

LAW, Joseph. Private who was recruited to serve in the Continental Army in 1780 [Ref: D-342].

LAWFER, Gudlip. Took the Oath of Allegiance in 1778 [Ref: L-2:28].

LAWRENCE, Sarah. See "James Allnutt, Sr.," q.v.

LAWS, Michael. Rendered aid by providing wheat for use of the military in 1781 [Ref: O-422].

LAWS, Thomas. Private, 3rd Class, 3rd Co., Middle Bn., Militia, July 15, 1780 [Ref: M-202].

LAYMAN (LAMAN), John. Private, 5th Co., Lower Bn., Militia, Aug., 1777 [Ref: M-199, T-5:48].

LAYMAN, William (1753-c1842). Served as an Ensign, and later as a Lieutenant, 1st Maryland Line, from April 10, 1777 until June 4, 1779, when he resigned [Ref: D-132]. Pensioned (S34954) in 1818 (aged 81 in 1835), dropped from the rolls in 1820, but restored in 1826. In 1840, aged 87, John was living in the household of Thomas Worthington in Montgomery County, 1st Division, and received half pay of a lieutenant [Ref: R-28:444, K-2:364, P-2033, Q-122]. On Feb. 12, 1842, Frances Valdenar, executor of William Layman, late of Montgomery County, deceased, was directed to be paid the amount due Layman at his death [Ref: Q-145].

LAZEAR (LAZIER, LAZURE), Henry. Private, 6th Co., Middle Bn., Militia, Aug., 1777 [Ref: M-197, T-5:41]. "Henry Lazier" was a private, 6th Co., Middle Bn., Militia, July 15, 1780 [Ref: M-203]. "Henry Lazier" took the Oath of Allegiance on Sep. 1, 1780, under the Act of May 12, 1780, having neglected to do so previously "due to ignorance of the duty owed the country." [Ref: R-27:115]. "Henry Lazure" lived in Linganore Hd. (one taxable) in 1777 [Ref: R-31:9].

LAZEAR (LAZIER), John. Private, Capt. Edward Burgess' Co., Lower District of Frederick (now Montgomery) County, Militia, July, 1776 [Ref: D-42, which listed the name as "John Lashyear (Layzare)"]. Private, 1st Co., Lower Bn., Militia, Sep., 1777 [Ref: M-198, T-5:44]. Took the Oath of Allegiance before the Hon. Edward Burgess on Feb. 28, 1778 [Ref: T-3:62, L-1:42]. "John Lazier" was a private, 7th Co., Lower Bn., Militia, July 15, 1780 [Ref: M-206].

LAZEAR (LAZURE), Joseph. Private, 1st Co., Lower Bn., Militia, Sep., 1777 [Ref: M-198, T-5:44]. Took the Oath of Allegiance before the Hon. Edward Burgess on Feb. 28, 1778 [Ref: T-3:61, L-1:42, which listed the name as "Joseph Lezlar"]. "Joseph Lazure" lived in the Lower Part of Newfoundland Hd. (two taxables) in 1777 [Ref: R-31:5].

LAZEAR (LAZIER), Joshua. Private, 7th Co., Lower Bn., Militia, July 15, 1780 [Ref: M-206].

LAZENBY, Alexander. Son of Robert Lazenby [Ref: V-82]. Private, Capt. Edward Burgess' Co., Lower District of Frederick (now Montgomery) County, Militia, July, 1776 [Ref: D-42]. Private, 1st Co., Lower Bn., Militia, Sep., 1777 [Ref: M-198, T-5:44]. Private, 7th Co., Lower Bn., Militia, July 15, 1780 [Ref: M-207]. Took the Oath of Allegiance before the Hon. Edward Burgess on Feb. 28, 1778 [Ref: T-3:58, L-1:42]. See "Joshua Lazenby," q.v.

LAZENBY, Elias (1752-1819). Son of Robert Lazenby [Ref: V-82]. Private, 1st Co., Lower Bn., Militia, Sep., 1777 [Ref: M-198, T-5:44]. Took the Oath of Allegiance before the Hon. Edward Burgess on Feb. 28, 1778 [Ref: T-3:62, L-1:42]. Rendered aid by hauling provisions for the military in 1781 [Ref: O-349]. "Elias Larenby" [Lasenby] lived in the Lower Part of Newfoundland Hd. (one taxable) in 1777 [Ref: R-31:5]. Elias Lazenby was born March 18, 1752, married Martha Jones, served as an ensign, and died July 31, 1819 [Ref: DAR-I:405]. See "Joshua Lazenby," q.v.

LAZENBY, Henry. Private, Capt. Edward Burgess' Co., Lower District of Frederick (now Montgomery) County, Militia, July, 1776 [Ref: D-42]. Private, 1st Co., Lower Bn., Militia, Sep., 1777 [Ref: M-198, T-5:44]. Private, 7th Co., Lower Bn., Militia, July 15, 1780 [Ref: M-206]. It appears that two men with this name took the Oath of Allegiance before the Hon. Edward Burgess on Feb. 28, 1778 [Ref: T-3:60, T-3:62, L-1:42]. One lived in Rock Creek Hd. (three taxables) in 1777 [Ref: R-31:16]. One was a son of "Robert Lazenby," q.v. [Ref: V-82]. See "Joshua Lazenby," q.v.

LAZENBY, John (c1750-c1787). Son of Robert Lazenby [Ref: V-82]. Took the Oath of Allegiance before the Hon. Joseph Wilson on Feb. 28, 1778 [Ref: T-3:66, L-1:42]. "John Larenberry" [Lasenberry] lived in Linganore Hd. (one taxable) in 1777. His wife was named Deborah ---- [Ref: R-31:9, DAR-I:405].

LAZENBY, Joshua (1759-1840). Son of Robert Lazenby [Ref: V-82]. Private, 1st Co., Lower Bn., Militia, Sep., 1777 [Ref: M-198, T-5:44]. Private, 7th Co., Lower Bn., Militia, July 15, 1780 [Ref: M-206]. Born in (now) Montgomery County, Maryland in 1759, he moved to Statesville, North Carolina between 1785 and 1790 and died there on Sep. 2, 1840. On Dec. 15, 1927, Mary E. Lazenby, of Washington, D. C., forwarded Joshua's original application (dated Aug. 22, 1832, in Iredell County, North Carolina) to the Pension Bureau "for the sake of posterity and not for the purpose of obtaining a pension." It stated that three of

Joshua's brothers also served in the war, namely Alexander, Henry, and Elias. It also stated they served with Daniel Lewis, the father-in-law of Joshua Lazenby's oldest son (name not stated). Joshua Lazenby married Keziah Belt and died on Sep. 2, 1840 [Ref: P-2034, DAR-I:405, and Henry C. Peden's *Marylanders to Carolina* (1994), pp. 98-99].

LAZENBY, Mary E. See "Thomas Belt" and "Joshua Lazenby," q.v.

LAZENBY, Robert. Private, 7th Co., Upper Bn., Militia, Aug. 30, 1777 [Ref: M-195]. One Robert Lazenby took the Oath of Allegiance before the Hon. Edward Burgess on Feb. 28, 1778 [Ref: T-3:59, L-1:42], and another took the Oath of Allegiance before the Hon. Aneas Campbell on March 2, 1778 [Ref: T-3:77, L-1:42]. Rendered aid by providing corn for use of the military in 1780 [Ref: O-283, O-286]. One "Robert Lazenby" lived in the Lower Part of Newfoundland Hd. (six taxables) in 1777 [Ref: R-31:5], and "Robert Larenby or Lazenby, aged 26" lived in Sugarland Hd. in 1776-1777 [Ref: K-1:211, R-31:12]. One Robert Lazenby died testate in Montgomery County (wife named Martha) in 1785 and mentioned a son Robert, among others [Ref: V-82]. One Robert Lazenby (1750-c1935) married Margery Ridgeway and served as a private soldier [Ref: DAR-I:405].

LAZENBY, Samuel. Private, 8th Co., Middle Bn., Militia, Sep., 1777 [Ref: M-198, T-5:43]. Private, 5th Co., Lower Bn., Militia, July 15, 1780 [Ref: M-206].

LAZENBY, Thomas (1755-1840). Private, 7th Co., Upper Bn., Militia, Aug. 30, 1777 [Ref: M-194]. Took the Oath of Allegiance before the Hon. Aneas Campbell on March 2, 1778 [Ref: T-3:77, L-1:42]. "Thomas Larenby or Lasenby, aged 21" lived in Sugarland Hd. in 1776-1777 [Ref: K-1:211, R-31:12]. Thomas Lazenby married Sarah Ridgeway, served as a private soldier, and died on April 5, 1840 [Ref: DAR-I:405].

LEACH (LEITCH), Benjamin. Took the Oath of Allegiance before the Hon. Gerrard Briscoe on March 2, 1778 [Ref: T-3:57, L-1:42]. "Benjamin Leitch" was a private, 5th Co., Upper Bn., Militia, Aug. 30, 1777 [Ref: M-194]. "Benjamin Leach" lived in Sugar Loaf Hd. (one taxable) in 1777 [Ref: R-31:10].

LEACH (LEITCH), James. (1) Private, 3rd Co., Upper Bn., Militia, Aug. 30, 1777 [Ref: M-193]. (2) Private, 1st Co., Middle Bn., Militia, Aug. 30, 1777 [Ref: M-195].

LEACH (LEECH, LEITCH), Jeremiah (b. 1749). "Jeremiah Leitch" was a private who enrolled in a company of militia for the service of the Flying Camp on Oct. 15, 1776 [Ref: B-353]. "Jeremiah Leech" lived in George Town Hd. in 1776 [Ref: K-1:194}, and "Jeamspile [?] Leach" [sic] lived in Sugar Loaf Hd. (one taxable) in 1777 [Ref: R-31:10].

LEACH (LEITCH), John. Private, 7th Co., Middle Bn., Militia, Sep., 1777 [Ref: M-197, T-5:42]. Took the Oath of Allegiance before the Hon. Gerrard Briscoe on March 2, 1778 [Ref: T-3:56, L-1:42]. Lived in Seneca Hd. (one taxable) in 1777 [Ref: R-31:8].

LEACH (LEITCH), Josiah. "Josiah Leitch" was a private, 5th Co., Upper Bn., Militia, Aug. 30, 1777 [Ref: M-194]. "Josiah Leach" took the Oath of Allegiance before the Hon. Gerrard Briscoe on March 2, 1778 [Ref: T-3:57, L-1:42]. Lived in Sugar Loaf Hd. (one taxable) in 1777 [Ref: R-31:10].
LEACH, Mary. See "John Edwards," q.v.
LEACH, Richard. Private, 7th Co., Middle Bn., Militia, Sep., 1777 [Ref: M-197, T-5:42].
LEACH (LEECH, LEITCH), Thomas (c1747-c1790). Son of William Leach [Ref: V-82]. "Thomas Leach" took the Oath of Allegiance before the Hon. Gerrard Briscoe on March 2, 1778 [Ref: T-3:56, L-1:42]. "Thomas Leitch" was a private, 1st Co., Middle Bn., Militia, Aug. 30, 1777 [Ref: M-195]. "Thomas Leech" was a private, 5th Co., Middle Bn., Militia, July 15, 1780 [Ref: M-203]. "Thomas Leach" lived in Seneca Hd. (one taxable) in 1777. He married Elizabeth Riggs [Ref: R-31:8, DAR-I:405].
LEACH (LEECH, LEITCH), William. (1) Private, 4th Co., Middle Bn., Militia, Sep., 1777 [Ref: M-196, T-5:39]. (2) Private, 3rd Co., Middle Bn., Militia, Sep., 1777 [Ref: M-196, T-5:38]. Private, 8th Class, 2nd Co., Middle Bn., Militia, July 15, 1780 [Ref: M-201]. (3) Private, 5th Co., Upper Bn., Militia, Aug. 30, 1777 [Ref: M-194]. "William Leach, Jr." and "William Leach, Sr." took the Oath of Allegiance before the Hon. Gerrard Briscoe on March 2, 1778 [Ref: T-3:56, L-1:42]. "William Leitch" took the Oath of Allegiance on Sep. 1, 1780, under the Act of May 12, 1780, having neglected to do so previously "due to ignorance of the duty owed the country." [Ref: R-27:115]. "William Leech" lived in the Upper Part of Newfoundland Hd. (one taxable), "William Leach, Sr." lived in Seneca Hd. (one taxable), "William Leach" (one taxable) lived in Sugar Loaf Hd. in 1777, and another "William Leach" lived in the Upper Part of Potomac Hd. (one taxable) in 1777 [Ref: R-31:6, R-31:8, R-31:10, R-31:14]. One rendered aid by providing wheat for use of the military in 1780 and 1781 [Ref: O-328, O-415]. "William Leach, Sr., planter" died testate in Montgomery County (wife named Mary) in 1781 and mentioned sons Thomas and William, Jr. [Ref: V-82].
LEAKE (LAKE), Nancy (Mary). See "Abraham Linthicum," q.v.
LEARY (LAREY), Daniel. "Daniel Leary" was a private, 4th Co., Middle Bn., Militia, Sep., 1777 [Ref: M-196, T-5:39]. "Daniel Lasey" [Larey] lived in the Upper Part of Newfoundland Hd. (one taxable) in 1777 [Ref: R-31:6].
LEATHER, John. Took the Oath of Allegiance in 1778 [Ref: L-2:28].
LEDSHARN, Paul. Took the Oath of Allegiance in 1778 [Ref: L-2:28].
LEE, Aaron. Took the Oath of Allegiance on Sep. 1, 1780, under the Act of May 12, 1780, having neglected to do so previously "due to ignorance of the duty owed the country." [Ref: R-27:115]. Lived in Sugar Loaf Hd. (two taxables) in 1777 [Ref: R-31:10].

LEE, Daniel (b. 1758). Son of John Lee, Sr. [Ref: V-82, K-1:223]. Private, 8th Co., Lower Bn., Militia, Sep., 1777, and Fourth Corporal, 6th Co., Lower Bn., July 15, 1780 [Ref: M-200, M-206, T-5:51]. Private, 6th Co., Lower Bn., Militia, July 15, 1780 [Ref: M-206]. Rendered aid by providing wheat for use of the military in 1780 [Ref: O-315].

LEE, James (b. 1761). Son of John Lee, Sr. [Ref: V-82, K-1:223]. Private, 6th Co., Lower Bn., Militia, July 15, 1780 [Ref: M-206]. Private, 8th Co., Lower Bn., Militia, Sep., 1777 [Ref: M-200, T-5:51]. Rendered aid by providing wheat for use of the military in 1780 [Ref: O-329].

LEE, John Jr. (b. 1755). Son of John Lee, Sr. [Ref: V-82]. Private, 8th Co., Lower Bn., Militia, Sep., 1777 [Ref: M-200, T-5:51]. Private, 6th Co., Lower Bn., Militia, July 15, 1780 [Ref: M-206]. Lived in North West Hd. in 1776-1777 [Ref: K-1:227, R-31:17].

LEE, John Sr. (1731-1819). Private, 8th Co., Lower Bn., Militia, Sep., 1777 [Ref: M-200, T-5:51]. Rendered aid by providing wheat for use of the military in 1780 [Ref: O-320]. Lived in North West Hd. in 1776 (wife named Elizabeth, aged 52) and had three taxables in 1777 [Ref: K-1:223, R-31:17]. Died testate in Montgomery County in 1819 [Ref: V-82].

LEE, Thomas Simm. See "Samuel Beall (of Richard)" and "Richard Johns," q.v.

LEE, William. Private, 5th Co., Upper Bn., Militia, Aug. 30, 1777 [Ref: M-194]. Took the Oath of Allegiance on Sep. 1, 1780, under the Act of May 12, 1780, having neglected to do so previously "due to ignorance of the duty owed the country." [Ref: R-27:115].

LEEK (LEEKE), Elizabeth. Widow of "Henry Leeke," q.v., who died in 1780 [Ref: V-83]. She rendered aid by providing wheat for use of the military in 1781 [Ref: O-379].

LEEK (LECK, LEEKE), Henry Sr. (died 1780). "Henry Leek" lived in the Upper Part of Newfoundland Hd. (three taxables) in 1777 [Ref: R-31:6]. "Henry Leck" took the Oath of Allegiance before the Hon. Edward Burgess on Feb. 28, 1778 [Ref: T-3:58, L-1:42]. "Henry Leeke" died testate in Montgomery County (wife named Elizabeth) in 1780 and mentioned his sons Henry, Joseph, and Obed [Ref: V-83].

LEEK (LEEKE, LEAKE), Henry (Jr.). "Henry Leek" was a corporal in the 2nd Maryland Line on Jan. 29, 1776 [Ref: D-7]. "Henry Leeke or Leake" was a sergeant in the 1st Maryland Line from April 17, 1777 to Dec. 10, 1779 [Ref: D-131]. He pensioned (S34395) in Montgomery County and in 1816 the Treasurer of Maryland was directed to pay "Henry Leeke," quarterly, the half pay of a sergeant. On Feb. 16, 1820, the balance due "Henry Leake," late of Montgomery County, deceased, was ordered paid to James Brown, of Montgomery County [Ref: J-38, P-2048, K-2:364, K-2:365, Q-122].

LEEK (LEEKE), Joseph. "Joseph Leck" took the Oath of Allegiance before the Hon. Edward Burgess on Feb. 28, 1778 [Ref: T-3:59, L-1:42]. "Joseph Leek" was an Ensign, 4th Co., Middle Bn., Militia, July 15, 1780

[Ref: M-202]. Lived in the Upper Part of Newfoundland Hd. (two taxables) in 1777 [Ref: R-31:6]. "Joseph Leeke, Jr." died testate in Montgomery County (wife named Elizabeth) in 1797 and mentioned a son Joseph. "Joseph Leeke" died testate in Montgomery County (wife named Casandrah) in 1805 [Ref: V-82, V-83]. See "Henry Leeke," q.v.

LEGG, Ann. See "John Davis," q.v.

LEGG, Arthur. Private, Capt. Edward Burgess' Co., Lower District of Frederick (now Montgomery) County, Militia, July, 1776 [Ref: D-42].

LEGG, John. Private, 5th Co., Middle Bn., Militia, July 15, 1780 [Ref: M-203]. Took the Oath of Allegiance on Sep. 1, 1780, under the Act of May 12, 1780, having neglected to do so previously "due to ignorance of the duty owed the country." [Ref: R-27:115]. Lived in Linganore Hd. (two taxables) in 1777 [Ref: R-31:9].

LEGG, Thomas. Private, 5th Co., Middle Bn., Militia, July 15, 1780 [Ref: M-203]. "Thomas Leg" took the Oath of Allegiance before the Hon. Gerrard Briscoe on March 2, 1778 [Ref: T-3:56, L-1:42]. "Thomas Legg" and "Thomas Logg" rendered aid by providing wheat for use of the military in 1780 and 1781 [Ref: O-314, O-403].

LEITCH, Benjamin, and others. See "Benjamin Leach," q.v.

LEMON, Andrew. Private, 1st or 32nd Bn., Militia (no date was given; possibly June, 1777). [Ref: T-5:2].

LEMON (LEMMON), John. Took the Oath of Allegiance in 1778 [Ref: L-2:28].

LENMAR (LENMAN), John. "John Lenmar" was a private, 2nd Co., Lower Bn., Militia, July 15, 1780 [Ref: T-5:19, M-204, which latter source listed the name as "John Len...?"]. "John Lemmar" took the Oath of Allegiance before the Hon. Samuel W. Magruder in 1778 [Ref: T-3:74, L-1:42]. "John Lenman" married Debora Reynolds in Montgomery County on Feb. 13, 1783 [Ref: K-2:522].

LEONARD, Robert. Private, 7th Maryland Line, 1780 [Ref: D-225].

LERNER, Val. Rendered aid by providing beef for use of the military in 1780 [Ref: O-345, O-355].

LERNOLD (LIRNOLD, LEONARD), William. Took the Oath of Allegiance before the Hon. Elisha Williams on March 2, 1778 [Ref: T-3:82].

LESLEY, John. Private, Capt. Price's Co., 3rd Maryland Line, 1781-1782 [Ref: D-453].

LESTER, Memory A. See "Asa Darby," q.v.

LETMAN (LEADMAN, LITMAN), George. "George Litman" lived in the Lower Part of Newfoundland Hd. (one taxable) in 1777 [Ref: R-31:5]. "George Leadman" took the Oath of Allegiance (made his "X" mark) before the Hon. Edward Burgess on Feb. 28, 1778 [Ref: T-3:62, L-1:42]. "George Letman" was a private, 4th Co., Lower Bn., Militia, July 15, 1780 [Ref: M-205]. "George Stetman" [sic] was a private, 7th Co., Lower Bn., Militia, Aug., 1777 [Ref: T-5:50 and M-200, which source questions if the name could have been "Letman"].

LEWIS, Alexander. See "Michael Downs" and "William Lewis," q.v.
LEWIS, Benjamin. Private, 3rd Co., Upper Bn., Militia, Aug. 30, 1777 [Ref: M-193].
LEWIS, Charles (b. 1747). Served as a Corporal, 4th Maryland Regiment, Dec. 18, 1776, a Sergeant, June 1, 1778, and was discharged Jan. 18, 1780 [Ref: D-134]. "Charles Lueas" [sic] lived in Sugarland Hd. in 1776-1777 [Ref: K-1:205, R-31:12].
LEWIS, Daniel (died 1787). Private, Capt. Edward Burgess' Co., Lower District of Frederick (now Montgomery) County, Militia, July, 1776 [Ref: D-42]. Private, 1st Co., Lower Bn., Militia, Sep., 1777 [Ref: M-198, T-5:44]. Took the Oath of Allegiance (made his "D" mark) before the Hon. Edward Burgess on Feb. 28, 1778 [Ref: T-3:58, L-1:42]. "Daniel Lewis, Sr." lived in the Lower Part of Newfoundland Hd. (one taxable) in 1777 [Ref: R-31:5]. "Daniel Lewis" married Margery Waters in Montgomery County on May 10, 1778 [Ref: K-2:522]. Died testate in Montgomery County (wife named Margaret) in 1787 [Ref: V-84].
LEWIS, Daniel Jr. Took the Oath of Allegiance (made his "X" mark) before the Hon. Edward Burgess on Feb. 28, 1778 [Ref: T-3:59, L-1:42].
LEWIS, David. Private, 2nd Co., Lower Bn., Militia, Sep., 1777 [Ref: M-198, T-5:45]. Took the Oath of Allegiance before the Hon. Edward Burgess on Feb. 28, 1778 [Ref: T-3:60, L-1:42]. Rendered aid by providing beef for use of the military in 1780 [Ref: O-343]. Lived in Rock Creek Hd. (two taxables) in 1777 [Ref: R-31:16].
LEWIS, Frances. See "Menum Beall," q.v.
LEWIS, Hopkins. Rendered aid by providing pork for use of the military in 1781 [Ref: O-384].
LEWIS, Isaac. Private, 3rd Co., Upper Bn., Militia, Aug. 30, 1777 [Ref: M-193]. Took the Oath of Allegiance on Sep. 1, 1780, under the Act of May 12, 1780, having neglected to do so previously "due to ignorance of the duty owed the country." [Ref: R-27:115].
LEWIS, Jeremiah (died 1822). Private, 2nd Co., Lower Bn., Militia, Aug., 1777 [Ref: M-198]. Private, 7th Co., Lower Bn., Militia, July 15, 1780 [Ref: M-206]. Took the Oath of Allegiance before the Hon. Edward Burgess on Feb. 28, 1778 [Ref: T-3:59, L-1:42]. Rendered aid by providing wheat for use of the military in 1781 [Ref: O-388]. Lived in Rock Creek Hd. (two taxables) in 1777 [Ref: R-31:16]. Died testate in Montgomery County (wife not named) in 1822 [Ref: V-84].
LEWIS, Jesse. Private, 5th Class, 4th Co., Middle Bn., Militia, July 15, 1780 [Ref: M-202].
LEWIS, John. Took the Oath of Allegiance before the Hon. Aneas Campbell on March 2, 1778 [Ref: T-3:77, L-1:42]. Lived in the Upper Part of Potomac Hd. (two taxables) in 1777 [Ref: R-31:14].
LEWIS, Jonathan. Private, 6th Co., Middle Bn., Militia, Aug., 1777 [Ref: M-197, T-5:41]. Private, 6th Co., Middle Bn., Militia, July 15, 1780 [Ref: M-203]. Took the Oath of Allegiance on Sep. 1, 1780, under the Act of

May 12, 1780, having neglected to do so previously "due to ignorance of the duty owed the country." [Ref: R-27:115]. Private, Capt. Price's Co., 3rd Maryland Line, 1781-1782 [Ref: D-453].

LEWIS, Joseph (died 1824). Private who enrolled into a company of militia for the service of the Flying Camp, Oct. 15, 1776 [Ref: B-352]. Private, 5th Co., Upper Bn., Militia, Aug. 30, 1777 [Ref: M-194]. Lived in Sugar Loaf Hd. (one taxable) in 1777 [Ref: R-31:10]. Died testate in Montgomery County (wife named Mary) in 1824 [Ref: V-84].

LEWIS, Margaret. See "Michael Downs," q.v.

LEWIS, Mary. Rendered aid by providing wheat for use of the military in 1781 [Ref: O-388]. Also see "John Treviss" and "Joseph Lewis," q.v.

LEWIS, Nancy. See "William Lewis," q.v.

LEWIS, Richard (b. 1749). Lived in Sugarland Hd. in 1776 [Ref: K-1:205]. Private, Flying Camp, enlisted on July 18, 1776, and a Corporal, 5th Maryland Line, 1778-1780 [Ref: D-49, D-223].

LEWIS, Samuel (b. 1741). Private, 6th Co., Upper Bn., Militia, Aug. 30, 1777 [Ref: M-194]. Lived in Sugarland Hd. (one taxable) in 1776-1777 [Ref: K-1:203, R-31:12].

LEWIS, Susannah. See "Richard Madden," q.v.

LEWIS, Thomas (b. 1742). Private, 2nd Co., Lower Bn., Militia, July 15, 1780 [Ref: M-204]. Took the Oath of Allegiance before the Hon. Samuel W. Magruder in 1778 [Ref: T-3:73, L-1:42]. Lived in Lower Potomac Hd. (two taxables) in 1776-1777, and owned a working plantation ("quarter") in Sugarland Hd. (nine taxables) in 1777 [Ref: R-31:4, R-31:12, K-1:184].

LEWIS, William (1756-1809). Private, 6th Co., Upper Bn., Militia, Aug. 30, 1777 [Ref: M-194]. Lived in Lower Potomac Hd. in 1776 with "Thomas Lewis," q.v., and was listed in Sugarland Hd. (one taxable) in 1777 [Ref: R-31:12, K-1:184]. William Lewis married Nancy Ellis (b. 1764) in Maryland and moved to Cynthiana, Kentucky in the 1780's. Died in Harrison County, Kentucky in 1809 and Nancy married Alexander Lewis who had moved with them from Maryland. Alexander died in 1841 in Harrison County, Kentucky. Nancy died in July, 1849, in West Feliciana Parish, Louisiana [Ref: *Kentucky Ancestor*, Vol. 16, p. 2, and *Maryland Genealogical Society Bulletin*, Vol. 26, No. 4 (1985), p. 440].

LIDARD, John. Private, 1st or 32nd Bn., Militia (no date was given; possibly June, 1777). [Ref: T-5:1].

LILLY, John. See "George Beckwith," q.v.

LILLY (LILLEY), William. Took the Oath of Allegiance (made his "X" mark) before the Hon. Joseph Wilson on Feb. 28, 1778 [Ref: T-3:64, L-1:42].

LINEBERRY (LIMBERY, LINBERG), Nicholas. See "Nicholas Lyenberger," q.v.

LINGAN, James (b. 1754). Lived in George Town Hd. in 1776 [Ref: K-1:194]. Served as a Lieutenant, Maryland Line, Rawlings' Regiment, and was an exchanged prisoner on Oct. 25, 1780 [Ref: D-616]. There was a "Capt. James McCubbin Lingan" in the Maryland Line from Dec., 1778 to Jan. 1, 1781 (supernumerary). [Ref: D-365, D-521, DAR-I:417].

LINGAN (LINGHAM), Nicholas (b. 1759). Lived in George Town Hd. in 1776 [Ref: K-1:194]. "Nicholas Lingham" was a private, 3rd Co., Lower Bn., Militia, Sep., 1777 [Ref: M-199, T-5:46]. "Nicholas Lingan, of George Town" was Assistant Commissary of Issues for the post of George Town, and took the Oath of Allegiance before the Hon. Richard Thompson on Feb. 26, 1778 [Ref: X-1146].

LINGAN, Thomas (1758-1825). "Thomas Lingan" was a Lieutenant, Maryland Line, who pensioned (S34962) in 1818, aged about 60, in Montgomery County, and died May 28, 1825, aged about 67 [Ref: J-38, K-2:366, P-2087, Q-123]. It appears that he served from Baltimore County in 1776 [Ref: D-52]. There was also a "Thomas Lingoe" (aged 16) in Lower Potomac Hd. in 1776 [Ref: K-1:184].

LINK, Nicholas. Took the Oath of Allegiance in 1778 [Ref: L-2:28].

LINSEY, Theophilus. Served as a Corporal, Capt. Price's Co., 3rd Maryland Line, 1781-1782 [Ref: D-452].

LINTON, George. Private, Capt. Price's Co., 3rd Maryland Line, 1781-1782 [Ref: D-453].

LINTHICUM, Ann. See "Edward Northcraft," q.v.

LINTHICUM, Archibald (c1757-1812). Private, 7th Co., Lower Bn., Militia, Aug., 1777 [Ref: M-200, T-5:50]. Took the Oath of Allegiance before the Hon. Edward Burgess on Feb. 28, 1778 [Ref: T-3:59, L-1:42]. His wife was named "Nancy (Mary) Leake (Lake)" [Ref: DAR-I:417].

LINTHICUM, Nathan. Served as an Ensign, Middle Bn., Militia, March 26, 1776, in the 2nd Co., Middle Bn., Sep. 4, 1777, and Second Lieutenant, April 21, 1779, and First Lieutenant, March 25, 1780, in the 3rd Co., Middle Bn., Militia, July 15, 1780 [Ref: M-97, M-98, M-195, A-287, C-373, E-357, F-120, M-202]. "Nathan Linthicum" rendered aid by providing corn for use of the military in 1780 [Ref: O-283]. "Nathan Linthecom" lived in Sugar Loaf Hd. (two taxables) in 1777 [Ref: R-31:10].

LINTHICUM, Nathan Jr. Private, 5th Class, 3rd Co., Middle Bn., Militia, July 15, 1780 [Ref: M-202].

LINTHICUM, Nathaniel. Private, 2nd Co., Middle Bn., Militia, Sep. 4, 1777 [Ref: M-196, T-5:37].

LINTHICUM, Sarah. See "John Prather," q.v.

LINTHICUM, Zachariah (1735-1808). Private, 2nd Co., Middle Bn., Militia, Sep. 4, 1777 [Ref: M-196, T-5:37]. Private, 1st Class, 3rd Co., Middle Bn., Militia, July 15, 1780 [Ref: M-202]. "Zacheriah Linthecom" lived in Sugar Loaf Hd. (five taxables) in 1777 [Ref: R-31:10]. "Zachariah Linthicum" died testate in Montgomery County (wife not named) in 1808 [Ref: V-85]. His first wife was Sarah Prather and his second wife was Ann Clagett [Ref: DAR-I:417].

LINTRIDGE (LINTRAGE), Samuel (b. 1749). Lived in Sugarland Hd. in 1776 [Ref: K-1:205]. Private, 7th Co., Upper Bn., Militia, Aug. 30, 1777 [Ref: M-195].
LITMAN, George. See "George Letman," q.v.
LITTON (LETTON), Grace. See "Benjamin Summers," q.v.
LITTON (LETTON, LYTTON, LYDDAN), Michael (died 1819). "Michael Lytton" was a private, 2nd Co., Lower Bn., Militia, Sep., 1777 [Ref: M-198, T-5:45]. "Michael Litton" was a private, 5th Co., Lower Bn., Militia, July 15, 1780 [Ref: M-206]. Took the Oath of Allegiance before the Hon. Samuel W. Magruder in 1778 [Ref: T-3:73, L-1:42]. Served as a petit juror in Nov., 1777 [Ref: R-31:18, which listed the name as "Sitton"]. Served as a grand juror in Aug., 1777 [Ref: R-31:17]. "Michael Litton" lived in the Upper Part of Potomac Hd. (four taxables) in 1777 [Ref: R-31:14]. "Michael Letton" died testate in Montgomery County (wife not named) in 1819 [Ref: V-84]. "Patrick Lyddan, Sr." died testate in 1815 and mentioned a son "Michael Lyddan," among others [Ref: V-87].
LITTON (LYDDAN, LYNDON), Nicholas (Nicolis). "Nicholas Lyddan" rendered aid by providing wheat for use of the military in 1780 [Ref: O-313, O-317, O-327]. "Nicolis Lyndon" lived in Rock Creek Hd. (one taxable) in 1777 [Ref: R-31:16].
LITTON, Tabitha. See "William Richards," q.v.
LLOYD, Daniel. Took the Oath of Allegiance before the Hon. Edward Burgess on Feb. 28, 1778 [Ref: T-3:62, L-1:42]. Private, 4th Co., Lower Bn., Militia, July 15, 1780 [Ref: M-205].
LLOYD, Samuel. Private, 4th Co., Lower Bn., Militia, July 15, 1780 [Ref: M-205].
LLOYD, Thomas. Took the Oath of Allegiance in 1778 [Ref: L-2:28].
LOCK, John. Private, 1st or 32nd Bn., Militia (no date was given; possibly June, 1777). [Ref: T-5:1].
LOCKER, John. Took the Oath of Allegiance (made his "I" mark) before the Hon. Samuel W. Magruder in 1778 [Ref: T-3:73, L-1:42].
LOCKER, Joseph (b. 1733). Lived in Sugarland Hd. in 1776 [Ref: K-1:205]. Private, 8th Co., Upper Bn., Militia, Aug. 30, 1777 [Ref: M-195]. Took the Oath of Allegiance before the Hon. Edward Burgess on Feb. 28, 1778 [Ref: T-3:63, L-1:42]. Served as a petit juror in Aug., 1777 [Ref: R-31:17], and rendered aid by providing wheat for use of the military in 1780 [Ref: O-317].
LOCKER, Shadrick or Shaderick (b. 1758). Lived in Sugarland Hd. in 1776 [Ref: K-1:205]. Private, 1st Co., Upper Bn., Militia, Aug. 30, 1777 [Ref: M-193]. Took the Oath of Allegiance before the Hon. Elisha Williams on March 2, 1778 [Ref: T-3:81, L-1:42]. "Shadreck Locker" married Eleanor Gentle in Montgomery County on April 30, 1778 [Ref: K-2:519].

LOCKER, Stephen. Took the Oath of Allegiance (made his "X" mark) before the Hon. Joseph Wilson on Feb. 28, 1778 [Ref: T-3:67, L-1:42, which source listed the name as "Lucker"].
LOCKER, Virlinda. See "George Gentle," q.v.
LODGE, William. Private, 5th Co., Lower Bn., Militia, Aug., 1777 [Ref: M-199, T-5:48]. "William Loodge" [sic] took the Oath of Allegiance before the Hon. Samuel W. Magruder in 1778 [Ref: T-3:73]. "William Lodge" lived in the Upper Part of Potomac Hd. (two taxables) in 1777 [Ref: R-31:14]. Private, 2nd Co., Lower Bn., Militia, July 15, 1780 [Ref: M-204].
LODGEADE, Marthew [sic]. Private, Capt. Edward Burgess' Co., Lower District of Frederick (now Montgomery) County, Militia, July, 1776 [Ref: D-42].
LODGET, Henry. Private, 7th Co., Middle Bn., Militia, July 15, 1780 [Ref: M-203].
LOGSDON, Edward. Took the Oath of Allegiance in 1778 [Ref: L-2:28].
LOGSDON, John Jr. Took the Oath of Allegiance in 1778 [Ref: L-2:28].
LOHR, Beltzer (1743-1827). Private in the Pennsylvania Line who pensioned in 1819, aged 76, in Montgomery County, Maryland, and died on Feb. 27, 1827 [Ref: J-38].
LONG, Jacob. Took the Oath of Allegiance in 1778 [Ref: L-2:28].
LONG, James. Private who enrolled into a company of militia for the service of the Flying Camp on Oct. 15, 1776 [Ref: B-353]. Took the Oath of Allegiance before the Hon. Richard Thompson in 1778 [Ref: T-3:75, L-1:42]. There was a James Long (aged 45) in Lower Potomac Hd. in 1776 and a James Long in George Town Hd. (one taxable) in 1777 [Ref: R-31:3, K-1:184].
LONGDON (LONGLAND), Thomas. "Thomas Longdon" was a private, 7th Co., Middle Bn., Militia, Sep., 1777 [Ref: M-197, T-5:42]. "Thomas Longland" took the Oath of Allegiance before the Hon. Gerrard Briscoe on March 2, 1778 [Ref: T-3:56, L-1:42]. "Thomas Longdon" lived in Seneca Hd. (one taxable) in 1777 [Ref: R-31:8].
LONGSWORTH, Solomon. Took the Oath of Allegiance in 1778 [Ref: L-2:28].
LORD, Thomas. Private, 2nd Co., Middle Bn., Militia, Sep. 4, 1777 [Ref: M-195]. Rendered aid by providing wheat for use of the military in 1780 [Ref: O-315]. Lived in Sugar Loaf Hd. (one taxable) in 1777 [Ref: R-31:10].
LOVE, David. Served as a Sergeant, 7th Maryland Line, 1779-1780 [Ref: D-225].
LOVE, Leonard (b. 1746). Private, 3rd Co., Upper Bn., Militia, Aug. 30, 1777 [Ref: M-193]. Took the Oath of Allegiance before the Hon. Elisha Williams on March 2, 1778 [Ref: T-3:81, L-1:42]. Lived in Sugarland Hd. (one taxable) in 1776-1777 [Ref: K-1:201, R-31:12].

LOVE, Samuel. Private, 2nd Co., Upper Bn., Militia, Aug. 30, 1777 [Ref: M-193]. Took the Oath of Allegiance before the Hon. Elisha Williams on March 2, 1778 [Ref: T-3:81, L-1:42].
LOVE, Thomas (b. 1749). Took the Oath of Allegiance before the Hon. Elisha Williams on March 2, 1778 [Ref: T-3:81, L-1:42]. Lived in Sugarland Hd. in 1776-1777 [Ref: K-1:201, R-31:10].
LOVELESS (LOVELACE, LOVELIS), Barton (b. 1757). "Barton Lovelis" lived in Sugarland Hd. in 1776 [Ref: K-1:198]. "Barton Lovelace" was a private, 7th Co., Upper Bn., Militia, Aug. 30, 1777 [Ref: M-194]. "Barton Loveless" took the Oath of Allegiance before the Hon. Elisha Williams on March 2, 1778 [Ref: T-3:81, L-1:42]. "Bartm. Loveless" married Lucy Watson in Montgomery County on June 11, 1778 [Ref: K-2:519].
LOVELESS (LOVELACE, LOVELIS), Benjamin. "Benjamin Lovelace" was a private, 2nd Co., Upper Bn., Militia, Aug. 30, 1777 [Ref: M-193]. "Benjamin Loveless" took the Oath of Allegiance before the Hon. Elisha Williams on March 2, 1778 [Ref: T-3:81, L-1:42]. Rendered aid by providing wheat for use of the military in 1781 [Ref: O-397]. "Benjamin Lovelis or Loveless" lived in Sugarland Hd. (three taxables) in 1776-1777 [Ref: K-1:198, R-31:12].
LOVELESS (LOVELACE), Elias (1755-1834). Born on Jan. 27, 1755, he lived in that part of Frederick County which became Montgomery County in 1776, but moved to Rowan County, North Carolina prior thereto. Elias married Anne Roby, daughter of Thomas, in 1775 and served in the military in North Carolina. In 1798 they moved to Butler County, Kentucky, where he died on Dec. 24, 1834. For more information on Elias and his brother Vachel, refer to Henry C. Peden's *Marylanders to Kentucky*, pp. 91-92, and Anderson C. Quisenberry's *Revolutionary Soldiers in Kentucky*, p. 113].
LOVELESS, Elisha. "Elisha Loveless" was a private, 1st Maryland Line, from May 22, 1778 to Jan. 16, 1779, at which time he was reported dead [Ref: D-132].
LOVELESS (LOVELACE, LOVELIS), Elkanah (b. 1755). "Elkanah Lovelace" was a private, 2nd Co., Upper Bn., Militia, Aug. 30, 1777 [Ref: M-193]. "Elkanah Loveless" took the Oath of Allegiance before the Hon. Elisha Williams on March 2, 1778 [Ref: T-3:81, L-1:42]. "Eleanah Lovelis" lived in Sugarland Hd. in 1776 and "Elkanah Lovelace" lived there in 1777 [Ref: K-1:198, R-31:12]. He was apparently a son of Benjamin Lovelace, q.v.
LOVELESS, Vachel. See "Elias Loveless (Lovelace)," q.v.
LOVELY, Thomas. Served as a musician (drum & fife) in Capt. Thomas Beall's Co., Maryland Line, 1780 [Ref: D-350].
LOWDEN (LEWDEN, LUTEN), Isaac. "Isaac Luten" was a private, 5th Co., Upper Bn., Militia, Aug. 30, 1777 [Ref: M-194].

LOWDEN (LOVEDEN?), John. "John Loveden" [Lowden?] was a private who was recruited to serve in the Continental Army in 1780 [Ref: D-341].

LOWDEN, Michael. Private, 1st Maryland Line, Dec. 10, 1776, and was taken prisoner on Aug. 16, 1780, at the Battle of Camden [Ref: D-131].

LOWDEN (LOADON), Nicholas. "Nichols Loaden" took the Oath of Allegiance before the Hon. Charles Jones on Jan. 10, 1778 [Ref: T-3:71, L-1:42].

LOWDEN (LEWDEN), William. "William Lewden" was a private who was recruited to serve in the Continental Army in 1780 [Ref: D-341].

LOWE, Daniel. Rendered aid by providing wheat for use of the military in 1780 [Ref: O-304].

LOWE (LOW), David. Private, 7th Co., Upper Bn., Militia, Aug. 30, 1777 [Ref: M-194]. Private, 3rd Co., Lower Bn., Militia, July 15, 1780 [Ref: M-205]. "David Lowe" rendered aid by providing wheat for use of the military in 1780 [Ref: O-305]. "David Low" took the Oath of Allegiance before the Hon. Joseph Wilson on Feb. 28, 1778 [Ref: T-3:64, L-1:42]. Lived in Sugarland Hd. (two taxables) in 1777 [Ref: R-31:12].

LOWE (LOW), Patrick. Took the Oath of Allegiance before the Hon. Joseph Wilson on Feb. 28, 1778 [Ref: T-3:66, L-1:42].

LOWE, William (b. 1746). Lived in North West Hd. (wife named Sarah, aged 18) in 1776 [Ref: K-1:226]. There were two men with this name who served in the 7th Maryland Regiment between 1777 and 1780, and it appears he may have been one of them [Ref: D-224].

LOWMAN, Thomas. Took the Oath of Allegiance (made his mark) before the Hon. Joseph Wilson on Feb. 28, 1778 [Ref: T-3:67, L-1:42].

LOWRY (LOWREY), John (b. 1756). Private, Flying Camp, enlisted Aug. 5, 1776 [Ref: D-44]. Lived in the household of Israel Case in Sugarland Hd. in 1776 [Ref: K-1:200].

LOWRY (LOWREY), William. Private, Flying Camp, enlisted July 29, 1776 [Ref: D-44]. Private, 7th Co., Middle Bn., Militia, Sep., 1777, and Third Sergeant, July 15, 1780 [Ref: M-197, M-203, T-5:42]. Took the Oath of Allegiance before the Hon. Joseph Wilson on Feb. 28, 1778 [Ref: T-3:67, L-1:42]. Lived in Seneca Hd. (one taxable) in 1777 [Ref: R-31:8].

LOYE, Frederick. Took the Oath of Allegiance in 1778 [Ref: L-2:28].

LUCAS, Ann. See "William Hickman," q.v.

LUCAS, Barton. Rendered aid by providing wheat for use of the military in 1780 [Ref: O-317].

LUCAS, Basil (1757-1841). Lived in the Lower Part of Newfoundland Hd. (two taxables) in 1777 [Ref: R-31:5]. Private, 7th Co., Lower Bn., Militia, Aug., 1777 [Ref: M-200, T-5:50], and Private, 1st or 32nd Bn., Militia (no date was given). [Ref: T-5:1]. Took the Oath of Allegiance before the Hon. Edward Burgess on Feb. 28, 1778 [Ref: T-3:59, L-1:42, DAR-I:427].

LUCAS, Charles (b. 1753). Private, 1st Co., Upper Bn., Militia, Aug. 30, 1777 [Ref: M-193]. Took the Oath of Allegiance before the Hon. Aneas

Campbell on March 2, 1778 [Ref: T-3:78, L-1:42]. Lived in Sugarland Hd. in 1776 and it appears that his mother was Mary Lucas who later married "Zephaniah Lucas," q.v. [Ref: K-1:219].

LUCAS, James. Private, 1st or 32nd Bn., Militia (no date was given; possibly June, 1777). [Ref: T-5:1].

LUCAS, Jonathan. Private, 6th Co., Lower Bn., Militia, July 15, 1780 [Ref: M-206].

LUCAS, Mary. See "Zephaniah Wood," q.v.

LUCAS, Thomas (b. 1751). Lived in Sugarland Hd. in 1776 [Ref: K-1:205]. Private, 5th Co., Lower Bn., Militia, Aug., 1777 [Ref: M-199, T-5:48].

LUCAS, William. (1) Private, 7th Co., Upper Bn., Militia, Aug. 30, 1777 [Ref: M-194]. (2) Private, 1st Maryland Line, from Feb. 1, 1777 to Jan. 21, 1778; reenlisted (no date given) and discharged Dec. 27, 1779 [Ref: D-132]. One William Lucas took the Oath of Allegiance before the Hon. Edward Burgess on Feb. 28, 1778 [Ref: T-3:62, L-1:42], and another took the Oath of Allegiance (made his "X mark) before the Hon. Aneas Campbell on March 2, 1778 [Ref: T-3:77, L-1:42]. One William Lucas lived in the Upper Part of Newfoundland Hd. (one taxable) in 1777 [Ref: R-31:6], and another lived in Sugarland Hd. (one taxable) in 1777 [Ref: R-31:12]. "William Lucas, aged 19" lived in Sugarland Hd. in 1776 and it appears that his mother was Mary Lucas who later married "Zepheniah Wood," q.v. [Ref: K-1:219].

LUCK, William Jr. Rendered aid by providing wheat for use of the military in 1780 [Ref: O-303].

LUCKETT, David and Susanna. See "William Luckett," q.v.

LUCKETT, Elizabeth. See "Thomas Offutt," q.v.

LUCKETT, Thomas Hussey. Served as Lieutenant in Rawlings' Regiment, Maryland Line, 1776, was promoted to captain on Jan. 1, 1777, captured (no date given), exchanged Oct. 25, 1780, and served through 1781 [Ref: D-365, D-521, D-616]. "Thomas Hussey Luckett" lived in Sugar Loaf Hd. (two taxables) in 1777 [Ref: R-31:10].

LUCKETT, William. Took the Oath of Allegiance before the Hon. Aneas Campbell on March 2, 1778 [Ref: T-3:77, L-1:42]. "Capt. William Luckett, aged 65" lived in Sugarland Hd. (wife named Charity) in 1776, and "William Luckett" lived in Sugarland Hd. (13 taxables) in 1777 [Ref: R-31:12, K-1:213]. One died testate in Montgomery County (naming his siblings, nieces and nephews) in 1799, and mentioned his parents David and Susanna Luckett [Ref: V-86].

LUESFORDE, John. Rendered aid by providing wheat for use of the military in 1781 [Ref: O-386].

LUTES (LUTTS), Alexander. "Alexander Lutes" was a private, 7th Co., Middle Bn., Militia, Sep., 1777 [Ref: T-5:42 and M-197, which latter source questions if name could have been "Sutes"]. "Alexander Lutts" lived in Sugar Loaf Hd. (one taxable) in 1777 [Ref: R-31:10].

LYDDAN, Nicholas. See "Nicholas Litton," q.v.

LYENBERGER (LEYENBERGER, LEGENBERGER, LINENBERY), Nicholas. Lived in George Town Hd. in 1776 and 1777 [Ref: K-1:194, R-31:3]. "Nicholas Legenberger or Leyenberger" took the Oath of Allegiance before the Hon. Richard Thompson in 1778 [Ref: T-3:76, L-1:42]. "Nicholas Limbery" [sic] was a private, 3rd Co., Lower Bn., Militia, Sep., 1777 [Ref: M-199, T-5:46].

LYLES, James. Private, Capt. Price's Co., 3rd Maryland Line, 1781-1782 [Ref: D-453].

LYNN, David. Took the Oath of Allegiance before the Hon. Charles Jones on Jan. 10, 1778 [Ref: T-3:71, L-1:42]. Rendered aid by providing wheat for use of the military in 1780 [Ref: O-311]. Lived in Rock Creek Hd. (ten taxables) and owned a working plantation ("quarter") in Seneca Hd. in 1777 [Ref: R-31:8, R-31:16].

LYNN, Elizabeth. See "Samuel Wade Magruder," q.v.

LYNN, John. Took the Oath of Allegiance before the Hon. Gerrard Briscoe on March 2, 1778 [Ref: T-3:56, L-1:42].

LYON, John. Private, 2nd Co., Lower Bn., Militia, Sep., 1777 [Ref: T-5:45].

LYON (LOGAN), Sarah. See "Samuel Griffith," q.v.

MACATEE (MACKETEE, MACCATTEE), Charles (b. 1760). Lived in Lower Potomac Hd. in 1776 [Ref: K-1:184]. Private, 4th Co., Lower Bn., Militia, Aug., 1777, and Private, 1st Co., Lower Bn., July 15, 1780 [Ref: T-5:47, M-204, M-199, which sources listed the name as "Chas. Mack...", "Charles McHettee," and "Charles Mackelter"].

MACATEE (MACKETEE, McATEE, MACKTEE), James. Private, 8th Co., Lower Bn., Militia, Sep., 1777 [Ref: M-200, T-5:51]. Took the Oath of Allegiance before the Hon. Samuel W. Magruder in 1778 [Ref: T-3:74, L-1:42, which latter source listed the name as "Mackabee"]. "James McAtee" took the Oath of Allegiance before the Hon. Edward Burgess on Feb. 28, 1778 [Ref: T-3:64, L-1:42]. "James Macktee" lived in North West Hd. (one taxable) in 1777 [Ref: R-31:17].

MACATEE (MACKETEE), Joseph. Private, 6th Co., Lower Bn., Militia, July 15, 1780 [Ref: M-206].

MACATEE (MACKETEE, MACCATTEE), Samuel (b. 1754). Lived in Lower Potomac Hd. in 1776 [Ref: K-1:184]. Private, 1st Co., Lower Bn., Militia, July 15, 1780 [Ref: M-204].

MACATEE (MACKETEE, McATEE), Walter (1758-1833). Served as a private in the Maryland Line. Applied for pension (S31945) in 1832, aged 75, in Nelson County, Kentucky, stating he was born in Charles County, Maryland, entered the service for about seven months in 1776 and 1777, and afterwards lived in Prince George's and Montgomery Counties. In 1781 he moved to Kentucky with his parents [Ref: Y-15, P-2239, Z-60]. "Walter Macatee or McAtee" died on Feb. 20, 1833, and "Mary McAtee" was an heir [Ref: P-2239, which indicates they moved to Nelson County, Kentucky in 1821]. Anderson C. Quisenberry's

Revolutionary Soldiers in Kentucky (page 133) mistakenly indicates he served in the Pennsylvania Militia.

MACCUBBIN (McCUBBIN), Thomas (b. 1748). Private, 4th Co., Lower Bn., Militia, Aug., 1777 [Ref: M-199, T-5:47]. Took the Oath of Allegiance before the Hon. Charles Jones on Jan. 10, 1778 [Ref: T-3:71, L-1:42]. Served as a grand juror in Aug., 1777 [Ref: R-31:17]. Rendered aid by providing wheat for use of the military in 1780 [Ref: O-299]. "Thomas McCubbin" was a private, 1st Co., Lower Bn., Militia, July 15, 1780 [Ref: M-204]. In March, 1780, the Collector of the Tax for Montgomery County was directed "to pay Thomas McCubbin, a Commissioner for said county, 500 pounds to enable him to carry into execution the Act for the immediate supply of flour and other provisions for the Army." [Ref: F-120]. "Thomas Maccubbin" lived in Lower Potomac Hd. in 1776 and "Thomas McCubbin" had 13 taxables in 1777 [Ref: K-1:184, R-31:4].

MACCUBBIN (McCUBBIN), Zachariah (b. 1752). Private, 5th Co., Lower Bn., Militia, Aug., 1777 [Ref: M-199, T-5:48]. Took the Oath of Allegiance before the Hon. Charles Jones on Jan. 10, 1778 [Ref: T-3:71, L-1:42]. He recruited John Davis Tulley in April, 1781 [Ref: R-33:156, X-1146]. Rendered aid by providing wheat for use of the military in 1780 [Ref: O-311]. "Zachariah McCubbin" was a private, 2nd Co., Lower Bn., Militia, July 15, 1780 [Ref: M-204]. "Zecheriah Maccubbin" lived in Lower Potomac Hd. in 1776 and "Zacheriah McCubbin" had nine taxables there in 1777 [Ref: K-1:184, R-31:4]. For a well-documented history see "The Maccubbin Family of Montgomery County, Maryland," by William M. LeoGrande and Jerome F. Collins, *Maryland Genealogical Society Bulletin*, Vol. 37, No. 1 (1996), pp. 67-92.

MACKALL, Thomas. Rendered aid by providing wheat for use of the military in 1781 [Ref: O-396].

MACKELFRESH, Abner. Private, 2nd Class, 4th Co., Middle Bn., Militia, July 15, 1780 [Ref: M-202].

MACKELFRESH, David. Private, 4th Co., Middle Bn., Militia, Sep., 1777 [Ref: M-196, T-5:39]. Private, 6th Co., Middle Bn., Militia, July 15, 1780 [Ref: M-203]. Took the Oath of Allegiance before the Hon. Edward Burgess on Feb. 28, 1778 [Ref: T-3:58, L-1:42].

MACKELFRESH, Elizabeth. See "Edward Burgess," q.v.

MACKELFRESH (MACKLEFISH), Henry. Private, 5th Class, 4th Co., Middle Bn., Militia, July 15, 1780 [Ref: M-202].

MACKELFRESH (MACKLEFISH), John. Private, 4th Co., Middle Bn., Militia, Sep., 1777 [Ref: M-196, T-5:39]. Took the Oath of Allegiance (made his "X" mark) before the Hon. Edward Burgess on Feb. 28, 1778 [Ref: T-3:58, L-1:42].

MACKELFRESH (MACKLEFISH), Richard. Private, 8th Co., Middle Bn., Militia, Sep., 1777 [Ref: M-198, T-5:43]. Private, 7th Class, 4th Co., Middle Bn., Militia, July 15, 1780 [Ref: M-202]. Two men with this name took the Oath of Allegiance before the Hon. Edward Burgess on Feb. 28, 1778 [Ref: T-3:58, L-1:42]. One made his "X" mark [Ref: T-3:59, L-1:42]. "Richard Mackilfish, Sr." rendered aid by providing wheat for use of the military in 1781 [Ref: O-395]. "Richard Maclefish" (three taxables) and "Richard Maclefish, Jr." (one taxable) lived in the Upper Part of Newfoundland Hd. in 1777 [Ref: R-31:6, R-31:7].

MACKELFRESH (MACKLEFONST), William. Private, 1st or 32nd Bn., Militia (no date was given; possibly June, 1777). [Ref: T-5:1].

MACKEY (MACKEE), William (b. 1746). "William Mackey" rendered aid by providing cornmeal for use of the military in 1781 [Ref: O-355]. "William Mackee" married Priscilla Jones in Montgomery County on June 13, 1779 [Ref: K-2:519]. "William Mackeay, Sert." [servant] lived in North West Hd. in 1776 [Ref: K-1:228].

MACMILLEN, Amith [sic]. See "Norman Bruce Magruder," q.v.

MADDEN (MADDIN), Ann. See "Nathan Collins," q.v.

MADDEN (MADDING), Benjamin (b. 1761). Son of Joseph Madding, of North West Hd., in 1776 [Ref: K-1:224]. Private, 8th Co., Lower Bn., Militia, Sep., 1777 [Ref: T-5:51]. Private, 1st Co., Lower Bn., Militia, July 15, 1780 [Ref: M-204].

MADDEN, Frederick. Took the Oath of Allegiance in 1778 [Ref: L-2:28].

MADDEN (MADDING), John. (1) Private, 6th Co., Upper Bn., Militia, Aug. 30, 1777 [Ref: M-194]. (2) Private, 8th Co., Lower Bn., Militia, Sep., 1777 [Ref: M-200, T-5:51]. Private, 1st Co., Lower Bn., Militia, July 15, 1780 [Ref: M-204]. (3) Took the Oath of Allegiance before the Hon. Elisha Williams on March 2, 1778 [Ref: T-3:80, L-1:42]. One "John Maddin" married Dolly Steward in Montgomery County on April 11, 1780 [Ref: K-2:519]. One John Maddin lived in Sugar Loaf Hd. (one taxable) in 1777 [Ref: R-31:10], and another lived in North West Hd. (one taxable) in 1777 [Ref: R-31:16]. "John Madding, aged 24" lived in Northwest Hd. in 1776 (wife named Margratt, aged 21) and was apparently a son of Joseph Madding, aged 48 [Ref: K-1:224]. "John Madding, aged 84" lived in North West Hd. (wife named Sarah, aged 68) in 1776 [Ref: K-1:226].

MADDEN (MADDING), Jonathan. Private, 7th Co., Upper Bn., Militia, Aug. 30, 1777 [Ref: M-194]. "Jonan. Madden" was a private, 6th Co., Upper Bn., Militia, Aug. 30, 1777 [Ref: M-194]. "Jonathan Madding, Sr." took the Oath of Allegiance before the Hon. Elisha Williams on March 2, 1778 [Ref: T-3:80, L-1:42]. "Jonathan Maddin" lived in Sugar Loaf Hd. (three taxables) in 1777 [Ref: R-31:10]. Also see "Jonathan Madden, Jr.," q.v.

MADDEN (MADDING, MADING), Jonathan Jr. "Jonathan Madding, Jr." took the Oath of Allegiance before the Hon. Elisha Williams on March 2, 1778 [Ref: T-3:80, L-1:42]. "Jonathan Mading" married Anne Patrick in Montgomery County on Nov. 4, 1779 [Ref: K-2:519].

MADDEN (MADDIN, MADDON), Joseph (b. 1757). Private, 8th Co., Lower Bn., Militia, Sep., 1777 [Ref: M-200, T-5:51]. "Joseph Maddin or Madden" applied for pension (S31237) in Fleming County, Kentucky, on Sep. 7, 1832, aged 75, stating he had enlisted in Frederick County, Maryland, in 1777 and for the past 29 years had lived in Fleming County [Ref: Z-35, P-2163]. "Joseph Maddon or Madding, aged 48" lived in North West Hd. (wife named Mary, aged 43) in 1776-1777, and had a son Joseph, aged 17, among many other children listed in 1776 [Ref: K-1:224, R-31:17].

MADDEN (MADDIN, MADDING), Richard. Private, 6th Co., Upper Bn., Militia, Aug. 30, 1777 [Ref: M-194]. "Richard Madding" took the Oath of Allegiance before the Hon. Elisha Williams on March 2, 1778 [Ref: T-3:80, L-1:42]. Richard Madding married Susannah Lewis in Montgomery County on Jan. 26, 1779 [Ref: K-2:519, which spelled the name "Modding"]. "Richard Maddin" lived in Sugar Loaf Hd. (one taxable) in 1777 [Ref: R-31:10].

MADDEN (MADDING), Thomas (b. 1762). Son of Joseph Madding, of North West Hd., in 1776 [Ref: K-1:224]. Served as a private in the Extra Regiment of the Continental Army in 1780 [Ref: D-342].

MADDEN, William. Served as a private when enrolled into a company of militia for the service of the Flying Camp on Oct. 15, 1776 [Ref: B-352].

MADDOX, James. Private, 6th Co., Lower Bn., Militia, July 15, 1780 [Ref: M-206].

MADDOX (MATTAX, MADOCK), Thomas (b. 1738). "Thomas Mattax" was a private, 4th Co., Lower Bn., Militia, Aug., 1777 [Ref: M-199, T-5:47]. "Thomas Maddox" took the Oath of Allegiance before the Hon. Samuel W. Magruder in 1778 [Ref: T-3:73]. "Thomas Maddox, aged 38" lived in North West Hd. in 1776 (wife named Jannet, aged 28) and "Thomas Madock" lived there in 1777 [Ref: K-1:224, R-31:16].

MADDOX, William. Private, 6th Co., Lower Bn., Militia, July 15, 1780 [Ref: M-206].

MAFFATT (MAFFITT, MUFFETT, MOFFITT, MUFFAT), Barney (b. 1746). Private, 5th Co., Lower Bn., Militia, Aug., 1777, and Private, 2nd Co., Lower Bn., July 15, 1780 [Ref: M-200, M-204, T-5:48]. Took the Oath of Allegiance (made his "B" mark) before the Hon. Samuel W. Magruder in 1778 [Ref: T-3:73, L-1:42, which source mistakenly listed the name as "Barney Mufphel"]. "Barney Maffatt" lived in Lower Potomac Hd. in 1776 and "Barney Muffat" had one taxable there in 1777 [Ref: K-1:184, R-31:4].

MAGARVY, James. Private, 1st or 32nd Bn., Militia (no date was given; possibly June, 1777). [Ref: T-5:2].

MAGILL, Thomas. Private, 5th Co., Middle Bn., Militia, July 15, 1780 [Ref: M-203].

MAGINNISS, Andrew. Private, 6th Co., Lower Bn., Militia, July 15, 1780 [Ref: M-206].

MAGINNISS, John. "John Maginniss" was a private, 2nd Class, 4th Co., Middle Bn., Militia, July 15, 1780 [Ref: M-202]. "John Maginnis" was recruited to serve in the Extra Regiment, Continental Army, in 1780 [Ref: D-342].

MAGINNISS, Neill (b. 1746). "Neill Maginniss" was a private, 4th Co., Upper Bn., Militia, Aug. 30, 1777 [Ref: M-194]. "Neal Maginnis or Meginias" lived in Sugarland Hd. in 1776-1777 [Ref: K-1:198, R-31:13].

MAGRATH (MAGROTH, McGREATH), William. "William Magrath" took the Oath of Allegiance before the Hon. Richard Thompson in 1778 [Ref: T-3:75, L-1:42]. "William and James Magroth" lived in the Upper Part of Potomac Hd. (two taxables) in 1777 [Ref: R-31:14]. "William McGreath" was a private, 3rd Class, 1st Co., Middle Bn., Militia, July 15, 1780 [Ref: M-201].

MAGRUDER, Alexander. See "Samuel and Nathaniel Magruder," q.v.

MAGRUDER, Aquila. See "Nathaniel Magruder," q.v.

MAGRUDER, Archibald (1751-1842). Lived in Lower Potomac Hd. in 1776 [Ref: K-1:184]. Private, 4th Co., Lower Bn., Militia, Aug., 1777 [Ref: M-199, T-5:47]. Took the Oath of Allegiance before the Hon. Samuel W. Magruder in 1778 [Ref: T-3:73]. Private, 1st Co., Lower Bn., Militia, July 15, 1780 [Ref: M-204]. Rendered aid by providing wheat for use of the military in 1780 [Ref: O-322, O-332]. Jane Magruder died testate in Montgomery County in 1787, naming only her son Archibald [Ref: V-90]. He was born on Nov. 4, 1751, married Cassandra Offutt, and died on Jan. 6, 1842 [Ref: DAR-I:433]. See "John Magruder," q.v.

MAGRUDER, Basil (died 1790). Private, 3rd Co., Middle Bn., Militia, Sep., 1777 [Ref: M-196, T-5:38]. Lived in the Upper Part of Potomac Hd. (eight taxables) in 1777 [Ref: R-31:14]. Died testate in 1790 in Montgomery County, naming his brother "George Frazer Magruder," q.v. [Ref: V-89].

MAGRUDER, Brook. See "Samuel Wade Magruder," q.v.

MAGRUDER, Bruce. See "Normand Bruce Magruder," q.v.

MAGRUDER, Catherine. See "Joseph Magruder," q.v.

MAGRUDER, Charles (b. 1761). Son of Samuel Wade Magruder [Ref: V-93]. Lived in Lower Potomac Hd. in 1776 [Ref: K-1:184]. Private, 5th Co., Lower Bn., Militia, Aug., 1777 [Ref: M-200, T-5:48], and private, 2nd Co., Lower Bn., Militia, July 15, 1780 [Ref: M-204].

MAGRUDER, Daniel (b. 1763 or 1764). Lived in Lower Potomac Hd. in 1776 [Ref: K-1:184]. Private, 1st Co., Lower Bn., Militia, July 15, 1780 [Ref: M-204].

MAGRUDER, Edward (1743-1819). Private, 4th Co., Lower Bn., Militia, Aug., 1777 [Ref: M-199, T-5:47]. Private, 1st Co., Lower Bn., Militia, July 15, 1780 [Ref: M-204]. Took the Oath of Allegiance before the Hon. Samuel W. Magruder in 1778 [Ref: T-3:73]. Recruited Joshua Baker in March, 1781 [Ref: R-33:155, X-1146]. Rendered aid by providing wheat for use of the military in 1780 and 1781 [Ref: O-315, O-412]. Lived in

Lower Potomac Hd. in 1776 and had three taxables in 1777 [Ref: K-1:184, R-31:4]. Died testate in Montgomery County (wife named Jane) in 1819 [Ref: V-90]. See "John Magruder," q.v.

MAGRUDER, Eleanor. See "John Magruder" and "Samuel Magruder" and "Kid Marquess" and "Samuel Beall Magruder," q.v.

MAGRUDER, Elias. (1) Son of "Samuel Magruder," q.v. [Ref: V-93]. Private, 3rd Co., Lower Bn., Militia, July 15, 1780 [Ref: M-205]. (2) Elias Magruder (b. 1726) lived in Lower Potomac Hd. in 1776 and had three taxables in 1777 [Ref: K-1:184, R-31:4]. Took the Oath of Allegiance before the Hon. Samuel W. Magruder in 1778 [Ref: T-3:73, L-1:42]. Rendered aid by providing wheat for use of the military in 1780 [Ref: O-341].

MAGRUDER, Elizabeth. See "Samuel W. Magruder" and "John Magruder," q.v.

MAGRUDER, Enoch (b. 1759). Private, 5th Co., Lower Bn., Militia, Aug., 1777 [Ref: M-199, T-5:48]. Private, 2nd Co., Lower Bn., Militia, July 15, 1780 [Ref: M-204]. Took the Oath of Allegiance before the Hon. Samuel W. Magruder in 1778 [Ref: T-3:73, L-1:42]. See "Nathaniel Magruder," q.v.

MAGRUDER, Ezekiel (b. 1757). Lived in Lower Potomac Hd. in 1776 [Ref: K-1:184]. Private, 4th Co., Lower Bn., Militia, Aug., 1777 [Ref: M-199, T-5:47].

MAGRUDER, George Beall. See "Samuel Wade Magruder," q.v.

MAGRUDER, George Frazer or Fraser (1733-c1793). Brother of "Basil Magruder," q.v. [Ref: V-89]. Rendered aid by providing wheat for use of the military in 1780 [Ref: O-314]. George Fraser Magruder married Eleanor Bowie [Ref: DAR-I:433].

MAGRUDER, Hezekiah (1729-1806). Served as a Lieutenant in the 4th Co., Lower Bn., Militia, Aug., 1777; First Lieutenant, 1st Co., Lower Bn., July 15, 1780; resigned May 7, 1782 [Ref: M-199, M-204, T-5:47, K-2:371]. Took the Oath of Allegiance before the Hon. Richard Thompson in 1778 [Ref: T-3:75, L-1:42]. Rendered aid by providing wheat for use of the military in 1780 [Ref: O-337]. Lived in Lower Potomac Hd. in 1776 and had six taxables in 1777 [Ref: K-1:184, R-31:4]. Died testate in Montgomery County (wife named Susanna Talbott) in 1806 [Ref: V-90, DAR-I:433].

MAGRUDER, Isaac (1755-1809). Son of Nathan Magruder [Ref: V-91]. Private, 2nd Co., Lower Bn., Militia, Sep., 1777 [Ref: M-198, T-5:45]. Took the Oath of Allegiance before the Hon. Joseph Wilson on Feb. 28, 1778 [Ref: T-3:66, L-1:42]. Lived in Seneca Hd. in 1777 and served as a constable in 1780 [Ref: R-31:8, W-1]. He married twice: (1) Sophia Baldwin, and (2) Ann Hill [Ref: DAR-I:433].

MAGRUDER, James (1723-1795). Lived in Sugar Loaf Hd. (six taxables) in 1777 [Ref: R-31:10]. Served as private, 2nd Co., Upper Bn., Militia, Aug. 30, 1777 [Ref: M-193]. Took the Oath of Allegiance before the Hon.

Elisha Williams on March 2, 1778 [Ref: T-3:80, L-1:42]. He married Mary Bowie [Ref: DAR-I:433]. Also see "Norman Bruce Magruder" and "John Magruder" and "Samuel Beall Magruder," q.v.

MAGRUDER, Jane. See "Archibald Magruder" and "John Magruder" and "Edward Magruder," q.v.

MAGRUDER, Jeffrey (1762-1805). Son of Nathan Magruder [Ref: V-91]. Private, 7th Co., Middle Bn., Militia, July 15, 1780 [Ref: M-204]. Jeffrey was born on April 21, 1762, married Susannah Bowie, and died on Oct. 31, 1805 [Ref: DAR-I:433].

MAGRUDER, John (1709-1782). Took the Oath of Allegiance before the Hon. Samuel W. Magruder in 1778 [Ref: T-3:73, L-1:43, L-2:28]. Lived in Lower Potomac Hd. in 1776 and had five taxables in 1777 [Ref: K-1:184, R-31:4]. Died testate in Montgomery County (wife not named) in 1782, and mentioned sons Ninian, Edward, Archibald, and James, and daughters Elizabeth, Eleanor, and Jane [Ref: V-90]. See "Kid Marquess," q.v.

MAGRUDER, John Beall. Son of Nathan Magruder [Ref: V-91]. Private, 2nd Co., Lower Bn., Militia, Sep., 1777 [Ref: M-198, T-5:46], and private, 7th Co., Middle Bn., Militia, July 15, 1780 [Ref: M-203]. "John B. Magruder" took the Oath of Allegiance before the Hon. Joseph Wilson on Feb. 7, 1778 [Ref: T-3:64, L-1:43]. Lived in Rock Creek Hd. (four taxables) in 1777 [Ref: R-31:16].

MAGRUDER, Joseph (1742-1793). Served as a Captain, 6th Co., 29th Bn., Militia, June 21, 1777, and Captain, 3rd Co., Lower Bn., July 15, 1780 [Ref: C-296, M-200, M-204, T-5:49, M-99, and C-373, which latter two listed his name as "Macgruder"]. Took the Oath of Allegiance before the Hon. Joseph Offutt on March 2, 1778 [Ref: T-3:70, L-1:43]. Served as a petit juror in Aug., 1777 [Ref: R-31:17]. Lived in the Upper Part of Potomac Hd. (five taxables) in 1777 [Ref: R-31:14]. He married twice: (1) Mary Jackson and (2) Catherine Flemming in Montgomery County on June 25, 1778 [Ref: K-2:519, V-90, DAR-I:433].

MAGRUDER, Josias or Josiah. Son of Samuel Magruder [Ref: V-93]. Served as an Ensign, 4th Co., Lower Bn., Militia, Aug., 1777, and Ensign, 1st Co., Lower Bn., July 15, 1780 [Ref: M-199, M-204, T-5:47]. "Josiah Magruder" took the Oath of Allegiance before the Hon. Samuel W. Magruder in 1778 [Ref: T-3:73, L-1:43]. "Josiah Magruder" (b. 1752) lived in Lower Potomac Hd. in 1776 and "Josias Magruder" (one taxable) lived there in 1777 [Ref: K-1:184, R-31:4].

MAGRUDER, Levin (b. 1759). Son of Samuel Wade Magruder [Ref: V-93]. Lived in Lower Potomac Hd. in 1776 [Ref: K-1:184]. Private, 5th Co., Lower Bn., Militia, Aug., 1777 [Ref: M-199, T-5:48]. Took the Oath of Allegiance before the Hon. Samuel W. Magruder in 1778 [Ref: T-3:73, L-1:43]. Private, 2nd Co., Lower Bn., Militia, July 15, 1780 [Ref: M-204].

MAGRUDER, Lloyd. See "Samuel Wade Magruder," q.v.

MAGRUDER, Mary and Nancy. See "Norman Bruce Magruder," q.v.

MAGRUDER, Nathaniel (Nathan). "Nathan Magruder" took the Oath of Allegiance before the Hon. Joseph Wilson on Feb. 28, 1778 [Ref: T-3:66, L-1:43]. "Nathaniel Magruder" rendered aid by providing wheat for use of the military in 1780 [Ref: O-307, O-311, O-329]. "Nathaniel Magruder, of Alexander" lived in Lower Potomac Hd. (nine taxables) in 1777 [Ref: R-31:4], and "Nathan Magruder" lived in Rock Creek Hd. (eight taxables) in 1777 [Ref: R-31:16]. "Nathan Magruder, planter" died testate in Montgomery County (wife not named) in 1786, naming sons Isaac Magruder, John Beall Magruder, Jeffrey Magruder, and Nathan Magruder (of Frederick County), and other children [Ref: V-91]. "Nathaniel Magruder, son of Alexander" (1716-1798) lived in Lower Potomac Hd. in 1776 and died testate in Montgomery County (wife not named) in 1798, mentioning sons Walter Magruder and Aquila Magruder, and other children [Ref: K-1:184, V-91]. There were two Nathaniel Magruders in Lower Potomac Hd. in 1776: Nathaniel Magruder (b. 1756) was listed in the household of Zechariah Magruder (b. 1711); and, Nathaniel Magruder, Jr. (b. 1761) was listed with Nathaniel Magruder, of Ninian (b. 1722), Ninian Magruder (b. 1752), and Enoch Magruder (b. 1759). [Ref: K-1:184, K-1:185. Also see Source DAR-I:433].

MAGRUDER, Nathaniel Beall. Served as an Ensign in the Maryland part of Col. Rawlings' Regiment, 1779-1780 [Ref: F-83].

MAGRUDER, Nathaniel, of Archibald. Took the Oath of Allegiance before the Hon. Samuel W. Magruder in 1778 [Ref: T-3:74, L-1:43].

MAGRUDER, Nathaniel, of Ninian. Took the Oath of Allegiance before the Hon. Samuel W. Magruder in 1778 [Ref: T-3:73, L-1:43]. "Nathaniel Magruder, of Ninian" (b. 1722) lived in Lower Potomac Hd. in 1776 and had seven taxables in 1777 [Ref: K-1:185, R-31:4].

MAGRUDER, Ninian. Private, 5th Co., Lower Bn., Militia, Aug., 1777, and Third Sergeant, 2nd Co., Lower Bn., July 15, 1780 [Ref: M-199, M-204, T-5:48]. Took the Oath of Allegiance before the Hon. Samuel W. Magruder in 1778 [Ref: T-3:73, L-1:43]. Served as a petit juror in Aug., 1777 [Ref: R-31:17]. Ninian Magruder (b. 1752) lived in Lower Potomac Hd. in 1776 and had five taxables in 1777 [Ref: K-1:185, R-31:4], and another Ninian Magruder lived in the Upper Part of Potomac Hd. (three taxables) in 1777 [Ref: R-31:14]. See "John Magruder" and "Samuel Magruder" and "Samuel Beall Magruder" and "Kid Marquess," q.v.

MAGRUDER, Ninian, of Ninian. Served as a grand juror in 1779 [Ref: W-1].

MAGRUDER, Ninian Beall (1735-1810). Son of Samuel Magruder [Ref: V-92]. Private, 5th Co., Lower Bn., Militia, Aug., 1777 [Ref: M-199, T-5:48], and private, 2nd Co., Lower Bn., Militia, July 15, 1780 [Ref: M-204]. Took the Oath of Allegiance before the Hon. Samuel W. Magruder in 1778 [Ref: T-3:73]. He was born on Nov. 22, 1735, married Rebecca Young, and died on May 7, 1810 [Ref: DAR-I:433].

MAGRUDER, Norman Bruce (1754-1836). Private, 1st Co., Lower Bn., Militia, July 15, 1780 [Ref: M-204]. Private, 4th Co., Lower Bn., Militia, Aug., 1777 [Ref: M-199, T-5:47]. "Normond Bruce Magruder" took the Oath of Allegiance before the Hon. Samuel W. Magruder in 1778 [Ref: T-3:73, L-1:43]. "Norman Bruce Magruder" applied for pension in 1832 in Switzerland County, Indiana, stating he had lived at Georgetown (now in D. C.) at time of enlistment and afterwards lived in Washington County, the part that became Allegany County, for 31 years. He married Nancy Paugh, daughter of Michael Paugh, on Dec. 25, 1783, and in 1814 they moved to Indiana. Norman died on Feb. 16, 1836, and Nancy applied for a pension (W9542) on Jan. 1, 1845, at Louisville, Jefferson County, Kentucky, while living with a granddaughter (not named). Different dates were given for her age, but she appeared to have been born circa 1767. Their children: Mary or Polly (b. Dec. 30, 1784, and died before 1814); James (b. Feb. 12, 1786, and died before 1814); and, Sarah or Sally (b. May 2, 1789, and married Amos Gilbert; both were deceased in 1845). In 1844 Amith MacMillen and Elijah Gilbert, grandchildren of the soldier, lived in Switzerland County, Indiana, and in 1845 a son of their granddaughter Nancy Magruder was mentioned (no name was given), as well as the half brother (no name ws given) of the widow Nancy in Ripley County, Indiana [Ref: P-2166, DAR-I:433]. "Normond Bruce Magruder, aged 22" lived in Lower Potomac Hd. in 1776 and "Bruce Magruder" lived in Lower Potomac Hd. (one taxable) in 1777 [Ref: K-1:184, R-31:4].

MAGRUDER, Patrick. See "Samuel Wade Magruder," q.v.

MAGUDER, Rebecca. See "Samuel Brewer Magruder," q.v.

MAGRUDER, Richard (b. 1750). Private, 4th Co., Lower Bn., Militia, Aug., 1777, and Third Sergeant, 1st Co., Lower Bn., July 15, 1780 [Ref: M-199, M-204, T-5:47]. Took the Oath of Allegiance before the Hon. Samuel W. Magruder in 1778 [Ref: T-3:73]. Served as a petit juror in Aug., 1777 [Ref: R-31:17]. Lived in Lower Potomac Hd. in 1776 and had two taxables in 1777 [Ref: K-1:184, R-31:4].

MAGRUDER, Samuel. Rendered aid by providing wheat for use of the military in 1780 and 1781 [Ref: O-256, O-315, O-393]. "Samuel Magruder" lived in Lower Potomac Hd. (nine taxables) in 1777 [Ref: R-31:4]. "Samuel Magruder, son of Ninian" died testate in Montgomery County (wife named Margaret) in 1786, mentioning sons Samuel Brewer Magruder and Ninian Beall Magruder, and other children [Ref: V-92]. "Samuel Magruder, Sr., planter" died testate in Montgomery County (wife named Eleanor) in 1779, naming sons Elias, Alexander, William, Josias, Samuel, and Zachariah, and other children [Ref: V-93]. Also, a "Samuel Jackson Magruder" died testate in Montgomery County (no wife or children; named only his three sisters) in 1793 [Ref: V-93].

MAGRUDER, Samuel 3rd (1707/8-1786). Lived in Lower Potomac Hd. in 1776 [Ref: K-1:184]. Took the Oath of Allegiance before the Hon.

Richard Thompson in 1778, and married Margaret Jackson [Ref: T-3:75, L-1:43, DAR-I:433].

MAGRUDER, Samuel Beall (c1759-1812). Private, 4th Co., Lower Bn., Militia, Aug., 1777, and Ensign, 5th Co., 29th Bn., Militia, Sep. 12, 1777, and First Lieutenant, 1st Co., Lower Bn., Militia, July 15, 1780 [Ref: M-100, M-199, M-204, T-5:47, T-5:48, C-373, F-248]. Took the Oath of Allegiance before the Hon. Samuel W. Magruder in 1778 [Ref: T-3:73].

MAGRUDER, Samuel Brewer (1744-1818). Son of Samuel Magruder [Ref: V-92]. "Samuel B. Magruder" lived in the Upper Part of Potomac Hd. (three taxables) in 1777 [Ref: R-31:14]. "Samuel Brewer Magruder" took the Oath of Allegiance before the Hon. Samuel W. Magruder in 1778 [Ref: T-3:73, L-1:43]. Served as a petit juror in Aug., 1777 [Ref: R-31:17]. "Samuel Bruce Magruder" [sic] lived in Lower Potomac Hd. in 1776 and "Samuel Bruer Magruder" [sic] lived in Lower Potomac Hd. (four taxables) in 1777 [Ref: K-1:184, R-31:4]. "Samuel B. Magruder" died testate in Montgomery County (wife named Eleanor) in 1818, naming sons Walter, James, Samuel, and Ninian Magruder, and daughter Charlotte Beall [Ref: V-93]. He was born on Oct. 14, 1744, married (1) Rebecca Magruder and (2) Eleanor Waring, and died on Jan. 20, 1818 [Ref: DAR-I:433].

MAGRUDER, Samuel Briscoe. Succeeded Jesse Willcoxen as captain of a militia company in the Lower Bn. of Montgomery County in Aug., 1780 [Ref: K-2:372, K-2:408].

MAGRUDER, Samuel Wade (1728-1792). Served as a Captain, 29th Bn., Militia, Nov. 20, 1776, and Second Major, June 21, 1777 [Ref: M-100, B-464, C-296, and A-522, which latter source listed him as "Capt. Wade Magruder"]. Justice of the Peace who administered the Oath of Allegiance in 1778, and Justice of the County Court, 1779-1781 [Ref: T-3:73, T-3:74, L-1:43, W-1, W-2, C-529]. Samuel Wade Magruder (1728-1792) married Lucy Beall (1738-1795) in 1758 and both are buried in Montgomery County. Their children were: Levin (b. 1759, married Elizabeth Lynn); Charles (b. 1761, married Eleanor ----); Sarah (b. 1763, married William Wilson); Brook (b. 1764 and died an infant); George Beall (b. 1766); Patrick (b. 1768, married Sally Turner); Lucy (b. 1770, married William W. Berry); Thomas Contee (b. 1771, married Elizabeth Magruder); Warren (b. 1777, married Harriet Holmes in 1803, and died 1834); and, Lloyd (b. 1781, married Elizabeth Turner). [Ref: S-3036, V-93]. Samuel Wade Magruder (b. 1728) lived in Lower Potomac Hd. in 1776 and had 13 taxables in 1777 [Ref: K-1:184, R-31:4]. Rendered aid by providing wheat for use of the military in 1780 [Ref: O-309, O-333]. (2) There was also a Samuel W. Magruder who was a private, 5th Co., Lower Bn., Militia, Aug., 1777 [Ref: M-200, T-5:48]. Also see Source DAR-I:433].

MAGRUDER, Sarah. See "Norman Bruce Magruder," q.v.

MAGRUDER, Thomas Contee. See "Samuel Wade Magruder," q.v.

MAGRUDER, Walter (b. 1760). Son of Nathaniel Magruder, of Alexander [Ref: V-91]. Lived in Lower Potomac Hd. in 1776 [Ref: K-1:184]. Private, 5th Co., Lower Bn., Militia, Aug., 1777 [Ref: M-199, T-5:48]. Private, 2nd Co., Lower Bn., Militia, July 15, 1780 [Ref: M-204]. Took the Oath of Allegiance before the Hon. Samuel W. Magruder in 1778 [Ref: T-3:73]. Rendered aid by providing wheat for use of the military in 1780 [Ref: O-303]. Walter Magruder married Margaret Orme in Montgomery County on June 14, 1782 [Ref: K-2:515]. See "Nathan Magruder" and "Samuel Beall Magruder," q.v.

MAGRUDER, Warren. See "Samuel Wade Magruder," q.v.

MAGRUDER, William Beall (b. 1737). Private, 4th Co., Lower Bn., Militia, Aug., 1777 [Ref: M-199, T-5:47]. Private, 1st Co., Lower Bn., Militia, July 15, 1780 [Ref: M-204]. Took the Oath of Allegiance before the Hon. Samuel W. Magruder in 1778 [Ref: T-3:73, L-1:43]. "William B. Magruder" rendered aid by providing wheat for use of the military in 1780 [Ref: O-313]. Lived in Lower Potomac Hd. in 1776 and had two taxables in 1777 [Ref: K-1:184, R-31:4].

MAGRUDER, William Offutt. Private, 5th Co., Lower Bn., Militia, Aug., 1777 [Ref: M-199, T-5:48]. Took the Oath of Allegiance before the Hon. Samuel W. Magruder in 1778 [Ref: T-3:73, L-1:43]. Private, 2nd Co., Lower Bn., Militia, July 15, 1780 [Ref: M-204]. Served as a grand juror in 1779 [Ref: W-1]. "William O. Magruder" lived in the Upper Part of Potomac Hd. (six taxables) in 1777 [Ref: R-31:14].

MAGRUDER, Zachariah (1711-c1789). Lived in Lower Potomac Hd. in 1776 and had seven taxables in 1777 [Ref: K-1:184, R-31:4]. Took the Oath of Allegiance before the Hon. Samuel W. Magruder in 1778 [Ref: T-3:73, L-1:43, DAR-I:433]. Also see "Samuel Magruder," q.v. [Ref: V-93].

MAGRUDER, Zadock (1729-1811). Lived in Rock Creek Hd. (twelve taxables) in 1777 [Ref: R-31:16], and owned a working plantation ("quarter") in Seneca Hd. in 1777 [Ref: R-31:8]. Served as Colonel, 16th Bn., Militia, from Jan. 6, 1776, through at least Sep. 12, 1777 [Ref: M-100, C-373]. "Zaak Magruder" took the Oath of Allegiance before the Hon. Joseph Wilson on Feb. 28, 1778 [Ref: T-3:64, L-1:43]. Zadock Magruder married Rachel (Pottinger) Bowie [Ref: DAR-I:433].

MAGUIRE, Andrew. Private, 6th Co., Lower Bn., Militia, Aug., 1777 [Ref: M-200, T-5:49]. Took the Oath of Allegiance before the Hon. Joseph Offutt on March 2, 1778 [Ref: T-3:70, L-1:43]. Lived in the Upper Part of Potomac Hd. (one taxable) in 1777 [Ref: R-31:14].

MAGUIRE, Peter. Private, 8th Co., Middle Bn., Militia, Sep., 1777 [Ref: M-198, T-5:43].

MAHOLL, Samuel. Took the Oath of Allegiance (made his "X" mark) before the Hon. Samuel W. Magruder in 1778 [Ref: T-3:73].

MAHOLL (MAHALL, MAYHALL), Stephen (b. 1739). "Stephen Maholl" took the Oath of Allegiance (made his "I" mark) before the Hon. Samuel

W. Magruder in 1778 [Ref: T-3:73, L-1:43]. "Stephen Mahall" lived in Lower Potomac Hd. in 1776 and "Stephen Mayhall" had two taxables there in 1777 [Ref: K-1:184, R-31:4].

MALONE (MALOWN), Thomas. Private, 4th Class, 2nd Co., Middle Bn., Militia, July 15, 1780 [Ref: M-201]. "Thomas Malown" took the Oath of Allegiance before the Hon. Gerrard Briscoe on March 2, 1778 [Ref: T-3:56, L-1:43]. "Thomas Malone" married Mary Harper in Montgomery County on Dec. 16, 1777 [Ref: K-2:519].

MANNING (MANHAN), Abraham. "Abraham Manhan, or Manning" was a Private, Capt. Price's Co., 3rd Maryland Line, 1781-1782 [Ref: D-453].

MANNING (MANNAN), Dennis. "Dennias Mannan" was a private who enrolled into a company of militia for the service of the Flying Camp on Oct. 15, 1776 [Ref: B-353].

MANNING (MANEN), James (b. 1741). Took the Oath of Allegiance before the Hon. Richard Thompson in 1778 [Ref: T-3:75, L-1:43]. "James Manning or Manen" lived in George Town Hd. (one taxable) in 1776-1777 [Ref: K-1:194, R-31:3].

MANTZ, Peter. Took the Oath of Allegiance in 1778 [Ref: L-2:28].

MARDON, James. Took the Oath of Allegiance before the Hon. Charles Jones on Jan. 10, 1778 [Ref: T-3:71, L-1:43].

MARDON, John. Took the Oath of Allegiance before the Hon. Charles Jones on Jan. 10, 1778 [Ref: T-3:71, L-1:43].

MARE, Silvanus. Private, 8th Co., Middle Bn., Militia, Sep., 1777 [Ref: M-198, T-5:43].

MARHAY, Dennis. Private, Capt. Edward Burgess' Co., Lower District of Frederick (now Montgomery) County, Militia, July, 1776 [Ref: D-42].

MARLOW, William. Private, Capt. Thomas Beall's Co., Maryland Line, 1780 [Ref: D-351]. Private, Capt. Price's Co., 3rd Maryland Line, 1781-1782 [Ref: D-453].

MARQUESS, Eleanor, James, and others. See "Kid Marquess," q.v.

MARQUESS (MARQUISS, MARQUIS, MARCUS), John. "John Marquiss" was a Second Lieutenant, 29th Bn., Militia, June 21, 1777 [Ref: M-101, C-296]. "John Marcus" was a Second Lieutenant, 3rd Co., Lower Bn., Militia, on July 15, 1780 [Ref: M-204]. "John Maquess" [sic] took the Oath of Allegiance before the Hon. Joseph Wilson on Feb. 28, 1778 [Ref: T-3:66, L-1:43]. "John Marquis" lived in the Upper Part of Potomac Hd. (one taxable) in 1777 [Ref: R-31:14]. He may have been a brother of "Kid Marquess," q.v.

MARQUESS (MARQUISS, MARQUES, MARCUS), Kid or Kidd (b. 1744). "Kid: Marcus" was a private, 1st Co., Lower Bn., Militia, July 15, 1780 [Ref: M-204]. The will of Margerit Smith, of Calvert County, Maryland, was probated on Feb. 8, 1774, naming her sons Kid, James, and John Marquess, among other children. The 1776 tax list of George Town Hd. in Frederick County (now Montgomery County), Maryland, enumerated on Aug. 22, 1776, listed "Kidd Marques" (age 32), Eleanor

Marques (age 30), James Marques (age 6), William Marques (age 4) and, Mary Marques (age 2). Some researchers have indicated that Kidd (or William Kidd) Marquess (1744-1812), son of John Marquess and Margerit Kidd (Marquess) Smith, married Eleanor Magruder (1746-1826), daughter of John Magruder and Jane Offutt, and are buried in Simpson County, Kentucky. They also note that Kid Marques, Sr. and Kidd Marques, Jr. were in Nelson County, Kentucky in 1795, and Christopher Kid Marques was in Hampshire County, Virginia in 1784. Some researchers believe he was the Christopher and/or Kid Marques in the Kentucky censuses of 1790 and 1800. Also, *The Yearbook of the American Clan Gregor Society*, Volume XLI, page 54 (1957), states, in part, "After a lengthy search over the period of several years one line has been successfully proven, and as a result we have a new member, Mrs. Effie Marquess Carmack, who descends from Ninian Magruder and Elizabeth Brewer through his son John who had a daughter Eleanor who married William Kidd Marquiss." However, it should be noted that attempts to obtain this documentation have not been successful; therefore, some of the information cited by Mrs. Carmack cannot be substantiated. A letter from an official in the American Clan Gregor Society in 1995 indicates, in part, "I have been unable to find any other documentation from Mrs. Carmack." [Ref: Research files of Fred W. Drogula, of Washington, D. C., Robert J. Hadeen, of Sunnyside, Washington, and Henry C. Peden, Jr., of Bel Air, Maryland].

MARQUIS, William. Private, 7th Maryland Line, from May 24, 1777 until May 12, 1780, when discharged [Ref: D-231]. Also see "Kid Marquess," q.v.

MARSH, Benjamin. Private, Capt. Price's Co., 3rd Maryland Line, 1781-1782 [Ref: D-452].

MARSHALL, Benjamin (1755-1834). Soldier in the Virginia Line who was born in 1755 in Prince George's County, Maryland, and lived in Hampshire County, Virginia, at the time of his enlistment. Applied for a pension in Hardy County, Virginia, in 1834, stating he had married Elizabeth ---- "about 1775 in Montgomery County, Maryland, where they both lived at that time." She applied for a pension (W4279) in 1838, stating Benjamin had died on March 29, 1834. She died on Oct. 10, 1845, leaving children: Hanson Marshall, Mary Tucker, Samuel Marshall (aged 43 in 1840), Elizabeth Marshall, Emily Marshall, and Thomas Marshall (who pre-deceased his mother). [Ref: P-2196, Q-127]. It should be noted that a "Benjamin Maskoll" [Masholl?] lived in Sugarland Hd. (two taxables) in 1777 [Ref: R-31:13]. See "Benjamin Greentree," q.v.

MARSHALL, Catharine. See "Elisha Williams," q.v.

MARSHALL, Elizabeth and Emily. See "Benjamin Marshall," q.v.

MARSHALL, George. Took the Oath of Allegiance in 1778 [Ref: L-2:28].

MARSHALL, Hanson. See "Benjamin Marshall," q.v.

MARSHALL, James. Private, 8th Co., Lower Bn., Militia, Sep., 1777 [Ref: M-200, T-5:51]. Private, 6th Co., Lower Bn., Militia, July 15, 1780 [Ref: M-206]. Took the Oath of Allegiance before the Hon. Charles Jones on Jan. 10, 1778 [Ref: T-3:71, L-1:43]. James Marshall lived in North West Hd. (one taxable) in 1777 [Ref: R-31:17].
MARSHALL, John. See "Clement Dowden," q.v.
MARSHALL, Samuel and Thomas. See "Benjamin Marshall," q.v.
MARTIN, Amelia. See "Burgess Gaither," q.v.
MARTIN, John (b. 1755). Lived in Sugarland Hd. in 1776 [Ref: K-1:200]. Private, Flying Camp, enlisted July 18, 1776 [Ref: D-49].
MARTIN, Samuel. Private, 3rd Co., Middle Bn., Militia, Sep., 1777 [Ref: M-196, T-5:38]. Took the Oath of Allegiance before the Hon. William Deakins, Jr. before March 3, 1778 [Ref: T-3:68, L-1:43]. Private, Capt. Thomas Beall's Co., Maryland Line, 1780 [Ref: D-350]. Two men named Samuel Martin lived in the Upper Part of Potomac Hd. (one with one taxable and one with two taxables) in 1777 [Ref: R-31:14]. One Samuel Martin married Jane Walker in Montgomery County on Sep. 5, 1779 [Ref: K-2:519].
MASON, --ngley (page torn). Private, 7th Co., Lower Bn., Militia, July 15, 1780 [Ref: M-206].
MASON, Alexander. Served as a private when enrolled into a company of militia for the service of the Flying Camp on Oct. 15, 1776 [Ref: B-353]. Private, 7th Co., Lower Bn., Militia, July 15, 1780 [Ref: M-206]. Took the Oath of Allegiance before the Hon. Edward Burgess on Feb. 28, 1778 [Ref: T-3:62, L-1:43]. Lived in the Lower Part of Newfoundland Hd. (one taxable) in 1777 [Ref: R-31:5].
MASON, Archibald. Private, 1st Co., Lower Bn., Militia, Sep., 1777, and Fourth Corporal, 7th Co., Lower Bn., July 15, 1780 [Ref: M-206, T-5:44, and M-198, which latter source listed the name as "Moson"].
MASON, Elizabeth Ann. See "Zachariah Downs," q.v.
MASON, Jonathan. Private, 1st Co., Lower Bn., Militia, Sep., 1777 [Ref: M-198, T-5:44]. Private, 7th Co., Lower Bn., Militia, July 15, 1780 [Ref: M-207]. Took the Oath of Allegiance before the Hon. Edward Burgess on Feb. 28, 1778 [Ref: T-3:60, L-1:43]. Jonathan Mason lived in the Lower Part of Newfoundland Hd. (two taxables) in 1777 [Ref: R-31:5].
MASON, Richard (died 1787). Took the Oath of Allegiance before the Hon. Edward Burgess on Feb. 28, 1778 [Ref: T-3:62, L-1:43]. Rendered aid by providing wheat for use of the military in 1780 [Ref: O-308]. Lived in the Lower Part of Newfoundland Hd. (four taxables) in 1777 [Ref: R-31:5]. Died testate in Montgomery County (wife named Ann) in 1787 [Ref: V-94].
MATTHEWS, Betsy. See "Samuel Griffith," q.v.
MATTHEWS, Conrad. Took the Oath of Allegiance in 1778 [Ref: L-2:28].
MATTHEWS, John. Took the Oath of Allegiance in 1778 [Ref: L-2:28].
MATTHEWS, Philip. Took the Oath of Allegiance in 1778 [Ref: L-2:28].

MATTHEWS, Thomas. Private who was recruited to serve in the Continental Army in 1780 [Ref: D-342].

MATTINGLY, Bernard. Private, 5th Co., Upper Bn., Militia, Aug. 30, 1777 [Ref: M-194].

MATTINGLY, James. Soldier under Gen. Green in the Revolutionary War, wounded at the Battle of Guilford Court House. Died in Georgetown, D. C., on April 29, 1842, in his 84th year [Ref: R-6:15, but he is not listed in *Archives of Maryland, Volume 18*].

MATTINGLY (MATTANLY), Joseph. "Joseph Mattingly" was a private, 5th Co., Upper Bn., Militia, Aug. 30, 1777 [Ref: M-194]. "Joseph Mattanly" was recruited to serve in the Continental Army in 1780 [Ref: D-341].

MATTINGLY, Moses. Private, 2nd Co., Upper Bn., Militia, Aug. 30, 1777 [Ref: M-193].

MAW (MAN?), James. Private, 3rd Co., Lower Bn., Militia, Sep., 1777 [Ref: M-199, T-5:46].

MAYHALL, Stephen. See "Stephen Maholl," q.v.

McBEE, Allen and Ninian. See "Allen and Ninian Mockbee," q.v.

McBRIDE, Thomas. Private who was recruited to serve in the Extra Regiment, Continental Army, in 1780 [Ref: D-342].

McBRYDE, John. Served as a musician (drum & fife) in Capt. Thomas Beall's Co., Maryland Line, 1780 [Ref: D-350].

McCABE, Henry Jr. Took the Oath of Allegiance before the Hon. Richard Thompson in 1778 [Ref: T-3:75, L-1:43].

McCALLAM, Elizabeth. See "John Owen," q.v.

McCANN, Patrick (b. 1758). "Patrick McCann" was a private, Maryland Line, Rawlings' Regiment, from Aug. 22, 1776 to July, 1777 [Ref: D-145, D-302]. "Patrick McCanna" lived in Sugarland Hd. in 1776 [Ref: K-1:201].

McCARTY (McCARTEE), Daniel. "Daniel McCartee" was a private, 6th Class, 2nd Co., Middle Bn., Militia, July 15, 1780 [Ref: M-201]. "Daniel McCarty" married Rebecca Carter in Montgomery County on Jan. 18, 1780 [Ref: K-2:519].

McCARTY, Jesse. Private who was recruited to serve in the Extra Regiment in the Continental Army in 1780 [Ref: D-342].

McCARTY (McCARTEY), William. Took the Oath of Allegiance in 1778 [Ref: L-2:28].

McCAULEY, Sarah. See "Thomas Owen," q.v.

McCAW, John and Margaret. See "Michael Downs," q.v.

McCLAIN, Joshua. Took the Oath of Allegiance in 1778 [Ref: L-2:28].

McCLEARY, John. Took the Oath of Allegiance before the Hon. Aneas Campbell on March 2, 1778 [Ref: T-3:77, L-1:43]. "John Melarve [McClarie?], aged 25" lived in Sugarland Hd. in 1776 [Ref: K-1:207].

McCOMB (MALCOM, MACUM), John (b. 1755). Lived in Sugarland Hd. in 1776 [Ref: K-1:212]. Private, 7th Maryland Regiment, from May 11,

1778 until Aug. 16, 1780, when reported missing at the Battle of Camden [Ref: D-233, D-515].

McCOOL, Miranda. See "Lodowick Davis," q.v.

McCORMACK (MACCORMICK), John (b. 1751 or 1752). "John McCormack" was a private, 6th Co., Lower Bn., Militia, Aug., 1777 [Ref: M-200, T-5:49]. "John McCornack" [sic] was a private, 3rd Co., Lower Bn., Militia, July 15, 1780 [Ref: M-205]. "John McLormack" [sic] took the Oath of Allegiance before the Hon. Edward Burgess on Feb. 28, 1778 [Ref: T-3:63, L-1:43]. "John McCormack" lived in Lower Potomac Hd. in 1776 and "John Maccormick" had one taxable there in 1777 [Ref: K-1:184, R-31:4].

McCOUNE, John. Private who was recruited to serve in the Extra Regiment, Continental Army, in 1780, in place of William Quinton [Ref: D-342].

McCOY, Sarah. See "William Buxton," q.v.

McCOY (MACOY), William. "William McCoy" was a private, 2nd Maryland Line, from April 30, 1778 until Aug. 16, 1780, when he was taken prisoner at the Battle of Camden [Ref: D-139]. "William Macoy" lived in Sugar Loaf Hd. (two taxables) in 1777 [Ref: R-31:10]. Also see "William McKay," q.v.

McCRAY (McCRAE), Zephaniah (b. 1746). Private, 6th Co., Upper Bn., Militia, Aug. 30, 1777 [Ref: M-194]. "Zephaniah McCrae" took the Oath of Allegiance before the Hon. Edward Burgess on Feb. 28, 1778 [Ref: T-3:64, L-1:43]. "Zephemiah [sic] McCray" married Mary Gatton in Montgomery County on Oct. 21, 1779 [Ref: K-2:519]. "Zaphaniah McCray" lived in Sugarland Hd. in 1776 as did "Mary Girton" [Gatton?] who was head of house in 1777 [Ref: K-1:202, R-31:12].

McCREARY (McCRORY), John. "John McCreary or McCrory is listed in the Revolutionary War list of pensioners from or having received pension in Montgomery County, and he may have resided in Montgomery County later, but the papers show that he applied in Baltimore County on Aug. 23, 1830, stating that he served in the regiment of light infantry in the Pennsylvania Line under Capt. John Lord's Co., that he resided formerly in York County, Pennsylvania and now resides in Baltimore County, Maryland, and has resided there in Baltimore County for 36 years." [Ref: Y-38].

McCUBBIN, Mary. See "Mathias Hempston," q.v.

McCUBBIN, Thomas. See "Thomas Maccubbin," q.v.

McCUBBIN, Zachariah. See "Zachariah Maccubbin," q.v.

McCULLUGH (McCULLOCH), James (b. 1750). Lived in Sugarland Hd. in 1776 [Ref: K-1:212]. Served as private, Flying Camp, enlisted July 13, 1776 [Ref: D-43].

McDADE (MacDADE), Daniel. (1) Private, 3rd Co., Upper Bn., Militia, Aug. 30, 1777 [Ref: M-193]. (2) Private, 6th Co., Upper Bn., Militia, Aug. 30, 1777 [Ref: M-194]. Took the Oath of Allegiance before the Hon.

William Deakins, Jr. before March 3, 1778 [Ref: T-3:68, L-1:43]. "Daniel McDade" rendered aid by providing wheat for use of the military in 1781 [Ref: O-380]. "Daniel Macdade" lived in Sugar Loaf Hd. (one taxable) in 1777 [Ref: R-31:10].

McDADE, James. Private, 6th Co., Upper Bn., Militia, Aug. 30, 1777 [Ref: M-194].

McDADE (MacDADE), John. Private, 2nd Co., Middle Bn., Militia, Sep. 4, 1777 [Ref: M-196, T-5:37], and Private, 3rd Class, 3rd Co., Middle Bn., Militia, July 15, 1780 [Ref: M-202], and Third Sergeant, 3rd Co., Middle Bn., Militia, July 15, 1780 [Ref: M-202]. "John McDade" rendered aid by providing corn for use of the military in 1780 [Ref: O-288]. "John Macdade" lived in Sugar Loaf Hd. (one taxable) in 1777 [Ref: R-31:10].

McDADE (MacDADE, McDEED), Patrick. "Patrick McDeed" took the Oath of Allegiance before the Hon. Elisha Williams on March 2, 1778 [Ref: T-3:80, L-1:43]. "Patrick Macdade" lived in Sugar Loaf Hd. (two taxables) in 1777 [Ref: R-31:10].

McDADE (McDEED), Robert. "Robert McDade" was a private, 6th Co., Upper Bn., Militia, Aug. 30, 1777 [Ref: M-194]. "Robert McDeed" took the Oath of Allegiance before the Hon. Elisha Williams on March 2, 1778 [Ref: T-3:80, L-1:43].

McDANIEL, Anguish (Anguis). "Anguish McDaniel" was a corporal in the 5th Maryland Regiment from Jan. 1, 1777 until Jan. 12, 1780, when discharged [Ref: D-226]. "Anguis McDaniel" lived in Sugarland Hd. (three taxables) in 1777 [Ref: R-31:13].

McDANIEL, Elisha (b. 1755). Lived in Sugarland Hd. in 1776-1777 [Ref: K-1:204, R-31:12]. Took the Oath of Allegiance before the Hon. William Deakins, Jr. before March 3, 1778 [Ref: T-3:68, L-1:43].

McDANIEL, Henry (b. 1757). Lived in Sugarland Hd. in 1776 [Ref: K-1:200]. Servd as a private, 1st Co., Upper Bn., Militia, Aug. 30, 1777 [Ref: M-193]. Took the Oath of Allegiance before the Hon. Elisha Williams on March 2, 1778 [Ref: T-3:82].

McDANIEL, John (b. 1752). Lived in Sugarland Hd. in 1776 [Ref: K-1:212]. Private, 7th Class, 3rd Co., Middle Bn., Militia, July 15, 1780 [Ref: M-202]. Took the Oath of Allegiance before the Hon. Charles Jones on Jan. 10, 1778 [Ref: T-3:71, L-1:43]. John McDaniel was also a private in the 5th Maryland Regiment from Jan. 30, 1777 until Jan. 10, 1780, when he was discharged [Ref: D-226].

McDANIEL, Mary. See "George Talbott," q.v.

McDANIEL, William Jr. (1753/54-1836). Private, 1st Co., Upper Bn., Militia, Aug. 30, 1777 [Ref: M-193]. Took the Oath of Allegiance before the Hon. Elisha Williams on March 2, 1778 [Ref: T-3:81, L-1:43]. Lived in Sugarland Hd. (four taxables) in 1776-1777 [Ref: K-1:200, R-31:13, DAR-I:452].

McDANIEL, William Sr. (b. 1729). Private, 7th Co., Upper Bn., Militia, Aug. 30, 1777 [Ref: M-194]. Took the Oath of Allegiance before the Hon.

Elisha Williams on March 2, 1778 [Ref: T-3:81, L-1:43]. Lived in Sugarland Hd. (one taxable) lived in Sugarland Hd. in 1776-1777 [Ref: K-1:200, R-31:13].

McDAVIT, James. Took the Oath of Allegiance before the Hon. Elisha Williams on March 2, 1778 [Ref: T-3:80, L-1:43].

McDAVIT, John. Took the Oath of Allegiance before the Hon. Gerrard Briscoe on March 2, 1778 [Ref: T-3:56, L-1:43].

McDEAKENS, Leonard. Took the Oath of Allegiance before the Hon. Aneas Campbell on March 2, 1778 [Ref: T-3:77, L-1:43].

McDERMET, Michael. Served as a Corporal, 5th Maryland Line, 1777 [Ref: D-226].

McDERMET (McDURMET, McDURMOTT), Patrick. Private, 2nd Co., Middle Bn., Militia, Sep. 4, 1777 [Ref: M-195]. Private, 5th Class, 3rd Co., Middle Bn., Militia, July 15, 1780 [Ref: M-202]. "Patrick McDermett" took the Oath of Allegiance before the Hon. Gerrard Briscoe on March 2, 1778 [Ref: T-3:56, L-1:43]. "Patrick Durmott" lived in Sugar Loaf Hd. (two taxables) in 1777 [Ref: R-31:10].

McDONACK (McDONOUGH), James. "James McDonack" was a private, 5th Co., Lower Bn., Militia, July 15, 1780 [Ref: M-206]. "James McDonough" married Judith Flinn in Montgomery County on July 29, 1778 [Ref: K-2:516].

McDONALD, George. Rendered aid by providing corn for use of the military in 1780 [Ref: O-285].

McDONALD, John (b. 1746). Lived in Lower Potomac Hd. in 1776 [Ref: K-1:184]. Private, 7th Co., Lower Bn., Militia, Aug., 1777 [Ref: M-200, T-5:50]. Private, 7th Co., Middle Bn., Militia, Sep., 1777 [Ref: M-197, T-5:42].

McDOUGAL (McDOUGLE), Alexander. Took the Oath of Allegiance on Sep. 1, 1780, under the Act of May 12, 1780, having neglected to do so previously "due to ignorance of the duty owed the country." [Ref: R-27:116]. "Alexander McDougle" was a private, 1st Co., Lower Bn., Militia, Sep., 1777 [Ref: M-198, T-5:44]. "Alexr. McDough" [Alexander McDougle?] was Second Sergeant, 7th Co., Middle Bn., Militia, July 15, 1780 [Ref: M-203].

McDOUGAL, James. Private, 8th Co., Lower Bn., Militia, July 15, 1780 [Ref: M-207].

McDOUGAL (MacDOUGLE, McDUGLE), John. "John MacDougle" took the Oath of Allegiance before the Hon. Edward Burgess on Feb. 28, 1778 [Ref: T-3:60, L-1:43]. "John McDogle" rendered aid by providing wheat for use of the military in 1781 [Ref: O-380]. "John McDugle" lived in the Lower Part of Newfoundland Hd. (three taxables) in 1777 [Ref: R-31:5. Source DAR-I:452 states that John McDougall was born on March 11, 1731, married Charity Duvall, served as a private, and died on July 1, 1778].

McDOUGAL (MacDOUGLE, McDOUGLE), Samuel. Private, 7th Co., Lower Bn., Militia, on July 15, 1780 [Ref: M-207]. "Samuel MacDougle" took the Oath of Allegiance (made his "X" mark) before the Hon. Edward Burgess on Feb. 28, 1778 [Ref: T-3:60, L-1:43]. "Samuel McDougle" was a private, 1st Co., Lower Bn., Militia, Sep., 1777 [Ref: M-198, T-5:44].

McFADDON (McFADDEN), Alexander (b. 1751). Served as a First Lieutenant, Lower District of Frederick County Militia, April 20, 1776, and Captain, 29th Bn. of Montgomery County Militia, from Sep. 12, 1777, to at least Aug. 11, 1779 [Ref: M-102, M-199, T-5:46, A-356, C-373]. "Alexander McFadon" took the Oath of Allegiance before the Hon. Richard Thompson in 1778 [Ref: T-3:75, L-1:43]. "Alexander McFadden" lived in George Town Hd. (six taxables) in 1776-1777 [Ref: K-1:194, R-31:3].

McFARDON, Joseph. Took the Oath of Allegiance before the Hon. Richard Thompson in 1778 [Ref: T-3:76, L-1:43].

McFARDON, Samuel. Took the Oath of Allegiance before the Hon. Richard Thompson in 1778 [Ref: T-3:76, L-1:43].

McFLOWERS, Samuel. Private, 8th Co., Lower Bn., Militia, July 15, 1780 [Ref: M-207].

McGINNIS, Neale. Took the Oath of Allegiance (made his "X" mark) before the Hon. Aneas Campbell on March 2, 1778 [Ref: T-3:77, L-1:43].

McGLIN, John. Private, Capt. Price's Co., 3rd Maryland Line, 1781-1782 [Ref: D-452].

McGLOCKLON (MAGROCKLEN), Henry. "Henry McGlocklon" took the Oath of Allegiance (made his "X" mark) before the Hon. Aneas Campbell on March 2, 1778 [Ref: T-3:78, L-1:43]. "Henry Magrocklen" lived in Sugarland Hd. (one taxable) in 1777 [Ref: R-31:12].

McGRAW, William. Rendered aid by providing wheat for use of the military in 1780 [Ref: O-308].

McGREE, Fauquhart. Private, 8th Co., Lower Bn., Militia, July 15, 1780 [Ref: M-207].

McGUIRE, Andrew. Private, 3rd Class, 1st Co., Middle Bn., Militia, July 15, 1780 [Ref: M-201].

McGUIRE, John. Private who was recruited to serve in the Extra Regiment, Continental Army, in 1780 [Ref: D-342].

McGUIRE, Patrick. Private, 8th Co., Lower Bn., Militia, July 15, 1780 [Ref: M-207].

McGUIRE, Peter. Private who was recruited to serve in the Continental Army in 1780 [Ref: D-341].

McINTOSH (McKINTOSH), Alexander (b. 1729). Private, 4th Co., Upper Bn., Militia, Aug. 30, 1777 [Ref: M-194]. Took the Oath of Allegiance before the Hon. William Deakins, Jr. before March 3, 1778 [Ref: T-3:68, L-1:43]. "Alexander Mcintoush" lived in Sugarland Hd. in 1776 [Ref: K-1:207].

McKANN, John. Private, Capt. Thomas Beall's Co., Maryland Line, 1780 [Ref: D-350].
McKAY, William (died 1797). Took the Oath of Allegiance before the Hon. Elisha Williams on March 2, 1778 [Ref: T-3:80, L-1:43]. Died testate in Montgomery County (wife named Ann) in 1797 [Ref: V-88].
McKEAN, Joseph. Took the Oath of Allegiance in 1778 [Ref: L-2:28].
McKEE, Archibald. See "David Beggarly," q.v.
McKINNEY, Roderick. Private, Capt. Thomas Beall's Co., Maryland Line, 1780 [Ref: D-350].
McKINRY (McKENERY, McKINSY), Thomas (b. 1746). Lived in George Town Hd. in 1776 [Ref: K-1:194]. Private, Capt. Thomas Beall's Co., Maryland Line, 1780 [Ref: D-350].
McKINSEY, Patrick. Private, Capt. Price's Co., 3rd Maryland Line, 1781-1782 [Ref: D-453].
McLAIN (McLANE), John. "John McLane" took the Oath of Allegiance in 1778 [Ref: L-2:28]. "John Macklain" died testate in Montgomery County (wife named Priscilla) in 1790 [Ref: V-89].
McLAIN, Joseph. Took the Oath of Allegiance in 1778 [Ref: L-2:28].
McLAMAR, Timothy, Recruited to serve in the Continental Army in 1780 [Ref: D-342].
McLEARY, John. Private, 8th Co., Upper Bn., Militia, Aug. 30, 1777 [Ref: M-195].
McLOCKLAND, Henry. Private, 4th Co., Upper Bn., Militia, Aug. 30, 1777 [Ref: M-194].
McMACKEN, Benjamin. Private, 1st or 32nd Bn., Militia (no date was given; possibly June, 1777). [Ref: T-5:1].
McMACKEN, Henry. Private, 1st or 32nd Bn., Militia (no date was given; possibly June, 1777). [Ref: T-5:1].
McMACKEN, Thomas. Private, 1st or 32nd Bn., Militia (no date was given; possibly June, 1777). [Ref: T-5:1].
McMAHONE, Andrew. Private who was recruited to serve in the Continental Army in 1780 [Ref: D-341].
McMANIS (MACKMANESS), Thomas (b. 1746). Lived in North West Hd. in 1776 [Ref: K-1:232]. Private, 7th Maryland Line, from June 4, 1777 until April 12, 1780, when discharged [Ref: D-231].
McMILLAN, Ruth. See "Gerrard Briscoe," q.v.
McMULLEN, Patrick. Took the Oath of Allegiance in 1778 [Ref: L-2:28].
McNEAR, Catherine. See "Robert Housley (Howsley)," q.v.
McNEAR, William. (1) Private, 2nd Co., Lower Bn., Militia, July 15, 1780 [Ref: M-204]. (2) Private, 1st Class, 1st Co., Middle Bn., Militia, July 15, 1780 [Ref: M-201].
McNEER, Jean. See "Elijah Cooke," q.v.
McNEILL (McNEAL), John. Took the Oath of Allegiance in 1778 [Ref: L-2:28]. "John McNeal" was a private in 1781 and a waggoner in 1782, Capt. Price's Co., 3rd Maryland Line [Ref: D-454].

McSHERRY, Hugh. Private, 5th Co., Upper Bn., Militia, Aug. 30, 1777 [Ref: M-194].

McTEL, Samuel. Took the Oath of Allegiance (made his "X" mark) before the Hon. Aneas Campbell on March 2, 1778 [Ref: T-3:77, L-1:43].

MECRAFT, Benjamin and Peter. See "Benjamin and Peter Becraft," q.v.

MEDLEY, William. Took the Oath of Allegiance before the Hon. Joseph Wilson on Feb. 28, 1778 [Ref: T-3:66, L-1:43]. "William Medly" was a private, 4th Class, 1st Co., Middle Bn., Militia, July 15, 1780 [Ref: M-201]. "William Medley, born in Maryland, about 17 years of age, 5 feet 2 or 3 inches high, smooth faced, light coloured hair, and well made, recruited by Philip Casey and David O'Neale on March 26, 1781." [Ref: R-33:155, X-1146]. William Medley lived in Linganore Hd. (one taxable) in 1777 [Ref: R-31:9].

MEEKS, George. Took the Oath of Allegiance before the Hon. Elisha Williams on March 2, 1778 [Ref: T-3:81, L-1:43].

MELOY, John. See "John Miloy," q.v.

MELTON, James. Took the Oath of Allegiance in 1778 [Ref: L-2:28].

MERCIER, Andrew. Private, 1st or 32nd Bn., Militia (no date was given; possibly June, 1777). [Ref: T-5:1].

MERCIER, Francis. Private, 1st or 32nd Bn., Militia (no date was given; possibly June, 1777). [Ref: T-5:1].

MERCIER, Joshua. Private, 1st or 32nd Bn., Militia (no date was given; possibly June, 1777). [Ref: T-5:1].

MERCIER, Luke. Private, 1st or 32nd Bn., Militia (no date was given; possibly June, 1777). [Ref: T-5:1].

MERCIER, Richard. Private, 1st or 32nd Bn., Militia (no date was given; possibly June, 1777). [Ref: T-5:1].

MESSENGER, Joseph Rev. See "Benjamin Burch," q.v.

METCALF (MEDCALF, MADCAP), Edward. Private, 3rd Co., Middle Bn., Militia, Sep., 1777 [Ref: M-196, T-5:38]. "Edward Metcalf" took the Oath of Allegiance before the Hon. Edward Burgess on Feb. 28, 1778 [Ref: T-3:63, L-1:43]. "Edward Medcalf" was a private, 1st Class, 2nd Co., Middle Bn., Militia, July 15, 1780 [Ref: M-201]. "Edward Madcap" lived in the Upper Part of Potomac Hd. (one taxable) in 1777 [Ref: R-31:14].

MEYER, Ronald B. See "William Byall," q.v.

MIDDLETON, William. Private, 6th Co., Lower Bn., Militia, Aug., 1777 [Ref: M-200, T-5:49].

MIDDOGH (MIDDAGH), John. "John Middogh" took the Oath of Allegiance before the Hon. Richard Thompson in 1778 [Ref: T-3:76, L-1:43]. "John Middagh" lived in George Town Hd. (one taxable) in 1777 [Ref: R-31:3].

MIFFORD, James. Took the Oath of Allegiance in 1778 [Ref: L-2:28].

MIKESELL, Andrew. Took the Oath of Allegiance in 1778 [Ref: L-2:28].

MILES, John (b. 1739). Private, 8th Co., Upper Bn., Militia, Aug. 30, 1777 [Ref: M-195]. Took the Oath of Allegiance before the Hon. Aneas Campbell on March 2, 1778 [Ref: T-3:78, L-1:43]. Lived in Sugarland Hd. (one taxable) in 1776-1777 [Ref: K-1:205, R-31:12].

MILES, Sarah. See "Mareen Duvall," q.v.

MILES, Thomas. Private, 8th Co., Middle Bn., Militia, Sep., 1777 [Ref: M-198, T-5:43]. Took the Oath of Allegiance before the Hon. Samuel W. Magruder in 1778 [Ref: T-3:73]. Private, 1st Co., Lower Bn., Militia, July 15, 1780 [Ref: M-204]. "Thomas Miles" was a private, 5th Maryland Regiment, on April 25, 1777, and corporal on Sep. 1, 1777, and sergeant on Nov. 1, 1778; reported missing on Aug. 16, 1780, at the Battle of Camden [Ref: D-226]. "Thomas Mills" [Miles?] lived in Rock Creek Hd. (one taxable) in 1777 [Ref: R-31:16]. "Thomas Miles" married Elizabeth King in Montgomery County on Feb. 7, 1779 [Ref: K-2:514].

MILLER, Adam. Took the Oath of Allegiance in 1778 [Ref: L-2:28].

MILLER, Anthony. Took the Oath of Allegiance in 1778 [Ref: L-2:28].

MILLER, Christian (b. 1752). Pensioner in 1840, aged 88, and head of household in Montgomery County, 5th Division [Ref: R-28:444]. His service during the war was with the 2nd Pennsylvania Line between Nov. 16, 1782(?) and June 26, 1783 [Ref: Y-40].

MILLER, Daniel. Took the Oath of Allegiance in 1778 [Ref: L-2:28].

MILLER, David. Private, 1st or 32nd Bn., Militia (no date was given; possibly June, 1777). [Ref: T-5:2].

MILLER, Eleanor and Jacob. See "John Miller," q.v.

MILLER, John (1762/3-1845). Applied for a pension in Cumberland County, Kentucky, on March 11, 1833, aged 71, stating he was born in Pennsylvania on July 16, 1762 or 1763, and lived in Montgomery County, Maryland when he enlisted at Fredericktown in 1781. In 1790 he moved to Surry County, North Carolina, and in 1812 moved to Kentucky. His widow Eleanor applied for pension (W2647) on Dec. 4, 1848 in Clinton County, Kentucky, stating John had died on Sep. 14, 1845. Her name was Eleanor Garner, daughter of John Garner, and she married John Miller in Surry County, North Carolina in the 17th year of her age. She was born March 16, 1779, and they were married on Sep. 7 or 17, 1796 at her father's house about seven miles from Shallow Ford on the Yadkin River, by Rev. Lazarus Whitehead, a Baptist preacher. Their children were: Jacob (b. Oct. 17, 1798, and died at the age of 5 years); Martin (b. Nov. 4, 1800); Nancy (b. Sep. 5, 1803, married ---- Peasey and was a widow by 1848); and, a fourth child who died in infancy [Ref: Y-10, P-2356, Z-32].

MILLER, Luds. Took the Oath of Allegiance in 1778 [Ref: L-2:28].

MILLER, Martin (b. 1754). Rendered aid by providing wheat for use of the military in 1781 [Ref: O-392]. Applied for pension (R7213) in Rockingham County, North Carolina, on July 11, 1844, aged 90, stating that he was born in Frederick County, Maryland in 1754 and served in the war in Frederick County. His claim was rejected "for further proof and explanation." John Miller, son of the "deceased soldier," also made affidavit in 1852 [Ref: P-2359, but he is not listed in *Archives of Maryland, Volume 18* nor Clements & Wright's *The Maryland Militia, Revolutionary War*]. See "John Miller," q.v.

MILLER, Michael. Took the Oath of Allegiance in 1778 [Ref: L-2:28].

MILLER, Nancy. See "John Miller," q.v.

MILLER, Thomas. Private, 2nd Co., Upper Bn., Militia, Aug. 30, 1777 [Ref: M-193]. Took the Oath of Allegiance before the Hon. Elisha Williams on March 2, 1778 [Ref: T-3:80, L-1:43].

MILLER, William. Took the Oath of Allegiance in 1778 [Ref: L-2:28].

MILLS, Charles. Took the Oath of Allegiance in 1778 [Ref: L-2:28].

MILLS, Jesse. Private, 2nd Co., Middle Bn., Militia, Sep. 4, 1777 [Ref: M-196, T-5:37]. Private, 3rd Class, 1st Co., Middle Bn., Militia, July 15, 1780 [Ref: M-201]. Took the Oath of Allegiance before the Hon. William Deakins, Jr. before March 3, 1778 [Ref: T-3:68, L-1:43].

MILLS, Thomas. See "Thomas Miles," q.v.

MILOY (MILEY), Frederick. Private, 8th Co., Lower Bn., Militia, July 15, 1780 [Ref: M-207].

MILOY (MILLEY), Jacob (b. 1758). Lived in George Town Hd. in 1776 [Ref: K-1:194]. Served as a private in the German Regiment in 1776 [Ref: D-266].

MILOY (MELOY), John. "John Meloy" was a private, 6th Co., Upper Bn., Militia, Aug. 30, 1777 [Ref: M-194]. "John Miloy" lived in Sugarland Hd. (one taxable) in 1777 [Ref: R-31:12].

MINN, Peter. See "George Beckwith," q.v.

MITCHELL (MICHILL), Benjamin. "Benjamin Michill" took the Oath of Allegiance before the Hon. Elisha Williams on March 2, 1778 [Ref: T-3:81, L-1:43].

MITCHELL, Joseph. Private, 2nd Co., Lower Bn., Militia, July 15, 1780 [Ref: M-204]. Rendered aid by providing wheat for use of the military in 1780 [Ref: O-318].

MITCHELL (MICHEL), Mordecai Miles. "Miles Mitchell" was a private in Capt. Edward Burgess' Co. in the Lower District of Frederick (now Montgomery) County, Militia, July, 1776 [Ref: D-42]. "Mordecai M. Mitchell" was a private, 7th Co., Middle Bn., Militia, Sep., 1777 [Ref: M-197, T-5:42]. "Mordaccai Miles Michel" lived in Seneca Hd. (one taxable) in 1777 [Ref: R-31:8]. One Mordecai Mitchell lived in the Lower Part of Newfoundland Hd. (three taxables) in 1777 and "Mordeca Mitchel, aged 50" lived in North West Hd. (wife named Sarah) in 1776 [Ref: R-31:5, K-1:228].

MITCHELL, Morrice. Took the Oath of Allegiance (made his "D" mark) before the Hon. Edward Burgess on Feb. 3, 1778 [Ref: T-3:58, L-1:43].

MITCHELL, Nancy. See "John Tucker," q.v.

MITCHELL, Nathan (Nathaniel). "Nathan Mitchell" was a private, 1st Co., Lower Bn., Militia, Sep., 1777 [Ref: M-198, T-5:44]. "Nathaniel Mitchell" was a private, 4th Co., Lower Bn., Militia, July 15, 1780 [Ref: M-205].

MITCHELL, Notley (b. 1763). Son of Mordecai and Sarah Mitchell, of North West Hd. [Ref: K-1:229]. Private, 6th Co., Lower Bn., Militia, July 15, 1780 [Ref: M-206].

MITCHELL, Robert. Took the Oath of Allegiance before the Hon. Elisha Williams on March 2, 1778 [Ref: T-3:80, L-1:43]. "Robert Mitchel" lived in Sugar Loaf Hd. (one taxable) in 1777 [Ref: R-31:10].

MITCHELL, Sarah. See "Notley Mitchell," q.v.

MITCHELL, Thomas. Private, 1st Co., Lower Bn., Militia, Sep., 1777 [Ref: M-198, T-5:44]. Took the Oath of Allegiance (made his "X" mark) before the Hon. Edward Burgess on Feb. 28, 1778 [Ref: T-3:59, L-1:43]. Private, 7th Co., Lower Bn., Militia, July 15, 1780 [Ref: M-207].

MITCHELL (MICHELL), Walter. "Walter Mitchell" was a private, 1st Co., Lower Bn., Militia, Sep., 1777 [Ref: M-198, T-5:44]. Private, 7th Co., Lower Bn., Militia, July 15, 1780 [Ref: M-206]. "Walter Michell" took the Oath of Allegiance on Sep. 1, 1780, under the Act of May 12, 1780, having neglected to do so previously "due to ignorance of the duty owed the country." [Ref: R-27:116].

MITCHELL, William. Private who was recruited to serve in the Continental Army in 1780 [Ref: D-342]. William Mitchell married Sarah Ashford in Montgomery County on Dec. 2, 1779 [Ref: K-2:514].

MOBBERLY (MOBLEY), Archibald. Private, 2nd Co., Middle Bn., Militia, Sep. 4, 1777 [Ref: M-196, T-5:37]. Private, 4th Class, 3rd Co., Middle Bn., Militia, July 15, 1780 [Ref: M-202]. Took the Oath of Allegiance (made his "X" mark) before the Hon. Edward Burgess on Feb. 28, 1778 [Ref: T-3:61, L-1:43]. Lived in Sugar Loaf Hd. (one taxable) in 1777 [Ref: R-31:10].

MOBBERLY (MOBLEY), Lewis. Served as an Ensign in the militia on Oct. 13, 1777 [Ref: M-104, which cited the Scharf Collection at the Maryland State Archives].

MOCKBEE (McBEE, MOCBE, MACKBEE), Allen (died 1796). "Allen Mockbee" was a private, 2nd Co., Middle Bn., Militia, Sep. 4, 1777 [Ref: M-196, T-5:37]. "Allen McBee" took the Oath of Allegiance before the Hon. Gerrard Briscoe on March 2, 1778 [Ref: T-3:56, L-1:43]. "Allen Mocbe" lived in Sugar Loaf Hd. (one taxable) in 1777 [Ref: R-31:10]. "Allen Mackbee" died testate in Montgomery County (wife named Deborah) in 1796 [Ref: V-89].

MOCKBEE (MACBEE, MOCKEBEY, MOCBE), Brock. "Brock Mockbee" was a Second Lieutenant, Middle Bn., Militia, March 26, 1776, and Second Lieutenant, 2nd Co., Middle Bn., Sep. 4, 1777, First Lieutenant, April 21, 1779, and Captain, March 25, 1780 [Ref: M-105, M-195, A-287, E-357, F-120, I-42, M-202, M-99, and C-373, which latter two sources misspelled the name as "Brock Macbee"]. "Brock Mockebey" took the Oath of Allegiance (made his circled "X" mark) before the Hon. Edward Burgess on Feb. 28, 1778 [Ref: T-3:59, L-1:43]. "Brock Mocbe" lived in Sugar Loaf Hd. (one taxable) in 1777 [Ref: R-31:10].

MOCKBEE (MACABEE, MOCKEBEE), John. Private, 7th Class, 2nd Co., Middle Bn., Militia, July 15, 1780 [Ref: M-201]. "John Mockebee" took the Oath of Allegiance before the Hon. William Deakins, Jr. before March 3, 1778 [Ref: T-3:68, L-1:43]. "John Mockbee" married Margaret Robinson in Montgomery County on Aug. 21, 1777 [Ref: K-2:522]. "John Macabee" lived in Seneca Hd. (one taxable) in 1777 [Ref: R-31:8].

MOCKBEE (McBEE, MOCBE, MOCKABOY), Ninian (died 1812). Private, 2nd Co., Middle Bn., Militia, Sep. 4, 1777 [Ref: M-196, T-5:37], and private, 1st Class, 3rd Co., Middle Bn., Militia, July 15, 1780 [Ref: M-202]. "Ninian McBee" took the Oath of Allegiance before the Hon. Gerrard Briscoe on March 2, 1778 [Ref: T-3:57, L-1:43]. "Ninian Mockaboy" rendered aid by providing wheat for use of the military in 1781 [Ref: O-378]. "Ninian Mocbe" lived in Sugar Loaf Hd. (two taxables) in 1777 [Ref: R-31:10]. "Ninian Mockbee" died testate in Montgomery County (wife named Mary) in 1812 [Ref: V-95].

MOCKBEE (MOCKEBY, MOCKBY), Zachariah (b. 1752). Lived in Lower Potomac Hd. in 1776 [Ref: K-1:184]. "Zachariah Mockbee" was a private, 8th Co., Lower Bn., Militia, Sep., 1777 [Ref: M-200, T-5:51]. "Zachariah Mockeby" took the Oath of Allegiance before the Hon. Charles Jones on Jan. 10, 1778 [Ref: T-3:71, L-1:43].

MOCKBEE (MOCKBE, MOCKBY), Zephaniah (1757-1805). Lived in Lower Potomac Hd. in 1776 [Ref: K-1:184]. Private, 4th Co., Lower Bn., Militia, Aug., 1777 [Ref: T-5:47]. Private, 1st Co., Lower Bn., Militia, July 15, 1780 [Ref: M-204]. "Zephaniah Mockbe" took the Oath of Allegiance before the Hon. Charles Jones on Jan. 10, 1778 [Ref: T-3:71, L-1:43]. "Zepheniah Mockbee" died testate in Montgomery County (wife not named) in 1805 [Ref: V-95].

MOLAND, James. Private who was recruited to serve in the Continental Army in 1780 [Ref: D-341].

MOLAND, William. Private, 3rd Co., Lower Bn., Militia, July 15, 1780 [Ref: M-205].

MONEY, Patrick. Private, 1st or 32nd Bn., Militia (no date was given; possibly June, 1777). [Ref: T-5:2].

MONTGOMERY, William. Private, 5th Co., Middle Bn., Militia, July 15, 1780 [Ref: M-203]. Took the Oath of Allegiance before the Hon. Gerrard Briscoe on March 2, 1778 [Ref: T-3:56, L-1:43].

MOODY, Levi. Private, Capt. Price's Co., 3rd Maryland Line, 1781, who was reported dead on Oct. 15, 1782 [Ref: D-452].

MOORE (MOOR), Barton. Private, 2nd Co., Lower Bn., Militia, July 15, 1780 [Ref: M-204]. Took the Oath of Allegiance before the Hon. Samuel

W. Magruder in 1778 [Ref: T-3:73]. Rendered aid by providing wheat for use of the military in 1780 [Ref: O-315].

MOORE, Benjamin (b. 1753). Private, 6th Co., Lower Bn., Militia, July 15, 1780 [Ref: M-206]. Private, 8th Co., Lower Bn., Militia, Sep., 1777 [Ref: M-200, T-5:51]. Lived in North West Hd. in 1776-1777 [Ref: K-1:227, R-31:17].

MOORE (MOOR), Elisha. Took the Oath of Allegiance (made his mark) before the Hon. Samuel W. Magruder in 1778 [Ref: T-3:73, L-1:43].

MOORE, George. Rendered aid by providing wheat for use of the military in 1780 [Ref: O-314].

MOORE, Isaac. Private, 7th Co., Lower Bn., Militia, July 15, 1780 [Ref: M-207].

MOORE, James. Private, 3rd Class, 2nd Co., Middle Bn., Militia, July 15, 1780 [Ref: M-201]. Private, 3rd Co., Middle Bn., Militia, Sep., 1777 [Ref: M-196, T-5:38]. One James Moore took the Oath of Allegiance before the Hon. William Deakins, Jr. before March 3, 1778 [Ref: T-3:68, L-1:43], and another took the Oath of Allegiance before the Hon. Samuel W. Magruder in 1778 [Ref: T-3:73, L-1:43]. Two men named James Moore lived in the Upper Part of Potomac Hd. (one with two taxables and the other with three taxables) in 1777 [Ref: R-31:14]. One rendered aid by providing wheat for use of the military in 1781 [Ref: O-387].

MOORE, John. Took the Oath of Allegiance in 1778 [Ref: L-2:28].

MOORE, John William. Private, 4th Co., Middle Bn., Militia, Sep., 1777 [Ref: M-196, T-5:39]. "John W. Moore" was a Second Lieutenant, Middle Bn., Militia, April 21, 1779. "Jonathan William Moore" was a First Lieutenant, Middle Bn., Militia, on March 25, 1780 [Ref: M-105, E-357, F-120]. "John William Moore" was a Captain, 4th Co., Middle Bn., Militia, July 15, 1780 [Ref: M-202]. "John Williams Moore" took the Oath of Allegiance before the Hon. Edward Burgess on Feb. 28, 1778 [Ref: T-3:59, L-1:43].

MOORE, Josias. Private, 5th Co., Middle Bn., Militia, July 15, 1780 [Ref: M-203].

MOORE, Mordecai. Took the Oath of Allegiance before the Hon. Edward Burgess on Feb. 28, 1778 [Ref: T-3:61, L-1:43]. Lived in the Lower Part of Newfoundland Hd. (one taxable) in 1777 [Ref: R-31:5].

MOORE, Nathan (b. 1749). Private, 6th Co., Upper Bn., Militia, Aug. 30, 1777 [Ref: M-194]. "Nathon More or Nathan Moore" lived in Sugarland Hd. (one taxable) in 1776-1777 [Ref: K-1:201, R-31:12].

MOORE, Robert. Private who enrolled into a company of militia for the service of the Flying Camp on Oct. 15, 1776 [Ref: B-353].

MOORE, Samuel (b. 1751). Private, 6th Co., Upper Bn., Militia, Aug. 30, 1777 [Ref: M-194]. Private, 1st Co., Lower Bn., Militia, Sep., 1777, and Fourth Sergeant, 7th Co., Lower Bn., July 15, 1780 [Ref: M-198, M-206, T-5:44]. Took the Oath of Allegiance before the Hon. Edward Burgess on Feb. 28, 1778 [Ref: T-3:59, L-1:43]. Lived in Sugarland Hd. (one taxable) in 1776-1777 [Ref: K-1:201, R-31:12].

MOORE, Silvanus. Private, 7th Co., Middle Bn., Militia, July 15, 1780 [Ref: M-203]. Took the Oath of Allegiance before the Hon. Edward Burgess on Feb. 28, 1778 [Ref: T-3:59, L-1:43].

MOORE, Thomas. Took the Oath of Allegiance before the Hon. Edward Burgess on Feb. 28, 1778 [Ref: T-3:60, L-1:43]. Lived in the Upper Part of Newfoundland Hd. (three taxables) in 1777 [Ref: R-31:7].

MOORE, William (died 1790). Private, 2nd Co., Lower Bn., Militia, July 15, 1780 [Ref: M-204]. Took the Oath of Allegiance before the Hon. Richard Thompson in 1778 [Ref: T-3:75, L-1:43]. Rendered aid by providing wheat for use of the military in 1780 [Ref: O-328]. A William Moore died testate in Montgomery County (wife named Mary) in 1790 [Ref: V-96].

MOORELAND, Mary. See "Elkanah (Aleanah) Watson," q.v.

MORAN, Patrick. Private, 7th Co., Lower Bn., Militia, July 15, 1780 [Ref: M-206].

MORGAN, Anne. See "Charles Burriss," q.v.

MORGAN, Dennis. Private, 8th Class, 4th Co., Middle Bn., Militia, July 15, 1780 [Ref: M-202].

MORGAN, Johnsey. Private, 4th Co., Middle Bn., Militia, Sep., 1777 [Ref: M-196, T-5:39]. Johnsey Morgan lived in the Upper Part of Newfoundland Hd. (one taxable) in 1777 [Ref: R-31:7].

MORGAN, Richard Jr. "Richard Morgan, Jr." was a private, 4th Co., Middle Bn., Militia, in Sep., 1777 [Ref: M-196, T-5:39]. "Richard Morgan" lived in the Upper Part of Newfoundland Hd. (two taxables) in 1777 [Ref: R-31:7].

MORRIS, Charles. Served as a Corporal in the New York Continental Line and was pensioned in Montgomery County, Maryland in 1831 and was subsequently paid in the District of Columbia [Ref: J-49].

MORRIS, Cornelius (Neel). Private, 6th Co., Lower Bn., Militia, Aug., 1777 [Ref: M-200, T-5:49], and was recruited and served in the 7th Maryland Regiment, Continental Army, in 1780 [Ref: D-234, D-341, F-114]. Applied for a pension (S40175) in Clark County, Ohio, on May 13, 1818, aged about 60, stating he enlisted in Montgomery County, Maryland in Feb., 1780, served in the Battles of Camden and Guilford and the Siege of Ninety-Six, and was discharged in June, 1783. In 1820 or 1821 his wife Sarah was aged 53 and they had these children: Jane (aged 19), Cornelius (aged 16), Harriet (aged 13), and Eliza (aged 10). Cornelius spent his last days in Lafayette, Indiana [Ref: P-2423. Although this latter source does not indicate it, he may have been related to Daniel Morris alias Morrison according to the abstract of his pension application by Mary K. Meyer published in *Maryland Genealogical Society Bulletin*, Vol. 35, No. 1 (1994), p. 56].

MORRIS, Elizabeth. See "John Taylor," q.v.

MORRIS, John. Served as a Lieutenant, 6th Co., Lower Bn., Militia, Aug., 1777 [Ref: M-200, T-5:49].

MORRISON (MARISON), John. Served as private, 1st or 32nd Bn., Militia (no date was given; possibly June, 1777). [Ref: T-5:2].

MORROW (MURROUGH), John (b. 1752). Lived in Sugarland Hd. in 1776 [Ref: K-1:214]. "John Morrow" was a private, 7th Maryland Regiment, 1776, and "John Murrough" was a corporal, 7th Maryland Regiment, from Jan. 5, 1777 to Aug., 1777 [Ref: D-15, D-232].

MOSES, Robert (b. 1741). Private, 3rd Co., Lower Bn., Militia, Sep., 1777 [Ref: M-199, T-5:46]. Private, 8th Co., Lower Bn., Militia, July 15, 1780 [Ref: M-207]. Lived in George Town Hd. (two taxables) in 1776-1777 [Ref: K-1:194, R-31:3].

MOSES, William. Private, 5th Co., Lower Bn., Militia, Aug., 1777 [Ref: M-199, T-5:48].

MOSS, Francis. Took the Oath of Allegiance before the Hon. Richard Thompson in 1778 [Ref: T-3:75, L-1:43].

MOSS, Robert. Took the Oath of Allegiance before the Hon. Richard Thompson in 1778 [Ref: T-3:75, L-1:43].

MOUNIKEY, Joseph. Took the Oath of Allegiance in 1778 [Ref: L-2:28].

MOUNT, Thomas. Took the Oath of Allegiance in 1778 [Ref: L-2:28].

MOUNTZ (MOUNTS, MOUNCE), John (b. 1740). Private, 3rd Co., Lower Bn., Militia, Sep., 1777 [Ref: M-199, T-5:46]. Took the Oath of Allegiance before the Hon. Richard Thompson in 1778 [Ref: T-3:76, L-1:43]. "John Mounts" was a private, 8th Co., Lower Bn., Militia, July 15, 1780 [Ref: M-207]. "John Mountz or Mounce" lived in George Town Hd. (two taxables) in 1776-1777 [Ref: K-1:194, R-31:3].

MOUNTZ, Michael. Private, 3rd Co., Lower Bn., Militia, Sep., 1777 [Ref: M-199, T-5:46].

MOXLEY, Daniel. Took the Oath of Allegiance before the Hon. Aneas Campbell on March 2, 1778 [Ref: T-3:78, L-1:43].

MOXLEY (MOXLY), John. Served as a First Lieutenant, 16th Bn., Militia, Sep. 12, 1777 [Ref: M-106, M-195, C-373]. "John Moxley" took the Oath of Allegiance before the Hon. Aneas Campbell on March 2, 1778 [Ref: T-3:78, L-1:43]. There was a "James Maxley, aged 31" in Sugarland Hd. in 1776 [Ref: K-1:209], and a "John Moxley" lived in Sugarland Hd. (one taxable) in 1777 [Ref: R-31:12]. "John Moxly" married Elizabeth Buchanan in Montgomery County on Nov. 30, 1780 [Ref: K-2:519]. See "William Moxley," q.v.

MOXLEY, Nehemiah (1737-1836). Lived at Elk Ridge, Maryland and had three sons who settled in Montgomery County: William, Ezekiel and Jacob. In the early 1800's their descendants moved to Kentucky and Ohio and other points west. Nehemiah Moxley participated in the burning of the brig "Peggy Stewart" in Annapolis in 1775 in the protest over tea taxes. For more information on the Moxley family see Mrs.

Allie May Moxley Burton's *Nehemiah Moxley: His Clagettsville Sons and Their Descendants* (1990), and Source DAR-I:486.

MOXLEY, William. Private, 8th Co., Upper Bn., Militia, Aug. 30, 1777 [Ref: M-195]. Lived in Sugarland Hd. (John Moxley, security) in 1777 [Ref: R-31:13]. See "Nehemiah Moxley," q.v.

MUCKLEROY, Robert. Private, enrolled into a company of militia for the service of the Flying Camp, Oct. 15, 1776 [Ref: B-353].

MUFPHEL, Barney. Took the Oath of Allegiance before the Hon. Samuel W. Magruder in 1778 [Ref: T-3:73, L-1:43].

MULLIKIN (MULLICAN), Archibald. "Archibald Mullikin" was a private, 2nd Co., Middle Bn., Militia, Sep. 4, 1777 [Ref: M-196, T-5:37. Also see Ref: D-44]. "Archd. Mullican" married Elizabeth Vincent in Montgomery County on March 19, 1778 [Ref: K-2:519]. "Archibald Mullikin" lived in Sugar Loaf Hd. (one taxable) in 1777 [Ref: R-31:10].

MULLIKIN, Basil (died 1803). Private, 4th Co., Middle Bn., Militia, Sep., 1777 [Ref: M-196, T-5:39]. Private, 6th Class, 4th Co., Middle Bn., Militia, July 15, 1780 [Ref: M-202]. Took the Oath of Allegiance before the Hon. Edward Burgess on Feb. 28, 1778 [Ref: T-3:59, L-1:43]. Lived in the Upper Part of Newfoundland Hd. (three taxables) in 1777 [Ref: R-31:7]. Died testate in Montgomery County (wife not named, nor children) in 1803 [Ref: V-96]. See "John Mullikin," q.v.

MULLIKIN, Elizabeth. See "John Smith," q.v.

MULLIKIN, John. (1) Private, 3rd Co., Upper Bn., Militia, Aug. 30, 1777 [Ref: M-193]. (2) Private, 2nd Co., Middle Bn., Militia, Sep. 4, 1777 [Ref: M-196, T-5:37]. Took the Oath of Allegiance before the Hon. Edward Burgess on Feb. 28, 1778 [Ref: T-3:64, L-1:43]. One John Mullikin lived in Sugar Loaf Hd. (two taxables) in 1777 [Ref: R-31:10], and another lived in the Upper Part of Potomac Hd. (one taxable) in 1777 [Ref: R-31:14]. One John Mullikin died testate in Montgomery County (wife named Ann) in 1778 and mentioned sons Basil and Willey, among other children. William Mullikin also died testate in Montgomery County (wife not named) in 1778 and mentioned sons William, John, and Basil. The wills of John Mullikin and William Mullikin were probated on the same day, March 21, 1778 [Ref: V-96, V-97].

MULLIKIN (MULLICAN, MULLAKIN), Lewis. "Lewis Mullican" served as a private, Flying Camp, on July 29, 1776 [Ref: D-44]. Private, 2nd Co., Middle Bn., Militia, on Sep. 4, 1777 [Ref: M-196, T-5:37, D-44]. "Lewis Mullikin" took the Oath of Allegiance before the Hon. Gerrard Briscoe on March 2, 1778 [Ref: T-3:56, L-1:43]. Private, 3rd Class, 3rd Co., Middle Bn., Militia, July 15, 1780 [Ref: M-202]. "Lewis Mullakin" married Susanna Jarvis in Montgomery County on Nov. 9, 1780 [Ref: K-2:520]. Lived in Sugar Loaf Hd. (two taxables) in 1777 [Ref: R-31:10].

MULLIKIN, Lewis Sr. Took the Oath of Allegiance before the Hon. Gerrard Briscoe on March 2, 1778 [Ref: T-3:57, L-1:43]. Also see "Lewis Mullikin," q.v.

237

MULLIKIN, William and Willey. See "John Mullikin," q.v.

MUMMART (MUMMERT), John. "John Mummart" took the Oath of Allegiance before the Hon. Edward Burgess on Feb. 28, 1778 [Ref: T-3:63, L-1:43]. "John Mummard" rendered aid by providing wheat for use of the military in 1780 [Ref: O-326, O-333]. "John Mummert" lived in Sugar Loaf Hd. (one taxable) in 1777 [Ref: R-31:10].

MUMMART (MUMMERT), Michael. "Michael Mummart" was a private, 7th Co., Middle Bn., Militia, Sep., 1777 [Ref: M-197, T-5:42]. "Michael Mummert" lived in Sugar Loaf Hd. (one taxable) in 1777 [Ref: R-31:10]. "Michael Murmet" married Mary Thomson [sic] in Montgomery County on Dec. 23, 1777 [Ref: K-2:516].

MUMMART, William. Private, 7th Co., Middle Bn., Militia, Sep., 1777 [Ref: M-197, T-5:42].

MURDOCK, John, Esq. (1734-1790). Served as Colonel, 29th Bn., Militia, from Jan. 6, 1776, and Lieutenant of Montgomery County through at least Nov. 5, 1781, on which date the Council of Maryland wrote to him as follows: "We are informed there are a number of the militia draughts and substitutes in and about George Town who are useless and an expense to the State, we therefore request you to give them a discharge and send them off to their respective homes." [Ref: G-662, M-106, M-198, M-204, C-373, B-558]. He also took the Oath of Allegiance before the Hon. Richard Thompson in 1778 [Ref: T-3:75, L-1:43]. "Col. John Murdock" lived in Lower Potomac Hd. in 1776 and had 25 taxables in 1777 [Ref: K-1:184, R-31:4]. "John Murdock, of Georgetown" died testate in Montgomery County (wife not named) in 1790 [Ref: V-97].

MURDOCK, William. Served as an Ensign, 6th Maryland Line, 1779, and Lieutenant, 2nd Maryland Line, 1780-1781 [Ref: D-231, D-363, R-33:157, X-1146].

MURPHY (MURPHEY), Anthony (b. 1748). "Antoney Murphey" lived in George Town Hd. in 1776 [Ref: K-1:194]. "Anthony Murphy" was a private who enrolled into a company of militia for the service of the Flying Camp on Oct. 15, 1776 [Ref: B-353].

MURPHY, Charles (died 1780). Private, 3rd Co., Lower Bn., Militia, July 15, 1780 [Ref: M-205]. Private, 6th Co., Lower Bn., Militia, Aug., 1777 [Ref: T-5:49]. Took the Oath of Allegiance before the Hon. Joseph Offutt on March 2, 1778 [Ref: T-3:70, L-1:43]. Served as a grand juror in Nov., 1777 [Ref: R-31:17]. Lived in the Upper Part of Potomac Hd. (three taxables) in 1777 [Ref: R-31:14]. "Charles Murphy, of Frederick County" died testate in Montgomery County (wife named Mary) in 1780 [Ref: V-97].

MURPHY, Darby. Private, 7th Class, 2nd Co., Middle Bn., Militia, July 15, 1780 [Ref: M-201]. Private, 3rd Co., Middle Bn., Militia, Sep., 1777 [Ref: M-196, T-5:38]. Took the Oath of Allegiance before the Hon. William Deakins, Jr. before March 3, 1778 [Ref: T-3:68, L-1:43]. Lived in the Upper Part of Potomac Hd. (one taxable) in 1777 [Ref: R-31:14].

MURPHY (MURPHEY), Francis. Private, 3rd Co., Upper Bn., Militia, Aug. 30, 1777 [Ref: M-193]. Took the Oath of Allegiance before the Hon. Elisha Williams on March 2, 1778 [Ref: T-3:80, L-1:43]. Francis Murphey lived in Sugar Loaf Hd. (two taxables) in 1777 [Ref: R-31:10].

MURPHY, James (1746-1789). Soldier, 1st Maryland Regiment, who lost a leg at the Battle of Long Island on Aug. 27, 1776. His invalid pension commenced April 10, 1781, aged 35, resident of Montgomery County, and he died in Aug., 1789 [Ref: D-632]. One James Murphy married Mary Craddock in Montgomery County on June 8, 1778 [Ref: K-2:520].

MURPHY, John. Private, 6th Co., Lower Bn., Militia, Aug., 1777 [Ref: M-200, T-5:49]. Private, 5th Co., Middle Bn., Militia, July 15, 1780 [Ref: M-203]. Took the Oath of Allegiance before the Hon. Joseph Offutt on March 2, 1778 [Ref: T-3:70, L-1:43]. Lived in the Upper Part of Potomac Hd. (one taxable) in 1777 [Ref: R-31:14].

MURPHY (MURPHEY), Joseph. Private, 7th Maryland Line, from March, 1779 until Aug. 16, 1780, when reported missing at the Battle of Camden [Ref: D-234].

MURPHY, Philip. Private, 3rd Co., Lower Bn., Militia, July 15, 1780 [Ref: M-205].

MURPHY, Sarah. See "William Gatton," q.v.

MURPHY, William. Private, 8th Co., Lower Bn., Militia, July 15, 1780 [Ref: M-207]. Private, 6th Co., Lower Bn., Militia, Aug., 1777 [Ref: M-200, T-5:49]. One William Murphy took the Oath of Allegiance before the Hon. Joseph Offutt on March 2, 1778 [Ref: T-3:70, L-1:43], and another took the Oath of Allegiance before the Hon. Richard Thompson in 1778 [Ref: T-3:75, L-1:43]. One rendered aid by providing wheat for use of the military in 1780 [Ref: O-311]. One William Murphy lived in the Upper Part of Potomac Hd. (six taxables) in 1777 [Ref: R-31:14].

MURRAY, Thompson. Private who was recruited and served in the 7th Maryland Regiment, Continental Army, from Feb. 12, 1780 to July 12, 1780, when he reportedly deserted [Ref: D-234, D-341, F-114].

MUSGROVE, Amos. See "John Musgrove," q.v.

MUSGROVE, John (died 1785). Took the Oath of Allegiance (made his "I" mark) before the Hon. Edward Burgess on Feb. 28, 1778 [Ref: T-3:59, L-1:43]. Rendered aid by providing wheat for use of the military in 1781 [Ref: O-391, O-395]. Lived in the Upper Part of Newfoundland Hd. (four taxables) in 1777 [Ref: R-31:7]. Died testate in Montgomery County (wife not named) in 1785 and mentioned sons Amos and Nathan Musgrove [Ref: V-97].

MUSGROVE, Nathan (1758-1823). Son of John Musgrove [Ref: V-97]. Private, Capt. Edward Burgess' Co., Lower District of Frederick (now Montgomery) County, Militia, July, 1776 [Ref: D-42]. Private, 4th Co., Middle Bn., Militia, Sep., 1777 [Ref: M-196, T-5:39]. Took the Oath of Allegiance before the Hon. Edward Burgess on Feb. 28, 1778. He married Ann Conner [Ref: T-3:59, L-1:43, DAR-I:488].

MUSGROVE, Samuel, of Anthony. Took the Oath of Allegiance before the Hon. Edward Burgess on Feb. 28, 1778 [Ref: T-3:60, L-1:43]. Private, 6th Co., Middle Bn., Militia, Aug., 1777 [Ref: M-197, T-5:41].

MUSGROVE, Samuel, of Samuel. Took the Oath of Allegiance before the Hon. Edward Burgess on Feb. 28, 1778 [Ref: T-3:59, L-1:43]. Private, 6th Co., Middle Bn., Militia, Aug., 1777 [Ref: M-197, T-5:41]. "Samuel Musgrove" (one taxable) and "Samuel Musgrove, of Samuel" (one taxable) lived in the Upper Part of Newfoundland Hd. in 1777 [Ref: R-31:7].

MYER, David. Took the Oath of Allegiance in 1778 [Ref: L-2:28].

MYER, Sebistan. Took the Oath of Allegiance in 1778 [Ref: L-2:28].

MYERS (MIRES), Adam (b. 1757). "Adam Mires" lived in Lower Potomac Hd. in 1776 [Ref: K-1:185]. "Adam Myers" was a private, 4th Co., Lower Bn., Militia, Aug., 1777 [Ref: M-199, T-5:47].

MYERS (MYRE, MIRES), Conrad (b. 1738). "Conrad Myers" was a private, 8th Co., Upper Bn., Militia, Aug. 30, 1777 [Ref: M-195]. "Conrad Myre" took the Oath of Allegiance (made his "X" mark) before the Hon. Aneas Campbell on March 2, 1778 [Ref: T-3:77, L-1:43]. "Conrod or Conrad Mires" lived in Sugarland Hd. in 1776-1777 [Ref: K-1:212, R-31:12].

MYERS, Felter. Private, 1st Co., Lower Bn., Militia, Sep., 1777, and Fourth Corporal, 7th Co., Lower Bn., July 15, 1780 [Ref: M-198, M-206, T-5:44].

MYERS, Henry. Took the Oath of Allegiance in 1778 [Ref: L-2:28].

MYERS (MIERS), Margaret. See "Weaver Waters," q.v.

MYERS (MIERS), Solomon. Private, 7th Co., Lower Bn., Militia, July 15, 1780 [Ref: M-206].

MYERS (MIRERS), Valentine. "Valentine Myers, Sr." lived in the Lower Part of Newfoundland Hd. (three taxables) in 1777 [Ref: R-31:5]. "Valentine Mirers" took the Oath of Allegiance before the Hon. Edward Burgess on Feb. 28, 1778 [Ref: T-3:58, L-1:43].

NABERS (NEIGHBOURS), John. Private who was recruited and served in the 7th Maryland Regiment, Continental Army, from Jan. 16, 1780 until Aug. 16, 1780, when reported missing at the Battle of Camden [Ref: D-235, D-341, F-86].

NABOURS, Nathan. Took the Oath of Allegiance before the Hon. Elisha Williams on March 2, 1778 [Ref: T-3:80, L-1:43].

NAYLOR, Joshua. Took the Oath of Allegiance before the Hon. Aneas Campbell on March 2, 1778 [Ref: T-3:78, L-1:43]. This may also refer to a "Joshua Nailor" of Prince George's County who served in the Maryland Line and then moved to Montgomery County, North Carolina (Ref: P-2468. For more details, consult *DAR Magazine*, Vol. 63, No. 2 (1929), p. 103, and Vol. 67, No. 4 (1933), p. 516].

NEALL (NEAL), Charles (b. 1705). Took the Oath of Allegiance before the Hon. Elisha Williams on March 2, 1778 [Ref: T-3:81, L-1:43]. "Dr.

Charles Neall" lived in Sugarland Hd. in 1776 [Ref: K-1:200]. See "Laurence O'Neal," q.v.

NEALL (NEALE, NEILL), Joseph. "Joseph Neill" was a private, 4th Co., Upper Bn., Militia, Aug. 30, 1777 [Ref: M-194]. "Joseph Neale or Neall" was a private, Capt. Thomas Beall's Co., Maryland Line, 1780 [Ref: D-351].

NEALL, Ralph (b. 1740). Lived in Sugarland Hd. in 1776 [Ref: K-1:200]. Private, 7th Co., Upper Bn., Militia, Aug. 30, 1777 [Ref: M-195].

NEALL, Thomas (1742-1781). Lived in Sugarland Hd. in 1776 [Ref: K-1:214]. "Thomas Neall" was a private, 3rd Maryland Regiment, 1781. "Thomas Neale" died on March 15, 1781 [Ref: D-394, D-550].

NEEDE, George. Took the Oath of Allegiance in 1778 [Ref: L-2:28].

NEEDHAM, William Abington. "William A. Needham" was a sergeant in the Maryland Line, Continental Army, "who was wounded by a musket ball which passed through his body and rendered him incapable of gaining a subsistence by labour." In Nov., 1791, the Treasurer of Maryland was directed to pay him, quarterly, the half pay of a sergeant. He was receiving $60 a year in 1808 and was still on the pension rolls in Montgomery County in 1835 [Ref: J-16, K-2:378, P-2475, Q-130, Y-42]. "William Abington Needham" was a son of William Needham who died testate in 1808 [Ref: V-98].

NEIGHBOURS, John. See "John Nabers (Neighbours)," q.v.

NELSON, Arthur. Rendered aid by providing pork for use of the military in 1781 [Ref: O-375].

NELSON, Henry (Harry). Private, 6th Co., Middle Bn., Militia, Aug., 1777 [Ref: M-197, T-5:41], and as an Ensign, Middle Bn., Militia, July 15, 1780 [Ref: M-106, M-203, F-248]. Took the Oath of Allegiance (made his "X" mark) before the Hon. Edward Burgess on Feb. 28, 1778 [Ref: T-3:59, L-1:43]. Rendered aid by providing wheat for use of the military in 1781 [Ref: O-449]. Lived in Linganore Hd. (one taxable) in 1777 [Ref: R-31:0].

NESBIT (NEZBIT, NISBETT), Bernard. "Bernard Nezbit" took the Oath of Allegiance before the Hon. Elisha Williams on March 2, 1778 [Ref: T-3:81, L-1:43]. "Bernard Nisbett" was a private, 3rd Co., Upper Bn., Militia, Aug. 30, 1777 [Ref: M-193].

NESBIT (NEZBIT, NISBETT), Charles (b. 1721). "Charles Nisbet" lived in Sugarland Hd. in 1776 [Ref: K-1:203]. "Charles Nezbit" took the Oath of Allegiance before the Hon. Elisha Williams on March 2, 1778 [Ref: T-3:81, L-1:43]. "Charles Nisbett" was a private, 7th Co., Upper Bn., Militia, Aug. 30, 1777 [Ref: M-194].

NEVITT, James. Private, 5th Co., Lower Bn., Militia, Aug., 1777 [Ref: M-199, T-5:48]. Took the Oath of Allegiance before the Hon. Charles Jones on Jan. 10, 1778 [Ref: T-3:71, L-1:43].

NEWCOMB, William. Private, 7th Co., Lower Bn., Militia, July 15, 1780 [Ref: M-206].

NEWCOMER, John. Took the Oath of Allegiance in 1778 [Ref: L-2:28].
NEWMAN, Benjamin. Private, 7th Co., Upper Bn., Militia, Aug. 30, 1777 [Ref: M-195]. Took the Oath of Allegiance (made his "X" mark) before the Hon. Aneas Campbell on March 2, 1778 [Ref: T-3:77, L-1:43].
NEWMAN, Harry Wright. See "Burgess Gaither," q.v.
NEWMAN, Jacob. Private, 7th Co., Upper Bn., Militia, Aug. 30, 1777 [Ref: M-195]. Took the Oath of Allegiance before the Hon. Aneas Campbell on March 2, 1778 [Ref: T-3:78, L-1:43].
NEWSTEP (NEWSTEEP, KNEWSTEP), Robert (died 1789). "Robert Newsteep" took the Oath of Allegiance (made his "X" mark) before the Hon. Edward Burgess on Feb. 28, 1778 [Ref: T-3:60, L-1:43]. "Robert Newslop" [Newstep] lived in Rock Creek Hd. (two taxables) in 1777 [Ref: R-31:16]. "Robert W. Knewstab" died testate in Montgomery County (wife named Tomoson) in 1789. "Thomason Knewstep" died testate in Montgomery County in 1809 and mentioned husband Robert Knewstep [Ref: V-78, V-79].
NEWTON, John 2nd. Private, Capt. Price's Co., 3rd Maryland Line, 1781-1782 [Ref: D-453].
NEWTON, Sarah. See "Stephen Newton Chiswell," q.v.
NEWTON (NUTON), Thomas. "Thomas Newton" was a private, 2nd Co., Upper Bn., Militia, Aug. 30, 1777 [Ref: M-193]. "Thomas Nuton" lived in Sugar Loaf Hd. (one taxable) in 1777 [Ref: R-31:10].
NEWTON, William. Private, 5th Co., Middle Bn., Militia, Sep., 1777 [Ref: M-197, T-5:40]. Private, 1st Class, 1st Co., Middle Bn., Militia, July 15, 1780 [Ref: M-201]. Rendered aid by providing wheat for use of the military in 1780 [Ref: O-313].
NEZDORFF, Samuel. Rendered aid by repairing the scales of the storehouse in April, 1781 [Ref: O-384].
NICHOLAS, Samuel. Rendered aid by providing wheat for use of the military in 1780 [Ref: O-313].
NICHOLAS, Thomas. Rendered aid by providing wheat for use of the military in 1780 [Ref: O-315].
NICHOLLS, Archibald. Private, 6th Co., Upper Bn., Militia, Aug. 30, 1777 [Ref: M-194]. Took the Oath of Allegiance before the Hon. Joseph Wilson on Feb. 28, 1778 [Ref: T-3:66, L-1:43]. His death notice was in the *Maryland Journal and True American* (Rockville) on Jan. 16, 1828: "Died at his residence near Hyatt's-town on Sunday the 6th instant, Archibald Nichols, aged inhabitant of this county, and patriot and soldier in the Continental Army." [Ref: F. Edward Wright's *Marriages and Deaths in the Newspapers of Frederick and Montgomery Counties, Maryland, 1820-1830*, p. 77].
NICHOLLS (NICOLS), Benjamin. "Benjamin Nicholls" was a private, 8th Co., Middle Bn., Militia, Sep., 1777 [Ref: M-198, T-5:43]. "Benjamin Nicols" lived in Rock Creek Hd. (three taxables) in 1777 [Ref: R-31:16].

NICHOLLS, Benjamin, of William. Took the Oath of Allegiance before the Hon. Joseph Wilson on Feb. 10, 1778 [Ref: T-3:64, L-1:43].

NICHOLLS, Daniel (b. 1763). Son of Thomas Nicholls, of North West Hd., in 1776 [Ref: K-1:232]. Served as a First Corporal, 2nd Co., Lower Bn., Militia, July 15, 1780 [Ref: M-204].

NICHOLLS, Edward. Took the Oath of Allegiance before the Hon. Joseph Wilson on Feb. 28, 1778 [Ref: T-3:64, L-1:43]. Rendered aid by providing wheat for use of the military in 1781 [Ref: O-384]. Lived in Sugar Loaf Hd. (three taxables) in 1777 [Ref: R-31:10].

NICHOLLS, James (b. 1726). Took the Oath of Allegiance before the Hon. Richard Thompson in 1778 [Ref: T-3:75, L-1:43]. Lived in Lower Potomac Hd. (one taxable) in 1776-1777 [Ref: K-1:185, R-31:4].

NICHOLLS, John. (1) Private, 3rd Co., Middle Bn., Militia, Sep., 1777 [Ref: M-196, T-5:38]. (2) Private, 5th Co., Middle Bn., Militia, Sep., 1777 [Ref: M-197, T-5:40]. (3) Private, Capt. Edward Burgess' Co., Lower District of Frederick (now Montgomery) County, Militia, July, 1776 [Ref: D-42]. Private, 4th Co., Lower Bn., Militia, Aug., 1777 [Ref: M-199, T-5:47]. Private, 1st Co., Lower Bn., Militia, July 15, 1780 [Ref: M-204]. One John Nicholls took the Oath of Allegiance in 1778 [Ref: L-2:28]. One John Nicholls (b. 1750) lived in Lower Potomac Hd. in 1776 and had one taxable in 1777, another lived in Sugar Loaf Hd. (one taxable), and another lived in the Upper Part of Potomac Hd. (one taxable) in 1777 [Ref: K-1:185, R-31:4, R-31:10, R-31:15].

NICHOLLS, John Hayman or Haymond. Served as private, Flying Camp, Frederick (now Montgomery) County, enlisted by Greenbury Gaither on July 29, 1776 [Ref: D-44]. Fourth Corporal, 1st Co., Middle Bn., Militia, July 15, 1780 [Ref: M-201]. Letter from John Murdock to the Governor and Council of Maryland, April 7, 1781, in part: "Mr. John Haymond Nicholls, son of the High Sheriff of this County [Montgomery], who never to my knowledge, held any commission in the militia, has had the influence to raise a number of volunteers to act as Select Militia, who have chosen him their Captain. I know Mr. Nicholls to be an active, spirited young man, therefore I could wish that he might obtain a commission and the whole be put under his command, if it can with propriety be done." [Ref: H-169, H-170]. Served as Captain, Select Militia, April 13, 1781 [Ref: M-107, G-396]. Took the Oath of Allegiance before the Hon. Joseph Wilson on Feb. 28, 1778 [Ref: T-3:64, L-1:43]. Deputy Sheriff of Montgomery County, 1781 [Ref: W-2], and elected Sheriff on Nov. 11, 1782 [Ref: I-301].

NICHOLLS, Ninian. Private, 6th Co., Upper Bn., Militia, Aug. 30, 1777 [Ref: M-194]. Took the Oath of Allegiance before the Hon. Joseph Wilson on Feb. 28, 1778 [Ref: T-3:66, L-1:43].

NICHOLLS, Samuel. Took the Oath of Allegiance before the Hon. Joseph Wilson on Feb. 28, 1778 [Ref: T-3:66, L-1:43]. Rendered aid by providing wheat for use of the military in 1780 and 1781 [Ref: O-309, O-398].

Lived in the Upper Part of Potomac Hd. (three taxables) in 1777 [Ref: R-31:15].

NICHOLLS, Simon. Served as High Sheriff of Montgomery County, 1779-1781 [Ref: W-1, W-2]. Lived in the Upper Part of Potomac Hd. (five taxables) in 1777 [Ref: R-31:15].

NICHOLLS, Thomas. Four men with this name took the Oath of Allegiance: one before the Hon. Charles Jones on Jan. 10, 1778; one before the Hon. Joseph Wilson on Feb. 28, 1778; one before the Hon. William Deakins, Jr. before March 3, 1778; and one before the Hon. Gerrard Briscoe on March 2, 1778 [Ref: T-3:56, T-3:64, T-3:68, T-3:71, L-1:43]. One rendered aid by providing wheat and corn for use of the military in 1780 [Ref: O-292, O-311]. One Thomas Nicholls (b. 1753) lived in Lower Potomac Hd. in 1776, another lived in Sugar Loaf Hd. (three taxables), another lived in the Upper Part of Potomac Hd. (two taxables), and another lived in North West Hd. (eleven taxables) in 1777 [Ref: R-31:10, R-31:14, R-31:17]. One Thomas Nicholls died testate in Montgomery County (wife not named) in 1803 [Ref: V-98]. "Thomas Nickolls, aged 47" lived in North West Hd. (wife named Cassandra, aged 39) in 1776 [Ref: K-1:232]. One Thomas Nicholls served as a petit juror in Aug., 1777 [Ref: R-31:17]. Military service was as follows: (1) Private, Capt. Edward Burgess' Co., Lower District of Frederick (now Montgomery) County, Militia, July, 1776 [Ref: D-42], Ensign, Upper Bn., Militia, April 21, 1779, Second Lieutenant, Middle Bn., Militia, March 25, 1780, Second Lieutenant, 3rd Co., Middle Bn., Militia, July 15, 1780, and Lieutenant, Select Militia, April 13, 1781 [Ref: M-107, M-202, E-357, F-120, G-396, R-33:155, X-1146]. (2) Private, 5th Co., Middle Bn., Militia, Sep., 1777 [Ref: M-197, T-5:40]. Private, 7th Class, 1st Co., Middle Bn., Militia, July 15, 1780 [Ref: M-201]. (3) Private, 2nd Co., Middle Bn., Militia, Sep., 1777 [Ref: M-195]. (4) Thomas Nicholls, Sr. was a private, 3rd Co., Middle Bn., Militia, Sep., 1777 [Ref: M-196, T-5:38].

NICHOLLS, Thomas Jr. Private, 3rd Co., Middle Bn., Militia, Sep., 1777 [Ref: M-196, T-5:38]. Took the Oath of Allegiance before the Hon. William Deakins, Jr. before March 3, 1778 [Ref: T-3:68, L-1:43].

NICHOLLS, William (b. 1759). Son of Thomas Nicholls, of North West Hd., in 1776 [Ref: K-1:232]. Private, 5th Co., Lower Bn., Militia, Aug., 1777 [Ref: M-199, T-5:48]. Took the Oath of Allegiance before the Hon. Richard Thompson in 1778 [Ref: T-3:75, L-1:43].

NICHOLLS, William, of Lin...(?). Private, 7th Class, 1st Co., Middle Bn., Militia, July 15, 1780 [Ref: M-201].

NICHOLLS, William, of Samuel. Private, 1st Class, 1st Co., Middle Bn., Militia, July 15, 1780 [Ref: M-201].

NICHOLSON, Joel. "Joel Nicholson, born in Maryland, between 16 and 17 years of age, 5 feet 6 inches high, short dark coloured hair and brown complexion, recruited by Capt. Thomas Edmonston on May 2, 1781." [Ref: R-33:156, X-1146].

NICHOLSON, John. Took the Oath of Allegiance on Sep. 1, 1780, under the Act of May 12, 1780, having neglected to do so previously "due to ignorance of the duty owed the country." [Ref: R-27:117]. Rendered aid by providing wheat for use of the military in 1781 [Ref: O-379].

NICHOLSON, Joseph. Took the Oath of Allegiance before the Hon. Edward Burgess on Feb. 28, 1778 [Ref: T-3:58, L-1:43]. Joseph Nicholson lived in the Upper Part of Newfoundland Hd. (one taxable) in 1777 [Ref: R-31:7].

NICHOLSON, Nicholas. Served as a Sergeant, Capt. Price's Co., 3rd Maryland Line, 1781-1782 [Ref: D-452].

NICHOLSON, Richard. Private, 5th Co., Lower Bn., Militia, July 15, 1780 [Ref: M-206]. Took the Oath of Allegiance before the Hon. Charles Jones on Jan. 10, 1778 [Ref: T-3:71, L-1:43]. "Richard Nicholasson" was a private, Capt. Edward Burgess' Co., Lower District of Frederick (now Montgomery) County, Militia, July, 1776 [Ref: D-42]. Richard Nicholson and Bridget Farelong were married by Bishop John Carroll (Roman Catholic) in Montgomery County on Oct. 18, 1777 [Ref: K-2:514].

NICHOLSON, William. Private, 4th Co., Middle Bn., Militia, Sep., 1777 [Ref: M-196, T-5:39]. Took the Oath of Allegiance before the Hon. Edward Burgess on Feb. 28, 1778 [Ref: T-3:59, L-1:43]. William Nicholson lived in the Upper Part of Newfoundland Hd. (three taxables) in 1777 [Ref: R-31:7].

NIGHOFF, Frederick. Took the Oath of Allegiance in 1778 [Ref: L-2:28].

NIXON, Hugh. Son of Jonathan Nixon, Sr. [Ref: V-99]. Private, 7th Co., Lower Bn., Militia, Aug., 1777 [Ref: M-200, T-5:50]. Took the Oath of Allegiance before the Hon. Edward Burgess on Feb. 28, 1778 [Ref: T-3:62, L-1:43]. Rendered aid by providing wheat for use of the military in 1780 [Ref: O-304]. Served as a grand juror in 1781 [Ref: W-2]. Lived in the Lower Part of Newfoundland Hd. (two taxables) in 1777 [Ref: R-31:5].

NIXON, James. Son of Jonathan Nixon, Sr. [Ref: V-99]. Private, 7th Co., Lower Bn., Militia, Aug., 1777, and Second Corporal, 4th Co., July 15, 1780 [Ref: M-200, M-205, T-5:50].

NIXON, Jonathan Jr. (b. 1757). Lived in North West Hd. in 1776 [Ref: K-1:229]. Private, 7th Co., Lower Bn., Militia, Aug., 1777, and Second Sergeant, 4th Co., Lower Bn., July 15, 1780 [Ref: M-200, M-205, T-5:50]. Took the Oath of Allegiance before the Hon. Edward Burgess on Feb. 28, 1778 [Ref: T-3:63, L-1:43].

NIXON, Jonathan Sr. Took the Oath of Allegiance before the Hon. Edward Burgess on Feb. 28, 1778 [Ref: T-3:62, L-1:43]. "Jonathan Nixon, Sr." lived in the Lower Part of Newfoundland Hd. (three taxables) in 1777 [Ref: R-31:5]. "Jonathan Nixon" died testate in Montgomery County (wife not named) in 1799 and mentioned sons Hugh, James, Jonathan, and Richard, among other children [Ref: V-99].

NIXON, Joshua. Private, 4th Co., Lower Bn., Militia, July 15, 1780 [Ref: M-205]. Private, 7th Co., Lower Bn., Militia, Aug., 1777 [Ref: M-200, T-5:50]. Took the Oath of Allegiance before the Hon. Edward Burgess on Feb. 28, 1778 [Ref: T-3:62, L-1:43]. Lived in the Lower Part of Newfoundland Hd. (one taxable) in 1777 [Ref: R-31:5].

NIXON, Martha. See "Benjamin Becraft," q.v.

NIXON, Richard. Son of Jonathan Nixon, Sr. [Ref: V-99]. Private, 4th Co., Lower Bn., Militia, July 15, 1780 [Ref: M-205]. Took the Oath of Allegiance before the Hon. Edward Burgess on Feb. 28, 1778 [Ref: T-3:63, L-1:43].

NOBBS (NOBB), John (b. 1712). "John Nobbs" lived in Sugarland Hd. in 1776 [Ref: K-1:212]. "John Nobb" took the Oath of Allegiance (made his "V" mark) before the Hon. Aneas Campbell on March 2, 1778 [Ref: T-3:77, L-1:43].

NODING, Alice. See "John Brown," q.v.

NOE, Peter. Private, 3rd Co., Middle Bn., Militia, Sep., 1777 [Ref: T-5:38 and M-196, which latter source questions if the name could be "Roe"]. Private, 3rd Class, 2nd Co., Middle Bn., Militia, July 15, 1780 [Ref: M-201]. Took the Oath of Allegiance before the Hon. William Deakins, Jr. before March 3, 1778 [Ref: T-3:68, L-1:43]. Lived in the Upper Part of Potomac Hd. (one taxable) in 1777 [Ref: R-31:15].

NOLLAND, John. Private, enrolled into a company of militia for the service of the Flying Camp, Oct. 15, 1776 [Ref: B-353].

NORFUT, Ann. See "Nathan Oden," q.v.

NORRIS, Benjamin (died 1786). Took the Oath of Allegiance before the Hon. Elisha Williams on March 2, 1778 [Ref: T-3:80, L-1:43]. Lived in Sugar Loaf Hd. (four taxables) in 1777 [Ref: R-31:10]. Died testate in Montgomery County (wife not named) in 1786 [Ref: V-99].

NORRIS, George (died 1789). Served as a Second Lieutenant, 16th Bn., Militia, March 26, 1776, and Second Lieutenant, 6th Co., Upper Bn., Sep. 12, 1777 [Ref: M-107, M-194, A-287, C-373]. Took the Oath of Allegiance before the Hon. Elisha Williams on March 2, 1778 [Ref: T-3:80, L-1:43]. Lived in Sugar Loaf Hd. (five taxables) in 1777 [Ref: R-31:10]. Died testate in Montgomery County (wife named Mary) in 1789 [Ref: V-99].

NORRIS, John. Served as a Second Lieutenant, 29th Bn., Militia, Sep. 12, 1777 [Ref: M-107, C-373].

NORRIS, William. Served as a First Lieutenant, 6th Co., 16th Bn., Militia, by Sep. 12, 1777, and Captain, Upper Bn., Militia, April 21, 1779 [Ref: M-107, M-194, C-373, E-356]. "William Norris" took the Oath of Allegiance before the Hon. Elisha Williams on March 2, 1778 [Ref: T-3:80, L-1:43]. "William Norris, Jr." lived in Sugar Loaf Hd. (four taxables) in 1777 [Ref: R-31:10]. "William Norris, of William" died testate in Montgomery County (wife named Elizabeth Margaret) in 1797, and "William Norris, of Belmont County, Ohio" died testate and his will was probated in Montgomery County, Maryland on Aug. 10, 1812 [Ref: V-100].

NORRIS, William, of Benjamin. Private who enrolled into a company of militia for the service of the Flying Camp on Oct. 15, 1776 [Ref: B-352].

NORTH, James. Private who was recruited to serve in the Continental Army in 1780 and subsequently reported dead (no date was given). [Ref: D-342].

NORTHCRAFT, Edward. "Edward Northcraft" was a private, 2nd Co., Middle Bn., Militia, Sep. 4, 1777 [Ref: M-196, T-5:37]. Private, 8th Class, 3rd Co., Middle Bn., Militia, July 15, 1780 [Ref: M-202]. "Edward North Craft" married Ann Linthicum in Montgomery County on March 11, 1779 [Ref: K-2:518].

NORTHCRAFT, Richard (died 1789). Private, 2nd Co., Middle Bn., Militia, Sep. 4, 1777 [Ref: M-196, T-5:37]. Private, 8th Class, 3rd Co., Middle Bn., Militia, July 15, 1780 [Ref: M-202]. Richard Northcraft lived in Sugar Loaf Hd. (three taxables) in 1777 [Ref: R-31:10]. "Richard Northcraft, planter and farmer" died testate in Montgomery County (wife not named) in 1789 [Ref: V-100].

NORWOOD, James. Private, 6th Co., Middle Bn., Militia, July 15, 1780 [Ref: M-203]. Took the Oath of Allegiance before the Hon. Edward Burgess on Feb. 28, 1778 [Ref: T-3:61, L-1:43]. Lived in Linganore Hd. (one taxable) in 1777 [Ref: R-31:9].

NORWOOD, Stephen. Private, 6th Co., Middle Bn., Militia, July 15, 1780 [Ref: M-203].

NOTLEY (NOTHEY), Samuel. Private, 8th Co., Lower Bn., Militia, July 15, 1780 [Ref: M-207].

NOWLAND, Thomas. Served as First Lieutenant, Lower District, Frederick County (now Montgomery), Militia, July 20, 1776 [Ref: D-42].

OARD, Iorasa or Jorasa. See "Josiah Hoskinson, Jr.," q.v.

O'BRIAN, Philip. Private, 8th Co., Lower Bn., Militia, July 15, 1780 [Ref: M-207]. "Philip O'Brien" took the Oath of Allegiance before the Hon. Richard Thompson in 1778 [Ref: T-3:75, L-1:43].

O'BRIAN, Richard. Private, 4th Co., Lower Bn., Militia, July 15, 1780 [Ref: M-205].

O'BRIEN, William. See "William Gibbons," q.v.

O'BRYAN, Edward. Took the Oath of Allegiance before the Hon. Edward Burgess on Feb. 28, 1778 [Ref: T-3:63, L-1:43].

O'DANIEL, Richard. Private, 6th Co., Upper Bn., Militia, Aug. 30, 1777 [Ref: M-194, D-43].

ODEL (ODLE, ODDELL), Barruck (1755-1789). Private, 5th Co., Lower Bn., Militia, Aug., 1777 [Ref: M-199, T-5:48]. Private, 2nd Co., Lower Bn., Militia, July 15, 1780 [Ref: M-204]. Took the Oath of Allegiance before the Hon. Samuel W. Magruder in 1778 [Ref: T-3:73, L-1:43, which source mistakenly listed the name as "Barruch Olel"]. "Baruch Odle" lived in Lower Potomac Hd. in 1776 and "Burch Oddell" lived in

Lower Potomac Hd. (two taxables) in 1777 [Ref: K-1:185, R-31:4].
"Baruck Odel" died testate in Montgomery County (wife named Margaret) in 1789, mentioning 6 unnamed minor children [Ref: V-100].

ODEL (ODLE), Rachel. See "John Prather," q.v.

ODEN (OWDEN), Gerard. Private, 7th Co., Middle Bn., Militia, Sep., 1777 [Ref: M-197, T-5:42].

ODEN, John David. Rendered aid by providing wheat for use of the military in 1780 [Ref: O-306]. John David Oden lived in Seneca Hd. (two taxables) in 1777 [Ref: R-31:8].

ODEN (OWDEN), Josias (Josiah). "Josias Owden" was a private, 7th Co., Middle Bn., Militia, Sep., 1777 [Ref: M-197, T-5:42]. "Josias Oden" rendered aid by providing wheat for use of the military in 1781 [Ref: O-380]. "Josiah Oden" lived in Seneca Hd. (one taxable) in 1777 [Ref: R-31:8]. See "Nathan Oden," q.v.

ODEN (OWDEN), Nathan. "Nathan Owden" was a private, 7th Co., Middle Bn., Militia, Sep., 1777 [Ref: M-197, T-5:42]. Private, 7th Co., Middle Bn., Militia, July 15, 1780 [Ref: M-203]. "Nathan Oden" took the Oath of Allegiance before the Hon. Edward Burgess on Feb. 28, 1778 [Ref: T-3:63, L-1:43]. Nathan Oden lived in Seneca Hd. (one taxable; Josiah Oden, security) in 1777 [Ref: R-31:8]. Nathan Oden married Ann Norfut in Montgomery County on Sep. 24, 1778 [Ref: K-2:520].

O'DONALD (O'DONNELL, O'DANIEL), Michael. "Michael O'Donald" took the Oath of Allegiance (made his "X" mark) before the Hon. Edward Burgess on Feb. 28, 1778 [Ref: T-3:60, L-1:43]. "Michael O'Donnell" rendered aid by providing wheat for use of the military in 1780 [Ref: O-320]. "Michael Odaniel" lived in Rock Creek Hd. (two taxables) in 1777 [Ref: R-31:16].

OFFUTT, Alexander (1736-1786). Private, 6th Co., Lower Bn., Militia, Aug., 1777 [Ref: M-200, T-5:49]. Private, 3rd Co., Lower Bn., Militia, July 15, 1780 [Ref: M-205]. Took the Oath of Allegiance before the Hon. Thomas Sprigg Wootton on March 3, 1778 [Ref: T-3:79, L-1:43, DAR-I:503]. Lived in the Upper Part of Potomac Hd. (four taxables) in 1777 [Ref: R-31:15]. Died testate in Montgomery County (wife not named) in 1786 [Ref: V-101].

OFFUTT, Cassandra. See "Archibald Magruder," q.v.

OFFUTT, Ezekiel. Private, 3rd Co., Lower Bn., Militia, July 15, 1780 [Ref: M-205].

OFFUTT, George. Private, 6th Co., Lower Bn., Militia, Aug., 1777 [Ref: M-200, T-5:49]. Served as a grand juror in Nov., 1777 [Ref: R-31:17]. Lived in the Upper Part of Potomac Hd. (two taxables) in 1777 [Ref: R-31:15].

OFFUTT, George H. Took the Oath of Allegiance before the Hon. Joseph Offutt on March 2, 1778 [Ref: T-3:70, L-1:43]. Served as First Sergeant, 3rd Co., Lower Bn., Militia, July 15, 1780 [Ref: M-204]. Served as a grand juror in 1781 [Ref: W-2].

OFFUTT, Henry. Private, 6th Co., Lower Bn., Militia, Aug., 1777 [Ref: M-200, T-5:49].
OFFUTT, Hezekiah (died 1789). Private, 3rd Co., Lower Bn., Militia, July 15, 1780 [Ref: M-205]. Took the Oath of Allegiance before the Hon. Joseph Offutt on March 2, 1778 [Ref: T-3:70, L-1:43]. Lived in the Upper Part of Potomac Hd. (two taxables) in 1777 [Ref: R-31:15]. Died testate in Montgomery County (wife named Sarah) in 1789 [Ref: V-101].
OFFUTT, James (1725-1802). Private, 6th Co., Lower Bn., Militia, Aug., 1777 [Ref: M-200, T-5:49]. Took the Oath of Allegiance before the Hon. Joseph Offutt on Feb. 6, 1778 [Ref: T-3:70, L-1:43]. Rendered aid by providing wheat for use of the military in 1781 [Ref: O-395]. Lived in the Upper Part of Potomac Hd. (six taxables) in 1777 [Ref: R-31:15]. James Offutt married Rebecca Offutt in Montgomery County on Feb. 14, 1782 [Ref: K-2:515, but Source DAR-I:503 states her name was Rebecca Magruder]. James died testate in Montgomery County (wife named Rebecca) in 1802 [Ref: V-101].
OFFUTT, James, of William. Private, 3rd Co., Lower Bn., Militia, July 15, 1780 [Ref: M-205]. Justice of the Peace, 1778-1780, and Justice of the County Court in 1781 [Ref: W-1, W-2, C-529].
OFFUTT, Jane. See "Kid Marquess," q.v.
OFFUTT, Jesse. Private, 3rd Co., Lower Bn., Militia, July 15, 1780 [Ref: M-205].
OFFUTT, John. Private, 3rd Co., Lower Bn., Militia, July 15, 1780 [Ref: M-205].
OFFUTT, Joseph. Justice who administered the Oath of Allegiance in 1778 [Ref: T-3:70, L-1:43].
OFFUTT, Molly. See "Thomas Sprigg Wootton," q.v.
OFFUTT, Mordecai. Private, 5th Co., Lower Bn., Militia, Aug., 1777 [Ref: M-199, T-5:48]. "Mordecai Offutt" took the Oath of Allegiance before the Hon. Joseph Offutt on March 2, 1778 [Ref: T-3:70, L-1:43].
OFFUTT, Mordecai Burgess (1744-1814). "Mordecai B. Offutt" lived in the Upper Part of Potomac Hd. (five taxables) in 1777 [Ref: R-31:15]. "Mordecai Burgess Offutt" was a constable in Middle Potomac Hd. in 1780 [Ref: W-1]. Source M-204 mistakenly listed "Mordecai Boffutt" as a private, 2nd Co., Lower Bn., July 15, 1780. Died testate in Montgomery County (wife not named) in 1814 [Ref: V-102]. He was born on Jan. 25, 1744, married Jane ----, rendered patriotic service, and died on March 7, 1814 [Ref: DAR-I:503].
OFFUTT, Nathan. (1) Private, 3rd Co., Middle Bn., Militia, Sep., 1777 [Ref: M-196, T-5:38]. Private, 7th Class, 2nd Co., Middle Bn., Militia, July 15, 1780 [Ref: M-201]. (2) Fourth Corporal, 3rd Co., Lower Bn., July 15, 1780 [Ref: M-205]. One Nathan Offutt took the Oath of Allegiance before the Hon. Edward Burgess on Feb. 28, 1778 [Ref: T-3:64, L-1:43]. Nathan Offutt lived in the Upper Part of Potomac Hd. (one taxable) in 1777 [Ref: R-31:15].

OFFUTT, Nathaniel. (1) Captain, 29th Bn., Militia, June 18, 1777 [Ref: M-108]. (2) Private, 3rd Co., Lower Bn., Militia, July 15, 1780 [Ref: M-205]. One Nathaniel Offutt rendered aid by providing wheat for use of the military in 1780 [Ref: O-311]. One Nathaniel Offutt lived in the Upper Part of Potomac Hd. (four taxables) in 1777 [Ref: R-31:15].

OFFUTT, Nathaniel Jr. Private, 5th Co., Middle Bn., Militia, Sep., 1777, and Private, 1st Class, 1st Co., Middle Bn., July 15, 1780 [Ref: M-201, M-197, T-5:40]. Took the Oath of Allegiance before the Hon. Joseph Offutt on March 2, 1778 [Ref: T-3:70, L-1:44].

OFFUTT, Nathaniel, of Samuel. Took the Oath of Allegiance before the Hon. Joseph Wilson on Feb. 28, 1778 [Ref: T-3:64, L-1:44, which latter source spelled the name "Offuth"]. "Nathaniel Offutt, of Sam" lived in the Upper Part of Potomac Hd. (three taxables) in 1777 [Ref: R-31:15].

OFFUTT, Natt., of Edward. Private, 6th Co., Lower Bn., Militia, Aug., 1777 [Ref: M-200, T-5:49].

OFFUTT, Rebecca. See "James Offutt," q.v.

OFFUTT, Rezin. Private, 6th Co., Lower Bn., Militia, Aug., 1777, and Second Sergeant, 3rd Co., Lower Bn., July 15, 1780 [Ref: M-200, M-204, T-5:49]. Took the Oath of Allegiance before the Hon. Joseph Offutt on March 2, 1778 [Ref: T-3:70, L-1:44].

OFFUTT, Samuel. (1) Private, 5th Co., Middle Bn., Militia, Sep., 1777 [Ref: M-197, T-5:40]. (2) Private, 3rd Co., Middle Bn., Militia, Sep., 1777 [Ref: M-196, T-5:38]. (3) Second Lieutenant, Middle Bn., Militia, April 21, 1779, and First Lieutenant, 2nd Co., Middle Bn., July 15, 1780 [Ref: M-108, M-201, E-357, F-248]. Took the Oath of Allegiance before the Hon. William Deakins, Jr. before March 3, 1778 [Ref: T-3:68, L-1:44]. Rendered aid by providing wheat for use of the military in 1780 [Ref: O-299, O-313]. One Samuel Offutt married Elizabeth Ray in Montgomery County on Oct. 22, 1778 [Ref: K-2:520]. "Samuel Offutt" lived in the Upper Part of Potomac Hd. (four taxables) in 1777 [Ref: R-31:15], and "Samuel Offutt, son of William" was a constable in the Upper Part of Potomac Hd., 1779-1781 [Ref: W-1, W-2]. "Samuel C. Offutt" died testate in Montgomery County (not married) in 1811 and mentioned his mother Margaret and deceased father (not named) and brothers Zephaniah Burgess Offutt and Zachariah Offutt [Ref: V-102].

OFFUTT, Sarah. See "John Young," q.v.

OFFUTT, Thomas. Private, 6th Co., Lower Bn., Militia, Aug., 1777 [Ref: M-200, T-5:49]. Took the Oath of Allegiance before the Hon. Joseph Offutt on March 2, 1778 [Ref: T-3:70, L-1:44].

OFFUTT, Thomas Jr. Private, 6th Co., Lower Bn., Militia, Aug., 1777 [Ref: M-200, T-5:49]. Private, 3rd Co., Lower Bn., Militia, July 15, 1780 [Ref: M-205].

OFFUTT, Thomas Sr. (c1731-1800). Private, 3rd Co., Lower Bn., Militia, July 15, 1780 [Ref: M-205]. Took the Oath of Allegiance before the Hon. Joseph Offutt on March 2, 1778 [Ref: T-3:70, L-1:44]. Died testate in

Montgomery County (wife not named) in 1800 [Ref: V-102]. Thomas Offutt married Elizabeth Luckett [Ref: DAR-I:503].

OFFUTT, William. Private, 6th Co., Lower Bn., Militia, Aug., 1777 [Ref: M-200, T-5:49]. Took the Oath of Allegiance before the Hon. Joseph Offutt on March 2, 1778 [Ref: T-3:70, L-1:44]. Private, 3rd Co., Lower Bn., Militia, July 15, 1780 [Ref: M-205]. Rendered aid by providing wheat for use of the military in 1780 [Ref: O-308]. "William Offutt (James)" [sic] lived in the Upper Part of Potomac Hd. (one taxable) in 1777 [Ref: R-31:15].

OFFUTT, William Jr. (died 1786). Took the Oath of Allegiance before the Hon. Joseph Offutt on March 2, 1778 [Ref: T-3:70, L-1:44]. Died testate in Montgomery County (wife not named) in 1786 [Ref: V-103].

OFFUTT, William 3rd (died 1810). Private, 6th Co., Lower Bn., Militia, Aug., 1777 [Ref: M-200 and T-5:49, which latter source listed the name as "William Offutt 2nd"]. "William Offutt 3rd" took the Oath of Allegiance before the Hon. Joseph Offutt on March 2, 1778 [Ref: T-3:70, L-1:44]. "William Offutt 3rd" lived in the Upper Part of Potomac Hd. (eight taxables) in 1777 [Ref: R-31:15]. "William Offutt III" died testate in Montgomery County (wife not named) in 1810 [Ref: V-103].

OFFUTT, William M. "William M. Offutt" was a private, 5th Co., Middle Bn., Militia, Sep., 1777 [Ref: M-197, T-5:40]. "William Mackle [Mockbe?] Offutt" took the Oath of Allegiance before the Hon. Joseph Wilson on Feb. 28, 1778 [Ref: T-3:64, L-1:44]. "William M. Offutt" rendered aid by providing wheat for use of the military in 1780 [Ref: O-315]. "William Mockbee Offutt" married Alley Thrift in Montgomery County on Nov. 26, 1778 [Ref: K-2:520]. "William M. Offutt" lived in the Upper Part of Potomac Hd. (two taxables) in 1777 [Ref: R-31:15].

OFFUTT, Zachariah. (1) Private, 5th Co., Middle Bn., Militia, Sep., 1777 [Ref: M-197, T-5:40]. (2) Private, 6th Co., Lower Bn., Militia, Aug., 1777 [Ref: M-200, T-5:49]. Served as a petit juror in Aug., 1777 [Ref: R-31:17]. Took the Oath of Allegiance before the Hon. Joseph Wilson on Feb. 28, 1778 [Ref: T-3:64, L-1:44]. "Zachy. Offutt" lived in the Upper Part of Potomac Hd. (six taxables) in 1777 [Ref: R-31:15]. "Zachariah Offutt" died testate in Montgomery County (unmarried) in 1815 [Ref: V-103]. See "Samuel Offutt," q.v.

OFFUTT, Zadock (Zadox). Private, 3rd Co., Lower Bn., Militia, July 15, 1780 [Ref: M-205]. "Zadox Offutt" took the Oath of Allegiance before the Hon. Joseph Offutt on March 2, 1778 [Ref: T-3:70, L-1:44]. Rendered aid by providing wheat for use of the military in 1780 and 1781 [Ref: O-313, O-395]. Constable in Middle Potomac Hd. in 1781 [Ref: W-2]. "Zadock Offutt" lived in the Upper Part of Potomac Hd. (two taxables) in 1777 [Ref: R-31:15].

OFFUTT, Zephaniah (1754-1796). Private, 6th Co., Lower Bn., Militia, Aug., 1777 [Ref: M-200, T-5:49]. Served as a grand juror in Nov., 1777 [Ref: R-31:18]. Took the Oath of Allegiance before the Hon. Thomas

Sprigg Wootton on March 3, 1778 [Ref: T-3:79, L-1:44]. Lived in the Upper Part of Potomac Hd. (three taxables) in 1777 [Ref: R-31:15]. Zephaniah was born on Aug. 14, 1754, married (1) Lucy Beall, and (2) Margaret Butler on Aug. 24, 1780, rendered civil and patriotic service, and died testate on Feb. 3, 1796 [Ref: K-2:520, DAR-I:503, V-104]. See "Samuel Offutt," q.v.

OGDEN, David (b. 1761 or 1762). Son of Hugh Ogden. Private, 7th Co., Upper Bn., Militia, Aug. 30, 1777 [Ref: M-195]. Lived in Sugarland Hd. in 1776 [Ref: K-1:216].

OGDEN, Hugh. Private, 7th Co., Upper Bn., Militia, Aug. 30, 1777 [Ref: M-195, which listed this name twice]. "Hugh Ogdon, or Heugh Ogden, aged 54" lived in Sugarland Hd. in 1776-1777 and had a son Hugh, aged 12, among others [Ref: K-1:216, R-31:13].

OGDEN, John. Private, 2nd Class, 2nd Co., Middle Bn., Militia, July 15, 1780 [Ref: M-201].

OGDEN, Joseph. Private, 1st Class, 2nd Co., Middle Bn., Militia, July 15, 1780 [Ref: M-201]. Joseph Ogden married Winfred Simms in Montgomery County on Jan. 10, 1781 [Ref: K-2:520].

OGDEN, Mary. See "William Sparrow," q.v.

OGDEN, Thomas. Private, 7th Co., Middle Bn., Militia, July 15, 1780 [Ref: M-203].

OGLE, Thomas. Took the Oath of Allegiance in 1778 [Ref: L-2:28].

O'HARRA, Patrick. Private, Capt. Thomas Beall's Co., Maryland Line, 1780 [Ref: D-350].

O'HAVIN, Christ. Took the Oath of Allegiance in 1778 [Ref: L-2:28].

O'HAVIN, Conrad. Took the Oath of Allegiance in 1778 [Ref: L-2:28].

OLIVER, John. Private, 7th Maryland Line, from Nov. 15, 1777 until Aug. 16, 1780, when reported missing at the Battle of Camden [Ref: D-236].

OLIVER, Laurence. Took the Oath of Allegiance before the Hon. Elisha Williams on March 2, 1778 [Ref: T-3:82].

OLIVER, William. Private, 2nd Co., Middle Bn., Militia, Sep. 4, 1777 [Ref: M-196, T-5:37]. Took the Oath of Allegiance before the Hon. Aneas Campbell on March 2, 1778 [Ref: T-3:77, L-1:44].

O'NEAL (O'NEILL, O'NEALE), Barton (b. 1760). Son of John O'Neal, of Sugarland Hd., in 1776 [Ref: K-1:219]. "Barton O'Neale" took the Oath of Allegiance before the Hon. Edward Burgess on Feb. 28, 1778 [Ref: T-3:63, L-1:43]. "Barton O'Neill" was a private, 7th Co., Upper Bn., Militia, Aug. 30, 1777 [Ref: M-194].

O'NEAL (O'NEALL), Charles. "Charles O'Neall" was a private, 1st Co., Middle Bn., Militia, Aug. 30, 1777 [Ref: M-195]. "Charles O'Neal" took the Oath of Allegiance before the Hon. Gerrard Briscoe on March 2, 1778 [Ref: T-3:56, L-1:43]. Lived in Seneca Hd. (one taxable) in 1777 [Ref: R-31:8].

O'NEAL (O'NEILL, O'NEALL, O'NEALE), David. "David O'Neall" was a private, 2nd Co., Lower Bn., Militia, July 15, 1780 [Ref: M-204]. "David

O'Neill" was a private, 5th Co., Lower Bn., Militia, Aug., 1777 [Ref: M-199, T-5:48]. "David O'Neale" recruited William Medley in March, 1781 [Ref: R-33:155, X-1146]. "David Oneal" lived in the Upper Part of Potomac Hd. (one taxable) in 1777 [Ref: R-31:15].

O'NEAL (O'NEILL, O'NEALL), Henry (died 1817). "Henry O'Neall" was an Ensign, Middle Bn., Militia, Sep. 12, 1777 [Ref: M-108, M-196, T-5:40, C-373], and First Lieutenant, 1st Co., Middle Bn., Militia, July 15, 1780 [Ref: M-201]. "Henry O'Neill" took the Oath of Allegiance before the Hon. Joseph Wilson on Feb. 28, 1778 [Ref: T-3:64, L-1:43]. "Henry Oneal" lived in the Upper Part of Potomac Hd. in 1777 [Ref: R-31:15]. "Henry O'Neale" died testate in Montgomery County (unmarried) in 1817 [Ref: V-104].

O'NEAL, James. Took the Oath of Allegiance before the Hon. Edward Burgess on Feb. 28, 1778 [Ref: T-3:63, L-1:43].

O'NEAL (O'NEILL, O'NAILL, O'NEALL), John. "John O'Neall" was a private, 5th Co., Middle Bn., Militia, Sep., 1777 [Ref: M-197, T-5:40], and a Private, 5th Class, 1st Co., Middle Bn., Militia, July 15, 1780 [Ref: M-201]. "John O'Naill" took the Oath of Allegiance (made his mark) before the Hon. Joseph Wilson on Feb. 28, 1778 [Ref: T-3:66, L-1:43]. "John O'Neill" rendered aid by providing wheat for use of the military in 1780 [Ref: O-304]. "John Oneal or O'Neal" lived in Sugarland Hd. in 1776 (wife named Margaret) and had three taxables in 1777 [Ref: K-1:219, R-31:13]. One John O'Neal married Mary Smith in Montgomery County on Dec. 23, 1777 [Ref: K-2:516]. One "John O'Neale" died testate in Montgomery County (wife not named) in 1785, and another "John O'Neale" died testate (wife named Eliza Henrietta) in 1818 [Ref: V-105].

O'NEAL (O'NEILL, O'NEALE), Laurence (1738-1815). Son of William O'Neale who probably immigrated from Pennsylvania to Prince George's County, Maryland, and married Elinor Ball, daughter of Thomas Ball, tailor. Laurence married Henrietta Brooke, widow of Clement Brooke, Jr., and daughter of Charles Neale (Neill) of Montgomery County, and had children: Henry, John, Mary Anne, and Eleanor. Laurence was Sheriff of Frederick County, 1773-1774, Tax Commissioner of Montgomery County, 1779, Court Justice, 1787-1797, and served in the Lower House from Montgomery County, 1780-1796. Lawrence took the Oath of Allegiance before the Hon. Elisha Williams on March 2, 1778, and also served as a militia recruiter in 1781 [Ref: T-3:81, L-1:43, N-623, which latter source contains more biographical information]. "Lawrence O'Neale" rendered aid by providing corn for use of the military in 1780 and 1781 [Ref: O-288, O-292, O-396]. "Lawrence O'Neill" rendered aid by providing wheat for use of the military in 1780 [Ref: O-334]. "Lawrance Oneal" owned a working plantation ("quarter") in the Upper Part of Potomac Hd. in 1777 [Ref: R-31:15].

O'NEAL (O'NEILL), Peter (b. 1754). Son of John O'Neal, of Sugarland Hd., in 1776 [Ref: K-1:219]. Took the Oath of Allegiance before the Hon.

Elisha Williams on March 2, 1778 [Ref: T-3:81, L-1:43]. "Peter O'Neill" was a private, 8th Co., Upper Bn., Militia, Aug. 30, 1777 [Ref: M-195].
O'NEAL (O'NEILL, O'NAILL, O'NEALL), William. "William O'Neall" was a private, 5th Co., Middle Bn., Militia, Sep., 1777 [Ref: M-197, T-5:40]. Private, 8th Class, 1st Co., Middle Bn., Militia, July 15, 1780 [Ref: M-201]. "William O'Naill" took the Oath of Allegiance before the Hon. Joseph Wilson on Feb. 28, 1778 [Ref: T-3:64, L-1:43]. "William O'Neal" was an invalid pensioner living in Montgomery County in 1835 [Ref: J-16]."William O'Neill" rendered aid by providing wheat for use of the military in 1780 [Ref: O-307, O-313, O-329]. "William Oneal" lived in the Upper Part of Potomac Hd. (four taxables) in 1777 [Ref: R-31:15]. See "Laurence O'Neal," q.v.
O'NEILL, Joshua. Rendered aid by providing wheat for use of the military in 1780 [Ref: O-313].
ONERAH, Christopher. Private who was recruited to serve in the Continental Army in 1780 [Ref: D-342].
ORME, Aaron. Private, 7th Co., Lower Bn., Militia, Aug., 1777 [Ref: M-200, T-5:50]. Took the Oath of Allegiance (made his "X" mark) before the Hon. Edward Burgess on Feb. 28, 1778 [Ref: T-3:62, L-1:44]. Private, 4th Co., Lower Bn., Militia, July 15, 1780 [Ref: M-205]. Lived in Rock Creek Hd. (one taxable) in 1777 [Ref: R-31:16].
ORME, Albert. Private, 8th Co., Lower Bn., Militia, July 15, 1780 [Ref: T-5:29].
ORME, Archibald (June 4, 1730 - May 9, 1812). Served as a Captain, 16th Bn., Militia, June 25, 1776, and Colonel, Middle Bn., from March 1, 1779, to at least July 15, 1780 [Ref: M-108, A-515, C-373, E-310, M-196, M-201]. Lived in the Upper Part of Potomac Hd. (ten taxables) in 1777 [Ref: R-31:15]. Took the Oath of Allegiance before the Hon. William Deakins, Jr. before March 3, 1778 [Ref: T-3:68, L-1:44]. Rendered aid by providing wheat for use of the military in 1781 [Ref: O-373], and appointed Surveyor of the County on March 20, 1782 [Ref: I-107]. He married Elizabeth Johns [Ref: DAR-I:506].
ORME, Charles. Private, 7th Co., Lower Bn., Militia, Aug., 1777 [Ref: M-200, T-5:50]. Private, 7th Maryland Line, 1778-1780 [Ref: D-236].
ORME, Eli (Ellry). "Eli (Ely) Orme" was a private, 7th Co., Lower Bn., Militia, Aug., 1777, and First Sergeant, 4th Co., Lower Bn., July 15, 1780 [Ref: M-200, M-205, T-5:50]. "Ellry [Elley?] Orme" took the Oath of Allegiance before the Hon. Charles Jones on Jan. 10, 1778 [Ref: T-3:71, L-1:44].
ORME (ORMES), James. "James Orme" took the Oath of Allegiance before the Hon. Joseph Wilson on Feb. 28, 1778 [Ref: T-3:64, L-1:44]. "James Ormes" lived in the Upper Part of Potomac Hd. (six taxables) in 1777 [Ref: R-31:15]. See "Moses Orme," q.v.
ORME, Jeremiah. Private, 7th Co., Lower Bn., Militia, Aug., 1777, and Ensign, 4th Co., Lower Bn., July 15, 1780 [Ref: M-200, M-205, T-5:50].

Took the Oath of Allegiance before the Hon. Edward Burgess on Feb. 28, 1778 [Ref: T-3:59, L-1:44]. Jeremiah Orme lived in the Lower Part of Newfoundland Hd. (six taxables) in 1777 [Ref: R-31:5].

ORME, John. Private, 8th Co., Lower Bn., Militia, July 15, 1780 [Ref: M-207]. See "Thomas Beall, of George," q.v.

ORME, Lucy. Rendered aid by providing bacon for use of the military in 1781 [Ref: O-406].

ORME, Margaret. See "Walter Magruder," q.v.

ORME, Moses (died 1782). Served as a grand juror in Nov., 1777 [Ref: R-31:18]. Took the Oath of Allegiance before the Hon. Charles Jones on Jan. 10, 1778 [Ref: T-3:71, L-1:44]. Rendered aid by providing wheat for use of the military in 1780 [Ref: O-308]. Served as a grand juror in 1781 [Ref: W-2]. Lived in Rock Creek Hd. (four taxables) in 1777 [Ref: R-31:16]. Died testate in Montgomery County (wife named Priscilla) in 1782 and mentioned sons James, Moses, and Samuel Taylor Orme, among other children [Ref: V-106]. "Moses Orme, Jr." married twice: (1) Verlinda Taylor, and (2) Priscilla Taylor [Ref: DAR-I:506].

ORME, Nancy. See "Thomas Beall, of George," q.v.

ORME, Nathan. Private, Capt. Edward Burgess' Co., Lower District of Frederick (now Montgomery) County, Militia, July, 1776 [Ref: D-42].

ORME (ORAM), Peter. Private, 6th Maryland Line, from Jan. 12, 1777 until Jan. 12, 1780, when discharged [Ref: D-236].

ORME, Philip. Lived in the Lower Part of Newfoundland Hd. (two taxables) in 1777 [Ref: R-31:6]. Served as a petit juror in Nov., 1777 [Ref: R-31:18]. Private, 4th Co., Lower Bn., Militia, July 15, 1780 [Ref: M-205]. Took the Oath of Allegiance before the Hon. Charles Jones on Jan. 10, 1778 [Ref: T-3:71, L-1:44].

ORME, Priscilla. See "Moses Orme," q.v.

ORME, Robert (1744-1820). Private, 1st Co., Lower Bn., Militia, Sep., 1777 [Ref: M-198, T-5:44]. Lived in the Lower Part of Newfoundland Hd. (two taxables) in 1777 [Ref: R-31:6]. Took the Oath of Allegiance before the Hon. Edward Burgess on Feb. 28, 1778 [Ref: T-3:61, L-1:44]. Private, 7th Co., Lower Bn., Militia, July 15, 1780 [Ref: M-206]. Robert was born on Aug. 12, 1744, married Priscilla Edmonston, and died on Sep. 13, 1820 [Ref: DAR-I:506].

ORME, Samuel J. Private, 7th Co., Lower Bn., Militia, Aug., 1777 [Ref: M-200 and T-5:50, which latter source listed the name as "Samuel I. Orme"].

ORME, Samuel Taylor (1750-1817). Son of Moses Orme [Ref: V-106]. Private, Capt. Edward Burgess' Co., Lower District of Frederick (now Montgomery) County, Militia, July, 1776 [Ref: D-42]. Samuel Taylor Orme married Mary Ransom [Ref: DAR-I:506].

ORME (ORUM), Zachariah. Private, 1st or 32nd Bn., Militia (no date was given; possibly June, 1777). [Ref: T-5:1].

ORNDORFF, Conrad. Took the Oath of Allegiance in 1778 [Ref: L-2:28].

255

ORR, John. Private, 8th Co., Lower Bn., Militia, July 15, 1780 [Ref: M-207].

OSBORN (OSBIN), Archibald (b. 1761). Son of William Osborn, of North West Hd., in 1776 [Ref: K-1:225]. Private, 6th Co., Lower Bn., Militia, July 15, 1780 [Ref: M-206].

OSBORN (ORSBON), William. "William Osborn" was a private, 3rd Maryland Regiment, from Aug. 15, 1777 until Jan. 24, 1778, when reported dead [Ref: D-148]. "William Ozburn, aged 53" lived in North West Hd. in 1776 [Ref: K-1:225], and "William Orsbon" lived in North West Hd. (one taxable) in 1777 [Ref: R-31:17].

OUCHTERLONY, Patrick. See "Patrick Auchterlony," q.v.

OWEN, Edward (died 1815). Private, 5th Co., Lower Bn., Militia, July 15, 1780 [Ref: M-206]. Died testate in Montgomery County (wife named Rachel) in 1815 [Ref: V-106].

OWEN, Eleanor. See "Robert Beall Crawford," q.v.

OWEN, John. Private, 6th Co., Middle Bn., Militia, July 15, 1780 [Ref: M-203]. Two men with this name took the Oath of Allegiance: one before the Hon. Elisha Williams on March 2, 1778 [Ref: T-3:80, L-1:44], and another before the Hon. Edward Burgess on Feb. 12, 1778 [Ref: T-3:59, L-1:44]. One John Owen married Elizabeth McCallam in Montgomery County on Feb. 2, 1778 [Ref: K-2:520]. "John Owen, Sr." lived in the Upper Part of Newfoundland Hd. (three taxables) in 1777 [Ref: R-31:7], and "John Owen, aged 70" lived in Sugarland Hd. (three taxables) in 1776-1777 [Ref: K-1:199, R-31:13].

OWEN, John Jr. Private, 6th Co., Middle Bn., Militia, Aug., 1777 [Ref: M-197, T-5:41]. Took the Oath of Allegiance before the Hon. Edward Burgess on Feb. 28, 1778 [Ref: T-3:59, L-1:44]. Also see "John Owen," q.v.

OWEN, Lawrence. "Lawrance Owen" was a private, 2nd Co., Upper Bn., Militia, Aug. 30, 1777 [Ref: M-193]. "Lawrence Owen" lived in Sugar Loaf Hd. (one taxable) in 1777 [Ref: R-31:10]. "Laurence Owen" married Sarah Hardy in Montgomery County on June 22, 1780 [Ref: K-2:520].

OWEN, Richard. Private, 2nd Co., Upper Bn., Militia, Aug. 30, 1777 [Ref: M-193].

OWEN, Robert. Served as a Captain, 16th Bn., Militia, May 20, 1776, and Major, Middle Bn., Militia, from March 1, 1779, to at least Jan. 31, 1781 [Ref: M-109, M-197, A-432, C-373, E-210, R-33:155, T-5:41]. "Captain Robert Owen" and another "Robert Owen" both took the Oath of Allegiance before the Hon. Edward Burgess on Feb. 28, 1778 [Ref: T-3:58, L-1:44]. "Major Robert Owen" rendered aid by providing wheat for use of the military in 1781 [Ref: O-383]. "Robert Owens" rendered aid by providing wheat for use of the military in 1780 [Ref: O-319]. "Robert Owen" lived in Rock Creek Hd. (nine taxables) in 1777 [Ref: R-31:16]. Major Robert Owen was born in 1730 or 1731 and died testate in

Montgomery County in 1779 (wife named Mary Ann Edmonston) and mentioned a son Robert, among others [Ref: V-107, DAR-I:509].

OWEN, Thomas. (1) Private, 2nd Co., Lower Bn., Militia, Sep., 1777 [Ref: M-198, T-5:45]. (2) Private, 8th Co., Upper Bn., Militia, Aug. 30, 1777 [Ref: M-195]. One was a Second Lieutenant, 6th Co., Middle Bn., July 15, 1780 [Ref: M-203]. One served as a petit juror in Nov., 1777 [Ref: R-31:18]. One took the Oath of Allegiance before the Hon. Edward Burgess on Feb. 28, 1778 [Ref: T-3:59, L-1:44]. One Thomas Owen married Sarah McCauley in Montgomery County on Nov. 25, 1780 [Ref: K-2:520]. "Thomas Owen, aged 17" lived in Sugarland Hd. in 1776, and a Thomas Owen lived in Rock Creek Hd. (four taxables) in 1777 [Ref: K-1:199, R-31:16].

OWEN, William. Private, 6th Co., Middle Bn., Militia, Aug., 1777 [Ref: M-197, T-5:41]. Took the Oath of Allegiance before the Hon. Edward Burgess on Feb. 28, 1778 [Ref: T-3:59, L-1:44]. Private, 6th Co., Middle Bn., Militia, July 15, 1780 [Ref: M-203]. Rendered aid by providing wheat for use of the military in 1781 [Ref: O-378]. Lived in Linganore Hd. (two taxables) in 1777 [Ref: R-31:9].

OWENS, John Sr. See "John Smith," q.v.

OWLER (OWLE), Daniel. Took the Oath of Allegiance in 1778 [Ref: L-2:28].

OWLER, Andrew. Took the Oath of Allegiance in 1778 [Ref: L-2:28].

OWLER, Philip. Took the Oath of Allegiance in 1778 [Ref: L-2:28].

OZMAN, Archibald. Rendered aid by providing wheat for use of the military in 1780 [Ref: O-256].

PACK, Richard. Private, 1st Co., Middle Bn., Militia, Aug. 30, 1777 [Ref: M-195]. Took the Oath of Allegiance before the Hon. Gerrard Briscoe on March 2, 1778 [Ref: T-3:57, L-1:44]. See "Thomas Pack," q.v.

PACK, Thomas. Private, 1st Co., Middle Bn., Militia, Aug. 30, 1777 [Ref: M-195, T-5:36]. Took the Oath of Allegiance before the Hon. Gerrard Briscoe on March 2, 1778 [Ref: T-3:56, L-1:44]. "Thomas Pack" lived in Seneca Hd. (two taxables) in 1777 [Ref: R-31:8]. "Thomas Pack, Sr." died testate in Montgomery County (wife named Christena) in 1804 and mentioned sons Thomas and Richard, among others [Ref: V-107].

PACK, Valentine. Private, 7th Co., Lower Bn., Militia, July 15, 1780 [Ref: M-206].

PACK, William Jr. Private, 1st Co., Middle Bn., Militia, Aug. 30, 1777 [Ref: M-195, T-5:36].

PACK, William Sr. Private, 1st Co., Middle Bn., Militia, Aug. 30, 1777 [Ref: M-195, T-5:36]. Took the Oath of Allegiance before the Hon. Gerrard Briscoe on March 2, 1778 [Ref: T-3:56, L-1:44]. "William Pack" lived in Seneca Hd. (one taxable) in 1777 [Ref: R-31:8].

PAGE, Jesse. Private, 6th Co., Middle Bn., Militia, Aug., 1777 [Ref: M-197, T-5:41]. "Jessey Page" took the Oath of Allegiance (made his "X" mark) before the Hon. Edward Burgess on Feb. 28, 1778 [Ref: T-3:60, L-1:44].

PAGNO, Nicholas. "Nichos Pigno(?)" [sic] was a private, 4th Class, 4th Co., Middle Bn., Militia, July 15, 1780 [Ref: M-202]. "Nicholas Pagno" died testate in Montgomery County (wife not named) in 1814 [Ref: V-107].

PAINTER, George. Took the Oath of Allegiance in 1778 [Ref: L-2:28].

PAINTER (PANTER), Jacob. Took the Oath of Allegiance in 1778 [Ref: L-2:28].

PAINTER (PANTER), Peter. Took the Oath of Allegiance in 1778 [Ref: L-2:28].

PALMER, Jacob. Private, Capt. Thomas Beall's Co., Maryland Line, 1780 [Ref: D-351].

PALMER, Jonathan. Private, 7th Co., Middle Bn., Militia, July 15, 1780 [Ref: M-203].

PALMER, Michael. Private, 6th Maryland Line, from May 31, 1777 until Aug. 16, 1780, when reported missing at the Battle of Camden [Ref: D-238].

PALMER, Samuel. Served as a Corporal, 6th Maryland Line, from April 5, 1777 until April 5, 1780, when he was discharged [Ref: D-238].

PANCOAST (PENCOAST), Adin (Oden). "Adin Pencoast" was a private, 3rd Co., Middle Bn., Militia, Sep., 1777 [Ref: M-196, T-5:38]. "Oden Pancoast" took the Oath of Allegiance before the Hon. William Deakins, Jr. before March 3, 1778 [Ref: T-3:68, L-1:44]. "Adin Pancoast" lived in the Upper Part of Potomac Hd. (four taxables) in 1777 [Ref: R-31:15].

PANCOAST (PENCOAST), John. "John Pancoast" lived in the Upper Part of Newfoundland Hd. (two taxables) in 1777 [Ref: R-31:7]. "John Pencoast" was a private, 8th Co., Middle Bn., Militia, Sep., 1777 [Ref: M-198, T-5:43]. "John Pancoast" was a private, 6th Class, 4th Co., Middle Bn., Militia, July 15, 1780 [Ref: M-202].

PANCOAST (PENCOAST), William. "William Pancoast" lived in the Upper Part of Newfoundland Hd. (one taxable) in 1777 [Ref: R-31:7]. "William Pencoast" was a private, 8th Co., Middle Bn., Militia, Sep., 1777 [Ref: M-198, T-5:43]. "William Pancoast" was a private, 7th Class, 4th Co., Middle Bn., Militia, July 15, 1780 [Ref: M-202].

PARADISE (PARIDICE), James. Private, 4th Co., Middle Bn., Militia, Sep., 1777 [Ref: M-196, T-5:39]. Private, 4th Class, 4th Co., Middle Bn., Militia, July 15, 1780 [Ref: M-202]. "James Paridice" took the Oath of Allegiance before the Hon. Edward Burgess on Feb. 28, 1778 [Ref: T-3:62, L-1:44]. "James Parradise" lived in the Upper Part of Newfoundland Hd. in 1777 [Ref: R-31:7].

PARADISE, William. Private, 2nd Class, 4th Co., Middle Bn., Militia, July 15, 1780 [Ref: M-202].

PARISH (PARISS), Nimrod. Private, 8th Co., Lower Bn., Militia, Sep., 1777 [Ref: M-200, T-5:51]. "Nimrod Parish" took the Oath of Allegiance before the Hon. Edward Burgess on Feb. 28, 1778 [Ref: T-3:62, L-1:44]. "Nimrod Pariss" lived in Rock Creek Hd. (one taxable) in 1777 [Ref: R-31:16].

PARKER, Doctor. Rendered aid by providing wheat for use of the military in 1780 [Ref: O-322].

PARKER, George. Private, Capt. Thomas Beall's Co., Maryland Line, 1780 [Ref: D-351].

PARKER, Mary. See "Vachel Harding," q.v.

PARKER, William. Served as a grand juror in Nov., 1777 [Ref: R-31:17]. Took the Oath of Allegiance before the Hon. Richard Thompson in 1778 [Ref: T-3:75, L-1:44]. There was a William Parker who was a private in the 7th Maryland Line from Jan. 16, 1777 until Jan. 12, 1780, when discharged [Ref: D-239]. "William Parker, R. C." (b. 1731) lived in Lower Potomac Hd. in 1776 and William Parker lived in Lower Potomac Hd. (five taxables) in 1777 [Ref: K-1:185, R-31:4].

PARRE, Alexander. Rendered aid by providing wheat for use of the military in 1781 [Ref: O-386].

PATRICK, Anne. See "Jonathan Madden," q.v.

PATRICK, John. Served as a private when enrolled into a company of militia for the service of the Flying Camp on Oct. 15, 1776 [Ref: B-352]. Private, 2nd Co., Upper Bn., Militia, Aug. 30, 1777 [Ref: M-193]. Took the Oath of Allegiance before the Hon. Elisha Williams on March 2, 1778 [Ref: T-3:80, L-1:44].

PATRICK (PARTRICK), William. "William Patrick" took the Oath of Allegiance before the Hon. Elisha Williams on March 2, 1778 [Ref: T-3:80, L-1:44]. "William Partrick" lived in Sugar Loaf Hd. (two taxables) in 1777 [Ref: R-31:10].

PATTERSON, John. Private, Capt. Price's Co., 3rd Maryland Line, 1781-1782 [Ref: D-453].

PATTERSON (PATERSON), Joseph. Took the Oath of Allegiance in 1778 [Ref: L-2:28].

PATTERSON (PATERSON), Robert. Took the Oath of Allegiance in 1778 [Ref: L-2:28].

PATTERSON, William. Private, 5th Co., Middle Bn., Militia, July 15, 1780 [Ref: M-203].

PAUGH, Michael and Nancy. See "Norman Bruce Magruder," q.v.

PAUL (PAULL), Nicholas (b. 1738). "Nicholas Paull" was a private, 3rd Co., Lower Bn., Militia, Sep., 1777 [Ref: M-199, T-5:46]. Took the Oath of Allegiance before the Hon. Richard Thompson in 1778 [Ref: T-3:76, L-1:44]. "Nicholas or Nicholls Paul" lived in George Town Hd. (two taxables) in 1776-1777 [Ref: K-1:194, R-31:3].

PAYNE, Frail [sic]. Took the Oath of Allegiance in 1778 [Ref: L-2:28].

PAYNE, Francis. Private, 2nd Class, 1st Co., Middle Bn., Militia, July 15, 1780 [Ref: M-201].

PAYNE (PAIN), George. Took the Oath of Allegiance in 1778 [Ref: L-2:28].

PAYNE (PAINE), John. Private, 8th Class, 1st Co., Middle Bn., Militia, July 15, 1780 [Ref: M-201]. One John Payne married Mary Bever in Montgomery County on July 16, 1780 [Ref: K-2:514].

PEAK (PEACK), Benjamin. Private, 2nd Class, 1st Co., Middle Bn., Militia, July 15, 1780 [Ref: M-201]. Private, 5th Co., Middle Bn., Militia, Sep., 1777 [Ref: M-197, T-5:40]. "Benjamin Peack" took the Oath of Allegiance before the Hon. Joseph Wilson on Feb. 28, 1778 [Ref: T-3:64, L-1:44]. "Benjamin Peak" married Cassandra Trail in Montgomery County on Dec. 14, 1779 [Ref: K-2:520].

PEAK, Hezekiah. Private, 5th Co., Middle Bn., Militia, July 15, 1780 [Ref: M-203].

PEAK (PEACK), James. "James Peak" was a private, 7th Co., Middle Bn., Militia, Sep., 1777 [Ref: M-197, T-5:42]. "James Peack" took the Oath of Allegiance (made his "X" mark) before the Hon. Joseph Wilson on Feb. 28, 1778 [Ref: T-3:67, L-1:44, which latter source misspelled the name "Peach"].

PEAK (PEACK), Lewis. "Lewis Peak" served as a private, 5th Co., Middle Bn., Militia, Sep., 1777 [Ref: M-197, T-5:40], and was Fourth Sergeant, 1st Co., Middle Bn., Militia, July 15, 1780 [Ref: M-201]. "Lewis Peack" took the Oath of Allegiance before the Hon. Joseph Wilson on Feb. 28, 1778 [Ref: T-3:64, L-1:44].

PEAK, Samuel. Private, 5th Co., Middle Bn., Militia, July 15, 1780 [Ref: M-203]. Private, 5th Co., Middle Bn., Militia, Sep., 1777 [Ref: M-197, T-5:40]. Lived in the Upper Part of Potomac Hd. (one taxable) in 1777 [Ref: R-31:15].

PEAK (PEACK), Thomas. Lived in the Upper Part of Potomac Hd. (two taxables) in 1777 [Ref: R-31:15]. Private, 7th Class, 1st Co., Middle Bn., Militia, July 15, 1780 [Ref: M-201]. Private, 5th Co., Middle Bn., Militia, Sep., 1777 [Ref: M-197, T-5:40]. "Thomas Peack" took the Oath of Allegiance before the Hon. Joseph Wilson on Feb. 28, 1778 [Ref: T-3:64, L-1:44]. He married Elizabeth Keymer in Montgomery County on Dec. 23, 1777 [Ref: K-2:516].

PEARCE, Benjamin Notley (1728-1792). Private, 3rd Co., Lower Bn., Militia, Sep., 1777 [Ref: M-199, T-5:46]. Took the Oath of Allegiance before the Hon. Richard Thompson in 1778 [Ref: T-3:75, L-1:44]. "Benjamin Nolley Pearce" [sic] lived in George Town Hd. in 1776 and "Benjamin N. Pearce" lived there (two taxables) in 1777 [Ref: K-1:194, R-31:3]. "Benjamin Notley Pearce, of Georgetown" died testate in Montgomery County (wife named Katherine) in 1792 [Ref: V-107].

PEARCE, Catherine. See "Ralph Knott," q.v.

PEARCE (PIERCE), Henry. "Henry Pearce" was a private, 7th Co., Lower Bn., Militia, Aug., 1777 [Ref: M-200, T-5:50]. "Henry Pierce" was a private, 6th Co., Lower Bn., Militia, July 15, 1780 [Ref: M-206].

PEARCE (PIERCE), Henry Culver (died 1814). "Henry Culver Pearce" was named in the will of "Benjamin Notley Pearce," q.v., as the eldest son of John Pearce, deceased [Ref: V-107]. "Henry Culver Pierce" rendered aid by providing wheat for use of the military in 1780 [Ref: O-332]. "Henry C. Peerce" died testate in Montgomery County (wife named Elizabeth) in 1814 and mentioned several children surnamed Peerce and Higdon who were in Kentucky when he wrote his will in March, 1812 [Ref: V-108].

PEARCE (PEIRCE), John Baptis or Babtis. "John Baptis Peirce, aged 22" lived in North West Hd. in 1776 and his mother Margratt, aged 55, was head of household [Ref: K-1:225]. "Babtis Pearce" was a private, 7th Co., Lower Bn., Militia, Aug., 1777 [Ref: M-200, T-5:50]. "John Baptist Peere" [sic] took the Oath of Allegiance before the Hon. Edward Burgess on Feb. 28, 1778 [Ref: T-3:62, L-1:44].

PEARCE (PIERCE), Nicholas (b. 1736). Lived in Lower Potomac Hd. in 1776 [Ref: K-1:185]. Private, 4th Co., Lower Bn., Militia, Aug., 1777 [Ref: M-199, T-5:47].

PEARCE (PIERCE), Thomas Jr. Private, 8th Co., Lower Bn., Militia, July 15, 1780 [Ref: M-207].

PEARRE, Alexander. See "Alexander Perry (Pearre)," q.v.

PEASEY, Nancy. See "John Miller," q.v.

PECK, Johan. See "Abraham Fields," q.v.

PECK, Mary and Richard. See "James Allnutt," q.v.

PECK, Thomas. Rendered aid by providing wheat for use of the military in 1780 [Ref: O-329].

PECK, William Sr. Private, 1st Class, 5th Co., Middle Bn., Militia, July 15, 1780 [Ref: M-202].

PECKINBAUGH, George Leonard. "George Lo. Pickenbaugh" took the Oath of Allegiance in 1778 [Ref: L-2:28]. See "Leonard Peckinbaugh," q.v.

PECKINBAUGH (BECKENBAUGH), Leonard (1761-1842). Rendered aid by providing flour for use by the military in 1780 in Montgomery County [Ref: O-344]. His military service is noted in his pension papers when he applied in Union County, Indiana on Sep. 9, 1833, aged 72, stating he had enlisted in Frederick County, Maryland, and 19 years after his discharge he moved to Fayette County, Pennsylvania, and in 1822 he moved to Union County, Indiana. He and wife, Catharine Shroyer, moved to Lebanon County, Ohio, in April, 1839, and he died there at his son Michael's home on Nov. 12, 1842. His widow applied for pension (W4122) on Aug. 30, 1848, aged 78, in Warren County, Ohio, stating they had married in 1786 when she was 16 years old. She died around May 6, 1857. Record also indicates Leonard Peckinbaugh (or Backenbaugh or Beckenbaugh), was a son of George Leonard Beckenbaugh of Frederick County, Maryland [Ref: P-107].

PECKINSON, Solomon. See "Solomon Dickerson (Dickenson)," q.v.

PEDDICOAT (PEDICORD), Caleb. Private, 1st or 32nd Bn., Militia (no date was given; possibly June, 1777). [Ref: T-5:1].
PEDDICOAT (PEDDICOART, PADDICORT), Jasper. Private, 7th Co., Middle Bn., Militia, Sep., 1777 [Ref: M-197, T-5:42]. "Jasper Paddicort" took the Oath of Allegiance before the Hon. Edward Burgess on Feb. 28, 1778 [Ref: T-3:60, L-1:44, which latter source misspelled the name "Paddicost"]. "Jasper Petticoat" lived in the Upper Part of Newfoundland Hd. (three taxables) in 1777 [Ref: R-31:7].
PEDDICOAT (PETTICOAT), Joseph. Rendered aid by providing wheat for use of the military in 1781 [Ref: O-380].
PEDDICOAT (PEDDICOART, PEDDICORD), Nicholas (b. 1750). Private, 8th Co., Upper Bn., Militia, Aug. 30, 1777 [Ref: M-195]. Took the Oath of Allegiance before the Hon. Aneas Campbell on March 2, 1778 [Ref: T-3:77, L-1:44, which source mistakenly listed his name as "Nicholas PeDeeomtz" probably due to illegible handwriting; it appears that the signature was actually "Pedecortz"]. "Nicholas Peddicoat" lived in Sugarland Hd. in 1776 and "Nicholas Peddicord" lived there and had three taxables in 1777 [Ref: K-1:214, R-31:13].
PEDDICOAT (PEDICORD), Thomas. Private, 1st or 32nd Bn., Militia (no date was given; possibly June, 1777). [Ref: T-5:1].
PEDDICOAT (PEDICORD), William. Private, 1st or 32nd Bn., Militia (no date was given; possibly June, 1777). [Ref: T-5:1].
PEDEN, Eva Coe. See "Solomon Dickerson," q.v.
PEDEN, Henry C. Jr. See "Mountjoy Bailey" and "Charles Beatty" and "Benjamin Burch" and "Michael Cochendorfer" and "Samuel Ellis" and "Benjamin Fitzgerald" and "Joshua Lazenby" and "Benjamin Penn" and "Jeremiah Plummer" and "Ninian Riley" and "John Smith" and "John Stinson" and "John Summers" and "Humphrey Beckett Tomlinson," q.v.
PEEK, Thomas. Rendered aid by providing wheat for use of the military in 1780 [Ref: O-307, O-313].
PEER, Philip. Took the Oath of Allegiance in 1778 [Ref: L-2:28].
PEGG, William. Private, 8th Co., Middle Bn., Militia, Sep., 1777 [Ref: M-197, T-5:43], and private, 7th Co., Middle Bn., Militia, July 15, 1780 [Ref: M-204].
PELLY, Calvert (Colbert). "Colbert Pelly" was a private, 1st Co., Middle Bn., Militia, Aug. 30, 1777 [Ref: M-195]. "Calvert Pelly" was a private, 5th Co., Middle Bn., Militia, July 15, 1780 [Ref: M-203]. "Calvert Pelley" lived in Seneca Hd. (two taxables) in 1777 [Ref: R-31:8].
PELLY (PELLA, PILLA), Harrison (died 1802). "Harrison Pelly" was a private, 3rd Co., Middle Bn., Militia, Sep., 1777 [Ref: M-196, T-5:38]. Took the Oath of Allegiance before the Hon. Edward Burgess on Feb. 28, 1778 [Ref: T-3:64, L-1:44]. "Harrisson Pella" was a private, 8th Class, 2nd Co., Middle Bn., Militia, July 15, 1780 [Ref: M-201]. "Harison Delly" [sic] rendered aid by providing wheat for use of the military in 1781 [Ref: O-392]. "Harrison Pilla" lived in the Upper Part of Potomac Hd.

(one taxable) in 1777 [Ref: R-31:15]. "Harrison Pelly" died testate in Montgomery County (wife named Mary) in 1802 [Ref: V-109].

PELLY (PILLA), James. Private, Flying Camp, Frederick (now Montgomery) County, enlisted by Greenbury Gaither on July 29, 1776 [Ref: D-44]. Private, 3rd Co., Middle Bn., Militia, Sep., 1777 [Ref: M-196, T-5:38]. Took the Oath of Allegiance before the Hon. William Deakins, Jr. before March 3, 1778 [Ref: T-3:68, L-1:44]. "James Pilla" lived in the Upper Part of Potomac Hd. (one taxable) in 1777 [Ref: R-31:15].

PENDER (PINDLE), Thomas (1757-1853). "Thomas Pender" was a private who was recruited to serve in the Extra Regiment of the Continental Army in 1780 [Ref: D-342]. "Thomas Pindle" lived in Sugar Loaf Hd. (eight taxables) in 1777 [Ref: R-31:10]. "Thomas Pender" applied for pension (R8085) on July 13, 1818, in Ohio County, Kentucky. In 1820 he was aged 63 and had one child of his own living with him (aged 2 years) and six stepchildren also with him (4 boys and 2 girls ranging in age from 6 to 21 years old), plus "his present wife Anna" who was aged 43. Thomas died on Jan. 14, 1853, in Ohio County, Kentucky, and his widow applied for pension on May 2, 1853, in Davies County, Kentucky, aged 80. She died on Aug. 3, 1853, leaving these children in 1854: Elijah C. Atherton, Miles M. Pender, and Rebecca Howard [Ref: P-2650, Y-15, Z-61].

PENDLEBERRY, Marmaduke. Took the Oath of Allegiance before the Hon. Edward Burgess on Feb. 28, 1778 [Ref: T-3:61, L-1:44]. Private, 3rd Maryland Line, from April 21, 1778 until Aug. 16, 1780, when reported missing at the Battle of Camden [Ref: D-152].

PENN (PEEN), Benjamin. (1) Private, 6th Co., Middle Bn., Militia, Aug., 1777 [Ref: M-197, T-5:41]. Private, 6th Co., Middle Bn., Militia, July 15, 1780 [Ref: M-203]. (2) Private, 1st Co., Lower Bn., Militia, Sep., 1777 [Ref: M-198, T-5:44]. Two men named "Benjamin Peen" took the Oath of Allegiance before the Hon. Edward Burgess on Feb. 28, 1778 [Ref: T-3:59, L-1:44], and one made his "B P" mark [Ref: T-3:60, L-1:44]. One Benjamin Penn married Rebecca Ryan in Montgomery County in 1774 (when she was 14 years old) and they subsequently moved to Henry County, Kentucky [Ref: Y-11, Z-37. For more information on this family, see Source P-2652, and *Marylanders to Kentucky, 1775-1825*, by Henry C. Peden, Jr. (1991), page 115, and *Revolutionary Patriots of Anne Arundel County, Maryland, 1775-1783*, by Henry C. Peden, Jr. (1992), page 150]. One Benjamin Penn lived in the Lower Part of Newfoundland Hd. (two taxables) in 1777 and another lived in Linganore Hd. (one taxable) in 1777 [Ref: R-31:6, R-31:9].

PENN (PEEN), Benjamin Davis. Private, 6th Co., Middle Bn., Militia, Aug., 1777 [Ref: M-197, T-5:41]. Private, 6th Co., Middle Bn., Militia, July 15, 1780 [Ref: M-203]. "Benjamin Davis Peen" took the Oath of

Allegiance before the Hon. Edward Burgess on Feb. 28, 1778 [Ref: T-3:60, L-1:44].

PENN, Caleb. Private, 6th Co., Middle Bn., Militia, Aug., 1777 [Ref: M-197, T-5:41]. Private, 6th Co., Middle Bn., Militia, July 15, 1780 [Ref: M-203]. Rendered aid by providing wheat for use of the military in 1781 [Ref: O-399].

PENN, Charles. (1) Second Lieutenant, 16th Bn., Militia, May 20, 1776 [Ref: M-110, A-432]. (2) Private, 6th Co., Middle Bn., Militia, Aug., 1777 [Ref: M-197, T-5:41]. Private, 6th Co., Middle Bn., Militia, July 15, 1780 [Ref: M-203]. One rendered aid by providing wheat for use of the military in 1781 [Ref: O-399]. One lived in the Upper Part of Newfoundland Hd. (five taxables) in 1777 [Ref: R-31:7].

PENN (PEEN), Edward. Private, 6th Co., Middle Bn., Militia, Aug., 1777 [Ref: M-197, T-5:41]. Private, 6th Co., Middle Bn., Militia, July 15, 1780 [Ref: M-203]. "Edward Peen" took the Oath of Allegiance before the Hon. Edward Burgess on Feb. 28, 1778 [Ref: T-3:59, L-1:44]. "Edward Penn" lived in the Upper Part of Newfoundland Hd. (three taxables) in 1777 [Ref: R-31:7].

PENN, Edward, of Edward. Private, 8th Co., Middle Bn., Militia, Sep., 1777 [Ref: M-197, T-5:43].

PENN (PEEN), John. Private, 6th Class, 4th Co., Middle Bn., Militia, July 15, 1780 [Ref: M-202]. Private, 4th Co., Middle Bn., Militia, Sep., 1777 [Ref: M-196, T-5:39]. "John Peen" took the Oath of Allegiance before the Hon. Edward Burgess on Feb. 28, 1778 [Ref: T-3:61, L-1:44]. "John Penn" rendered aid by providing wheat for use of the military in 1781 [Ref: O-421]. John Penn lived in the Upper Part of Newfoundland Hd. (two taxables) in 1777 [Ref: R-31:7].

PENN, Joseph. Private, 6th Co., Middle Bn., Militia, July 15, 1780 [Ref: M-203]. Private, 6th Co., Middle Bn., Militia, Aug., 1777 [Ref: M-197, T-5:41]. Rendered aid by providing wheat for use of the military in 1781 [Ref: O-399].

PENN, Michael. Private, 7th Maryland Line, 1780 [Ref: D-239].

PENN (PEEN), Shadrach (Shadrech). Private, Capt. Edward Burgess' Co., Lower District of Frederick (now Montgomery) County, Militia, July, 1776 [Ref: D-42].

PENNIFIELD (PENEFILL, PINFOLD), Thomas (1760-1832). "Thomas Pennifield" was a private, 2nd Maryland Line, who was recruited to serve in the Extra Regiment of the Continental Army in 1780, and "Thomas Pinfold" was a private, 3rd Maryland Regiment, in 1781 [Ref: D-342, D-355, D-393]. "Thomas Penefill" pensioned in 1818 and was aged 72 when he died on Dec. 15, 1832. "Heister Pennefill" was a pensioner in 1840, aged 71, living in the household of Asa Clagett in Montgomery County's Third Division [Ref: J-38, R-28:444]. In 1818, aged 57, Thomas stated he enlisted in 1780 under Capt. Benjamin Price and served in the 2nd Maryland Line for 3 years, during which time he was on board the sloop "Porpoise" as a marine and was in two battles at sea. He was also at the siege of Yorktown and was discharged in Annapolis in Aug., 1783. In 1820, aged 60, he stated he had a wife Eastor, aged 45, and 11 children: William (aged 29); Lucy (aged 26); Jane (aged 22); Thomas (aged 21); Martha (aged 19); Catharine (aged 17); Levy (aged 15); Joseph (aged 13); Anne (aged 11); Eleassor (aged 7); and, Airy (aged 5). Thomas died on Dec. 15, 1832, and his widow applied for pension (W9224) on July 1, 1839, in Montgomery County, Maryland, aged 64. She also applied for his bounty land warrant #29741-160-55 on May 4, 1855 [Ref: P-2651, Y-45, Y-46].

PENNY, John. Private, 2nd Maryland Line, 1780 [Ref: D-151].

PENNY (PENNA, PENNE), Joseph. "Joseph Penny" was a private, 2nd Co., Middle Bn., Militia, Sep. 4, 1777 [Ref: M-196, T-5:37]. Took the Oath of Allegiance before the Hon. Edward Burgess on Feb. 28, 1778 [Ref: T-3:63, L-1:44]. "Joseph Penna" was a private, 4th Class, 3rd Co., Middle Bn., Militia, July 15, 1780 [Ref: M-202]. "Joseph Penne" lived in Sugar Loaf Hd. (one taxable) in 1777 [Ref: R-31:10].

PERRY (PEARRE), Alexander (died 1804). Served as a petit juror in Aug., 1777 [Ref: R-31:17]. "Alexander Perry" lived in Sugar Loaf Hd. (three taxables) in 1777 [Ref: R-31:10]. "Alexander Pearre, Sr." died testate in Montgomery County (wife not named) in 1804 [Ref: V-108].

PERRY, Charles. Private, 3rd Co., Middle Bn., Militia, Sep., 1777 [Ref: M-196, T-5:38], and private, 2nd Maryland Line, from May 20, 1778 until March, 1779, when he was discharged [Ref: D-151]. Took the Oath of Allegiance before the Hon. Joseph Wilson on Feb. 28, 1778 [Ref: T-3:67, L-1:44]. One Charles Perry lived in Seneca Hd. (eight taxables) in 1777 [Ref: R-31:8], and another lived in Sugarland Hd. (one taxable) in 1777 [Ref: R-31:13]. One Charles Perry died testate in Montgomery County (wife named Priscilla) in 1819. "Priscilla Perry, relict of Charles Perry" died testate in Montgomery County in 1825 [Ref: V-109, V-110].

PERRY, Erasmus. Private, 2nd Co., Lower Bn., Militia, Sep., 1777 [Ref: M-198, T-5:45]. Private, 5th Co., Lower Bn., Militia, July 15, 1780 [Ref: M-205]. Took the Oath of Allegiance before the Hon. Edward Burgess on Feb. 28, 1778 [Ref: T-3:60, L-1:44]. Erasmus Perry married Elizabeth Harding in Montgomery County on Jan. 13, 1778 [Ref: K-2:516].

PERRY, James. Private, 3rd Co., Middle Bn., Militia, Sep., 1777 [Ref: M-196, T-5:38]. Served as petit juror in Nov., 1777 [Ref: R-31:18]. Two men with this name took the Oath of Allegiance: one before the Hon. Joseph Wilson on Feb. 28, 1778 [Ref: T-3:66, L-1:44, which latter source listed the name as "James Perry (coroner)"], and one made his "I P" mark before the Hon. Edward Burgess on Feb. 28, 1778 [Ref: T-3:59]. Rendered aid by providing wheat for use of the military in 1781 [Ref: O-379]. One James Perry lived in Linganore Hd. (four taxables) in 1777 [Ref: R-31:9], and another lived in Sugarland Hd. (one taxable) in 1777 [Ref: R-31:13]. One James Perry died testate in Montgomery County (wife named Hanner) in 1784 and mentioned sons James and John, among others [Ref: V-109]. Another James Perry died testate in Montgomery County (wife named Rachel) in 1802, but mentioned no children in his will [Ref: V-109, V-110].

PERRY, Jane. See "Elisha Beall," q.v.

PERRY, John. Private, 6th Co., Middle Bn., Militia, Aug., 1777 [Ref: M-197, T-5:41]. Private, 6th Co., Middle Bn., Militia, July 15, 1780 [Ref: M-203]. Took the Oath of Allegiance before the Hon. Edward Burgess on Feb. 28, 1778 [Ref: T-3:63, L-1:44]. See "James Perry," q.v.

PERRY, Joseph (died 1797). Took the Oath of Allegiance before the Hon. Edward Burgess on Feb. 28, 1778 [Ref: T-3:59, L-1:44]. Lived in the Lower Part of Newfoundland Hd. (six taxables) in 1777 [Ref: R-31:6]. "Joseph Perry, planter" died testate in Montgomery County (wife named Jemima) in 1797 [Ref: V-110].

PERRY, Joshua. Private, 6th Co., Upper Bn., Militia, Aug. 30, 1777 [Ref: M-194]. Took the Oath of Allegiance before the Hon. Edward Burgess on Feb. 28, 1778 [Ref: T-3:63, L-1:44].

PERRY, Priscilla. See "Clement Perry," q.v.

PERRY, Rebeckah. See "James Fyffe," q.v.

PERRY, Thomas. Private, 4th Co., Lower Bn., Militia, July 15, 1780 [Ref: M-205].

PERRY, Zadock (died 1812). Rendered aid by providing corn for use of the military in 1780 [Ref: O-288]. Died testate in Montgomery County (wife named Ann) in 1812 [Ref: V-111].

PETER (PETOR, PETERS), John (1756-1804?). Lived in George Town Hd. in 1776 and was apparently a son of "Robert Peter or Petor," q.v., aged 50 [Ref: K-1:194]. Served as Second Lieutenant, Lower District of Frederick County Militia, on April 20, 1776, and First Lieutenant, 29th Bn. of Montgomery County Militia, Sep. 12, 1777 [Ref: M-111, M-199, A-356, C-373, T-5:46]. "John S. Peters" died testate in Montgomery County (wife not named) in 1804 [Ref: V-112, V-113].

PETER (PETOR), Robert Jr. (b. 1757). Lived in George Town Hd. in 1776 and was apparently a son of "Robert Peter or Petor," q.v. [Ref: K-1:194]. Private, 3rd Co., Lower Bn., Militia, Sep., 1777 [Ref: M-199, T-5:46]. Took the Oath of Allegiance before the Hon. Richard Thompson in 1778 [Ref: T-3:75, L-1:44].

PETER (PETOR, PETERS), Robert Sr. Private, 3rd Co., Lower Bn., Militia, Sep., 1777 [Ref: M-199, T-5:46]. Took the Oath of Allegiance before the Hon. Richard Thompson in 1778 [Ref: T-3:75, L-1:44]. "Robert Peter" rendered aid by providing wheat for use of the military in 1780 [Ref: O-309]. "Robert Peters" rendered aid by providing wheat and corn for use of the military in 1780 [Ref: O-297, O-316]. "Robert Peter" lived in George Town Hd. (ten taxables) in 1777 [Ref: R-31:3], and owned a working plantation ("quarter") in Sugarland Hd. (seven taxables) in 1777 [Ref: R-31:13]. One "Robert Peter, of Georgetown,

Washington County and District of Columbia" died testate in Montgomery County (wife not named) in 1806, leaving a will and several codicils that named numerous heirs. Another "Robert Peter, of Washington County, District of Columbia" died testate in Montgomery County in 1809 (unmarried), naming numerous family members [Ref: V-111, V-112]. One "Robert Petor or Peter, aged 50" lived in George Town Hd. in 1776 and had a large family [Ref: K-1:194].

PETERS, Mary. See "Richard Smith," q.v.

PHERSON, Joseph. Served as a Corporal, Capt. Price's Co., 3rd Maryland Line, 1781-1782 [Ref: D-452].

PHILLIPS (FILLIPE), Charles. Served as an Ensign, 8th Co., 29th Bn., Militia, June 21, 1777 [Ref: M-111, M-200, T-5:51, C-286, C-373]. "Charles Phillips" was a private, 6th Co., Lower Bn., Militia, July 15, 1780 [Ref: M-206]. "Charles Fillipe" lived in Rock Creek Hd. (one taxable) in 1777 [Ref: R-31:16].

PHILLIPS, James. Private, Capt. Price's Co., 3rd Maryland Line, 1781-1782 [Ref: D-453].

PHILLIPS, John. Private, 7th Co., Middle Bn., Militia, Sep., 1777 [Ref: M-197, T-5:42].

PHILLIPS, Samuel. Private, 7th Co., Middle Bn., Militia, Sep., 1777 [Ref: M-197, T-5:42].

PHILPOTT, Barton. Took the Oath of Allegiance in 1778 [Ref: L-2:28].

PHILPOTT, Thomas. Private, 6th Co., Upper Bn., Militia, Aug. 30, 1777 [Ref: M-194].

PICKERING, John. Private who was recruited to serve in the Extra Regiment, Continental Army, in 1780 [Ref: D-342].

PIERCE, Henry, and others. See "Henry Pearce" and others, q.v.

PIGMAN, Eliza. See "Weaver Barnes," q.v.

PIGMAN, Ignatius. Son of Matthew Pigman [Ref: V-113]. Took the Oath of Allegiance on Sep. 1, 1780, under the Act of May 12, 1780, having neglected to do so previously "due to ignorance of the duty owed the country." [Ref: R-27:118]. Ignatius Pigman married Susanna Lamar in Montgomery County on Aug. 3, 1777 [Ref: K-2:516].

PIGMAN, Matthew (died 1784). Took the Oath of Allegiance before the Hon. Edward Burgess on Feb. 28, 1778 [Ref: T-3:58, L-1:44]. "Matthew Pigmam" [sic] lived in the Upper Part of Newfoundland Hd. (five taxables) in 1777 [Ref: R-31:7]. "Matthew Pigman" died testate in Montgomery County (wife named Dorcas) in 1784 [Ref: V-113].

PIGMAN, Nacy. Private, 7th Co., Middle Bn., Militia, Sep., 1777 [Ref: M-197, T-5:42]. Private, 7th Co., Middle Bn., Militia, July 15, 1780 [Ref: M-203].

PIGMAN, Nathaniel (c1735-1801). Lived in Rock Creek Hd. (five taxables) in 1777 [Ref: R-31:16], and married Ann Waters [Ref: DAR-I:535]. Served as a Captain, 29th Bn., Militia, May 14, 1776, Captain, Middle Bn., Sep. 12, 1777, Lieutenant Colonel, March 1, 1779, and

Colonel, 1781 [Ref: M-111, A-424, C-373, E-310, R-33:157, X-1146, M-196, which latter source mistakenly listed the name as "Nathl. Pagman"]. See "Thomas Gordon" and "Charles Tracy," q.v.

PILES, Osburn. Private, 1st Class, 2nd Co., Middle Bn., Militia, July 15, 1780 [Ref: M-201].

PINCHBACK, John. Private, 2nd Co., Middle Bn., Militia, Sep. 4, 1777 [Ref: M-196, T-5:37]. Took the Oath of Allegiance before the Hon. Gerrard Briscoe on March 2, 1778 [Ref: T-3:56, L-1:44]. John Pinchback lived in Sugar Loaf Hd. (three taxables) in 1777 [Ref: R-31:10].

PINKERTON, William. Served as a Lieutenant, 1st or 32nd Bn., Militia (no date was given; possibly June, 1777). [Ref: T-5:1].

PINN, Charles. Took the Oath of Allegiance on Sep. 1, 1780, under the Act of May 12, 1780, having neglected to do so previously "due to ignorance of the duty owed the country." [Ref: R-27:118].

PINN, Joseph. Took the Oath of Allegiance on Sep. 1, 1780, under the Act of May 12, 1780, having neglected to do so previously "due to ignorance of the duty owed the country." [Ref: R-27:118].

PLUMMER, Charity. See "Jeremiah Plummer" and "Mathias Hempston," q.v.

PLUMMER, Jeremiah (c1741-1809). Lived in Sugar Loaf Hd. (one taxable) in 1777 [Ref: R-31:10]. Private, 6th Co., Upper Bn., Militia, Aug. 30, 1777 [Ref: M-194]. Took the Oath of Allegiance before the Hon. Elisha Williams on March 2, 1778 [Ref: T-3:80, L-1:44]. He appears to have been the Jeremiah Plummer, son of William, who was born circa 1741 in Frederick County, Maryland, married Nancy Banfield, and died in 1809 in Abbott's Station, Kentucky. Their son Zephaniah Plummer married Charity Hempston (Hemstone), daughter of "Mathias Hempston," q.v., in 1791 [Ref: Research files of Herbert F. Smith, of Lawrenceburg, Indiana, and Margaret V. Williams, of Baltimore, Maryland, and Henry C. Peden, Jr., of Bel Air, Maryland. For more information on the Plummers of Maryland, see *Early Families of Southern Maryland, Volume II*, by Elise Greenup Jourdan, 1993].

PLUMMER, John. Private, 8th Co., Middle Bn., Militia, Sep., 1777 [Ref: M-197, T-5:43], and private, 8th Class, 4th Co., Middle Bn., Militia, on July 15, 1780 [Ref: M-202].

PLUMMER, Mahala. See "Mathias Hempston," q.v.

PLUMMER, Obed. Private, 2nd Maryland Line, 1780 [Ref: D-151].

PLUMMER, Philemon. Lived in the Upper Part of Newfoundland Hd. (three taxables) in 1777 [Ref: R-31:7]. "Philamon Plummer" was a private, 8th Co., Middle Bn., Militia, Sep., 1777 [Ref: M-197, T-5:43]. "Philliman Plummer" took the Oath of Allegiance before the Hon. Edward Burgess on Feb. 28, 1778 [Ref: T-3:58, L-1:44]. Rendered aid by providing wheat for use of the military in 1781 [Ref: O-384]. One Philemon Plummer died testate in Montgomery County (wife not named) in 1820 and mentioned a son Philemon, among other children [Ref: V-114].

PLUMMER, William. See "Jeremiah Plummer," q.v.

PLUMMER, Zephaniah. See "Jeremiah Plummer" and "Mathias Hempston," q.v.

PLUNKETT, Rev. See "Lawson Beall," q.v.

POCK (POCH), Phillip. Lived in the Lower Part of Newfoundland Hd. (one taxable) in 1777 [Ref: R-31:6]. Took the Oath of Allegiance before the Hon. Edward Burgess on Feb. 28, 1778 [Ref: T-3:59, L-1:44].

POCK, Felter. Private, 1st Co., Lower Bn., Militia, Sep., 1777 [Ref: M-198, T-5:44].

POLHOWER, Sand. Took the Oath of Allegiance in 1778 [Ref: L-2:28].

POLLARD, William. Served as a private when enrolled into a company of militia for the service of the Flying Camp on Oct. 15, 1776 [Ref: B-353], and private, 8th Co., Lower Bn., Militia, Sep., 1777 [Ref: M-200, T-5:51]. "William Poland" [Polard?] lived in Lower Potomac Hd. in 1776, aged 20 [Ref: K-1:185].

POOL, Amos. Private, 1st or 32nd Bn., Militia (no date was given; possibly June, 1777). [Ref: T-5:1].

POOL, Basil. Took the Oath of Allegiance on Sep. 1, 1780, under the Act of May 12, 1780, having neglected to do so previously "due to ignorance of the duty owed the country." [Ref: R-27:118].

POOL (POOLE), Benjamin. Private, 3rd Maryland Line, from April 3, 1778 until Nov. 1, 1778, when he was discharged [Ref: D-152].

POOL, Charles. Private, 1st or 32nd Bn., Militia (no date was given; possibly June, 1777). [Ref: T-5:1].

POOL (POOLE), Eliza Sprigg. See "Leonard Hays," q.v.

POOL (POOLE), John (1733-1816). "John Poole" was a private, 7th Co., Upper Bn., Militia, Aug. 30, 1777 [Ref: M-194]. "John Pool" lived in Sugarland Hd. in 1776 (wife named Sary) and had two taxables in 1777 [Ref: K-1:221, R-31:13]. "John Poole, planter," died testate in Montgomery County (wife not named) in 1816 and left all his land to his son John [Ref: V-114, V-115]. "John Pool" married Sarah Collier [Ref DAR-I:540].

POOL, John W. Private, 1st or 32nd Bn., Militia (no date was given; possibly June, 1777). [Ref: T-5:1].

POOL (POOLE), Joseph (b. 1738). "Joseph Poole" was a private, 1st Co., Upper Bn., Militia, Aug. 30, 1777 [Ref: M-193]. Took the Oath of Allegiance before the Hon. Elisha Williams on March 2, 1778 [Ref: T-3:80, L-1:44]. "Joseph Pool" lived in Sugarland Hd. in 1776 (wife named Mary) and had two taxables in 1777 [Ref: K-1:221, R-31:13].

POOL, Lloyd. Private, 1st or 32nd Bn., Militia (no date was given; possibly June, 1777). [Ref: T-5:1].

POOL, Philemon. Private, 1st or 32nd Bn., Militia (no date was given; possibly June, 1777). [Ref: T-5:1].

PORMER (FARMER?), Jon or John. Private, 6th Co., Middle Bn., Militia, July 15, 1780 [Ref: M-203].
PORTERFIELD, James. Took the Oath of Allegiance before the Hon. Edward Burgess on Feb. 28, 1778 [Ref: T-3:61, L-1:44].
POST, Val. Took the Oath of Allegiance in 1778 [Ref: L-2:28].
POTTER, William. Served as a Corporal, Capt. Price's Co., 3rd Maryland Line, 1781-1782 [Ref: D-452].
POTTINGER, Elizabeth. See "Allen Bowie," q.v.
POWER, Joshua. Private, Capt. Gray's Co., Maryland Line, 1780 [Ref: D-603].
POWER, Nicholas. Took the Oath of Allegiance before the Hon. Elisha Williams on March 2, 1778 [Ref: T-3:81, L-1:44].
PRATHER, Aaron (c1739-c1797). Lived in Rock Creek Hd. (one taxable) in 1777 [Ref: R-31:16]. Private, 2nd Co., Lower Bn., Militia, Sep., 1777 [Ref: M-198, T-5:45]. Served as a petit juror in Nov., 1777 [Ref: R-31:18]. Took the Oath of Allegiance before the Hon. Joseph Wilson on Feb. 28, 1778 [Ref: T-3:66, L-1:44]. Private, 5th Co., Lower Bn., Militia, July 15, 1780 [Ref: M-206]. Aaron Prather married Mary Swearingen [Ref: DAR-I:545].
PRATHER, Azariah (Aseriah). Private, 2nd Co., Lower Bn., Militia, Sep., 1777, and Second Sergeant, 5th Co., Lower Bn., July 15, 1780 [Ref: M-198, M-205, T-5:45]. Took the Oath of Allegiance before the Hon. Joseph Wilson on Feb. 28, 1778 [Ref: T-3:66, L-1:44].
PRATHER (PRATOR), Baruch (1742-1822). Private, 2nd Co., Lower Bn., Militia, Sep., 1777, and First Sergeant, 5th Co., Lower Bn., July 15, 1780 [Ref: M-198, M-205, T-5:45]. Took the Oath of Allegiance before the Hon. Charles Jones on Jan. 10, 1778 [Ref: T-3:71, L-1:44]. "Baruch Prator" rendered aid by providing wheat for use of the military in 1780 [Ref: O-304]. "Banich Prather" [sic] lived in the Upper Part of Potomac Hd. (two taxables) in 1777 [Ref: R-31:15]. "Baruch William Prather" was the twin of "William Basil Prather." Married Sarah Higgins on Nov. 15, 1775 and they were in Fayette County, Kentucky by 1810. He died on Oct. 7, 1822. They are buried in the Prather Cemetery near Spears, Kentucky [Ref: *Kentucky Ancestor*, Vol. 8 (1973), p. 211, and DAR-I:545].
PRATHER (PRATOR), Basil. Fourth Corporal, 5th Co., Lower Bn., Militia, July 15, 1780 [Ref: M-205]. "Basil Prator" rendered aid by providing wheat for use of the military in 1780 [Ref: O-315]. See "Baruch Prather," q.v.
PRATHER, Benjamin (died 1778). Took the Oath of Allegiance before the Hon. Edward Burgess on Feb. 28, 1778 [Ref: T-3:62, L-1:44]. Lived in the Lower Part of Newfoundland Hd. (two taxables) in 1777 [Ref: R-31:6]. Died testate in Montgomery County (wife not named) in May, 1778 [Ref: V-115].
PRATHER, Eleanor. See "Elisha Williams," q.v.

PRATHER (PRATHAR), John (1715-1805). Lived in the Upper Part of Newfoundland Hd. (six taxables) in 1777 [Ref: R-31:7]. Took the Oath of Allegiance before the Hon. Edward Burgess on Feb. 28, 1778 [Ref: T-3:62, L-1:44]. "John Prathar" rendered aid by providing wheat for use of the military in 1781 [Ref: O-388]. "John Prather, planter" died testate in Montgomery County (wife not named) in 1805 and mentioned his son Thomas Prather and daughters Sarah Linthicum and Mary Duvall [Ref: V-115]. John Prather married Rachel Odle or Odel [Ref: DAR-I:545].

PRATHER, Lucy. See "Joseph Estep," q.v.

PRATHER, Philip. See "Elisha Williams," q.v.

PRATHER, Thomas. Private, 2nd Co., Middle Bn., Militia, Sep. 4, 1777 [Ref: M-196, T-5:37]. Thomas Prather lived in Seneca Hd. (two taxables) in 1777 [Ref: R-31:8]. See "John Prather" and "Elisha Williams," q.v.

PRATHER, Virlinda. See "Joshua Saffle," q.v.

PRATHER, Walter. Private, 2nd Co., Lower Bn., Militia, Sep., 1777 [Ref: M-198, T-5:45]. Private, 5th Co., Lower Bn., Militia, July 15, 1780 [Ref: M-206]. Took the Oath of Allegiance before the Hon. Joseph Wilson on Feb. 28, 1778 [Ref: T-3:67, L-1:44]. Walter Prather lived in Rock Creek Hd. (two taxables) in 1777 [Ref: R-31:16]. Walter Prather married Ann Higgins in Montgomery County on April 9, 1778 [Ref: K-2:522].

PRATHER, William. Private, 5th Co., Lower Bn., Militia, July 15, 1780 [Ref: M-206]. See "Baruch Prather," q.v.

PRATHER (PRATER), Zachariah (c1752-c1814). Private, 2nd Co., Lower Bn., Militia, Sep., 1777 [Ref: M-198, T-5:45]. Private, 5th Co., Lower Bn., Militia, July 15, 1780 [Ref: M-206]. "Zach. Prather" was a sergeant, 2nd Maryland Line, 1780 [Ref: D-151]. "Zaccai Prater" took the Oath of Allegiance before the Hon. Joseph Wilson on Feb. 28, 1778 [Ref: T-3:67, L-1:44]. Zachariah Prather lived in Rock Creek Hd. (one taxable) in 1777 [Ref: R-31:16]. He married Ruth Allison in Montgomery County on Aug. 25, 1778 [Ref: K-2:516, DAR-I:545].

PREDIX, John. "John Predix, alias Matthias Risley, an American born, about 5 feet 8 inches high, hair trimmed on the top of the head, brown complexion, smooth faced, black eyes, a remarkable scar between his shoulders, a well set man, recruited by Capt. John Johnson, James Fyfe, and Arthur Steel on Feb. 5, 1781." [Ref: R-33:155, X-1146].

PRESTON, William. Private, enrolled into a company of militia for the service of the Flying Camp, Oct. 15, 1776 [Ref: B-353].

PRICE, John. Private, 1st or 32nd Bn., Militia (no date was given; possibly June, 1777). [Ref: T-5:1].

PRICE, Mary. See "John Barrett," q.v.

PRICE, Richard. Private, 3rd Class, 4th Co., Middle Bn., Militia, July 15, 1780 [Ref: M-202]. Private, 2nd Co., Lower Bn., Militia, July 15, 1780 [Ref: M-204]. Took the Oath of Allegiance before the Hon. Samuel W. Magruder in 1778 [Ref: T-3:73]. Richard Price married Anne Randall in Montgomery County on Feb. 15, 1779 [Ref: K-2:520].

PRICE, Sarah. See "James Allnutt," q.v.
PRICE, Thomas (b. 1753). Lived in Sugarland Hd. in 1776 [Ref: K-1:219]. Served as a Lieutenant and Paymaster in the 3rd Maryland Regiment, from 1777 until Feb. 11, 1780, when discharged [Ref: D-152]. Also see "Richard Johns," q.v.
PRICE, William. See "James Allnutt," q.v.
PRICKERS, Charles. Rendered aid by providing wheat for use of the military in 1781 [Ref: O-395].
PRIEST (PREAST), Henry. Private, 1st Co., Lower Bn., Militia, July 15, 1780 [Ref: M-204]. "Henry Preast" took the Oath of Allegiance (made his "H" mark) before the Hon. Samuel W. Magruder in 1778 [Ref: T-3:73]. "Henry Preast" lived in the Upper Part of Potomac Hd. (one taxable) in 1777 [Ref: R-31:15].
PRIEST, John. Private, 1st Maryland Regiment, 1777 [Ref: D-150].
PRIEST, Thomas. Private, 8th Class, 1st Co., Middle Bn., Militia, July 15, 1780 [Ref: T-5:4 and M-201, which latter source listed the name as ".... Priest"].
PRIEST, William. Private, 5th Class, 1st Co., Middle Bn., Militia, July 15, 1780, and Corporal, Maryland Line, until discharged on Nov. 29, 1783 [Ref: M-201, D-551].
PRINGLE, John (b. 1748). Lived in George Town Hd. in 1776 [Ref: K-1:194]. Private, 8th Co., Lower Bn., Militia, July 15, 1780 [Ref: M-207].
PRITCHETT (PRITCHET, PREECHET), Charles. Son of Thomas Pritchett who died testate in 1778 [Ref: V-115]. Private, 1st Class, 1st Co., Middle Bn., Militia, July 15, 1780 [Ref: M-201], and a private, 5th Co., Middle Bn., Militia, Sep., 1777 [Ref: T-5:40, M-197]. Took the Oath of Allegiance (made his "C" mark) before the Hon. Joseph Wilson on Feb. 28, 1778 [Ref: T-3:66, L-1:44]. "Charles Pritchet" lived in the Upper Part of Potomac Hd. (one taxable) in 1777 [Ref: R-31:15].
PRITCHETT (PRITCHET, PREECHET), Elias (Lyas). Son of Thomas Pritchett who died testate in 1778 [Ref: V-115]. Private, 4th Class, 1st Co., Middle Bn., Militia, July 15, 1780 [Ref: M-201]. Private, 5th Co., Middle Bn., Militia, Sep., 1777 [Ref: T-5:40, M-197]. Took the Oath of Allegiance before the Hon. Charles Jones on Jan. 10, 1778 [Ref: T-3:71, L-1:44]. Rendered aid by providing wheat for use of the military in 1780 and 1781 [Ref: O-317, O-391]. "Lyas Pritchet" lived in the Upper Part of Potomac Hd. (one taxable) in 1777 [Ref: R-31:15].
PRITCHETT (PREECHET), William. Son of Thomas Pritchett who died testate in 1778 [Ref: V-115]. Private, 7th Class, 1st Co., Middle Bn., Militia, July 15, 1780 [Ref: M-201]. Private, 5th Co., Middle Bn., Militia, Sep., 1777 [Ref: T-5:40, M-197]. Took the Oath of Allegiance before the Hon. Joseph Wilson on Feb. 28, 1778 [Ref: T-3:64, L-1:44].
PRUITT (PRUETT), William. Private who enrolled into a company of militia for the service of the Flying Camp on Oct. 15, 1776 [Ref: B-353].

PURDAM (PURDOM, PUDAM), John (b. 1739). "John Pudam" was a private, 3rd Co., Upper Bn., Militia, Aug. 30, 1777 [Ref: M-193]. "John Purdom" took the Oath of Allegiance before the Hon. Edward Burgess on Feb. 28, 1778 [Ref: T-3:63, L-1:44]. "John Purdum or Purdom" lived in Sugarland Hd. (one taxable) in 1776-1777 [Ref: K-1:201, R-31:13].

PURDEN (PERDEN), Josiah. Served as a First Corporal, 7th Co., Middle Bn., Militia, July 15, 1780 [Ref: M-203].

PURDY (PURDEY), Charles. Took the Oath of Allegiance before the Hon. Richard Thompson in 1778 [Ref: T-3:75, L-1:44].

PURDY (PURDIE), Edward. "Edward Purdie" was a private, 3rd Maryland Line, from March 5, 1777 until Aug. 16, 1780, when reported missing at the Battle of Camden [Ref: D-152]. "Edward Purdy" was a private, 6th Maryland Line, 1780 [Ref: D-238].

PURDY, Henry (died 1833). Private, 6th Maryland Line, 1780 [Ref: D-238, D-439, noting he may have initially served from Prince George's County]. He was born in Maryland and went to what is now Marion County, Kentucky "in an early day." He married three times, had 21 children, and died in 1833 [Ref: Thomas C. Westerfield's *Kentucky Biography and Genealogy*, Volume 5, p. 240].

PURDY, John. Served as a Sergeant, 2nd Maryland Line, 1778, and reportedly "deserted" on March 4, 1778 [Ref: D-151]. He may have returned because there was a John Purdy who was a private in the 6th Maryland Line in 1780 [Ref: D-238].

PURDY (PURDIE), Richard (b. 1731). "Richard Purdie" was a private, 6th Co., Upper Bn., Militia, Aug. 30, 1777 [Ref: M-194]. "Richard Purdy" took the Oath of Allegiance before the Hon. Elisha Williams on March 2, 1778 [Ref: T-3:81, L-1:44]. "Richard Purdy or Purdey" lived in Sugarland Hd. (one taxable) in 1776-1777 [Ref: K-1:202, R-31:13].

PURNELL (PURNAL), Samuel. Private, Capt. Edward Burgess' Co., Lower District of Frederick (now Montgomery) County, Militia, July, 1776 [Ref: D-42]. Private, 7th Maryland Line, from Feb. 11, 1777 until Feb. 8, 1780, when he was discharged [Ref: D-239]. This or perhaps another Samuel Purnell was a private, 6th Co., Lower Bn., Militia, on July 15, 1780 [Ref: M-206].

QUARDON (QUORDREN), John. "John Quardon" was a private, 6th Co., Middle Bn., Militia, July 15, 1780 [Ref: M-203]. Private, 6th Co., Middle Bn., Militia, Aug., 1777 [Ref: M-197, T-5:41]. "John Quordren" took the Oath of Allegiance before the Hon. Edward Burgess on Feb. 28, 1778 [Ref: T-3:59, L-1:44]. "John Quordren" lived in Linganore Hd. (one taxable) in 1777 [Ref: R-31:9].

QUARY (QUIRY, QUEARY), Daniel. Son of Nicholas Quary who died testate in 1788 [Ref: V-116]. "Daniel Quary" was a private, 6th Class, 2nd Co., Middle Bn., Militia, July 15, 1780 [Ref: M-201]. "Daniel Quiry" acted in the roll of a commissary in 1781 [Ref: O-383]. "Daniel Queary" married Eve Wilfree in Montgomery County on Nov. 9, 1779 [Ref: K-2:520].

QUEEN, John. Served as a Corporal, 4th Maryland Regiment, 1778 [Ref: D-154]. Rendered aid by providing beef for use of the military in 1781 [Ref: O-352].

QUEEN, William. Took the Oath of Allegiance in 1778 [Ref: L-2:28].

QUINN, Patrick. Private, Maryland Line, Rawlings' Regiment, from Oct. 15, 1776 to Jan. 1, 1777, when reported deserted; yet he was "sick and present" in the 4th Maryland line in July, 1778, and served in Capt. Thomas Beall's Co. in 1780 [Ref: D-154, D-302, D-350].

QUINTON (QUINTUM), William. Private who was recruited to serve in the Extra Regiment, Continental Army, in 1780, was then reported subsequently to be a deserter, and afterwards joined on Oct. 1, 1780 and was present on Nov. 1, 1780, in the 7th Maryland Regiment [Ref: D-240, D-341, D-342].

QUISENBERRY, Anderson C. See "Elias Loveless" and "Walter Macatee," q.v.

RAGAN, Darby. Private, 7th Maryland Line, 1777 [Ref: D-242].

RAGLAND, James. See "Charles Tracy," q.v.

RAMEY, Annie Jane. See "Samuel Clagett," q.v.

RAMSEY, William. Took the Oath of Allegiance in 1778 [Ref: L-2:28].

RANDALL, Anne. See "Richard Price," q.v.

RANDEL, Isaac. Private, 1st or 32nd Bn., Militia (no date was given; possibly June, 1777). [Ref: T-5:1].

RANDELL (RANDAL, RANDLE, RANDOLS), John (b. 1737). "John Randal or Randle" lived in George Town Hd. (three taxables) in 1776-1777 [Ref: K-1:194, R-31:3]. "John Randols" was a private, 3rd Co., Lower Bn., Militia, Sep., 1777 [Ref: M-199, T-5:46]. "John Randell" took the Oath of Allegiance before the Hon. Joseph Wilson on Feb. 28, 1778 [Ref: T-3:66, L-1:44]. Private, 2nd Class, 1st Co., Middle Bn., Militia, July 15, 1780 [Ref: M-201].

RANDOL, Eleanor and Jemima. See "Josiah Earp," q.v.

RANSOM, Mary. See "Samuel Taylor Orme," q.v.

RATLEAF (RATCLIFF), Francis. "Francis Ratleaf" was a private, 7th Co., Lower Bn., Militia, Aug., 1777 [Ref: M-200, T-5:50]. Private, 4th Co., Lower Bn., Militia, July 15, 1780 [Ref: M-205]. "Francis Rattes" [Ratlef?] took the Oath of Allegiance before the Hon. Edward Burgess on Feb. 28, 1778 [Ref: T-3:62, L-1:44]. "Francis Ratcliff" lived in the Lower Part of Newfoundland Hd. (one taxable) in 1777 [Ref: R-31:6].

RAVENSCROFT, Francis. Private, Maryland Line, Gist's Regiment, 1777-1780 [Ref: D-601]. Although Francis was not listed, there was a John Ravenscroft, aged 42, listed in the 1776 tax list of George Town Hd. [Ref: K-1:194].

RAWLINGS, Anna. See "Leonard Hays," q.v.

RAWLINGS (ROLLINS, ROLLINGS, ROWLEN), Aaron. "Aaron Rollings" was a private, 8th Co., Middle Bn., Militia, Sep., 1777 [Ref: M-198, T-5:43]. "Aaron Rowlen" was a private, 3rd Co., Lower Bn., Militia, July 15, 1780 [Ref: M-205]. "Aaron Rollins" lived in the Upper Part of Newfoundland Hd. (one taxable) in 1777 [Ref: R-31:7].

RAWLINGS (ROLLINS, RAWLINS), John (died 1784). "John Rollins" was a private, 1st Co., Middle Bn., Militia, Aug. 30, 1777 [Ref: M-195]. "John Rawlings" took the Oath of Allegiance before the Hon. Gerrard Briscoe on March 2, 1778 [Ref: T-3:56, L-1:44]. Rendered aid by providing wheat for use of the military in 1781 [Ref: O-434]. Lived in Seneca Hd. (five taxables) in 1777 [Ref: R-31:8]. "John Rawlins" died testate in Montgomery County (wife named Mary) in 1784 [Ref: V-116].

RAWLINGS (ROLLINS), Thomas. "Thomas Rollins" was a private, 1st Co., Middle Bn., Militia, Aug. 30, 1777 [Ref: M-195]. "Thomas Rawlings" was Fourth Sergeant, 5th Co., Middle Bn., Militia, July 15, 1780 [Ref: M-202].

RAY, Benjamin. Lived in the Upper Part of Potomac Hd. (three taxables) in 1777 [Ref: R-31:15]. Private, 3rd Co., Middle Bn., Sep., 1777; First Lieutenant, Middle Bn., Militia, April 21, 1779; Captain, 2nd Co., Middle Bn., March 25, 1780 [Ref: M-114, M-196, M-201, E-357, F-120, T-5:38]. Took the Oath of Allegiance before the Hon. William Deakins, Jr. before March 3, 1778 [Ref: T-3:68, L-1:44]. Rendered aid by providing wheat for use of the military in 1780 and 1781 [Ref: O-328, O-383].

RAY, Elizabeth. See "Caleb Darby" and "Samuel Offutt," q.v.

RAY, George. Private, 2nd Class, 1st Co., Middle Bn., Militia, July 15, 1780 [Ref: M-201].

RAY, James (1724-1807). Took the Oath of Allegiance (made his "R" mark) before the Hon. Samuel W. Magruder in 1778 [Ref: T-3:73]. Rendered aid by providing wheat for use of the military in 1780 [Ref: O-321]. Lived in Lower Potomac Hd. (three taxables) in 1776-1777 [Ref: K-1:185, R-31:4]. Died testate in Montgomery County (wife named Mary) in 1807 [Ref: V-116].

RAY, John (June 24, 1732 - 1811). Served as a private in Capt. Edward Burgess' Co., Lower District of Frederick (now Montgomery) County, Militia, July, 1776, and First Lieutenant, Middle Bn., Militia, Sep. 12, 1777, and Captain on April 21, 1779, 1st Co., Middle Bn., Militia, through at least July 15, 1780 [Ref: D-42, M-114, M-196, M-210, C-373, E-357, T-5:40]. Served as a petit juror in Aug., 1777 [Ref: R-31:17]. Took the Oath of Allegiance before the Hon. Edward Burgess on Feb. 28, 1778 [Ref: T-3:62, L-1:44]. Lived in the Upper Part of Potomac Hd. (one taxable) in 1777 [Ref: R-31:15]. John Ray married Martha Wood [Ref: DAR-I:558].

RAY, John Jr. Took the Oath of Allegiance before the Hon. Gerrard Briscoe on March 2, 1778 [Ref: T-3:56, L-1:44].

RAY, Joseph (b. 1755). Private, 2nd Maryland Line, Dec. 24, 1776 to Nov. 1, 1780. He pensioned (S35040) in 1818, aged 60 (65?), and was still on the pension rolls in 1835 [Ref: D-156, J-38, Q-134, K-2:384, P-2821]. An affidavit of his Revolutionary War service is recorded in *Montgomery County Wills Liber 3* (folio 107), dated Sep. 12, 1820, stating he was then aged 65 and he had enlisted in 1776 as a private in Capt. Benjamin Price's Co., 2nd Maryland Regiment. He fought in the battles of Camden, Monmouth Plains, and Eutaw Springs, and was wounded in the left knee [Ref: V-116].

RAY, Nicholas. (1) Second Lieutenant, Middle Bn., Militia, Sep. 12, 1777, and Captain from April 21, 1779, to at least March 25, 1780 [Ref: M-114, M-197, C-373, E-333, E-357, T-5:41]. Took the Oath of Allegiance before the Hon. Edward Burgess on Feb. 28, 1778 [Ref: T-3:61, L-1:44]. (2) Private, 6th Co., Middle Bn., Militia, July 15, 1780 [Ref: M-203]. Rendered aid by providing wheat for use of the military in 1781 [Ref: O-378]. One Nicholas Ray lived in Linganore Hd. (four taxables) in 1777 [Ref: R-31:9]. Captain Nicholas Ray was born on Sep. 19, 1747, and died in 1819 [Ref: DAR-I:558].

RAY, Thomas (b. 1721). Took the Oath of Allegiance before the Hon. Richard Thompson in 1778 [Ref: T-3:75, L-1:44]. Thomas Ray lived in Lower Potomac Hd. (one taxable) in 1776-1777 [Ref: K-1:185, R-31:4].

RAY, William. (1) Private, 5th Co., Middle Bn., Militia, Sep., 1777 [Ref: M-197, T-5:40]. Private, 5th Class, 1st Co., Middle Bn., Militia, July 15, 1780 [Ref: M-201]. Took the Oath of Allegiance before the Hon. Elisha Williams on March 2, 1778 [Ref: T-3:80, L-1:44]. (2) Private, 2nd Co., Upper Bn., Militia, Aug. 30, 1777 [Ref: M-193]. Took the Oath of Allegiance before the Hon. Edward Burgess on Feb. 28, 1778 [Ref: T-3:63, L-1:44]. One William Ray lived in Linganore Hd. (two taxables), another lived in Sugar Loaf Hd. (one taxable), and another lived in the Upper Part of Potomac Hd. (three taxables) in 1777 [Ref: R-31:9, R-31:11, R-31:15]. One William Ray was born in 1705 and died in July, 1778; wife named Anne [Ref: DAR-I:558].

RAYMAR, Eleanor. See "James Veatch," q.v.

RAYNOR, William. Rendered aid by providing pork for use of the military in 1781 [Ref: O-356].

RAYON, John. Took the Oath of Allegiance before the Hon. Aneas Campbell on March 2, 1778 [Ref: T-3:78, L-1:44].

READ, Alexander. Private, enrolled into a company of militia for the service of the Flying Camp, Oct. 15, 1776 [Ref: B-352]. Alexander Read married Rebecca Stevens in Montgomery County on Nov. 27, 1777 [Ref: K-2:520].

READ, Christopher. See "Christopher Reed," q.v.

READ, George, and others. See "George Reed" and others, q.v.

READING, Patrick. Private, Capt. Price's Co., 3rd Maryland Line, 1781, and "then Smith at Annapolis" in 1782 [Ref: D-454].

REDMAN, Benjamin. Private, 4th Co., Middle Bn., Militia, Sep., 1777 [Ref: M-196, T-5:39]. Private, 5th Class, 4th Co., Middle Bn., Militia, July 15, 1780 [Ref: M-202]. Rendered aid by providing wheat for use of the military in 1781 [Ref: O-417].
REDMAN, Charles. Private, 2nd Class, 4th Co., Middle Bn., Militia, July 15, 1780 [Ref: M-202].
REDMAN, Francis. Private, 4th Co., Middle Bn., Militia, Sep., 1777 [Ref: M-196, T-5:39]. Private, 7th Class, 4th Co., Middle Bn., Militia, July 15, 1780 [Ref: M-202]. "Frances Redman" rendered aid by providing wheat for use of the military in 1781 [Ref: O-407]. "Francis Redmon" lived in Seneca Hd. (one taxable) in 1777 [Ref: R-31:8].
REDMAN, Joseph. Private, 5th Class, 4th Co., Middle Bn., Militia, July 15, 1780 [Ref: M-202]. Joseph Redman married Sarah Windsor in Montgomery County on April 24, 1778 [Ref: K-2:522].
REDMAN, Lucy. See "William Burriss," q.v.
REDMAN, Robert. "Robert Redman" was a private, 4th Co., Middle Bn., Militia, Sep., 1777 [Ref: M-196, T-5:39]. "Robert Redmon" lived in Seneca Hd. (one taxable) in 1777 [Ref: R-31:8].
REDMAN, William. Private, 4th Co., Middle Bn., Militia, Sep., 1777 [Ref: M-196, T-5:39]. Private, 1st Class, 4th Co., Middle Bn., Militia, July 15, 1780 [Ref: M-202]. "William Redman" rendered aid by providing wheat for use of the military in 1781 [Ref: O-417]. "William Redmand" lived in the Upper Part of Newfoundland Hd. (one taxable) in 1777 [Ref: R-31:7].
REED (READ), Christopher. "Christopher Read" was a private, 7th Maryland Line, from May 15, 1777 until May 5, 1780, when discharged [Ref: D-242]. "Christr. Reed" was a soldier whose invalid pension commenced on Aug. 20, 1784, in Montgomery County, and he was still on the rolls on Nov. 1, 1789 [Ref: D-632].
REED, Cynthia. See "John Howard," q.v.
REED (READ), George (b. 1749). Private, Maryland Line, and applied for pension (S30669) in Breckenridge County, Kentucky, on Sep. 17, 1832, aged 83, stating he was born in Feb., 1749, and enlisted in Montgomery County, Maryland, near Bladensburg, in 1775 [sic]. Thomas Sullivan made affidavit that he knew George Reed during the war and lived with his family [Ref: P-2835, Y-7, Z-16, which latter two sources mistakenly stated he applied for pension on March 4, 1831]. "George Read" was a private, 1st Co., Lower Bn., Militia, July 15, 1780 [Ref: M-204]. Took the Oath of Allegiance before the Hon. Charles Jones on Jan. 10, 1778 [Ref: T-3:71, L-1:44]. "George Reed" was a private, 4th Co., Lower Bn., Militia, Aug., 1777 [Ref: M-199, T-5:47]. "George Reed, aged 23" lived in Lower Potomac Hd. in 1776 and had three taxables in 1777 [Ref: K-1:185, R-31:4].
REED (READ, REID), John (died 1811). "John Read" took the Oath of Allegiance before the Hon. William Deakins, Jr. before March 3, 1778

[Ref: T-3:68, L-1:44]. "John Reed" was a private, 6th Co., Upper Bn., Militia, Aug. 30, 1777 [Ref: M-194]. Lived in Sugar Loaf Hd. (two taxables) in 1777 [Ref: R-31:11]. "John Reid, of Frederick County" died testate in Montgomery County (wife named Ann) in 1811 [Ref: V-117].
REED (READ), Jonathan. Took the Oath of Allegiance before the Hon. Elisha Williams on March 2, 1778 [Ref: T-3:80, L-1:44].
REED (READ), Matthew (died 1802). "Matthew Read" was a private who enrolled into a company of militia for the service of the Flying Camp on Oct. 15, 1776 [Ref: B-352]. "Matthew Reed" took the Oath of Allegiance before the Hon. Elisha Williams on March 2, 1778 [Ref: T-3:80, L-1:44]. Died testate in Montgomery County (wife named Eleanor) in 1802 [Ref: V-117].
REED (READ), Patrick. Private, Capt. Price's Co., 3rd Maryland Line, 1781-1782 [Ref: D-453].
REED (READ), Thomas. "Thomas Read, clerk" took the Oath of Allegiance before the Hon. Gerrard Briscoe on March 2, 1778 [Ref: T-3:56, L-1:44]. "Thomas Reed" recruited Alexander Bonney to serve in the military in Feb., 1781 [Ref: R-33:155, X-1146].
REEDER, Benjamin and Elizabeth. See "Robert Green," q.v.
REEDER, Francis, Henry, Hezekiah, John. See "Simon Reeder," q.v.
REEDER (READER), Mike. Took the Oath of Allegiance in 1778 [Ref: L-2:28].
REEDER (READER), Simon. "Simon Reeder" was a private, 2nd Co., Upper Bn., Militia, Aug. 30, 1777 [Ref: M-193]. Served as a petit juror in Aug., 1777 [Ref: R-31:17]. "Simon Reader "took the Oath of Allegiance before the Hon. Elisha Williams on March 2, 1778 [Ref: T-3:80, L-1:44]. "Simon Reeder" lived in Sugar Loaf Hd. (four taxables) in 1777 [Ref: R-31:10]. When Francis Reeder wrote his will in Montgomery County in 1791 (no wife or children named) he mentioned "Simon Reeder, Sr., of Charles County" and his three youngest brothers John, Hezekiah and Henry (residences not stated). [Ref: V-117].
REESE, Andrew. Took the Oath of Allegiance in 1778 [Ref: L-2:28].
REESE, Frederick. Took the Oath of Allegiance in 1778 [Ref: L-2:28].
REESE, Henry. Private, 7th Maryland Line, 1777-1780 [Ref: D-243].
REINTZEL, Andrew. See "Andrew Rhintzell" and others, q.v.
RELLY, David. Private, Capt. Price's Co., 3rd Maryland Line, 1781-1782 [Ref: D-453].
REMINGTON, James. See "Michael Downs," q.v.
REMINGTON (REMINTON, RIMINGTON, RAMINGTON), John. Private, 6th Co., Lower Bn., Militia, Aug., 1777 [Ref: T-5:49 and M-200, which latter source listed the name as "John Remin..."]. Private, 3rd Co., Lower Bn., Militia, July 15, 1780 [Ref: M-205]. Took the Oath of Allegiance before the Hon. Joseph Offutt on March 2, 1778 [Ref: T-3:70, L-1:44]. Rendered aid by providing wheat for use of the military in 1780 and 1781 [Ref: O-315, O-386]. "John Rimington" was a private, 7th

Maryland Line, from June 6, 1778 until March 16, 1779, when discharged [Ref: D-242]. "John Ramington" (b. 1752) lived in Lower Potomac Hd. in 1776 and "John Reminton" lived in the Upper Part of Potomac Hd. (one taxable) in 1777 [Ref: K-1:185, R-31:15].

RENEGAR (RENNAGER, RYNAGOR), George. Private, 3rd Co., Middle Bn., Militia, Sep., 1777 [Ref: M-196, T-5:38]. "George Rennager" was a private, 8th Class, 2nd Co., Middle Bn., Militia, July 15, 1780 [Ref: M-201]. "George Rynagon" [Rynagor] took the Oath of Allegiance before the Hon. Edward Burgess on Feb. 28, 1778 [Ref: T-3:63, L-1:44].

RENEGAR (RENIGAR), Harman. "Harman Renegar" was a private, 3rd Co., Middle Bn., Militia, Sep., 1777 [Ref: M-196, T-5:38]. "Harmon Renigar" was a private, 2nd Class, 2nd Co., Middle Bn., Militia, July 15, 1780 [Ref: M-201].

RENEGAR (RYNEGAR), Henry. "Henry Rynegar" took the Oath of Allegiance before the Hon. Edward Burgess on Feb. 28, 1778 [Ref: T-3:63, L-1:44].

RENEGAR (RUNEGAR), Joseph. "Joseph Renegar" was a private, 2nd Co., Upper Bn., Militia, Aug. 30, 1777 [Ref: M-193]. "Joseph Runegar" lived in Sugar Loaf Hd. (one taxable) in 1777 [Ref: R-31:11].

RERESIDE, Andrew (died 1782). Private, Capt. Price's Co., 3rd Maryland Line, 1781-1782, and died on Dec. 16, 1782 [Ref: D-454].

REYES, John. Took the Oath of Allegiance before the Hon. Edward Burgess on Feb. 28, 1778 [Ref: T-3:59, L-1:44].

REYNOLDS, Caleb Rev. See "Robert Cumming," q.v.

REYNOLDS, Charles. Private, 8th Co., Lower Bn., Militia, July 15, 1780 [Ref: M-207], and was recruited to serve in the Continental Army in 1780 [Ref: D-342]. Two men with this name took the Oath of Allegiance: one before the Hon. Edward Burgess on Feb. 28, 1778 [Ref: T-3:59, L-1:44], and the other before the Hon. Charles Jones on Jan. 10, 1778 [Ref: T-3:71, L-1:44]. "Charles Rennals, Jr." was a private, 7th Co., Lower Bn., Militia, Aug., 1777 [Ref: M-200, T-5:50]. One Charles Reynolds lived in the Lower Part of Newfoundland Hd. (three taxables) in 1777 [Ref: R-31:6].

REYNOLDS, Charles Maccubin. Private, Capt. Edward Burgess' Co., Lower District of Frederick (now Montgomery) County, Militia, July, 1776 [Ref: D-42].

REYNOLDS, Debora. See "John Lenmar (Lenman)," q.v.

REYNOLDS, John. Private, enrolled into a company of militia for the service of the Flying Camp, Oct. 15, 1776 [Ref: B-352]. "John Rennals" was a private, 7th Co., Middle Bn., Militia, Sep., 1777 [Ref: M-197, T-5:42].

REYNOLDS, Thomas. Private, 4th Co., Lower Bn., Militia, July 15, 1780 [Ref: M-205].

REYNOLDS, William. Private, 8th Class, 2nd Co., Middle Bn., Militia, July 15, 1780 [Ref: M-201]. Took the Oath of Allegiance before the Hon.

William Deakins, Jr. before March 3, 1778 [Ref: T-3:68, L-1:44]. "William Rennalls" was a private, 3rd Co., Middle Bn., Militia, Sep., 1777 [Ref: M-196, T-5:38]. William Reynolds married Elizabeth Stevens in Montgomery County on Dec. 25, 1780 [Ref: K-2:520].
RHINE, Henry. See "Mathias Hempston," q.v.
RHINTZELL (RHENTZELL, REINTZEL, RANSELL), Andrew. "Andrew Rhintzell" was a private, 7th Co., Middle Bn., Militia, Sep., 1777 [Ref: M-197, T-5:42]. "Andrew Rhentzell" was a private, 8th Co., Lower Bn., Militia, July 15, 1780 [Ref: M-207]. "Andrew Reintzel" took the Oath of Allegiance before the Hon. Joseph Wilson on Feb. 28, 1778 [Ref: T-3:66, L-1:44]. Served as a grand juror in 1781 [Ref: W-2]. "Andrew Reintzel" lived in George Town Hd. (one taxable) in 1777 and "Andrew Ransell" lived in the Upper Part of Potomac Hd. (one taxable) in 1777 [Ref: R-31:3, R-31:15].
RHINTZELL (RHENTZELL, REINTZELL), Anthony. "Anthony Rhintzell" was a private, 8th Co., Lower Bn., Militia, July 15, 1780 [Ref: M-207]. "Anthony Rhentzell" was a Second Lieutenant, 8th Co., Lower Bn., Militia, Aug. 4, 1780 [Ref: M-115, M-207, F-248]. "Anthony Reintzell" took the Oath of Allegiance in 1778 [Ref: L-2:28].
RHINTZELL (RHENTZELL, REINTZEL), Daniel (b. 1756). "Daniel Rhintzell" was a private, 3rd Co., Lower Bn., Militia, Sep., 1777 [Ref: M-199, T-5:46]." Daniel Reintzel" took the Oath of Allegiance before the Hon. Richard Thompson in 1778 [Ref: T-3:75, L-1:44]. "Daniel Rhentzell" was a Captain, 8th Co., Lower Bn., Militia, Aug. 4, 1780 [Ref: M-115, F-248]. "Daniel Reinztel" lived in George Town Hd. (one taxable) in 1776-1777 [Ref: R-31:3], and was apparently a son of "Valentine Rhintzell," q.v. [Ref: K-1:194, which mistakenly listed the name as "Runhel"].
RHINTZELL (REINTZEL, RANSELL), Jacob. "Jacob Rhintzell" was a private, 5th Co., Middle Bn., Militia, Sep., 1777 [Ref: M-196, T-5:40]. "Jacob Reintzel" was a private, 8th Co., Lower Bn., Militia, July 15, 1780 [Ref: M-207]. "Jacob Reintzel" took the Oath of Allegiance before the Hon. Joseph Wilson on Feb. 28, 1778 [Ref: T-3:66, L-1:44]. "Jacob Ransell" lived in the Upper Part of Potomac Hd. (two taxables) in 1777 [Ref: R-31:15].
RHINTZELL (REINTZEL), Valentine (b. 1720). "Valentine Rhintzell" was a private, 8th Co., Lower Bn., Militia, July 15, 1780 [Ref: M-207]. "Valentine Reintzel" took the Oath of Allegiance before the Hon. Richard Thompson in 1778 [Ref: T-3:75, L-1:44]. "Valentine Reinztel" lived in George Town Hd. in 1776-1777 [Ref: R-31:3], and had sons Daniel (aged 20), Valentine, Jr. (aged 15), and John (aged 9). [Ref: K-1:194, which mistakenly listed the name as "Valentine Runhel"].
RHOADES (RHOADS), Elisha. Son of Nicholas Rhoades [Ref: V-118]. Served as private, 5th Co., Upper Bn., Militia, Aug. 30, 1777 [Ref: M-194].

RHOADES (RHOADS, RHODES, ROADS), Jacob. "Jacob Roads" lived in Sugar Loaf Hd. (one taxable) in 1777 [Ref: R-31:10]. Private, 5th Co., Upper Bn., Militia, Aug. 30, 1777 [Ref: M-194]. "Jacob Rhodes" was an Ensign, Upper Bn., Militia, on April 21, 1779 [Ref: M-115, E-357]. "Jacob Rhoades" took the Oath of Allegiance before the Hon. Joseph Wilson on Feb. 28, 1778 [Ref: T-3:64, L-1:44].

RHOADES (RHOADS), John. Son of Nicholas Rhoades [Ref: V-118]. Private, 5th Co., Upper Bn., Militia, Aug. 30, 1777 [Ref: M-194]. "John Rhoades" took the Oath of Allegiance (made his "R" mark) before the Hon. Joseph Wilson on Feb. 28, 1778 [Ref: T-3:66, L-1:44].

RHOADES (RHOADS, RHODES, RODES), Nicholas (died 1780). "Nicholas Rodes" was a private who enrolled into a company of militia for the service of the Flying Camp, Oct. 15, 1776 [Ref: B-353]. "Nicholas Rhodes" was a private, 5th Co., Upper Bn., Militia, Aug. 30, 1777 [Ref: M-194]. "Nicholas Rhoades, of Frederick County" died testate in Montgomery County (wife named Jane) in 1780, naming sons John, Elisha and Nicholas [Ref: V-118].

RHOADES (RHOADS, RODES), Nicholas Jr. Son of Nicholas Rhoades [Ref: V-118]. Served as a private when enrolled into a company of militia for the service of the Flying Camp on Oct. 15, 1776 [Ref: B-353].

RICHARDS, Elizabeth. See "John Hill," q.v.

RICHARDS, John (b. 1753). Private, 3rd Co., Upper Bn., Militia, Aug. 30, 1777 [Ref: M-193]. Took the Oath of Allegiance before the Hon. Edward Burgess on Feb. 28, 1778 [Ref: T-3:63, L-1:44]. Private, 5th Co., Middle Bn., Militia, July 15, 1780 [Ref: M-203]. Rendered aid by providing wheat for use of the military in 1781 [Ref: O-449]. Lived in Sugarland Hd. in 1776 and in the Upper Part of Potomac Hd. in 1777 [Ref: K-1:211, R-31:15].

RICHARDS, Leonard. "Leonard Richards" lived in Seneca Hd. (one taxable) in 1777 [Ref: R-31:8]. "Len Richards" was a private, 1st Co., Middle Bn., Militia, Aug. 30, 1777 [Ref: M-195]. "Leonard Richards" was a private, 5th Co., Middle Bn., Militia, July 15, 1780 [Ref: M-203]. Took the Oath of Allegiance before the Hon. Edward Burgess on Feb. 28, 1778 [Ref: T-3:63, L-1:44].

RICHARDS, William. Private, 5th Co., Lower Bn., Militia, July 15, 1780 [Ref: M-205]. William Richards married Tabitha Litton in Montgomery County on Sep. 29, 1778 [Ref: K-2:522].

RICHARDSON, Edward. See "Clement Dowden," q.v.

RICHARDSON, Thomas (b. 1741). Private, 3rd Co., Lower Bn., Militia, Sep., 1777 [Ref: M-199, T-5:46]. "Thomas Richardson, of George Town" was Commissary of Purchases for the Continental Army and took the Oath of Allegiance before the Hon. Richard Thompson on Feb. 26, 1778 [Ref: X-1146, F-215, F-222, E-529, which latter source stated he was commissioned "Assistant Deputy Quarter Master General of the Army of the United States in Montgomery County" on July 1, 1778]. He also rendered aid by providing wheat for use of the military in 1780 [Ref: O-307, O-313]. Thomas Richardson lived in George Town Hd. (three taxables) in 1776-1777 [Ref: K-1:194, R-31:3].

RICKER, Peter. Took the Oath of Allegiance in 1778 [Ref: L-2:28].

RICKETTS, Andrew. Private, 7th Maryland Line, from May 13, 1779 until Aug. 16, 1780, when reported missing at the Battle of Camden [Ref: D-24].

RICKETTS, Anthony (Oct. 4, 1725 - 1794). Lived in Seneca Hd. (three taxables) in 1777 [Ref: R-31:8]. Took the Oath of Allegiance before the Hon. Gerrard Briscoe on March 2, 1778 [Ref: T-3:57, L-1:44] Rendered aid by providing wheat for use of the military in 1780 and 1781 [Ref: O-308, O-380]. The nuncupative will of "Anthony Ricketts, Sr." (wife named Mary) was prepared by Benjamin Ricketts on Feb. 4, 1793 and probated in Montgomery County on April 8, 1794 [Ref: V-118, DAR-I:570]. See "Benjamin Ricketts," q.v.

RICKETTS, Anthony Jr. "Anthony Rickets, Jr." was a private, 7th Co., Middle Bn., Militia, Sep., 1777, and "Anthony Rickets" was a First Sergeant on July 15, 1780 [Ref: M-197, M-203, T-5:42].

RICKETTS, Benjamin. There were three men with this name. "Benjamin Ricketts Jr." took the Oath of Allegiance before the Hon. Joseph Wilson on Feb. 28, 1778. "Benjamin Ricketts, Sr." took the Oath of Allegiance before the Hon. Edward Burgess on Feb. 28, 1778 [Ref: T-3:63, T-3:64, L-1:44]. "Benjamin Ricketts, Sr." (eight taxables) and "Benjamin Ricketts, Jr." (one taxable) and "Benjamin Ricketts, of Anthony" (Richard Ricketts, security) all lived in Seneca Hd. in 1777 [Ref: R-31:8]. "Benjamin Ricketts, Sr." died testate in Montgomery County (wife not named) in 1788 [Ref: V-118, DAR-I:570, which latter source states Benjamin and Benjamin Jr. both died in 1788?]. Military service: Private, 7th Co., Middle Bn., Militia, Sep., 1777 [Ref: M-197, T-5:42]. Second Lieutenant, Middle Bn., Militia, April 21, 1779, and First Lieutenant, Upper Bn., March 25, 1780, and Captain, 7th Co., Middle Bn., July 15, 1780 [Ref: M-115, M-203, E-357, F-120, F-248]. Also see Source DAR-I:570, and "Anthony Ricketts," q.v.

RICKETTS, Jacob. Private, 7th Co., Middle Bn., Militia, Sep., 1777 [Ref: M-197, T-5:42]. Took the Oath of Allegiance (made his "X" mark) before the Hon. Joseph Wilson on Feb. 28, 1778 [Ref: T-3:66, L-1:44].

RICKETTS, Joseph. Private, 2nd Co., Lower Bn., Militia, Sep., 1777 [Ref: M-198, T-5:45]. Private, 7th Co., Middle Bn., Militia, July 15, 1780 [Ref: M-203]. Ensign, 7th Co., Middle Bn., Militia, Aug. 4, 1780 [Ref: M-115, M-203, F-248]. Took the Oath of Allegiance before the Hon. Edward Burgess on Feb. 28, 1778 [Ref: T-3:60, L-1:44].

RICKETTS, March or Merchant. "March Rickets" was a private, 1st Co., Lower Bn., Militia, Sep., 1777, and "Mark Ricketts" was a private, 7th Co., Middle Bn., Militia, July 15, 1780 [Ref: M-198, M-203, T-5:44]. "Merchant Ricketts" took the Oath of Allegiance (made his "X" mark) before the Hon. Edward Burgess on Feb. 28, 1778 [Ref: T-3:58, L-1:44]. "March Ricketts" rendered aid by providing wheat for use of the military in 1781 [Ref: O-400]. "Merchant Ricketts" lived in the Lower Part of Newfoundland Hd. (one taxable) in 1777 [Ref: R-31:6].

RICKETTS, Mary. See "Anthony Ricketts," q.v.

RICKETTS, Richard. Private, 7th Co., Middle Bn., Militia, Sep., 1777 [Ref: M-197, T-5:42]. Took the Oath of Allegiance (made his "R R" mark) before the Hon. Edward Burgess on Feb. 28, 1778 [Ref: T-3:60, L-1:44, which latter source listed the name as "Richard Rickket (attorney)"]. "Richard Rickets" was a private, 7th Co., Middle Bn., Militia, July 15, 1780 [Ref: M-203]. Rendered aid by providing wheat for use of the military in 1781 [Ref: O-398]. One Richard Ricketts lived in Seneca Hd. (two taxables) in 1777 [Ref: R-31:8], and another lived in Rock Creek Hd. (three taxables) in 1777 [Ref: R-31:16]. One Richard Ricketts died testate in Montgomery County (wife named Elizabeth) in 1819 [Ref: V-119], and Richard Ricketts (c1754-1830) married Elizabeth Welch [Ref: DAR-I:570]. See "Benjamin Ricketts," q.v.

RICKETTS, Robert. Private, 7th Co., Middle Bn., Militia, Sep., 1777 [Ref: M-197, T-5:42]. Private, 7th Co., Middle Bn., Militia, July 15, 1780 [Ref: M-203]. Lived in Seneca Hd. (one taxable) in 1777 [Ref: R-31:8]. Robert Ricketts married Ellian. [sic] Allison in Montgomery County on Oct. 4, 1778 [Ref: K-2:520].

RICKETTS, Sarah. Rendered aid by providing wheat for use of the military in 1781 [Ref: O-406, O-445].

RICKETTS, Thomas (1753-1828). Private, 1st Co., Lower Bn., Militia, Sep., 1777 [Ref: M-198, T-5:44]. Took the Oath of Allegiance before the Hon. Joseph Wilson on Feb. 28, 1778 [Ref: T-3:67, L-1:44]. Thomas Ricketts married Ruth Adamson in Montgomery County on June 7, 1778 [Ref: K-2:520]. He was born on Nov. 23, 1753, married secondly to Martha Wilson, and died on Aug. 22, 1828 [Ref: DAR-I:570].

RICKETTS, William. Private, 7th Co., Middle Bn., Militia, Sep., 1777 [Ref: T-5:42]. Took the Oath of Allegiance before the Hon. Edward Burgess on Feb. 28, 1778 [Ref: T-3:60, L-1:44]. Rendered aid by providing wheat for use of the military in 1781 [Ref: O-395]. Lived in Seneca Hd. (two taxables) in 1777 [Ref: R-31:8].

RICKETTS, William Jr. Private, 7th Co., Middle Bn., Militia, July 15, 1780 [Ref: M-203].

RIDGELY, Helen W. See "Jeremiah Crabb" and "Robert Doyne Dawson" and "Richard Green" and "Philemon Griffith" and "Samuel Griffith" and "William Hempston" and "Henry Hillary" and "John Trundle" and "James White," q.v.

RIDGELY, Henry. There was a Henry Ridgely in the 3rd Maryland Line, 1777-1780, but it appears he was from Anne Arundel County. He entered the service as a cadet in 1776 and rose to the rank of captain [Ref: D-5, D-39, D-157]. There was also a Henry Ridgely who lived in

Linganore Hd. (six taxables) in Montgomery County in 1777 [Ref: R-31:9].
RIDGELY, Sarah. See "Charles Greenbury Griffith," q.v.
RIDGEWAY, Isaac (b. 1752). Son of Robert Ridgeway [Ref: V-119]. Lived in Lower Potomac Hd. in 1776 [Ref: K-1:185]. Private, 5th Co., Lower Bn., Militia, Aug., 1777, and Fourth Corporal, 2nd Co., Lower Bn., July 15, 1780 [Ref: M-199, M-204, T-5:48]. Took the Oath of Allegiance (made his "X" mark) before the Hon. Samuel W. Magruder in 1778 [Ref: T-3:73]. Rendered aid by providing wheat for use of the military in 1780 [Ref: O-311].
RIDGEWAY, Margery. See "Robert Lazenby," q.v.
RIDGEWAY, Masham (Masum, Mussum). "Mussum Ridgeway" was a private, 2nd Co., Lower Bn., Militia, Sep., 1777 [Ref: M-198, T-5:45]. "Masham Ridgeway" was a private, 5th Co., Lower Bn., Militia, July 15, 1780 [Ref: M-206]. "Masum Ridgeway" took the Oath of Allegiance before the Hon. Edward Burgess on Feb. 28, 1778 [Ref: T-3:58, L-1:44]. "Masham Ridgeway" rendered aid by providing wheat for use of the military in 1780 [Ref: O-328].
RIDGEWAY, Robert. (1) Robert Ridgeway or Ridgway (1716-1781) lived in Lower Potomac Hd. (three taxables) in 1776-1777 [Ref: R-31:4, K-1:185]. Took the Oath of Allegiance before the Hon. Edward Burgess on Feb. 28, 1778 [Ref: T-3:63, L-1:44]. Died testate in Montgomery County (wife named Sarah) in July, 1781 [Ref: V-119]. (2) Robert Ridgway or Ridgeway lived in the Upper Part of Newfoundland Hd. (one taxable) in 1777 [Ref: R-31:7]. Private, 7th Co., Middle Bn., Militia, Sep., 1777 [Ref: M-197, T-5:42], and private, 7th Co., Middle Bn., Militia, July 15, 1780 [Ref: M-203]. It appears that another served at the same time as a private, 3rd Co., Lower Bn., Militia, July 15, 1780 [Ref: M-205].
RIDGEWAY, Sarah. See "Thomas Lazenby," q.v.
RIDGEWAY, William. Private, 8th Co., Upper Bn., Militia, Aug. 30, 1777 [Ref: M-195]. Took the Oath of Allegiance before the Hon. Edward Burgess on Feb. 28, 1778 [Ref: T-3:58, L-1:44]. One "William Rigeaway, aged 30" lived in Sugarland Hd. in 1776 and "William Ridgway" lived there (one taxable) in 1777 [Ref: R-31:13]. Another "William Ridgeway" lived in Rock Creek Hd. (four taxables) in 1777 [Ref: R-31:16].
RIGDON, John. Took the Oath of Allegiance before the Hon. Edward Burgess on Feb. 28, 1778 [Ref: T-3:63, L-1:44].
RIGDON, Thomas (b. 1747). Private, 8th Co., Lower Bn., Militia, July 15, 1780 [Ref: M-207]. Private, 4th Co., Lower Bn., Militia, Aug., 1777 [Ref: T-5:47 and M-199, which latter source listed the name as "Thos. Reg..on"]. Took the Oath of Allegiance before the Hon. Richard Thompson in 1778 [Ref: T-3:75, L-1:44]. Lived in George Town Hd. (two taxables) in 1776-1777 [Ref: K-1:194, R-31:3]. A Thomas Rigdon married Lucy Jennings in Montgomery County on May 20, 1779 [Ref: K-2:514].

RIGGS, Amon (1748-1822). Served as a Captain, 2nd Co., 16th (or Middle) Bn., Militia, from March 26, 1776, to at least April 21, 1779 [Ref: A-287, C-373, M-195, E-357, C-362, and M-115, which latter two sources listed his first name as "Aaron" and "Amos" instead of "Amon"]. Took the Oath of Allegiance on Sep. 1, 1780, under the Act of May 12, 1780, having neglected to do so previously "due to ignorance of the duty owed the country." [Ref: R-27:119]. Lived in Linganore Hd. (four taxables) in 1777 [Ref: R-31:9]. Amon was born on April 21, 1748, married Ruth Griffith, served as a captain, and died testate in Montgomery County on March 16, 1822 [Ref: V-119, DAR-I:571].

RIGGS, Azeriah (b. 1754). Took the Oath of Allegiance (made his "V" mark) before the Hon. Aneas Campbell on March 2, 1778 [Ref: T-3:78, L-1:44]. Lived in Sugarland Hd. in 1776-1777 [Ref: K-1:220, R-31:13].

RIGGS, Benjamin (b. 1731). Private, 4th Co., Upper Bn., Militia, Aug. 30, 1777 [Ref: M-194]. Took the Oath of Allegiance (made his "X" mark) before the Hon. Aneas Campbell on March 2, 1778 [Ref: T-3:78, L-1:44]. "Benjamin Rigg or Riggs" lived in Sugarland Hd. in 1776-1777 [Ref: K-1:211, R-31:13].

RIGGS, Edmund or Edmond (died 1784). Rendered aid by providing wheat for use of the military in 1781 [Ref: O-390]. "Edmond Riggs" lived in Sugar Loaf Hd. (two taxables) in 1777 [Ref: R-31:10]. "Edmund Riggs" died testate in Montgomery County (wife named Ruth) in 1784 [Ref: V-119].

RIGGS, Greenbury or Greenberry (1757-1844). Son of Edmund Riggs [Ref: V-119]. Private, 3rd Co., Upper Bn., Militia, Aug. 30, 1777 [Ref: M-193]. Greenbury Riggs was born on Oct. 7, 1757, married Ann Hardy in Montgomery County on Jan. 25, 1781, and died on Aug. 30, 1744 [Ref: K-2:520, DAR-I:571].

RIGGS, John. Private, 6th Co., Upper Bn., Militia, Aug. 30, 1777 [Ref: M-194]. Two men with this name took the Oath of Allegiance: one before the Hon. Edward Burgess on Feb. 28, 1778 [Ref: T-3:60, L-1:44], and another before the Hon. Elisha Williams on March 2, 1778 [Ref: T-3:80, L-1:44]. One John Riggs was a drummer, 7th Maryland Line from Dec. 6, 1777 until Dec. 8, 1779, when discharged, and this or perhaps another John Riggs was a fifer in the 7th Maryland Line in 1780 [Ref: D-242, D-243]. One John Riggs married Mary Eleaner in Montgomery County on Feb. 13, 1781 [Ref: K-2:520]. One John Riggs lived in the Upper Part of Newfoundland Hd. (three taxables) in 1777 and another lived in Sugar Loaf Hd. (two taxables) in 1777 [Ref: R-31:7, R-31:11]. One was a son of "Edmund Riggs," q.v. [Ref: V-119]. Source DAR-I:571 lists three men named John Riggs in Maryland.

RIGGS, Samuel. (1) Served as a Second Lieutenant, 29th Bn., Militia, May 14, 1776, to at least Sep., 1777 [Ref: M-116, M-196, A-424]. Took the Oath of Allegiance before the Hon. Edward Burgess on Feb. 28, 1778 [Ref: T-3:58, L-1:44]. Lived in the Upper Part of Newfoundland

Hd. (seven taxables) in 1777 and was a Constable in 1780 [Ref: W-1, R-31:7]. He was born on Oct. 6, 1740, married Amelia Dorsey, and died testate in Montgomery County on May 25, 1814 [Ref: V-120, DAR-I:571]. (2) There was also a Samuel Riggs who was a private, 7th Co., Upper Bn., Militia, Aug. 30, 1777 [Ref: M-195].

RIGGS, Susan. See "Robert Hurdle," q.v.

RIGGS, Thomas (1745-1797). Took the Oath of Allegiance (made his "X" mark) before the Hon. Edward Burgess on Feb. 28, 1778 [Ref: T-3:60, L-1:44]. Lived in Sugarland Hd. in 1776-1777 [Ref: K-1:220, R-31:13]. Died testate in Montgomery County in 1797 [Ref: V-120].

RIGGS, Thomas Whiting (or Whelan). "Thomas Whiting Riggs" was a private, 2nd Co., Upper Bn., Militia, Aug. 30, 1777 [Ref: M-193]. "Thomas Whelan Riggs" took the Oath of Allegiance before the Hon. Aneas Campbell on March 2, 1778 [Ref: T-3:78, L-1:44]. "Thomas Riggs" lived in the Upper Part of Newfoundland Hd. (two taxables) in 1777 [Ref: R-31:7].

RIGGS, Virlinda. See "John Clayton," q.v.

RIGGS, William. Private, 7th Maryland Line, who transferred to the 2nd Maryland Line on Jan. 11, 1779 [Ref: D-243].

RIGNEY, Terrence (b. 1730). Private, 1st Co., Upper Bn., Militia, Aug. 30, 1777 [Ref: M-193]. Took the Oath of Allegiance before the Hon. Edward Burgess on Feb. 28, 1778 [Ref: T-3:63, L-1:44]. Rendered aid by providing corn for use of the military in 1780 [Ref: O-301]. "Turrance Rigne or Terance Rigney"" lived in Sugarland Hd. (one taxable) in 1776-1777 [Ref: K-1:199, R-31:13].

RILEY, Anne. See "Isaac Windsor," q.v.

RILEY (RIELY), Barney. Private, 7th Maryland Regiment, from Dec. 12, 1776 until Aug. 22, 1777, when reported killed [Ref: K-1:185].

RILEY, Elijah. Private, 2nd Class, 3rd Co., Middle Bn., Militia, July 15, 1780 [Ref: M-202].

RILEY (REILY), Elizabeth. "Elizabeth Riley" lived in Sugar Loaf Hd. (four taxables) in 1777 [Ref: R-31:10]. "Elizabeth Reily" rendered aid by providing wheat for use of the military in 1781 [Ref: O-391]. See "Ninian Riley," q.v.

RILEY, Garrard. See "Ninian Riley," q.v.

RILEY (REILY), Hugh (1726-1804). Took the Oath of Allegiance before the Hon. Samuel W. Magruder in 1778 [Ref: T-3:73, L-1:44]. "Hugh Reily" rendered aid by providing wheat for use of the military in 1780 [Ref: O-317]. "Hugh Riley" lived in Lower Potomac Hd. (seven taxables) in 1776-1777 [Ref: K-1:185, R-31:4]. Died testate in Montgomery County (wife not named) in 1804 [Ref: V-120, V-121]. See "James Riley," q.v.

RILEY, James. (1) Private, 2nd Co., Middle Bn., Militia, Sep. 4, 1777 [Ref: M-196, T-5:37]. Private, 2nd Co., Lower Bn., Militia, July 15, 1780 [Ref: M-204]. Took the Oath of Allegiance before the Hon. Gerrard Briscoe on March 2, 1778 [Ref: T-3:56, L-1:44]. (2) Private, 7th Class, 3rd Co.,

Middle Bn., Militia, July 15, 1780 [Ref: M-202]. He appears to have been born in 1763, a son of "Hugh Riley," q.v. [Ref: K-1:185]. See "Ninian Riley," q.v.

RILEY, Jeremiah. Private, 2nd Co., Middle Bn., Militia, Sep. 4, 1777 [Ref: M-196, T-5:37]. Took the Oath of Allegiance before the Hon. Gerrard Briscoe on March 2, 1778 [Ref: T-3:56, L-1:44]. Private, 7th Class, 3rd Co., Middle Bn., Militia, July 15, 1780 [Ref: M-202].

RILEY (RIELY), John. Private, 7th Maryland Regiment, from April 25, 1778 until Feb. 20, 1780, when he reportedly "deserted" [Ref: D-243]. Private, Capt. Thomas Beall's Co., Maryland Line, 1780 [Ref: D-350]. See "Nnian Riley," q.v.

RILEY, Mark. Private, 4th Co., Middle Bn., Militia, Sep., 1777 [Ref: M-196, T-5:39]. Private, 1st Class, 4th Co., Middle Bn., Militia, July 15, 1780 [Ref: M-202].

RILEY, Martha. See "Joseph White," q.v.

RILEY, Mary. See "Solomon Dickerson" and "William Allnut," q.v.

RILEY (REILY), Ninian. Took the Oath of Allegiance before the Hon. Samuel W. Magruder in 1778 [Ref: T-3:73, L-1:44]. "Ninian Reily" rendered aid by providing wheat for use of the military in 1780 [Ref: O-302]. "Ninian Riley" lived in the Upper Part of Potomac Hd. (one taxable) in 1777 [Ref: R-31:15]. The children of Ninian Riley and Elizabeth Taylor were all born in Maryland: James Taylor, Ninian, Jr., Garrard, John, Sarah, Mary, Ann, Lucy, and another daughter (name not stated). Family records and the diary of Nancy Riley (daughter of Garrard) indicate that Garrard Riliey was 17 years old when the family left Maryland and went to North Carolina (circa 1783 or 1784). James Riley bought land on Nov. 24, 1784 on the north side of the South Fork of Hunting Creek in Rowan County. The deed also stated he was from Montgomery County, Maryland [Ref: Research files of Helen Scholl, of Indianapolis, Indiana (1994), and Henry C. Peden's *Marylanders to Carolina* (1994), p. 180].

RILEY, Ninian Jr. Private, 2nd Co., Lower Bn., Militia, July 15, 1780 [Ref: M-204]. See "Ninian Riley," q.v.

RILEY, Patrick (b. 1752). Lived in Sugarland Hd. in 1776 [Ref: K-1:214]. Served as a Corporal, 7th Maryland Regiment, 1776-1780 [Ref: D-242]. He may have been the "Patrick Riely" who was recruited to serve in the Continental Army in 1780 [Ref: D-342].

RILEY, Walter (1752-1777). Lived in Lower Potomac Hd. in 1776 [Ref: K-1:185]. Private, 7th Maryland Regiment, from Dec. 5, 1776 until Oct. 4, 1777, when reported killed [Ref: D-242].

RILEY, Zachariah. Private, 2nd Co., Middle Bn., Militia, Sep. 4, 1777 [Ref: M-196, T-5:37]. Took the Oath of Allegiance before the Hon. Gerrard Briscoe on March 2, 1778 [Ref: T-3:57, L-1:44]. Private, 1st Class, 3rd Co., Middle Bn., Militia, July 15, 1780 [Ref: M-202].

RINER, George. Took the Oath of Allegiance in 1778 [Ref: L-2:28].

RISENER (REISNER), Jacob (b. 1750). Private, 3rd Co., Lower Bn., Militia, Sep., 1777 [Ref: M-199, T-5:46]. Private, 8th Co., Lower Bn., Militia, July 15, 1780 [Ref: M-207]. "Jacob Risener or Risoner" lived in George Town Hd. (one taxable) in 1776-1777 [Ref: K-1:194, R-31:3]. "Jacob Reisner" took the Oath of Allegiance before the Hon. Richard Thompson in 1778 [Ref: T-3:76, L-1:44].

RISLEY, Matthias. See "John Predix," q.v.

ROADABUSH, Dan. Took the Oath of Allegiance in 1778 [Ref: L-2:28].

ROADEN, Richard (negro). Private, 8th Co., Lower Bn., Militia, July 15, 1780 [Ref: M-207].

ROBERTS, Alexander. Private, 6th Co., Lower Bn., Militia, July 15, 1780 [Ref: M-206].

ROBERTS, Basil. Private, 1st Co., Upper Bn., Militia, Aug. 30, 1777 [Ref: M-193]. Served as a grand juror in Aug., 1777 [Ref: R-31:17]. Took the Oath of Allegiance before the Hon. Joseph Wilson on Feb. 28, 1778 [Ref: T-3:66, L-1:44]. He was paid for recruiting services in 1780 by the Collector of the Tax in Montgomery County [Ref: F-54]. Basil Robert lived in Sugar Loaf Hd. (five taxables) in 1777 [Ref: R-31:11].

ROBERTS, Billingsley (died 1791). "Billingsley Roberts" rendered aid by providing wheat for use of the military in 1781 [Ref: O-413]. "Billinsby Roberts" [sic] lived in the Upper Part of Potomac Hd. (six taxables) in 1777 [Ref: R-31:15]. "Billingsly Roberts" died testate in Montgomery County (wife not named) in 1791 and mentioned son Richard Roberts in Kentucky and left land there on the north fork of the Holson River to sons Richard, John, Henry, Joseph, James, and William [Ref: V-121].

ROBERTS, Henry. See "Billingsley Roberts," q.v.

ROBERTS, Hezekiah. Private, 1st Co., Upper Bn., Militia, Aug. 30, 1777 [Ref: M-193]. "Ezekiah Roberts" took the Oath of Allegiance before the Hon. Gerrard Briscoe on March 2, 1778 [Ref: T-3:56, L-1:44]. "Hezekiah Roberts" lived in Sugar Loaf Hd. (one taxable) in 1777 [Ref: R-31:11]. He married Cloe Coffee in Montgomery County on July 7, 1778 [Ref: K-2:516].

ROBERTS, Horatio. Private, 3rd Co., Upper Bn., Militia, Aug. 30, 1777 [Ref: M-193]. Private, 7th Maryland Line, from Feb. 2, 1780 until Aug. 16, 1780, when reported missing at the Battle of Camden [Ref: D-243, D-341].

ROBERTS, James. Took the Oath of Allegiance before the Hon. Elisha Williams on March 2, 1778 [Ref: T-3:81, L-1:44]. James Roberts lived in Sugar Loaf Hd. (four taxables) in 1777 [Ref: R-31:10]. See "Billingsley Roberts," q.v.

ROBERTS, John. Private, 7th Class, 2nd Co., Middle Bn., Militia, July 15, 1780 [Ref: M-201]. Took the Oath of Allegiance in 1778 [Ref: L-2:28]. See "Billingsley Roberts," q.v.

ROBERTS, Joseph. See "Billingsley Roberts," q.v.

ROBERTS, Richard. Private, 6th Co., Lower Bn., Militia, Aug., 1777 [Ref: M-200, T-5:49]. Private, 3rd Co., Lower Bn., Militia, July 15, 1780 [Ref: M-205]. Took the Oath of Allegiance before the Hon. William Deakins, Jr. before March 3, 1778 [Ref: T-3:68, L-1:44]. Rendered aid by providing wheat for use of the military in 1781 [Ref: O-413]. Richard Roberts married Catherine Clements in Montgomery County on Nov. 26, 1778 [Ref: K-2:520]. See "Billingsley Roberts," q.v.
ROBERTS, Sarah. See "Benjamin Greentree," q.v.
ROBERTS, Thomas. Private, 4th Class, 2nd Co., Middle Bn., Militia, July 15, 1780 [Ref: M-201].
ROBERTS, William (died 1816). Private, 8th Class, 2nd Co., Middle Bn., Militia, July 15, 1780 [Ref: M-201]. Died testate in Montgomery County (unmarried) in 1816 [Ref: V-121]. See "Billingsley Roberts," q.v.
ROBERTS, Zephaniah. Took the Oath of Allegiance before the Hon. Elisha Williams on March 2, 1778 [Ref: T-3:81, L-1:44].
ROBERTSON, Basil. Private, 7th Co., Middle Bn., Militia, Sep., 1777 [Ref: M-197, T-5:42]. Lived in Seneca Hd. (one taxable) in 1777 [Ref: R-31:8].
ROBERTSON (ROBERSON, ROBESON), George. Lived in Rock Creek Hd. (eight taxables) in 1777 [Ref: R-31:16]. Took the Oath of Allegiance before the Hon. Edward Burgess on Feb. 28, 1778 [Ref: T-3:64, L-1:44]. "George Roberson" was a private, 8th Co., Middle Bn., Militia, Sep., 1777 [Ref: M-198, T-5:43].
ROBERTSON, Isaac. Private, 7th Maryland Line, 1777-1779 [Ref: D-242].
ROBERTSON (ROBESON), James. Lived in Sugarland Hd. (one taxable) in 1777 [Ref: R-31:13]. Private, 1st Class, 3rd Co., Middle Bn., Militia, July 15, 1780 [Ref: M-202]. Took the Oath of Allegiance before the Hon. Elisha Williams on March 2, 1778 [Ref: T-3:82, L-1:44]. "James Robeson" was a private, 7th Co., Upper Bn., Militia, Aug. 30, 1777 [Ref: M-194].
ROBERTSON (ROBESON), John. Lived in Sugarland Hd. (two taxables) in 1777 [Ref: R-31:13]. Took the Oath of Allegiance before the Hon. Elisha Williams on March 2, 1778 [Ref: T-3:81, L-1:45]. "John Robeson" was a private, 1st Co., Upper Bn., Militia, Aug. 30, 1777 [Ref: M-193].
ROBERTSON (ROBERSON), Nathan or Nathaniel (b. 1752). "Nathan Robeson or Robertson" lived in Lower Potomac Hd. (one taxable) in 1776-1777 [Ref: K-1:185, R-31:4]. "Nathaniel Robertson" was a private, 4th Co., Lower Bn., Militia, Aug., 1777 [Ref: M-199, T-5:47]. "Nathan Robertson" was a private, 1st Co., Lower Bn., Militia, July 15, 1780 [Ref: M-204]. "Nathan Roberson" took the Oath of Allegiance before the Hon. Charles Jones on Jan. 10, 1778 [Ref: T-3:71, L-1:44].
ROBERTSON, Robert (b. 1742). Lived in Lower Potomac Hd. in 1776 [Ref: K-1:185]. Private, 1st Co., Lower Bn., Militia, July 15, 1780 [Ref: M-204].
ROBERTSON (ROBERSON), William. (1) Served as a Second Lieutenant, Middle Bn., Militia, Sep. 12, 1777 [Ref: M-116, C-373]. Took the Oath

of Allegiance before the Hon. Joseph Wilson on Feb. 28, 1778 [Ref: T-3:67, L-1:45]. (2) "William Roberson" was a private, 2nd Co., Lower Bn., Militia, Sep., 1777 [Ref: M-198, T-5:45]. "William Robertson" lived in Rock Creek Hd. (six taxables) in 1777 [Ref: R-31:16].

ROBERTSON (ROBERSON), Zachariah. "Zachariah Robertson, aged 14" lived in Lower Potomac Hd. in 1776 and "Zachariah Roberson, aged 15" lived in George Town Hd. in 1776 [Ref: K-1:185, K-1:194]. One served as a private, 1st Co., Lower Bn., Militia, July 15, 1780 [Ref: M-204], and private, Capt. Price's Co., 3rd Maryland Line, 1781-1782 [Ref: D-452].

ROBINS (ROBBINS), John. Private, Maryland Line, when recruited to serve in the Continental Army in 1780. He pensioned (S35051) in Montgomery County in 1818, aged about 60, and was still on rolls in 1835, aged about 72 [Ref: D-342, J-38, K-2:386, Q-135, P-2902].

ROBINSON, James. Private, 4th Co., Lower Bn., Militia, July 15, 1780 [Ref: M-205]. In 1776 "James Robinson, aged 49" lived in Sugarland Hd. with a large family [Ref: K-1:199].

ROBINSON, Leonard. Took the Oath of Allegiance before the Hon. Edward Burgess on Feb. 28, 1778 [Ref: T-3:63, L-1:45]. Rendered aid by providing wheat for use of the military in 1781 [Ref: O-435].

ROBINSON, Margaret. See "John Mockbee," q.v.

ROBINSON, Robert. Private, enrolled into a company of militia for the service of the Flying Camp, Oct. 15, 1776 [Ref: B-353].

ROBY, Absolam. Rendered aid by providing wheat for use of the military in 1780 [Ref: O-329, O-344].

ROBY, Anne. See "Elias Loveless (Lovelace)," q.v.

ROBY, Berry. Private, 2nd Co., Lower Bn., Militia, Sep., 1777 [Ref: M-198, T-5:45]. Took the Oath of Allegiance before the Hon. Edward Burgess on Feb. 28, 1778 [Ref: T-3:60, L-1:45]. Private, 5th Co., Lower Bn., Militia, July 15, 1780 [Ref: M-206]. "Beary Roby" lived in Rock Creek Hd. (one taxable) in 1777 [Ref: R-31:16].

ROBY, Ignatius. Private, 2nd Co., Lower Bn., Militia, Sep., 1777 [Ref: M-198, T-5:45]. Served as a petit juror in Nov., 1777 [Ref: R-31:18]. Took the Oath of Allegiance before the Hon. Edward Burgess on Feb. 28, 1778 [Ref: T-3:63, L-1:45]. Lived in Rock Creek Hd. (four taxables) in 1777 [Ref: R-31:16].

ROBY (ROBEY, ROBIE), John. Private, 4th Co., Upper Bn., Militia, Aug. 30, 1777 [Ref: M-194]. "John Robie" took the Oath of Allegiance (made his "X" mark) before the Hon. Aneas Campbell on March 2, 1778 [Ref: T-3:78, L-1:45]. In 1815 the Treasurer of Maryland was directed to pay to John Roby, during life, the half pay of a private for his Revolutionary War services [Ref: K-2:386]. A "Taylor John Robey" [John Robey, taylor?] lived in Sugarland Hd. (two taxables) in 1777 [Ref: R-31:13].

ROBY, Patrick. Private, 4th Co., Upper Bn., Militia, Aug. 30, 1777 [Ref: M-194].

ROBY, Thomas. See "Elias Loveless (Lovelace)," q.v.

ROCKFORD (ROCHFORD), Edward (b. 1748). Lived in Sugarland Hd. in 1776 [Ref: K-1:199]. "Edward Rochford" was a private, 7th Maryland Regiment, from April 23, 1778 until Aug. 27, 1780, when he reportedly "deserted" [Ref: D-243].

ROGERS, Francis. Substitute from Montgomery County in the 7th Maryland Line who served as a private under Capt. Lloyd Beall in 1780, in the Extra Regiment in 1781, and in the 3rd Maryland Line from 1781 to July, 1782 [Ref: D-394, D-442, G-238, G-332].

ROGERS, William. Private, 8th Co., Lower Bn., Militia, July 15, 1780 [Ref: M-207].

ROLLINS, Aaron, and others. See "Aaron Rawlings," q.v.

RONEY, James. Private, 1st or 32nd Bn., Militia (no date was given; possibly June, 1777). [Ref: T-5:2].

RONEY, John. Private, 1st or 32nd Bn., Militia (no date was given; possibly June, 1777). [Ref: T-5:1].

ROSE, George. Private, 5th Co., Middle Bn., Militia, July 15, 1780 [Ref: M-203].

ROSENSTEEL, George. Rendered aid by providing pork for use of the military in 1780 [Ref: O-344].

ROSS, Alexander (b. 1751). Lived in Lower Potomac Hd. in 1776 [Ref: K-1:185]. Served as a private in the 7th Maryland Regiment, Feb. 11, 1777 to 1780, and a private, 1st Maryland Regiment, 1780-1781 [Ref: D-242, D-356].

ROSS, John. Took the Oath of Allegiance before the Hon. Elisha Williams on March 2, 1778 [Ref: T-3:82].

ROUSTRIDGE (ROUGHSIDGE), William. "William Roustridge" was a private, 8th Co., Lower Bn., Militia, July 15, 1780 [Ref: M-207]. "William Roughsidge" took the Oath of Allegiance before the Hon. Richard Thompson in 1778 [Ref: T-3:75, L-1:45].

ROWE (ROE), Robert (b. 1755). "Robert Rowe" was a private, 2nd Maryland Regiment, from 1777 until discharged on Dec. 12, 1779 [Ref: D-155, D-156]. "Robert Roe" lived in North West Hd. in 1776 [Ref: K-1:228].

ROWWEN, Paul. Private, Capt. Price's Co., 3rd Maryland Line, 1781-1782 [Ref: D-454, although the index shows "Timothy Rowwen"]. There was a "Daniel Rowwen, aged 22" in George Town Hd. in 1776, but Paul Rowwen was not listed [Ref: K-1:194].

ROZAN, Nathan. Private, 1st Co., Lower Bn., Militia, Sep., 1777 [Ref: M-198, T-5:44].

RUGLASS (RUGGLES, ROUGHLESS), James. "James Ruglass" took the Oath of Allegiance (made his "X" mark) before the Hon. Edward Burgess on Feb. 28, 1778 [Ref: T-3:58, L-1:45]. "James Roughless" lived in the Lower Part of Newfoundland Hd. (one taxable) in 1777 [Ref: R-31:6]. "James Ruggles, Sr." applied for pension (R9067) in Greenup County, Kentucky, stating he served in Capt. Bell's Co. in Maryland in 1777. He had filed on May 5, 1834, but was apparently rejected in 1836 (due to lack of proof and the original papers lost in Annapolis). James Ruggles (1784-1857), probably a son of James Ruggles, Sr., was born in Maryland, lived in Mason County, Kentucky (where he married Sarah Conway in 1804, and second to Margaret Clancy in 1813 in Fleming County, Kentucky). Died in Indiana in 1857 [Ref: P-2975 and *Kentucky Ancestor*, Vol. 5, No. 1 (1969), p. 49].

RUGLESS, William. Private, 7th Co., Lower Bn., Militia, July 15, 1780 [Ref: M-207].

RUNKLE, Jacob. Took the Oath of Allegiance in 1778 [Ref: L-2:28].

RUNKLE, William Rev. See "Ninian Beall," q.v.

RUSSELL, Aaron (1759-1780). Lived in Lower Potomac Hd. in 1776 [Ref: K-1:185]. Private, 7th Maryland Regiment, from May 30, 1778 until Feb. 20, 1780, when reported dead [Ref: D-243].

RUSSELL, Henry. Private, 3rd Co., Upper Bn., Militia, Aug. 30, 1777 [Ref: M-193]. "Henry Russell" took the Oath of Allegiance before the Hon. Edward Burgess on Feb. 28, 1778 [Ref: T-3:63, L-1:45]. "Henry Rusett" [sic] lived in the Upper Part of Potomac Hd. (one taxable) in 1777 [Ref: R-31:15].

RUSSELL, Thomas (b. 1758). Lived in Sugarland Hd. in 1776 [Ref: K-1:215]. Private, 3rd Maryland Regiment, enlisted on May 16, 1778, for the duration [Ref: D-157, D-297].

RYAN, John. Private, Capt. Edward Burgess' Co., Lower District of Frederick (now Montgomery) County, Militia, July, 1776 [Ref: D-42].

RYAN, Rebecca. See "Benjamin Penn," q.v.

RYAN, William. Private, 7th Co., Middle Bn., Militia, Sep., 1777 [Ref: M-197, T-5:42]. Private, 4th Co., Lower Bn., Militia, July 15, 1780 [Ref: M-205]. Took the Oath of Allegiance before the Hon. Edward Burgess on Feb. 28, 1778 [Ref: T-3:58, L-1:45]. "William Ryon" took the Oath of Allegiance on Sep. 1, 1780, under the Act of May 12, 1780, having neglected to do so previously "due to ignorance of the duty owed the country." [Ref: R-27:119].

SAFFLE (SAFFELL), Charles (1751-1836). Private, Flying Camp, Frederick (now Montgomery) County, enlisted by Greenbury Gaither on July 29, 1776 [Ref: D-44]. Private, 1st Co., Middle Bn., Militia, Aug. 30, 1777 [Ref: M-195]. Private, 5th Co., Middle Bn., Militia, July 15, 1780 [Ref: M-203]. Took the Oath of Allegiance before the Hon. Gerrard Briscoe on March 2, 1778 [Ref: T-3:56, L-1:45]. "Charles Saffell" was a musician, Maryland Militia, who applied for pension (S7442) in Montgomery County on March 23, 1833, aged 82, stating he enlisted on June 15, 1776, in Baltimore, Maryland, and served six months as a drummer in Col. Griffith's Maryland Regiment of the Flying Camp. He reenlisted immediately and served in the 7th Maryland Line until discharged in the fall of 1778. His father (name not given) died while he was in the service. Charles died on March 31, 1836, and final payment was made to his surviving children (none named). [Ref: P-2996, J-49, Y-51]. Charles Saffle married Sophia Segar in Montgomery County on Oct. 5, 1780 [Ref: K-2:520]. Also see "George Beckwith," q.v.

SAFFLE (SAFFEL, SAFFIELD), James. Private, 1st Co., Middle Bn., Militia, Aug. 30, 1777 [Ref: M-195]. Private, 5th Co., Middle Bn., Militia, July 15, 1780 [Ref: M-203]. "James Saffield" lived in Seneca Hd. (one taxable) in 1777 [Ref: R-31:8].

SAFFLE (SAFFEL), Joshua. "Joshua Saffle" was a private, 5th Co., Middle Bn., Militia, July 15, 1780 [Ref: M-203]. "Joshua Saffel" married Virlinda Prather in Montgomery County on July 24 1777 [Ref: K-2:516].

SAFFLE (SAFFEL, SAFFIELD), William. Private, 1st Co., Middle Bn., Militia, Aug. 30, 1777 [Ref: M-195]. Took the Oath of Allegiance before the Hon. Gerrard Briscoe on March 2, 1778 [Ref: T-3:56, L-1:45]. Private, 5th Co., Middle Bn., Militia, July 15, 1780 [Ref: M-203]. "William Saffel" rendered aid by providing wheat for use of the military in 1781 [Ref: O-394]. "William Saffield" lived in Seneca Hd. (one taxable) in 1777 [Ref: R-31:8].

SAGE, Thomas. Took the Oath of Allegiance in 1778 [Ref: L-2:28].

SANDERS, Charles (b. 1731). Lived in Sugarland Hd. in 1776 and had two taxables in 1777 [Ref: K-1:220, R-31:13]. Private, 8th Co., Upper Bn., Militia, Aug. 30, 1777 [Ref: M-195]. Took the Oath of Allegiance before the Hon. Aneas Campbell on March 2, 1778 [Ref: T-3:77, L-1:45].

SANDERS, John and Thomas. See "Asa Darby," q.v.

SANGO (SANG), James Perry. "James Perry Sango" rendered aid by providing wheat for use of the military in 1781 [Ref: O-448]. There was a "James Sung or Sang?" (b. 1761) who lived in Lower Potomac Hd. in 1776 [Ref: K-1"186].

SANSBERRY (SANSBURY), Richard. Private, 4th Maryland Regiment, discharged Dec. 14, 1779 [Ref: D-165].

SANSBERRY (SANSBURY), Thomas (b. 1748). "Thomas Sansbury" was a private, 5th Co., Middle Bn., Militia, Sep., 1777 [Ref: M-197, T-5:40]. Took the Oath of Allegiance (made his "T" mark) before the Hon. Joseph Wilson on Feb. 28, 1778 [Ref: T-3:64, L-1:45]. "Thomas Sansberry or Sandsbery" lived in Lower Potomac Hd. (one taxable) in 1776-1777 [Ref: K-1:185, R-31:4].

SANSBERRY (SANSBURY), William. "William Sansbury" was a private, 1st Co., Middle Bn., Militia, Aug. 30, 1777 [Ref: M-195]. "William Sansberry" took the Oath of Allegiance before the Hon. Gerrard Briscoe on March 2, 1778 [Ref: T-3:57, L-1:45].

SARGEANT, Elisha. Took the Oath of Allegiance in 1778 [Ref: L-2:28].

SARGEANT, James Sr. Took the Oath of Allegiance in 1778 [Ref: L-2:28].

SARGEANT, Richard. This may be the "Richard Sarjeant, Jr." who enlisted in Frederick County on July 22, 1776 [Ref: D-49]. See "William Sargeant," q.v.

SARGEANT, Thomas. Private, 2nd Maryland Line, April 24, 1778 to Nov. 20, 1778, when reported dead [Ref: D-162, D-294]. See "William Sargeant," q.v.

SARGEANT, William (b. 1760). Private, Maryland Line, who applied for pension (S38356) on April 21, 1834, aged 74, in Bracken County, Kentucky, stating he was born in 1760 in Montgomery County, Maryland and enlisted in Frederick County on Sep. 17, 1777. Prior to the war he lived in Montgomery and Frederick Counties, Maryland, and Loudoun County, Virginia. Since the war he removed to Madison County (another source stated Butler County), Kentucky from Loudoun County, Virginia. He stated that his brothers Richard and Thomas and father William all died while serving in the war [Ref: P-3017, Y-6, Z-15, D-49, D-159, D-162, D-294].

SARGEANT, William Sr. Private, 1st Maryland Line, from Dec. 10, 1776 to March 6, 1778, when he reportedly "deserted;" however, his son William stated that his father William died while serving in the war [Ref: P-3017]. See "William Sargeant," q.v.

SCHLIGO, William. Private, 7th Co., Middle Bn., Militia, Sep., 1777 [Ref: M-197, T-5:42].

SCHNERTZELL, George. Took the Oath of Allegiance in 1778 [Ref: L-2:28].

SCHOOLFIELD, David. Rendered aid by providing mutton for use of the military in 1781 [Ref: O-373].

SCHOOLFIELD, John (b. 1721). Rendered aid by providing wheat for use of the military in 1781 [Ref: O-397]. John Schoolfield lived in George Town Hd. in 1776-1777 [Ref: K-1:194, R-31:3].

SCHOOLFIELD (SCHOFIELD), Joseph. Private, 3rd Co., Lower Bn., Militia, Sep., 1777 [Ref: M-199, T-5:46].

SCHOOLFIELD (SCHOFIELD, SCOFFIELD), William (b. 1736). Private, 3rd Co., Lower Bn., Militia, Sep., 1777 [Ref: M-199, T-5:46], and private, 8th Co., Lower Bn., Militia, July 15, 1780 [Ref: M-207]. "William Schofield" lived in Lower Potomac Hd. in 1776 [Ref: K-1:185].

SCISSELL, John, and others. See "John Cecil" and others, q.v.

SCOTT, Agnes. See "Thomas Hoy," q.v.

SCOTT, Amos. See "Thomas Scott," q.v.

SCOTT, Charles. Private, 2nd Co., Upper Bn., Militia, Aug. 30, 1777 [Ref: M-193]. Took the Oath of Allegiance (made his mark) before the Hon. Aneas Campbell on March 2, 1778 [Ref: T-3:77, L-1:45]. Charles Scott lived in Sugar Loaf Hd. (one taxable) in 1777 [Ref: R-31:11].

SCOTT, George. Took the Oath of Allegiance in 1778 [Ref: L-2:28]. Lived in Sugar Loaf Hd. (seven taxables) and also owned a working plantation ("quarter") there in 1777 [Ref: R-31:11, R-31:13].

SCOTT, Samuel. Took the Oath of Allegiance in 1778 [Ref: L-2:28].

SCOTT, Thomas. (1) Ensign, 6th Co., 29th Bn., Militia, June 21, 1777, and Ensign, 3rd Co., Lower Bn., July 15, 1780 [Ref: M-119, M-200, M-

204, T-5:49, C-296, C-373]. Took the Oath of Allegiance before the Hon. Joseph Offutt on March 2, 1778 [Ref: T-3:70, L-1:45]. (2) Private, 1st or 32nd Bn., Militia (no date was given; possibly June, 1777). [Ref: T-5:2]. One Thomas Scott lived in the Upper Part of Potomac Hd. (one taxable) in 1777 [Ref: R-31:15]. One died testate in Montgomery County (wife named Margaret) in 1820 and mentioned sons Amos, Thomas and William, among other children [Ref: V-122, V-123].

SCOTT, William. Substitute from Montgomery County who was discharged from the Maryland Line on Dec. 3, 1781 [Ref: I-11]. See "Thomas Scott," q.v.

SCRIBNER, Sarah. See "Henry Gue," q.v.

SCRIVENOR, William. See "George Snell," q.v.

SEABORN (SEABURN, SEBON), John (b. 1750). "John Seaburn" was a private, 8th Co., Upper Bn., Militia, Aug. 30, 1777 [Ref: M-195]. "John Seaborn" took the Oath of Allegiance before the Hon. Elisha Williams on March 2, 1778 [Ref: T-3:80, L-1:45]. "John Sebon, aged 26" lived in Sugarland Hd. in 1776 [Ref: K-1:217].

SEAGER (SEAGAR), John (died 1785). "John Seager" took the Oath of Allegiance before the Hon. Gerrard Briscoe on March 2, 1778 [Ref: T-3:56, L-1:45]. "John Seagar" died testate in Montgomery County (wife not named) in 1785 [Ref: V-123].

SEALY, Edward. See "Asa Darby," q.v.

SEAR (SEARS), James. (1) Private, 7th Co., Upper Bn., Militia, Aug. 30, 1777 [Ref: M-195]. (2) Private, 4th Co., Upper Bn., Militia, Aug. 30, 1777 [Ref: M-194]. Two men with this name took the Oath of Allegiance before the Hon. Aneas Campbell on March 2, 1778 [Ref: T-3:77, L-1:45], and one made his "X" mark [Ref: T-3:78, L-1:45]. One "James Sear" lived in Sugarland Hd. (one taxable) in 1777 [Ref: R-31:13], and "James Seares, aged 16" lived there in 1776, a son of William Seares, Jr. [Ref: K-1:215]. "James Seares, aged 78" lived in Sugarland Hd. (wife named Elizabeth) in 1776 [Ref: K-1:215].

SEAR (SEYER), Richard. Rendered aid by providing wheat for use of the military in 1780 [Ref: O-317].

SEAR (SEARS, SEAYER), William. Private, 8th Co., Upper Bn., Militia, Aug. 30, 1777 [Ref: M-195]. Took the Oath of Allegiance before the Hon. Aneas Campbell on March 2, 1778 [Ref: T-3:77, L-1:45]. "William Sear" lived in Sugarland Hd. (two taxables) in 1777 [Ref: R-31:13]. "William Seares, Jr., aged 48" lived in Sugarland Hd. in 1776 (wife named Elizabeth) and he had a son William, aged 14, among others [Ref: K-1:215]. "William Seayer" (Jr.?) was a private, 5th Co., Lower Bn., Militia, July 15, 1780 [Ref: M-206]. "William Sear" (Sr.?) died testate in Montgomery County (wife not named) in 1803 [Ref: V-124].

SEDWICK (SEDGEWICK), Benjamin. Private, 7th Co., Middle Bn., Militia, Sep., 1777 [Ref: M-197, T-5:42]. "Benjamin Sedgewick" was a private, 7th Co., Middle Bn., Militia, July 15, 1780 [Ref: M-203].

"Benjamin Sedwick" lived in Seneca Hd. (two taxables) in 1777 [Ref: R-31:8].
SEDWICK (SEDGEWICK, SEGGICK), John. Private, 5th Co., Lower Bn., Militia, Aug., 1777 [Ref: T-5:48]. "John Sedwick" took the Oath of Allegiance before the Hon. Samuel W. Magruder in 1778 [Ref: T-3:73]. "John Sedgewick" was a private, 2nd Co., Lower Bn., Militia, July 15, 1780 [Ref: M-204]. "John Seggick" lived in the Upper Part of Potomac Hd. (one taxable) in 1777 [Ref: R-31:15].
SEDWICK (SEDGEWICK), William. Private, 5th Co., Lower Bn., Militia, Aug., 1777 [Ref: T-5:48]. Took the Oath of Allegiance (made his "W" mark) before the Hon. Samuel W. Magruder in 1778 [Ref: T-3:73]. "William Sedgewick" was a private, 2nd Co., Lower Bn., Militia, July 15, 1780 [Ref: M-204].
SEGAR, Sarah. See "Nathaniel Ducker," q.v.
SEGAR, Sophia. See "Charles Saffle," q.v.
SELBY, Ely. Private, 1st or 32nd Bn., Militia (no date was given; possibly June, 1777). [Ref: T-5:1].
SELBY (SEBLEY), James (1760-1801). "James Selby" was a private, 7th Co., Upper Bn., Militia, Aug. 30, 1777 [Ref: M-194]. "James Sebley" [sic] lived in Sugarland Hd. (one taxable) in 1777 [Ref: R-31:13]. He married (1) Elizabeth Selby and (2) Mary Hickman Bell [Ref: DAR-I:603].
SELBY, John (1755?-1813). Private, 7th Co., Lower Bn., Militia, Aug., 1777 [Ref: M-200, T-5:50]. Lived in the Lower Part of Newfoundland Hd. (three taxables) in 1777 [Ref: R-31:6]. There was a "John Celbe, aged 21" who was a servant of Frances Larrow in North West Hd. in 1776 [Ref: K-1:230, which mistakenly listed the name as "Colbo"]. "John Selby" died testate in Montgomery County (wife not named) in 1813 [Ref: V-124].
SELBY, Richard. Son of Thomas Selby, Sr. [Ref: V-125]. Private, 1st Co., Middle Bn., Militia, Aug. 30, 1777 [Ref: M-195]. Took the Oath of Allegiance before the Hon. Gerrard Briscoe on March 2, 1778 [Ref: T-3:57, L-1:45]. Private, 5th Co., Middle Bn., Militia, July 15, 1780 [Ref: M-203]. Rendered aid by providing wheat for use of the military in 1780 and 1781 [Ref: O-308, O-396]. Lived in Seneca Hd. (one taxable) in 1777 [Ref: R-31:8].
SELBY, Samuel. Private, 4th Co., Middle Bn., Militia, Sep., 1777 [Ref: M-196, T-5:39]. Took the Oath of Allegiance before the Hon. Edward Burgess on Feb. 28, 1778 [Ref: T-3:58, L-1:45]. Lived in the Upper Part of Newfoundland Hd. (two taxables) in 1777 [Ref: R-31:7].
SELBY, Thomas Jr. Son of Thomas Selby, Sr. [Ref: V-125]. Took the Oath of Allegiance before the Hon. Gerrard Briscoe on March 2, 1778 [Ref: T-3:56, L-1:45]. Private, 5th Co., Middle Bn., Militia, July 15, 1780 [Ref: M-203]. Lived in Seneca Hd. (one taxable) in 1777 [Ref: R-31:8].
SELBY, Thomas Sr. Private, 1st Co., Middle Bn., Militia, Aug. 30, 1777 [Ref: M-195]. Took the Oath of Allegiance before the Hon. Gerrard

Briscoe on March 2, 1778 [Ref: T-3:57, L-1:45]. Rendered aid by providing wheat for use of the military in 1781 [Ref: O-396]. "Thomas Selby" lived in Seneca Hd. (two taxables) in 1777 [Ref: R-31:8]. "Thomas Selby, Sr." died testate in Montgomery County (wife named Rebekah) in 1793 [Ref: V-125].

SELBY, Thomas, of Joseph. Private, 1st Co., Middle Bn., Militia, Aug. 30, 1777 [Ref: M-195]. Thomas Selby, of Joseph, lived in Seneca Hd. (two taxables) in 1777 [Ref: R-31:8].

SELBY, Zachariah. Son of Zachariah Selby [Ref: V-125]. Private, 1st Co., Middle Bn., Militia, Aug. 30, 1777 [Ref: M-195]. Took the Oath of Allegiance before the Hon. Gerrard Briscoe on March 2, 1778 [Ref: T-3:57, L-1:45].

SELF, John (b. 1760). Lived in Sugarland Hd. in 1776 [Ref: K-1:212]. Private, Flying Camp, enlisted July 25, 1776 [Ref: D-50]. Private, 3rd Maryland Regiment, from April 25, 1778 until Sep. 28, 1778, when he was discharged [Ref: D-165].

SELLMAN, Babar(?). Took the Oath of Allegiance in 1778 [Ref: L-2:28].

SELLMAN, Benjamin Jr. Private, 8th Co., Lower Bn., Militia, July 15, 1780 [Ref: M-207].

SELLMAN, Benjamin Sr. Private, 8th Co., Lower Bn., Militia, July 15, 1780 [Ref: M-207].

SEYBERT, George. Private, 2nd Co., Middle Bn., Militia, Sep. 4, 1777 [Ref: M-196, T-5:37]. Took the Oath of Allegiance before the Hon. Gerrard Briscoe on March 2, 1778 [Ref: T-3:56, L-1:45]. George Seybert married Mary Shepherd in Montgomery County on Jan. 21, 1781 [Ref: K-2:520].

SEYBERT (SIBERT), Henry. "Henry Seybert" was a private, 2nd Co., Middle Bn., Militia, Sep. 4, 1777 [Ref: M-196, T-5:37]. "Henry Sibert" took the Oath of Allegiance before the Hon. Gerrard Briscoe on March 2, 1778 [Ref: T-3:57, L-1:45]. "Henry Sibert" lived in Sugar Loaf Hd. (one taxable) in 1777 [Ref: R-31:11].

SEYBERT (SYBERT), Nicholas. "Nicholas Scybert" was an Ensign in the Lower District of Frederick County (now Montgomery), July 20, 1776 [Ref: D-42]. "Nicholas Seybert" served in the 1st Co., Middle Bn., Militia, Aug. 30, 1777 [Ref: M-195]. "Nicholas Sybert" lived in Seneca Hd. (one taxable) in 1777 [Ref: R-31:8].

SEYER, Richard. See "Richard Sear," q.v.

SEYLE (SEYL, SOYL), John. "John Seyl" lived in George Town Hd. (one taxable) in 1777 [Ref: R-31:3]. "John Soyl" was a private, 3rd Co., Lower Bn., Militia, Sep., 1777 [Ref: M-199, T-5:46]. "John Seyle" took the Oath of Allegiance before the Hon. Richard Thompson in 1778 [Ref: T-3:75, L-1:45].

SHAFFER, Conrad. Took the Oath of Allegiance in 1778 [Ref: L-2:28].

SHAFTS, James. Private, 7th Co., Middle Bn., Militia, July 15, 1780 [Ref: M-203].

SHALER, George. Took the Oath of Allegiance in 1778 [Ref: L-2:28].
SHALER, Peter. Took the Oath of Allegiance in 1778 [Ref: L-2:28].
SHASTO, James (Doctor). Private, 8th Co., Middle Bn., Militia, Sep., 1777 [Ref: M-198, T-5:43]. Took the Oath of Allegiance before the Hon. Edward Burgess on Feb. 28, 1778 [Ref: T-3:62, L-1:45].
SHAVER, Adam. Took the Oath of Allegiance in 1778 [Ref: L-2:28].
SHAW, Basil. Private, 7th Co., Lower Bn., Militia, Aug., 1777 [Ref: M-200, T-5:50], and Sergeant, Capt. Thomas Beall's Co., Maryland Line, 1780 [Ref: D-350].
SHAW, Benjamin. Private, Capt. Price's Co., 3rd Maryland Line, 1781-1782 [Ref: D-453].
SHAW, James. Private, 5th Co., Lower Bn., Militia, July 15, 1780 [Ref: M-206]. Took the Oath of Allegiance before the Hon. Edward Burgess on Feb. 28, 1778 [Ref: T-3:60, L-1:45]. Rendered aid by providing wheat for use of the military in 1780 [Ref: O-333]. James Shaw lived in Rock Creek Hd. (one taxable) in 1777 [Ref: R-31:16].
SHAW, John. Private, 5th Co., Middle Bn., Militia, July 15, 1780 [Ref: M-203]. Took the Oath of Allegiance (made his mark) before the Hon. Joseph Wilson on Feb. 28, 1778 [Ref: T-3:67, L-1:45]. Rendered aid by providing wheat for use of the military in 1781 [Ref: O-380].
SHAW, Sally. See "Thomas Bateman (Batman)," q.v.
SHAW, Thomas. Private, 8th Co., Middle Bn., Militia, Sep., 1777 [Ref: M-198, T-5:43].
SHAW, William (died 1779). Took the Oath of Allegiance before the Hon. Edward Burgess on Feb. 28, 1778 [Ref: T-3:60, L-1:45]. Lived in Rock Creek Hd. (four taxables) in 1777 [Ref: R-31:16]. Died testate in Montgomery County (wife named Rebecca) in 1779 [Ref: V-125].
SHEARBUTT (SHABORD), Samuel (b. 1745). Private, 8th Co., Upper Bn., Militia, Aug. 30, 1777 [Ref: M-195]. Took the Oath of Allegiance (made his "X" mark) before the Hon. Aneas Campbell on March 2, 1778 [Ref: T-3:77, L-1:45]. Samuel Shearbutt lived in Sugarland Hd. (two taxables) in 1777 [Ref: R-31:13]. He was probably the "Samuel Shabord, aged 31" who lived there with his family in 1776 [Ref: K-1:214].
SHEARBUTT (SHERBUTT, SHERBOTT), Thomas. "Thomas Shearbutt" was a private, 3rd Co., Middle Bn., Militia, Sep., 1777 [Ref: M-196, T-5:38]. "Thomas Sherbutt" took the Oath of Allegiance before the Hon. William Deakins, Jr. before March 3, 1778 [Ref: T-3:68, L-1:45]. "Thomas Sherbott" was a private, 8th Class, 2nd Co., Middle Bn., Militia, July 15, 1780 [Ref: M-201].
SHEARLOCK (SHERLOCK, SHARLOCK), James (1745-1792). "James Shearlock" was a private, 5th Co., Lower Bn., Militia, Aug., 1777 [Ref: T-5:48]. Private, 2nd Co., Lower Bn., Militia, July 15, 1780 [Ref: M-204]. "James Sharlock" took the Oath of Allegiance before the Hon. Samuel W. Magruder in 1778 [Ref: T-3:73]. "James Sherlock" died testate in

Montgomery County (wife not named) in 1792 [Ref: V-126]. "James Shearlock" lived in Lower Potomac Hd. in 1776 [Ref: K-1:185].

SHEARS, Thomas. Private who was recruited to serve in the Extra Regiment, Continental Army, in 1780 [Ref: D-342].

SHEARWOOD, John. Private, 2nd Class, 4th Co., Middle Bn., Militia, July 15, 1780 [Ref: M-202].

SHECKELL (SHEKELLS, SHECKLES), Abraham. Took the Oath of Allegiance before the Hon. Gerrard Briscoe on March 2, 1778 [Ref: T-3:56, L-1:45]. "Abraham Shekell or Shekells" was a private, 6th Co., Middle Bn., Militia, from Aug., 1777, to at least July 15, 1780 [Ref: M-203]. [Ref: M-197, T-5:41]. "Abraham Shekell" rendered aid by providing wheat for use of the military in 1781 [Ref: O-379]. "Abraham Sheckles" lived in Linganore Hd. (two taxables) in 1777 [Ref: R-31:9].

SHECKELL (SHEKELLS, SHECKLES), John. Private, Capt. Edward Burgess' Co., Lower District of Frederick (now Montgomery) County, Militia, July, 1776 [Ref: D-42, which listed the name as "John Sheekels (or Shukels)"]. "John Sheckles" was an Ensign, 29th Bn., Militia, Sep. 12, 1777 [Ref: M-120, C-296, C-373]. "John Shekell or Shekells" was a private, 1st Co., Lower Bn., Militia, Sep., 1777, and Second Lieutenant, 7th Co., Lower Bn., July 15, 1780 [Ref: M-198, M-206, T-5:44]. Two men with this name took the Oath of Allegiance before the Hon. Edward Burgess on Feb. 28, 1778 [Ref: T-3:58, L-1:45, T-3:61, L-1:45]. "John Shekels" served as a grand juror in 1781 [Ref: W-2]. "John Sheckells" lived in the Lower Part of Newfoundland Hd. (five taxables) in 1777 [Ref: R-31:6].

SHECKELL (SHEKELL), Richard. Private, 6th Co., Middle Bn., Militia, July 15, 1780 [Ref: M-203].

SHECKELL (SHEEKELS), Thomas. "Thomas Sheekels (Shukels)" was a private, Capt. Edward Burgess' Co., Lower District of Frederick (now Montgomery) County, Militia, July, 1776 [Ref: D-42].

SHEHORN (SHEHON), David. "David Shehon" was a private, 5th Co., Lower Bn., Militia, Aug., 1777 [Ref: M-199, T-5:48. Source M-204 listed a "David Shepone" as a private, 2nd Co., Lower Bn., July 15, 1780; perhaps the reference could be to David Shehon rather than David Shepone?]. "David Shehorn" lived in Lower Potomac Hd. (one taxable) in 1777 [Ref: R-31:5].

SHEHORN (SHEHONE), James (b. 1721). Lived in Lower Potomac Hd. in 1776 [Ref: K-1:185]. Took the Oath of Allegiance (made his mark) before the Hon. Samuel W. Magruder in 1778 [Ref: T-3:74, L-1:45].

SHEHORN (SHEAHORN), Joseph. Private, 1st or 32nd Bn., Militia (no date was given; possibly June, 1777). [Ref: T-5:1].

SHEKLEWORTH (SHECKELSWORTH, SHUTTLEWORTH), Phillip (b. 1748). "Philip Shekleworth" was a private, 7th Co., Upper Bn., Militia, Aug. 30, 1777 [Ref: M-194]. "Philip Shuttleworth" took the Oath of Allegiance before the Hon. Aneas Campbell on March 2, 1778 [Ref: T-

3:77, L-1:45]. "Philip Shekelworth or Sheckelsworth" lived in Sugarland Hd. (wife named Luranah) in 1776-1777 [Ref: K-1:216, R-31:13].

SHEPHERD, James. Private, Capt. Price's Co., 3rd Maryland Line, 1781-1782 [Ref: D-453].

SHEPHERD, Jonathan. Private, Capt. Thomas Beall's Co., Maryland Line, 1780 [Ref: D-351].

SHEPHERD, Mary. See "George Seybert," q.v.

SHEPHERD (SHEPPARD), Thomas. Private, 2nd Co., Middle Bn., Militia, Sep. 4, 1777 [Ref: M-196, T-5:37]. Rendered aid by providing wheat for use of the military in 1781 [Ref: O-398].

SHEPONE, David. See "David Shehon," q.v.

SHIELDS (SHEALS), Thomas. Private, 6th Co., Lower Bn., Militia, Aug., 1777 [Ref: M-200, T-5:49]. Private, 3rd Co., Lower Bn., Militia, July 15, 1780 [Ref: M-205]. "Thomas Shields" took the Oath of Allegiance before the Hon. Joseph Offutt on March 2, 1778 [Ref: T-3:70, L-1:45]. "Thomas Sheals" lived in the Upper Part of Potomac Hd. (one taxable) in 1777 [Ref: R-31:15].

SHILLING, Conrad. Took the Oath of Allegiance in 1778 [Ref: L-2:28].

SHIPLEY, Elias. Private, 1st or 32nd Bn., Militia (no date was given; possibly June, 1777). [Ref: T-5:1].

SHIPLEY, George H. Private, 1st or 32nd Bn., Militia (no date was given; possibly June, 1777). [Ref: T-5:1].

SHIPLEY, George O. Private, 1st or 32nd Bn., Militia (no date was given; possibly June, 1777). [Ref: T-5:1].

SHIPLEY, Vachel, of William. Private, 1st or 32nd Bn., Militia (no date was given; possibly June, 1777). [Ref: T-5:1].

SHOEMAKER (SHUMAKER), Joshua (b. 1753). Private, 4th Co., Lower Bn., Militia, Aug., 1777 [Ref: M-199, T-5:47]. Private, 1st Co., Lower Bn., Militia, July 15, 1780 [Ref: M-204]. Took the Oath of Allegiance before the Hon. Charles Jones on Jan. 10, 1778 [Ref: T-3:71, L-1:45]. Lived in Lower Potomac Hd. (one taxable) in 1776-1777 [Ref: K-1:186, R-31:5].

SHOEMAKER, Peter. Private, 7th Maryland Line, from May 17, 1778 until Aug. 16, 1780, when reported killed at the Battle of Camden [Ref: D-249].

SHORT, George. Private, 7th Co., Lower Bn., Militia, Aug., 1777 [Ref: M-200, T-5:50]. George Short lived in the Lower Part of Newfoundland Hd. (one taxable) in 1777 [Ref: R-31:6]. "George Shirts" [Shorts?] took the Oath of Allegiance in 1778 [Ref: L-2:28].

SHORT, Hezekiah. Private, 7th Co., Lower Bn., Militia, Aug., 1777 [Ref: M-200, T-5:50]. Hezekiah Short lived in the Lower Part of Newfoundland Hd. (one taxable) in 1777 [Ref: R-31:6].

SHORT, John. Private, 7th Co., Lower Bn., Militia, Aug., 1777 [Ref: M-200, T-5:50].

SHORT, Richard (b. 1754). Lived in Sugarland Hd. in 1776 [Ref: K-1:201]. Private, Flying Camp, Frederick (now Montgomery) County, enlisted by Greenbury Gaither on July 29, 1776 [Ref: D-44].
SHROYER, Catharine. See "Leonard Peckinbaugh," q.v.
SHUTTER, Christian. Took the Oath of Allegiance in 1778 [Ref: L-2:28].
SHUTTLEWORTH, Philip. See "Philip Shekleworth," q.v.
SIBERT, Henry, and others. See "Henry Seybert" and others, q.v.
SIBLEY (SIBLE, SIBBEY), James (b. 1751). "James Sibley" took the Oath of Allegiance before the Hon. Aneas Campbell on March 2, 1778 [Ref: T-3:77, L-1:45]. "James Sible, aged 25" lived in Sugarland Hd. in 1776 [Ref: K-1:211]. "James Sibbey" married Amelia Wiley in Montgomery County on Sep. 28, 1777 [Ref: K-2:517].
SIGERFOOSE, George. Took the Oath of Allegiance in 1778 [Ref: L-2:28. This same source also stated "George Seihfeet (Seigfeet)" took the Oath of Allegiance in 1778].
SIGIRT, George. Took the Oath of Allegiance in 1778 [Ref: L-2:28].
SILK, Samuel. Private, Capt. Price's Co., 3rd Maryland Line, 1781, and "then Armourer at Annapolis" in 1782 [Ref: D-454].
SILLINGS (STILLINGS), Richard. "Richard Sillings" took the Oath of Allegiance (made his "X" mark) before the Hon. Edward Burgess on Feb. 28, 1778 [Ref: T-3:60, L-1:45]. "Richard Stillings" married Mary Dailey in Montgomery County on June 6, 1778 [Ref: K-2:517].
SILVER, George (c1751-1839). Private, German Regiment, 1778-1780, and private, 3rd Maryland Line, 1780-1781 [Ref: D-250, D-268, D-395]. He married Ann Nancy Griffin [Ref: DAR-I:617].
SILVER, Nathaniel. Took the Oath of Allegiance before the Hon. Charles Jones on Jan. 10, 1778 [Ref: T-3:71, L-1:45].
SIMMONS, Eleanor. See "Leonard Hays," q.v.
SIMMONS, Aaron. Private, Capt. Gray's Co., Maryland Line, 1780 [Ref: D-603].
SIMMONS, Samuel. Private, 6th Co., Upper Bn., Militia, Aug. 30, 1777 [Ref: M-194]. Rendered aid by providing corn and rye for use of the military in 1780 [Ref: O-287, O-295]. Samuel Simmons lived in Sugar Loaf Hd. (three taxables) in 1777 [Ref: R-31:11].
SIMMONS (SIMMONDS), Thomas (b. 1756). Lived in Lower Potomac Hd. in 1776 [Ref: K-1:186]. Private, 4th Maryland Regiment, 1778 [Ref: D-166].
SIMMS, Elexious (Alexcious). "Alexcious Simms" was a private in Capt. Edward Burgess' Co., Lower District of Frederick (now Montgomery) County, Militia, July, 1776 [Ref: D-42]. "Elexious Simms" was a private, 8th Co., Middle Bn., Militia, Sep., 1777 [Ref: M-198, T-5:43]. "Elixus Sims" was a private, 6th Co., Lower Bn., Militia, July 15, 1780 [Ref: M-206].
SIMMS, Joseph. Private, 8th Co., Middle Bn., Militia, Sep., 1777 [Ref: M-198, T-5:43]. Took the Oath of Allegiance before the Hon. Edward

Burgess on Feb. 28, 1778 [Ref: T-3:62, L-1:45]. "Joseph Sims" rendered aid by providing wheat for use of the military in 1780 [Ref: O-306]. "Joseph Simms" lived in Rock Creek Hd. (four taxables) in 1777 [Ref: R-31:16].

SIMMS, Winfred. See "Joseph Ogden," q.v.

SIMPSON, James. Private, 2nd Co., Middle Bn., Militia, Sep. 4, 1777 [Ref: M-196, T-5:37]. One James Simpson took the Oath of Allegiance before the Hon. Elisha Williams on March 2, 1778 [Ref: T-3:80, L-1:45], and another took the Oath of Allegiance before the Hon. Gerrard Briscoe on March 2, 1778 [Ref: T-3:56, L-1:45]. One "James Simpson" lived in Sugar Loaf Hd. (three taxables) in 1777 [Ref: R-31:11]. "James Stimpson" [sic] served as a grand juror in Aug., 1777 [Ref: R-31:17].

SIMPSON, John D. Private, 1st or 32nd Bn., Militia (no date was given; possibly June, 1777). [Ref: T-5:1].

SIMPSON, Richard. Took the Oath of Allegiance in 1778 [Ref: L-2:28].

SIMPSON, Solomon. See "Solomon Stimpson (Stympson)," q.v.

SINCLAIR (SINCLEAR, SINKLER), Duncan (b. 1750). Took the Oath of Allegiance before the Hon. Elisha Williams on March 2, 1778 [Ref: T-3:81, L-1:45]. "Duncan Sinclear" was a private, 8th Co., Upper Bn., Militia, Aug. 30, 1777 [Ref: M-195]. "Dunkin Sinkler or Sinclear" lived in Sugarland Hd. (one taxable) in 1776-1777 [Ref: K-1:199, R-31:13].

SINN, Jacob. Took the Oath of Allegiance in 1778 [Ref: L-2:28].

SISILEND, William. Took the Oath of Allegiance before the Hon. Joseph Wilson on Feb. 28, 1778 [Ref: T-3:64, L-1:45].

SIX, Henry. Served as a private in Capt. Wiley's Co., Rawlings Regiment, Maryland Line. Applied for and received pension (S9481) on Sep. 24, 1833, aged 82, stating he was born near Emmitsburg, Maryland, and resided there at the time of his service (and application for pension). Appears to have been a substitute once and drafted twice (no dates were given) and guarded prisoners at Fort Frederick, Maryland, and Harpers Ferry, Virginia, and York, Pennsylvania. Notes indicate he became a sergeant, but his pension was as a private. An affidavit dated Feb. 24, 1836, stated he was 84 years of age [Ref: P-3149]. Henry Six was from Frederick County, not Montgomery County. His name had been unintentionally omitted from my book *Revolutionary Patriots of Frederick County, 1775-1783*. He has been included here in order to preserve the record of his service as submitted by Mrs. William (Gladys) Six, of Frederick, Maryland. It should be noted that Henry Six is not listed in *Archives of Maryland, Volume 18*, nor is he in Clements and Wright's *Maryland Militia in the Revolutionary War*, which explains the initial oversight. HCP].

SKEPPAN, Thomas. Took the Oath of Allegiance before the Hon. Gerrard Briscoe on March 2, 1778 [Ref: T-3:56, L-1:45].

SKINNER, Leonard. Private, 5th Co., Middle Bn., Militia, July 15, 1780 [Ref: M-203].

SLACK, John. Took the Oath of Allegiance before the Hon. Richard Thompson in 1778 [Ref: T-3:75, L-1:45].

SLATER, Jonathan. Rendered aid by providing wheat for use of the military in 1780 [Ref: O-329, O-337].

SLATOR, Thomas. Rendered aid by providing wheat for use of the military in 1781 [Ref: O-415].

SLEAGLE, Henry. Took the Oath of Allegiance in 1778 [Ref: L-2:28].

SLICER (SLYCER), James (b. 1751). "James Slicer" took the Oath of Allegiance before the Hon. Charles Jones on Jan. 10, 1778 [Ref: T-3:71, L-1:45]. "James Slycer" was a private, 4th Co., Lower Bn., Militia, Aug., 1777 [Ref: T-5:47]. "James Slicer" lived in Lower Potomac Hd. (one taxable) in 1776-1777 [Ref: K-1:185, R-31:5].

SMALLWOOD, William. Lived in the Upper Part of Potomac Hd. (one taxable) in 1777 [Ref: R-31:15]. Private, 3rd Co., Middle Bn., Militia, Sep., 1777 [Ref: M-196, T-5:38]. Took the Oath of Allegiance before the Hon. Edward Burgess on Feb. 28, 1778 [Ref: T-3:63, L-1:45].

SMITH, Annastatia. See "Josias Willcoxen," q.v.

SMITH, Archibald (b. 1760). Private, 3rd Co., Upper Bn., Militia, Aug. 30, 1777 [Ref: M-193]. Lived in Sugarland Hd. in 1776 [Ref: K-1:201].

SMITH, Basil. Private, 2nd Co., Middle Bn., Militia, Sep. 4, 1777 [Ref: M-196, T-5:37]. Private, 2nd Class, 3rd Co., Middle Bn., Militia, July 15, 1780 [Ref: M-202]. Took the Oath of Allegiance before the Hon. Joseph Wilson on Feb. 28, 1778 [Ref: T-3:66, L-1:45]. Lived in Linganore Hd. (one taxable) in 1777 [Ref: R-31:9].

SMITH, Benjamin. "Benjamin Smith, born in Maryland, about 21 years of age, 6 feet 2 inches high, black hair, good complexion and had the smallpox, recruited by Joseph White for John Clagett, Sr. on May 12, 1781." [Ref: R-33:156, X-1146]. Private, Capt. Price's Co., 3rd Maryland Line, 1781-1782 [Ref: D-452].

SMITH, Catherine. See "John Buller," q.v.

SMITH, Charles. Took the Oath of Allegiance before the Hon. Elisha Williams on March 2, 1778 [Ref: T-3:81, L-1:45].

SMITH, Curtis. See "Robert Housley (Howsley)," q.v.

SMITH, Daniel. Two men with this name took the Oath of Allegiance: one before the Hon. Edward Burgess on Feb. 28, 1778 [Ref: T-3:60, L-1:45], and another before the Hon. Charles Jones on Jan. 10, 1778 [Ref: T-3:71, L-1:45]. One Daniel Smith lived in Rock Creek Hd. (two taxables) in 1777 [Ref: R-31:16].

SMITH, Daniel Jr. Private, 2nd Co., Lower Bn., Militia, Sep., 1777 [Ref: M-198, T-5:45]. Private, 7th Co., Middle Bn., Militia, July 15, 1780 [Ref: M-203]. Took the Oath of Allegiance before the Hon. Edward Burgess on Feb. 28, 1778 [Ref: T-3:60, L-1:45].

SMITH, David (1736-1800). Lived in Lower Potomac Hd. (one taxable) in 1776-1777 [Ref: K-1:186, R-31:5]. Private, Maryland Line, discharged

March 1, 1781 [Ref: D-554]. Died testate in Montgomery County (wife named Sarah) in 1800 [Ref: V-127].

SMITH, Eli or Ali (b. 1757). "Eli Smith" was a private, Flying Camp, enlisted on July 29, 1776 [Ref: D-44]. "Ali Smith" lived in Sugarland Hd. in 1776 [Ref: K-1:201].

SMITH, Elizabeth. See "John Smith," q.v.

SMITH, Esther. See "Joseph Belt," q.v.

SMITH, Gerrard. Private, 2nd Class, 1st Co., Middle Bn., Militia, July 15, 1780 [Ref: M-201].

SMITH, Godfrey. Took the Oath of Allegiance in 1778 [Ref: L-2:28].

SMITH, Herbert F. See "Jeremiah Plummer," q.v.

SMITH, James. Took the Oath of Allegiance (made his "I" mark) before the Hon. Samuel W. Magruder in 1778 [Ref: T-3:73]. James Smith lived in the Upper Part of Potomac Hd. (six taxables) in 1777 [Ref: R-31:15]. "James Smith, now a resident of Montgomery County" wrote his will in 1788 (wife named Sicilly) and it was probated in Feb., 1789 [Ref: V-127]. See "Robert Hurdle," q.v.

SMITH, James Edward. Private, 3rd Co., Lower Bn., Militia, July 15, 1780 [Ref: M-205].

SMITH, Jarrett (Mrs.). See "Burch Allison," q.v.

SMITH, John. (1) Private, 4th Co., Lower Bn., Militia, Aug., 1777 [Ref: M-199, T-5:47]. (2) Private, 7th Co., Lower Bn., Militia, Aug., 1777 [Ref: M-200, T-5:50]. (3) Private, 6th Class, 3rd Co., Middle Bn., Militia, July 15, 1780 [Ref: M-202]. One John Smith took the Oath of Allegiance before the Hon. Gerrard Briscoe on March 2, 1778 [Ref: T-3:56, L-1:45]. One John Smith was a private who enrolled into a company of militia for the service of the Flying Camp, Oct. 15, 1776 [Ref: B-352], and another was recruited to serve in the Extra Regiment, Continental Army, in 1780 [Ref: D-342]. One John Smith was born in (now) Montgomery County on Feb. 2, 1753, and lived there at the time of his enlistment. He entered the service twice, once as a substitute and once as a volunteer. He participated in the Battle of Germantown, which can be verified by his fellow soldiers George Heathman and John Owens, Sr. In 1796 John Smith married Elizabeth Mullikin and left for Kentucky on May 12, 1796, arriving in Clark County on June 16, 1796. He applied for a pension (S1255) in 1832, aged 79, and died in Clark County on July 22, 1835. His widow applied for a pension (W8741) on Feb. 2, 1843, mentioning her elder son John M. Smith, born Oct. 10, 1791 [sic], who lived in Tennessee. She also referred to her other children in Tennessee and Indiana (no names were given). Elias and Susannah Browning (no relationship stated) made affidavits in Clark County, Kentucky, in 1843. Elizabeth (widow) also applied for bounty land in 1856 [Ref: Y-8, Z-28, P-3199]. Another John Smith served in the Pennsylvania Line and applied for pension (S3741) in 1818, aged 63, stating he was born in Hagerstown, Maryland, where he enlisted in 1776, but he lived in

Pennsylvania prior to the war and in Montgomery County, Maryland thereafter [Ref: Y-14, Z-58, P-3199, which latter source contains information on other John Smiths from western Maryland. Also see *Revolutionary Patriots of Frederick County, Maryland, 1775-1783*, by Henry C. Peden, Jr., 1995]. One John Smith (b. 1726) lived in Lower Potomac Hd. in 1776, another lived in the Lower Part of Newfoundland Hd. (one taxable) in 1777 and another lived in Sugar Loaf Hd. (one taxable) in 1777 [Ref: K-1:186, R-31:6, R-31:11. Source DAR-I:627 lists four John Smiths].

SMITH, John 3rd. Private, Capt. Price's Co., 3rd Maryland Line, 1781-1782 [Ref: D-453].

SMITH (SMYTH), John 4th. Private, Capt. Price's Co., 3rd Maryland Line, 1781-1782 [Ref: D-453].

SMITH, Joseph (Doctor). Private, 8th Co., Lower Bn., Militia, July 15, 1780 [Ref: M-207].

SMITH, Margerit. See "Kid Marquess," q.v.

SMITH, Mary. See "John O'Neal" and "Asa Darby" and "Jacob Holland," q.v.

SMITH, Matthew (b. 1751). Lived in Lower Potomac Hd. in 1776 [Ref: K-1:185]. Served as a private in the 3rd Maryland Regiment in 1778 [Ref: D-165].

SMITH, Nathan (b. 1735). Lived in Sugarland Hd. (two taxables) in 1776-1777 [Ref: K-1:201, R-31:13]. Private, 3rd Co., Upper Bn., Militia, Aug. 30, 1777 [Ref: M-193]. Took the Oath of Allegiance before the Hon. Elisha Williams on March 2, 1778 [Ref: T-3:81, L-1:45].

SMITH, Nicholas. Private, 5th Co., Middle Bn., Militia, Sep., 1777 [Ref: M-197, T-5:40]. "Nicholas Smith" took the Oath of Allegiance (made his "N" mark) before the Hon. Joseph Wilson on Feb. 28, 1778 [Ref: T-3:66, L-1:45]. "Nichols Smith" [sic] lived in the Upper Part of Potomac Hd. (one taxable) in 1777 [Ref: R-31:15].

SMITH, Patrick. Private who was recruited to serve in the Extra Regiment, Continental Army, in 1780 [Ref: D-342].

SMITH, Peter. Private, 4th Co., Upper Bn., Militia, Aug. 30, 1777 [Ref: M-194]. Took the Oath of Allegiance before the Hon. William Deakins, Jr. before March 3, 1778 [Ref: T-3:68, L-1:45].

SMITH, Philip. Took the Oath of Allegiance in 1778 [Ref: L-2:28].

SMITH, R. G. See "Leonard Hays," q.v.

SMITH, Rebecca. Rendered aid by providing wheat for use of the military in 1781 [Ref: O-403]. Rebecca Smith lived in the Upper Part of Potomac Hd. (three taxables) in 1777 [Ref: R-31:15].

SMITH, Richard (1750-1788). Served as a Captain, 16th Bn., Militia, March 26, 1776, and Captain of a company of militia enrolled for the service of the Flying Camp, Oct. 15, 1776, and Colonel, Upper Bn., Militia, March 1, 1779 [Ref: M-122, M-193, A-287, C-373, E-310, B-352]. Took the Oath of Allegiance before the Hon. Elisha Williams on March

2, 1778 [Ref: T-3:80, L-1:45]. Rendered aid by providing wheat for use of the military in 1780 [Ref: O-338]. Justice of the County Court in 1781 [Ref: W-2]. Lived in Sugar Loaf Hd. (seven taxables) in 1777 [Ref: R-31:11]. Richard Smith married Mary Peters [Ref: DAR-I:629].

SMITH, Rob (attorney). Took the Oath of Allegiance in 1778 [Ref: L-1:45].

SMITH, Samuel. Private, 3rd Co., Middle Bn., Militia, Sep., 1777 [Ref: M-196, T-5:38]. Took the Oath of Allegiance before the Hon. William Deakins, Jr. before March 3, 1778 [Ref: T-3:68, L-1:45]. Lived in the Upper Part of Potomac Hd. (one taxable) in 1777 [Ref: R-31:15].

SMITH, Sarah W. See "Robert Hurdle," q.v.

SMITH, Stephen (b. 1733). Lived in Lower Potomac Hd. in 1776 [Ref: K-1:185]. Took the Oath of Allegiance before the Hon. Aneas Campbell on March 2, 1778 [Ref: T-3:77, L-1:45].

SMITH, Thomas. (1) Private, 4th Co., Middle Bn., Militia, Sep., 1777 [Ref: M-196, T-5:39]. Private, 7th Class, 4th Co., Middle Bn., Militia, July 15, 1780 [Ref: M-202]. (2) Private, 6th Co., Middle Bn., Militia, Aug., 1777 [Ref: M-197, T-5:41]. Private, 6th Co., Middle Bn., Militia, July 15, 1780 [Ref: M-203]. One Thomas Smith took the Oath of Allegiance (made his "X" mark) before the Hon. Edward Burgess on Feb. 28, 1778 [Ref: T-3:59, L-1:45], and another took the Oath of Allegiance on Sep. 1, 1780, under the Act of May 12, 1780, having neglected to do so previously "due to ignorance of the duty owed the country." [Ref: R-27:120]. One Thomas Smith (b. 1750) lived in Lower Potomac Hd. in 1776 [Ref: K-1:186]. Thomas Smith married Leah Hill in Montgomery County on Aug. 28, 1779 [Ref: K-2:515].

SMITH, Vachel. Took the Oath of Allegiance before the Hon. Gerrard Briscoe on March 2, 1778 [Ref: T-3:56, L-1:45]. Lived in Sugar Loaf Hd. (one taxable) in 1777 [Ref: R-31:11].

SMITH, Walter. (1) Physician who lived in George Town Hd. (five taxables) in 1776-1777 and owned a working plantation ("quarter") in Lower Potomac Hd. in 1777 [Ref: K-1:194, R-31:3, R-31:5]. He was born in 1744, married Esther Belt, and died on Aug. 29, 1796 [Ref: DAR-I:630]. Served as Supervisor of Roads, 1777 [Ref: R-31:18]. "Dr. Walter Smith, Jr., Surgeon of the Continental Hospital at George Town in the Middle Department" took the Oath of Allegiance before the Hon. Richard Thompson on April 21, 1778 [Ref: X-1146]. (2) Private, 3rd Co., Lower Bn., Militia, Sep., 1777 [Ref: M-199, T-5:46]. Took the Oath of Allegiance before the Hon. Richard Thompson in 1778 [Ref: T-3:75, L-1:45]. Private, 8th Co., Lower Bn., Militia, July 15, 1780 [Ref: M-207].

SMITH, William. Private, 4th Class, 3rd Co., Middle Bn., Militia, July 15, 1780 [Ref: M-202]. Rendered aid by providing wheat for use of the military in 1780 [Ref: O-325].

SNELL, George. Private, 1st Co., Lower Bn., Militia, Sep., 1777 [Ref: M-198, T-5:44]. Private, 7th Co., Lower Bn., Militia, July 15, 1780 [Ref: M-

206]. Took the Oath of Allegiance before the Hon. Edward Burgess on Feb. 28, 1778 [Ref: T-3:60, L-1:45]. Lived in the Lower Part of Newfoundland Hd. (six taxables) in 1777 [Ref: R-31:6]. "Elizabeth Snell, widow of George Snell" died testate in Montgomery County in 1800 and mentioned her brother William Scrivenor, deceased [Ref: V-128].

SNOWDEN, Ann. See "Richard Crabb" and "Jeremiah Crabb," q.v.

SNOWFER, John. Took the Oath of Allegiance in 1778 [Ref: L-2:28].

SNUKE, John. Took the Oath of Allegiance in 1778 [Ref: L-2:28].

SNYDER, Mike. Took the Oath of Allegiance in 1778 [Ref: L-2:28].

SOLOMON (SOLAMON), Samuel. Private, Capt. Edward Burgess' Co., Lower District of Frederick (now Montgomery) County, Militia, July, 1776 [Ref: D-42]. Private, 6th Maryland Regiment, from Dec. 5, 1776 until April 13, 1777, when reported "deserted" [Ref: D-290].

SOPER (SOAPER), Basil (died 1825). Private, 5th Co., Upper Bn., Militia, Aug. 30, 1777 [Ref: M-194]. Took the Oath of Allegiance on Sep. 1, 1780, under the Act of May 12, 1780, having neglected to do so previously "due to ignorance of the duty owed the country." [Ref: R-27:120]. "Basil Saper" [sic] rendered aid by providing wheat for use of the military in 1781 [Ref: O-379]. "Basil Soper" lived in Linganore Hd. (four taxables) in 1777 [Ref: R-31:9]. "Basil Soaper, Sr." died testate in Montgomery County (wife not named) in 1825 [Ref: V-128].

SOPER (SUPER), Christopher. Took the Oath of Allegiance in 1778 [Ref: L-2:28].

SOPER (SOAPER), James (b. 1732). Private, 1st Co., Upper Bn., Militia, Aug. 30, 1777 [Ref: M-193]. Took the Oath of Allegiance before the Hon. Elisha Williams on March 2, 1778 [Ref: T-3:82]. Lived in Sugarland Hd. in 1776 and had three taxables in 1776-1777 [Ref: K-1:219, R-31:13].

SOPER (SOAP), John. "John Soap" was a private, 4th Maryland Line, from Aug. 2 to Aug. 18, 1778, when he reportedly "deserted" [Ref: D-289]. "John Soper" moved to Kentucky circa 1799 and had a son James Soper (1792-1861) who lived in Jessamine County [Ref: Westerfield's *Kentucky Biography and Genealogy*, Vol. 5, p. 263].

SOPER (SOAPER), Zadock (b. 1751). Lived in Lower Potomac Hd. in 1776 [Ref: K-1:186]. Private, 4th Co., Lower Bn., Militia, Aug., 1777 [Ref: M-199, T-5:47].

SOUTHERN, Alexander. Private, 3rd Co., Lower Bn., Militia, July 15, 1780 [Ref: M-205].

SPACE, Catherine. See "George Heater," q.v.

SPACE (SPECE?), Zadock. Private, 5th Co., Middle Bn., Militia, July 15, 1780 [Ref: M-203].

SPARROW, Benjamin. Private, 5th Co., Lower Bn., Militia, Aug., 1777 [Ref: M-200, T-5:48]. Private, 5th Class, 2nd Co., Middle Bn., Militia, July 15, 1780 [Ref: M-201]. Took the Oath of Allegiance (made his "X" mark) before the Hon. Samuel W. Magruder in 1778 [Ref: T-3:73, L-1:45]. Benjamin Sparrow lived in Lower Potomac Hd. (one taxable) in

1777 [Ref: R-31:5]. Benjamin Battey Sparrow (b. 1753) lived in Lower Potomac Hd. in 1776 [Ref: K-1:185].

SPARROW, Jonathan (1746-1807). Private, 5th Co., Lower Bn., Militia, Aug., 1777 [Ref: M-199, T-5:48]. Private, 5th Class, 2nd Co., Middle Bn., Militia, July 15, 1780 [Ref: M-201]. Took the Oath of Allegiance (made his "I" mark) before the Hon. Samuel W. Magruder in 1778 [Ref: T-3:73, L-1:45]. Lived in Lower Potomac Hd. (one taxable) in 1776- 1777 [Ref: K-1:185, R-31:5]. Died testate in Montgomery County (wife not named) in 1807 [Ref: V-129].

SPARROW, Mary. See "Alexander Campbell," q.v.

SPARROW, Thomas. Private, 3rd Co., Middle Bn., Militia, Sep., 1777 [Ref: M-196, T-5:38]. Took the Oath of Allegiance before the Hon. Samuel W. Magruder in 1778 [Ref: T-3:73, L-1:45]. Thomas Sparrow lived in the Upper Part of Potomac Hd. (one taxable) in 1777 [Ref: R-31:15]. One Thomas Sparrow died testate in Montgomery County (wife named Ann) in 1792, and another was a son of" Jonathan Sparrow," q.v., who died in 1807 [Ref: V-129].

SPARROW, William. Private, 1st Class, 2nd Co., Middle Bn., Militia, July 15, 1780 [Ref: M-201]. Private, 3rd Co., Middle Bn., Militia, Sep., 1777 [Ref: M-196, T-5:38]. Took the Oath of Allegiance (made his "X" mark) before the Hon. Samuel W. Magruder in 1778 [Ref: T-3:73, L-1:45]. Lived in the Upper Part of Potomac Hd. (one taxable) in 1777 [Ref: R-31:15]. William Sparrow married Mary Ogden in Montgomery County on Nov. 6, 1781 [Ref: K-2:520].

SPAULDING, Eleanor. See "Mathias Hempston," q.v.

SPEAKS (SPEAK), Charles. Took the Oath of Allegiance before the Hon. Elisha Williams on March 2, 1778 [Ref: T-3:81, L-1:45]. "Charles Speaks" lived in Sugar Loaf Hd. (one taxable) in 1777 [Ref: R-31:11].

SPEAKS (SPEAK), Eleanor, and others. See "Hezekiah Speaks," q.v.

SPEAKS (SPEAKE), George. Served as a Corporal, Capt. Gray's Co., Maryland Line, 1780 [Ref: D-603].

SPEAKS (SPEAK, SPEAKE), Hezekiah (1757-1837). Private, 4th Co., Lower Bn., Militia, Aug., 1777 [Ref: M-199, T-5:47], and Second Corporal, 1st Co., Lower Bn., July 15, 1780 [Ref: M-204]. "Hezekiah Speake" was a private in Capt. Grayson's Co., Maryland Line, 1780 [Ref: D-603]. Took the Oath of Allegiance before the Hon. Charles Jones on Jan. 10, 1778 [Ref: T-3:71, L-1:45]. "Hezekiah Speaks" applied for pension in Bourbon County, Kentucky, on Sep. 17, 1832, aged 75, stating he was born in Prince George's County, Maryland, and lived in Montgomery County, Maryland, at the time of enlistment in 1776. He served in the Maryland Line and fought in the Battle of Germantown. Ann Hughes made affidavit on Sep. 25, 1833, stating she was well acquainted with Hezekiah Speaks in Montgomery County during the revolution and he had lived at the home of her uncle (name not stated). Hezekiah died on Jan. 1, 1837, and his widow Eleanor applied for pension (W8748) on Dec. 30, 1842, aged 80, stating she is a daughter of Edward Tucker of Montgomery County, Maryland (which is show in an indenture in Montgomery County dated Feb. 23, 1785), and she had married Hezekiah about the first of the year in 1783 in Georgetown, Maryland, which is now Washington, D. C. In 1842 she was living with a daughter Ally Ashford, aged 40, wife of Michael Ashford. The children of Hezekiah and Eleanor Speaks in 1842 were: John (if alive, aged 59); Elizabeth (aged 58); William (if alive, aged 54); Sarah (aged 51); Eleanor (aged 49); Nancy (aged 47); Mary (if alive, aged 45); Casey (if alive, aged 42); and, Ally (aged 40). Also mentioned was a John Tucker, of Bourbon County, Kentucky, in 1832, but no relationship was stated [Ref: P-3261, Y-5, Z-12].

SPEAKS (SPEAK), Ignatius. Private, 3rd Co., Lower Bn., Militia, July 15, 1780 [Ref: M-205]. Private, 6th Co., Lower Bn., Militia, Aug., 1777 [Ref: M-200, T-5:49]. Took the Oath of Allegiance before the Hon. Joseph Offutt on March 2, 1778 [Ref: T-3:70, L-1:45]. "Ignatious Speak" married Catherine McCloud in Montgomery County on Jan. 21, 1779 [Ref: K-2:520].

SPEAKS (SPEAK), Martin. Private, 6th Co., Lower Bn., Militia, July 15, 1780 [Ref: M-206]. Private, 6th Co., Lower Bn., Militia, Aug., 1777 [Ref: M-200, T-5:49]. Took the Oath of Allegiance before the Hon. Edward Burgess on Feb. 28, 1778 [Ref: T-3:63, L-1:45]. Martin Speak lived in the Upper Part of Potomac Hd. (one taxable) in 1777 [Ref: R-31:15].

SPEAKS (SPEAK), Nathaniel. Private, 6th Maryland Line, 1778-1780 [Ref: D-246].

SPEAKS (SPEAK), Nicholas. Private, 1st Co., Middle Bn., Militia, Aug. 30, 1777 [Ref: M-195]. Took the Oath of Allegiance before the Hon. Gerrard Briscoe on March 2, 1778 [Ref: T-3:56, L-1:45]. "Nicholas Speaks" lived in Seneca Hd. (one taxable) in 1777 [Ref: R-31:8].

SPEAKS (SPEAK), Richard. Private, 6th Co., Lower Bn., Militia, Aug., 1777 [Ref: M-200, T-5:49]. Took the Oath of Allegiance before the Hon. Joseph Offutt on March 2, 1778 [Ref: T-3:70, L-1:45]. Richard Speak lived in the Upper Part of Potomac Hd. (two taxables) in 1777 [Ref: R-31:15].

SPEAKS (SPEAK, SPEAKE), William (Jr.?). "William Speak" lived in the Upper Part of Potomac Hd. (one taxable) in 1777 [Ref: R-31:15]. "William Speake" was a private, Capt. Grayson's Co., Maryland Line, 1780 [Ref: D-603].

SPEAKS, William (Sr.?). Took the Oath of Allegiance before the Hon. Gerrard Briscoe on March 2, 1778 [Ref: T-3:56, L-1:45]. "William Speaks, aged 60" lived in North West Hd. in 1776 [Ref: K-1:226].

SPEARS, John. Rendered aid by providing wheat for use of the military in 1781 [Ref: O-396].

SPEIGHT (SPATES), Robert (b. 1739). "Robert Spates" was a private, 6th Co., Upper Bn., Militia, Aug. 30, 1777 [Ref: M-194]. "Robert Speight" took the Oath of Allegiance before the Hon. Elisha Williams on March 2, 1778 [Ref: T-3:82]. "Robert Speight, aged 37" lived in Sugarland Hd. in 1776 and "Robert Spates" lived there in 1777 [Ref: K-1:217, R-31:13].

SPIERS, Asenath. See "Abraham Holland," q.v.

SPIERS, Nancy. See "Basil Adamson," q.v.

SPIERS (SPIRES), Richard. Served as a private in Capt. Price's Co., 3rd Maryland Line, 1781-1782 [Ref: D-453].

SPRAGUE, Stuart Seely. See "William Hocker," q.v.

SPRIGG, Elizabeth. See "Thomas Sprigg Wootton," q.v.

SPRIGG, Frederick (1749-1791). Served as Captain, 5th Co., Upper Bn., Militia, Aug. 30, 1777, and Major, March 1, 1779 [Ref: M-124, M-194, E-310, E-356]. Took the Oath of Allegiance before the Hon. Elisha Williams on March 2, 1778 [Ref: T-3:80, L-1:45]. Lived in Sugar Loaf Hd. (one taxable) in 1777 [Ref: R-31:11]. He was born in 1749, married Deborah Woodward, and died on Oct. 15, 1791 [Ref: DAR-I:638].

SPRIGG, James (died 1778). Took the Oath of Allegiance before the Hon. Elisha Williams on March 2, 1778 [Ref: T-3:80, L-1:45]. Lived in Sugar Loaf Hd. (three taxables) in 1777 [Ref: R-31:11]. Died testate in Montgomery County (wife named Elizabeth) in May, 1778 [Ref: V-130].

SPRIGG, Thomas. Ensign who enrolled in a company of militia for the service of the Flying Camp, Oct. 15, 1776, and Captain, 6th Co., 16th Bn., Militia, by Sep. 12, 1777 [Ref: B-352, M-124, M-194, C-373]. Took the Oath of Allegiance before the Hon. Elisha Williams on March 2, 1778 [Ref: T-3:80, L-1:45]. Rendered aid by providing wheat for use of the military in 1781 [Ref: O-439]. Lived in Sugar Loaf Hd. (two taxables) in 1777 [Ref: R-31:11]. Thomas Sprigg married Elizabeth Belt in Montgomery County on Feb. 8, 1780 [Ref: K-2:514].

SPYKER, Benjamin. Served as a Captain, Lower District, Frederick County (now Montgomery), Militia, July 20, 1776 [Ref: D-42].

STACKS, John. Private, Capt. Thomas Beall's Co., Maryland Line, 1780 [Ref: D-350].

STAFFORD, Elizabeth. See "William Byall," q.v.

STALEY, Henry. Took the Oath of Allegiance in 1778 [Ref: L-2:28].

STALLINGS, Griffith (b. 1749). "Griffon Stallons" lived in North West Hd. in 1776 [Ref: K-1:226]. "Griffith Stallings" was a private, 8th Co., Lower Bn., Militia, Sep., 1777 [Ref: M-200, T-5:51].

STALLINGS (STALLONS), Jacob (b. 1751). "Jacob Stallings" was a private, 3rd Maryland Line, until discharged on Jan. 15, 1778 [Ref: D-164]. "Jacob Stalling or Stallons" lived in North West Hd. in 1776 and had two taxables in 1777 [Ref: K-1:226, R-31:17].

STALLINGS (STALLONS), Joseph. Private, 2nd Co., Upper Bn., Militia, Aug. 30, 1777 [Ref: M-193]. He was probably a son of "Joseph Stallons or Stallings, aged 60" who lived in North West Hd. (wife named Elezebeth, aged 53) in 1776 and had five taxables in 1777 [Ref: K-1:229, R-31:17]. "Joseph Stallings, Sr." died testate in Montgomery County (wife named Elizabeth) in 1797 and mentioned his children, but none were named [Ref: V-130].

STALLINGS (STALLIONS), Thomas (b. 1757). Son of Joseph Stallings, of North West Hd., in 1776 [Ref: K-1:229]. "Thomas Stallings" was a private, 3rd Maryland Line, until discharged on Jan. 15, 1778 [Ref: D-164]. "Thomas Stallions" was a private, 6th Co., Lower Bn., Militia, on July 15, 1780 [Ref: M-206].

STALLINGS (STALONS), William (b. 1757). "William Stalons" lived in Sugarland Hd. in 1776 [Ref: K-1:204]. "William Stallings or Stalion" was a private, Flying Camp, who enlisted on July 18, 1776 [Ref: D-49].

STALLIONS, Margaret. See "John Howard," q.v.

STAMP (STAMPS), William. Private, 6th Co., Middle Bn., Militia, Aug., 1777 [Ref: M-197, T-5:41]. Took the Oath of Allegiance before the Hon. Edward Burgess on Feb. 28, 1778 [Ref: T-3:61, L-1:45]. Private, 6th Co., Middle Bn., Militia, July 15, 1780 [Ref: M-203].

STANDIFORD, Eleanor. See "Charles Hoskinson," q.v.

STANLEY (STANDLEY, STANDLER), Michael. "Michael Stanley" took the Oath of Allegiance before the Hon. Gerrard Briscoe on March 2, 1778 [Ref: T-3:56, L-1:45], which misspelled the name "Stanby"]. "Michael Standley" lived in Sugar Loaf Hd. (one taxable) in 1777 [Ref: R-31:11]. "Michael Standler" was a private, 2nd Co., Upper Bn., Militia, Aug. 30, 1777 [Ref: M-193, T-5:53].

STARR, Henry. Private, 2nd Co., Upper Bn., Militia, Aug. 30, 1777 [Ref: M-193]. Lived in Sugar Loaf Hd. (one taxable) in 1777 [Ref: R-31:11].

STEEL (STEALL), Arthur. Lived in Sugarland Hd. (one taxable) in 1777 [Ref: R-31:13]. Private, 8th Co., Upper Bn., Militia, Aug. 30, 1777 [Ref: M-195]. He recruited John Predix in Feb., 1781 [Ref: R-33:155, X-1146]. "Arthur Steep" [Steel?] took the Oath of Allegiance (made his "X" mark) before the Hon. Aneas Campbell on March 2, 1778 [Ref: T-3:78, L-1:45].

STEEL, George. Took the Oath of Allegiance in 1778 [Ref: L-2:28].

STEEL (STEALL), James (b. 1750). Private, 4th Co., Upper Bn., Militia, Aug. 30, 1777 [Ref: M-194]. Took the Oath of Allegiance before the Hon. Edward Burgess on Feb. 28, 1778 [Ref: T-3:64, L-1:45]. "James Steel or Steall" lived in Sugarland Hd. in 1776-1777 [Ref: K-1:204, R-31:13].

STEEL (STEALL), John (b. 1755). Served as Ensign, Upper Bn., Militia, March 25, 1780 [Ref: M-124, E-120]. Took the Oath of Allegiance before the Hon. Edward Burgess on Feb. 28, 1778 [Ref: T-3:64, L-1:45]. "John Steel or Steall" lived in Sugarland Hd. in 1776-1777 [Ref: K-1:204, R-31:13].

STEEL (STEALL), William. Private, 4th Co., Lower Bn., Militia, Aug., 1777. Private, 1st Co., Lower Bn., July 15, 1780 [Ref: M-199, M-204, T-5:47]. One William Steel (or Steal) took the Oath of Allegiance (made his "W" mark) before the Hon. Samuel W. Magruder in 1778 [Ref: T-3:73], and another took the Oath of Allegiance before the Hon. Edward Burgess on Feb. 28, 1778 [Ref: T-3:64, L-1:45]. One William Steel (b.

1743) lived in Lower Potomac Hd. in 1776 [Ref: K-1:185], and "William Steall, aged 67" lived in Sugarland Hd. in 1776 and had a large family [Ref: K-1:204].

STEINER (STEIN), Jacob. "Jacob Steiner" took the Oath of Allegiance in 1778 [Ref: L-2:28]. "Jacob Stein" rendered aid by providing corn for use of the military in 1780 [Ref: O-300]. Also see "Jacob Stoner," q.v.

STEPHENS, Benjamin. Private, 3rd Co., Middle Bn., Militia, Sep., 1777 [Ref: M-196, T-5:38]. Took the Oath of Allegiance before the Hon. Edward Burgess on Feb. 28, 1778 [Ref: T-3:63, L-1:45]. Benjamin Stephens lived in the Upper Part of Potomac Hd. (one taxable) in 1777 [Ref: R-31:15].

STEPHENS, Edward. Private, 2nd Co., Upper Bn., Militia, Aug. 30, 1777 [Ref: M-193]. Took the Oath of Allegiance before the Hon. Elisha Williams on March 2, 1778 [Ref: T-3:80, L-1:45].

STEPHENS, John. Private, 2nd Co., Upper Bn., Militia, Aug. 30, 1777 [Ref: M-193]. Also see "John Stevens," q.v.

STEPHENS, Lewis. Private, 8th Co., Upper Bn., Militia, Aug. 30, 1777 [Ref: M-195]. Took the Oath of Allegiance before the Hon. Aneas Campbell on March 2, 1778 [Ref: T-3:77, L-1:45]. Lived in Sugarland Hd. (one taxable) in 1777 [Ref: R-31:13].

STEPHENS, Michael. Took the Oath of Allegiance before the Hon. William Deakins, Jr. before March 3, 1778 [Ref: T-3:68, L-1:45]. Lived in the Upper Part of Potomac Hd. (four taxables) in 1777 [Ref: R-31:15].

STEPHENS (STEPHEN), Richard. "Richard Stephens" was a private, 4th Co., Middle Bn., Militia, Sep., 1777 [Ref: M-196, T-5:39]. "Richard Stephen" lived in the Upper Part of Newfoundland Hd. (two taxables) in 1777 [Ref: R-31:7]. Also see "Richard Stephens," q.v.

STEVENS, Andrew. Private, 1st or 32nd Bn., Militia (no date was given; possibly June, 1777). [Ref: T-5:1].

STEVENS, Elizabeth. See "William Reynolds," q.v.

STEVENS, John. Took the Oath of Allegiance before the Hon. Samuel W. Magruder in 1778 [Ref: T-3:73, L-1:45].

STEVENS, Oliver. Private, 5th Class, 1st Co., Middle Bn., Militia, July 15, 1780 [Ref: M-201]. "Oliver Stevens, an Englishman born, 24 years of age, about 5 feet 4 or 5 inches high, black hair, brown complexion, and black eyes, recruited by Benedict Woodward on March 12, 1781." [Ref: R-33:155, X-1146].

STEVENS, Rebecca. See "Alexander Read," q.v.

STEVENS, Richard. Served as a Second Sergeant, 4th Co., Middle Bn., Militia, July 15, 1780 [Ref: M-202]. Richard Stevens married Elizabeth Jennings in Montgomery County on Sep. 26, 1780 [Ref: K-2:520]. Also see "Richard Stephens," q.v.

STEVENSON, John. See "John Stinson" and "Charles Tracy," q.v.

STEWARD, Dolly. See "John Madden," q.v.

STEWART (STEUART), Brian (b. 1749). Lived in Lower Potomac Hd. in 1776 [Ref: K-1:185]. Took the Oath of Allegiance before the Hon. Charles Jones on Jan. 10, 1778 [Ref: T-3:71, L-1:45].

STEWART, Charles. Private who enrolled into a company of militia for the service of the Flying Camp, Oct. 15, 1776 [Ref: B-353], and served as a private, 2nd Co., Middle Bn., Militia, Sep. 4, 1777 [Ref: M-196, T-5:37].

STEWART, James 2nd. Private, Capt. Price's Co., 3rd Maryland Line, 1781-1782 [Ref: D-453].

STEWART, Mordecai. Lived in the Upper Part of Potomac Hd. (two taxables) in 1777 [Ref: R-31:15]. Private, 5th Co., Middle Bn., Militia, Sep., 1777 [Ref: M-197, T-5:40]. Took the Oath of Allegiance before the Hon. Joseph Wilson on Feb. 28, 1778 [Ref: T-3:66, L-1:45]. Rendered aid by providing wheat for use of the military in 1780 and 1781 [Ref: O-306, O-396].

STEWART (STEUART), William. Private, 7th Co., Middle Bn., Militia, Sep., 1777 [Ref: M-197, T-5:42]. Private, 2nd Class, 2nd Co., Middle Bn., Militia, July 15, 1780 [Ref: M-201]. "William Stewart" was a private who was recruited to serve in the Extra Regiment of the Continental Army in 1780 [Ref: D-342]. "William Steuart" lived in the Upper Part of Newfoundland Hd. (one taxable) in 1777 [Ref: R-31:7].

STEWART (STEUART, STUART), William Veale. Took the Oath of Allegiance before the Hon. Richard Thompson in 1778 [Ref: T-3:75, L-1:45]. "William Veal Steuart" was a private, enrolled into a company of militia for the service of the Flying Camp, Oct. 15, 1776 [Ref: B-353]. Private, 3rd Co., Lower Bn., Militia, Sep., 1777 [Ref: M-199, T-5:46]. "William V. Stewart" was a private, 8th Co., Lower Bn., Militia, July 15, 1780 [Ref: M-207]. "William Veale Stewart, born in Maryland, about 28 or 29 years of age, 5 feet 10 inches high, dark hair, black eyes, and red beard, recruited by Thomas Beall (of George) on April 28, 1781." [Ref: R-33:156, X-1146]. "William X. Stuart" [sic] lived in George Town Hd. (one taxable) in 1777 [Ref: R-31:3].

STILES (STYLES), William (b. 1735). Private, 1st Co., Lower Bn., Militia, July 15, 1780 [Ref: M-204]. Took the Oath of Allegiance (made his "X" mark) before the Hon. Samuel W. Magruder in 1778 [Ref: T-3:73]. "William Styles" lived in Lower Potomac Hd. in 1776-1777 [Ref: K-1:186, R-31:5]. "William Stiles" rendered aid by providing wheat for use of the military in 1781 [Ref: O-424].

STILLINGS, Richard. See "Richard Sillings," q.v.

STILLY (STILLEY), Peter. Rendered aid by providing hay for use of the military in 1780 [Ref: O-336]. "Peter Stilley, or Stilbey," took the Oath of Allegiance in 1778 [Ref: L-2:28].

STIMPSON (STYMPSON, STIMPSON), Solomon (1736-1804). "Capt. Solomon Stimpson" lived in Sugarland Hd. (wife named Dorkus) in 1776 and "Solomon Simpson" lived there and had four taxables in 1777 [Ref:

K-1:218, R-31:13]. "Solomon Simpson" was a Captain, 16th Bn., Militia, Sep. 12, 1777, and Major, Oct. 7, 1777 [Ref: M-121, M-193, C-373, C-392]. "Solomon Simpson" rendered aid by providing wheat for use of the military and acted in roll of a commissary to acquire flour and grain for the use of the military in 1780 [Ref: O-299, O-261, F-105, F-120, which latter source spelled the name "Solomon Stympson"]. "Sollomon Stimpson" took the Oath of Allegiance before the Hon. Elisha Williams on March 2, 1778 [Ref: T-3:81, L-1:45]. "Solomon Stympson" was paid by the Collector of the Tax in Montgomery County for recruiting services in 1780 [Ref: F-54]. "Col. Solomon Stympson" was Contractor for Wagons and Teams in Montgomery County in Sep., 1780 [Ref: F-286]. "Solomon Simpson" died testate in Montgomery County (wife named Dorcas) in 1804 [Ref: V-126]. It should be noted that neither Solomon Simpson, Stimpson, nor Stympson are listed in *Archives of Maryland, Volume 18*].

STINSON (STEVENSON), John (b. 1755). "John Stinson or Stevenson" was a private in the Maryland Line who applied for pension (S30717) in Clark County, Kentucky, in 1832, stating he was born in Bucks County, Pennsylvania on July 6, 1755, and at the age of 9 moved to Maryland with his father (no name given). He enlisted in Frederick County, moved to Virginia in 1783, leaving his father in Maryland, and in 1793 he moved to Kentucky. He also made a statement to support the pension application of "Charles Tracy," q.v., stating they served in the war together from Montgomery County, Maryland [Ref: P-3346, P-3529, Y-9, Z-29. Also see *Revolutionary Patriots of Frederick County, Maryland, 1775-1783*, by Henry C. Peden, Jr., 1995].

STOFFLE, John. Private, Capt. Price's Co., 3rd Maryland Line, 1781-1782 [Ref: D-453].

STONER, Abraham. Private, 3rd Class, 1st Co., Middle Bn., Militia, July 15, 1780 [Ref: M-201].

STONER, Jacob. Private, 5th Co., Middle Bn., Militia, Sep., 1777 [Ref: M-197, T-5:40]. Took the Oath of Allegiance before the Hon. Joseph Wilson on Feb. 28, 1778 [Ref: T-3:67, L-1:45]. Lived in the Upper Part of Potomac Hd. (one taxable) in 1777 [Ref: R-31:15]. "Jacob Stoner, blacksmith" died testate in Montgomery County (wife named Margaret) in 1781 [Ref: V-130]. Also see "Jacob Steiner," q.v.

STONESTREET, Butler (b. 1757). Lived in George Town Hd. in 1776 [Ref: K-1:195]. Private, 3rd Co., Lower Bn., Militia, Sep., 1777 [Ref: M-199, T-5:46].

STORY, Henry (died 1793). Private, 6th Co., Middle Bn., Militia, Aug., 1777 [Ref: M-197, T-5:41]. "Henry Storres" [Storry?] took the Oath of Allegiance before the Hon. Edward Burgess on Feb. 28, 1778 [Ref: T-3:62, L-1:45]. "Henry Story" lived in Linganore Hd. (one taxable) in 1777 [Ref: R-31:9], and died testate in Montgomery County in 1793 (no family mentioned, but he freed his slaves). [Ref: V-131].

STRAHAN, Mary. See "John Herring," q.v.
STREET (STREAT), Francis. "Francis Street" took the Oath of Allegiance before the Hon. Elisha Williams on March 2, 1778 [Ref: T-3:81, L-1:45]. "Francis Streat" lived in Sugar Loaf Hd. (one taxable) in 1777 [Ref: R-31:11].
STREET, John. Took the Oath of Allegiance before the Hon. Charles Jones on Jan. 10, 1778 [Ref: T-3:71, L-1:45].
STUART, William. See "William Stewart," q.v.
STUDEY, Peter. Took the Oath of Allegiance in 1778 [Ref: L-2:28].
STULL, Christiana. See "Ninian Beall," q.v.
SUCKSBERRY, Joseph. Private who was recruited to serve in the Continental Army in 1780 [Ref: D-341].
SUDELEY, William. Private, 6th Co., Middle Bn., Militia, Aug., 1777 [Ref: M-197, T-5:41].
SUGER (SUGARS, SHUGAR), William (b. 1758). "William Suger" lived in Sugarland Hd. in 1776 [Ref: K-1:218]. "William Shugar" was a private, Flying Camp, enlisted on July 18, 1776 [Ref: D-35]. "William Sugars" was a private, 3rd Maryland Regiment, enlisted on April 25, 1778, for the duration of the war [Ref: D-165, D-396].
SULLIVAN, Cornelius. Private, 4th Co., Middle Bn., Militia, Sep., 1777 [Ref: M-196, T-5:39]. Took the Oath of Allegiance before the Hon. Edward Burgess on Feb. 28, 1778 [Ref: T-3:60, L-1:45]. "Cornelious Sullivan" lived in the Upper Part of Newfoundland Hd. (one taxable) in 1777 [Ref: R-31:7].
SULLIVAN, Jeremiah. Private, Capt. Price's Co., 3rd Maryland Line, 1781-1782 [Ref: D-453].
SULLIVAN, Philip. Private who was recruited to serve in the Continental Army in 1780 [Ref: D-341].
SULLIVAN, Thomas (b. 1753). Lived in Lower Potomac Hd. in 1776 [Ref: K-1:168]. Private, 3rd Maryland Regiment, 1780 [Ref: D-165]. See "George Reed," q.v.
SUMMERS (SOMMERS), Benjamin (c1783-1783). Served as a Second Lieutenant, 16th Bn., 3rd Co., Militia, Sep. 12, 1777, and a First Lieutenant, Upper Bn., March 25, 1780 [Ref: M-123, M-193, C-373, E-120]. Took the Oath of Allegiance before the Hon. Edward Burgess on Feb. 28, 1778 [Ref: T-3:64, L-1:45]. Lived in Sugar Loaf Hd. (four taxables) in 1777 [Ref: R-31:11]. Benjamin Summers married Grace Litton or Letton [Ref: DAR-I:659].
SUMMERS, Caleb. Private, 3rd Co., Upper Bn., Militia, Aug. 30, 1777 [Ref: M-193]. Private, 7th Class, 1st Co., Middle Bn., Militia, July 15, 1780 [Ref: M-201]. Caleb Summers married Rachel Crawford in Montgomery County on March 2, 1780 [Ref: K-2:520].
SUMMERS, Cassandra Ellis. See "Humphrey Beckett Tomlinson," q.v.
SUMMERS, Clement. Private, 7th Co., Middle Bn., Militia, July 15, 1780 [Ref: M-204].

SUMMERS, Dent (died 1809). Rendered aid by providing wheat for use of the military in 1780 [Ref: O-309]. Took the Oath of Allegiance on Sep. 1, 1780, under the Act of May 12, 1780, having neglected to do so previously "due to ignorance of the duty owed the country." [Ref: R-27:121]. Lived in North West Hd. (two taxables) in 1777 [Ref: R-31:17]. Previously, in 1776, the census taker noted that "Dent Sumers family is 9 but he won't make a return of names nor ages." [Ref: K-1:232]. "Dent Summers, of Frederick County" died testate in Montgomery County (wife not named) in 1809 [Ref: V-131].

SUMMERS, Dorcus (Dorkus). See "Zachariah Jacobs," q.v.

SUMMERS, George. Private, 3rd Co., Upper Bn., Militia, Aug. 30, 1777 [Ref: M-193].

SUMMERS, Hezekiah (b. 1750). Son of Dent Summers [Ref: V-131]. Private, 1st Co., Lower Bn., Militia, July 15, 1780 [Ref: M-204]. Rendered aid by providing wheat for use of the military in 1780 [Ref: O-309]. Lived in North West Hd. (wife "Rebacker, aged 32") in 1776-1777 [Ref: K-1:230, R-31:17].

SUMMERS (SOMMERS), John. (1) "John Sommers" was a Second Lieutenant, 16th Bn., 2nd Co., Militia, Sep. 12, 1777. "John Summers" was a First Lieutenant, Upper Bn., Militia, April 21, 1779, and Captain, March 25, 1780 [Ref: M-123, M-193, C-373, E-356, F-120]. (2) Private, 3rd Co., Upper Bn., Militia, Aug. 30, 1777. Private, 6th Co., Lower Bn., Militia, July 15, 1780 [Ref: M-193, M-206]. One John Summers married Jean Hoskinson in Montgomery County on Dec. 8, 1781, and another John Summers married Sarah Howard in Montgomery County on Feb. 8, 1780 [Ref: K-2:515, K-2:520]. Another John Summers married Ann Clagett on Dec. 8, 1774 in Frederick, Maryland, and their children were Charles Clagett (b. Sep. 7, 1775), Mary (b. Sep., 1777), John (b. Nov. 24, 1779), Ruth (b. March 17, 1782), Basil (b. Sep. 11, 1783), Ann (b. Nov. 14, 1785), Joseph (b. March 15, 1789), Solomon (b. April 21, 1792), and William (b. Oct. 1, 1794). Near the end of the Revolutionary War, John moved to Rowan County, North Carolina and died on April 17, 1808, in Iredell County. His widow applied for pension (R10303) on June 24, 1844, aged 91, but it was suspended because the "period, length and grade of service, and name of company and field officers were required." Ann Summers died in 1856 [Ref: P-3389, and Henry C. Peden's *Marylanders to Carolina* (1994), pp. 152-153]. One John Summers lived in Sugar Loaf Hd. (one taxable) in 1777 [Ref: R-31:11]. One was a son of "Dent Summers," q.v. [Ref: V-131].

SUMMERS, Margaret. See "Josiah Hoskinson," q.v.

SUMMERS, Mary. See "Edward Jacobs" and "Jonathan Johnson," q.v.

SUMMERS, Paul. Son of Dent Summers [Ref: V-131]. Private, 4th Co., Lower Bn., Militia, Aug., 1777 [Ref: M-199, T-5:47]. Private, 1st Co., Lower Bn., Militia, July 15, 1780 [Ref: M-204].

SUMMERS, Thomas. Private, 3rd Co., Upper Bn., Militia, Aug. 30, 1777 [Ref: M-193]. Took the Oath of Allegiance before the Hon. Elisha Williams on March 2, 1778 [Ref: T-3:81, L-1:45]. One "Thomas Summers, aged 25" lived in George Town Hd. in 1776 [Ref: K-1:194], and Thomas Summers lived in Sugar Loaf Hd. (one taxable) in 1777 [Ref: R-31:11].

SUMMERS, Thomas Jr. Private, 3rd Co., Upper Bn., Militia, Aug. 30, 1777 [Ref: M-193].

SUMMERS, Thomas Sr. Private, 3rd Co., Upper Bn., Militia, Aug. 30, 1777 [Ref: M-193].

SUMMERS, Valentine. Rendered aid by providing beef for use of the military in 1781 [Ref: O-393].

SUMMERS, William Jr. "William Summers, Jr." was an Ensign, 2nd Co., Upper Bn., Militia, from Aug. 30, 1777, to at least April 21, 1779 [Ref: M-123, M-193, E-356]. Took the Oath of Allegiance before the Hon. Elisha Williams on March 2, 1778 [Ref: T-3:81, L-1:45]. "William Summers" married Rebecca Jacobs in Montgomery County on Oct. 1, 1778 [Ref: K-2:521]. William Summers (b. 1751) is listed twice in Lower Potomac Hd. in 1776 [Ref: K-1:186].

SUMMERS, William Sr. "William Summers, Sr." was a private, 2nd Co., Upper Bn., Militia, Aug. 30, 1777 [Ref: M-193]. Took the Oath of Allegiance before the Hon. Elisha Williams on March 2, 1778 [Ref: T-3:81, L-1:45]. "William Summers" was a private who enrolled into a company of militia for the service of the Flying Camp on Oct. 15, 1776 [Ref: B-352]. Rendered aid by providing wheat for use of the military in 1780 and 1781 [Ref: O-309, O-447]. "William Summers" lived in Sugar Loaf Hd. (four taxables) in 1777 [Ref: R-31:11]. Also see "William Summers, Jr." and "Humphrey Beckett Tomlinson," q.v.

SUTER (SUITER), George. "George Suter" was a private, 5th Co., Lower Bn., Militia, July 15, 1780 [Ref: M-206]. Rendered aid by providing wheat for use of the military in 1781 [Ref: O-399]. "George Suiter" married Mary Beall in Montgomery County on Jan. 7, 1779 [Ref: K-2:520].

SUTER (SUITOR), James (died 1815). Private, 4th Class, 1st Co., Middle Bn., Militia, July 15, 1780 [Ref: M-201]. Took the Oath of Allegiance before the Hon. Joseph Wilson on Feb. 28, 1778 [Ref: T-3:66, L-1:45]. Rendered aid by providing wheat for use of the military in 1780 [Ref: O-304]. "James Suitor" lived in the Upper Part of Potomac Hd. (six taxables) in 1777 [Ref: R-31:15]. "James Suter" died testate in Montgomery County (wife not named) in 1815 [Ref: V-131].

SUTER (SUITER), John (died 1794). Served as a Second Lieutenant, 7th Co., Middle Bn., Militia, Sep. 12, 1777 [Ref: M-127, M-197, C-373, T-5:41]. Took the Oath of Allegiance before the Hon. Gerrard Briscoe on March 2, 1778 [Ref: T-3:56, L-1:45]. Rendered aid by providing wheat for use of the military in 1780 [Ref: O-304]. "John Suiter" lived in

Seneca Hd. (two taxables) in 1777 [Ref: R-31:8]. "John Suter, of Georgetown" died testate in Montgomery County (wife named Sarah) in 1794 and mentioned a son John, among others [Ref: V-131].

SUTHERLAND, Alexander. Took the Oath of Allegiance before the Hon. Joseph Offutt on March 2, 1778 [Ref: T-3:70, L-1:45].

SUTTON, John (b. 1747). Lived in Lower Potomac Hd. in 1776 [Ref: K-1:186]. Private, 3rd Co., Lower Bn., Militia, Sep., 1777 [Ref: M-199, T-5:46]. Private, 5th Class, 1st Co., Middle Bn., July 15, 1780 [Ref: M-201].

SUTTON, Robert (b. 1749). Private, 3rd Co., Lower Bn., Militia, Sep., 1777 [Ref: M-199, T-5:46]. Private, 8th Co., Lower Bn., Militia, July 15, 1780 [Ref: M-207]. Lived in Lower Potomac Hd. (one taxable) in 1776-1777 [Ref: K-1:186, R-31:5]. Robert Sutton married Judith Canady in Montgomery County on Dec. 1, 1779 [Ref: K-2:514].

SUTTON (SUTTEN), William (b. 1736). "William Sutten" lived in Sugarland Hd. in 1776 [Ref: K-1:203]. "William Sutton" was a private who enrolled into a company of militia for the service of the Flying Camp on Oct. 15, 1776 [Ref: B-353].

SWAIN, Joshua. Private, 7th Co., Lower Bn., Militia, July 15, 1780 [Ref: M-207].

SWAIN, Robert. Took the Oath of Allegiance before the Hon. Edward Burgess on Feb. 28, 1778 [Ref: T-3:60, L-1:45]. Robert Swain lived in the Upper Part of Newfoundland Hd. (one taxable) in 1777 [Ref: R-31:7].

SWANN (SWAIN), Thomas (b. 1761). "Thomas Swann" lived in Sugarland Hd. in 1776 [Ref: K-1:202]. "Thomas Swain" was a private who was drafted in Prince George's County in 1781 [Ref: D-382].

SWANN (SWAN), Zephaniah (b. 1740). Private, 1st Co., Upper Bn., Militia, Aug. 30, 1777 [Ref: M-193]. "Zephaniah Swann" took the Oath of Allegiance before the Hon. Elisha Williams on March 2, 1778 [Ref: T-3:82]. "Zepheniah Swan" lived in Sugarland Hd. (two taxables) in 1776-1777 [Ref: K-1:201, R-31:13].

SWEARINGEN, Mary. See "Aaron Prather" and "George Willcoxen," q.v.

SWEARINGEN, Obediah. Son of Thomas Swearingen [Ref: V-132]. Served as First Corporal, 5th Co., Lower Bn., Militia, July 15, 1780 [Ref: M-205].

SWEARINGEN, Samuel. Served as an Ensign, 16th Bn., Militia, May 14, 1776, Ensign, 29th (Lower) Bn., Militia, Sep. 12, 1777, and Captain, 5th Co., Lower Bn., by July 15, 1780 [Ref: F-120, M-127, M-198, M-205, T-5:45, A-424, C-373]. Took the Oath of Allegiance before the Hon. Edward Burgess on Feb. 28, 1778 [Ref: T-3:60, L-1:45]. Lived in Rock Creek Hd. (two taxables) in 1777 [Ref: R-31:16].

SWEARINGEN, Thomas Jr. Private, 2nd Co., Lower Bn., Militia, Sep., 1777 [Ref: M-198, T-5:45]. Took the Oath of Allegiance before the Hon. Edward Burgess on Feb. 28, 1778 [Ref: T-3:61, L-1:45].

SWEARINGEN, Thomas Sr. (died 1794). "Thomas Swearingen, Sr." was a private, 2nd Co., Lower Bn., Militia, Sep., 1777 [Ref: M-198, T-5:45]. Took the Oath of Allegiance before the Hon. Joseph Wilson on Feb. 28, 1778 [Ref: T-3:66, L-1:45, which latter source spelled the name "Sweararinger"]. "Thomas Swearingen" rendered aid by providing wheat for use of the military in 1780 [Ref: O-315]. Lived in Rock Creek Hd. (seven taxables) in 1777 [Ref: R-31:16], and served as a constable in 1779 [Ref: W-1]. Died testate in Montgomery County (wife named Mary) in 1794 [Ref: V-132].

SWEARINGEN, Van (b. 1747). Private, 4th Co., Upper Bn., Militia, Aug. 30, 1777 [Ref: M-194]. "Van Swarigen" took the Oath of Allegiance before the Hon. Richard Thompson in 1778 [Ref: T-3:75, L-1:45]. "Van Swearinger or Swearingin" lived in Sugarland Hd. (two taxables) in 1776-1777 [Ref: K-1:205, R-31:13]. "Van Swearingen" rendered aid by providing flour for use of the military in 1781 [Ref: O-374]. See "George Beckwith," q.v.

SWEENY (SWENEY, SWEANEY), Owen. "Owen Sweaney" lived in Seneca Hd. (one taxable) in 1777 [Ref: R-31:8]. "Owen Sweny" was a private, 6th Maryland Line, from May 23, 1778, until Aug. 16, 1780, when reported missing at the Battle of Camden [Ref: D-247]. "Owen Sweny" took the Oath of Allegiance (made his "X" mark) before the Hon. Joseph Wilson on Feb. 28, 1778 [Ref: T-3:66, L-1:45].

TALBOTT (TALBERT, TOLBERT), Basil (b. 1754). "Basil Tolbert" was a private, 8th Co., Upper Bn., Militia, Aug. 30, 1777 [Ref: M-195]. "Basil Talbott" took the Oath of Allegiance before the Hon. Elisha Williams on March 2, 1778 [Ref: T-3:81, L-1:45]. "Basil Talbott or Tolbert" lived in Sugarland Hd. (one taxable) in 1776-1777 [Ref: K-1:199, R-31:13].

TALBOTT (TALBUTT, TOLBERT), George (b. 1760). "George Talbott" was a private, 8th Co., Upper Bn., Militia, Aug. 30, 1777 [Ref: M-195]. "George Tolbert" lived in Sugarland Hd. in 1776 [Ref: K-1:199]. "George Talbutt" married Mary McDaniel in Montgomery County on Aug. 6, 1778 [Ref: K-2:521].

TALBOTT (TALBERT), John. Took the Oath of Allegiance before the Hon. Richard Thompson in 1778 [Ref: T-3:75, L-1:45]. "John Talbert" lived in George Town Hd. (one taxable) in 1777 [Ref: R-31:3].

TALBOTT, Mary. See "William Allnutt," q.v.

TALBOTT (TALBERT), Notley. Private, 1st Co., Upper Bn., Militia, Aug. 30, 1777 [Ref: M-193]. "Notly Talbot" took the Oath of Allegiance before the Hon. Elisha Williams on March 2, 1778 [Ref: T-3:81, L-1:45]. "Notley Talbert" lived in Sugarland Hd. (one taxable) in 1777 [Ref: R-31:13].

TALBOTT, Susannah. See "Hezekiah Magruder," q.v.

TALBOTT (TOLBERT), Thomas (died 1810). Private, 6th Co., Upper Bn., Militia, Aug. 30, 1777 [Ref: M-194]. Took the Oath of Allegiance before the Hon. Elisha Williams on March 2, 1778 [Ref: T-3:80, L-1:45]. "Thomas Tolbert" was a private, 8th Co., Upper Bn., Militia, Aug. 30,

1777 [Ref: M-195]. "Thomas Talbott" lived in Sugar Loaf Hd. (one taxable) in 1777 [Ref: R-31:11]. Died testate in Montgomery County (wife not named) in 1810 and had a son Thomas, among other children [Ref: V-132].

TALBOTT (TALBERT), William (b. 1741). "William Talbott" was a private, 5th Co., Lower Bn., Militia, Aug., 1777 [Ref: M-199, T-5:48]. "William Talbert" was a Second Lieutenant, 2nd Co., Lower Bn., Militia, July 15, 1780 [Ref: F-248, M-127, M-204]. Took the Oath of Allegiance before the Hon. Samuel W. Magruder in 1778 [Ref: T-3:73, L-1:45]. "William Talbert" served as a petit juror in Aug., 1777 [Ref: R-31:17]. "William Talbott" rendered aid by providing wheat for use of the military in 1780 [Ref: O-313, O-316]. Served as a grand juror in 1779 [Ref: W-1]. "William Talbutt or Talbot" lived in Lower Potomac Hd. (five taxables) in 1776-1777 [Ref: K-1:186, R-31:5].

TALL (TAUL), Arthur (b. 1748). "Arther Tall" was a private, 3rd Co., Upper Bn., Militia, Aug. 30, 1777 [Ref: M-193]. "Arthur Thomas Taul" took the Oath of Allegiance before the Hon. Elisha Williams in 1778 [Ref: T-3:81, L-1:45]. "Arthur Tall" lived in Sugarland Hd. in 1776 and had one taxable in 1777 [Ref: R-31:13, K-1:207, which latter source questions if the name was "Tall" or "Lall?"].

TALL (TOLE), Stephen. "Stephen Tall" was a private, 5th Co., Lower Bn., Militia, July 15, 1780 [Ref: M-206]. "Stephen Tole" took the Oath of Allegiance (made his "X" mark) before the Hon. Joseph Wilson on Feb. 28, 1778 [Ref: T-3:66, L-1:45].

TANNEHILL, Adamson. Served as a Captain, Maryland Line, 1778-1779, and Captain in Col. Rawlings' Regiment in 1780 [Ref: D-350, F-83].

TANNEHILL, John. Took the Oath of Allegiance before the Hon. Edward Burgess on Feb. 28, 1778 [Ref: T-3:60, L-1:45]. Lived in Rock Creek Hd. (two taxables) in 1777 [Ref: R-31:16].

TANNEHILL, Josias. Served as Adjutant in the Maryland part of Col. Rawlings' Regiment in 1780 [Ref: F-83].

TANNEHILL (TAWNEYHILL), Malcham. Private, 5th Co., Lower Bn., Militia, July 15, 1780 [Ref: M-206].

TANNEHILL (TANNIHILL), Ninian. "Ninian Tannehill" took the Oath of Allegiance before the Hon. Joseph Offutt on March 2, 1778 [Ref: T-3:70, L-1:45]. "Ninian Tannihill" lived in the Upper Part of Potomac Hd. (three taxables) in 1777 [Ref: R-31:15].

TANNEHILL, William (b. 1721). Took the Oath of Allegiance before the Hon. Edward Burgess on Feb. 28, 1778 [Ref: T-3:62, L-1:45]. Served as a petit juror in Nov., 1777 [Ref: R-31:18]. Lived in North West Hd. (wife named Sarah, aged 59) in 1776 and had four taxables in 1777 [Ref: K-1:229, R-31:17].

TANNEHILL (TAWNEYHILL), William Harris (b. 1760). "William Harres Tannehill" was a son of William and Sarah Tannehill, of North West Hd., in 1776 [Ref: K-1:299]. "William Tannehill" was a private, 8th Co., Lower

Bn., Militia, Sep., 1777 [Ref: M-200, T-5:51]. "William Harris Tawneyhill" was Fourth Sergeant, 6th Co., Lower Bn., Militia, July 15, 1780 [Ref: M-206].

TANNER, Thomas. See "Thomas Tennett," q.v.

TAPLIN, John. See "John Toplin," q.v.

TASDEN, Joshua. Took the Oath of Allegiance on Sep. 1, 1780, under the Act of May 12, 1780, having neglected to do so previously "due to ignorance of the duty owed the country." [Ref: R-27:121].

TAYLOR, Elizabeth. See "Ninian Taylor," q.v.

TAYLOR, Griffin (b. 1748). "Griffin Taylor" lived in Sugarland Hd. in 1776 [Ref: K-1:214]. "Griffith Taylor" was a private, 3rd Maryland Regiment, from April 20, 1778 to at least Nov. 1, 1780 [Ref: D-170]. "Griffin Taylor" was a corporal in the Maryland Line who was "wounded at Eutaw [Springs] and not heard of since June [1781?] muster." [Ref: D-435].

TAYLOR, James. Private, 3rd Co., Upper Bn., Militia, Aug. 30, 1777 [Ref: M-193]. Took the Oath of Allegiance before the Hon. Gerrard Briscoe on March 2, 1778 [Ref: T-3:57, L-1:45]. James Taylor lived in Sugar Loaf Hd. (three taxables) in 1777 [Ref: R-31:11].

TAYLOR, Jane. See "Joseph Woodard," q.v.

TAYLOR, John. Private, 8th Co., Upper Bn., Militia, Aug. 30, 1777 [Ref: M-195]. Took the Oath of Allegiance before the Hon. Aneas Campbell on March 2, 1778 [Ref: T-3:77, L-1:45]. One John Taylor married Ruth Bailey on March 16, 1780, and a John Taylor married Elizabeth Morris on May 3, 1780, both in Montgomery County [Ref: K-2:521]. The petition of a John Taylor, Montgomery County, dated Aug. 26, 1781, to the Governor and Council of Maryland stated, in part": "Whereas your petitioner hath continued in the above mentioned county, pursuant to the Order of your Excellency and Honors, your petitioner now impelled by the duty he owes to his distressed wife and family, who are reduced to the most pitiable circumstances by reason of his absence, requests your Excellency and Honors, that he may be permitted to return to St. Mary's County where his wife resides in order to settle his affairs there and remove her into Montgomery County. This your petitioner humbly presumes will be granted him, as he hath agreeable to your desire given bond with security to Col. Richard Barnes for his beheavour as a good citizen. And your petitioner as in duty bound will ever pray." [Ref: H-449]. "John Taylor, aged 24" lived in Sugarland Hd. in 1776 and had five taxables in 1777 [Ref: K-1:204, R-31:13], and "John Taylor, aged 28" also lived in Sugarland Hd. in 1776 [Ref: K-1:210].

TAYLOR (TAILOR), Mary. Listed as a pensioner in 1840, aged 78, and living in Montgomery County's 5th Division, but the name of her husband was not given [Ref: R-28:445]. See "Zachariah Butt," q.v.

TAYLOR, Priscilla. See "Moses Orme," q.v.

TAYLOR, Richard. Private, 3rd Co., Lower Bn., Militia, Sep., 1777 [Ref: T-5:46, M-199, which latter source questions if name could be "Tyler"].

"Richard Taylor, aged 15," lived in George Town Hd. in 1776 [Ref: K-1:195]. He may have been the Richard Taylor who was recruited to serve as a private in the Continental Army in 1780 [Ref: D-341].

TAYLOR, Robert. Private, 8th Co., Middle Bn., Militia, Sep., 1777 [Ref: M-198, T-5:43].

TAYLOR, Samuel. Private, Capt. Edward Burgess' Co., Lower District of Frederick (now Montgomery) County, Militia, July, 1776 [Ref: D-42].

TAYLOR, Thomas. Private, 8th Co., Lower Bn., Militia, July 15, 1780 [Ref: M-207].

TAYLOR, Verlinda. See "Moses Orme," q.v.

TAYLOR, Walter (died 1786). Took the Oath of Allegiance (made his "X" mark) before the Hon. Samuel W. Magruder in 1778 [Ref: T-3:73]. Died testate in Montgomery County (wife named Mary) in 1786 [Ref: V-133].

TAYLOR, William (b. 1762). Lived in Lower Potomac Hd. in 1776 [Ref: K-1:186]. Private, Capt. Thomas Beall's Co., Maryland Line, 1780 [Ref: D-351].

TENNETT (TANNER), Thomas. "Thomas Tennett" lived in the Lower Part of Newfoundland Hd. (one taxable) in 1777 [Ref: R-31:6]. "Thomas Tanner" was a private in the 7th Maryland Line from April 22, 1778 until Aug. 16, 1780, when reported missing at the Battle of Camden [Ref: D-253]. "Thomas Tanner" was also a private in Capt. Price's Co., 3rd Maryland Line, in 1781, and reported dead on Jan. 3, 1782 [Ref: D-453].

TERNEN, Dennis. Private who was recruited to serve in the Continental Army in 1780 [Ref: D-341].

TERRY, James. Private, Capt. Price's Co., 3rd Maryland Line, 1781-1782 [Ref: D-453].

THAWING, William. Private, 4th Co., Lower Bn., Militia, Aug., 1777 [Ref: M-199, T-5:47].

THOMAS, Amelia. See "Samuel Griffith," q.v.

THOMAS, Evan. Son of "Samuel Thomas," q.v. [Ref: V-134]. Private, Maryland Line, between Jan. 1, 1782 and Nov. 15, 1783 [Ref: D-558]. Lived in the Lower Part of Newfoundland Hd. (seven taxables) in 1777 [Ref: R-31:6].

THOMAS, Gabriel (1721-1794). Took the Oath of Allegiance in 1778 [Ref: L-2:28]. Buried in the German Thomas Family Cemetery at Mountain, Frederick County, Maryland [Ref: S-1993].

THOMAS, James. Private, 7th Co., Upper Bn., Militia, Aug. 30, 1777 [Ref: M-195].

THOMAS, John. (1) Private, 3rd Co., Middle Bn., Militia, Sep., 1777 [Ref: M-196, T-5:38]. (2) Private, 1st Co., Lower Bn., Militia, Sep., 1777 [Ref: M-198, T-5:44]. Private, 7th Co., Lower Bn., Militia, July 15, 1780 [Ref: M-206]. One John Thomas took the Oath of Allegiance in 1778 [Ref: L-2:28]. One John Thomas lived in the Lower Part of Newfoundland Hd.

(ten taxables) in 1777 [Ref: R-31:6], and another lived in the Upper Part of Potomac Hd. (one taxable) in 1777 [Ref: R-31:15].

THOMAS, Martin (b. 1751). Private, 4th Co., Upper Bn., Militia, Aug. 30, 1777 [Ref: M-194]. "Martain Thomas" took the Oath of Allegiance (made his "X" mark) before the Hon. Aneas Campbell on March 2, 1778 [Ref: T-3:78, L-1:45]. "Martin Thomas" lived in Sugarland Hd. (one taxable) in 1776-1777 [Ref: K-1:206, R-31:13].

THOMAS, Notley (b. 1755). Private, 7th Co., Upper Bn., Militia, Aug. 30, 1777 [Ref: M-194]. Lived in Sugarland Hd. in 1776 [Ref: K-1:200].

THOMAS, Richard Jr. Private, 1st Co., Lower Bn., Militia, Sep., 1777 [Ref: M-198, T-5:44]. Took the Oath of Allegiance (affirmed) before the Hon. Edward Burgess on March 10, 1778 [Ref: T-3:64, L-1:45]. Private, 7th Co., Lower Bn., Militia, July 15, 1780 [Ref: M-206].

THOMAS, Richard Sr. "Richard Thomas, Sr." lived in the Lower Part of Newfoundland Hd. (eleven taxables) in 1777 [Ref: R-31:6]. "Richard Thomas" was a private in the 5th Maryland Regiment from June 4, 1778 until March 20, 1779, when discharged [Ref: D-251]. "Richard Thomas" owned two working plantations ("quarters") in the Upper Part of Newfoundland Hd. in 1777: one with five taxables ("upper quarter") and one with nine taxables ("lower quarter") [Ref: R-31:7]. One "Richard Thomas, Quaker" died testate in Montgomery County (wife not named) in 1806 [Ref: V-133].

THOMAS, Robert. Private, 4th Co., Lower Bn., Militia, Aug., 1777 [Ref: M-199, T-5:47]. Private, 1st Co., Lower Bn., Militia, July 15, 1780 [Ref: M-204]. Took the Oath of Allegiance before the Hon. Charles Jones on Jan. 10, 1778 [Ref: T-3:71, L-1:45]. Rendered aid by providing wheat for use of the military in 1780 [Ref: O-308].

THOMAS, Samuel (died 1783). Private, 1st Co., Lower Bn., Militia, Sep., 1777 [Ref: M-198, T-5:44]. Rendered aid by providing corn, rye, and flour for use of the military in 1781 [Ref: O-404]. "Samuel Thomas, Sr." lived in the Lower Part of Newfoundland Hd. (six taxables) in 1777 [Ref: R-31:6]. "Samuel Thomas" died testate in Montgomery County in 1783, naming only a son Evan in his will [Ref: V-134].

THOMAS, Samuel 3rd. "Samuel Thomas 3rd" took the Oath of Allegiance before the Hon. Edward Burgess on Jan. 24, 1778 [Ref: T-3:64, L-1:45]. "Samuel Thomas III" acted in roll of a commissary to acquire flour and grain for the use of the military in 1780 [Ref: O-258, O-271, D-105, which latter source listed the name as "Samuel Thomas 3rd, Esq., Commissioner of Montgomery County"]. He was also Contractor for Horses in Montgomery County in Oct., 1780 [Ref: F-321]. "Samuel Thomas 3rd" lived in the Lower Part of Newfoundland Hd. (four taxables) in 1777 [Ref: R-31:6].

THOMAS, William. Private, 7th Co., Upper Bn., Militia, Aug. 30, 1777 [Ref: M-195, which source listed this name twice]. One took the Oath of Allegiance before the Hon. Elisha Williams on March 2, 1778 [Ref: T-

3:82]. William Thomas lived in Sugarland Hd. (two taxables) in 1777 [Ref: R-31:13].

THOMPSON, Babtis (Baptist). "Babtis Thompson" was a private, 6th Co., Upper Bn., Militia, Aug. 30, 1777 [Ref: M-194]. "Baptist Thomson" lived in Sugar Loaf Hd. (one taxable) in 1777 [Ref: R-31:11]. See "John Baptist Thompson," q.v.

THOMPSON, George. Private, 6th Class, 3rd Co., Middle Bn., Militia, July 15, 1780 [Ref: M-202].

THOMPSON, James. Private, 4th Co., Middle Bn., Militia, Sep., 1777 [Ref: M-196, T-5:39]. Private, 6th Class, 4th Co., Middle Bn., Militia, July 15, 1780 [Ref: M-202].

THOMPSON, John. (1) Private, 3rd Co., Middle Bn., Militia, Sep., 1777 [Ref: M-196, T-5:38]. Private, 3rd Class, 2nd Co., Middle Bn., Militia, July 15, 1780 [Ref: M-201]. (2) Private, 8th Co., Lower Bn., Militia, July 15, 1780 [Ref: M-207]. (3) Private, 4th Class, 2nd Co., Middle Bn., Militia, July 15, 1780 [Ref: M-201]. Took the Oath of Allegiance before the Hon. William Deakins, Jr. before March 3, 1778 [Ref: T-3:68, L-1:45], and served as a grand juror in Nov., 1777 [Ref: R-31:17]. One John Thompson lived in the Upper Part of Potomac Hd. (two taxables) in 1777 [Ref: R-31:15]. One "John Thompson, aged 15" lived in Sugarland Hd. in 1776 [Ref: K-1:206].

THOMPSON, John Baptist. Served as a Lieutenant, Flying Camp, in 1776 [Ref: D-44, D-46]. Took the Oath of Allegiance before the Hon. Elisha Williams on March 2, 1778 [Ref: T-3:80, L-1:45]. Rendered aid by providing wheat for use of the military in 1781 [Ref: O-444]. Also see "Babtis Thompson," q.v.

THOMPSON, Joseph. Private, 8th Co., Lower Bn., Militia, July 15, 1780 [Ref: M-207].

THOMPSON (THOMSON), Mary. See "Michael Mummart," q.v.

THOMPSON, Nathan. Private, 5th Co., Middle Bn., Militia, Sep., 1777 [Ref: M-197, T-5:40].

THOMPSON, Richard. (1) Private, 3rd Co., Lower Bn., Militia, Sep., 1777 [Ref: M-199, T-5:46]. (2) Private, 4th Class, 1st Co., Middle Bn., Militia, July 15, 1780 [Ref: M-201]. (3) Quartermaster, 29th Bn., Militia, Jan. 6, 1776 [Ref: M-129]. Justice of the Peace who administered the Oath of Allegiance in 1778, and Justice of the County Court, 1779-1781 [Ref: T-3:76, L-1:45, X-1146, W-1, W-2, C-529]. "Richard Tomson, aged 38" lived in George Town Hd. in 1776 and "Richard Thompson, Esq." lived there (eight taxables) in 1777 [Ref: K-1:195, R-31:3].

THOMPSON, Thomas. Private, 7th Maryland Line, enlisted Jan. 28, 1777. Private, 2nd Maryland Line, April 2, 1778 until Dec. 4, 1780, when discharged [Ref: D-169, D-305]. Ed. Note: This might be two different Thomas Thompsons]. One Thomas Thompson lived in Seneca Hd. (two taxables) in 1777 [Ref: R-31:8].

THOMPSON, William. Private, 5th Co., Middle Bn., Militia, Sep., 1777 [Ref: M-197, T-5:40]. Private, 5th Class, 1st Co., Middle Bn., Militia, July 15, 1780 [Ref: M-201]. One William Thompson took the Oath of Allegiance before the Hon. William Deakins, Jr. by March 3, 1778 [Ref: T-3:68, L-1:45], and another before the Hon. Richard Thompson in 1778 [Ref: T-3:75, L-1:45]. One rendered aid by providing wheat for use of the military in 1781 [Ref: O-389]. One "William Thompson, aged 37" lived in Sugarland Hd. in 1776 and had two taxables in 1777 [Ref: K-1:206, R-31:13]. One William Thompson married Martha Easton in Montgomery County on Feb. 24, 1778 [Ref: K-2:517].

THOMPSON (TOMSON), Zachariah (died 1824). Private, 5th Co., Middle Bn., Militia, Sep., 1777 [Ref: M-197, T-5:40]. Served as a petit juror in Aug., 1777 [Ref: R-31:17]. "Zachariah Tomson" took the Oath of Allegiance (made his mark) before the Hon. Joseph Wilson on Feb. 28, 1778 [Ref: T-3:66, L-1:45]. "Zachy. Thompson" lived in the Upper Part of Potomac Hd. (four taxables) in 1777 [Ref: R-31:15]. "Zachariah Thompson, Sr." died testate in Montgomery County (wife not named) in 1824 [Ref: V-134].

THRASHER, Mary. See "Philip Tracy," q.v.

THRASHER, Robert. Rendered aid by providing wheat for use of the military in 1780 [Ref: O-311].

THRASHER (THRESHER), John. "John Thresher" took the Oath of Allegiance in 1778 [Ref: L-2:28]. A "John Thrasher" was a son of William Thrasher who died testate in Jan., 1801 [Ref: V-134, V-135].

THRASHER, William. See "John Thrasher" and "Philip Tracy," q.v. William Thrasher's daughter Mary married Philip Tracy [Ref: V-134]. "William Tharasher, aged 45" lived in North West Hd. in 1776 (wife named Margrett, aged 39) and had a daughter Mary, aged 17, among other children [Ref: K-1:224].

THRELKELD (THRELKIELD), Henry (b. 1716). Took the Oath of Allegiance before the Hon. Richard Thompson in 1778 [Ref: T-3:75, L-1:45]. "Henry Threlkeld or Threlkield" lived in George Town Hd. (twelve taxables) in 1776-1777 and also owned a working plantation ("quarter") in Lower Potomac Hd. [Ref: K-1:195, R-31:3, R-31:5].

THRELKELD (THULKELD), Hugh. Rendered aid by providing wheat for use of the military in 1780 [Ref: O-338].

THRELKELD (THRELKIELD), John (b. 1759). "John Threlkeld" took the Oath of Allegiance before the Hon. Richard Thompson in 1778 [Ref: T-3:75, L-1:45]. "John Threlkield" was a private, 3rd Co., Lower Bn., Militia, Sep., 1777 [Ref: M-199, T-5:46]. "John Threlkild, aged 17" lived in George Town Hd. in 1776 [Ref: K-1:195].

THRELKELD, Joseph. Took the Oath of Allegiance before the Hon. William Deakins, Jr. before March 3, 1778 [Ref: T-3:68, L-1:45]. Lived in the Upper Part of Potomac Hd. (six taxables) in 1777 [Ref: R-31:15].

"Joseph Threlkeld, V.D.M., of Prince George's County" died testate in Montgomery County (wife named Jane) in 1783 [Ref: V-135].
THRELKELD, Rev. See "Michael Downs," q.v.
THRIFT, Alley. See "William M. Offutt," q.v.
THRIFT, Samuel. See "Francis Hutchinson," q.v.
TILLARD, Edward. Served as a Major and then as Lieutenant Colonel, 6th Maryland Line, from Feb. 20, 1777 until Jan. 1, 1781 [Ref: D-252, D-365]. Received bounty land warrant #2207-450-4 in March, 1800. On Jan. 6, 1812, the Treasurer of Maryland was directed to pay to Edward Tillard of Montgomery County, $125 a year in quarterly payments. In 1819 Sarah Tillard, widow of Lt. Col. Tillard, received, during life, "a sum of money equal to half pay of a captain." In 1834 an Otho Thomas Tillard, of Frederick County, received the balance due the heirs of Sarah Tillard at the time of her death [Ref: K-2:349, K-2:399, P-3500, Q-113, Q-143].
TILLARD, Elizabeth. See "Leonard Hays," q.v.
TILLARD, Otho and Sarah. See "Edward Tillard," q.v.
TIPPERY, Jacob. Took the Oath of Allegiance in 1778 [Ref: L-2:28].
TISUE, Jacob. Private, 1st Class, 2nd Co., Middle Bn., Militia, July 15, 1780 [Ref: M-201].
TOLBERT, Basil, and other. See "Basil Talbott" and others, q.v.
TOMLINSON, Grove. Private, 1st Co., Upper Bn., Militia, Aug. 30, 1777 [Ref: M-193]. Draught who was discharged from the Maryland Line in 1781 [Ref: D-412].
TOMLINSON (TOMBLINSON), Hugh (1752 - died after 1790). "Heugh or Hugh Tomlinson" lived in Sugarland Hd. in 1776-1777 [Ref: K-1:218, R-31:13]. Served as a private and corporal, 1st Co., Upper Bn., Militia, Aug. 30, 1777 [Ref: M-193, DAR-I:682]. "Hugh Tomblinson" took the Oath of Allegiance before the Hon. Elisha Williams on March 2, 1778 [Ref: T-3:81, L-1:45]. Rendered aid by providing corn and wheat for use of the military in 1780 [Ref: O-283, O-286, O-328]. See "Humphrey Beckett Tomlinson," q.v.
TOMLINSON, Humphrey Beckett (1744-1825). "Humphry B. Tomlinson" was a private, 2nd Co., Upper Bn., Militia, Aug. 30, 1777 [Ref: M-193]. He took the Oath of Allegiance before the Hon. Elisha Williams on March 2, 1778 [Ref: T-3:80, L-1:45]. "Humphry Becket Tomlinson" lived in Sugar Loaf Hd. (three taxables) in 1777 [Ref: R-31:11]. "Humphrey Beckett Tomlinson," son of Hugh Tomlinson and Johanna Beckett, was born on Nov. 14 or 24, 1744 in Frederick County, Maryland. He was married thrice: (1) Tabitha Wheat, daughter of John Wheat; (2) Unknown; and, (3) Cassandra (Ellis) Summers, widow of William Summers and daughter of Samuel Ellis. Humphrey's children included John (1768-1848), William, Sarah, Mary, Wiley, and Notley (who changed the name to "Tomlin" after his father's death). In 1787 Humphrey bought a plantation on Rocky Creek in Rowan County, North

Carolina, having been preceded there by his younger brother Hugh Tomlinson, Jr. [Ref: DAR-I:682, and research files of Robert E. Hedgcock, of Fruitland Park, Florida (1944), and Henry C. Peden's *Marylanders to Carolina* (1994), p. 184].

TOMLINSON (TOMBLINSON), William (b. 1750). Private, 1st Co., Upper Bn., Militia, Aug. 30, 1777 [Ref: M-193]. "William Tomblinson" took the Oath of Allegiance before the Hon. Elisha Williams on March 2, 1778 [Ref: T-3:81, L-1:45]. "William Tomlinson" lived in Sugarland Hd. in 1776 and had two taxables in 1777 [Ref: K-1:220, R-31:13]. Served as a constable in 1781 [Ref: W-2].

TOMLINSON, Zadock. Private, 7th Maryland Line, from June 8, 1778 until March 30, 1779, when discharged [Ref: D-253].

TOOL (TOOLE), James. Private, 6th Co., Middle Bn., Militia, July 15, 1780 [Ref: M-203]. Private, 6th Co., Middle Bn., Militia, Aug., 1777 [Ref: M-197, T-5:41]. Lived in the Upper Part of Newfoundland Hd. (one taxable) in 1777 [Ref: R-31:7].

TOOL, Sarah. See "Tobias Butler," q.v.

TOPLIN, John. Private who was recruited and served in the 7th Maryland Regiment, Continental Army, in 1780 [Ref: D-341, F-114, which latter source listed the name as "John Taplin"].

TOPPING, James (1714-1787). Took the Oath of Allegiance before the Hon. Charles Jones on Jan. 10, 1778 [Ref: T-3:71, L-1:45]. Lived in Lower Potomac Hd. (four taxables) in 1776-1777 [Ref: K-1:186, R-31:5]. Died testate in Montgomery County (wife Margaret Leadsom Topping, deceased) in 1787 [Ref: V-136].

TOWNLEY, Henry. Private, Capt. Price's Co., 3rd Maryland Line, 1781-1782 [Ref: D-452].

TOWNSEND (TOWNSHEND), Joseph (1752-1780). Lived in Lower Potomac Hd. in 1776 [Ref: K-1:186]. Private, 7th Maryland Regiment, from May 9, 1777 until April 1, 1780 when reported dead [Ref: D-253].

TOWSTER, Alicia E. See "Jesse Willcoxen (Wilcoxon)," q.v.

TRACY, Alexander. Lived in the Upper Part of Potomac Hd. (two taxables) in 1777 [Ref: R-31:15]. Took the Oath of Allegiance before the Hon. William Deakins, Jr. before March 3, 1778 [Ref: T-3:68, L-1:45].

TRACY, Charles (1759-1834). Private, 3rd Co., Middle Bn., Militia, Sep., 1777 [Ref: M-196, T-5:38]. Private, 7th Class, 2nd Co., Middle Bn., Militia, July 15, 1780 [Ref: M-201]. Took the Oath of Allegiance before the Hon. William Deakins, Jr. before March 3, 1778 [Ref: T-3:68, L-1:45]. He applied for pension (S31437) in Clarke County, Kentucky, on July 11, 1832, stating that he was born in Nov., 1759, on Cabin John Creek in (now) Montgomery County, Maryland, and lived there at the time of enlistment. He served served as a substitute for Mordecai Oxford under Capt. Nathaniel Pigman and Capt. Thomas Beall in the Maryland Line, and participated in the Battles of Germantown and Paoli. He also served on the western frontier near Pittsburgh and was discharged at Fort Lawrence. In 1781 he served again under Capt. Nicholls and guarded at Fort Frederick, Maryland. He also stated he once lived with Col. John Beall at his quarters on the Potomac River, and the moved to Fayette County, Kentucky circa 1789. He married Sarah Noe, daughter of Peter Now, and their children were Catherine, Lobiada, Telatha, Asa, Obediah, Noland, Jerusha, Naomi, Rosana, and Winifred. In 1832 Charles lived in Clark County, being supported mainly by his son-in-law (name not stated) who had a large family and was an uncle of his wife (no name given). James Stevenson (or Stinson) also made affidavit in 1832 in Kentucky that he had known Charles Tracey since 1793 and they served in the war together. James Ragland also stated that about 30 years ago he often heard his father and Tracey talk about the Revolutionary War. Charles died on March 19, 1834 [Ref: P-3529, Y-9, Z-29, *Kentucky Ancestor*, Vol. 16. No. 1 (1980), p. 57, and Edward H. West's *Tracy Families in Maryland*, 1960].

TRACY, Philip (b. 1757). Son of William Tracy, of North West Hd., in 1776 [Ref: K-1:223]. Private, 8th Co., Lower Bn., Militia, Sep., 1777, and First Sergeant, 6th Co., Lower Bn., July 15, 1780 [Ref: M-200, M-206, T-5:51]. Took the Oath of Allegiance before the Hon. Charles Jones on Jan. 10, 1778 [Ref: T-3:71, L-1:46]. Philip Tracy married Mary Thrasher in Montgomery County on Dec. 12, 1782 [Ref: K-2:522]. See "William Thrasher," q.v.

TRACY (TRACEY), William. (1) Private, 5th Co., Middle Bn., Militia, from Sep., 1777, to at least July 15, 1780 [Ref: M-197, M-203, T-5:40]. (2) Private, 6th Class, 1st Co., Middle Bn., Militia, July 15, 1780 [Ref: M-201]. One William Tracey took the Oath of Allegiance before the Hon. Samuel W. Magruder in 1778 [Ref: T-3:73], and another took the Oath of Allegiance before the Hon. Gerrard Briscoe on March 2, 1778 [Ref: T-3:56, L-1:46]. "William Tracy" lived in the Upper Part of Potomac Hd. (one taxable) in 1777 [Ref: R-31:15], and "William Tracey" lived in Rock Creek Hd. (one taxable) in 1777 [Ref: R-31:16]. "William Tracy, aged 53" lived in North West Hd. (wife named Elenorr, aged 53) in 1776 [Ref: K-1:223].

TRAIL, Ann. See "William Trail," q.v.

TRAIL, Archibald. Son of James Trail, Sr. [Ref: V-137]. Private, 1st Co., Middle Bn., Militia, Aug. 30, 1777 [Ref: M-195]. Took the Oath of Allegiance before the Hon. Gerrard Briscoe on March 2, 1778 [Ref: T-3:57, L-1:46]. Private, 6th Class, 3rd Co., Middle Bn., Militia, July 15, 1780 [Ref: M-202].

TRAIL, Basil. Son of David Trail, Sr. [Ref: V-136]. Private, 1st Co., Middle Bn., Militia, Aug. 30, 1777 [Ref: M-195]. Private, 5th Co., Middle Bn., Militia, July 15, 1780 [Ref: M-203]. Took the Oath of Allegiance before the Hon. Gerrard Briscoe on March 2, 1778 [Ref: T-3:56, L-1:46]. Lived in Sugar Loaf Hd. (one taxable) in 1777 [Ref: R-31:11].

TRAIL, Cassandra. See "Benjamin Peak," q.v.

TRAIL, David Jr. Son of David Trail, Sr. [Ref: V-136]. Took the Oath of Allegiance before the Hon. Gerrard Briscoe on March 2, 1778 [Ref: T-3:56, L-1:46]. Private, 1st Co., Middle Bn., Militia, Aug. 30, 1777 [Ref: M-195]. Rendered aid by providing wheat for use of the military in 1781 [Ref: O-383].

TRAIL, David Sr. (1726-1781) "David Trail, Sr." took the Oath of Allegiance before the Hon. Gerrard Briscoe on March 2, 1778 [Ref: T-3:56, L-1:46]. Rendered aid by providing wheat for use of the military in 1780 [Ref: O-314]. Lived in Sugar Loaf Hd. (one taxable) in 1777 [Ref: R-31:11]. "David Trail, Sr., of Frederick County, planter" died testate in Montgomery County (wife named Margaret) in 1781 [Ref: V-136, DAR-I:685].

TRAIL, David, of James. "David Trail, of James" was a private, 1st Class, 5th Co., Middle Bn., Militia, July 15, 1780 [Ref: M-202]. "David Trail" lived in Seneca Hd. (three taxables) in 1777 [Ref: R-31:8].

TRAIL, James. Son of James Trail, Sr. [Ref: V-136]. Private, 2nd Co., Middle Bn., Militia, Sep. 4, 1777 [Ref: M-196, T-5:37]. Private, 7th Class, 3rd Co., Middle Bn., Militia, July 15, 1780 [Ref: M-202]. Took the Oath of Allegiance before the Hon. Edward Burgess on Feb. 28, 1778 [Ref: T-3:63, L-1:46]. Lived in Sugar Loaf Hd. (one taxable) in 1777 [Ref: R-31:11]. See "James Trail, Sr." and "David Trail, of James," q.v.

TRAIL, James Sr. (died 1798). Took the Oath of Allegiance before the Hon. Gerrard Briscoe on March 2, 1778 [Ref: T-3:56, L-1:46]. Lived in Seneca Hd. (three taxables) in 1777 [Ref: R-31:8]. Died testate in Montgomery County (wife named Rachel) in 1798 [Ref: V-136]. "James Traile, Sr." died testate in Montgomery County (wife named Mary Ann) in 1823 [Ref: V-137].

TRAIL, Margery. See "Walter Fryer," q.v.

TRAIL, Nathan. Private, Flying Camp, Frederick (now Montgomery) County, enlisted by Greenbury Gaither, July 29, 1776 [Ref: D-44].

TRAIL, Osborn. Son of James Trail [Ref: V-137]. "Orsban Trail" was Second Sergeant, 5th Co., Middle Bn., Militia, July 15, 1780 [Ref: M-202]. "Osborn Trail" married Francis Fryer in Montgomery County on Oct. 9, 1781 [Ref: K-2:521].

TRAIL, William. Private, 2nd Co., Middle Bn., Militia, Sep. 4, 1777 [Ref: M-196, T-5:37]. Took the Oath of Allegiance before the Hon. Gerrard Briscoe on March 2, 1778 [Ref: T-3:56, L-1:46]. Lived in Sugar Loaf Hd. (five taxables) in 1777 [Ref: R-31:11]. Ann Trail died testate in Montgomery County (wife of William Trail) in 1808 and her will indicated she had married a Belt prior to marrying William Trail [Ref: V-136]. See "Leonard Hays," q.v.

TRAMMEL, Elizabeth. See "Josiah (Josias) Barnes," q.v.

TRAY, Alexander. Private, 3rd Co., Middle Bn., Militia, Sep., 1777 [Ref: M-196, T-5:38].

TREVISS (TREVIS), John. Private, Capt. Thomas Beall's Co., Maryland Line, 1780 [Ref: D-351]. Private, 6th Co., Lower Bn., Militia, Aug., 1777 [Ref: M-200, T-5:49, which questions if the name could have been "Trevere?"]. "John Trevis" married Mary Lewis in Montgomery County on May 23, 1778 [Ref: K-2:514].

TRISSLER (TRISLER), Jacob (b. 1744). Private who enrolled into a company of militia for the service of the Flying Camp, Oct. 15, 1776 [Ref: B-353, which source misspelled the name as "Irissler"]. Private, 3rd Co., Lower Bn., Militia, Sep., 1777 [Ref: M-199, T-5:46]. Private, 8th Co., Lower Bn., Militia, July 15, 1780 [Ref: M-207]. "Jacob Trissler" took the Oath of Allegiance before the Hon. Richard Thompson in 1778 [Ref: T-3:76, L-1:46]. "Jacob Trissler or Trissoler" lived in George Town Hd. in 1776-1777 [Ref: K-1:195, R-31:3].

TROTT, Henry. Private, 2nd Co., Middle Bn., Militia, Sep. 4, 1777 [Ref: M-196, T-5:37]. Private, 3rd Class, 3rd Co., Middle Bn., Militia, July 15, 1780 [Ref: M-202]. Took the Oath of Allegiance before the Hon. Gerrard Briscoe on March 2, 1778 [Ref: T-3:57, L-1:46]. Henry Trott lived in Sugar Loaf Hd. (one taxable) in 1777 [Ref: R-31:11].

TROTT, James. Private, 2nd Co., Middle Bn., Militia, Sep. 4, 1777 [Ref: M-196, T-5:37]. James Trott lived in Sugar Loaf Hd. (two taxables) in 1777 [Ref: R-31:11].

TROTTER, Louden. Served as a Corporal, Capt. Thomas Beall's Co., Maryland Line, 1780 [Ref: D-350].

TROUT, Edmond (Edward). "Edward Trout" was a private, Capt. Edward Burgess' Co., Lower District of Frederick (now Montgomery) County, Militia, July, 1776 [Ref: D-42]. "Edmond Trout" was a private, 8th Co., Lower Bn., Militia, Sep., 1777 [Ref: M-200, T-5:51]. "Edmund Trout" took the Oath of Allegiance before the Hon. Charles Jones on Jan. 10, 1778 [Ref: T-3:71, L-1:46].

TROUT, Jacob. Rendered aid by providing hay for use of the military in 1780 [Ref: O-336].

TROUT, Mike. Took the Oath of Allegiance in 1778 [Ref: L-2:28].

TROY, Jeremiah. Substitute from Montgomery County who was discharged from the Maryland Line on Dec. 8, 1781 [Ref: I-17].

TRUNDLE, John (March 6, 1753 - March 25, 1810). Private, 8th Co., Lower Bn., Militia, Sep., 1777, and Second Lieutenant, 6th Co., Lower Bn., July 15, 1780 [Ref: M-200, M-206, T-5:51]. Took the Oath of Allegiance before the Hon. Charles Jones on Jan. 10, 1778 [Ref: T-3:71, L-1:46]. Rendered aid by providing wheat for use of the military in 1780 [Ref: O-308]. Lived in North West Hd. in 1776 and had two taxables in 1777 [Ref: K-1:226, R-31:17]. John and wife Ann are buried at Dickerson Station in the Barnesville District of Montgomery County [Ref: *Historic Graves of Maryland and the District of Columbia*, by Helen W. Ridgely (1908), p. 181].

TRUNDLE, Josiah. Private, 6th Co., Lower Bn., Militia, July 15, 1780 [Ref: M-206]. Private, 8th Co., Middle Bn., Militia, Sep., 1777 [Ref: M-198, T-5:43]. Took the Oath of Allegiance before the Hon. Charles Jones on Jan. 10, 1778 [Ref: T-3:71, L-1:46].

TRUNDLE (TRUNDELL), Thomas. Private, 7th Co., Lower Bn., Militia, Aug., 1777 [Ref: M-200, T-5:50]. Private, 4th Co., Lower Bn., Militia, July 15, 1780 [Ref: M-205]. Took the Oath of Allegiance before the Hon. Edward Burgess on Feb. 28, 1778 [Ref: T-3:62, L-1:46]. "Thomas Trunell" [sic] rendered aid by providing wheat for use of the military in 1781 [Ref: O-380, O-452]. "Thomas Trundell" lived in the Lower Part of Newfoundland Hd. (one taxable) and "Thomas Trundle" lived in North West Hd. (eight taxables) in 1777 [Ref: R-31:6, R-31:17]. One "Thomas Trundle, Sr." died testate in Montgomery County (wife named Hannah) in 1792 and mentioned his unmarried son Thomas, and another "Thomas Trundle" died testate in Montgomery County (wife named Rachell) in 1795 and mentioned a son Thomas, among other children [Ref: V-137, V-138]. "Thomas Trundle, aged 65" lived in North West Hd. (wife named Johanah, aged 43) in 1776 [Ref: K-1:223].

TUCKER, Alexander (b. 1755). Lived in Lower Potomac Hd. in 1776 [Ref: K-1:186]. Private, Capt. Edward Burgess' Co., Lower District of Frederick (now Montgomery) County, Militia, July, 1776 [Ref: D-42]. Private, 5th Co., Lower Bn., Militia, Aug., 1777, and Second Sergeant, 2nd Co., Lower Bn., July 15, 1780 [Ref: M-199, M-204, T-5:48].

TUCKER, Benjamin (b. 1754). Lived in Lower Potomac Hd. in 1776 [Ref: K-1:186]. Private, Capt. Edward Burgess' Co., Lower District of Frederick (now Montgomery) County, Militia, July, 1776 [Ref: D-42].

TUCKER, David. Private, 7th Co., Lower Bn., Militia, Aug., 1777 [Ref: M-200, T-5:50]. Took the Oath of Allegiance before the Hon. Edward Burgess on Feb. 28, 1778 [Ref: T-3:59, L-1:46]. David Tucker lived in the Lower Part of Newfoundland Hd. (one taxable) in 1777 [Ref: R-31:6].

TUCKER, Edward (b. 1720). Rendered aid by providing wheat for use of the military in 1780 [Ref: O-308]. Edward Tucker lived in Lower Potomac Hd. (two taxables) in 1776-1777 [Ref: K-1:186, R-31:5]. See "Hezekiah Speaks," q.v.

TUCKER, George. Private, 5th Co., Lower Bn., Militia, Aug., 1777 [Ref: M-199, T-5:48]. Two men named George Tucker lived in the Upper Part of Potomac Hd. (one taxable each) in 1777 [Ref: R-31:15].

TUCKER, Gregory Page. "Gregory Page Tucker" was a private, 1st Co., Middle Bn., Militia, Aug. 30, 1777 [Ref: M-195]. "Gregory Tucker" lived in Seneca Hd. (one taxable) in 1777 [Ref: R-31:8].

TUCKER, Henry (b. 1759). Lived in North West Hd. in 1776 [Ref: K-1:229]. Private, 8th Co., Lower Bn., Militia, Sep., 1777 [Ref: M-200, T-5:51].

TUCKER, Hezekiah (b. 1751). Private, 4th Co., Lower Bn., Militia, Aug., 1777 [Ref: M-199, T-5:47]. Lived in Lower Potomac Hd. (one taxable) in 1776-1777 [Ref: K-1:186, R-31:5].
TUCKER, Jacob. Private, 6th Co., Lower Bn., Militia, Aug., 1777 [Ref: T-5:49]. Private, 3rd Co., Lower Bn., Militia, July 15, 1780 [Ref: M-205]. Took the Oath of Allegiance before the Hon. Joseph Offutt on March 2, 1778 [Ref: T-3:70, L-1:46]. Lived in the Upper Part of Potomac Hd. (one taxable) in 1777 [Ref: R-31:15].
TUCKER, Jeremiah. See "John Tucker," q.v.
TUCKER, John. (1) Private, 3rd Co., Middle Bn., Militia, Sep., 1777 [Ref: M-196, T-5:38]. Took the Oath of Allegiance before the Hon. William Deakins, Jr. before March 3, 1778 [Ref: T-3:68, L-1:46]. (2) Private, Capt. Edward Burgess' Co., Lower District of Frederick (now Montgomery) County, Militia, July, 1776 [Ref: D-42]. Private, 1st Co., Lower Bn., Militia, Sep., 1777 [Ref: M-198, T-5:44]. Took the Oath of Allegiance before the Hon. Edward Burgess on Feb. 28, 1778 [Ref: T-3:59, L-1:46]. Two men named John Tucker were recruited to serve in the Continental Army in 1780 [Ref: D-341], and one was subsequently reported to have been a deserter [Ref: D-342]. One John Tucker lived in the Upper Part of Potomac Hd. (one taxable) in 1777 [Ref: R-31:15]. One John Tucker applied for pension in Bracken County, Kentucky, on Nov. 14, 1828, and in 1833 stated he was aged 83 (another source indicated April 15, 1833, aged 87, stating he was born in the United States and enlisted in Montgomery County in 1777). He had married Nancy Mitchell on Jan. 10, 1818, in Bracken County, Kentucky, in the town of Aug.a. Died on March 25, 1834, or March 24, 1835, and his widow applied for pension (W2279) on Dec. 29, 1851, in Mason County, Kentucky, at which time she lived with Jeremiah Tucker (no relationship stated, but probably a son). In 1853 she was aged 70 [Ref: P-3549, Y-6, Z-14]. Another John Tucker, of Maryland or Virginia, served in the war, moved to Spartanburg, South Carolina, and died in Franklin County, Georgia in Nov., 1807 [Ref: P-3549, but it did not indicate if he was from Montgomery County]. Also see "Hezekiah Speaks," q.v.
TUCKER, John, of Edward. Took the Oath of Allegiance before the Hon. William Deakins, Jr. before March 3, 1778 [Ref: T-3:68, L-1:46]. Private, 3rd Co., Middle Bn., Militia, Sep., 1777 [Ref: M-196, T-5:38]. See "Hezekiah Speaks," q.v.
TUCKER, Jonathan (b. 1738). Lived in Sugarland Hd. (three taxables) in 1776-1777 [Ref: K-1:203, R-31:13]. Private, 1st Co., Upper Bn., Militia, Aug. 30, 1777 [Ref: M-193]. Took the Oath of Allegiance before the Hon. William Deakins, Jr. before March 3, 1778 [Ref: T-3:68, L-1:46]. Rendered aid by providing corn for use of the military in 1780 [Ref: O-289].
TUCKER, Joseph (b. 1751). Private, 8th Co., Lower Bn., Militia, Sep., 1777 [Ref: M-200, T-5:51]. Private, 6th Co., Lower Bn., Militia, July 15,

1780 [Ref: M-206]. Private, 4th Co., Lower Bn., Aug., 1777 [Ref: M-199, T-5:47]. Took the Oath of Allegiance before the Hon. Edward Burgess on Feb. 28, 1778 [Ref: T-3:63, L-1:46]. Rendered aid by providing wheat for use of the military in 1780 and 1781 [Ref: O-316, O-395]. One Joseph Tucker lived in Lower Potomac Hd. (one taxable) in 1776-1777, and another lived in the Lower Part of Newfoundland Hd. (one taxable) in 1777 [Ref: K-1:186, R-31:5, R-31:6].

TUCKER, Mary. See "Benjamin Marshall," q.v.

TUCKER, Nicholas. Private, 3rd Co., Lower Bn., Militia, Sep., 1777 [Ref: M-199, T-5:46].

TUCKER, Sarah. See "Jacob Burton," q.v.

TUCKER, Stephen. Private, 1st Co., Middle Bn., Militia, Aug. 30, 1777 [Ref: M-195]. Stephen Tucker lived in Seneca Hd. (one taxable) in 1777 [Ref: R-31:8].

TUCKER, Thomas. Private, 7th Co., Lower Bn., Militia, Aug., 1777 [Ref: M-200 and T-5:50, which sources listed this name twice on the company's muster rolls]. Private, 4th Co., Lower Bn., Militia, July 15, 1780 [Ref: M-205]. Took the Oath of Allegiance before the Hon. Edward Burgess on Feb. 28, 1778 [Ref: T-3:62, L-1:46], and also served as a petit juror in Nov., 1777 [Ref: R-31:18]. One Thomas Tucker (b. 1717) lived in George Town Hd. (two taxables) in 1776-1777 [Ref: K-1:195, R-31:3], and another lived in Rock Creek Hd. (three taxables) in 1777 [Ref: R-31:16].

TUCKER, Walter (b. 1742). Private, 1st Co., Lower Bn., Militia, July 15, 1780 [Ref: M-204]. Private, 4th Co., Lower Bn., Militia, Aug., 1777 [Ref: M-199, T-5:47]. Rendered aid by providing wheat for use of the military in 1780 and 1781 [Ref: O-316, O-379]. Lived in Lower Potomac Hd. (one taxable) in 1776-1777 [Ref: K-1:186, R-31:5].

TUCKER, William. (1) Private, 4th Co., Lower Bn., Militia, Aug., 1777 [Ref: M-199, T-5:47]. Private, 1st Co., Lower Bn., Militia, July 15, 1780 [Ref: M-204]. (2) Private, 2nd Co., Lower Bn., Militia, Sep., 1777 [Ref: M-198, T-5:45]. Private, 2nd Co., Lower Bn., Militia, July 15, 1780 [Ref: M-204]. One William Tucker took the Oath of Allegiance (made his "X" mark) before the Hon. Samuel W. Magruder in 1778 [Ref: T-3:73]. One rendered aid by providing wheat for use of the military in 1780 [Ref: O-309]. "William Tucker, Sr., aged 63" (wife named Elizabeth, aged 49) and "William Tucker, Juner, aged 29" (wife named Margary, aged 25) all lived in North West Hd. in 1776 [Ref: K-1:229]. "William Tucker" lived in Rock Creek Hd. (one taxable) in 1777 [Ref: R-31:16], and "William Tucker, Sr." (two taxables) and "William Tucker, Jr." (one taxable) both lived in North West Hd. in 1777 [Ref: R-31:16].

TULLEY, John Davis (Davies). "John Davis Tulley, born in Canada, a seaman, says he is about 23 years of age, 5 feet 2 or 3 inches high, dark coloured hair tied behind, marked with the smallpox, recruited by James Wallace and Zachariah Maccubbin [in Montgomery County] on April 26,

1781, and sent to Annapolis under the care of Lt. William Murdock on April 29, 1781." [Ref: R-33:156, X-1146]. "Jno. Davies Tulley" was a private, 3rd Maryland Regiment, 1781 [Ref: D-394].

TUPLE (TUPPLE, TIEPLE), Isaac. "Isaac Tuple" was a private, 1st Co., Middle Bn., Militia, Aug. 30, 1777 [Ref: M-195]. "Isaac Tieple" took the Oath of Allegiance before the Hon. Gerrard Briscoe on March 2, 1778 [Ref: T-3:56, L-1:46]. "Isaac Tupple" lived in Seneca Hd. (one taxable) in 1777 [Ref: R-31:8].

TURLEY, Benjamin. Private, 1st Class, 5th Co., Middle Bn., Militia, July 15, 1780 [Ref: M-202].

TURNER, Charles. Took the Oath of Allegiance in 1778 [Ref: L-2:28].

TURNER, Elizabeth. See "Samuel Wade Magruder," q.v.

TURNER, John. Private, 7th Co., Middle Bn., Militia, Sep., 1777 [Ref: M-197, T-5:42].

TURNER, Mary. See "John Holmes," q.v.

TURNER, Samuel (died 1809). Lived in the Upper Part of Potomac Hd. (eight taxables) in 1777 [Ref: R-31:15]. Served as a petit juror in Aug., 1777 [Ref: R-31:17]. Took the Oath of Allegiance before the Hon. Richard Thompson in 1778 [Ref: T-3:75, L-1:46]. Rendered aid by providing wheat for use of the military in 1781 [Ref: O-390, O-413]. Samuel died testate in Montgomery County (wife not named) in 1809 [Ref: V-138].

TURNER, Sally. See "Samuel Wade Magruder," q.v.

TURNER, Thomas. On Feb. 19, 1819, the Treasurer of Maryland was directed to pay to Thomas Turner, of Montgomery County, a soldier of the revolution, half pay of a private for his services during that war [Ref: K-2:401, Q-144].

TURNER, William (b. 1754). Lived in Lower Potomac Hd. in 1776 [Ref: K-1:186]. Private, Capt. Price's Co., 3rd Maryland Line, 1781-1782 [Ref: D-453].

TUTTLE, Baptist. Private, 1st Co., Lower Bn., Militia, July 15, 1780 [Ref: M-204].

TWINCH, George. Served as a musician (drum & fife) in Capt. Thomas Beall's Co., Maryland Line, 1780, and also as a sergeant in Capt. Thomas Beall's Co., Maryland Line, 1780 [Ref: D-350].

UMBLE, George. Private, 3rd Co., Lower Bn., Militia, July 15, 1780 [Ref: M-205].

UMSTATTD (UMSTAD, UMSLADT), Abraham. "Abraham Umstattd or Umstad" rendered aid by providing wheat for use of the military in 1780 and 1781 [Ref: O-333, O-388]. "Abraham Umsladt" married Mary Howard in Montgomery County on Dec. 28, 1780 [Ref: K-2:521].

UPRIGHT, Jacob (b. 1722). Lived in George Town Hd. in 1776 [Ref: K-1:195]. Served as a petit juror in Aug., 1777 [Ref: R-31:17].

VALDENAR, Frances. See "William Layman," q.v.

VANLANDINGHAM, George. See "Clement Dowden," q.v.

VANSICKLE, Phebe. See "John Gebhart," q.v.
VEARS (VEIRS, VIERS), Daniel (1756-1787). Took the Oath of Allegiance before the Hon. Elisha Williams on March 2, 1778 [Ref: T-3:81, L-1:46, which source misspelled the name as "Daniel Veaes"]. "Daniel Veares" lived in Sugarland Hd. in 1776 and "Daniel Vears" lived in Sugar Loaf Hd. (five taxables) in 1777 [Ref: K-1:201, R-31:11]. "Daniel Bucy Viers" married Ann Williamson in Montgomery County on Jan. 9, 1781 [Ref: K-2:521]. "Daniel Veirs" died testate in Montgomery County (wife not named) in 1787 [Ref: V-139].
VEARS (VIERS), Elijah. "Elijah Vears" was a private, 3rd Co., Upper Bn., Militia, Aug. 30, 1777 [Ref: M-193]. "Elijah Viers" took the Oath of Allegiance before the Hon. Elisha Williams on March 2, 1778 [Ref: T-3:81, L-1:46].
VEARS (VIERS), John. "John Vears" was a private, 3rd Co., Upper Bn., Militia, Aug. 30, 1777 [Ref: M-193]. "John Viers" rendered aid by providing wheat for use of the military in 1780 [Ref: O-309].
VEARS (VEARES, VEIRS, VIERS), William (1735-1811). "William Vears" was a Captain, 16th Bn., 3rd Co., Militia, Sep. 12, 1777, and Lieutenant Colonel, Upper Bn., Militia, March 1, 1779 [Ref: C-373, E-310, M-131. Also, Source M-193 listed a "Capt. William Vears" on Aug. 30, 1777, and Source F-120 listed a "Capt. William Vearse" on March 25, 1780]. "William Viers" took the Oath of Allegiance before the Hon. Elisha Williams on March 2, 1778 [Ref: T-3:81, L-1:46], and rendered aid by providing wheat for use of the military in 1780 [Ref: O-308]. "Capt. William Veares, aged 41" lived in Sugarland Hd. in 1776 and he had a son William, aged 15, among others [Ref: K-1:202]. "William Veirs" died testate in Montgomery County (wife named Mary) in 1811 [Ref: V-139].
VEATCH, Abram. Private, German Regiment, 1780 [Ref: D-254].
VEATCH, Eleanor, Elias, and Isaac. See "James Veatch," q.v.
VEATCH (VEACH, VEITCH), Hezekiah. Private, 2nd Co., Upper Bn., Militia, Aug. 30, 1777 [Ref: M-193], Ensign, 16th Bn., Sep. 12, 1777, Second Lieutenant, Upper Bn., April 21, 1779, and First Lieutenant, March 25, 1780 [Ref: M-131, C-373, E-356, F-120]. Took the Oath of Allegiance before the Hon. Elisha Williams on March 2, 1778 [Ref: T-3:80, L-1:46]. Lived in Sugar Loaf Hd. (four taxables) in 1777 [Ref: R-31:11].
VEATCH, James (III). Son of James Veatch, Jr. and Eleanor Raymar. He was born June 27, 1762 on Pickleton's Rest, Frederick (now upper Montgomery) County, Maryland, and his family moved to Rowan County, North Carolina, when he was 5 years old. Just prior to the American Revolution they moved to the Camden area of South Carolina. James served in the war and participated in the Battle of Camden on Aug. 16, 1780. "James Veatch, Jr., was mortally wounded; his son, Isaac, also, died a prisoner; and, a third member of the family, Elias, wounded in the thigh and taken a prisoner. How James, III, fared, we are not

informed; at any rate, he escaped the British." [Ref: *We Veitches, Veatches, Veaches, Veeches*, by Laurence R. Guthrie (Redmond, Oregon: Midstate Printing, Inc., 1974, p. 599].

VEATCH (VEACH, VEITCH), John. Private, 8th Co., Upper Bn., Militia, Aug. 30, 1777 [Ref: M-195]. Took the Oath of Allegiance before the Hon. Elisha Williams on March 2, 1778 [Ref: T-3:82]. There was also a John Veach who enlisted in the 2nd Maryland Line on March 5, 1776 [Ref: D-8].

VEATCH (VEACH), Nathan. Took the Oath of Allegiance before the Hon. Elisha Williams on March 2, 1778 [Ref: T-3:80, L-1:46]. Nathan Veach lived in Sugar Loaf Hd. (two taxables) in 1777 [Ref: R-31:11].

VEATCH (VEACH, VEITCH), Ninian (died 1798). Private, 7th Co., Upper Bn., Militia, Aug. 30, 1777 [Ref: M-195]. Two men with this name took the Oath of Allegiance before the Hon. Elisha Williams on March 2, 1778 [Ref: T-3:81, L-1:46, T-3:82]. Lived in Sugarland Hd. (five taxables) in 1777 [Ref: R-31:13]. Died testate in Montgomery County (wife not named) in 1798 [Ref: V-138].

VEATCH, Ninian Jr. Private, 7th Co., Upper Bn., Militia, Aug. 30, 1777 [Ref: M-195]. See "Ninian Veatch (Veach)," q.v.

VEATCH (VEACH, VEITCH), Richard (b. 1742). Private, 8th Co., Upper Bn., Militia, Aug. 30, 1777 [Ref: M-195]. Took the Oath of Allegiance before the Hon. Aneas Campbell on March 2, 1778 [Ref: T-3:77, L-1:46]. Lived in Sugarland Hd. (wife named Sary) in 1776 [Ref: K-1:215].

VEATCH, Silas (1731-1806). Private, 8th Co., Upper Bn., Militia, Aug. 30, 1777 [Ref: M-195]. Silas Veatch, aged 45, lived in Sugarland Hd. in 1776 and had three taxables in 1777 [Ref: K-1:215, R-31:13]. Died testate in Montgomery County (wife named Elizabeth) in 1806, and mentioned that "some of his children lived in Kentucky and some on the northwest side of the Ohio." [Ref: V-138].

VEATCH, Solomon. Son of Ninian Veatch [Ref: V-138]. Private, 7th Co., Upper Bn., Militia, Aug. 30, 1777 [Ref: M-195].

VEATCH (VEACH, VEITCH), Thomas (1736-1819). Private, 1st Co., Upper Bn., Militia, Aug. 30, 1777 [Ref: M-193]. Took the Oath of Allegiance before the Hon. Elisha Williams on March 2, 1778 [Ref: T-3:81, L-1:46]. Thomas Veatch, aged 40, lived in Sugarland Hd. in 1776 (wife named Lurana) and had four taxables in 1777 [Ref: K-1:215, R-31:13]. "Thomas Veatch, Sr." died testate in Montgomery County (wife deceased) in 1819 and mentioned some of his children living in North Carolina [Ref: V-139].

VEATCH, William (b. 1756). Private, Flying Camp, enlisted July 18, 1776 [Ref: D-49]. Lived in Sugarland Hd. in 1776 [Ref: K-1:215].

VENABLE (VENNABLES, VENEBILS), John. "John Venable" lived in the Upper Part of Newfoundland Hd. (one taxable) in 1777 [Ref: R-31:7]. "John Vennables" was a private, 4th Co., Middle Bn., Militia, Sep., 1777, and Fourth Sergeant, July 15, 1780 [Ref: M-196, M-202, T-5:39].

"John Venebils" took the Oath of Allegiance before the Hon. Edward Burgess on Feb. 28, 1778 [Ref: T-3:63, L-1:46]. "John Venables" rendered aid by providing wheat for use of the military in 1781 [Ref: O-407].

VERMILLION, Ben. Private, 2nd Maryland Line, enlisted on Feb. 3, 1776 [Ref: D-8].

VERMILLION, Hanson. Private, 1st Co., Lower Bn., Militia, July 15, 1780 [Ref: M-204].

VERNALL, Henry. Private, 3rd Co., Lower Bn., Militia, July 15, 1780 [Ref: M-205].

VILEY, George. Took the Oath of Allegiance before the Hon. Joseph Offutt on March 2, 1778 [Ref: T-3:70, L-1:46]. Served as a Second Corporal, 3rd Co., Lower Bn., Militia, July 15, 1780 [Ref: M-205]. Lived in the Upper Part of Potomac Hd. (one taxable) in 1777 [Ref: R-31:15].

VINCENT, Benjamin. Private, 1st Class, 2nd Co., Middle Bn., Militia, July 15, 1780 [Ref: M-201]. Private, 3rd Co., Middle Bn., Militia, Sep., 1777 [Ref: M-196, T-5:38]. Took the Oath of Allegiance before the Hon. Edward Burgess on Feb. 28, 1778 [Ref: T-3:63, L-1:46]. One Benjamin Vincent was a private in the 5th Maryland Line from May 22, 1779 until Oct. 1, 1779, when he reportedly "deserted" [Ref: D-254]. "Benjamin Vincet" [sic] lived in the Upper Part of Potomac Hd. (one taxable) in 1777 [Ref: R-31:15].

VINCENT, Elizabeth. See "Archibald Mullikin," q.v.

VINCENT (VINSON), John. "John Vinson" was a private, 5th Co., Upper Bn., Militia, Aug. 30, 1777 [Ref: M-194]. "John Vincent" was a private in the 2nd Maryland Line from May 6, 1778 to May 6, 1781, when he was discharged [Ref: D-172]. "John Vinson" lived in Sugar Loaf Hd. (two taxables) in 1777 [Ref: R-31:11]. See "Stephen Warman," q.v.

VINSON (VINCENT), William (1752-1840). Private, 2nd Co., Middle Bn., Militia, Sep. 4, 1777. "William Vincent" was a private in the German Regiment in 1778 [Ref: D-254, D-266, M-196, T-5:37]. "William Vinson died at his farm *Seneca* in Montgomery County, Maryland, on May 30, 1840, aged 88 years, a Whig of '76." [Ref: R-10:56].

WADE, John. Private, 6th Co., Lower Bn., Militia, Aug., 1777 [Ref: T-5:49 and M-200, which latter source listed the name as "John W..."]. John Wade lived in the Upper Part of Potomac Hd. (two taxables) in 1777 [Ref: R-31:15].

WAGONER, Michael Jr. Took the Oath of Allegiance in 1778 [Ref: L-2:28].

WAGONER (WAGGONER), Rebecca. See "John Yost," q.v.

WALKER, George. Private, 6th Co., Middle Bn., Militia, July 15, 1780 [Ref: M-203].

WALKER, Jane. See "Samuel Martin," q.v.

WALKER, Richard. Private, 1st Co., Middle Bn., Militia, Aug. 30, 1777 [Ref: M-195]. Richard Walker lived in Seneca Hd. (one taxable) in 1777 [Ref: R-31:8].
WALKER, Robert. Private, 2nd Co., Upper Bn., Militia, Aug. 30, 1777 [Ref: M-193]. Took the Oath of Allegiance before the Hon. Elisha Williams on March 2, 1778 [Ref: T-3:80, L-1:46]. Robert Walker lived in Sugar Loaf Hd. (two taxables) in 1777 [Ref: R-31:11].
WALKER (WARKER), Thomas (b. 1737). Private, 8th Co., Upper Bn., Militia, Aug. 30, 1777 [Ref: M-195]. "Thomas Warker or Walker" lived in Sugarland Hd. (one taxable) in 1776-1777 [Ref: K-1:198, R-31:13].
WALKER (WORKER), William. (1) Private, 7th Co., Lower Bn., Militia, Aug., 1777 [Ref: M-200, T-5:50]. (2) Private, 2nd Co., Upper Bn., Militia, Aug. 30, 1777 [Ref: M-193]. One took the Oath of Allegiance before the Hon. Elisha Williams on March 2, 1778 [Ref: T-3:80, L-1:46]. One William Walker lived in the Lower Part of Newfoundland Hd. (one taxable) in 1777 [Ref: R-31:6]. A "William Worker" [Walker?], aged 21, lived in Sugarland Hd. in 1776 [Ref: K-1:218].
WALLACE (WALLISE), Alexander. "Alexander Wallace" was Third Corporal, 2nd Co., Lower Bn., Militia, July 15, 1780 [Ref: M-204]. "Alexander Wallise" took the Oath of Allegiance before the Hon. Edward Burgess on Feb. 28, 1778 [Ref: T-3:63, L-1:46].
WALLACE, Herbert (b. 1726). "Harburt Wallace" took the Oath of Allegiance before the Hon. Samuel W. Magruder in 1778 [Ref: T-3:74, L-1:46]. "Harbert Wallace" served as a grand juror in Aug., 1777 [Ref: R-31:17]. "Harbert or Herbert Wallace" lived in Lower Potomac Hd. (ten taxables) in 1776-1777 [Ref: K-1:186, R-31:5].
WALLACE, Herbert Alexander (b. 1756). Son of Herbert Wallace [Ref: K-1:186]. "Herbert Alexander Wallace" was a private who enrolled into a company of militia for the service of the Flying Camp on Oct. 15, 1776 [Ref: B-353]. "Harbert A. Wallace" was a private, 5th Co., Lower Bn., Militia, Aug., 1777 [Ref: M-199, T-5:48].
WALLACE, James. Served as a Lieutenant, 29th Bn., Militia, Nov. 20, 1776 (which may have been the date of resignation). [Ref: M-132, B-464]. Took the Oath of Allegiance before the Hon. Richard Thompson in 1778 [Ref: T-3:75, L-1:46]. Served as a petit juror in Aug., 1777 [Ref: R-31:17]. He recruited John Davis Tulley in April, 1781 [Ref: R-33:156, X-1146]. Lived in Lower Potomac Hd. (six taxables) in 1777 [Ref: R-31:5]. There were two James Wallace's in Lower Potomac Hd. in 1776: one was aged 24 and the other was aged 39 [Ref: K-1:186]. One died testate in Montgomery County (wife not named) in 1825 [Ref: V-140].
WALLACE, James Jr. Private, 5th Co., Lower Bn., Militia, Aug., 1777 [Ref: M-199, T-5:48]. Took the Oath of Allegiance before the Hon. Samuel W. Magruder in 1778 [Ref: T-3:73].
WALLACE, Nathaniel. Took the Oath of Allegiance before the Hon. Samuel W. Magruder in 1778 [Ref: T-3:73]. "Natt. Wallace" was a

private, 5th Co., Lower Bn., Militia, Aug., 1777 [Ref: M-199, T-5:48]. Nathaniel Wallace lived in Lower Potomac Hd. (six taxables) in 1776-1777 [Ref: K-1:186, R-31:5].

WALLACE (WALLIS), Thomas. Private, Capt. Edward Burgess' Co., Lower District of Frederick (now Montgomery) County, Militia, July, 1776 [Ref: D-42].

WALLACE (WALLIS), William. (1) Private, 7th Co., Upper Bn., Militia, Aug. 30, 1777 [Ref: M-195]. (2) Private, 5th Co., Lower Bn., Militia, Aug., 1777 [Ref: M-199 and T-5:48, which sources listed the name twice on this company's rolls]. Private, 2nd Co., Lower Bn., Militia, July 15, 1780 [Ref: M-204]. (3) Private, enrolled into a company of militia for the service of the Flying Camp, Oct. 15, 1776 [Ref: B-352]. Three men with this name took the Oath of Allegiance: two before the Hon. Samuel W. Magruder in 1778 [Ref: T-3:73], and one before the Hon. Elisha Williams on March 2, 1778 [Ref: T-3:81, L-1:46]. There were four William Wallace's in Lower Potomac Hd. in 1776: one was aged 40, another was aged 19, another was aged 18, and another was aged 12 [Ref: K-1:186, K-1:187]. Also, one lived there in 1777 and had six taxables [Ref: R-31:5]. "William Wallase, aged 52" lived in Sugarland Hd. in 1776 and "William Wallis" lived there (one taxable) in 1777 [Ref: R-31:13]. One William Wallace died testate in Montgomery County (wife not named) in 1806 and he also had a son William, among others [Ref: V-140].

WALLACE, Zephaniah (b. 1752). Served as a private when enrolled into a company of militia for the service of the Flying Camp on Oct. 15, 1776 [Ref: B-353], and private, 5th Co., Lower Bn., Militia, Aug., 1777 [Ref: M-199, T-5:48]. Served as a petit juror in Aug., 1777 [Ref: R-31:17]. Took the Oath of Allegiance before the Hon. Samuel W. Magruder in 1778 [Ref: T-3:73, L-1:46]. Lived in Lower Potomac Hd. in 1776 and in the Upper Part of Potomac Hd. (four taxables) in 1777 [Ref: K-1:186, R-31:15].

WALLER, Mariam. See "Paul Hoy," q.v.

WALLING, John. See "John Welling," q.v.

WALTER, Clement (b. 1744). Private, 4th Co., Upper Bn., Militia, Aug. 30, 1777 [Ref: M-194]. Took the Oath of Allegiance before the Hon. William Deakins, Jr. before March 3, 1778 [Ref: T-3:68, L-1:46]. Lived in Sugarland Hd. in 1776 and had one taxable in 1777 [Ref: K-1:207, R-31:13].

WALTER (WALTERS), David (b. 1741). Served as Ensign, 4th Co., 16th Bn., Militia, by Sep. 12, 1777 [Ref: C-373, M-194, and M-133, which latter source listed him as a captain and an ensign on the same day, Sep. 12, 1777]. "David Walter" took the Oath of Allegiance before the Hon. Elisha Williams on March 2, 1778 [Ref: T-3:82]. "David Walters" took the Oath of Allegiance before the Hon. Edward Burgess on Feb. 28, 1778 [Ref: T-3:62, L-1:46], and rendered aid by providing wheat for use of the military in 1781 [Ref: O-395]. "David Walter" lived in Sugarland Hd. (two taxables) in 1776-1777 [Ref: K-1:200,R-31:13]. "David Walter" married Elizabeth Allison in Montgomery County on July 1, 1781 [Ref: K-2:521].

WALTER, George. Served as a First Lieutenant, 16th Bn., 4th Co., Militia, Sep. 12, 1777, and Captain, Upper Bn., Militia, March 25, 1780 [Ref: M-133, M-194, C-373, F-120]. Took the Oath of Allegiance before the Hon. Aneas Campbell on March 2, 1778 [Ref: T-3:77, L-1:46]. Lived in Sugarland Hd. (four taxables) in 1777 [Ref: R-31:13]. "George Walter, planter" died testate in Montgomery County (wife not named) in 1785 [Ref: V-140]. There was also a "George Walter, aged 88" in Sugarland Hd. in 1776 [Ref: K-1:208].

WALTER, John. Private, 8th Co., Lower Bn., Militia, July 15, 1780 [Ref: M-207].

WALTER, John or Jonathan (b. 1733). "John Walter" was a Captain, 16th Bn., Militia, by Sep. 12, 1777. "Jonathan Walter" was a Captain, Upper Bn., Militia, on March 25, 1780 [Ref: M-133, M-194, C-373, F-120]. "John Walter, aged 43" lived in Sugarland Hd. in 1776 and had three taxables in 1777 [Ref: K-1:209, R-31:13].

WALTER (WALTERS), Levy (b. 1749). "Levy Walter" was a private, 4th Co., Upper Bn., Militia, Aug. 30, 1777 [Ref: M-194]. Rendered aid by providing corn for use of the military in 1780 [Ref: O-288]. "Levy Walters" took the Oath of Allegiance before the Hon. Aneas Campbell on March 2, 1778 [Ref: T-3:77, L-1:46]. "Levy Walter" lived in Sugarland Hd. (one taxable) in 1776-1777 [Ref: K-1:204, R-31:13]. He married Priscilla Fletcher in Montgomery County on Sep. 14, 1779 [Ref: K-2:521].

WALTER, Matthew. Private, 7th Maryland Line, 1777-1778 [Ref: D-258].

WALTER, Sarah. See "Mark Elliott," q.v.

WALTERS (WOLTERS), Ephraim. Private, 7th Maryland Line, from May 4, 1778 until Dec., 1779, when he reportedly deserted [Ref: D-258].

WALTERS, Josephus. Took the Oath of Allegiance before the Hon. Edward Burgess on Feb. 28, 1778 [Ref: T-3:61, L-1:46].

WALTERS, Sarah. Rendered aid by providing wheat for use of the military in 1781 [Ref: O-400].

WALTERS, Thomas. Took the Oath of Allegiance before the Hon. Edward Burgess on Feb. 28, 1778 [Ref: T-3:64, L-1:46].

WALTERS, Weavour. Took the Oath of Allegiance before the Hon. Edward Burgess on Feb. 28, 1778 [Ref: T-3:60, L-1:46].

WALTERS, William. Took the Oath of Allegiance before the Hon. Edward Burgess on Feb. 28, 1778 [Ref: T-3:60, L-1:46].

WALTON, John. Private who was recruited to serve in the Continental Army in 1780 [Ref: D-341].

WARBLE, Philip. Took the Oath of Allegiance in 1778 [Ref: L-2:28].

WARD, Benjamin (b. 1754). Private, 1st Co., Upper Bn., Militia, Aug. 30, 1777 [Ref: M-193]. Private, 2nd Class, 2nd Co., Middle Bn., Militia, July 15, 1780 [Ref: M-201]. Lived in Sugarland Hd. in 1776 and served as a constable in 1780 [Ref: K-1:203, W-1].

WARD, Benjamin, of Joseph. Took the Oath of Allegiance before the Hon. William Deakins, Jr. before March 3, 1778 [Ref: T-3:68, L-1:46].

WARD, Edward (died 1820). Private, 5th Co., Upper Bn., Militia, Aug. 30, 1777 [Ref: M-194]. Lived in Sugar Loaf Hd. (two taxables) in 1777 [Ref: R-31:11]. Died testate in Montgomery County (wife not named) in 1820 [Ref: V-141].

WARD, John. Private, 8th Co., Middle Bn., Militia, Sep., 1777 [Ref: M-198, T-5:43]. Took the Oath of Allegiance before the Hon. Samuel W. Magruder in 1778 [Ref: T-3:73]. Lived in Rock Creek Hd. (one taxable) in 1777 [Ref: R-31:16]. Also see "Benjamin Greentree," q.v.

WARD, Joseph (died 1781). Lived in Sugarland Hd. (nine taxables) in 1777 [Ref: R-31:13]. Took the Oath of Allegiance (affirmed) before the Hon. Edward Burgess on March 10, 1778 [Ref: T-3:64, L-1:46]. Died testate in Montgomery County (wife named Anne Mary) in 1781 [Ref: V-141].

WARD, Lloyd. Private, 6th Co., Middle Bn., Militia, Aug., 1777, and private, 6th Co., Middle Bn., Militia, July 15, 1780 [Ref: M-197, M-203, T-5:41]. "Lloyd Ward" took the Oath of Allegiance on Sep. 1, 1780, under the Act of May 12, 1780, having neglected to do so previously "due to ignorance of the duty owed the country." [Ref: R-27:122]. "Lord Ward" lived in Linganore Hd. (one taxable) in 1777 [Ref: R-31:9].

WARFIELD, Elizabeth. See "Joseph Warfield," q.v.

WARFIELD, John Worthington (died 1811). Rendered aid by providing wheat for use of the military in 1780 and 1781 [Ref: O-325, O-380]. Died testate in Montgomery County (wife named Mary) in 1811 [Ref: V-142].

WARFIELD, Joseph (1758-1837). Lieutenant in the Maryland Line who made his pension application in Montgomery County on Jan. 6, 1833. He stated he was born on Feb. 19, 1758, in Anne Arundel County, Maryland, where he also enlisted in the war; however, his service is not listed in *Archives of Maryland, Volume 18*. Joseph married on Aug. 6, 1778 to Elizabeth Dorsey (b. Dec. 6, 1761), daughter of Nicholas Dorsey (who died Sep. 27, 1792) and wife Elizabeth (who died Nov. 17, 1803). The children of Joseph and Elizabeth Warfield were Eliza (b. June 4, 1782), Juliet (b. May 18, 1785), Harriet (b. July 2, 1787), Nicholas D. (b. May 25, 1789), Elizabeth D. (b. Sep. 10, 1791), Charlotte (b. Oct. 25, 1793), and Sarah (b. Sep. 25, 1798). [Ref: J-49, P-3676, which latter source contains much more detailed family information]. Joseph died Oct. 17, 1837, and Elizabeth applied for pension (W8978) on March 8, 1839. She was listed as a pensioner in 1840, aged 86, living in the house of N. D. Warfield in Montgomery County's 5th Division [Ref: R-28:445].

WARFIELD, Levin. Took the Oath of Allegiance in 1778 [Ref: L-2:28].

WARGER, Richard. Took the Oath of Allegiance (made his "X" mark) before the Hon. Joseph Wilson on Feb. 28, 1778 [Ref: T-3:67, L-1:46].

WARING, Eleanor. See "Samuel Brewer Magruder," q.v.

WARMAN (WORMAN), John. Rendered aid by providing wheat for use of the military in 1781 [Ref: O-390].

WARMAN, Stephen (died 1799). Private, 5th Co., Upper Bn., Militia, Aug. 30, 1777 [Ref: M-194]. Took the Oath of Allegiance before the Hon. Elisha Williams on March 2, 1778 [Ref: T-3:80, L-1:46]. Lived in Sugar Loaf Hd. (two taxables) in 1777 [Ref: R-31:11]. Died testate in Montgomery County (wife not named) in 1799, mentioned his deceased son Thomas, and left all his land in Maryland, Kentucky and Virginia to his son-in-law John Vinson [Ref: V-142].

WARMAN, Stephen Jr. Took the Oath of Allegiance before the Hon. Elisha Williams on March 2, 1778 [Ref: T-3:81, L-1:46].

WARNER, Peter Jr. Took the Oath of Allegiance in 1778 [Ref: L-2:28].

WARNER, Peter Sr. Took the Oath of Allegiance in 1778 [Ref: L-2:28].

WARNER, Samuel. Served as a Sergeant, 7th Maryland Line, from March 25, 1777 until Feb., 1778 [Ref: D-257]. "Samuel Warner, aged 57" lived in Sugarland Hd. in 1776 and had two taxables in 1777 [Ref: K-1:214, R-31:13]. "Samuel Warner, Sr." took the Oath of Allegiance before the Hon. Aneas Campbell on March 2, 1778 [Ref: T-3:77, L-1:46].

WARNER, Thomas. Private, 7th Co., Upper Bn., Militia, Aug. 30, 1777 [Ref: M-195]. Took the Oath of Allegiance before the Hon. Aneas Campbell on March 2, 1778 [Ref: T-3:77, L-1:46]. Lived in Sugarland Hd. (one taxable) in 1777 [Ref: R-31:13].

WARREN (WARRING), George (1722-1780). Took the Oath of Allegiance before the Hon. Elisha Williams on March 2, 1778 [Ref: L-1:46, T-3:81]. "George Warren" lived in Sugarland Hd. (three taxables) in 1777 [Ref: R-31:13]. Died testate in Montgomery County (wife named Mary) in 1780 and he had sons John, aged 24, and George, age 21, among other children [Ref: V-142].

WARREN (WARRING), George Jr. (b. 1755). Took the Oath of Allegiance before the Hon, Elisha Williams on March 2, 1778 [Ref: Y-3:80, L-1:46]. "George Warring" was a private, 7th Co., Upper Bn., Militia, Aug. 30, 1777 [Ref: M-194].

WARREN (WARRING), James. Private, 6th Co., Middle Bn., Militia, Aug., 1777 [Ref: M-197, T-5:41]. Private, 6th Co., Middle Bn., Militia, July 15, 1780 [Ref: M-203].

WARREN (WARRING), John (b. 1752). "John Warring" was a private, 1st Co., Upper Bn., Militia, Aug. 30, 1777 [Ref: M-193]. "John Warren" took the Oath of Allegiance before the Hon. Elisha Williams on March 2, 1778 [Ref: T-3:81, L-1:46]. "Johan Warren, aged 24" lived in Sugarland Hd. in 1776 [Ref: K-1:218].

WARREN (WARRING), Thomas (b. 1750). "Thomas Warring" was a private, 1st Co., Upper Bn., Militia, Aug. 30, 1777 [Ref: M-193]. "Thomas

Warren, Sr." took the Oath of Allegiance before the Hon. Elisha Williams on March 2, 1778 [Ref: T-3:81, L-1:46]. "Thomas Warren" lived in Sugarland Hd. in 1776-1777 [Ref: K-1:218, R-31:13].

WARTHIN (WORTHIN), Ignatius. "Ignatius Warthin" was a private, 6th Co., Upper Bn., Militia, Aug. 30, 1777 [Ref: M-194]. "Ignatious Worthin" lived in Sugar Loaf Hd. (two taxables) in 1777 [Ref: R-31:11].

WARUM, Isaac. Private, 1st or 32nd Bn., Militia (no date was given; possibly June, 1777). [Ref: T-5:1].

WASKEY, Aug.us. Took the Oath of Allegiance in 1778 [Ref: L-2:28].

WATERS, Ann. See "Nathaniel Pigman," q.v.

WATERS, Azel (Ozell). Son of Joseph Waters, Sr. [Ref: V-143]. Took the Oath of Allegiance on Sep. 1, 1780, under the Act of May 12, 1780, having neglected to do so previously "due to ignorance of the duty owed the country." [Ref: R-27:122].

WATERS, Basil. Son of William Waters, Sr. [Ref: V-145]. Served as Second Corporal, 4th Co., Middle Bn., Militia, July 15, 1780 [Ref: M-202].

WATERS, Benjamin (died 1825). Took the Oath of Allegiance on Sep. 1, 1780, under the Act of May 12, 1780, having neglected to do so previously "due to ignorance of the duty owed the country." [Ref: R-27:122]. Died testate in Montgomery County (wife named Hannah) in 1825 [Ref: V-142].

WATERS, Isaac. Private, 2nd Co., Middle Bn., Militia, Sep. 4, 1777 [Ref: M-195], and First Sergeant, 3rd Co., Middle Bn., Militia, July 15, 1780 [Ref: M-202]. Took the Oath of Allegiance before the Hon. Gerrard Briscoe on March 2, 1778 [Ref: T-3:56, L-1:46]. Rendered aid by providing wheat for use of the military in 1780 [Ref: O-309]. Lived in Sugar Loaf Hd. (one taxable) in 1777 [Ref: R-31:11].

WATERS, James (1746-1815). Private, 4th Co., Upper Bn., Militia, Aug. 30, 1777 [Ref: M-194]. Took the Oath of Allegiance before the Hon. William Deakins, Jr. before March 3, 1778 [Ref: T-3:68, L-1:46]. "James Warters" lived in Sugarland Hd. in 1776 [Ref: K-1:221]. "James Waters" died testate in Montgomery County in 1815 (unmarried) and left his land to various relatives with the surnames of Allison and Hickman [Ref: V-143].

WATERS, John. Lived in George Town Hd. in 1777 [Ref: R-31:4]. One John Waters was a private in the 6th Maryland Line from April 3, 1778 to Aug. 23, 1778, when reported dead [Ref: D-256].

WATERS, Joseph. Private, 5th Co., Upper Bn., Militia, Aug. 30, 1777 [Ref: M-194]. Took the Oath of Allegiance on Sep. 1, 1780, under the Act of May 12, 1780, having neglected to do so previously "due to ignorance of the duty owed the country." [Ref: R-27:122]. Rendered aid by providing wheat for use of the military in 1781 [Ref: O-443, which listed the name as "Joseph Warters"]. On July 5, 1781, the Council of Maryland wrote to the Lieutenant of Montgomery County, as follows:

"We enclose you the petition of Joseph Watters which has been handed to this Board; as we are totally unacquainted with the signers to the petition, think it proper to refer the matter to you. If it should appear to you that he is not fit for service, you will then discharge him." [Ref: G-495]. Joseph Waters lived in Linganore Hd. (four taxables) in 1777 [Ref: R-31:9]. "Joseph Waters, Sr." died testate in Montgomery County (wife not named) in 1820 [Ref: V-143].

WATERS, Josephus. Private, 1st Co., Lower Bn., Militia, Sep., 1777 [Ref: M-198, T-5:44]. Private, 7th Co., Lower Bn., Militia, July 15, 1780 [Ref: M-207]. Lived in the Lower Part of Newfoundland Hd. (two taxables) in 1777 [Ref: R-31:6]. Joseph Waters (1742-c1800) and Josephus Burton Waters (1753-1837) were both from Maryland [Ref: DAR-I:721].

WATERS, Margery. See "Daniel Lewis," q.v.

WATERS, Nacey. Son of Richard Waters, Sr. [Ref: V-144]. Private, 5th Co., Middle Bn., Militia, July 15, 1780 [Ref: M-204]. Took the Oath of Allegiance before the Hon. Gerrard Briscoe on March 2, 1778 [Ref: T-3:56, L-1:46]. "Nacy Water" was a private, 7th Co., Middle Bn., Militia, Sep., 1777 [Ref: M-197, T-5:42].

WATERS, Nathan. Private, Capt. Edward Burgess' Co., Lower District of Frederick (now Montgomery) County, Militia, July, 1776 [Ref: D-42].

WATERS, Richard. Private, 7th Co., Middle Bn., Militia, July 15, 1780 [Ref: M-203]. Took the Oath of Allegiance (made his mark) before the Hon. Edward Burgess on Feb. 28, 1778 [Ref: T-3:62, L-1:46]. Rendered aid by providing wheat for use of the military in 1781 [Ref: O-435]. "Richard Waters" died testate in Montgomery County (wife named Margaret) in 1810. "Richard Waters, Sr." died testate in Montgomery County (wife not named) in 1797 and he had a son Richard, among other children [Ref: V-144]. One Richard Waters lived in the Lower Part of Newfoundland Hd. (six taxables) and another lived in Seneca Hd. (four taxables) in 1777 [Ref: R-31:6, R-31:8]. Both are listed as patriots in Source DAR-I:721.

WATERS, Thomas. (1) Private, 2nd Co., Middle Bn., Militia, Sep. 4, 1777 [Ref: M-196, T-5:37]. (2) Private, 1st Co., Lower Bn., Militia, Sep., 1777 [Ref: M-198, T-5:44]. Private, 7th Co., Lower Bn., Militia, July 15, 1780 [Ref: M-207]. One Thomas Waters lived in the Lower Part of Newfoundland Hd. (four taxables) in 1777 [Ref: R-31:6].

WATERS, Weaver (Wevour). Private, Capt. Edward Burgess' Co., Lower District of Frederick (now Montgomery) County, Militia, July, 1776 [Ref: D-42]. Private, 7th Co., Lower Bn., Militia, July 15, 1780 [Ref: M-207]. Private, 1st Co., Lower Bn., Militia, Sep., 1777 [Ref: M-198, T-5:44]. "Weaver Waters" married Margaret Miers in Montgomery County on April 3, 1782 [Ref: K-2:515].

WATERS, William. Private, 2nd Co., Middle Bn., Militia, Sep. 4, 1777 [Ref: M-196, T-5:37]. Took the Oath of Allegiance before the Hon. Gerrard Briscoe on March 2, 1778 [Ref: T-3:56, L-1:46]. "William

Waters" lived in the Upper Part of Newfoundland Hd. (eight taxables) in 1777 and "William Waters, Jr." lived in Sugar Loaf Hd. (four taxables) in 1777 [Ref: R-31:7, R-31:11]. "William Waters" died testate in Montgomery County (unmarried) in 1825, and "William Waters, Sr., planter" died testate in Montgomery County (wife named Mary Harris) in 1788 and he had a son William, among other children [Ref: V-145, DAR-I:721].

WATERS, Zachariah (died 1825). Eldest son of "William Waters, Sr.," q.v. Lived in Sugar Loaf Hd. (six taxables) in 1777 [Ref: R-31:11]. Took the Oath of Allegiance before the Hon. Gerrard Briscoe on March 2, 1778 [Ref: T-3:56, L-1:46]. "Zachariah Warters" rendered aid by providing wheat for use of the military in 1781 [Ref: O-384]. Died testate in Montgomery County (wife named Anna) in 1825 [Ref: V-145].

WATKINS, Ann and Benjamin. See "Leonard Watkins," q.v.

WATKINS, John. Served as Ensign, 16th Bn., Militia, Sep. 12, 1777 [Ref: M-134, C-373]. Served as a petit juror in 1777 [Ref: R-31:17, R-31:18]. Lived in the Upper Part of Potomac Hd. (four taxables) in 1777 [Ref: R-31:15].

WATKINS, John Jr. Took the Oath of Allegiance before the Hon. William Deakins, Jr. before March 3, 1778 [Ref: T-3:68, L-1:46].

WATKINS, Leonard (c1758-1828). Private, 4th Co., Upper Bn., Militia, Aug. 30, 1777 [Ref: M-194]. Took the Oath of Allegiance before the Hon. Aneas Campbell on March 2, 1778 [Ref: T-3:77, L-1:46]. On Feb. 28, 1839, the Treasurer of Maryland was directed to pay to Mary Watkins, of Montgomery County, widow of Leonard, a sergeant of the Revolutionary War, during life, quarterly, half pay of a sergeant, commencing Jan. 1, 1839 [Ref: K-2:405, Q-146]. Leonard applied for pension on April 22, 1818 in Anne Arundel County, stating he had enlisted on Jan. 20, 1776, and served two years in the 1st Maryland Line. One May 23, 1778, he enlisted for three years and served as a Sergeant in the 6th Maryland Line. He participated in the battles of Long Island (where he was wounded), York Island, White Plains, and Monmouth. He was discharged on May 11, 1780, in Frederick, Maryland. He married Mary Higdon in Dec., 1781, and moved to Montgomery County in 1820, aged 66, with wife Mary, aged 60, and an orphaned female named Sarah Smith, aged 14 or 15. Mary Watkins applied for a pension (W8976) on March 16, 1839, aged 78, stating that Leonard Watkins had died on Oct. 10, 1828. She also referred to her children born before 1794: Benjamin Watkins, Ann Elizabeth Watkins, and William Watkins (b. Nov. 2, 1792, and of Montgomery County in 1839), and Thomas Watkins (living in 1839). [Ref: U-36:121, U-36:122, P-3699]. Mary was a pensioner in 1840, aged 81, living in the household of Thomas Watkins in Montgomery County, 5th Division [Ref: R-28:445]. Leonard Watkins married Mary Higden in Montgomery County on Dec. 19, 1780 [Ref: K-2:521].

WATKINS, Margaret. See "Basil Gaither," q.v.

WATKINS, Mary, Thomas, and William. See "Leonard Watkins," q.v.

WATSON, Elkahan (b. 1756). "Elkahan Watson" was a private, 4th Co., Upper Bn., Militia, Aug. 30, 1777 [Ref: M-194]. "Elkanah Watson" lived in Sugarland Hd. in 1776 and was apparently a son of "Samuel Watson," q.v. [Ref: K-1:198]. "Aleanah Watson" married Mary Mooreland in Montgomery County on June 11, 1779 [Ref: K-2:521].

WATSON, Henry. Took the Oath of Allegiance before the Hon. Joseph Wilson on Feb. 28, 1778 [Ref: T-3:66, L-1:46]. Henry Watson lived in Rock Creek Hd. (five taxables) in 1777 [Ref: R-31:16].

WATSON, John (b. 1734). Private, 8th Co., Lower Bn., Militia, Sep., 1777 [Ref: M-200, T-5:51]. Took the Oath of Allegiance before the Hon. Samuel W. Magruder in 1778 [Ref: T-3:73, L-1:46]. Lived in North West Hd. (wife named Sarah) in 1776 and had six taxables in 1777 [Ref: K-1:231, R-31:17].

WATSON, Lucy. See "Barton Loveless," q.v.

WATSON, Samuel. Served as an Ensign, 16th Bn., Militia, June 20, 1777, Second Lieutenant by Sep. 12, 1777, and First Lieutenant, Upper Bn., March 25, 1780 [Ref: M-134, M-194, C-373, F-120]. Served as a petit juror in Aug., 1777 [Ref: R-31:17]. Two men with this name took the Oath of Allegiance before the Hon. Elisha Williams on March 2, 1778 [Ref: T-3:81, L-1:46]. One Samuel Watson, aged 48, lived in Sugarland Hd. (two taxables) in 1776-1777 [Ref: K-1:198, R-31:13].

WATTS, John. Private, 2nd Co., Middle Bn., Militia, Sep. 4, 1777 [Ref: M-196, T-5:37]. Took the Oath of Allegiance before the Hon. Joseph Wilson on Feb. 28, 1778 [Ref: T-3:64, L-1:46]. Private, 2nd Class, 3rd Co., Middle Bn., Militia, July 15, 1780 [Ref: M-202]. Lived in Sugar Loaf Hd. (two taxables) in 1777 [Ref: R-31:11].

WAYMAN (WEYMAN), Ann. See "William Holland," q.v.

WAYMAN (WEYMAN), Dorcus. See "John Harris," q.v.

WAYMAN, Edward (Edmond). "Edward Wayman" was a private, 6th Co., Upper Bn., Militia, Aug. 30, 1777 [Ref: M-194]. "Edmond Wayman" rendered aid by providing wheat for use of the military in 1781 [Ref: O-400].

WAYMAN, Leonard. Private, 2nd Co., Upper Bn., Militia, Aug. 30, 1777 [Ref: M-193]. Leonard Wayman lived in Sugar Loaf Hd. (five taxables) in 1777 [Ref: R-31:11].

WAYMAN, Thomas. Private, 2nd Co., Upper Bn., Militia, Aug. 30, 1777 [Ref: M-193]. Took the Oath of Allegiance before the Hon. Elisha Williams on March 2, 1778 [Ref: T-3:80, L-1:46]. Thomas Wayman lived in Sugar Loaf Hd. (one taxable) in 1777 [Ref: R-31:11].

WAYNER, Bernard N. Took the Oath of Allegiance in 1778 [Ref: L-2:28].

WEAVER, Conrad. Took the Oath of Allegiance in 1778 [Ref: L-2:28].

WEAVER, James. Took the Oath of Allegiance in 1778 [Ref: L-2:28].

WEBBER, Robert. Private, 4th Co., Upper Bn., Militia, Aug. 30, 1777 [Ref: M-194]. Took the Oath of Allegiance before the Hon. Edward Burgess on Feb. 28, 1778 [Ref: T-3:63, L-1:46].

WEDGE, Anthony. Private who was recruited to serve in the Continental Army in 1780 [Ref: D-342].

WEDGE, Samuel. Private, 7th Maryland Line, from Feb. 2, 1780 until Aug. 16, 1780, when reported missing at the Battle of Camden. He apparently returned and served to 1783 [Ref: D-258, D-560].

WEDGE, William. Private, 7th Maryland Line, from March 14, 1778 until March 15, 1781, when discharged [Ref: D-258, D-560].

WEEDEN, Jonathan. Served as a Sergeant, Capt. Thomas Beall's Co., Maryland Line, 1780 [Ref: D-350].

WEEDON, Richard. Private, 6th Co., Middle Bn., Militia, July 15, 1780 [Ref: M-203].

WELLER, Henry. Took the Oath of Allegiance in 1778 [Ref: L-2:28].

WELLER, John. Took the Oath of Allegiance in 1778 [Ref: L-2:28].

WELLER, John Jr. Took the Oath of Allegiance in 1778 [Ref: L-2:28].

WELLER, Philip. Took the Oath of Allegiance in 1778 [Ref: L-2:28].

WELLING (WILLING, WALLING), John. "John Willing" was a private, 2nd Co., Middle Bn., Militia, Sep. 4, 1777 [Ref: M-196, T-5:37]. "John Welling" rendered aid by providing wheat for use of the military in 1781 [Ref: O-386]. "John Welling" lived in the Upper Part of Newfoundland Hd. (one taxable) in 1777 [Ref: R-31:7]. "John Walling" took the Oath of Allegiance before the Hon. Gerrard Briscoe on March 2, 1778 [Ref: T-3:57, L-1:46].

WELLMAN, Bennet. Private, 3rd Co., Upper Bn., Militia, Aug. 30, 1777 [Ref: M-193]. "Bennett Wellman" was a private, 3rd Co., Middle Bn., Militia, Sep., 1777 [Ref: T-5:38 and M-196, which latter source questions if the name could have been "Weltman"]. "Bennett Wellman" took the Oath of Allegiance before the Hon. Edward Burgess on Feb. 28, 1778 [Ref: T-3:64, L-1:46].

WELLMAN (WILLMAN), Jeremiah. Private, 4th Co., Middle Bn., Militia, Sep., 1777 [Ref: T-5:39 and M-196, which latter source listed the name as "Jerre Willman"]. Private, 5th Class, 4th Co., Middle Bn., Militia, July 15, 1780 [Ref: M-202]. Took the Oath of Allegiance (made his "X" mark) before the Hon. Edward Burgess on Feb. 28, 1778 [Ref: T-3:60, L-1:46]. "Jeremiah Willman" lived in the Upper Part of Newfoundland Hd. (one taxable) in 1777 [Ref: R-31:7].

WELLMAN (WELLMON), John. "John Wellman" was a private, 3rd Co., Upper Bn., Militia, Aug. 30, 1777 [Ref: M-193]. "John Wellmon" lived in Sugar Loaf Hd. (one taxable) in 1777 [Ref: R-31:11].

WELLMORE, Robert. Took the Oath of Allegiance before the Hon. Edward Burgess on Feb. 28, 1778 [Ref: T-3:59, L-1:46].

WERTENBAKER, Adam. Took the Oath of Allegiance in 1778 [Ref: L-2:28].

WERTZ, Jasper. Rendered aid by providing wheat for use of the military in 1780 [Ref: O-319].

WESLEY, Humphry. Took the Oath of Allegiance (made his "X" mark) before the Hon. Edward Burgess on Feb. 28, 1778 [Ref: T-3:60, L-1:46].

WEST, Alexander. Private who was recruited to serve in the Continental Army in 1780 [Ref: D-341].

WEST, Basil. Private, 5th Co., Middle Bn., Militia, Sep., 1777 [Ref: M-196, M-197, T-5:40], and First Sergeant, 1st Co., Middle Bn., Militia, July 15, 1780 [Ref: M-201]. Took the Oath of Allegiance before the Hon. Joseph Wilson on Feb. 28, 1778 [Ref: T-3:64, L-1:46]. Rendered aid by providing wheat for use of the military in 1780 and 1781 [Ref: O-301, O-403]. Lived in Seneca Hd. (two taxables) in 1777 [Ref: R-31:8].

WEST, Benjamin. Two men with this name were privates, 5th Co., Middle Bn., Militia, Sep., 1777 [Ref: M-196, M-197, T-5:40]. One was a private, 3rd Class, 1st Co., Middle Bn., Militia, July 15, 1780 [Ref: M-201]. One Benjamin West lived in Seneca Hd. (four taxables) in 1777 [Ref: R-31:8], and another lived in the Upper Part of Potomac Hd. (one taxable) in 1777 [Ref: R-31:15].

WEST, Edward. Private, 5th Co., Middle Bn., Militia, Sep., 1777 [Ref: M-197, T-5:40].

WEST, Edward H. See "Charles Tracy," q.v.

WEST, Erasmus. Private, 1st Co., Middle Bn., Militia, Aug. 30, 1777 [Ref: M-195].

WEST, Henry. Private, 4th Co., Lower Bn., Militia, Aug., 1777 [Ref: T-5:47].

WEST, John. Private who was recruited to serve in the Continental Army in 1780 [Ref: D-341].

WEST, Joseph. (1) Private, 5th Co., Middle Bn., Militia, Sep., 1777 [Ref: M-197, T-5:40]. (2) Private, 5th Co., Upper Bn., Militia, Aug. 30, 1777 [Ref: M-194]. Two men with this name took the Oath of Allegiance: one before the Hon. Gerrard Briscoe on March 2, 1778 [Ref: T-3:57, L-1:46], and another (made his "W" mark) before the Hon. Joseph Wilson on Feb. 28, 1778 [Ref: T-3:66, L-1:46]. One Joseph West lived in Linganore Hd. (one taxable) in 1777 [Ref: R-31:9], and another lived in the Upper Part of Potomac Hd. (three taxables) in 1777 [Ref: R-31:15].

WEST, Joseph Sr. Private, 1st Co., Middle Bn., Militia, Aug. 30, 1777 [Ref: M-195]. Joseph West, Sr. lived in Seneca Hd. (ten taxables) in 1777 [Ref: R-31:8].

WEST, Nicholas. Served as a Second Sergeant, 1st Co., Middle Bn., Militia, July 15, 1780 [Ref: M-201].

WEST, Osborn (Osburn). Private, Flying Camp, Frederick (now Montgomery) County, enlisted by Greenbury Gaither on July 29, 1776 [Ref: D-44]. "Osburn West" was a private, 5th Co., Middle Bn., Militia, Sep., 1777 [Ref: M-197, T-5:40]. "Osborn West" took the Oath of Allegiance before the Hon. Joseph Wilson on Feb. 28, 1778 [Ref: T-3:64,

L-1:46], and rendered aid by providing wheat for use of the military in 1780 [Ref: O-305]. "Osburn West" rendered aid by providing wheat for use of the military in 1781 [Ref: O-403]. "Osborn West" lived in Seneca Hd. (two taxables) in 1777 [Ref: R-31:8]. He married Dorkus Trail in Montgomery County on Nov. 19, 1778 [Ref: K-2:521].

WEST, Richard. Lived in the Upper Part of Potomac Hd. (one taxable) in 1777 [Ref: R-31:15]. Private, 5th Co., Middle Bn., Militia, Sep., 1777 [Ref: M-196, T-5:40], and Ensign, 1st Co., Middle Bn., Militia, July 15, 1780 [Ref: M-201]. Rendered aid by providing wheat for use of the military in 1780 [Ref: O-305, O-307, O-315].

WEST, Samuel. Served as a Captain, Middle Bn., Militia, from Sep. 12, 1777, to at least April 21, 1779 [Ref: M-135, M-196, C-373, E-357, T-5:40]. Lived in the Upper Part of Potomac Hd. (one taxable) in 1777 [Ref: R-31:15]. A Samuel West died testate in Montgomery County (wife named Sarah) in Feb., 1778, and he had a son Samuel, among other children [Ref: V-146, V-147].

WEST, Thomas. Private, 4th Class, 1st Co., Middle Bn., Militia, July 15, 1780 [Ref: M-201]. Private, 1st Co., Middle Bn., Militia, Aug. 30, 1777 [Ref: M-195]. Took the Oath of Allegiance before the Hon. Gerrard Briscoe on March 2, 1778 [Ref: T-3:57, L-1:46].

WEST, William. Private, 5th Co., Middle Bn., Militia, Sep., 1777 [Ref: M-197, T-5:40]. Private, 6th Class, 1st Co., Middle Bn., Militia, July 15, 1780 [Ref: M-201]. Rendered aid by providing wheat for use of the military in 1780 and 1781 [Ref: O-302, O-403]. William West lived in Seneca Hd. (two taxables) in 1777 [Ref: R-31:8].

WEST, William, of John. Took the Oath of Allegiance before the Hon. Joseph Wilson on Feb. 28, 1778 [Ref: T-3:64, L-1:46].

WESTLEY, Humphrey. "Humphrey Westley" was a private, 7th Co., Lower Bn., Militia, July 15, 1780 [Ref: M-207]. "Humphry Westly" was a private, 7th Co., Lower Bn., Militia, Aug., 1777 [Ref: M-200, T-5:50].

WESTLICK, William. Private who was recruited to serve in the Continental Army in 1780 [Ref: D-341].

WETZEL, Frederick. Took the Oath of Allegiance before the Hon. Richard Thompson in 1778 [Ref: T-3:75, L-1:46]. "Frederick Wetzell" was a private, 8th Co., Lower Bn., Militia, July 15, 1780 [Ref: M-207]. "Frederick Wetzill" was a private, 3rd Co., Lower Bn., Militia, Sep., 1777 [Ref: M-199, T-5:46]. Frederick Wetzel lived in George Town Hd. (two taxables) in 1777 [Ref: R-31:3].

WEYMAN, Ann. See "William Holland," q.v.

WEYMAN, Darcus. See "John Harris," q.v.

WHEAT, Azariah. Took the Oath of Allegiance before the Hon. Gerrard Briscoe on March 2, 1778 [Ref: T-3:57, L-1:46].

WHEAT, Basil. Private, 2nd Co., Lower Bn., Militia, Sep., 1777 [Ref: M-198, T-5:45].

349

WHEAT, Hezekiah. Private, 6th Co., Upper Bn., Militia, Aug. 30, 1777 [Ref: M-194]. Hezekiah Wheat lived in Sugar Loaf Hd. (one taxable) in 1777 [Ref: R-31:11].

WHEAT, John. Private, 2nd Co., Middle Bn., Militia, Sep. 4, 1777 [Ref: M-195]. Private, 2nd Class, 3rd Co., Middle Bn., Militia, July 15, 1780 [Ref: M-202]. Took the Oath of Allegiance before the Hon. Gerrard Briscoe on March 2, 1778 [Ref: T-3:57, L-1:46]. Lived in Sugar Loaf Hd. (one taxable) in 1777 [Ref: R-31:11]. See "Humphrey B. Tomlinson," q.v.

WHEAT, Joseph. Private, 4th Class, 3rd Co., Middle Bn., Militia, July 15, 1780 [Ref: M-202]. Took the Oath of Allegiance before the Hon. Gerrard Briscoe on March 2, 1778 [Ref: T-3:57, L-1:46]. Rendered aid by providing wheat for use of the military in 1781 [Ref: O-388]. Lived in Sugar Loaf Hd. (four taxables) in 1777 [Ref: R-31:11], and served as Constable in 1780-1781 [Ref: W-2].

WHEAT, Tabitha. See "Humphrey Beckett Tomlinson," q.v.

WHEAT, Zachariah. Private, 3rd Class, 3rd Co., Middle Bn., Militia, July 15, 1780 [Ref: M-202].

WHEELER, Edward. Served as a Second Lieutenant, 7th Co., 29th (Lower) Bn., Militia, Sep. 12, 1777 [Ref: M-135, M-200, T-5:50, C-373]. Took the Oath of Allegiance before the Hon. Edward Burgess on Feb. 28, 1778 [Ref: T-3:59, L-1:46]. Served as a petit juror in Nov., 1777 [Ref: R-31:18].

WHEELER, John Hanson. "John Hanson Wheeler" was a private, Capt. Edward Burgess' Co., Lower District of Frederick (now Montgomery) County, Militia, July, 1776 [Ref: D-42]. "Hanson Wheeler" was a private, 8th Co., Upper Bn., Militia, Aug. 30, 1777 [Ref: M-195]. "John Hanson Wheeler" took the Oath of Allegiance before the Hon. Aneas Campbell on March 2, 1778 [Ref: T-3:77, L-1:46].

WHEELER (WHEALER), Leonard. "Leonard Wheeler" was a private, 8th Co., Upper Bn., Militia, Aug. 30, 1777 [Ref: M-195]. "Leonard Whealer" lived in Sugarland Hd. (one taxable) in 1777 [Ref: R-31:13]. See "Lawrence Hurdle," q.v.

WHEELER, Nicholas. See "Nicholas Whelan (Whealer)," q.v.

WHEELER, Samuel. Private, Capt. Edward Burgess' Co., Lower District of Frederick (now Montgomery) County, Militia, July, 1776 [Ref: D-42].

WHEELER, William. Private, 7th Co., Lower Bn., Militia, Aug., 1777 [Ref: M-200, T-5:50]. Private, 4th Co., Lower Bn., Militia, July 15, 1780 [Ref: M-205]. Took the Oath of Allegiance (made his "X" mark) before the Hon. Edward Burgess on Feb. 28, 1778 [Ref: T-3:62, L-1:46]. "William Whealer" lived in the Lower Part of Newfoundland Hd. (one taxable) in 1777 [Ref: R-31:6].

WHELAN (WHELAND, WHEALEN, WHALAND, WHALING), Daniel (b. 1746). "Daniel Whelan" took the Oath of Allegiance before the Hon. Elisha Williams on March 2, 1778 [Ref: T-3:80, L-1:46]. "Daniel Wheland" rendered aid by providing wheat for use of the military in 1781 [Ref: O-

397]. "Daniel Whaling" was a private, 7th Co., Upper Bn., Militia, Aug. 30, 1777 [Ref: M-194]. "Daniel Whaland" rendered aid by providing corn for use of the military in 1780 [Ref: O-287, O-301]. "Daniel Whalen or Whealen" lived in Sugarland Hd. (one taxable) in 1776-1777 [Ref: K-1:204, R-31:13].

WHELAN (WHELAND), John. Private who was recruited to serve in the Extra Regiment, Continental Army, in 1780 [Ref: D-342].

WHELAN (WHALEN), Mark (b. 1761). Son of Michael Whelan, of North West Hd., in 1776 [Ref: K-1:228]. Private, 6th Co., Lower Bn., Militia, July 15, 1780 [Ref: M-206].

WHELAN, Mary. See "Joseph Clewley," q.v.

WHELAN (WHELAND, WHELEN), Matthew (b. 1756). Took the Oath of Allegiance before the Hon. Charles Jones on Jan. 10, 1778 [Ref: T-3:71, L-1:46]. "Matthew Wheland" was a private, 6th Co., Lower Bn., Militia, July 15, 1780 [Ref: M-206]. "Matthew Whelen or Whallen" lived in North West Hd. (one taxable) in 1776-1777, a son of Michael Whelan [Ref: K-1:228, R-31:17].

WHELAN (WHEALING, WHELEN), Michael (b. 1716). Took the Oath of Allegiance before the Hon. Charles Jones on Jan. 10, 1778 [Ref: T-3:71, L-1:46]. "Michael Whealing" rendered aid by providing wheat for use of the military in 1780 [Ref: O-335]. "Michel Whallen" lived in North West Hd. (wife named Bridgett) in 1776 and "Michael Whelen" lived there in 1777 [Ref: K-1:228, R-31:17].

WHELAN (WHEALER), Nicholas. "Nicholas Whelan" took the Oath of Allegiance before the Hon. Charles Jones on Jan. 10, 1778 [Ref: T-3:71, L-1:46]. "Nicholas Whealer" lived in the Lower Part of Newfoundland Hd. (one taxable) in 1777 [Ref: R-31:6].

WHELAN (WHEELING), Richard. "Richard Wheeling" rendered aid by providing wheat for use of the military in 1780 [Ref: O-317].

WHELAN (WHEYLIN), William. "William Wheylin" was a private, Capt. Price's Co., 3rd Maryland Line, 1781-1782 [Ref: D-452].

WHIPS, Benjamin. Private, 1st or 32nd Bn., Militia (no date was given; possibly June, 1777). [Ref: T-5:1].

WHIPS, Ezekiel. Private, 1st or 32nd Bn., Militia (no date was given; possibly June, 1777). [Ref: T-5:1].

WHITAKER, Alexander (b. 1746). Private, 8th Co., Upper Bn., Militia, Aug. 30, 1777 [Ref: M-195]. Took the Oath of Allegiance before the Hon. Joseph Wilson on Feb. 28, 1778 [Ref: T-3:64, L-1:46]. Lived in Sugarland Hd. in 1776 and had four taxables in 1777 [Ref: K-1:218, R-31:13].

WHITAKER (WHITEKAR), Francis. Private who was recruited to serve in the Continental Army in 1780 [Ref: D-341].

WHITE, Alexander. Private, 3rd Co., Lower Bn., Militia, Sep., 1777 [Ref: M-199, T-5:46]. Took the Oath of Allegiance before the Hon. Richard Thompson in 1778 [Ref: T-3:75, L-1:46]. Private, 8th Co., Lower Bn.,

Militia, July 15, 1780 [Ref: M-207]. Lived in George Town Hd. (one taxable) in 1777 [Ref: R-31:3].

WHITE, Basil. Private, 8th Co., Lower Bn., Militia, Sep., 1777 [Ref: M-200, T-5:51]. Lived in North West Hd. (one taxable) in 1777 [Ref: R-31:17]. Previously, in 1776, it was noted by the census taker that "Bazil White won't make a return of neither number, names nor ages, but I think 8 [is] in his family." [Ref: K-1:232].

WHITE, Burgess. Private, 4th Co., Lower Bn., Militia, Aug., 1777 [Ref: M-199, T-5:47].

WHITE, Eleanor. See "Joseph Newton Chiswell (Chissell)," q.v.

WHITE, James (c1759-1829). Private, 8th Co., Lower Bn., Militia, Sep., 1777 [Ref: M-200, T-5:51]. Invalid (disability) pension commenced in 1789. On May 27, 1815, he also applied for pension (S25481) at Baltimore, Maryland, and applied again on July 12, 1825, aged about 66 (another source states aged 78 or 79), in Washington, D. C., stating he had enlisted in 1779 and served in the 7th Maryland Line. Affidavit by Richard Anderson in Montgomery County, Maryland, on May 3, 1825, stated that James White, of the Maryland Line, enlisted for the duration, was wounded in the arm at the second Battle of Camden on April 25, 1781, and was furloughed thereafter. James died Oct. 21, 1829, and in 1830 the Treasurer of Maryland was directed to pay to Henry Harding for the use of Priscilla White, widow of the late James White, the $22.33 balance due him at his death [Ref: D-632, J-16, K-2:406, K-2:407, P-3789, Y-61]. One "James White, aged 16" lived in North West Hd. and his mother Mary White, aged 45, was head of household in 1776 [Ref: K-1:225]. "Mary White, consort of Capt. James White of Montgomery County" is buried in the Monocacy Cemetery (no dates given). [Ref: *Historic Graves of Maryland and the District of Columbia*, by Helen W. Ridgely (1908), p. 172].

WHITE, John. Private, 5th Co., Middle Bn., Militia, Sep., 1777 [Ref: M-197, T-5:40]. Private, 3rd Co., Lower Bn., Militia, July 15, 1780 [Ref: M-205]. Took the Oath of Allegiance before the Hon. Thomas Sprigg Wootton on March 3, 1778 [Ref: T-3:79, L-1:46]. Lived in the Upper Part of Potomac Hd. (one taxable) in 1777 [Ref: R-31:15].

WHITE, Joseph. Served as a First Lieutenant, 6th Co., 29th Bn., Militia, June 21, 1777, and First Lieutenant, 3rd Co., Lower Bn., July 15, 1780 [Ref: M-136, M-200, M-204, T-5:49, C-296, C-373]. Took the Oath of Allegiance before the Hon. Samuel W. Magruder in 1778 [Ref: T-3:73, L-1:46]. Served as a petit juror in Aug., 1777 [Ref: R-31:17]. Lived in the Upper Part of Potomac Hd. (four taxables) in 1777 [Ref: R-31:15]. One Joseph White married Martha Riley on Dec. 22, 1778, and Joseph White married Jean Baer in Montgomery County on Oct. 31, 1782 [Ref: K-2:515, K-2:521].

WHITE, Mary and Priscilla. See "James White," q.v.

WHITE, Samuel. Took the Oath of Allegiance before the Hon. Elisha Williams on March 2, 1778 [Ref: T-3:80, L-1:46]. Lived in Sugar Loaf Hd. (Walter White, security) in 1777 [Ref: R-31:11]. One Samuel White died testate in Montgomery County (wife not named) in 1798 [Ref: V-148].

WHITE, Samuel Jr. Private, 2nd Co., Lower Bn., Militia, Sep., 1777 [Ref: M-198, T-5:45]. Took the Oath of Allegiance before the Hon. Edward Burgess on Feb. 28, 1778 [Ref: T-3:60, L-1:46]. Also see "Samuel White," q.v.

WHITE, Samuel Beall (1759-1832). Private, Capt. Edward Burgess' Co., Lower District of Frederick (now Montgomery) County, Militia, July, 1776 [Ref: D-42]. Took the Oath of Allegiance before the Hon. Edward Burgess on Feb. 28, 1778 [Ref: T-3:58, L-1:46]. Private, 5th Co., Lower Bn., Militia, July 15, 1780 [Ref: M-206]. Private, 1st Maryland Regiment (possibly 3rd Maryland Line), who was wounded in the left kidney, abdomen, and back at the second Battle of Camden on April 25, 1781. His disability pension (S25482) commenced on June 9, 1789, aged 30, resident of Montgomery County. He was considered totally disabled by his physicians Jacob Baer and W. Bradley Tyler, of Frederick County, Maryland, on Oct. 4, 1823. Samuel died on Jan. 18, 1832 and the Treasurer of Maryland was directed to pay to Sarah White, of Montgomery County, during her widowhood, the half pay of a private, for her husband's services [Ref: D-632, J-16, K-2:407, P-3796, Q-147, Y-59, Y-60]. It should be noted also that there was a Samuel Beall White who died testate in Montgomery County (wife named Nancy) in 1790 [Ref: V-148].

WHITE, Sarah. See "Samuel Beall White," q.v.

WHITE (WIGHTT), Trueman or Truman (c1755-1781). "Truman White" lived in Sugarland Hd. (eight taxables) in 1777 [Ref: R-31:13]. "Trewman White" was a private, 8th Co., Upper Bn., Militia, Aug. 30, 1777 [Ref: M-195]. "Trueman White" rendered aid by providing corn for use of the military in 1780 [Ref: O-294]. "Truman Wightt" died testate in Montgomery County (unmarried) in 1781 and left his property to his sister Ann Wheeler and "brother" Samuel Wheeler [Ref: V-148].

WHITE, Walter. (1) Lieutenant, enrolled into a company of militia for the service of the Flying Camp, Oct. 15, 1776 [Ref: B-352, A-287]. (2) Private, 2nd Co., Upper Bn., Militia, Aug. 30, 1777 [Ref: M-193]. Ensign, Upper Bn., Militia, April 21, 1779, and Second Lieutenant, March 25, 1780 [Ref: M-136, E-356, F-120]. One served as a petit juror in Aug., 1777 [Ref: R-31:17]. Took the Oath of Allegiance before the Hon. Elisha Williams on March 2, 1778 [Ref: T-3:80, L-1:46]. Rendered aid by providing corn for use of the military in 1780 [Ref: O-300]. One Walter White lived in Sugar Loaf Hd. (four taxables) in 1777 [Ref: R-31:11]. See "Samuel White," q.v.

WHITE, Zachariah Jr. Private, 6th Co., Lower Bn., Militia, July 15, 1780 [Ref: M-206].

WHITEHEAD, Lazarus Rev. See "John Miller," q.v.

WHITEHEAD, Timothy (b. 1709). Lived in North West Hd. in 1776 [Ref: K-1:228]. Took the Oath of Allegiance before the Hon. Charles Jones on Jan. 10, 1778 [Ref: T-3:71, L-1:46].

WIETT, Alexander and James. See "Alexander and James Wyatt," q.v.

WILEY, Amelia. See "James Sibbey (Sibley)," q.v.

WILEY (WHILEY), Richard. Private who was recruited to serve in the Continental Army in 1780 [Ref: D-342].

WILFREE, Eve. See "Daniel Quiry," q.v.

WILKINSON (WILKERSON), William (b. 1749). Private, 7th Co., Upper Bn., Militia, Aug. 30, 1777 [Ref: M-195]. Took the Oath of Allegiance (made his "W" mark) before the Hon. Aneas Campbell on March 2, 1778 [Ref: T-3:78, L-1:46]. "William Wilkerson" lived in Sugarland Hd. in 1776 [Ref: K-1:211].

WILLCOXEN (WILCOXON), Ann. See "Josias (Josias) Hoskinson," q.v.

WILLCOXEN (WILCOXEN), Anthony. Private, 2nd Co., Lower Bn., Militia, Sep., 1777 [Ref: M-198, T-5:45]. Second Lieutenant, 5th Co., Lower Bn., Militia, March 25, 1780 [Ref: M-137, M-205, F-120]. Took the Oath of Allegiance before the Hon. Edward Burgess on Feb. 28, 1778 [Ref: T-3:60, L-1:46, which latter source mistakenly listed the name as "Anthony Nittcoxen"]. Served as a petit juror in Nov., 1777 [Ref: R-31:18].

WILLCOXEN (WILCOXEN), George. Served as an Ensign, Lower Bn., Militia, March 25, 1780 [Ref: M-137, M-205, F-120]. Took the Oath of Allegiance before the Hon. Edward Burgess on Feb. 28, 1778 [Ref: T-3:60, L-1:46]. George Wilcoxen married Mary Swearingen in Montgomery County on Jan. 22, 1778 [Ref: K-2:517]. See "Josiah Hoskinson, Jr.," q.v.

WILLCOXEN (WILCOXEN), Henry. Private, 3rd Co., Upper Bn., Militia, Aug. 30, 1777 [Ref: M-193]. Took the Oath of Allegiance before the Hon. Elisha Williams on March 2, 1778 [Ref: T-3:81, L-1:46].

WILLCOXEN (WILCOXEN, WILLCOXON), Jesse (1738-1812). Served as a First Lieutenant, 5th Co., Lower Bn., Militia, Dec. 7, 1776, and First Lieutenant, 29th Bn., Militia, Sep. 12, 1777, and Captain, Lower Bn., Militia, from July 15, 1780, until May, 1782, when he resigned [Ref: M-136, M-137, M-199, M-204, T-5:48, B-464, B-511, C-373, F-248, K-2:408]. Took the Oath of Allegiance before the Hon. Samuel W. Magruder in 1778 [Ref: T-3:73, L-1:46]. Rendered aid by providing wheat for use of the military in 1780 [Ref: O-303]. Lived in Lower Potomac Hd. (four taxables) in 1776-1777 [Ref: K-1:186, R-31:5]. "Jesse Wilcoxon" was born on Jan. 30, 1738, married Elizabeth Clagett (1752-1835), and died testate in Montgomery County on Dec. 11, 1811 [Ref: V-148, V-149, DAR-I:743. The Bible record of his son "Horatio Wilcoxon"

(1795-1844) has been published in the *Maryland Genealogical Society Bulletin*, Vol. 36, No. 3 (1995), pp. 495-496, contributed by Alicia E. Towster].

WILLCOXEN (WILCOXEN), John Jr. Private, 2nd Co., Lower Bn., Militia, Sep., 1777 [Ref: M-198, T-5:45]. Took the Oath of Allegiance before the Hon. Edward Burgess on Feb. 28, 1778 [Ref: T-3:60, L-1:46]. "John Wilcoxon." aged 20, lived in Lower Potomac Hd. in 1776 [Ref: K-1:186]. "John Wilcoxen, Jr." lived in Rock Creek Hd. (one taxable) in 1777 [Ref: R-31:16].

WILLCOXEN (WILCOXEN), John Sr. Private, Capt. Edward Burgess' Co., Lower District of Frederick (now Montgomery) County, Militia, July, 1776 [Ref: D-42]. Private, 2nd Co., Lower Bn., Militia, Sep., 1777 [Ref: M-198, T-5:45], and Fourth Sergeant, 5th Co., Lower Bn., July 15, 1780 [Ref: M-205]. Took the Oath of Allegiance before the Hon. Edward Burgess on Feb. 28, 1778 [Ref: T-3:60, L-1:46]. Served as a petit juror in Nov., 1777 [Ref: R-31:18]. Lived in Rock Creek Hd. (seven taxables) in 1777 [Ref: R-31:16].

WILLCOXEN (WILCOXEN), Josiah or Josias (b. 1758). Private, 4th Class, 3rd Co., Middle Bn., Militia, July 15, 1780 [Ref: M-202, which source mistakenly listed the name as "Josiah W. Coxen"]. Took the Oath of Allegiance before the Hon. Edward Burgess on Feb. 28, 1778 [Ref: T-3:63, L-1:46]. "Josias Willcoxen" was a private, 5th Co., Lower Bn., Militia, Aug., 1777 [Ref: M-200, T-5:48]. Josias Wilcoxen married Annastatia Smith in Montgomery County on Nov. 19, 1779 [Ref: K-2:515].

WILLCOXEN (WILCOXEN, WILLCOXON), Lewis. Private, 2nd Co., Lower Bn., Militia, July 15, 1780 [Ref: M-204]. Took the Oath of Allegiance before the Hon. Charles Jones on Jan. 10, 1778 [Ref: T-3:71, L-1:46]. "Lewis Wilcoxon" was constable in Lower Potomac Hd. in 1780 [Ref: W-1]. Lewis Willcoxon lived in Lower Potomac Hd. (three taxables) in 1777 [Ref: R-31:5].

WILLCOXEN (WILLCOXON), William. Rendered aid by providing wheat for use of the military in 1780 and 1781 [Ref: O-307, O-380]. One William Willcoxon lived in Lower Potomac Hd. (three taxables) in 1777 [Ref: R-31:5], and another lived in Sugarland Hd. (one taxable) in 1777 [Ref: R-31:13]. "William Wilcoxon" died testate in Montgomery County (wife named Rebeckah) in 1804, and "William Wilcoxon, Sr." died testate in Montgomery County (no wife or children named) in 1811 [Ref: V-149].

WILLETT (WILLET), Benjamin (1744-1835). Private, 5th Co., Middle Bn., Militia, Sep., 1777 [Ref: M-197, T-5:40]. Private, 6th Class, 1st Co., Middle Bn., Militia, July 15, 1780 [Ref: M-201]. Took the Oath of Allegiance before the Hon. Joseph Wilson on Feb. 28, 1778 [Ref: T-3:66, L-1:46]. "Benjamin Willet" lived in the Upper Part of Potomac Hd. (one taxable) in 1777 [Ref: R-31:15]. Rendered aid by providing wheat for use of the military in 1780 and 1781 [Ref: O-316, O-393]. The children of Benjamin and Mary Willett were: Ann (b. May 10, 1770); Essay (Esther, born April 19, 1772); Thomas (b. Feb. 21, 1774); William (b. June 16, 1776); Ibby (Isabella, born July 8, 1778); Babby (Barbara, born July 9, 1780); Mary (b. Aug. 20, 1782, and married Eleven Fish); Elizabeth (b. March 11, 1784); Benjamin (b. July 25, 1786); and, John (b. May 16, 1789). [Ref: "The Benjamin Willett Family of Montgomery County, Maryland," by Mrs. Frederick L. Allman, *Western Maryland Families*, edited by Raymond B. Clark, Jr. (1987), p. 61]. Also see "Thomas Hays," q.v.

WILLETT, Griffith (b. 1750). Lived in Sugarland Hd. in 1776 [Ref: K-1:222]. Private, 1st Co., Upper Bn., Militia, Aug. 30, 1777 [Ref: M-193]. Took the Oath of Allegiance before the Hon. Aneas Campbell on March 2, 1778 [Ref: T-3:77, L-1:46]. Served as Constable, 1779 [Ref: W-1].

WILLETT, Mary, and others. See "Benjamin Willett," q.v.

WILLETT (WILLET), Ninian. Private, 5th Co., Lower Bn., Militia, Aug., 1777 [Ref: M-199, T-5:48]. Took the Oath of Allegiance before the Hon. Samuel W. Magruder in 1778 [Ref: T-3:73]. Private, 2nd Co., Lower Bn., Militia, July 15, 1780 [Ref: M-204]. Rendered aid by providing wheat for use of the military in 1780 [Ref: O-318]. Lived in the Upper Part of Potomac Hd. (one taxable) in 1777 [Ref: R-31:15].

WILLETT (WILLET), William (died 1785). Private, 5th Co., Lower Bn., Militia, Aug., 1777 [Ref: M-199, T-5:48]. Took the Oath of Allegiance before the Hon. Samuel W. Magruder in 1778 [Ref: T-3:73]. Private, 2nd Co., Lower Bn., Militia, July 15, 1780 [Ref: M-204]. Served as a grand juror in Nov., 1777 [Ref: R-31:18]. "William Willet" lived in the Upper Part of Potomac Hd. (two taxables) in 1777 [Ref: R-31:15]. Died testate in Montgomery County (wife not named) in 1785 [Ref: V-149]. See "Benjamin Willett," q.v.

WILLIAMS, Amos. Son of William Williams [Ref: V-151, V-152]. Private, 1st Co., Middle Bn., Militia, Aug. 30, 1777 [Ref: M-195], and private, 5th Co., Middle Bn., Militia, July 15, 1780 [Ref: M-203]. Took the Oath of Allegiance before the Hon. Joseph Wilson on Feb. 28, 1778 [Ref: T-3:66, L-1:46]. Rendered aid by providing wheat for use of the military in 1780 and 1781 [Ref: O-315, O-331, O-445]. Lived in Seneca Hd. (two taxables) in 1777 [Ref: R-31:8].

WILLIAMS, Andrew (b. 1740). Private, 8th Co., Upper Bn., Militia, Aug. 30, 1777 [Ref: M-195]. Lived in Sugarland Hd. in 1776-1777 [Ref: K-1:211, R-31:13].

WILLIAMS, Benjamin. Private, 1st Co., Middle Bn., Militia, Aug. 30, 1777 [Ref: M-195]. Took the Oath of Allegiance before the Hon. Gerrard Briscoe on March 2, 1778 [Ref: T-3:56, L-1:46]. Private, 5th Co., Middle Bn., Militia, July 15, 1780 [Ref: M-203]. Rendered aid by providing wheat for use of the military in 1781 [Ref: O-406]. Lived in Seneca Hd. (three taxables) in 1777 [Ref: R-31:8].

WILLIAMS, Charles. Private, 1st Co., Middle Bn., Militia, Aug. 30, 1777 [Ref: M-195], and Second Corporal, 5th Co., Middle Bn., July 15, 1780 [Ref: M-202]. One Charles Williams took the Oath of Allegiance before the Hon. Joseph Wilson on Feb. 28, 1778, and another took the Oath of Allegiance before the Hon. Edward Burgess on Feb. 28, 1778 [Ref: T-3:58, T-3:66, L-1:46]. One (or both) rendered aid by providing wheat for use of the military in 1780 and 1781 [Ref: O-304, O-315, O-444]. One lived in the Lower Part of Newfoundland Hd. (four taxables) in 1777 and another in Seneca Hd. (three taxables) in 1777 [Ref: R-31:6, R-31:8]. One Charles Williams died testate in Montgomery County (wife named Sarah) in 1785 [Ref: V-150].

WILLIAMS, Clement. Son of Charles Williams [Ref: V-150]. Private, 7th Co., Lower Bn., Militia, July 15, 1780 [Ref: M-207]. Private, 1st Co., Lower Bn., Militia, Sep., 1777 [Ref: M-198, T-5:44]. Took the Oath of Allegiance before the Hon. Edward Burgess on Feb. 28, 1778 [Ref: T-3:58, L-1:46]. Lived in the Lower Part of Newfoundland Hd. (two taxables) in 1777 [Ref: R-31:6].

WILLIAMS, Daniel (b. 1756). Private, 8th Co., Lower Bn., Militia, Sep., 1777, and Second Sergeant, 6th Co., Lower Bn., July 15, 1780 [Ref: M-200, M-206, T-5:51]. Took the Oath of Allegiance before the Hon. Charles Jones on Jan. 10, 1778 [Ref: T-3:71, L-1:46]. Lived in North West Hd. in 1776-1777, with Ann Williams, aged 60, who was head of household in 1776 [Ref: K-1:227, R-31:17].

WILLIAMS, Edward Owen. Private, 8th Co., Middle Bn., Militia, Sep., 1777 [Ref: M-198, T-5:43]. Took the Oath of Allegiance before the Hon. Joseph Wilson on Feb. 28, 1778 [Ref: T-3:64, L-1:46, which listed his name as "Elisha Owen Williams"].

WILLIAMS, Elisha. There were two, and possibly three, men named Elisha Williams in 1776: (1) Son of Thomas Williams (1693-1749) and Eleanor Prather. "Elisha Williams, aged 41" lived in Sugarland Hd. in 1776 [Ref: K-1:217]. He married Ann ---- by 1759 and had these children: John, Thomas, Jarred, Elisha, Hazel [male], Mary, and Martha. Elisha served in the 9th Maryland Convention in 1776 (Frederick County) and in the Lower House from Montgomery County, 1777-1778; Second Lieutenant, Lower District, Frederick County (now Montgomery), Militia, July 20, 1776, and Captain, 7th Regiment, Dec. 10, 1776, until he resigned Nov. 28, 1778 [Ref: N-891, D-42, D-257]. He was also a Justice of the Peace who administered the Oath of Allegiance in 1778 [Ref: T-3:80, T-3:82, L-1:46, C-529]. On Feb. 27, 1832, the Treasurer of Maryland was directed to pay to Harriet [sic] Williams, of Georgetown, D. C., in consideration of services rendered by her deceased husband, Elisha Williams, a captain in the Revolutionary War, during her life, quarterly, a sum equal to the half pay of a captain [Ref: K-2:408, Q-147]. "By Nov., 1778, Elisha Williams had sold virtually all of his land and does not appear again in Maryland records. There is a strong possibility that he may have joined other family members out of the state. A cousin, Thomas Prather, settled in Louisville, Kentucky, and became a merchant in 1794. An uncle, Philip Prather, settled in Guilford County, North Carolina, in 1756." [Ref: N-891]. Harriet Williams applied for pension (W26019) on Sep. 1, 1838, aged 69, in Georgetown, D. C., stating she was the widow of Elisha Williams who was born in Frederick (now Montgomery County), Maryland. He enlisted in the spring of 1776 in the Revolutionary War, served as a captain in the 7th Maryland Line from Dec. 10, 1776 to Nov. 28, 1777, was wounded at the Battle of Germantown, and resigned his commission. They were married on May 6, 1784 (her maiden name was Harriet Beall) at Georgetown (now in the District of Columbia) by Rev. Stephen B. Balch. Elisha died on Dec. 14, 1805. The only child named in the claim was Margaret A. Johns, and also mentioned was Catharine Marshall, sister of Harriet (Beall) Williams, in 1838. Harriet Williams died on Dec. 14, 1865, in Georgetown [Ref: P-3852, U-34:70, U-34:71]. One Elisha Williams, aged 41, lived in Sugarland Hd. in 1776 and had two taxables in 1777 [Ref: K-1:217, R-31:13]. "Elisha O. Williams, of Georgetown, District of Columbia" died testate in Montgomery County (wife not named) in 1806 [Ref: V-150]. (2) Private, 5th Co., Lower Bn., Militia, Aug., 1777 [Ref: M-199, T-5:48]. Private, 2nd Co., Lower Bn., Militia, July 15, 1780 [Ref: M-204]. (3) Private, 1st Co., Upper Bn., Militia, Aug. 30, 1777 [Ref: M-193]. One Elisha Williams took the Oath of Allegiance (made his "X" mark) before the Hon. Samuel W. Magruder in 1778 [Ref: T-3:73].

WILLIAMS, Francis. Took the Oath of Allegiance on Sep. 1, 1780, under the Act of May 12, 1780, having neglected to do so previously "due to ignorance of the duty owed the country." [Ref: R-27:123, which source listed this name twice]. Francis Williams lived in Sugarland Hd. (one taxable) in 1777 [Ref: R-31:13].

WILLIAMS, Gabriel. Served as a Sergeant, 7th Maryland Line, 1780, and was also involved in the recruiting service until discharged Feb. 6, 1783 [Ref: D-258, D-389, D-560].

WILLIAMS, Harriet. See "Elisha Williams," q.v.

WILLIAMS, Hazel (b. 1758). Son of Elisha and Ann Williams, of Sugarland Hd. [Ref: K-1:217]. "Hazel Williams" was a private, 1st Co., Upper Bn., Militia, Aug. 30, 1777 [Ref: M-193]. "Hazael Williams" married Mary Gore Hardy in Montgomery County on Oct. 13, 1778 [Ref: K-2:521]. "Hazle Williams" was a drummer in Capt. Moore's Co., Maryland Line, Gist's Regiment, in 1781 [Ref: D-601].

WILLIAMS, Jacob (died 1804). Private, 2nd Co., Middle Bn., Militia, Sep. 4, 1777 [Ref: M-196, T-5:37]. Rendered aid by providing wheat for use of the military in 1780 [Ref: O-314]. Died testate in Montgomery County (wife named Elizabeth) in 1804 [Ref: V-151].

WILLIAMS, James (b. 1753). Lived in Sugarland Hd. in 1776 [Ref: K-1:204]. Served as private, Flying Camp, enlisted July 18, 1776 [Ref: D-49]. Private, Maryland Line, 1782-1783 [Ref: D-561].

WILLIAMS, Jarvis. Private, 1st Class, 5th Co., Middle Bn., Militia, July 15, 1780 [Ref: M-202]. Private, Maryland Line, 1780-1783 [Ref: D-561].

WILLIAMS, John. (1) Private, 8th Co., Lower Bn., Militia, Sep., 1777 [Ref: M-200, T-5:51]. (2) Private, 4th Co., Lower Bn., Militia, Aug., 1777 [Ref: M-199, T-5:47]. (3) Private, 1st Co., Lower Bn., Militia, Sep., 1777 [Ref: M-198, T-5:44]. (4) First Sergeant, 7th Co., Lower Bn., Militia, July 15, 1780 [Ref: M-206]. (5) Private, 8th Co., Upper Bn., Militia, Aug. 30, 1777 [Ref: M-195, and which source listed the name twice]. One John Williams took the Oath of Allegiance before the Hon. Aneas Campbell on March 2, 1778 [Ref: T-3:77, L-1:46], and another took the Oath of Allegiance (made his "O" mark) before the Hon. Joseph Wilson on Feb. 28, 1778 [Ref: T-3:66, L-1:46]. One rendered aid by providing corn for use of the military in 1780 [Ref: O-285]. One John Williams was constable in Lower Newfoundland Hd. in 1780 [Ref: W-1]. One John Williams married Sarah Stewart in Montgomery County on July 29, 1779 [Ref: K-2:514]. There were two men named John Williams, both aged 48, in 1776: one lived in Lower Potomac Hd. (one taxable) in 1776-1777 and the other lived in Sugarland Hd. (three taxables) in 1776-1777 (and had a son John J. [Jr.?], aged 17). Other men named John Williams lived in the Lower Part of Newfoundland Hd. (seven taxables), the Upper Part of Potomac Hd. (one taxable), and North West Hd. (one taxable) in 1777 [Ref: K-1:187, K-1:212, R-31:5, R-31:6, R-31:13, R-31:15, R-31:17]. "John Williams, aged 35" lived in Northwest Hd. (wife named Mary, aged 32) in 1776 [Ref: K-1:223].

WILLIAMS, Leonard (died 1819). Private, 3rd Co., Upper Bn., Militia, Aug. 30, 1777 [Ref: M-193]. Took the Oath of Allegiance before the Hon. Edward Burgess on Feb. 28, 1778 [Ref: T-3:62, L-1:46]. Private, 6th Co., Lower Bn., Militia, July 15, 1780 [Ref: M-206]. Lived in Sugarland Hd. (one taxable) in 1777 [Ref: R-31:13]. Died testate in Montgomery County (wife not named) in 1819 [Ref: V-151].

WILLIAMS, Margaret V. See "Jeremiah Plummer," q.v.

WILLIAMS, Richard. Private, 1st Co., Lower Bn., Militia, Sep., 1777, and Second Corporal, 7th Co., Lower Bn., July 15, 1780 [Ref: M-198, M-206, T-5:44].

WILLIAMS, Samuel. Private, 7th Co., Lower Bn., Militia, Aug., 1777 [Ref: M-200, T-5:50]. "Samuel Williams (cooper)" lived in the Lower Part of Newfoundland Hd. (one taxable) in 1777 [Ref: R-31:6].

WILLIAMS, Thomas. Took the Oath of Allegiance in 1778 [Ref: L-2:28]. Owned a working plantation ("quarter") in Sugarland Hd. in 1777 [Ref: R-31:13]. See "Elisha Williams," q.v

WILLIAMS, William. (1) Private, 6th Co., Upper Bn., Militia, Aug. 30, 1777 [Ref: M-194]. Private, 4th Class, 2nd Co., Middle Bn., Militia, July

15, 1780 [Ref: M-201]. (2) Second Lieutenant, 5th Co., Middle Bn., Militia, July 15, 1780 [Ref: M-202]. One William Williams took the Oath of Allegiance in 1778 [Ref: L-2:28], and William Williams, Sr. took the Oath of Allegiance before the Hon. Joseph Wilson on Feb. 28, 1778 [Ref: T-3:66, L-1:46]. One William Williams rendered aid by providing wheat for use of the military in 1780 and 1781 [Ref: O-314, O-322, O-444]. One William Williams lived in Sugar Loaf Hd. (one taxable) in 1777 [Ref: R-31:11]. One William Williams died testate in Montgomery County (wife named Verlenda) in 1788 and he had sons William and Amos and a daughter Eleanor [Ref: V-151]. See "William Williams, Jr.," q.v.

WILLIAMS, William Jr. Private, 1st Co., Middle Bn., Militia, Aug. 30, 1777, and Second Lieutenant, Middle Bn., Militia, Aug. 4, 1780 [Ref: M-138, M-195, F-248]. Took the Oath of Allegiance before the Hon. Joseph Wilson on Feb. 28, 1778 [Ref: T-3:64, L-1:46]. William Williams, Jr. lived in Seneca Hd. (three taxables) in 1777 [Ref: R-31:8, which source listed this same name and this same information twice; perhaps one should have been "Sr." rather than "Jr."].

WILLIAMS, William Naler. "William N. Williams" was a private, 8th Co., Middle Bn., Militia, Sep., 1777 [Ref: M-198, T-5:43]. "William Naler Williams" lived in Rock Creek Hd. (one taxable) in 1777 [Ref: R-31:16].

WILLIAMS, William Prather. Private, 2nd Co., Lower Bn., Militia, Sep., 1777 [Ref: M-198, T-5:45]. "William Prather Williams" took the Oath of Allegiance before the Hon. Edward Burgess on Feb. 28, 1778 [Ref: T-3:60, L-1:46]. "William Prator Williams" rendered aid by providing wheat for use of the military in 1780 [Ref: O-328].

WILLIAMSON, Alexander. Took the Oath of Allegiance before the Hon. Richard Thompson in 1778 [Ref: T-3:75, L-1:46]. Rendered aid by providing flour for use of the military in 1781 [Ref: O-378]. "Revd. Alexander Williamson" lived in Lower Potomac Hd. (six taxables) in 1777 [Ref: R-31:5]. Alexander Williamson died testate in Montgomery County (wife not named) in 1787 [Ref: V-152].

WILLIAMSON, Ann. See "Daniel Vears (Viers)," q.v.

WILLIAMSON, William. Took the Oath of Allegiance before the Hon. Elisha Williams on March 2, 1778 [Ref: T-3:80, L-1:46].

WILLMOT, Robert. Private, 7th Co., Lower Bn., Militia, Aug., 1777 [Ref: M-200, T-5:50].

WILLMOTT (WILMOT), Thomas. Private, 7th Co., Lower Bn., Militia, Aug., 1777 [Ref: M-200, T-5:50]. Private, 4th Co., Lower Bn., Militia, July 15, 1780 [Ref: M-205]. Took the Oath of Allegiance before the Hon. Charles Jones on Jan. 10, 1778 [Ref: T-3:71, L-1:46]. One "Thomas Wilmot" married Anne Gill in Montgomery County on May 20, 1779 [Ref: K-2:514]. "Thomas Willmutt" lived in the Lower Part of Newfoundland Hd. (two taxables) in 1777 [Ref: R-31:6].

WILMORE (WILLMORE), John. Private, 4th Co., Lower Bn., Militia, July 15, 1780 [Ref: M-205].

WILMORE (WILLMORE), Robert. Private, 4th Co., Lower Bn., Militia, July 15, 1780 [Ref: M-205]. Robert Willmore lived in the Lower Part of Newfoundland Hd. (one taxable) in 1777 [Ref: R-31:6].

WILSON, Agnes. See "Samuel Johnson," q.v.

WILSON (WILLSON), Alexander (Exander). Private, 1st Co., Middle Bn., Militia, Aug. 30, 1777 [Ref: M-195]. Private, 5th Co., Middle Bn., Militia, July 15, 1780 [Ref: M-203]. Took the Oath of Allegiance before the Hon. Joseph Wilson on Feb. 28, 1778 [Ref: T-3:67, L-1:46]. "Alexander Wilson" rendered aid by providing wheat for use of the military in 1780 [Ref: O-309]. "Exander Willson" rendered aid by providing wheat for use of the military in 1781 [Ref: O-396]. "Alexander Willson" lived in Seneca Hd. (two taxables) and "Alexander Wilson" lived in the Upper Part of Potomac Hd. (two taxables) in 1777 [Ref: R-31:8, R-31:15].

WILSON, Ann, Caroline, and others. See "Zadock Wilson," q.v.

WILSON, Elizabeth, and others. See "John Wilson," q.v.

WILSON, Ephraim. Private, 1st or 32nd Bn., Militia (no date was given; possibly June, 1777). [Ref: T-5:1].

WILSON (WILLSON), George (1746-1809). Private, 1st Co., Upper Bn., Militia, Aug. 30, 1777 [Ref: M-193]. Took the Oath of Allegiance (made his "X" mark) before the Hon. Edward Burgess on Feb. 28, 1778 [Ref: T-3:62, L-1:46]. Private, 8th Class, 1st Co., Middle Bn., Militia, July 15, 1780 [Ref: M-201]. "George Willson" lived in Sugarland Hd. (one taxable) in 1776-1777 [Ref: K-1:199, R-31:13]. "George Wilson" died testate in Montgomery County (unmarried) in 1809 [Ref: V-153].

WILSON, George, of William. Private, 4th Co., Lower Bn., Militia, July 15, 1780 [Ref: M-205].

WILSON, Henry, and others. See "Zadock Wilson" and others, q.v.

WILSON (WILLSON), James. (1) Private, 8th Co., Lower Bn., Militia, Sep., 1777 [Ref: M-200, T-5:51]. (2) Private, 3rd Co., Upper Bn., Militia, Aug. 30, 1777 [Ref: M-193]. (3) Private, 7th Co., Upper Bn., Militia, Aug. 30, 1777 [Ref: M-194]. One James Wilson married Ann Johnston in Montgomery County on Oct. 16, 1777 [Ref: K-2:521]. "James Willson, aged 16" (son of Wadsworth Willson) lived in Sugarland Hd. in 1776 and another lived in Sugar Loaf Hd. (one taxable) in 1777. (3) "James Wilson, aged 13" lived in North West Hd. in 1776-1777 [Ref: K-1:226, R-31:17]. He was apparently the James Wilson who applied for pension (W35727) in Clark County, Kentucky, on Jan. 26, 1824, aged 61, stating he was born on March 12, 1763, and entered the service at Frederick, Maryland, on March 2, 1781. In 1824 he had a wife (aged 48, no name given) and these children living with them: Rachel (aged 23); Thomas (aged 16); Elizabeth (aged 13); Moses (aged 10); and, Susan (aged 5). He also mentioned his brother-in-law Samuel Constable who lived in Illinois over 300 miles from Clark County, Kentucky, but was unable to get his deposition [Ref: P-3887, Z-29].

WILSON (WILLSON), John. (1) Private, 6th Co., Upper Bn., Militia, Aug. 30, 1777 [Ref: M-194]. (2) Private, 7th Co., Upper Bn., Militia, Aug. 30, 1777 [Ref: M-194]. (3) Private, 1st Co., Middle Bn., Militia, Aug. 30, 1777 [Ref: M-195]. (4) Private, 7th Co., Lower Bn., Militia, Aug., 1777 [Ref: M-200, T-5:50]. (5) Private, 8th Co., Lower Bn., Militia, Sep., 1777 [Ref: M-200, T-5:51]. One John Wilson took the Oath of Allegiance before the Hon. Elisha Williams on March 2, 1778 [Ref: T-3:81, L-1:46], another took the Oath of Allegiance before the Hon. Joseph Offutt on March 2, 1778 [Ref: T-3:70, L-1:46], and another took the Oath of Allegiance before the Hon. Gerrard Briscoe on March 2, 1778 [Ref: T-3:57, L-1:46]. Rendered aid by providing corn for use of the military in 1780 [Ref: O-298]. One John Willson lived in Seneca Hd. (one taxable), another lived in Sugar Loaf Hd. (eleven taxables), and "John Wilson" lived in the Upper Part of Potomac Hd. (one taxable) in 1777 [Ref: R-31:8, R-31:11, R-31:15]. One John Wilson, of Montgomery County, Maryland, married Elizabeth ----, and died in Woodford County, Kentucky in 1831. Their children were Samuel, William, Joshua, Lawrence (b. 1779 in Maryland), Mary, Sally, Margaret, Nancy, and Ruth [Ref: *Maryland Genealogical Society Bulletin*, Vol. 20, No. 2 (1979), p. 175].

WILSON, John, of Henry. Private, 4th Co., Lower Bn., Militia, July 15, 1780 [Ref: M-205].

WILSON, John Maddox. Private, 6th Co., Lower Bn., Militia, July 15, 1780 [Ref: M-206].

WILSON (WILLSON), Jonathan (died 1806). Private, 6th Co., Lower Bn., Militia, July 15, 1780 [Ref: M-206]. Took the Oath of Allegiance before the Hon. Joseph Wilson on Feb. 7, 1778 [Ref: T-3:64, L-1:46]. "Jonathan Willson" lived in Sugar Loaf Hd. (seven taxables) in 1777 [Ref: R-31:11]. Died testate in Montgomery County (wife not named) in 1806 [Ref: V-152].

WILSON (WILLSON), Joseph. Justice of the Peace who administered the Oath of Allegiance in 1778, and Justice of the County Court, 1779-1781 [Ref: T-3:64, T-3:67, L-1:46, W-1, W-2, C-529]. Rendered aid by providing wheat for use of the military in 1780 [Ref: O-332]. "Joseph Willson" lived in Seneca Hd. (19 taxables) in 1777 [Ref: R-31:8]. "Joseph Wilson" died testate in Montgomery County (wife not named) in 1791 [Ref: V-153, V-154].

WILSON (WILLSON), Josiah (b. 1731). "Josiah Wilson" was a private, 8th Co., Upper Bn., Militia, Aug. 30, 1777 [Ref: M-195]. "Josiah Willson" lived in Sugarland Hd. in 1776 and had one taxable in 1777 [Ref: K-1:214, R-31:13].

WILSON, Kilbreth. Private, Capt. Thomas Beall's Co., Maryland Line, 1780 [Ref: D-351].

WILSON, Levin and Lorenzo. See "Zadock Wilson," q.v.

WILSON, Martha. See "Thomas Ricketts," q.v.

WILSON (WILLSON), Matthew. (1) Private, 5th Co., Middle Bn., Militia, July 15, 1780 [Ref: M-203]. (2) Private, 1st Co., Upper Bn., Militia, Aug. 30, 1777, and Ensign, March 25, 1780 [Ref: M-138, M-193, F-120]. (3) Took the Oath of Allegiance before the Hon. Elisha Williams on March 2, 1778 [Ref: T-3:81, L-1:46]. Private, 1st or 32nd Bn., Militia (no date was given; possibly June, 1777). [Ref: T-5:1]. "Matthew Willson, aged 35" lived in Sugarland Hd. (wife named Rachel) in 1776-1777 [Ref: K-1:218, R-31:13].

WILSON, Noah. Private, 8th Co., Lower Bn., Militia, July 15, 1780 [Ref: M-207].

WILSON, Obed. Private, Capt. Edward Burgess' Co., Lower District of Frederick (now Montgomery) County, Militia, July, 1776 [Ref: D-42].

WILSON (WILLSON), Robert. Took the Oath of Allegiance before the Hon. Elisha Williams on March 2, 1778 [Ref: T-3:81, L-1:46]. Rendered aid by providing wheat for use of the military in 1781 [Ref: O-379]. "Robert Willson" lived in Sugar Loaf Hd. (two taxables) in 1777 [Ref: R-31:11]. "Robert Wilson, Sr." died testate in Montgomery County (wife not named) in 1794 [Ref: V-154].

WILSON, Sarah. See "Zadock Wilson" and "Matthew Fitzgerald," q.v.

WILSON, Stephen. Private, 7th Co., Lower Bn., Militia, Aug., 1777 [Ref: M-200, T-5:50]. Private, 4th Co., Lower Bn., Militia, July 15, 1780 [Ref: M-205].

WILSON (WILLSON), Thomas. Private, 8th Co., Lower Bn., Militia, Sep., 1777 [Ref: M-200, T-5:51]. Private, 6th Co., Middle Bn., Militia, July 15, 1780 [Ref: M-203]. Took the Oath of Allegiance before the Hon. Elisha Williams on March 2, 1778 [Ref: T-3:81, L-1:46]. Rendered aid by providing wheat for use of the military in 1780 [Ref: O-328]. One "Thomas Willson" lived in Sugar Loaf Hd. (two taxables) in 1777 [Ref: R-31:11], and "Thomas Wilson" lived in Rock Creek Hd. (three taxables) in 1777 [Ref: R-31:16].

WILSON, Thomas, of Henry. "Thomas Wilson, aged 13" was a son of Henry and Verlinda Wilson who lived in North West Hd. in 1776 [Ref: K-1:226]. Private, 6th Co., Lower Bn., Militia, July 15, 1780 [Ref: M-206]. See "Zadock Wilson," q.v.

WILSON, Verlinda. See "Zachariah Wilson" and "Zadock Wilson," q.v.

WILSON (WILLSON), Wadsworth (1725-1802). "Wadsworth Wilson" took the Oath of Allegiance before the Hon. Elisha Williams on March 2, 1778 [Ref: T-3:80, L-1:46]. "Wodsworth Willson" lived in Sugarland Hd. in 1776 and "Wadsworth Willson" lived there (three taxables) in 1777 [Ref: K-1:214, R-31:13]. "Wadsworth Wilson" died testate in Montgomery County (wife named Eleanor) in 1802 [Ref: V-154].

WILSON (WILLSON), William. (1) Private, 8th Co., Lower Bn., Militia, Sep., 1777 [Ref: M-200, T-5:51]. (2) Private, 3rd Co., Lower Bn., Militia, Sep., 1777 [Ref: M-199, T-5:46]. (3) Private, Capt. Thomas Beall's Co., Maryland Line, 1780 [Ref: D-351]. One William Wilson served as a grand juror in 1781 [Ref: W-2]. One "William Wilson, aged 20" lived in George Town Hd. in 1776 [Ref: K-1:95] and may have been the same "William Willson" who lived there (four taxables) in 1777. Two William Willson's (one had one taxable and the other had two taxables) lived in the Lower Part of Newfoundland Hd. in 1777 [Ref: R-31:3, R-31:6]. "William Willson, aged 43" lived in Sugarland Hd. in 1776 and died testate in Montgomery County (wife named Elizabeth) in 1777 and mentioned his children, but only named a son Hezekiah. The rest are listed in the 1776 tax list [Ref: V-153, K-1:214]. See "Samuel Wade Magruder," q.v.

WILSON, William, of George. Took the Oath of Allegiance before the Hon. Edward Burgess on Feb. 28, 1778 [Ref: T-3:62, L-1:46].

WILSON, Wilson [sic]. Served as First Corporal, 6th Co., Lower Bn., Militia, July 15, 1780 [Ref: M-206].

WILSON, Zachariah (b. 1731). Lived in North West Hd. in 1776, with Verlander Wilson, aged 80, who was head of household [Ref: K-1:228]. Zachariah Wilson was drafted in Prince George's County on July 13, 1781 [Ref: D-382].

WILSON, Zadock (1757-1826). Private, 8th Co., Lower Bn., Militia, Sep., 1777 [Ref: M-200, T-5:51]. Private, 6th Co., Lower Bn., Militia, July 15, 1780 [Ref: M-206]. "Zadock Wilson" was the eldest son of Henry Wilson, aged 51, and Forlander (Verlinda) Wilson, aged 47, of North West Hd., in 1776. He was born in 1757 in Frederick County and married twice: first to Ann Beall and had three children; and second to Ann Clark (who died in Loudoun County, Virginia, in 1834) and had four more children: Thomas Noble, Henry Griffin, Anne, Levin Jefferson, Caroline, Lorenzo Madison, and Sarah Evaline. "Zadok Wilson" died testate in the District of Columbia in 1826 [Ref: K-1:226, and "The Wilson Family of Georgetown and Montgomery County, Maryland," by George E. Bushnell, *Western Maryland Families*, edited by Raymond B. Clark, Jr. (1987), pp. 62-66]. There was also a Zadock Wilson who was a private, 5th Co., Middle Bn., Militia, Sep., 1777 [Ref: M-197, T-5:40].

WILSON, Zedekiah. Took the Oath of Allegiance (made his mark) before the Hon. Samuel W. Magruder in 1778 [Ref: T-3:73, L-1:46].

WINDOM (WINDAM), George (b. 1760). Lived in Sugarland Hd. in 1776 [Ref: K-1:201]. "George Windom" was a private who enrolled into a company of militia for the service of the Flying Camp on Oct. 15, 1776 [Ref: B-352]. "George Windham" was a private, 7th Co., Upper Bn., Militia, Aug. 30, 1777 [Ref: M-194].

WINDOM (WINDHAM), William. "William Windham" was a private, 1st Co., Lower Bn., Militia, July 15, 1780 [Ref: M-204]. "William Windsom" (Windom?) rendered aid by providing wheat for use of the military in 1780 [Ref: O-313].

WINDSOR, Basil. Private, 8th Co., Middle Bn., Militia, Sep., 1777 [Ref: M-198, T-5:43], and private, 7th Co., Middle Bn., Militia, July 15, 1780

[Ref: M-204]. Lived in the Upper Part of Newfoundland Hd. (one taxable) in 1777 [Ref: R-31:7].

WINDSOR (WINSOR), Isaac. Private, 3rd Co., Middle Bn., Militia, Sep., 1777 [Ref: M-196, T-5:38]. Took the Oath of Allegiance before the Hon. William Deakins, Jr. before March 3, 1778 [Ref: T-3:68, L-1:46, which latter source spelled the name as "Winson"]. "Isaac Winsor" was a private, 8th Class, 2nd Co., Middle Bn., Militia, July 15, 1780 [Ref: M-201]. "Isaac Windsor" married Anne Riley in Montgomery County on March 2, 1779 [Ref: K-2:521]. "Isaac Winsor" lived in the Upper Part of Potomac Hd. (three taxables) in 1777 [Ref: R-31:15].

WINDSOR (WINSOR), John. Private, 4th Co., Middle Bn., Militia, Sep., 1777 [Ref: M-196, T-5:39]. "John Windsor" was a private, 6th Class, 4th Co., Middle Bn., Militia, July 15, 1780 [Ref: M-202]. "John Winsor" lived in Rock Creek Hd. (one taxable) in 1777 [Ref: R-31:16].

WINDSOR, John S. Private, 8th Co., Middle Bn., Militia, Sep., 1777 [Ref: M-198, T-5:43].

WINDSOR (WINSOR), Rebeccah. See "John Chambers," q.v.

WINDSOR (WINSER), Samuel Queen. "Samuel Queen Windsor" enrolled as a private in a company of militia (Flying Camp) under Capt. Richard Smith on Oct. 15, 1776 [Ref: B-352, D-648]. "Samuel Q. Winser" served in the artillery under Capt. John Fulford in Annapolis on Dec. 12, 1776 [Ref: D-572].

WINDSOR, Sarah. See "Joseph Redman," q.v.

WINDSOR (WINSOR), Thomas (died 1810). Private, 6th Co., Middle Bn., Militia, Aug., 1777 [Ref: M-197, T-5:41]. Private, 6th Co., Middle Bn., Militia, July 15, 1780 [Ref: M-203]. Took the Oath of Allegiance on Sep. 1, 1780, under the Act of May 12, 1780, having neglected to do so previously "due to ignorance of the duty owed the country." [Ref: R-27:123]. Rendered aid by providing wheat for use of the military in 1781 [Ref: O-443]. Lived in the Upper Part of Newfoundland Hd. (one taxable) in 1777 [Ref: R-31:7]. "Thomas Winsor" died testate in Montgomery County (wife named Catherine) in 1810 [Ref: V-154].

WINEBERGER (WIENBERGER, WINBUGAR, WEYNBERGER, WINBARGLE), George (b. 1746). "George Winberger" was a private, 8th Co., Lower Bn., Militia, July 15, 1780 [Ref: M-207]. "George Winbugar" was a private, 3rd Co., Lower Bn., Militia, Sep., 1777 [Ref: M-199, T-5:46]. "George Weynberger" took the Oath of Allegiance before the Hon. Richard Thompson in 1778 [Ref: T-3:76, L-1:46]. "George Winbargle" lived in George Town Hd. in 1776 [Ref: K-1:915]. "George Wienberger" lived in George Town Hd. (one taxable) in 1777 [Ref: R-31:3].

WINROD, Francis. Took the Oath of Allegiance on Sep. 1, 1780, under the Act of May 12, 1780, having neglected to do so previously "due to ignorance of the duty owed the country." [Ref: R-27:123].

WISE (WIES), John (b. 1740). Took the Oath of Allegiance before the Hon. Richard Thompson in 1778 [Ref: T-3:75, L-1:46]. Private, Capt.

Price's Co., 3rd Maryland Line, 1781, sick in Boon's Hospital on March 4, 1782, and reportedly "deserted" on May 4, 1782 [Ref: D-454]. "John Wies or Wise" lived in George Town Hd. (two taxables) in 1776-1777 [Ref: K-1:195, R-31:3].

WISE, Thomas. Private, Flying Camp, Frederick (now Montgomery) County, enlisted on Aug. 5, 1776 [Ref: D-44].

WITMAN, Andrew. Private, 8th Co., Lower Bn., Militia, July 15, 1780 [Ref: M-207].

WOCK, John. Took the Oath of Allegiance in 1778 [Ref: L-2:28].

WOLVERTON, Charles. Took the Oath of Allegiance in 1778 [Ref: L-2:28].

WOLVERTON, Isaac. Took the Oath of Allegiance in 1778 [Ref: L-2:28].

WOOD, Aaron. Private, Flying Camp, Frederick (now Montgomery) County, enlisted by Greenbury Gaither on July 29, 1776 [Ref: D-44]. In pension application W6566 it was noted that Aaron was born in Loudoun County, Virginia, and moved with his parents (not named) to Halifax County, North Carolina when he was a young boy. In June, 1776, he was living with relatives in Maryland when he enlisted in the war and served 8 months under Capt. Benjamin Speaks in the Flying Camp. He later moved to South Carolina [Ref: P-3924, and Henry C. Peden's *Marylanders to Carolina* (1994), pp. 178-179, which should be consulted for more family information].

WOOD, Aristarchus (Aristarcus). Took the Oath of Allegiance before the Hon. Elisha Williams on March 2, 1778 [Ref: T-3:80, L-1:46]. "Aristarcus Wood" was a private, 2nd Co., Upper Bn., Militia, Aug. 30, 1777 [Ref: M-193]. "Arristarcus Wood" lived in Sugar Loaf Hd. (one taxable) in 1777 [Ref: R-31:11].

WOOD, James. "James Wood, aged 32" lived in Lower Potomac Hd. in 1776 [Ref: K-1:186]. "James Wood, aged 19" lived in Sugarland Hd. in 1776 [Ref: K-1:218]. One James Wood was a private, 3rd Maryland Regiment, 1781 [Ref: D-395]. "James Wood, 1st" was a sergeant, Maryland Line, 1780-1783 [Ref: D-561], and "James Wood, 2nd" was a private, Maryland Line, 1780-1783 [Ref: D-560].

WOOD, John. (1) Private, 8th Class, 2nd Co., Middle Bn., Militia, July 15, 1780 [Ref: M-201]. Took the Oath of Allegiance before the Hon. Elisha Williams on March 2, 1778 [Ref: T-3:82]. (2) Private, 1st Co., Middle Bn., Militia, Aug. 30, 1777 [Ref: T-5:54]. Took the Oath of Allegiance before the Hon. Edward Burgess on Feb. 28, 1778 [Ref: T-3:62, L-1:46]. One John Wood lived in North West Hd. (one taxable) in 1777 [Ref: R-31:17], and "John Wood, aged 47" lived in Sugarland Hd. (wife named Anna) in 1776 [Ref: K-1:218, K-1:219].

WOOD, Leonard. Private, Capt. Edward Burgess' Co., Lower District of Frederick (now Montgomery) County, Militia, July, 1776 [Ref: D-42].

WOOD, Martha. See "John Ray," q.v.

WOOD, Rebecca. See "Samuel Jones," q.v.

WOOD, Stephen (b. 1751). Private, 6th Co., Upper Bn., Militia, Aug. 30, 1777 [Ref: M-194]. Took the Oath of Allegiance before the Hon. Elisha Williams on March 2, 1778 [Ref: T-3:80, L-1:46]. Lived in Sugarland Hd. in 1776-1777 [Ref: K-1:221, R-31:13].

WOOD, Thomas. Private, Capt. Edward Burgess' Co., Lower District of Frederick (now Montgomery) County, Militia, July, 1776 [Ref: D-42]. Private, 7th Co., Lower Bn., Militia, Aug., 1777 [Ref: M-200, T-5:50]. Thomas Wood lived in North West Hd. (one taxable) in 1777 [Ref: R-31:17]. "Thomas Wood, aged 58" lived in North West Hd. in 1776 [Ref: K-1:223]. One Thomas Wood married Ann Hall in Montgomery County on Aug. 11, 1782 [Ref: K-2:515].

WOOD, Zephaniah (b. 1744). Private, 1st Co., Upper Bn., Militia, Aug. 30, 1777 [Ref: M-193]. "Zephaniah Wood" took the Oath of Allegiance before the Hon. Elisha Williams on March 2, 1778 [Ref: T-3:81, L-1:46]. "Jephaniah Wood" [sic] married Mary Lucas in Montgomery County on Aug. 14, 1777 [Ref: K-2:517]. "Zepheniah or Zophonioh Wood" lived in Sugarland Hd. in 1776-1777 [Ref: K-1:218, R-31:13]. "Mary Lucas, aged 43" also lived in Sugarland Hd. and was head of head of household in 1776. She was listed after "Zophonioh Wood, aged 32" in the 1776 tax list [Ref: K-1:218].

WOODARD (WOODWARD), Benedict (b. 1754). "Benedict Woodward" took the Oath of Allegiance before the Hon. Samuel W. Magruder in 1778 [Ref: T-3:73, L-1:47]. "Benedict Woodard" was a private, 2nd Co., Lower Bn., Militia, July 15, 1780 [Ref: M-204]. "Benedict Woodward" recruited Oliver Stevens in March, 1781 [Ref: R-33:155, X-1146]. Lived in Lower Potomac Hd. (two taxables) in 1776-1777 [Ref: K-1:186, R-31:5].

WOODARD (WOODWARD), Bennett. "Bennet Woodard" was a private, 5th Co., Lower Bn., Militia, Aug., 1777 [Ref: M-199, T-5:48]. "Bennett Woodward" married Elizabeth Cecil in Montgomery County on Dec. 17, 1778 [Ref: K-2:515].

WOODARD, Francis (b. 1757). Son of "Frances or Francis Woodard, aged 63" who lived in North West Hd. in 1776-1777 [Ref: K-1:231, R-31:17]. Private, 8th Co., Lower Bn., Militia, Sep., 1777 [Ref: M-200, T-5:51]. Private, 8th Class, 3rd Co., Middle Bn., Militia, July 15, 1780 [Ref: M-202].

WOODARD, Hezekiah (b. 1760). Son of "Frances or Francis Woodard, aged 63" of North West Hd. in 1776 [Ref: K-1:231, R-31:17]. Private, 8th Co., Lower Bn., Militia, Sep., 1777 [Ref: M-200, T-5:51]. Private, 6th Co., Lower Bn., Militia, July 15, 1780 [Ref: M-206].

WOODARD, Jesse and John. See "Jesse and John Woodyard," q.v.

WOODARD (WOODWARD), John (b. 1708). "John Woodard" took the Oath of Allegiance before the Hon. Samuel W. Magruder in 1778 [Ref: T-3:73, L-1:46]. "John Woodward" lived in Lower Potomac Hd. (one taxable) in 1776-1777 [Ref: K-1:186, R-31:5]. Also see "John Woodyard," q.v.

WOODARD (WOODWARD), Joseph. "Joseph Woodard" was a private, 6th Class, 2nd Co., Middle Bn., Militia, July 15, 1780 [Ref: M-201]. "Joseph Woodward" married Jane Taylor in Montgomery County on March 7, 1779 [Ref: K-2:514].

WOODARD (WOODWARD), Thomas (b. 1746). "Thomas Woodward" lived in Lower Potomac Hd. in 1776 [Ref: K-1:186]. "Thomas Woodward" was a private, 8th Co., Lower Bn., Militia, Sep., 1777 [Ref: M-200, T-5:51].

WOODARD (WOODYARD), William (b. 1744). "William Woodgerd" [Woodyard?] lived in Sugarland Hd. in 1776 and "William Woodard" lived in Sugarland Hd. (one taxable) in 1777 [Ref: K-1:206, R-31:13]. "William Woodyard" was a private, 8th Co., Upper Bn., Militia, Aug. 30, 1777 [Ref: M-195]. "William Woodard" took the Oath of Allegiance (made his mark) before the Hon. Aneas Campbell on March 2, 1778 [Ref: T-3:78, L-1:46].

WOODARD, Zachariah (b. 1763). Son of "Frances or Francis Woodard, age 63," of North West Hd., 1776-1777 [Ref: K-1:231, R-31:17]. Private, 6th Co., Lower Bn., Militia, July 15, 1780 [Ref: M-206].

WOODS, William. Took the Oath of Allegiance before the Hon. Charles Jones on Jan. 10, 1778 [Ref: T-3:71, L-1:46].

WOODWARD, Deborah. See "Frederick Sprigg," q.v.

WOODYARD, Jesse (b. 1751). Lived in Sugarland Hd. in 1776 [Ref: K-1:204]. Private, 1st Maryland Line, 1779 [Ref: E-350].

WOODYARD, John (b. 1756). "John Woodyard" lived in Sugarland Hd. in 1776 [Ref: K-1:205]. "John Woodward" was a private in the 2nd Maryland Line from May 20, 1778 until Aug. 16, 1780, when he was reported missing at the Battle of Camden [Ref: D-175]. Also see "John Woodard," q.v.

WOOLF, George. Took the Oath of Allegiance in 1778 [Ref: L-2:28].
WOOLF, Isaac. Took the Oath of Allegiance in 1778 [Ref: L-2:28].
WOOLF, Peter. Took the Oath of Allegiance in 1778 [Ref: L-2:28].
WOOTSELL, Jacob. Took the Oath of Allegiance in 1778 [Ref: L-2:29].

WOOTTON, Richard. Private, 5th Co., Middle Bn., Militia, Sep., 1777 [Ref: M-197, T-5:40]. Took the Oath of Allegiance before the Hon. Joseph Wilson on Feb. 28, 1778 [Ref: T-3:64, L-1:47]. Rendered aid by providing wheat for use of the military in 1780 [Ref: O-306]. One Richard Wootton lived in Sugar Loaf Hd. (three taxables) and another lived in the Upper Part of Potomac Hd. (one taxable) in 1777 [Ref: R-31:11, R-31:15]. One Richard Wootton died testate in Montgomery County (wife named Martha) in 1817 and he had a son Richard, among other children [Ref: V-154, V-155].

WOOTTON, Thomas Sprigg. Son of Turner Wootton and Elizabeth Sprigg. He married Molly Offutt, "who was said to have been murdered, and probably died without progeny." Thomas held numerous civil offices in Frederick County prior to the Revolutionary War and many in Montgomery County during the war, including Court Justice, 1768-1777, Committee of Correspondence, 1774, Committee of Observation, 1774, Justice of the Orphans' Court, 1777-1778, and Speaker of the Lower House, 1777. He was a Justice of the Peace who administered the Oath of Allegiance in 1778 and a Justice of the Orphans Court in 1778 [Ref: N-910, N-911, T-3:79, L-1:47, C-529]. "T. S. Wootten, doctor" was a private in the 5th Co., Middle Bn., Militia, in Sep., 1777 [Ref: M-197, T-5:40]. "Dr. Thomas Sprigg Wootton" recruited Archibald Casey in May, 1781 [Ref: R-33:156, X-1146]. "Thomas Wootton" owned a working plantation ("quarter") in the Upper Part of Potomac Hd. (six taxables) in 1777 [Ref: R-31:15]. "Thomas S. Wootton" died testate in Montgomery County (no wife or children named) in 1789 [Ref: V-155].

WOOTTON, Turner. See "Thomas Sprigg Wootton," q.v.

WORKER, Thomas. See "Thomas Walker (Warker)," q.v.

WORKER, William. See "William Walker (Worker)," q.v.

WORNELL, William. Private, 1st Class, 3rd Co., Middle Bn., Militia, July 15, 1780 [Ref: M-202].

WORSLEY, John. Private who was recruited and served in the Continental Army in 1780 [Ref: D-341].

WORTH, Andrew. Rendered aid by providing wheat for use of the military in 1780 [Ref: O-331].

WORTHINGTON, Thomas. See "William Layman," q.v.

WRIGHT (WRIT), Alexander. "Alexander Wright" was a private, 5th Co., Middle Bn., Militia, July 15, 1780 [Ref: M-203]. "Alexander Writ" lived in Seneca Hd. (James Writ, security) in 1777 [Ref: R-31:8].

WRIGHT, F. Edward. See "Archibald Nicholls" and "Edward House" and "Robert Cumming" and "Richard Harry" and "Thomas Cramphin," q.v.

WRIGHT (WRIT), James. "James Wright" was a private, 5th Co., Middle Bn., Militia, July 15, 1780 [Ref: M-203]. "James Writ" lived in Seneca Hd. (two taxables) in 1777 [Ref: R-31:8]. See "Alexander Wright," q.v.

WRIGHT, Joseph. Private, 7th Class, 4th Co., Middle Bn., Militia, July 15, 1780 [Ref: M-202].

WRIGHT, Robert. Private, 7th Co., Lower Bn., Militia, Aug., 1777 [Ref: M-200, T-5:50].

WRIGHT, Thomas. (1) Private, 4th Co., Middle Bn., Militia, Sep., 1777 [Ref: M-196, T-5:39]. Private, 6th Class, 4th Co., Middle Bn., Militia, July 15, 1780 [Ref: M-202]. (2) Private, 7th Co., Lower Bn., Militia, July 15, 1780 [Ref: M-207]. One Thomas Wright took the Oath of Allegiance (made his "X" mark) before the Hon. Edward Burgess on Feb. 28, 1778 [Ref: T-3:60, L-1:47]. One Thomas Wright lived in the Upper Part of Newfoundland Hd. (one taxable) in 1777 [Ref: R-31:7]. One Thomas Wright died testate in Montgomery County (no wife or children named) in 1800 [Ref: V-155].

WRIGHT, William Jr. Private, 7th Co., Middle Bn., Militia, Sep., 1777 [Ref: M-197, T-5:42].

WRIGHT, William Sr. Private, 7th Co., Middle Bn., Militia, Sep., 1777 [Ref: M-197, T-5:42]. "William Wright, Sr." took the Oath of Allegiance before the Hon. Edward Burgess on Feb. 28, 1778 [Ref: T-3:60, L-1:47]. "William Wright" lived in the Upper Part of Newfoundland Hd. (three taxables) in 1777 [Ref: R-31:7].

WYATT (WIETT), Alexander. Private, 1st Co., Middle Bn., Militia, Aug. 30, 1777 [Ref: M-195].

WYATT (WIETT), James. Private, 1st Co., Middle Bn., Militia, Aug. 30, 1777 [Ref: M-195].

WYGNAN, Philip C. Took the Oath of Allegiance in 1778 [Ref: L-2:29].

WYNCHAN, William. Took the Oath of Allegiance before the Hon. Edward Burgess on Feb. 28, 1778 [Ref: T-3:64, L-1:47].

WYNN, Robert. Took the Oath of Allegiance before the Hon. Aneas Campbell on March 2, 1778 [Ref: T-3:77, L-1:47].

WYVELL (WYVILL, WIFEWILL), Edward. "Edward Wyvell" was a private, 6th Co., Upper Bn., Militia, Aug. 30, 1777 [Ref: M-194]. "Edward Hale Wyvill" took the Oath of Allegiance before the Hon. Elisha Williams on March 2, 1778 [Ref: T-3:80, L-1:47]. "Edward Wifewill" lived in Sugar Loaf Hd. (one taxable) in 1777 [Ref: R-31:11].

YATES (YEATS), Ignatius. Private, 8th Co., Upper Bn., Militia, Aug. 30, 1777 [Ref: M-195]. "Ignatius Yates" took the Oath of Allegiance before the Hon. Aneas Campbell on March 2, 1778 [Ref: T-3:78, L-1:47]. "Ignatius Yeats" lived in Sugarland Hd. (one taxable) in 1777 [Ref: R-31:13].

YATES (YEATES), John (b. 1751). Private, 5th Co., Upper Bn., Militia, Aug. 30, 1777 [Ref: M-194]. "John Yeates, Sr., aged 25" lived in Sugarland Hd. in 1776 [Ref: K-1:218]. One John Yates served as a Corporal, Sergeant, and then Quartermaster Sergeant in the 7th Maryland Regiment, 1777-1780 [Ref: D-259].

YATES, Joseph (b. 1750). Lived in George Town Hd. in 1776 [Ref: K-1:195]. Served as private, 8th Co., Lower Bn., Militia, July 15, 1780 [Ref: M-207].

YATES, Josiah. Took the Oath of Allegiance before the Hon. Richard Thompson in 1778 [Ref: T-3:75, L-1:47].

YATES, Philip. Took the Oath of Allegiance in 1778 [Ref: L-2:29].

YATES, Robert (1754-1823). Served as a Corporal, 7th Maryland Line, Dec. 15, 1776, Sergeant on April 1, 1778, and discharged on Jan. 6, 1780 [Ref: D-259]. He had enlisted in Montgomery County and applied for a pension (S35754) in Washington County, Kentucky on Nov. 10, 1818, aged 64. In 1850 it was stated he had died in 1823 and his widow died about 5 years later; although children were mentioned, none were named [Ref: P-3986, and Anderson C. Quisenberry's *Revolutionary Soldiers in Kentucky*, p. 164].

YATES (YEATS), Thomas. Private, 8th Co., Upper Bn., Militia, Aug. 30, 1777 [Ref: M-195]. "Thomas Yates" took the Oath of Allegiance in 1778 [Ref: L-2:29]. "Thomas Yeats" lived in Sugarland Hd. (three taxables) in 1777 [Ref: R-31:13].
YESTERDAY, Christian. Took the Oath of Allegiance in 1778 [Ref: L-2:29].
YESTERDAY, Christian Jr. Took the Oath of Allegiance in 1778 [Ref: L-2:29].
YESTERDAY, Martin. Took the Oath of Allegiance in 1778 [Ref: L-2:29].
YONST (YOUST), Susanna. See "Frederick Cochantofer," q.v.
YOST, George. Served as a Drummer, 7th Maryland Line, from May 4, 1777 until May 20, 1780, when discharged [Ref: D-259].
YOST (YOUST), John (1743-1806). Took the Oath of Allegiance before the Hon. Richard Thompson in 1778 [Ref: T-3:76, L-1:47, L-2:29, which listed the name as "John H. D. Yost"]. "John Youst" rendered aid by providing wheat for use of the military in 1781 [Ref: O-392]. "John Youst" lived in George Town Hd. in 1776 and "John Yost" was constable there in 1779 [Ref: K-1:195, W-1]. In a letter from John Murdock, Lieutenant of Montgomery County, to the Governor and Council of Maryland on July 16, 1781, he stated, in part, "John Yost, who has already repaired several public arms, and is now employed about repairing those you last sent to this county, has made frequent applications to me for money, and he now tells me that he cannot go on with the work, nor longer maintain his family without regular payments, so that he must stop unless he can be paid for it." [Ref: H-351, H-352]. He married Rebecca Waggoner [Ref: DAR-I:768].
YOST, Lodowick. Private, 1st Co., Middle Bn., Militia, Aug. 30, 1777 [Ref: M-195]. Took the Oath of Allegiance before the Hon. Gerrard Briscoe on March 2, 1778 [Ref: T-3:57, L-1:47]. Served as a Captain, 5th Co., Middle Bn., Militia, July 15, 1780 [Ref: M-202]. Lived in Seneca Hd. (one taxable) in 1777 [Ref: R-31:8].
YOST, Tobias (b. 1755). Private, 3rd Co., Lower Bn., Militia, Sep., 1777, and First Lieutenant, 8th Co., Lower Bn., July 15, 1780, and Captain, Lower Bn., Aug. 4, 1780 [Ref: M-140, M-199, M-207, F-248, T-5:46]. Took the Oath of Allegiance before the Hon. Gerrard Briscoe on March 2, 1778 [Ref: T-3:56, L-1:47]. "Tobias Yost or Youst" lived in George Town Hd. (one taxable) in 1776-1777 [Ref: K-1:195, R-31:4].
YOUNG, Abraham (b. 1751). Served as a Second Lieutenant, 5th Co., Lower Bn., Militia, July 12, 1776, and Second Lieutenant, 29th Bn., Sep. 12, 1777 [Ref: M-140, M-199, T-5:48, C-373, B-464, B-511]. Took the Oath of Allegiance before the Hon. Samuel W. Magruder in 1778 [Ref: T-3:73]. Lived in Lower Potomac Hd. in 1776 and in the Upper Part of Potomac Hd. (four taxables) in 1777 [Ref: K-1:187, R-31:15].
YOUNG, Casper. Took the Oath of Allegiance in 1778 [Ref: L-2:29].

YOUNG, George (b. 1748). Lived in George Town Hd. in 1776 [Ref: K-1:195]. He may have been the George Young who enlisted in 1782 and served in the First Partizan Legion commanded by General Armand, Marquis de la Rouerie [Ref: D-394, D-395].

YOUNG, Isaac. Served as a Drummer, Capt. Price's Co., 3rd Maryland Line, 1781-1782 [Ref: D-452].

YOUNG, James (b. 1751). Lived in Lower Potomac Hd. in 1776 [Ref: K-1:187]. Took the Oath of Allegiance in 1778 [Ref: L-2:29].

YOUNG, John. (1) Private, 1st Co., Upper Bn., Militia, Aug. 30, 1777 [Ref: M-193]. Took the Oath of Allegiance before the Hon. Edward Burgess on Feb. 28, 1778 [Ref: T-3:62, L-2:29]. (2) Private, 7th Co., Lower Bn., Militia, Aug., 1777 [Ref: M-200, T-5:50]. One took the Oath of Allegiance before the Hon. Elisha Williams on March 2, 1778 [Ref: T-3:80, L-1:47]. One John Young recruited James Creighton in April, 1781 [Ref: R-33:156, X-1146]. One John Young lived in the Lower Part of Newfoundland Hd. (one taxable) in 1777 [Ref: R-31:6]; another "John Young, aged 33" lived in Sugarland Hd. in 1776 and had four taxables in 1777; and "John Young, aged 54" lived in North West Hd. in 1776 [Ref: K-1:205, K-1:225, R-31:13]. John Young married Sarah Offutt in Montgomery County on April 29, 1781 [Ref: K-2:521]. One John Young died testate in Montgomery County (wife not named) in 1820 and he had a son John, among other heirs [Ref: V-155].

YOUNG, John Jr. Took the Oath of Allegiance in 1778 [Ref: L-2:29]. See "John Young," q.v.

YOUNG, Joshua. Private, 1st or 32nd Bn., Militia (no date was given; possibly June, 1777). [Ref: T-5:1].

YOUNG, Notley. Rendered aid by providing wheat for use of the military in 1781 [Ref: O-393, O-395].

YOUNG, Peter (b. 1759). Lived in Lower Potomac Hd. in 1776 [Ref: K-1:187]. Private, 4th Co., Lower Bn., Militia, Aug., 1777 [Ref: M-199, T-5:47]. Private, 1st Co., Lower Bn., Militia, July 15, 1780 [Ref: M-204, D-413]. Took the Oath of Allegiance (made his mark) before the Hon. Samuel W. Magruder in 1778 [Ref: T-3:73, L-2:29].

YOUNG, Thomas (b. 1743). Lived in George Town Hd. in 1776 [Ref: K-1:195]. Private, 7th Maryland Regiment, on June 4, 1777, hospitalized at Reading on Nov. 17, 1777, and transferred to the invalids corps on Nov. 1, 1780 [Ref: D-259, D-618].

YOUNG, William. Lived in Sugar Loaf Hd. (three taxables) in 1777 [Ref: R-31:11]. Private, 7th Co., Upper Bn., Militia, Aug. 30, 1777 [Ref: M-194]. Private, 7th Maryland Line, 1777-1780 [Ref: D-259]. Served as a substitute from Montgomery County until discharged from the Maryland Line on Dec. 3, 1781 [Ref: I-11].

ZACHARIAS, Daniel. Took the Oath of Allegiance in 1778 [Ref: L-2:29].

ZACHARIUS, Frederick. Private, 7th Maryland Line, from June 4, 1778 until March 30, 1779, when discharged [Ref: D-260].

Heritage Books by Henry C. Peden, Jr. :
A Closer Look at St. John's Parish Registers [Baltimore County, Maryland], 1701–1801
A Collection of Maryland Church Records
A Guide to Genealogical Research in Maryland: 5th Edition, Revised and Enlarged
Abstracts of the Ledgers and Accounts of the Bush Store and Rock Run Store, 1759–1771
Abstracts of the Orphans Court Proceedings of Harford County, 1778–1800
Abstracts of Wills, Harford County, Maryland, 1800–1805
Baltimore City [Maryland] Deaths and Burials, 1834–1840
Baltimore County, Maryland, Overseers of Roads, 1693–1793
Bastardy Cases in Baltimore County, Maryland, 1673–1783
Bastardy Cases in Harford County, Maryland, 1774–1844
Bible and Family Records of Harford County, Maryland Families: Volume V
Children of Harford County: Indentures and Guardianships, 1801–1830
Colonial Delaware Soldiers and Sailors, 1638–1776
Colonial Families of the Eastern Shore of Md.: Vols. 5, 6, 7, 8, 9, 11, 12, 13, 14, and 16
Colonial Maryland Soldiers and Sailors, 1634–1734
Dr. John Archer's First Medical Ledger, 1767–1769, Annotated Abstracts
Early Anglican Records of Cecil County
Early Harford Countians, Individuals Living in Harford Co., Md. in Its Formative Years Volume 1: A to K, Volume 2: L to Z, and Volume 3: Supplement
Harford County Taxpayers in 1870, 1872 and 1883
Harford County, Maryland Divorce Cases, 1827–1912: An Annotated Index
Heirs and Legatees of Harford County, Maryland, 1774–1802
Heirs and Legatees of Harford County, Maryland, 1802–1846
Inhabitants of Baltimore County, Maryland, 1763–1774
Inhabitants of Cecil County, Maryland, 1649–1774
Inhabitants of Harford County, Maryland, 1791–1800
Inhabitants of Kent County, Maryland, 1637–1787
Joseph A. Pennington & Co., Havre De Grace, Maryland Funeral Home Records: Volume II, 1877–1882, 1893–1900
Maryland Bible Records, Volume 1: Baltimore and Harford Counties
Maryland Bible Records, Volume 2: Baltimore and Harford Counties
Maryland Bible Records, Volume 3: Carroll County
Maryland Bible Records, Volume 4: Eastern Shore
Maryland Deponents, 1634–1799
Maryland Deponents: Volume 3, 1634–1776
Maryland Public Service Records, 1775–1783: A Compendium of Men and Women of Maryland Who Rendered Aid in Support of the American Cause against Great Britain during the Revolutionary War
Marylanders to Carolina: Migration of Marylanders to North Carolina and South Carolina prior to 1800

Marylanders to Kentucky, 1775–1825
Methodist Records of Baltimore City, Maryland: Volume 1, 1799–1829
Methodist Records of Baltimore City, Maryland: Volume 2, 1830–1839
Methodist Records of Baltimore City, Maryland: Volume 3, 1840–1850 (East City Station)
More Maryland Deponents, 1716–1799
More Marylanders to Carolina: Migration of Marylanders to North Carolina and South Carolina prior to 1800
More Marylanders to Kentucky, 1778–1828
Outpensioners of Harford County, Maryland, 1856–1896
Presbyterian Records of Baltimore City, Maryland, 1765–1840
Quaker Records of Baltimore and Harford Counties, Maryland, 1801–1825
Quaker Records of Northern Maryland, 1716–1800
Quaker Records of Southern Maryland, 1658–1800
Revolutionary Patriots of Anne Arundel County, Maryland
Revolutionary Patriots of Baltimore Town and Baltimore County, 1775–1783
Revolutionary Patriots of Calvert and St. Mary's Counties, Maryland, 1775–1783
Revolutionary Patriots of Caroline County, Maryland, 1775–1783
Revolutionary Patriots of Cecil County, Maryland
Revolutionary Patriots of Charles County, Maryland, 1775–1783
Revolutionary Patriots of Delaware, 1775–1783
Revolutionary Patriots of Dorchester County, Maryland, 1775–1783
Revolutionary Patriots of Frederick County, Maryland, 1775–1783
Revolutionary Patriots of Harford County, Maryland, 1775–1783
Revolutionary Patriots of Kent and Queen Anne's Counties
Revolutionary Patriots of Lancaster County, Pennsylvania
Revolutionary Patriots of Maryland, 1775–1783: A Supplement
Revolutionary Patriots of Maryland, 1775–1783: Second Supplement
Revolutionary Patriots of Montgomery County, Maryland, 1776–1783
Revolutionary Patriots of Prince George's County, Maryland, 1775–1783
Revolutionary Patriots of Talbot County, Maryland, 1775–1783
Revolutionary Patriots of Worcester and Somerset Counties, Maryland, 1775–1783
Revolutionary Patriots of Washington County, Maryland, 1776–1783
St. George's (Old Spesutia) Parish, Harford County, Maryland: Church and Cemetery Records, 1820–1920
St. John's and St. George's Parish Registers, 1696–1851
Survey Field Book of David and William Clark in Harford County, Maryland, 1770–1812
The Crenshaws of Kentucky, 1800–1995
The Delaware Militia in the War of 1812
Union Chapel United Methodist Church Cemetery Tombstone Inscriptions, Wilna, Harford County, Maryland